FOLIUM

FOLIUM

JEANNE BATISTE

Smith Street Books

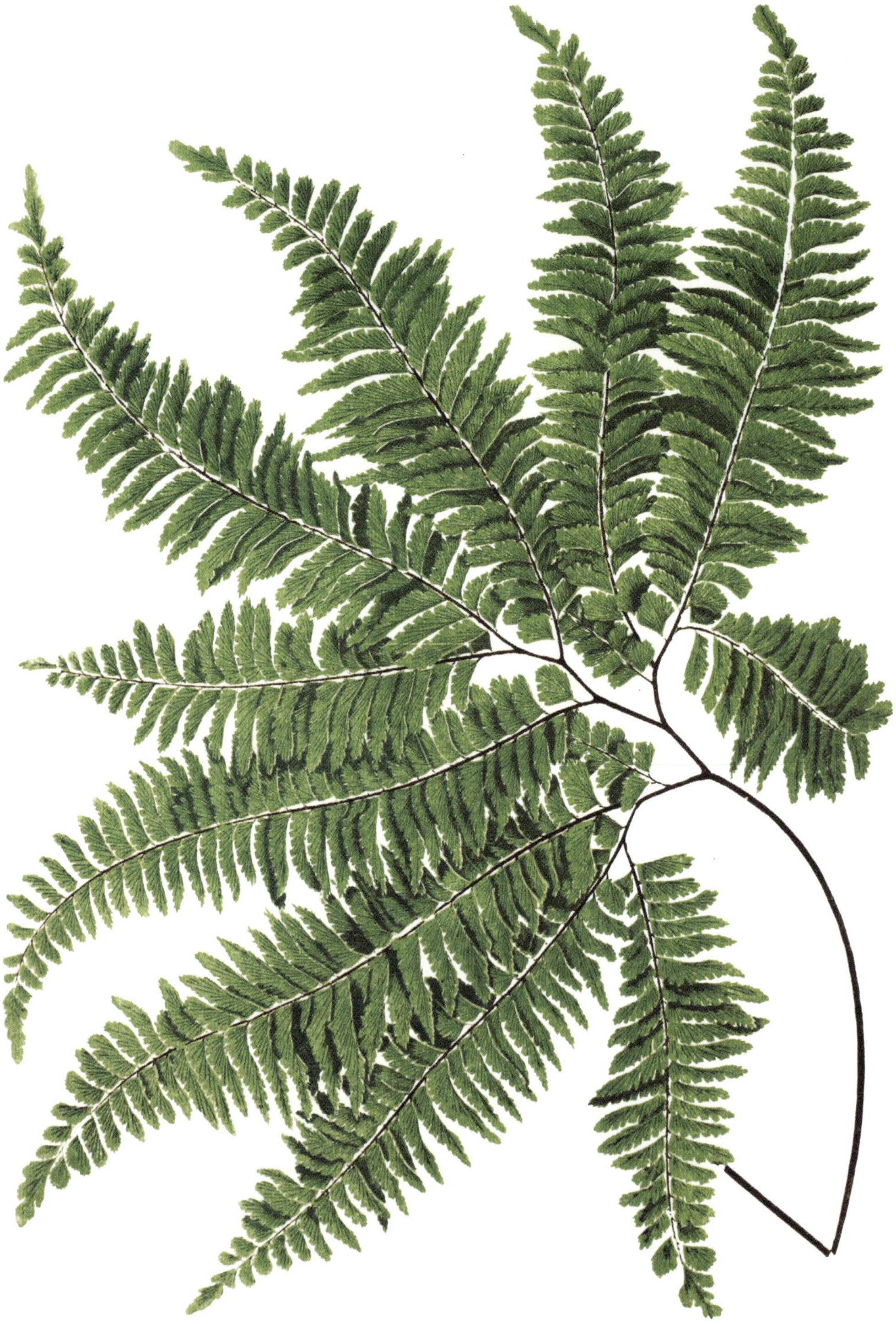

Adiantum curvatum
by Pierre-Joseph Redouté

maidenhair fern

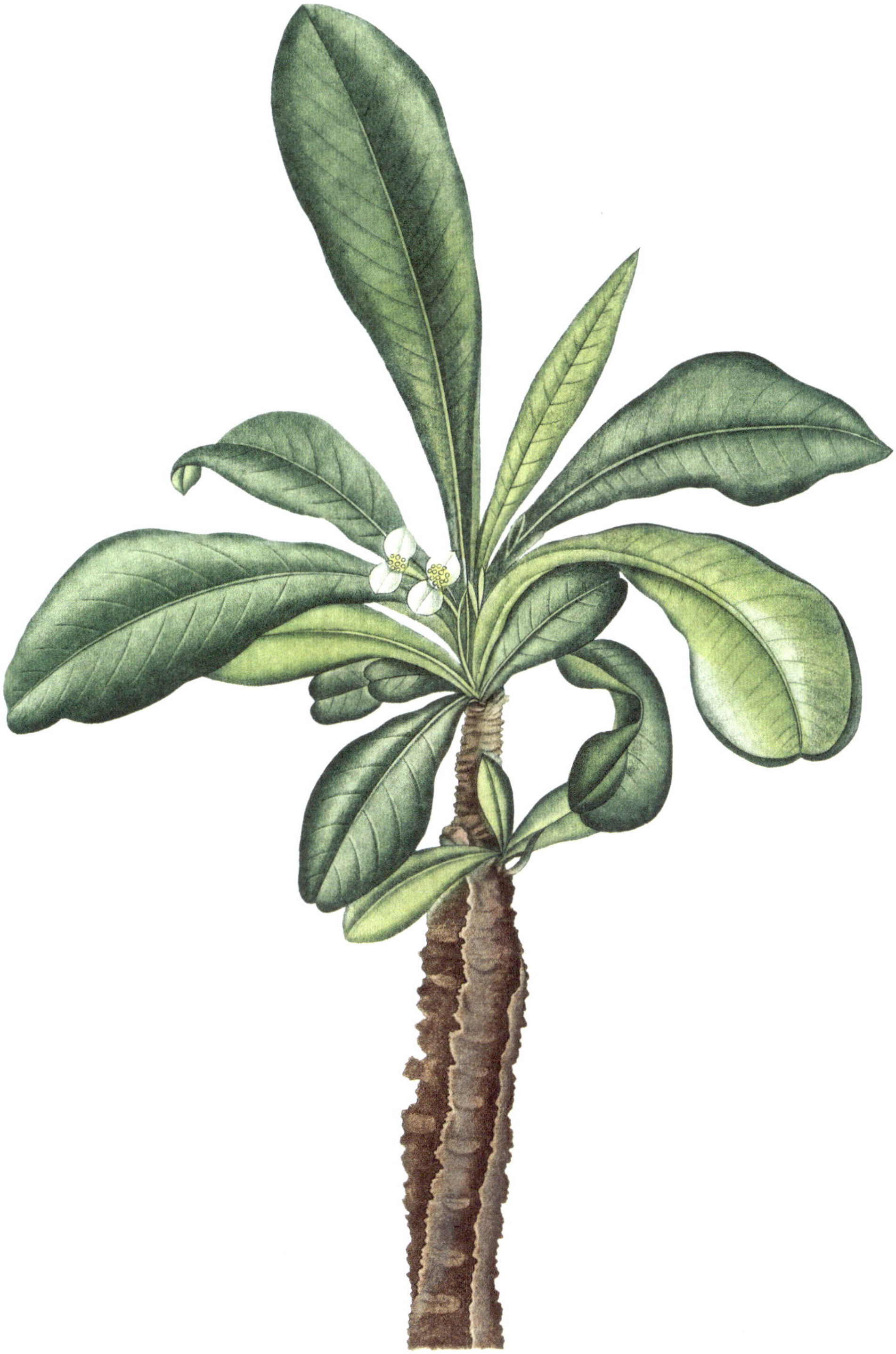

Euphorbia lophogona
by Pierre-Joseph Redouté

Madagascar jewel | white crown of thorns

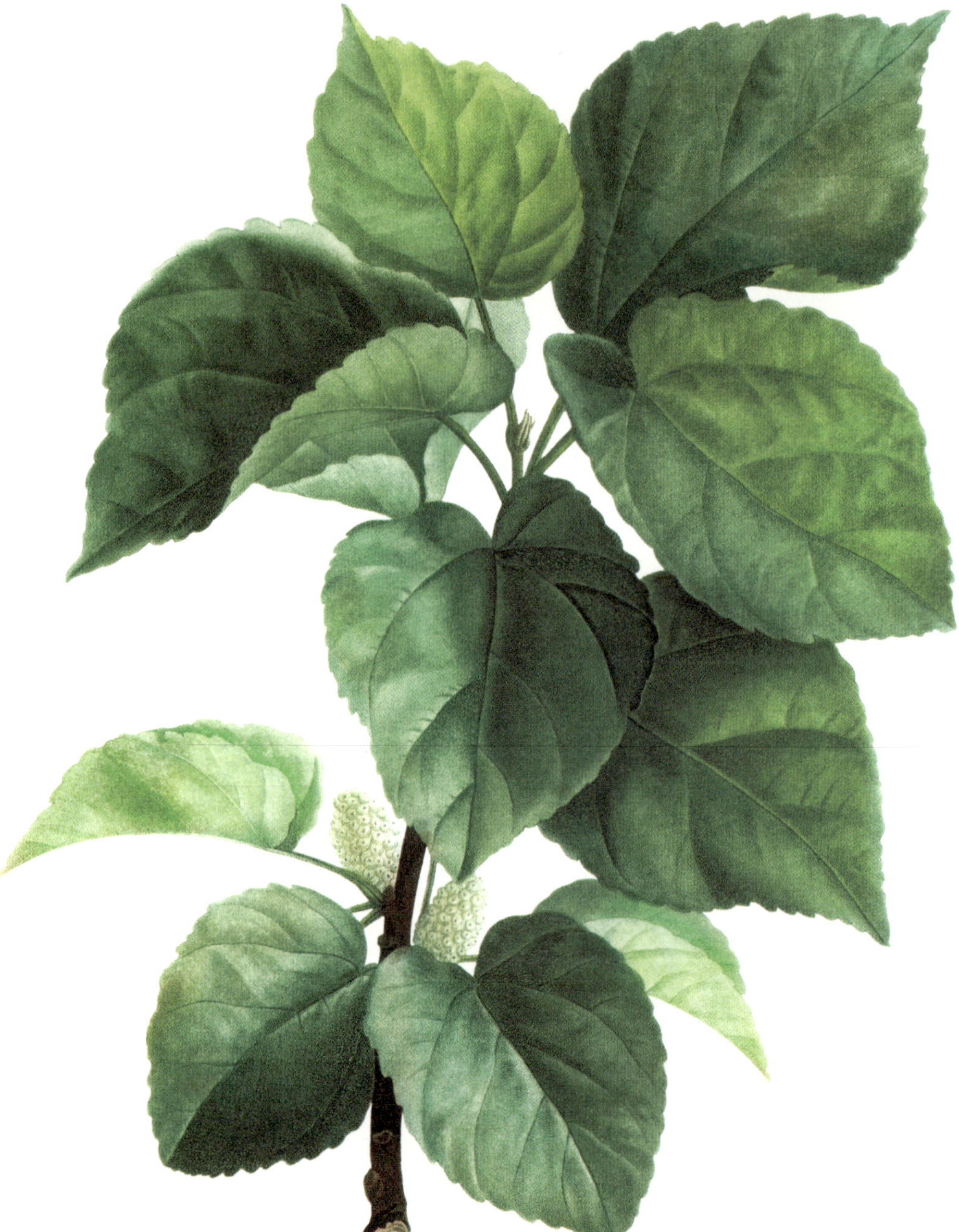

Morus alba
by Pierre-Joseph Redouté

white mulberry | common mulberry | silkworm mulberry

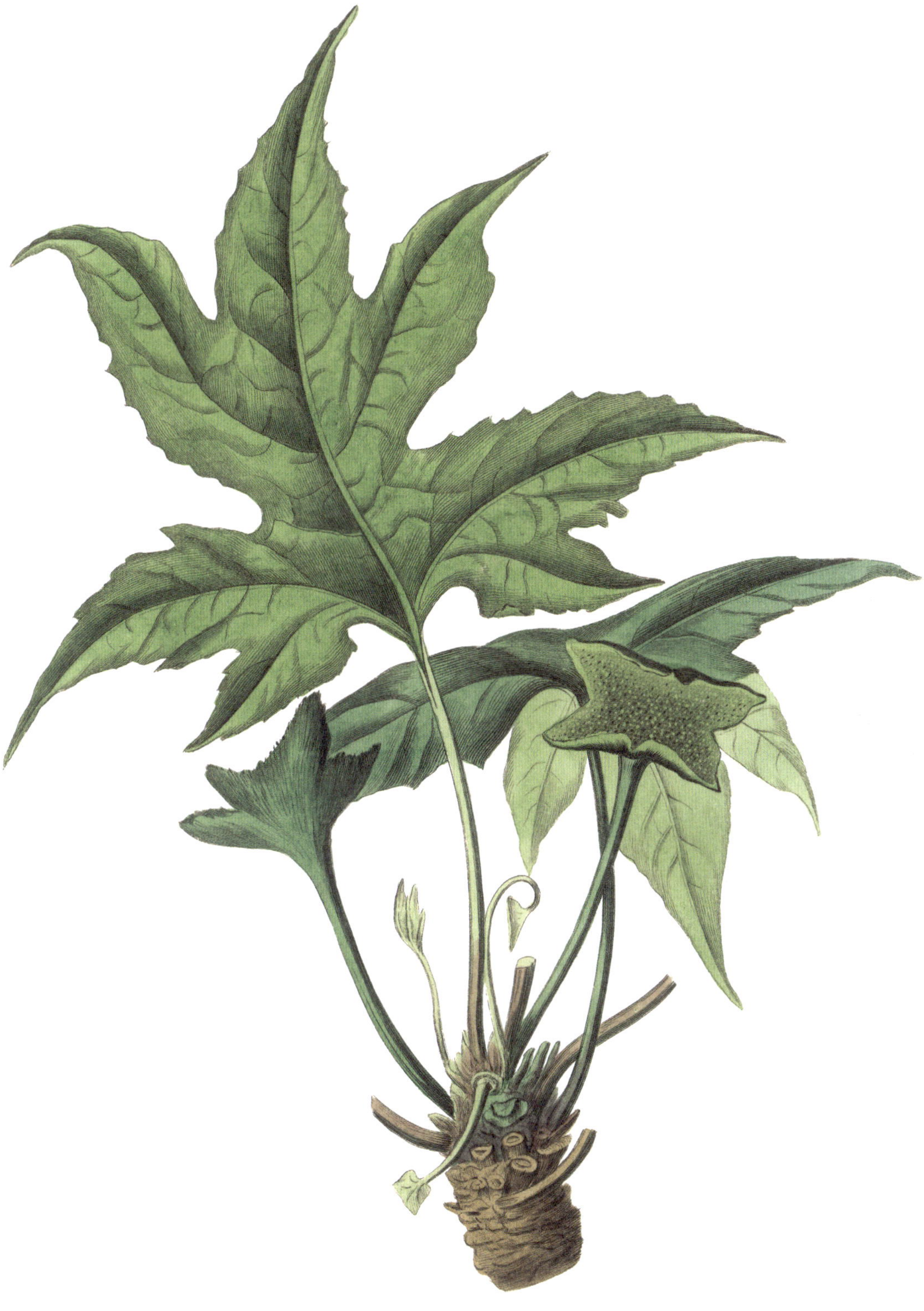

Dorstenia contrajerva
by John Stephenson & James Morss Churchill

snakewort

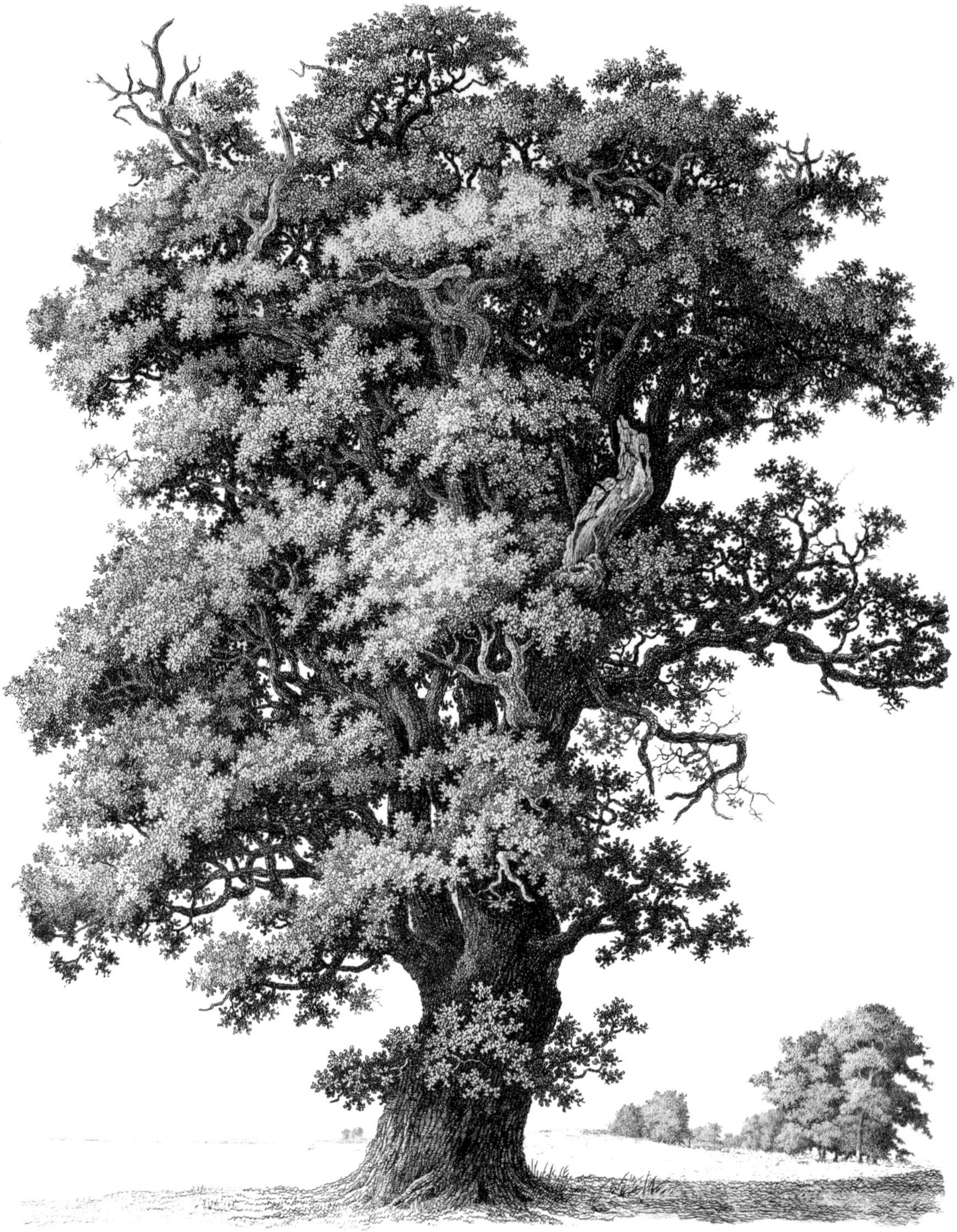

Quercus robur subsp. *robur*
by Søren Henrik Petersen

common oak | English oak | pedunculate oak

Trees are poems
that the earth writes
upon the sky.

FROM *Sand and Foam* BY KAHLIL GIBRAN

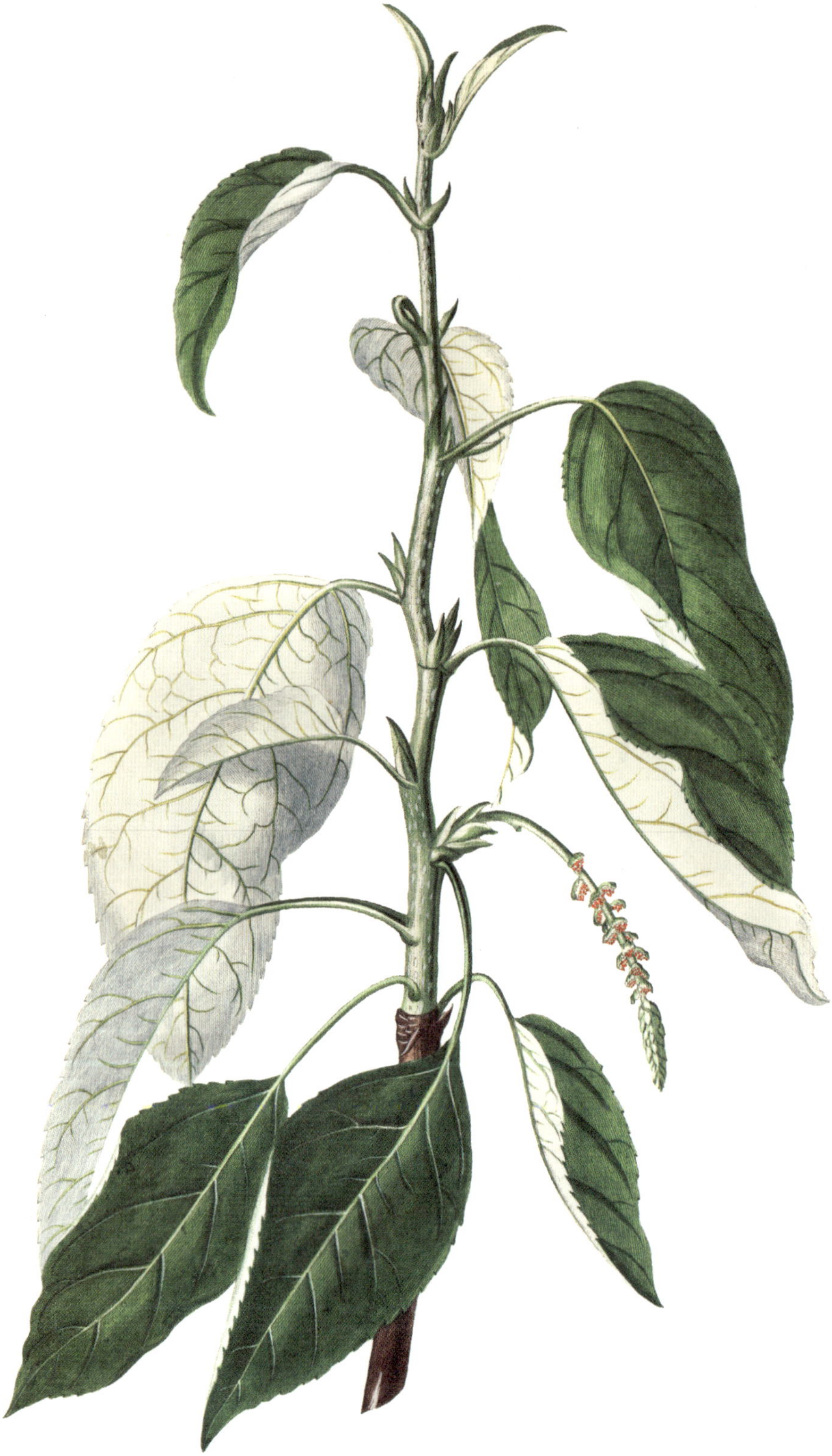

Populus balsamifera
by Georg Dionysius Ehret

balsam poplar | bam | bamtree | eastern balsam-poplar

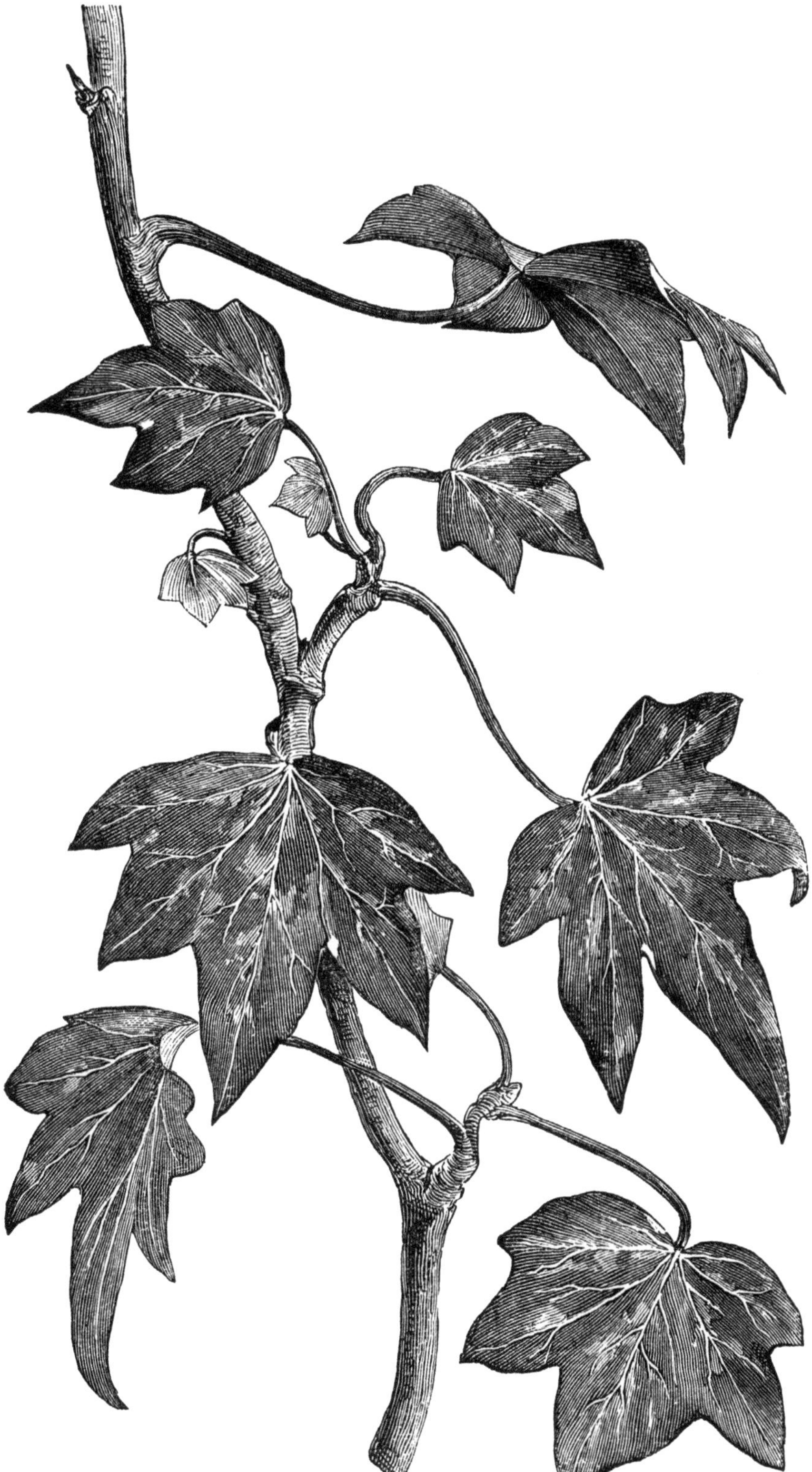

Hedera helix
by James Shirley Hibberd

common ivy | English ivy | European ivy

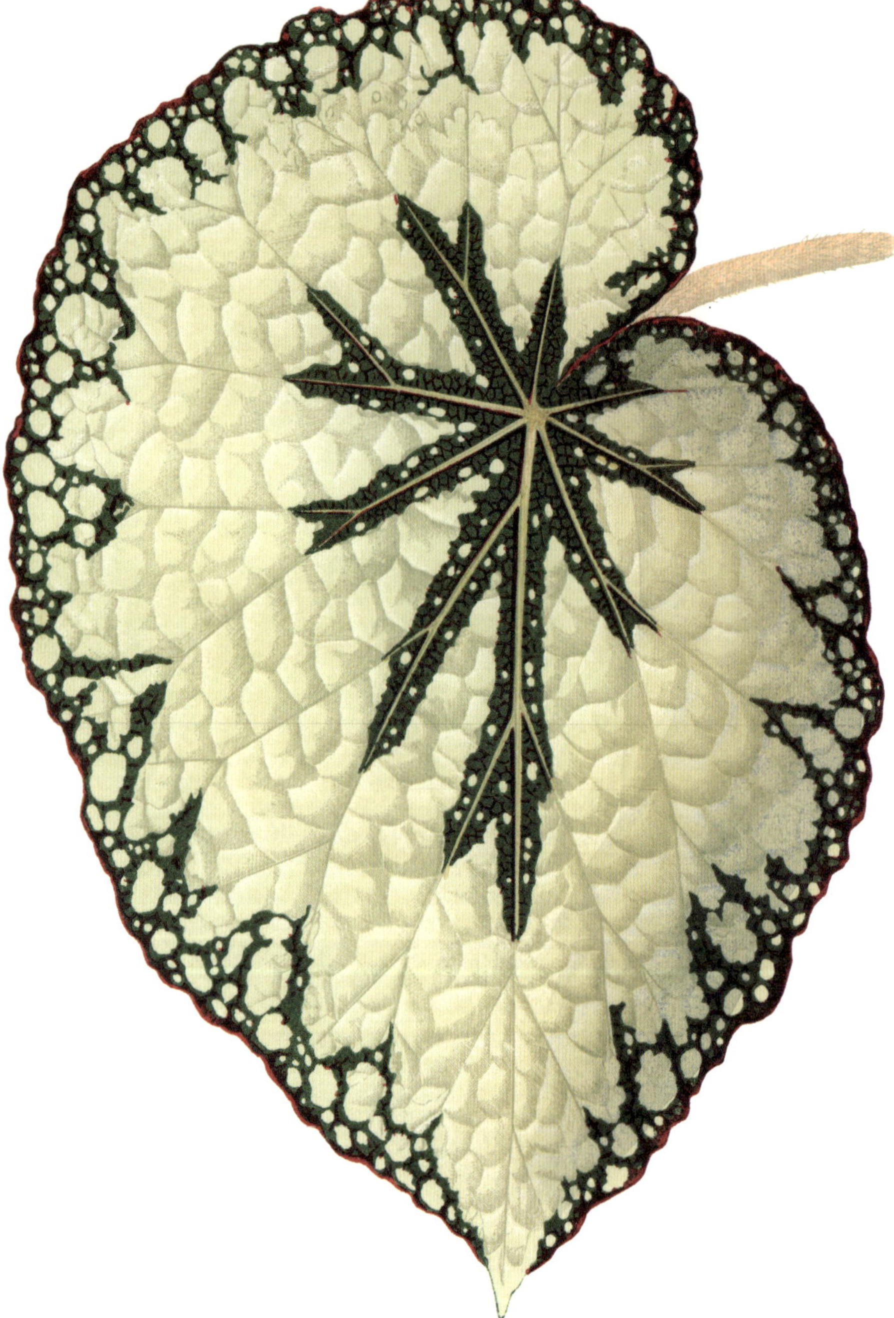

Begonia
by ALEXANDER FRANCIS LYDON & BENJAMIN FAWCETT

begonia (unknown variety)

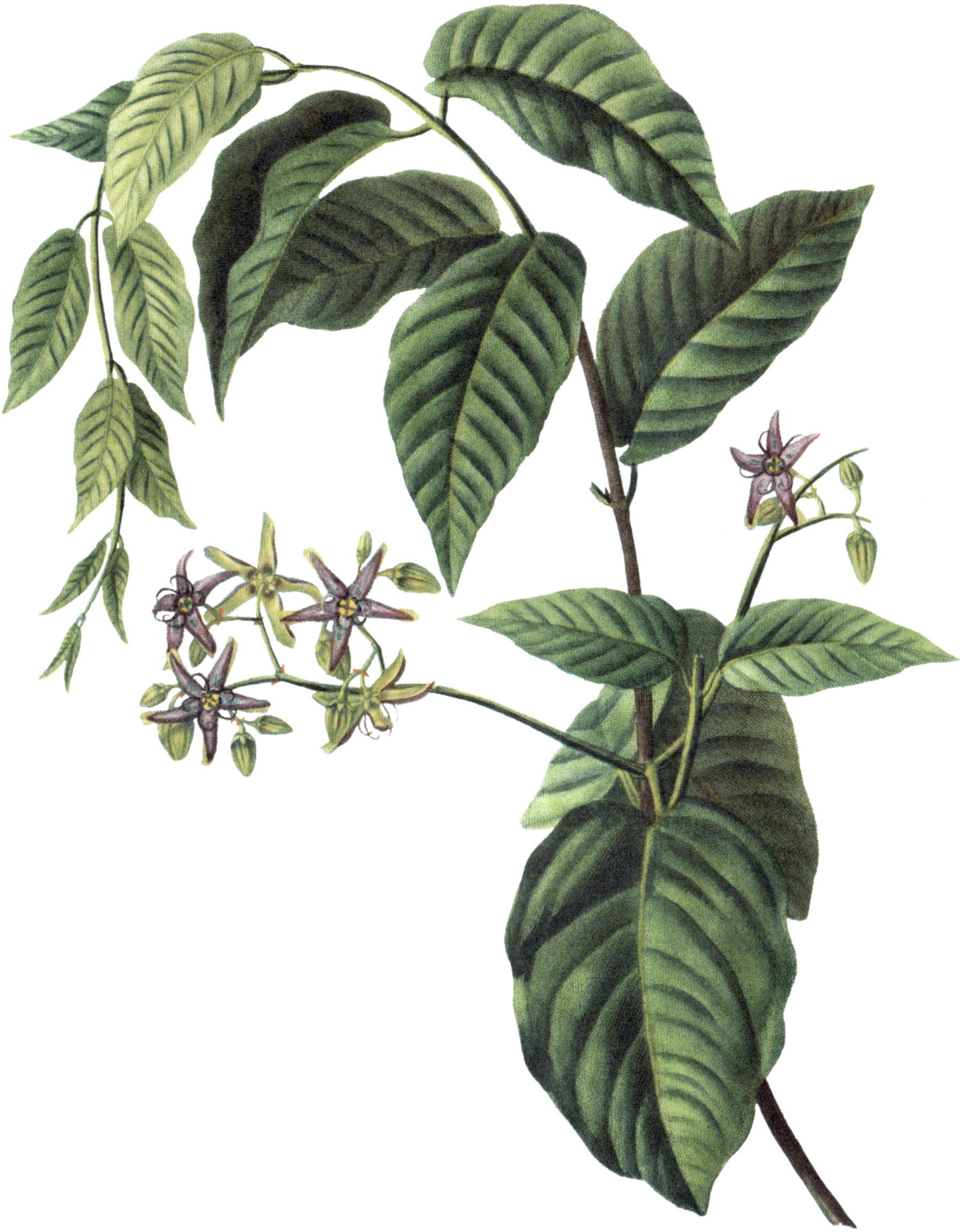

Periploca graeca
by Pierre-Joseph Redouté

silkvine

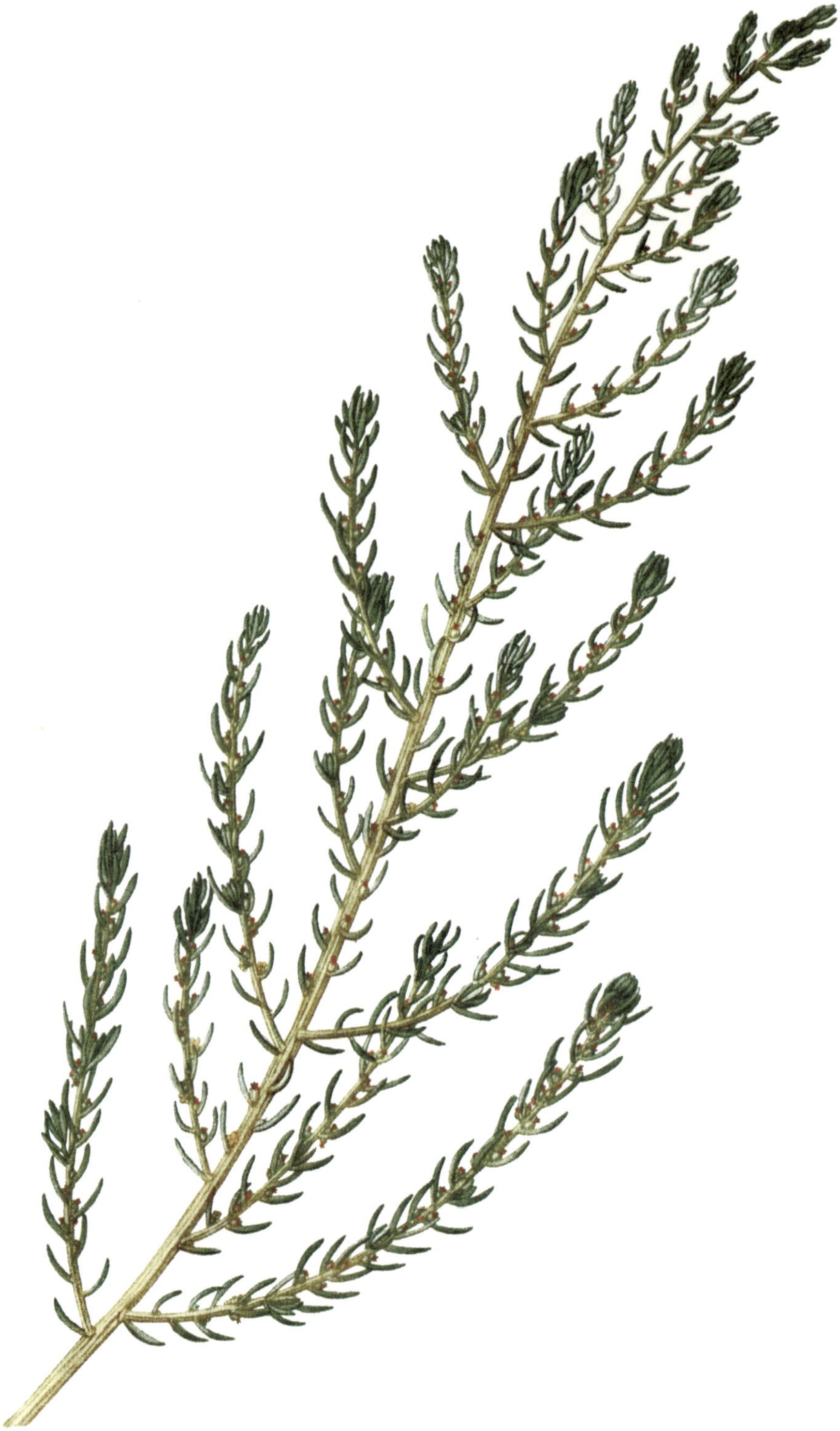

Suaeda vera
by Pierre-Joseph Redouté

shrubby seablite | alkali seepweed

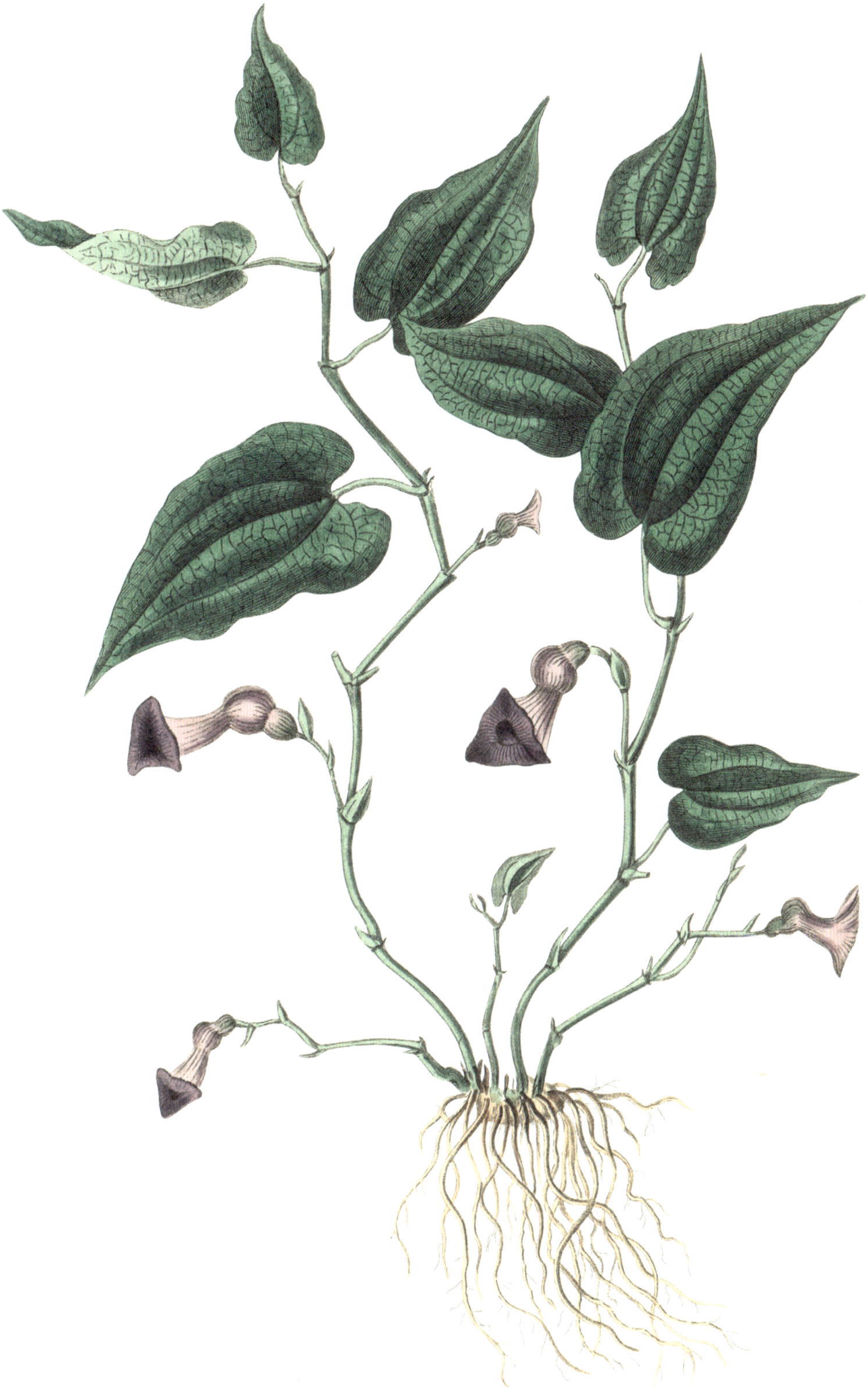

Aristolochia serpentaria
by John Stephenson & James Morss Churchill

Virginia snakeroot

One touch of
nature makes the
whole world kin.

WILLIAM SHAKESPEARE

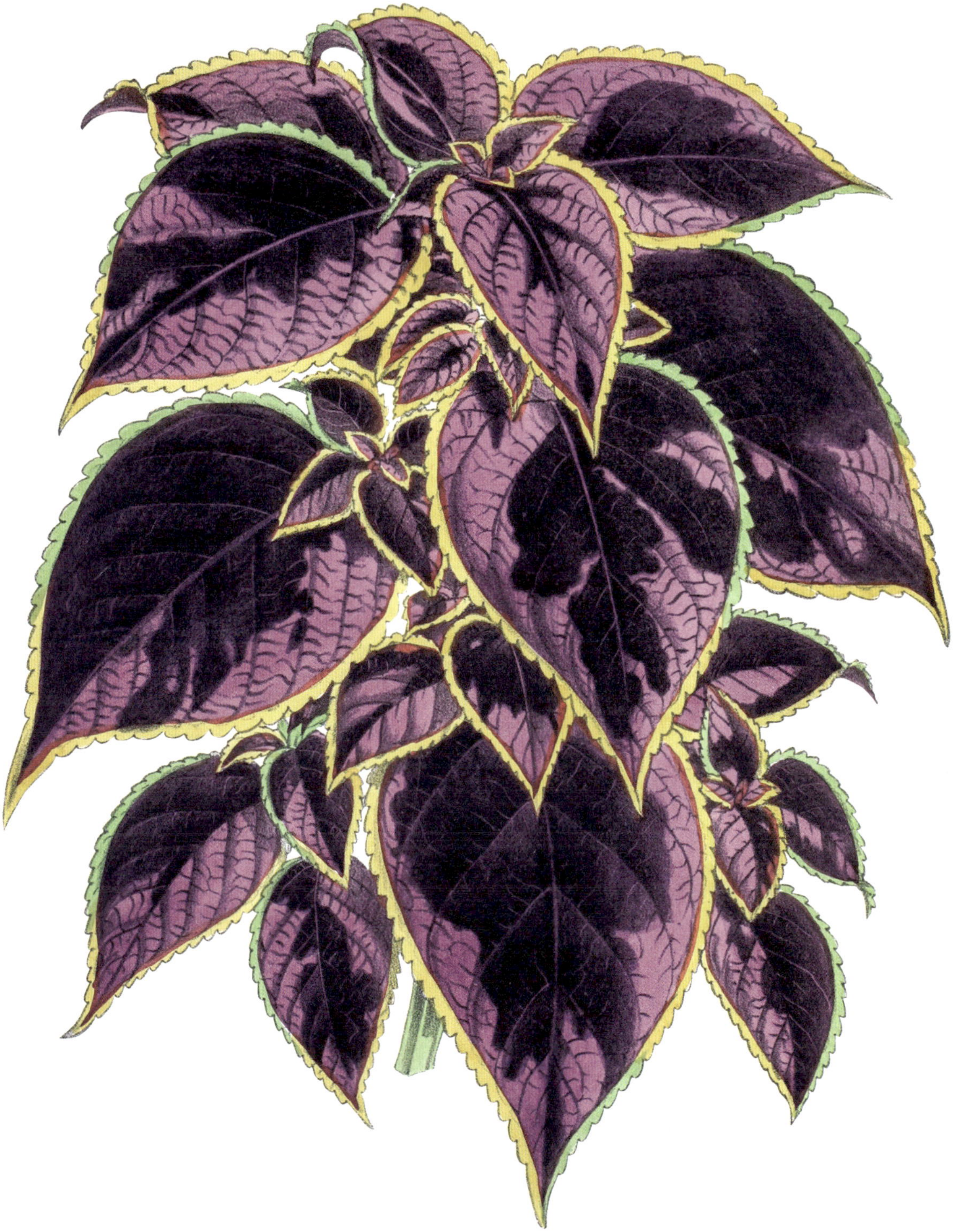

17

Coleus
by Worthington G. Smith

spurflower | flybush | hedgehog flower | hullwort

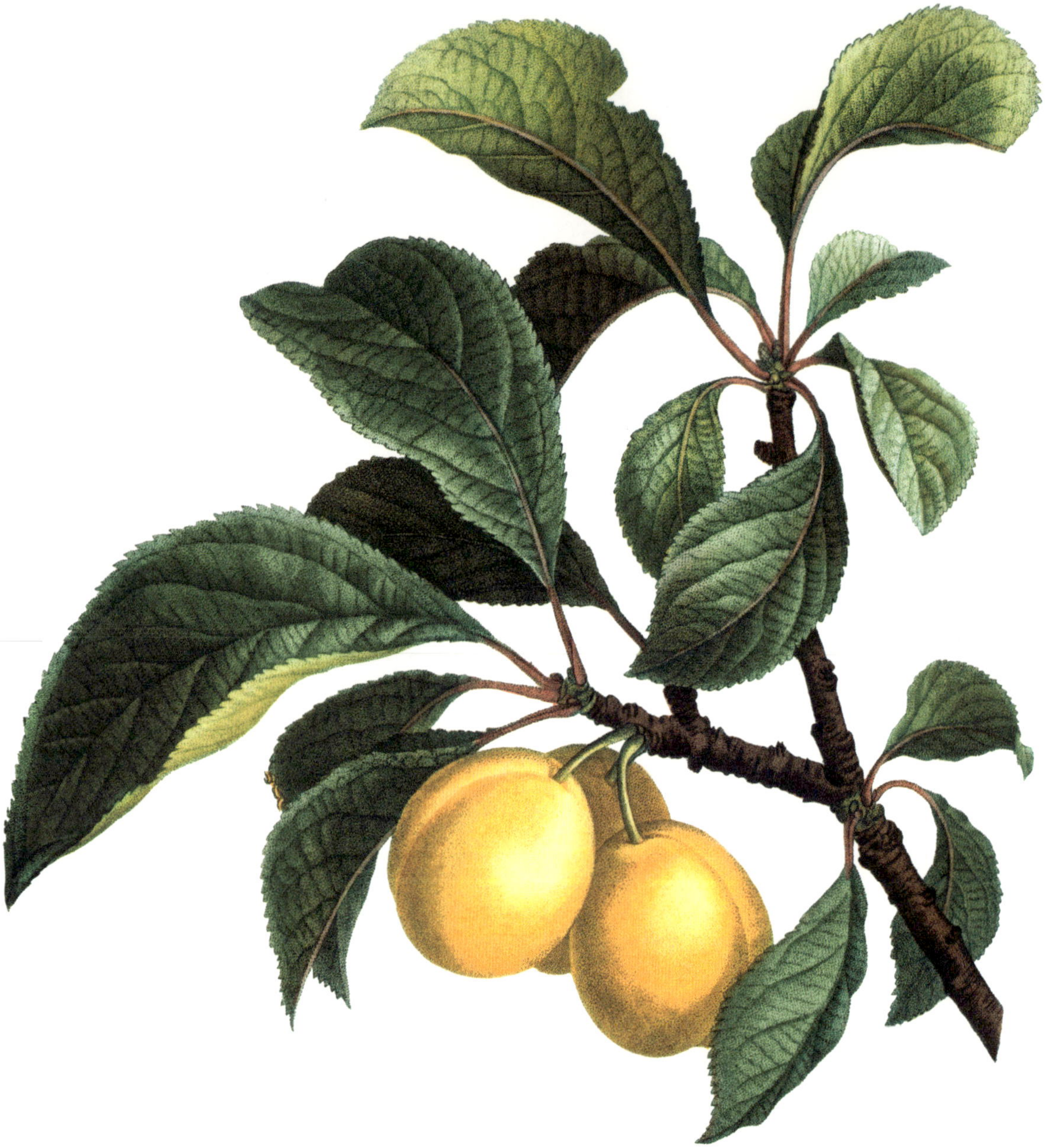

Prunus domestica 'Ste Catherine'
by Pierre-Joseph Redouté

St Catherine plum

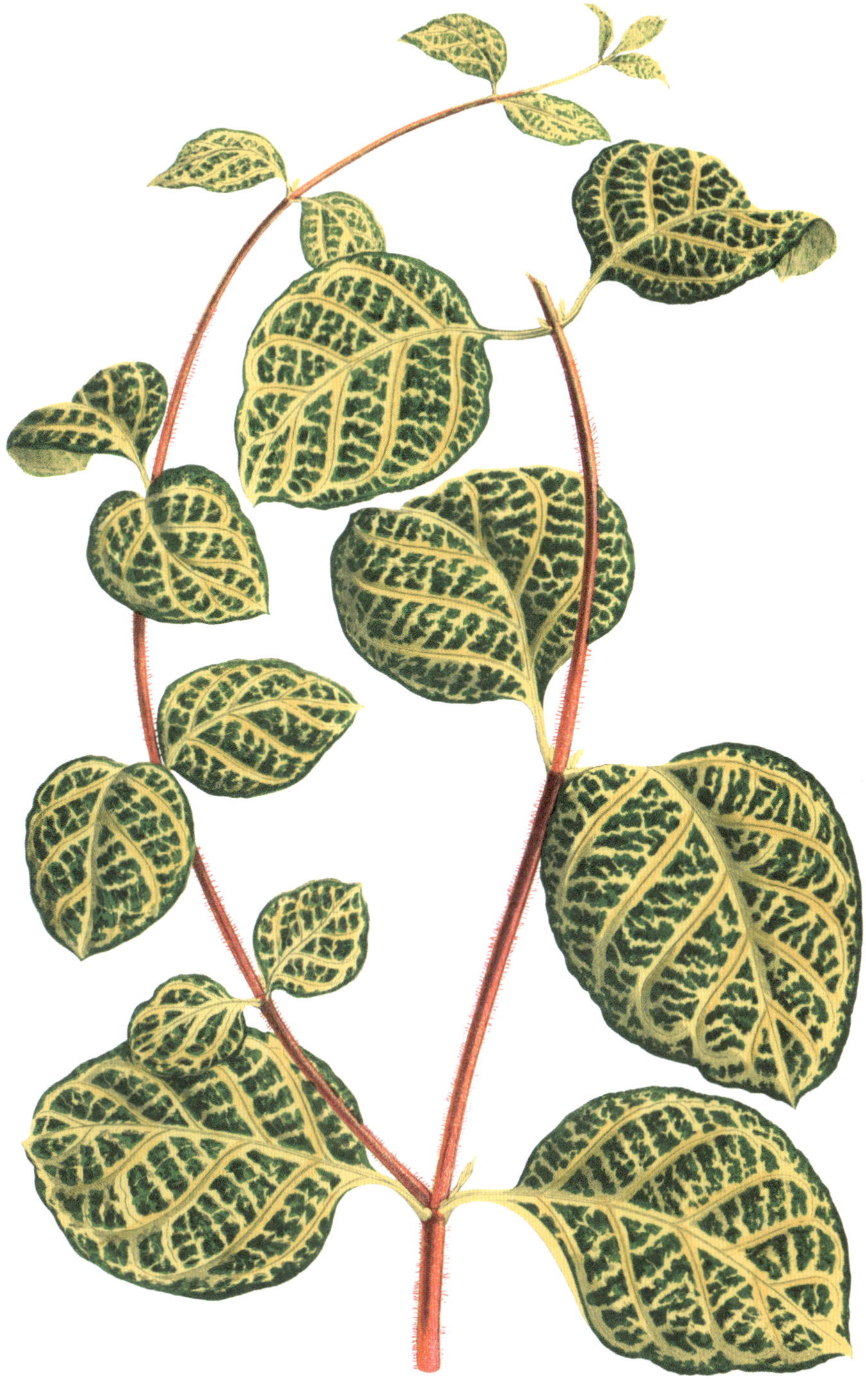

Lonicera japonica
by Alexander Francis Lydon & Benjamin Fawcett

Japanese honeysuckle | golden-and-silver honeysuckle

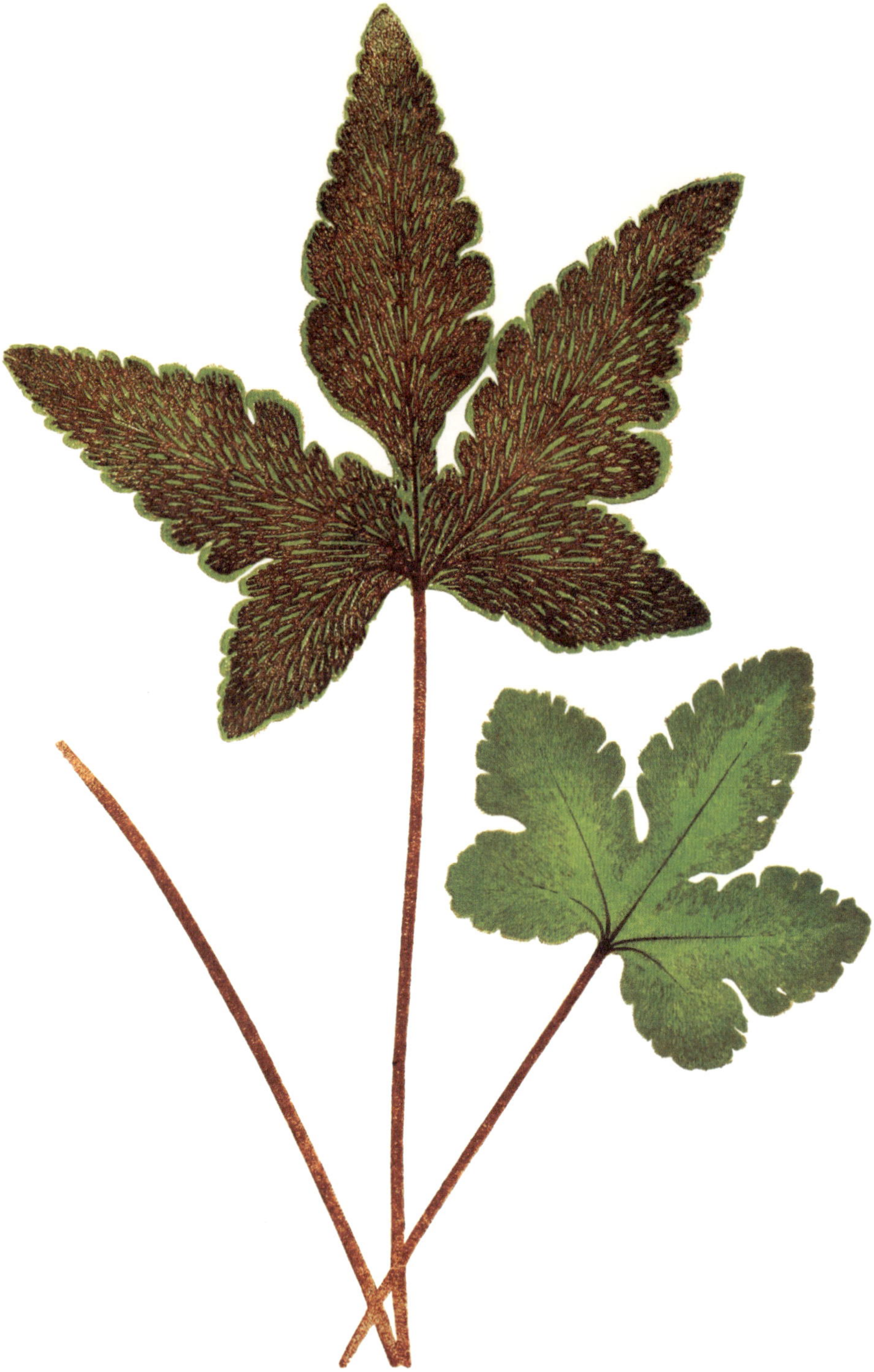

Hemionitis palmata
by Edward Joseph Lowe

star fern

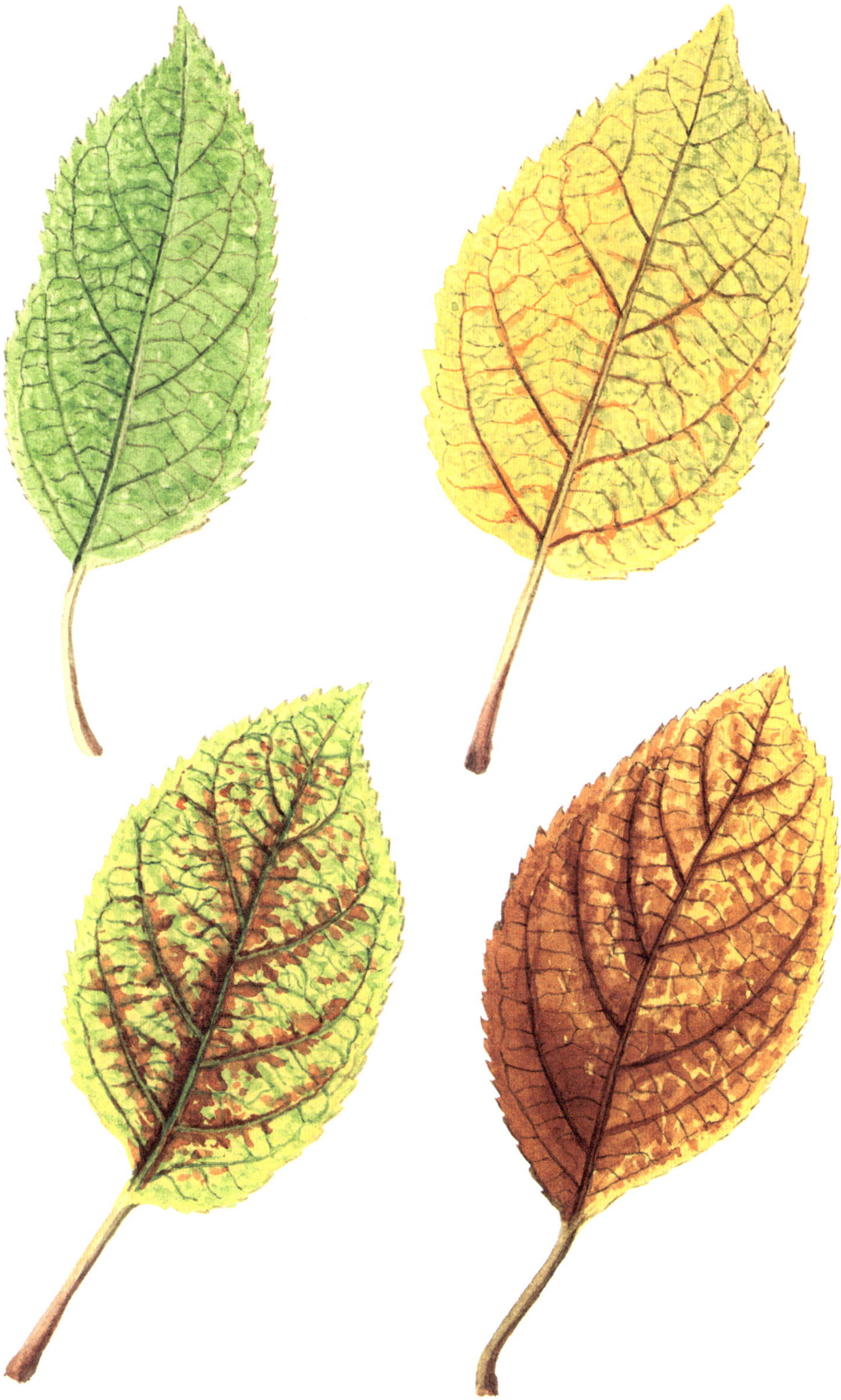

Malus domestica
by JAMES MARION SHULL

apple

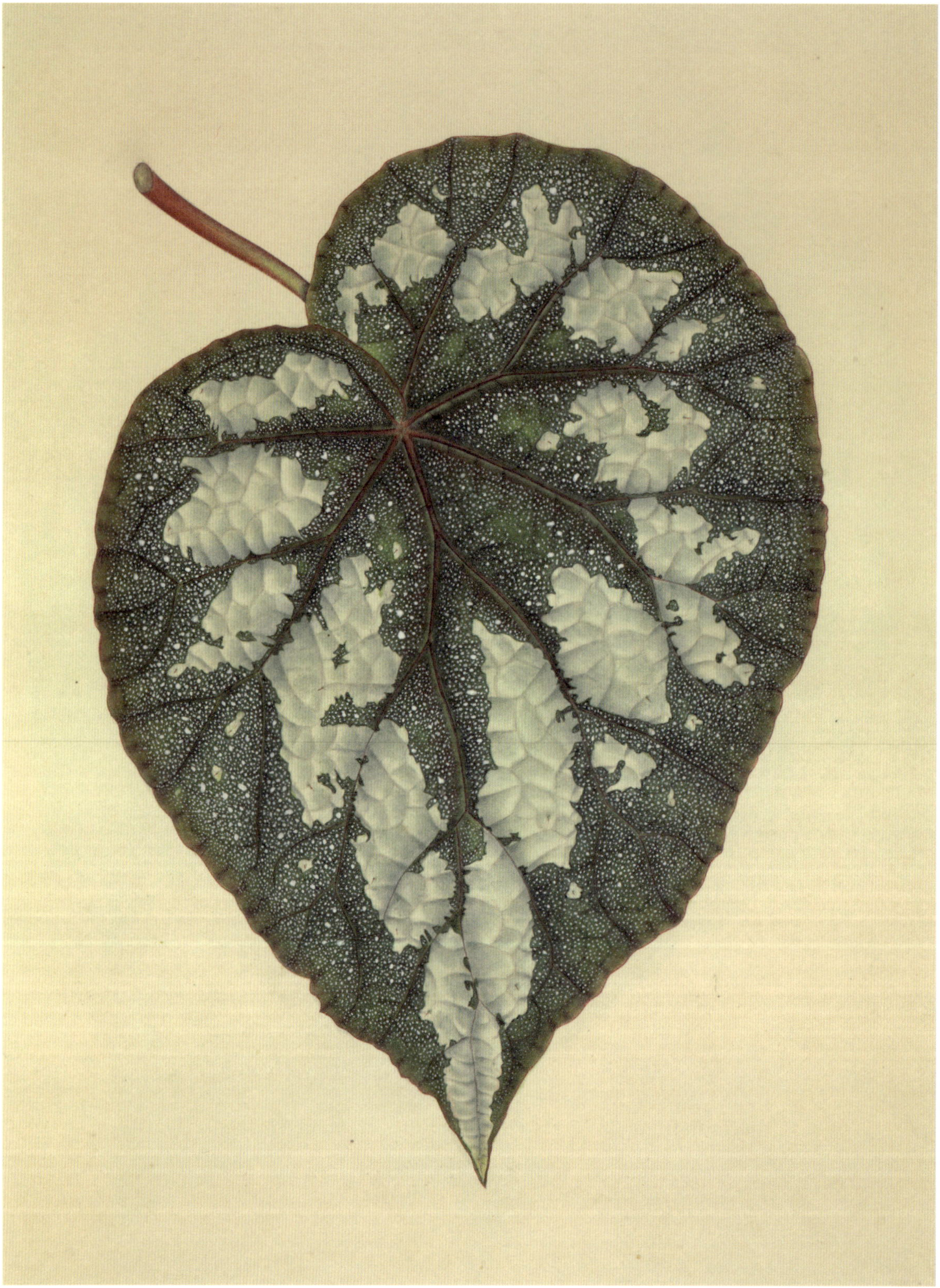

Begonia rex
by George De Alwis

king begonia | fancy-leaf begonia | painted-leaf begonia

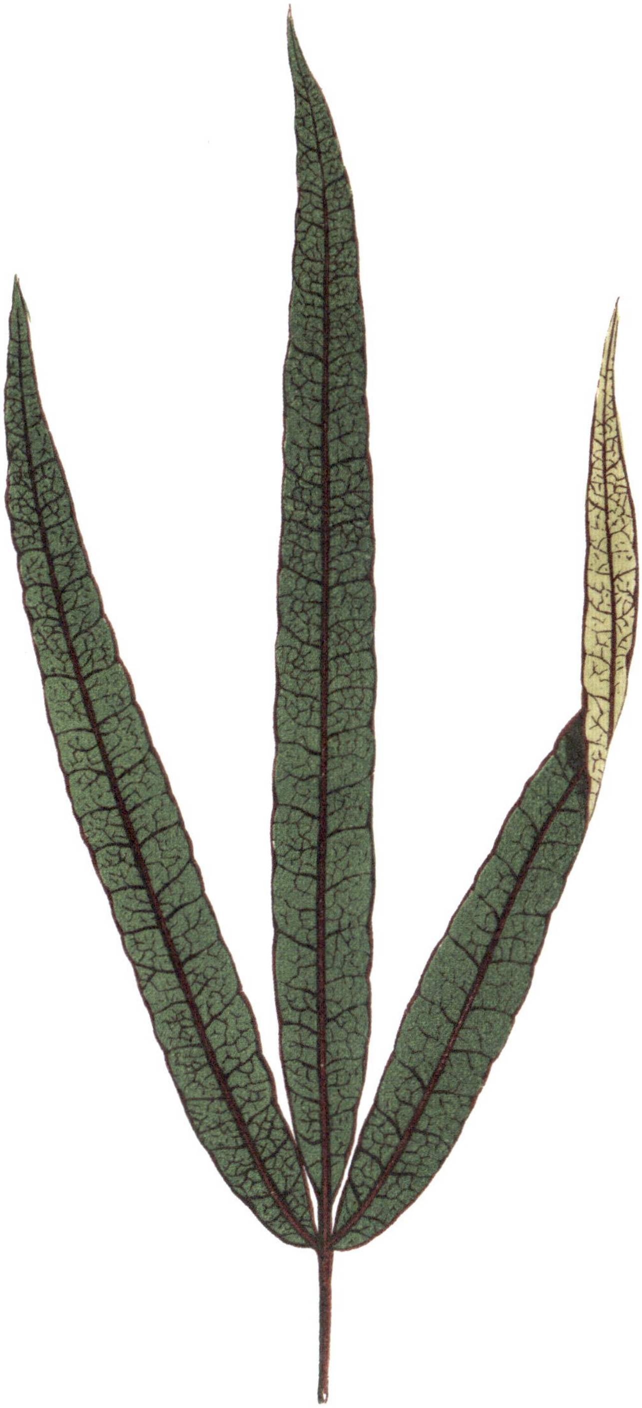

Pteris cretica
by Alexander Francis Lydon & Benjamin Fawcett

cretan brake fern

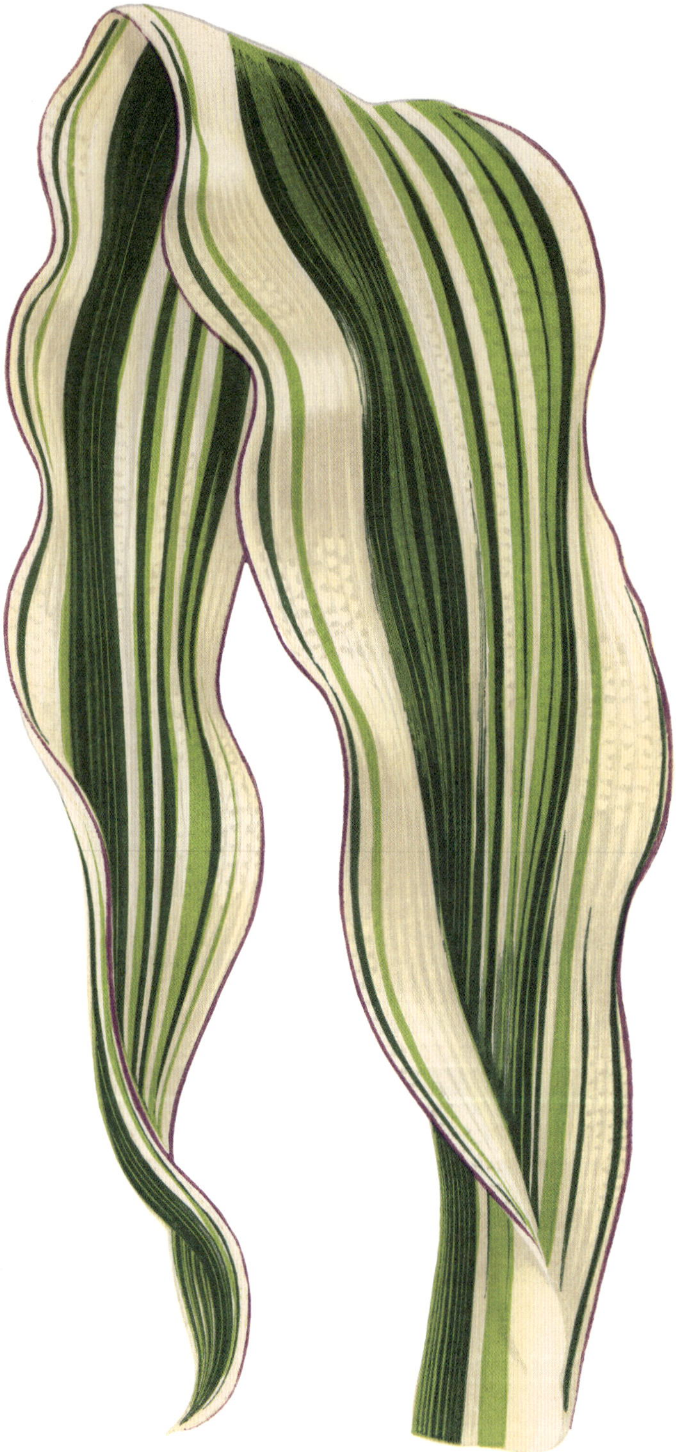

Zea mays var. *japonica*
by Alexander Francis Lydon & Benjamin Fawcett

Japanese maize

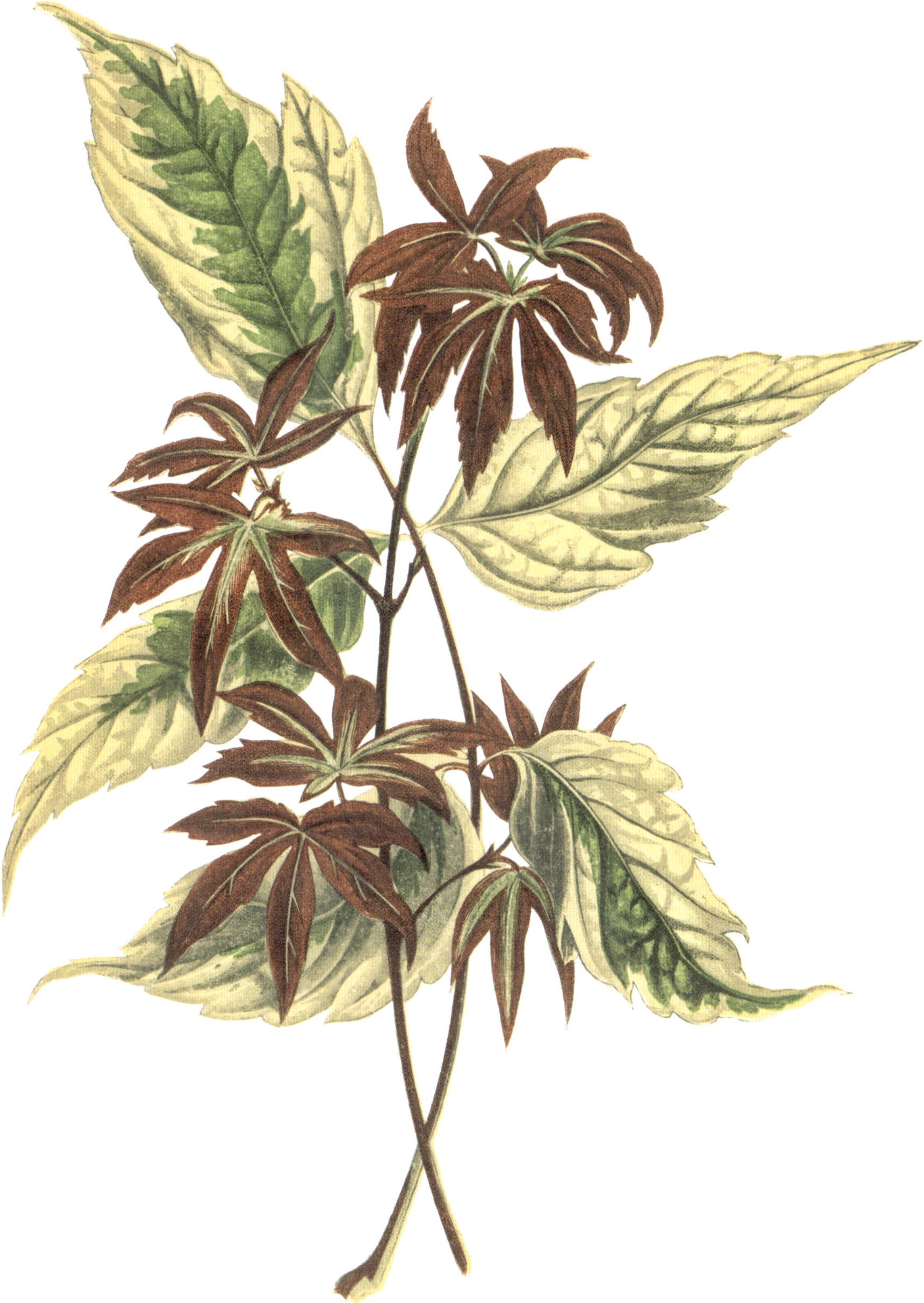

Acer
by Benjamin Fawcett & James Shirley Hibberd

maple (unknown variety)

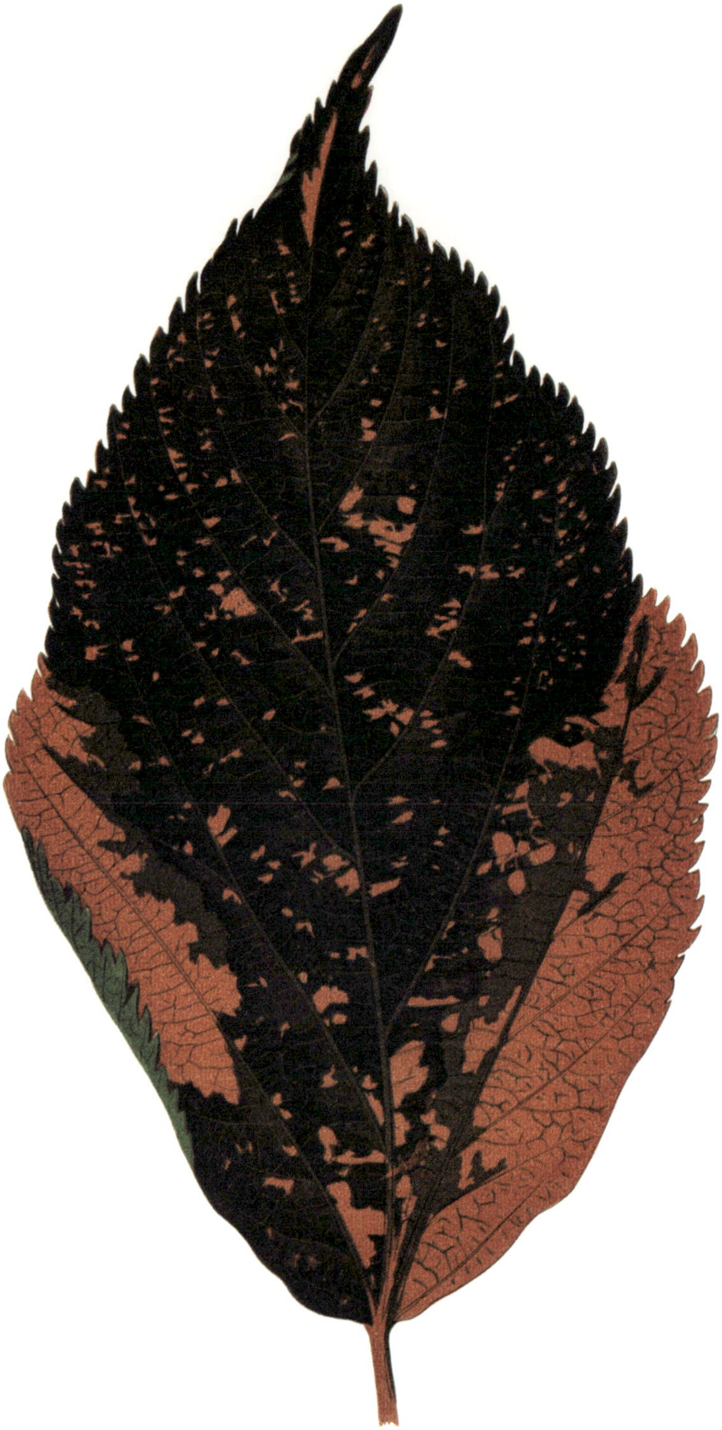

Acalypha wilkesiana
by Benjamin Fawcett & James Shirley Hibberd

copperleaf | Jacob's coat | flamengueira

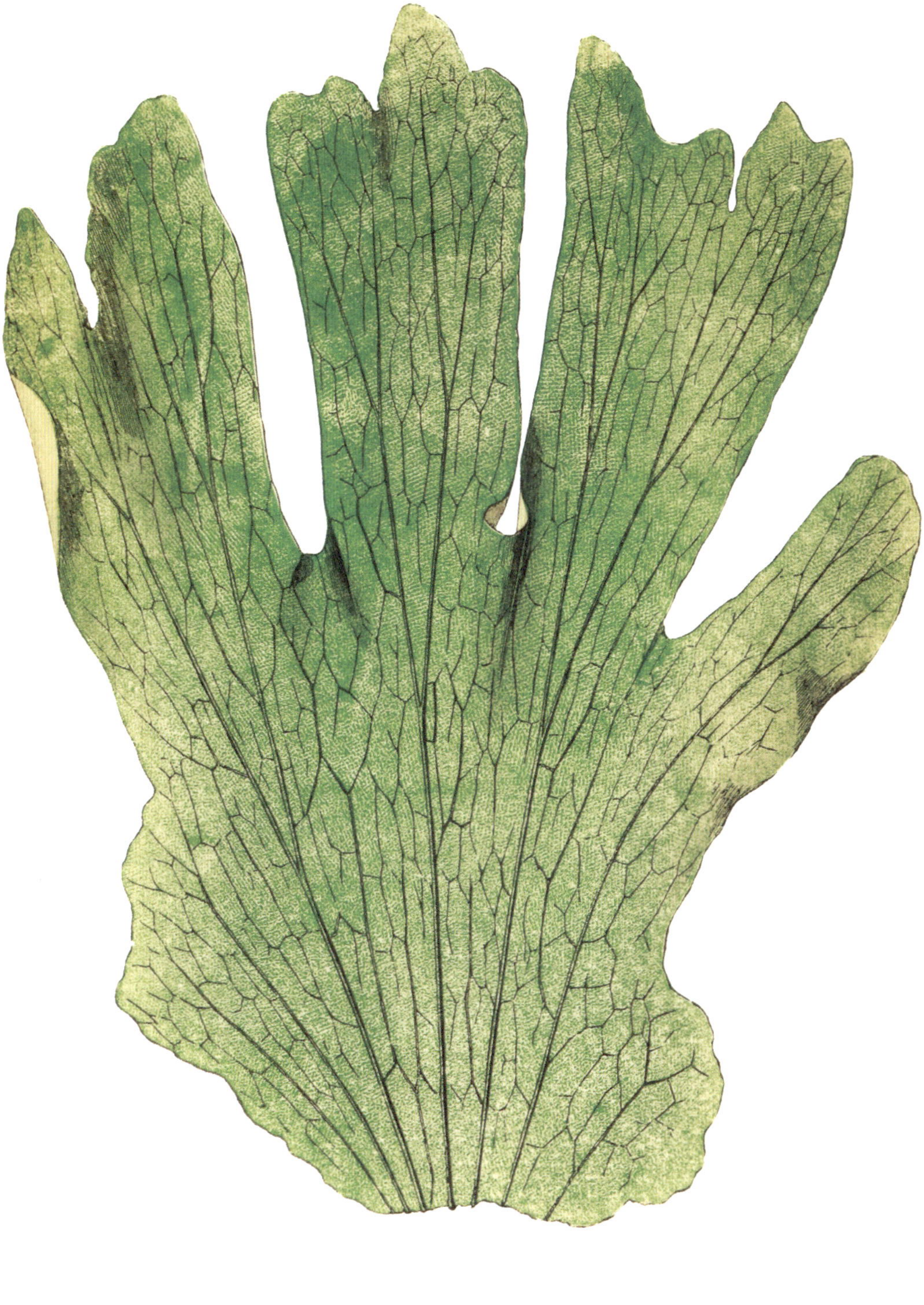

Platycerium grande
by Edward Joseph Lowe

giant staghorn fern

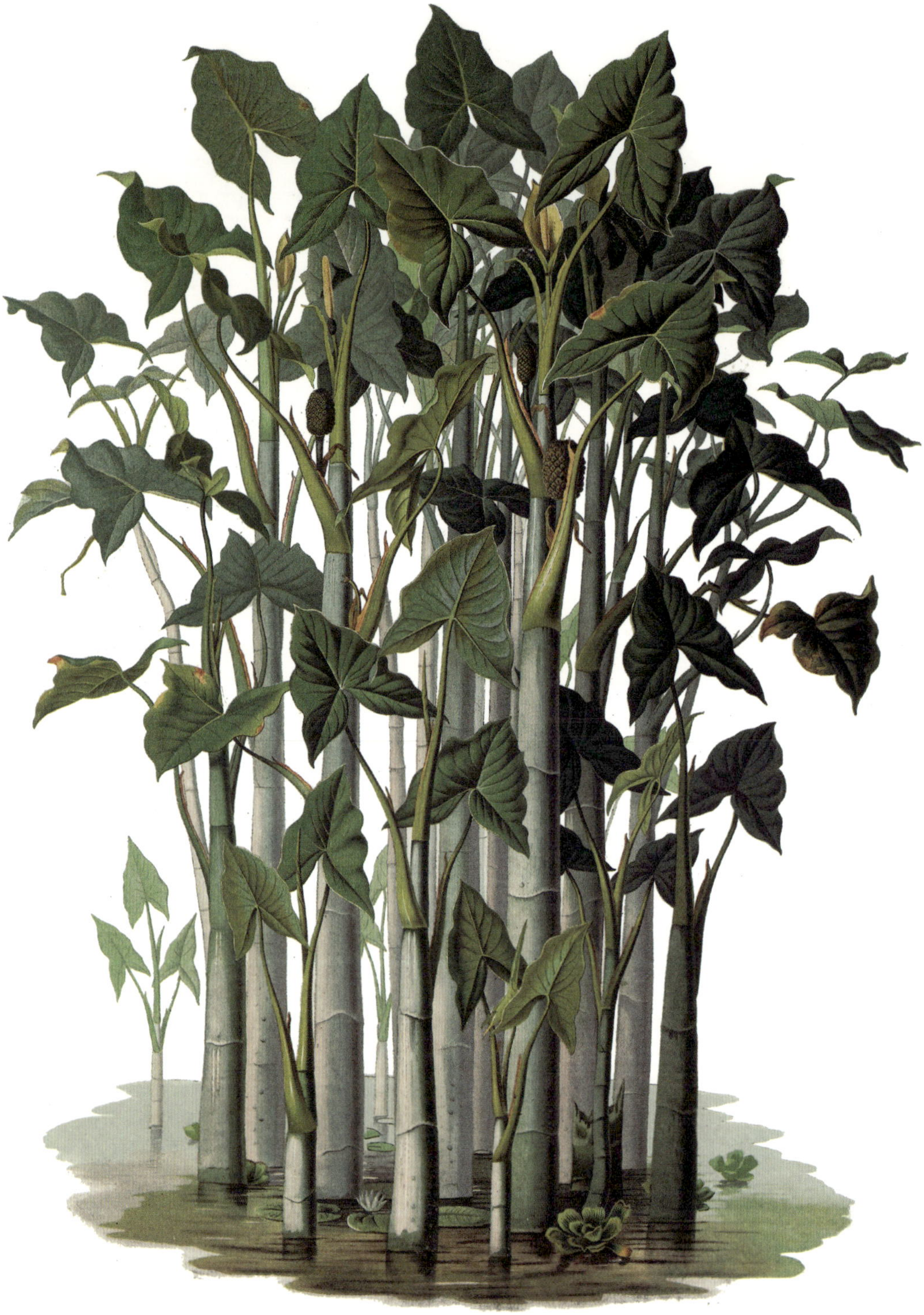

Montrichardia linifera
by HEINRICH WILHELM SCHOTT

aninga

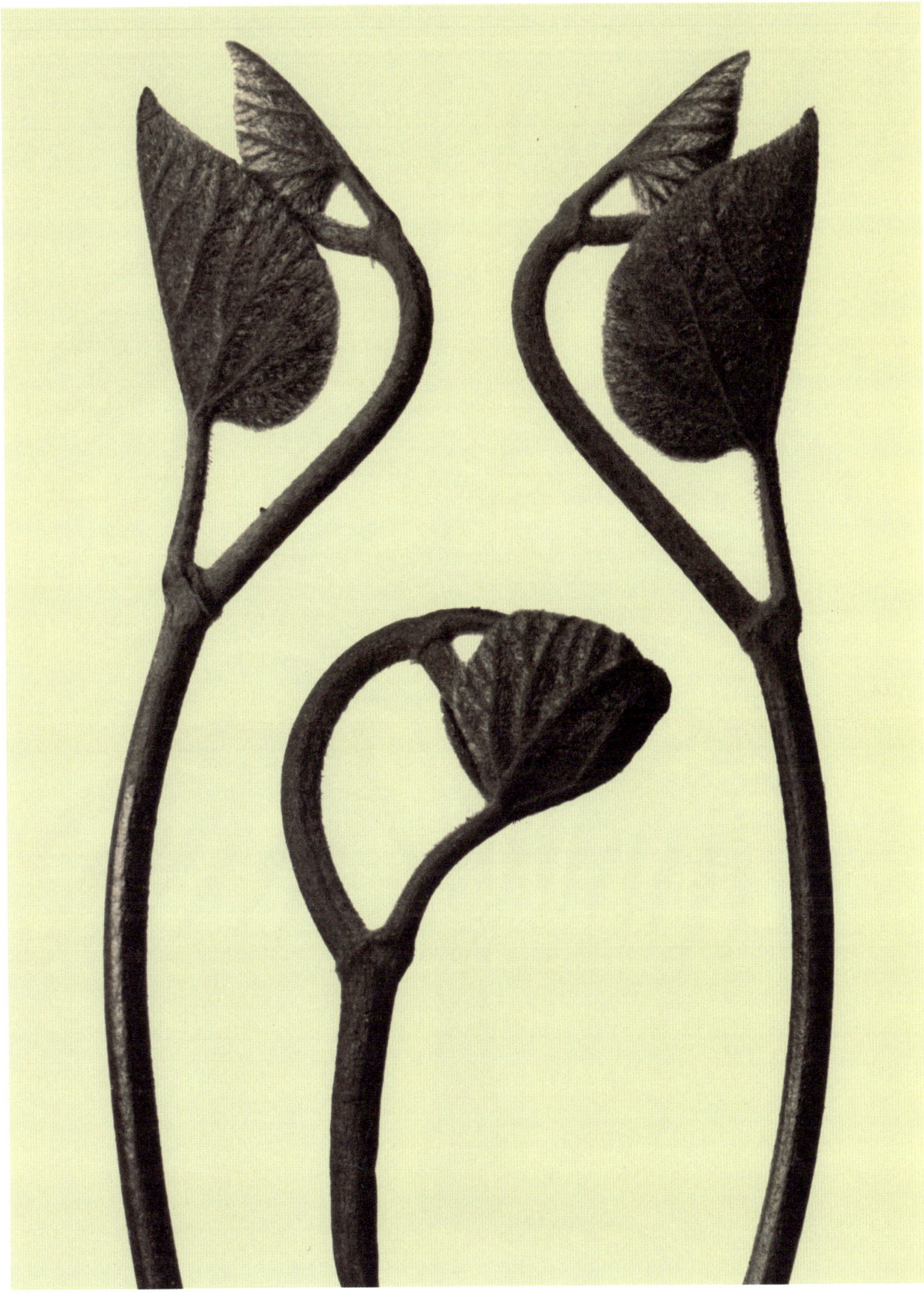

Aristolochia
by Karl Blossfeldt

aristolochia (unknown variety)

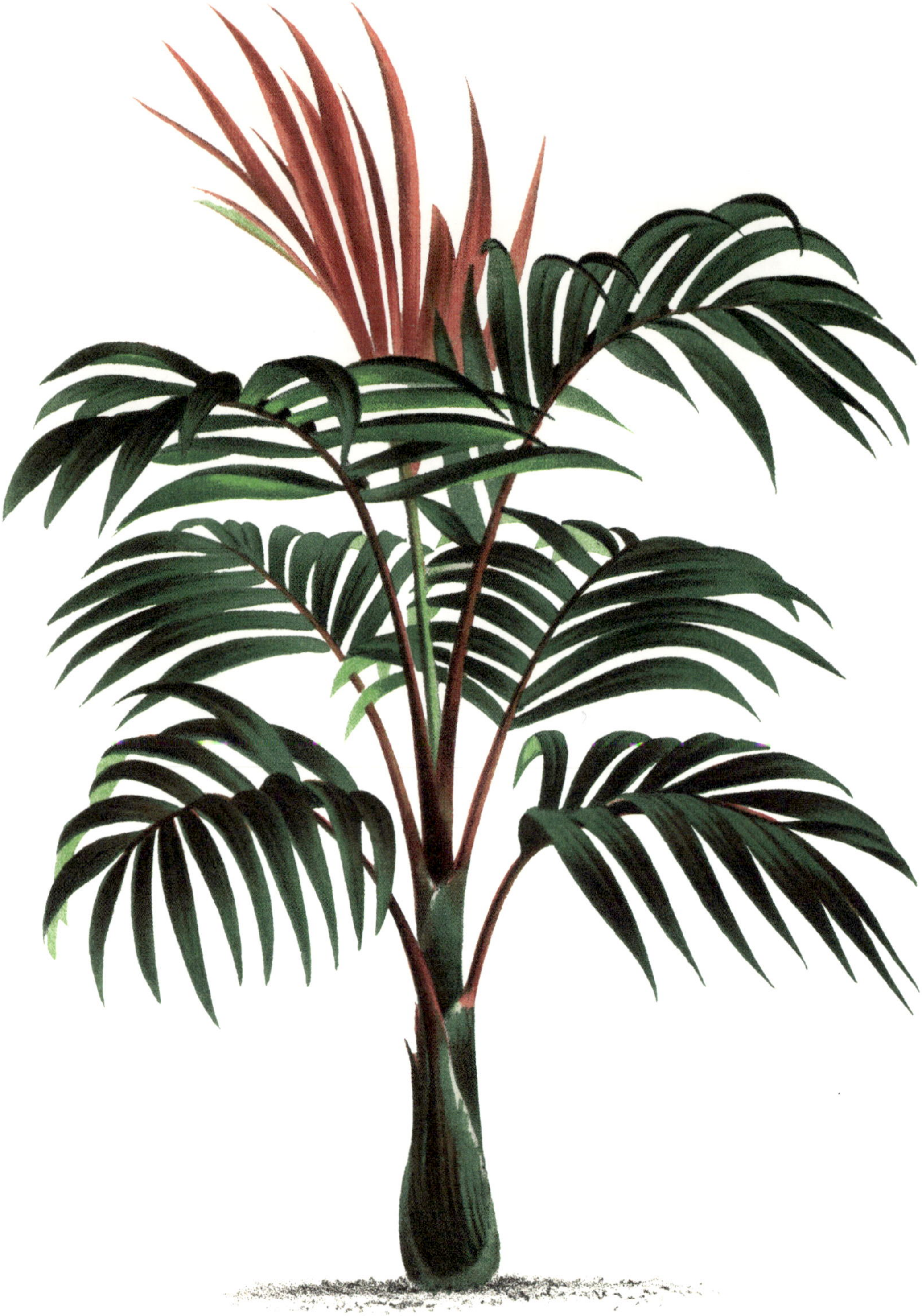

Chambeyronia macrocarpa
by Oswald de Kerchove de Denterghem

red leaf palm | flamethrower palm

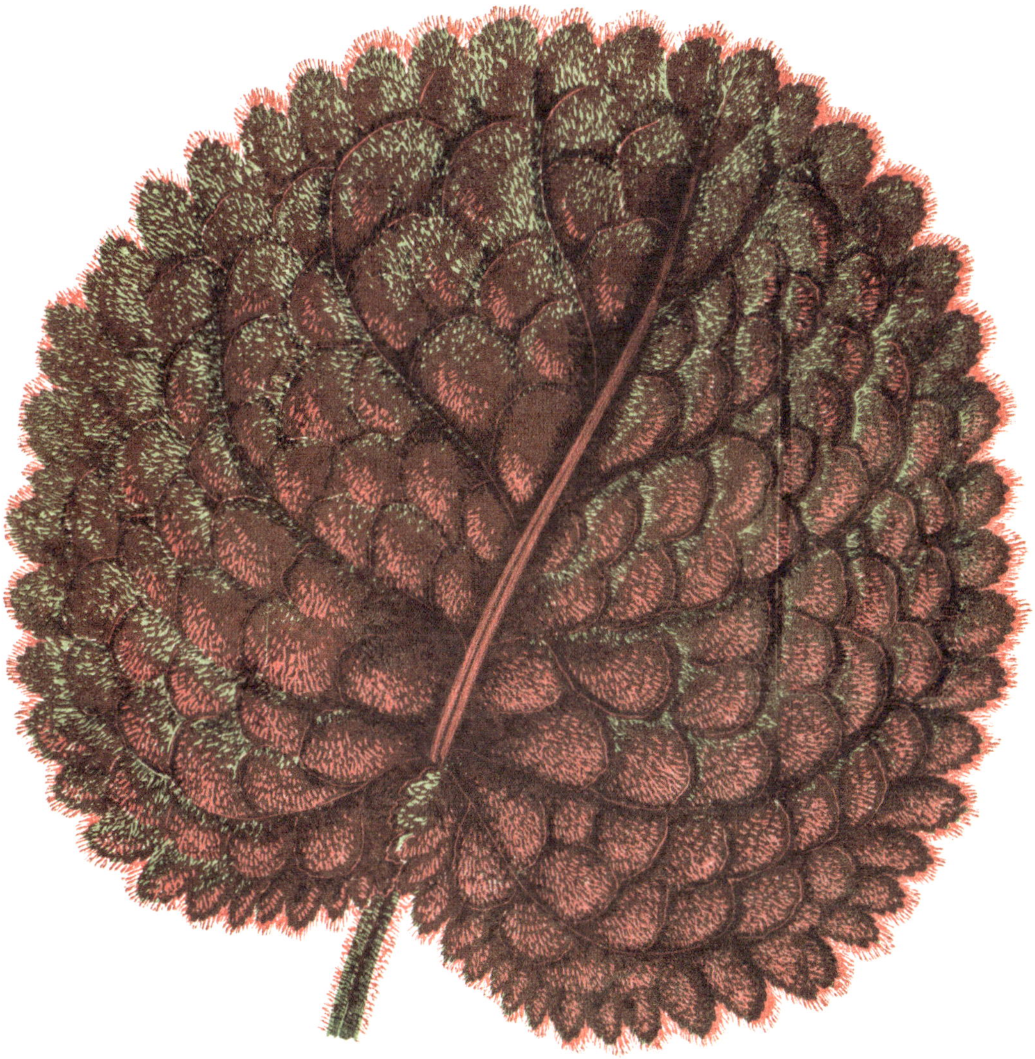

Ulmus glabra 'Exoniensis'
by BENJAMIN FAWCETT & JAMES SHIRLEY HIBBERD

Exeter elm

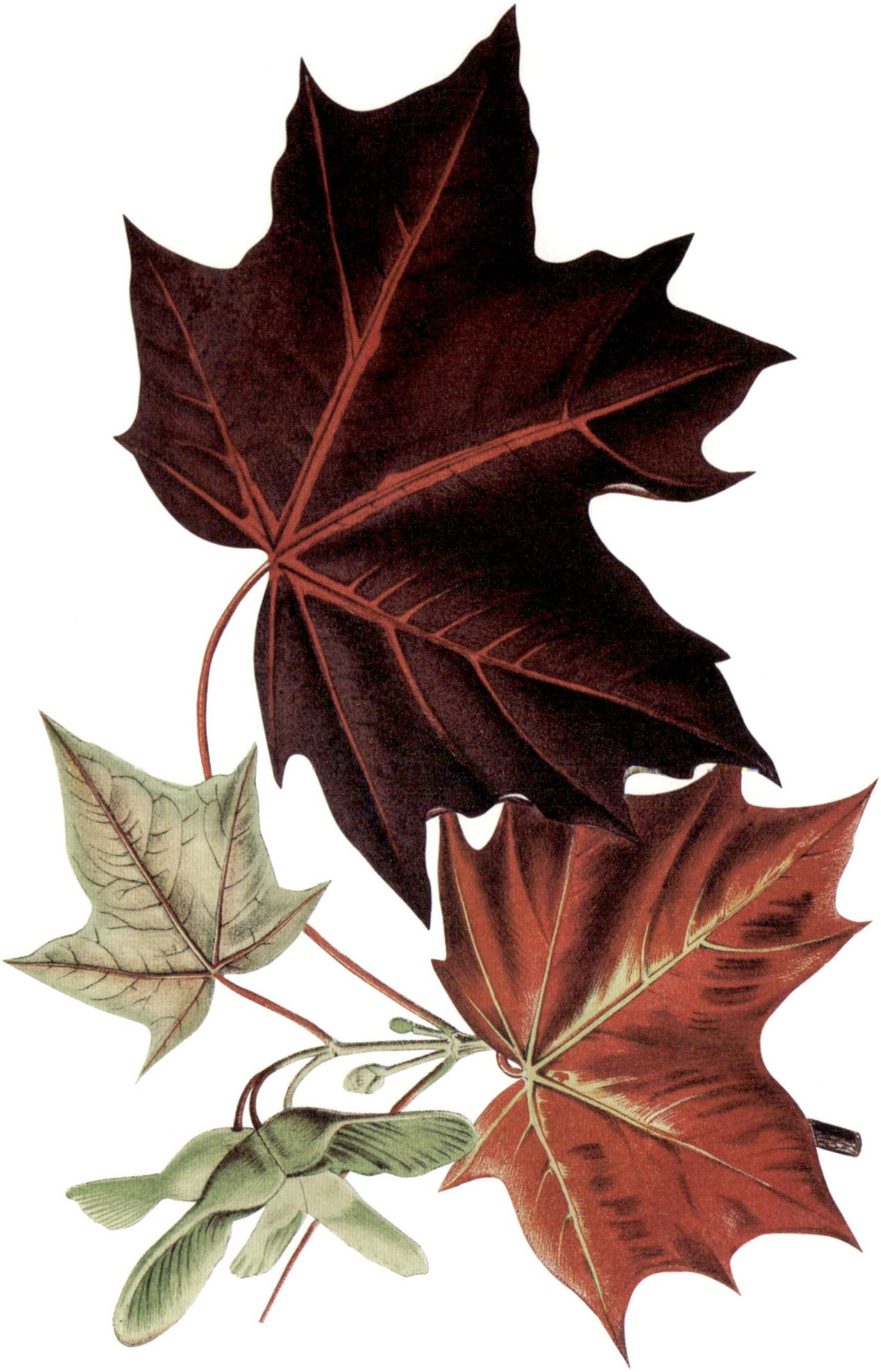

Acer rubrum
from Biodiversity Heritage Library

red maple

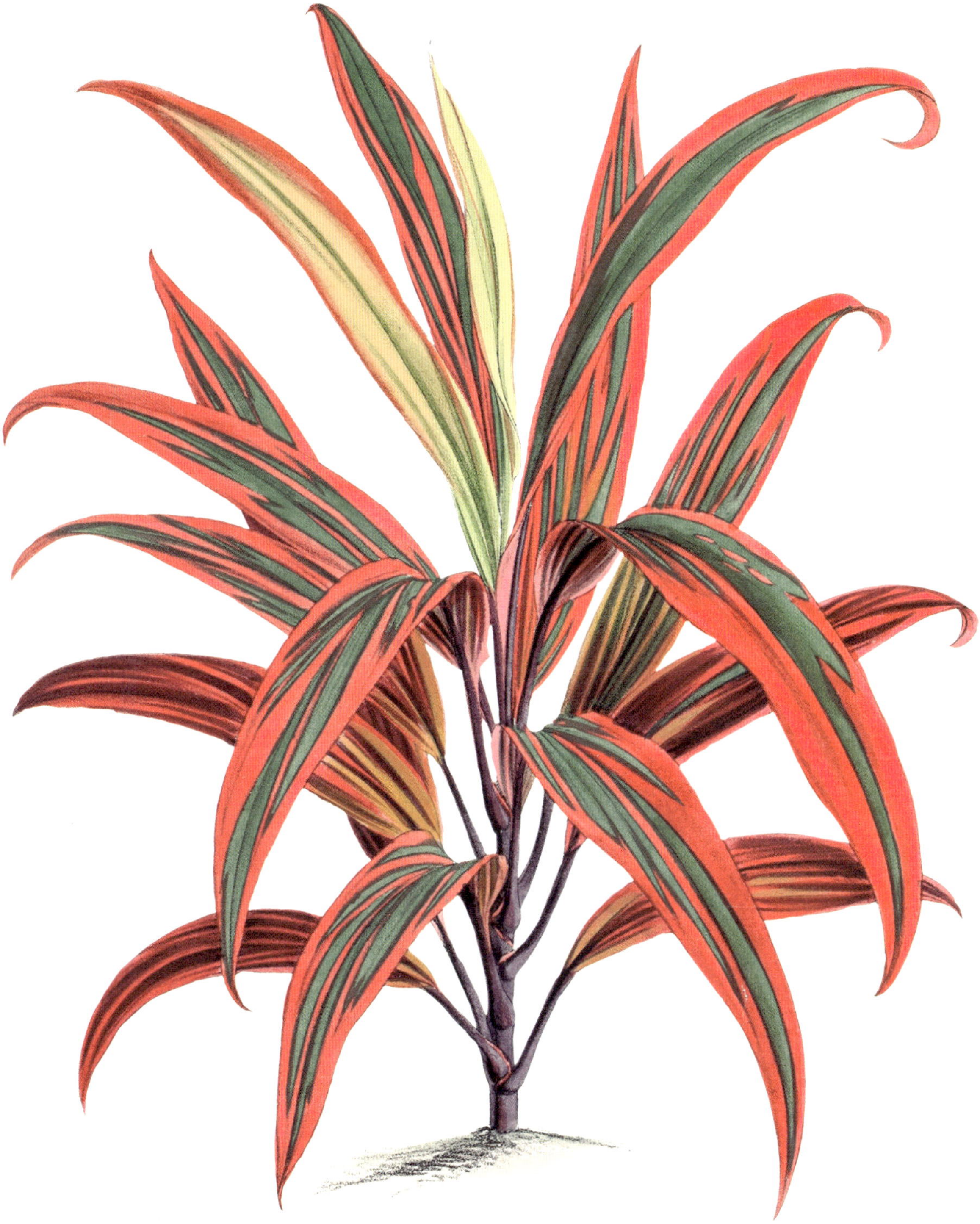

Cordyline fruticosa
from Biodiversity Heritage Library

ti plant | palm lily | cabbage palm

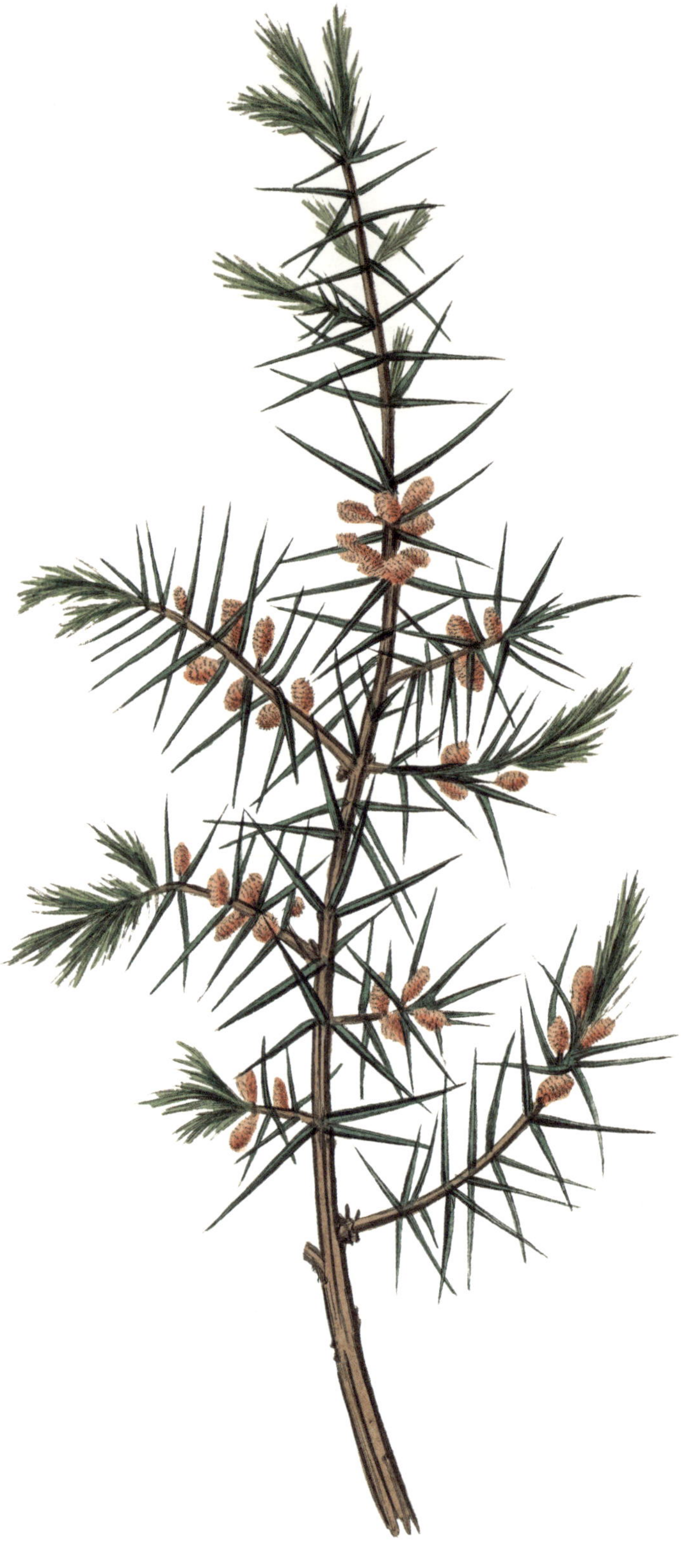

Juniperus communis
by John Stephenson & James Morss Churchill

common juniper

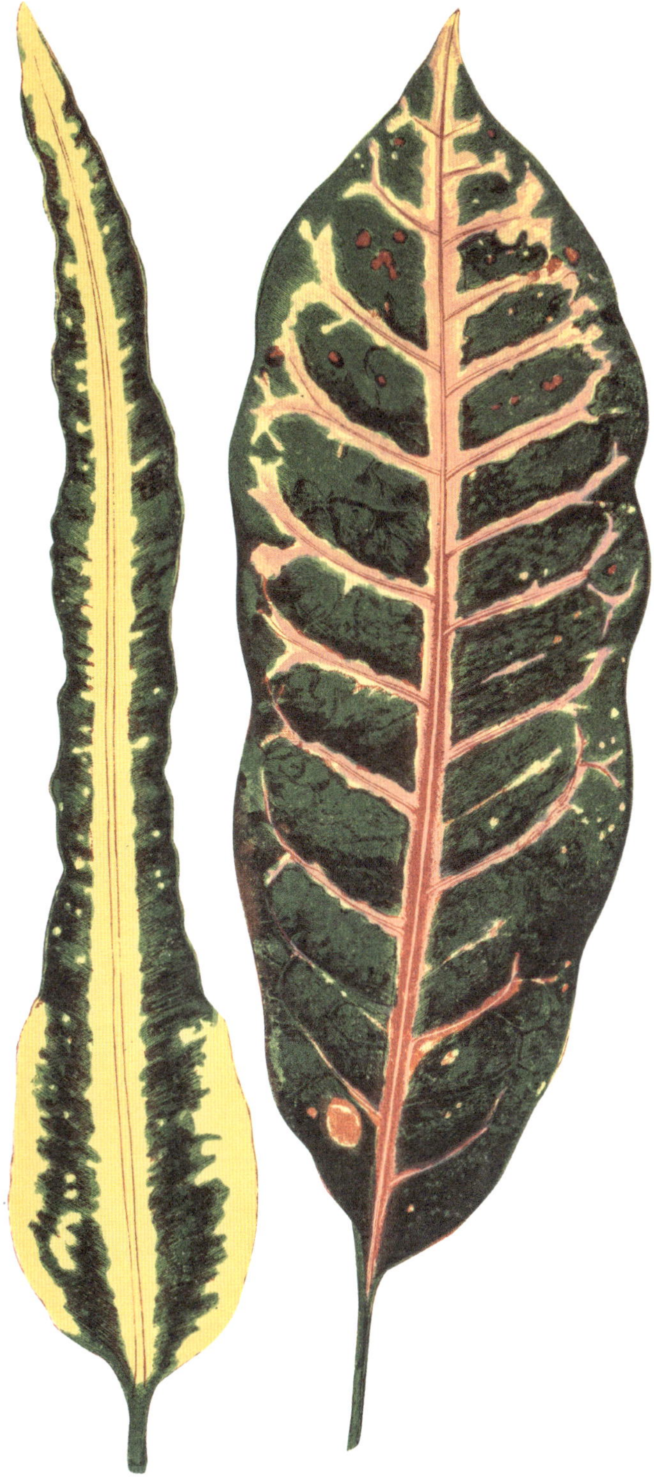

Codiaeum variegatum
by BENJAMIN FAWCETT & JAMES SHIRLEY HIBBERD

croton | variegated croton | garden croton | Joseph's coat

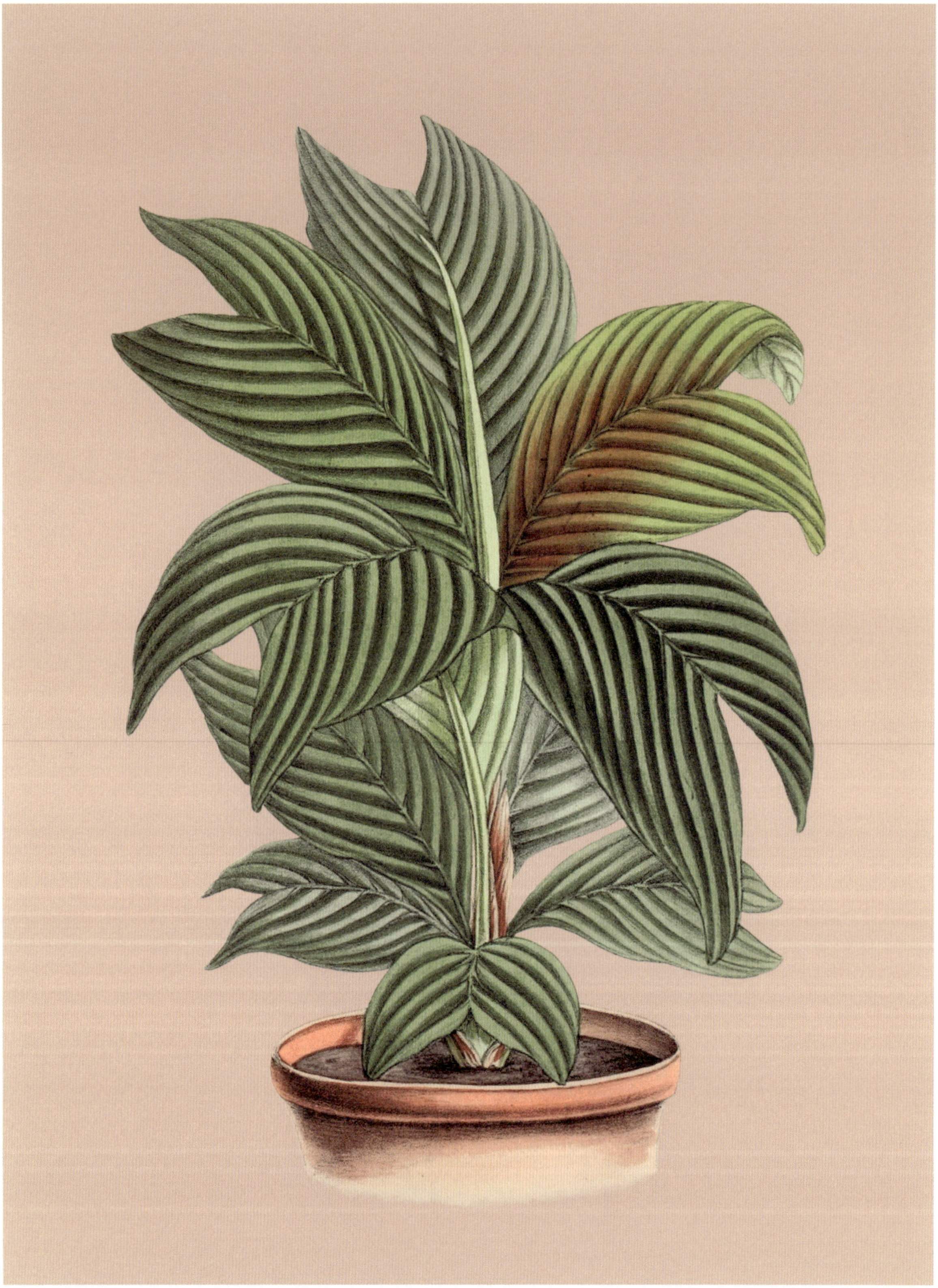

Goeppertia orbifolia
from Biodiversity Heritage Library

orb-leafed prayer plant | orbifolia calathea

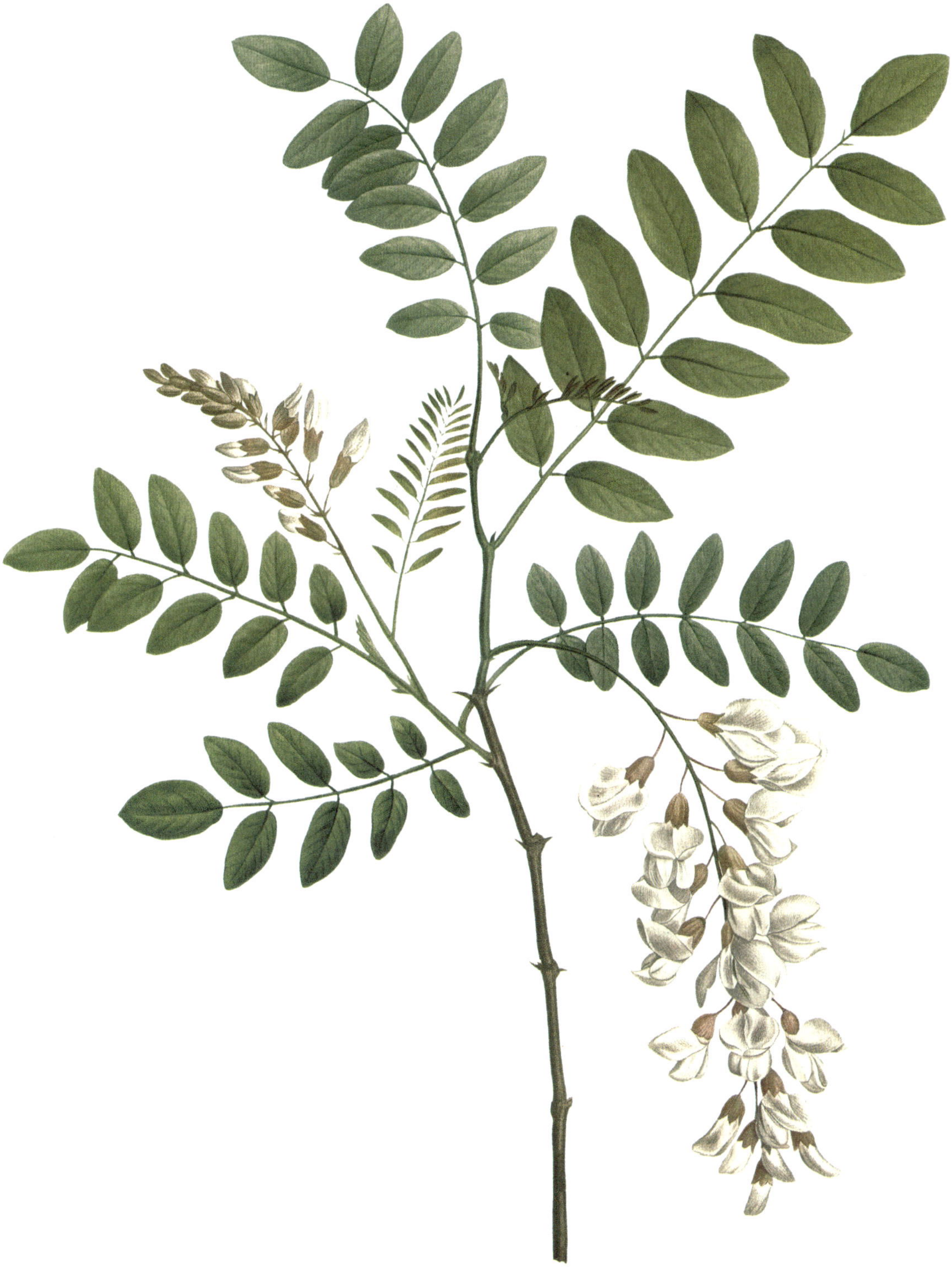

Robinia pseudoacacia
by Pierre-Joseph Redouté

black locust

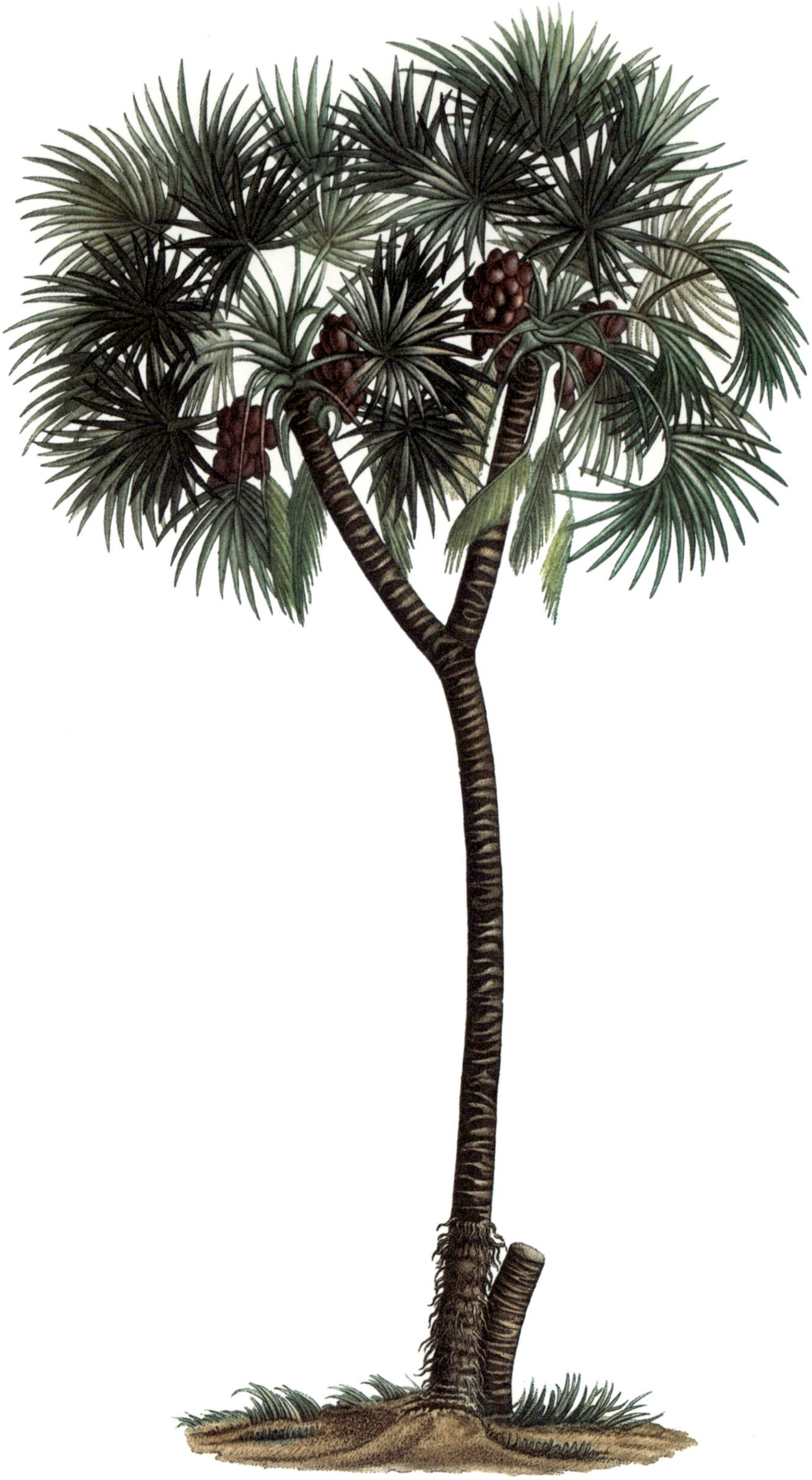

Phoenix dactylifera
by Pierre-Joseph Redouté

date palm

Palm-tree: single-legged giant,
topping other trees,
peering at the firmament –
It longs to pierce the black cloud-ceiling
and fly away, away,
if only it had wings.

The tree seems to express its wish
in the tossing of its head:
its fronds heave and swish –
It thinks, Maybe my leaves are feathers,
and nothing stops me now
from rising on their flutter.

FROM 'Palm Tree' BY RABINDRANATH TAGORE

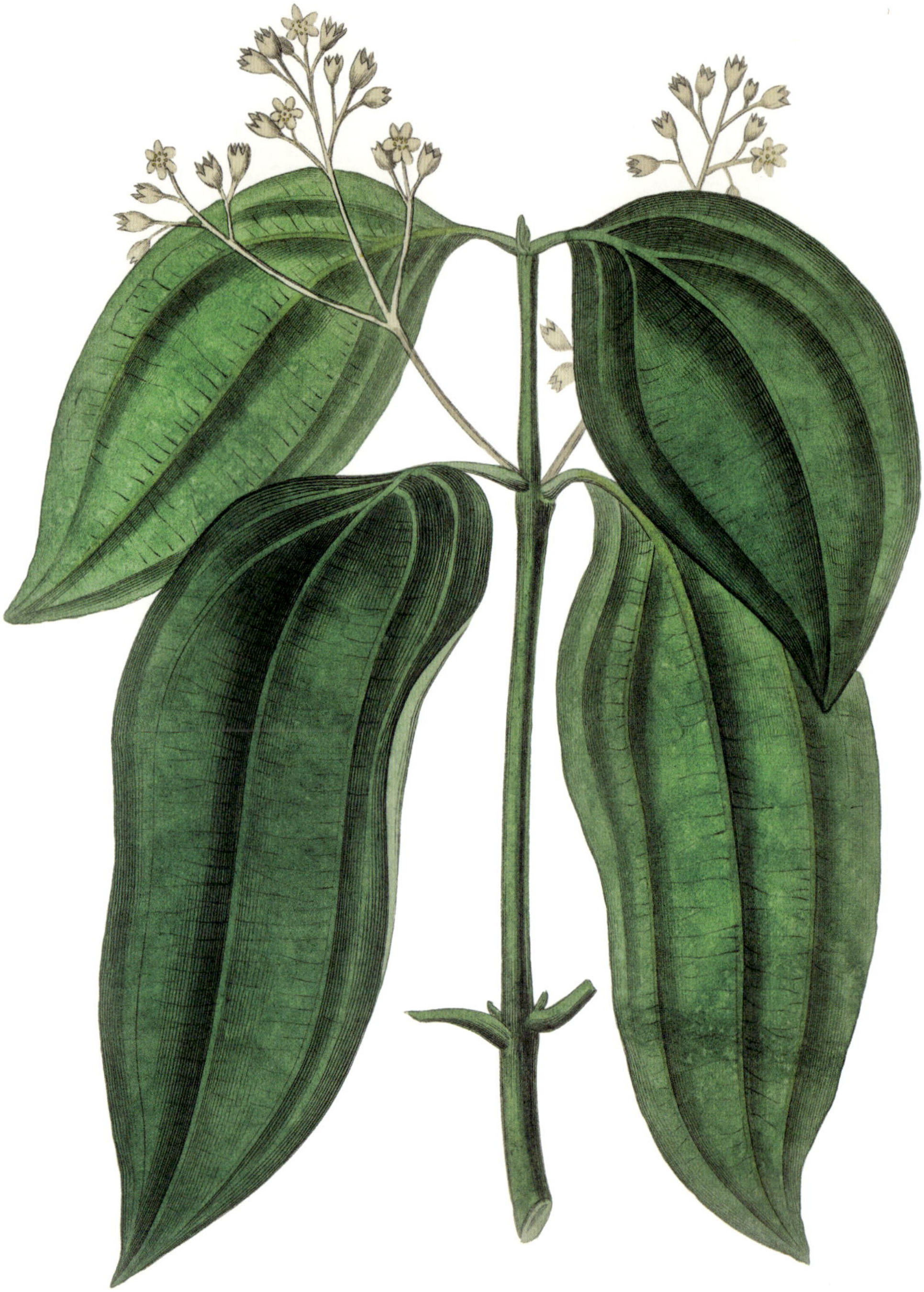

Cinnamomum verum
by JOHN STEPHENSON & JAMES MORSS CHURCHILL

true cinnamon | Ceylon cinnamon

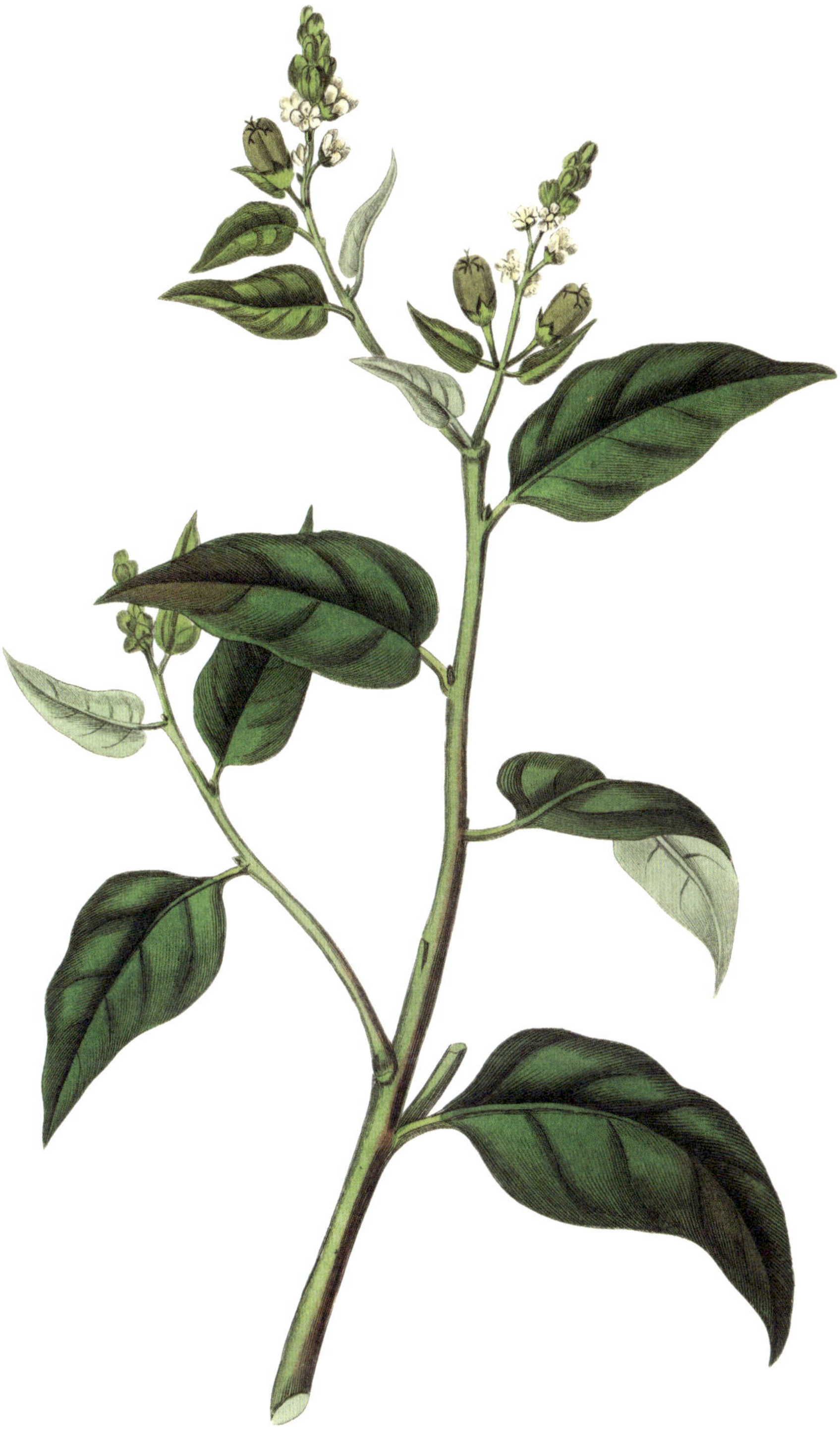

Croton eluteria
by John Stephenson & James Morss Churchill

cascarilla

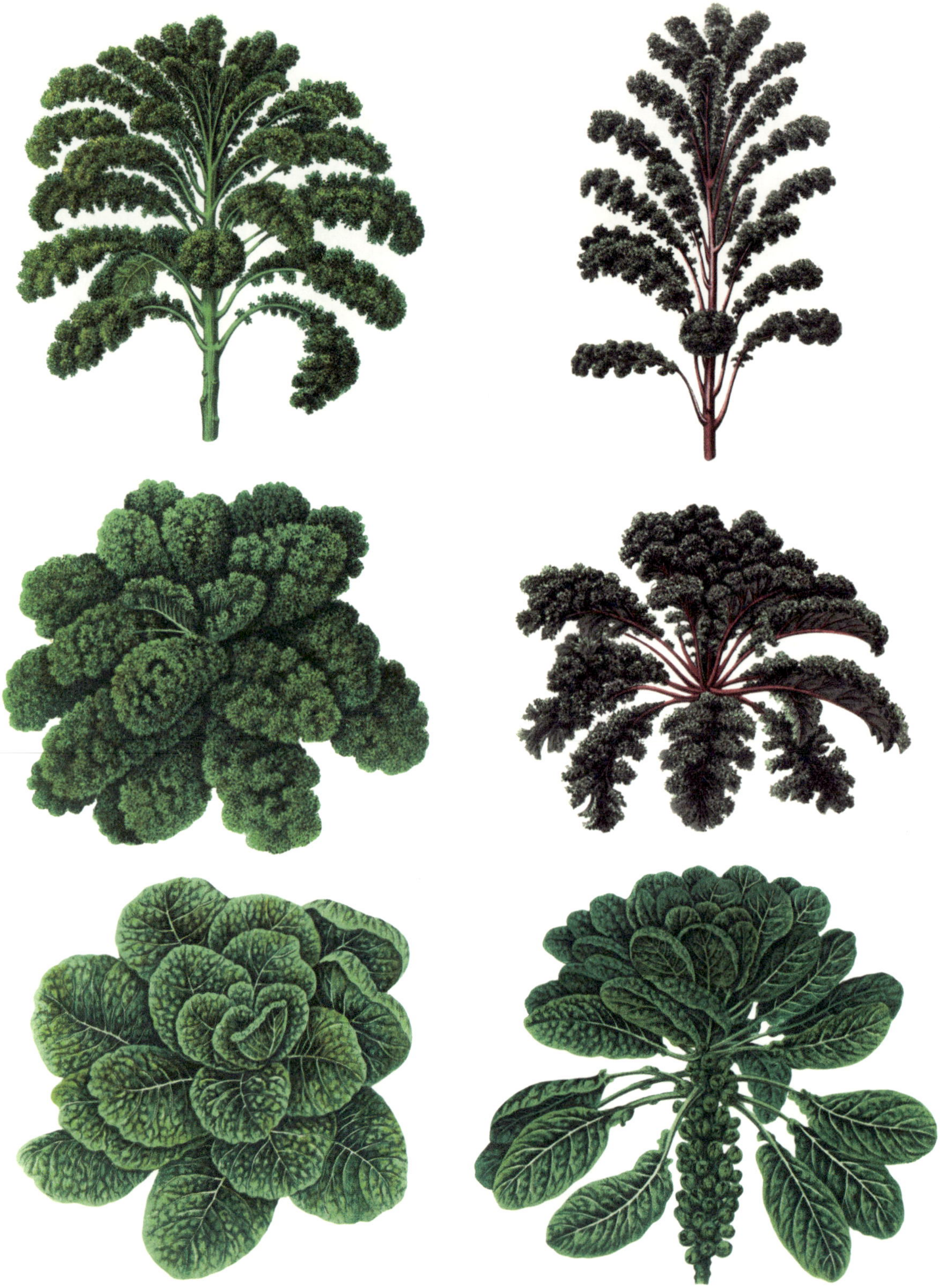

Brassicaceae
by Ernst Benary

brassica (various)

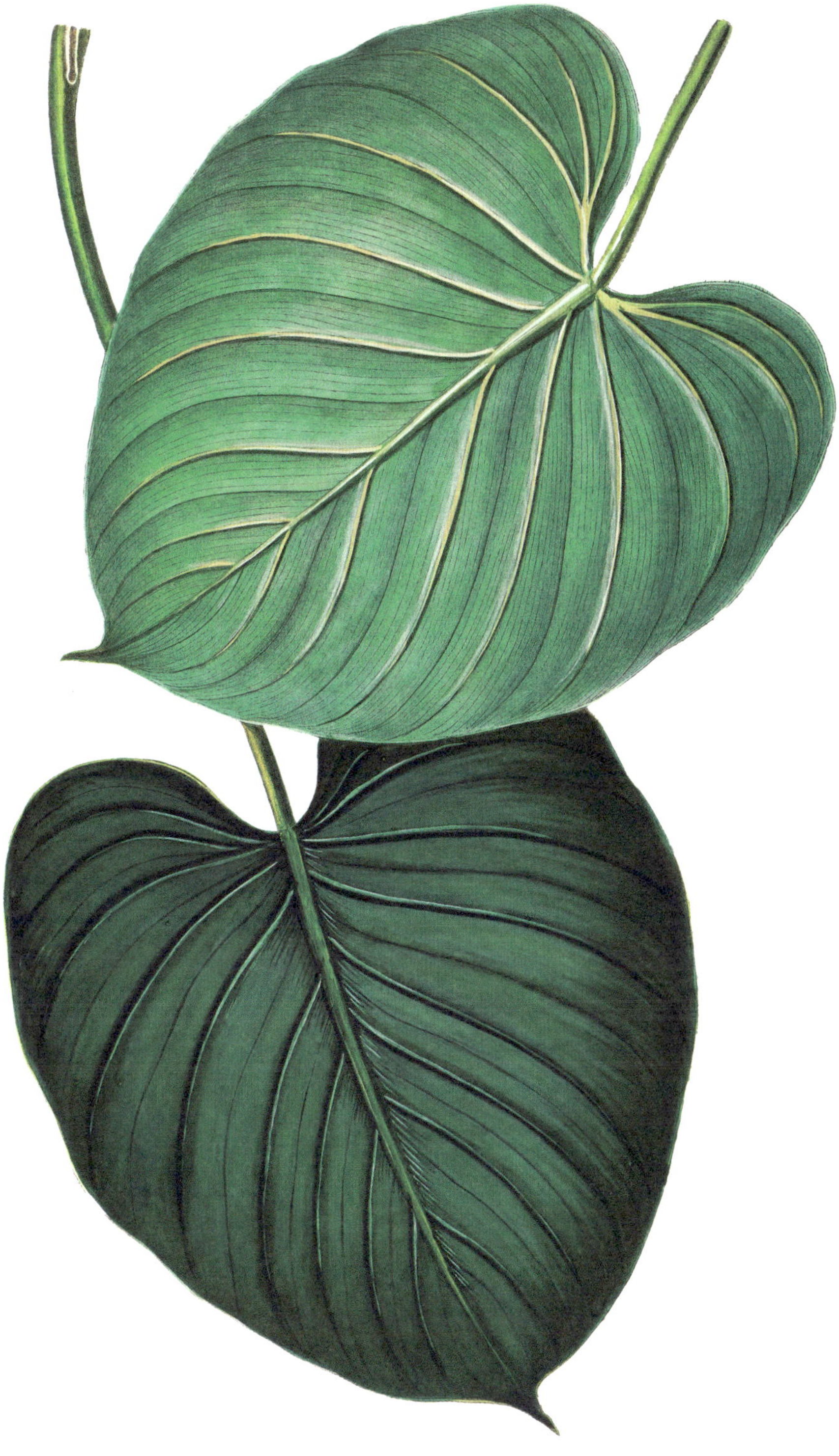

Philodendron eximium
by Heinrich Wilhelm Schott

philodendron eximium

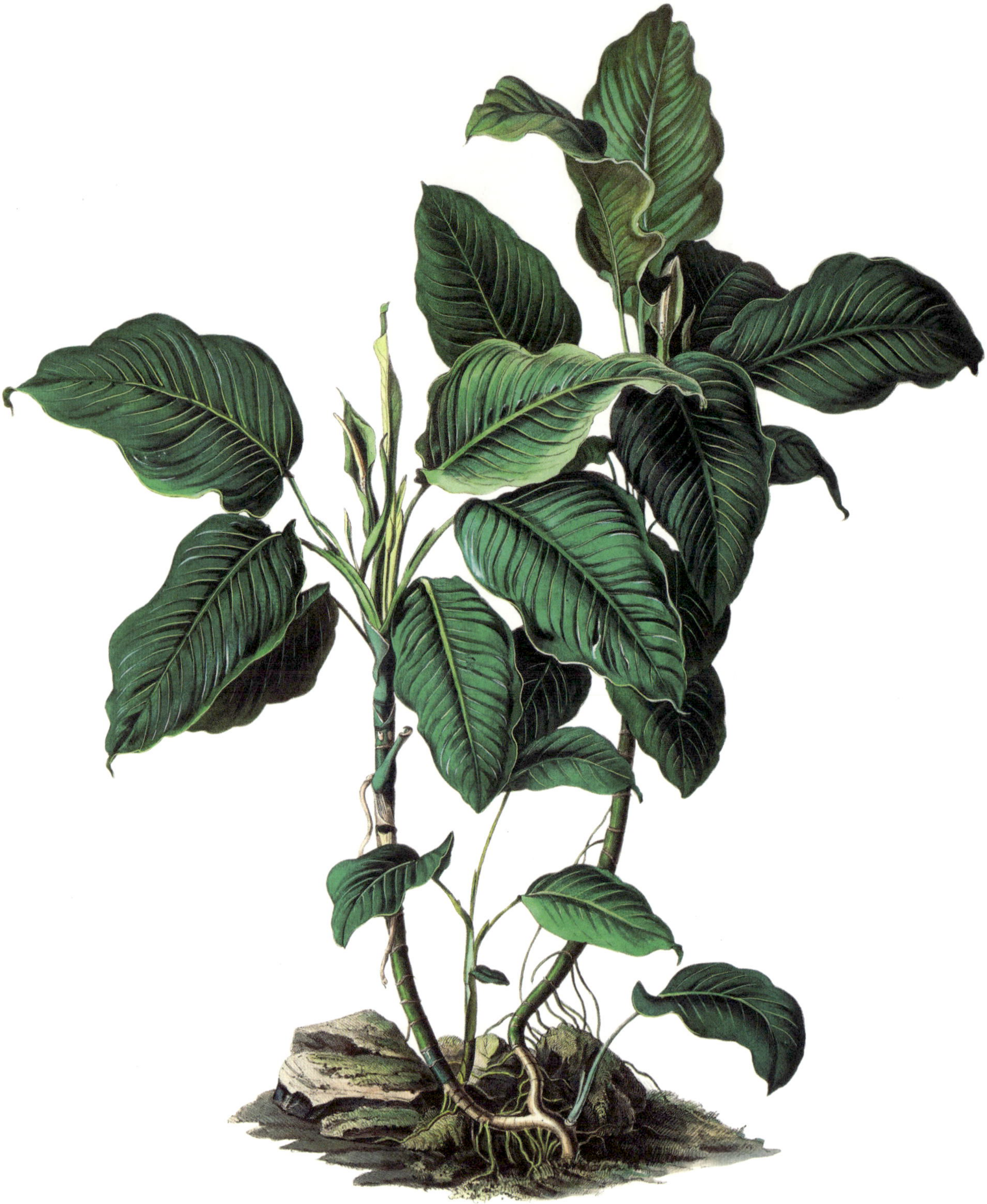

Dieffenbachia macrophylla
by Heinrich Wilhelm Schott

dumb cane

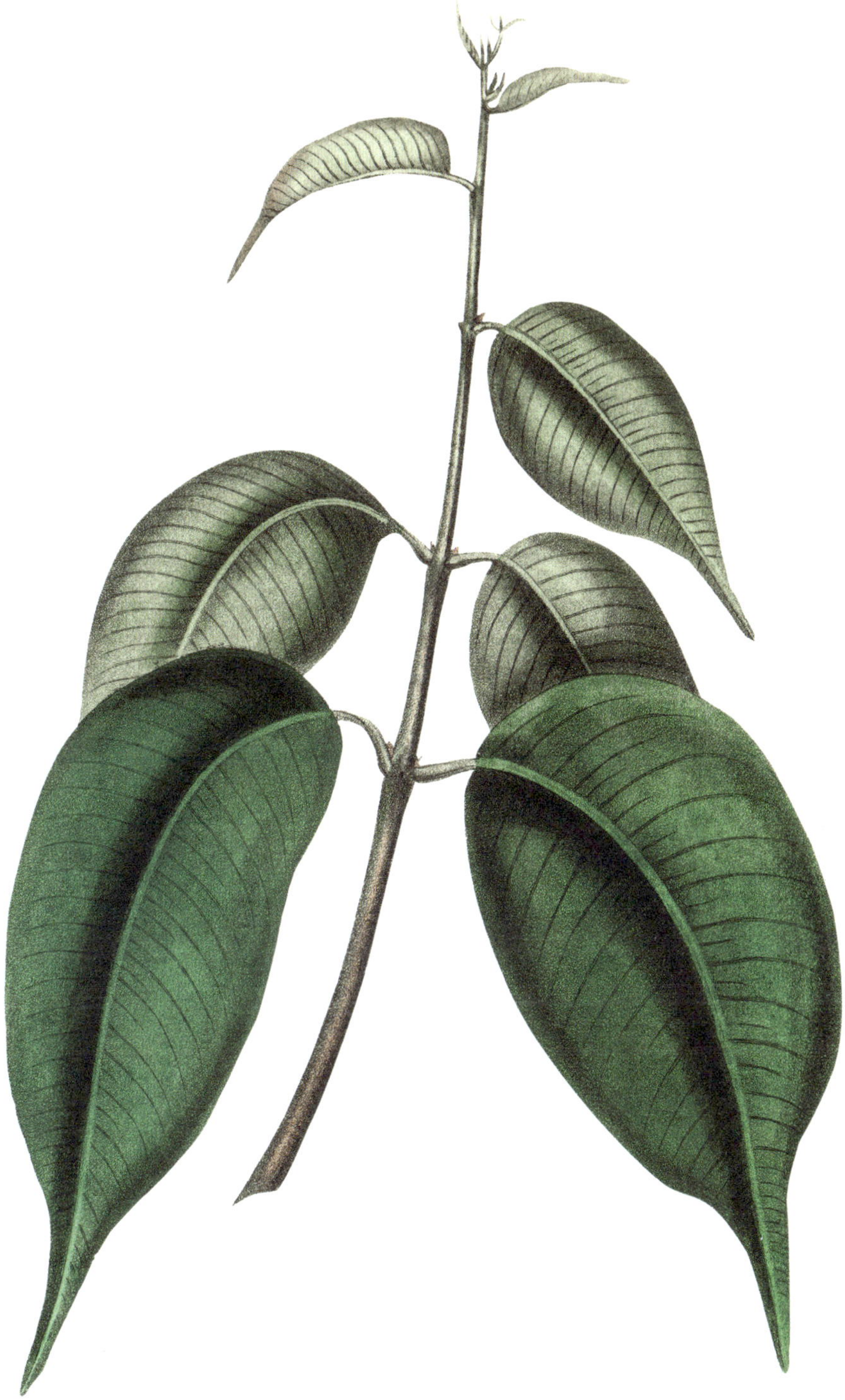

Dryobalanops aromatica
by John Stephenson & James Morss Churchill

Borneo camphor | camphor tree | Malay camphor | Sumatran camphor

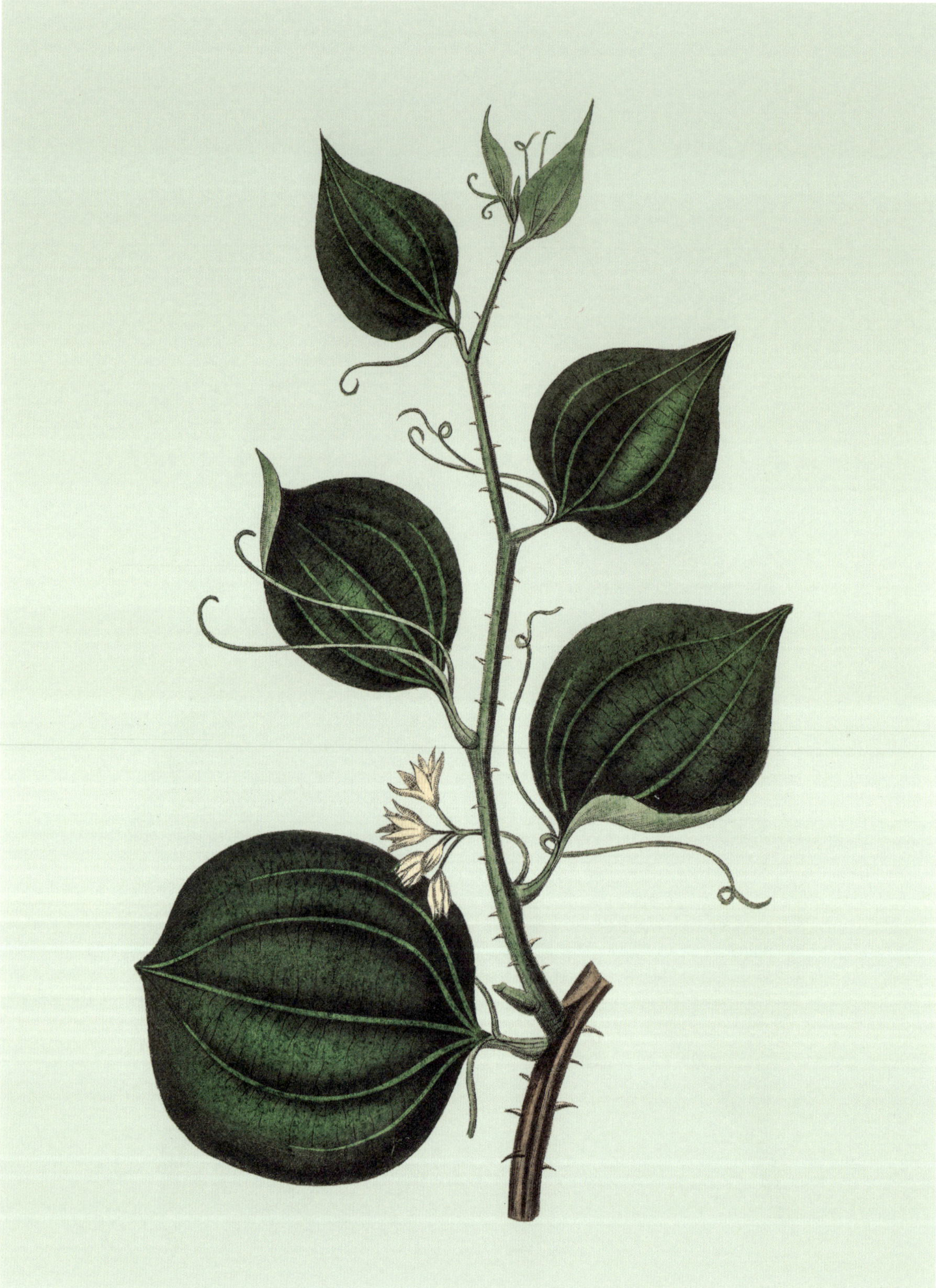

Smilax ornata
by John Stephenson & James Morss Churchill

sarsaparilla | Honduran sarsaparilla | Jamaican sarsaparilla | West African sarsaparilla

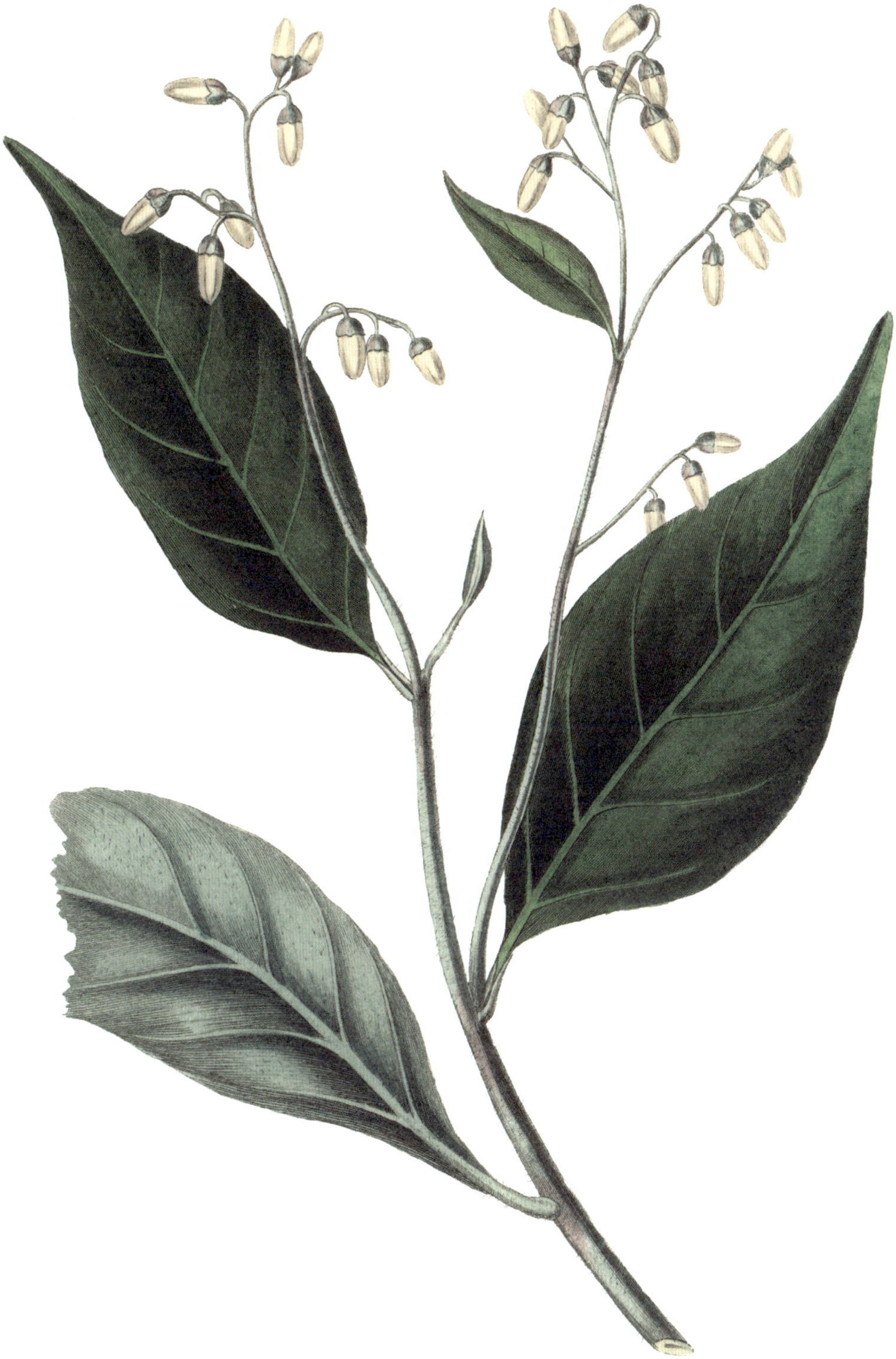

Styrax benzoin
by JOHN STEPHENSON & JAMES MORSS CHURCHILL

gum benjamin tree | benzoin | Sumatra benzoin tree

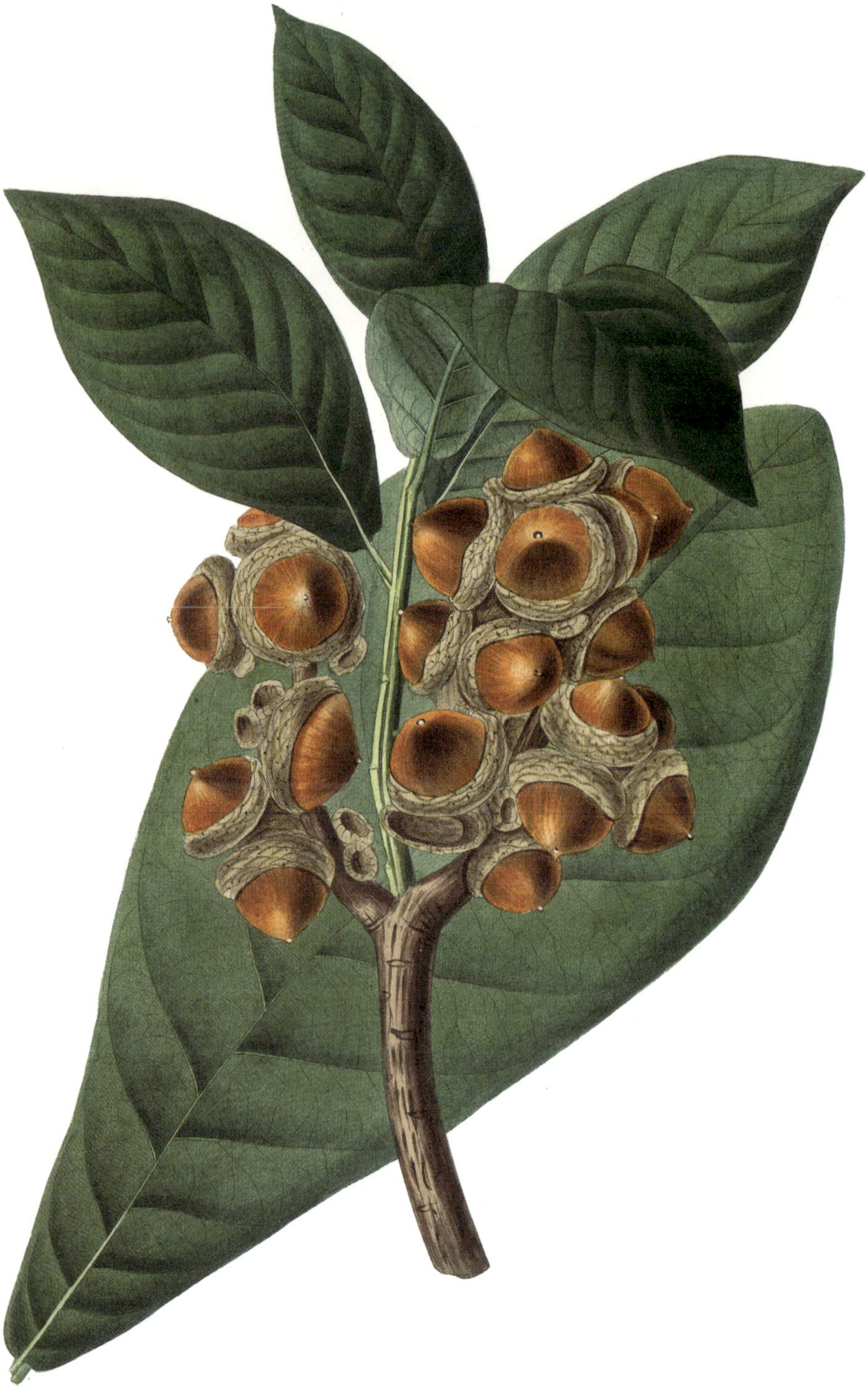

Lithocarpus elegans
by Aylmer Bourke Lambert

spike oak

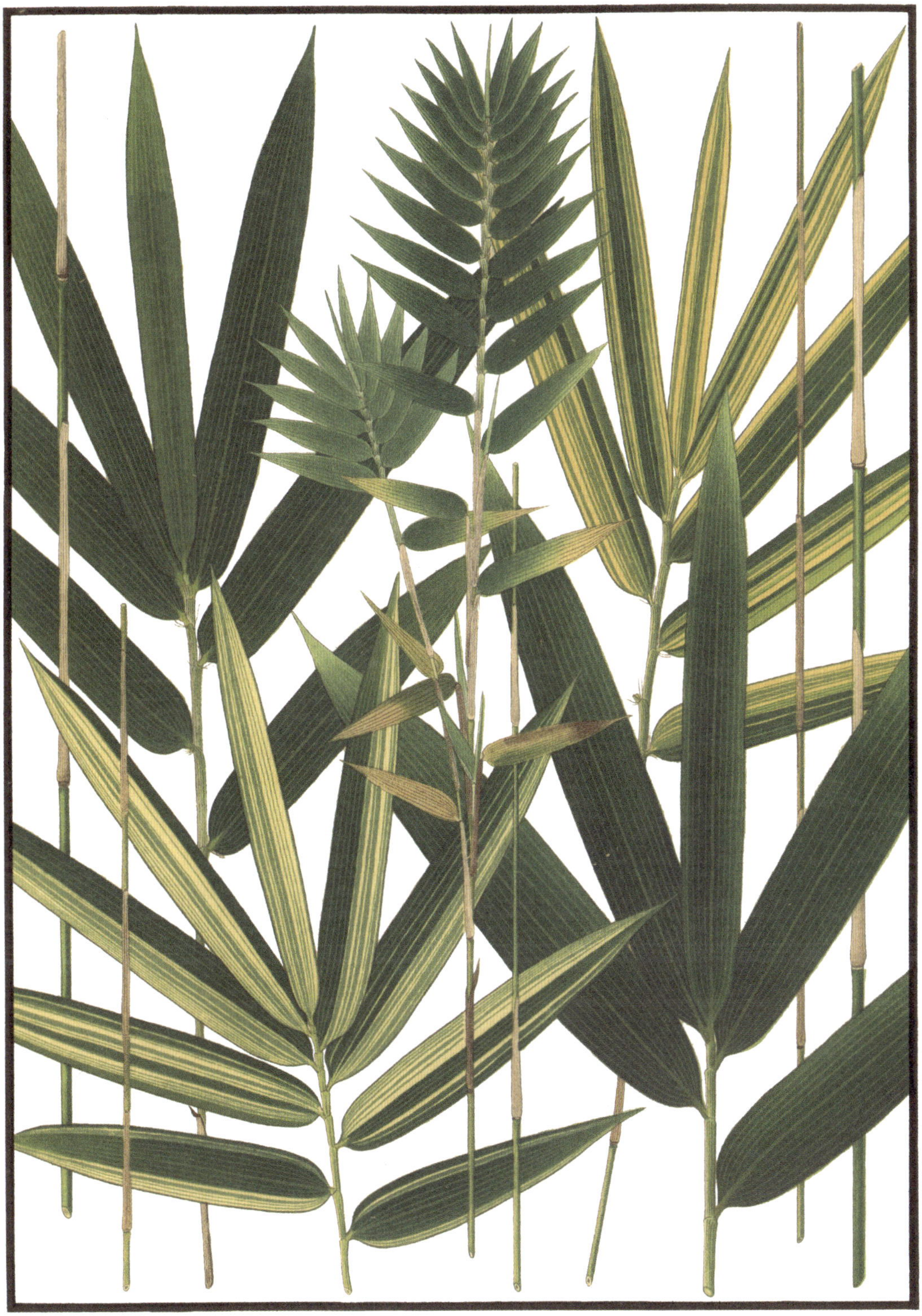

Pleioblastus
by YASUYOSHI SHIRASAWA

bamboo (various)

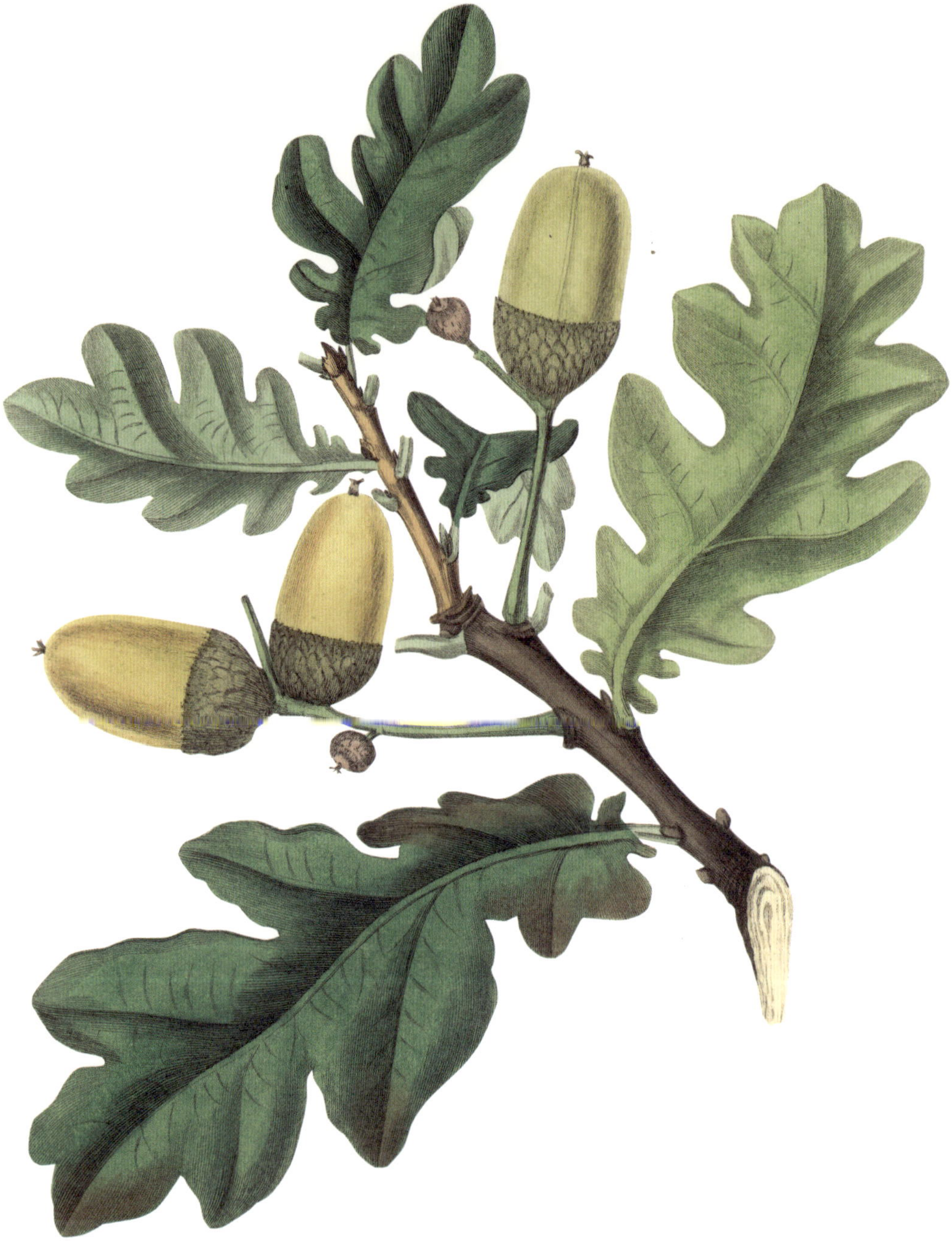

Quercus robur subsp. *robur*
by John Stephenson & James Morss Churchill

common oak | English oak | pedunculate oak

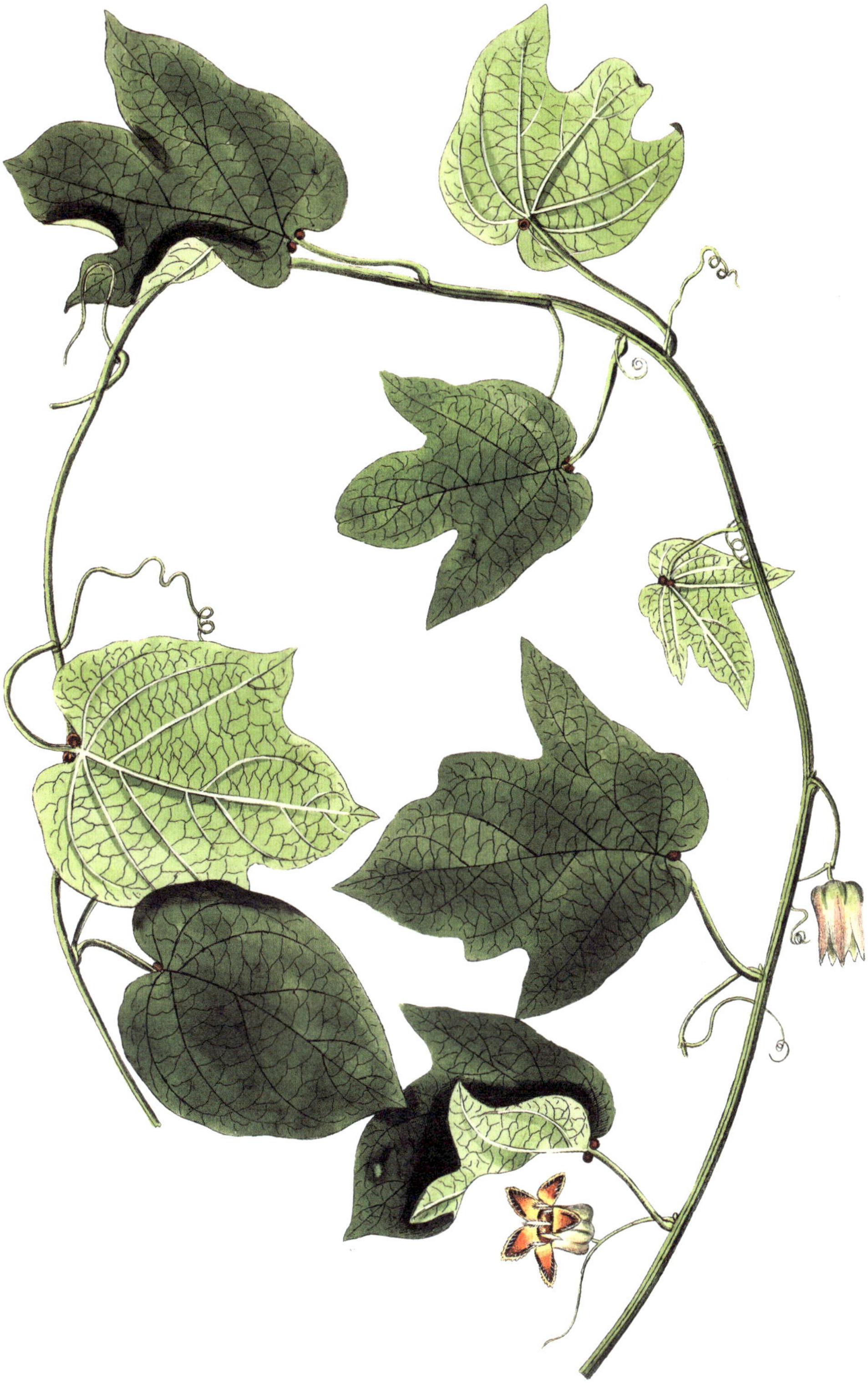

Adenia lobata
by UNKNOWN

Adenia lobata

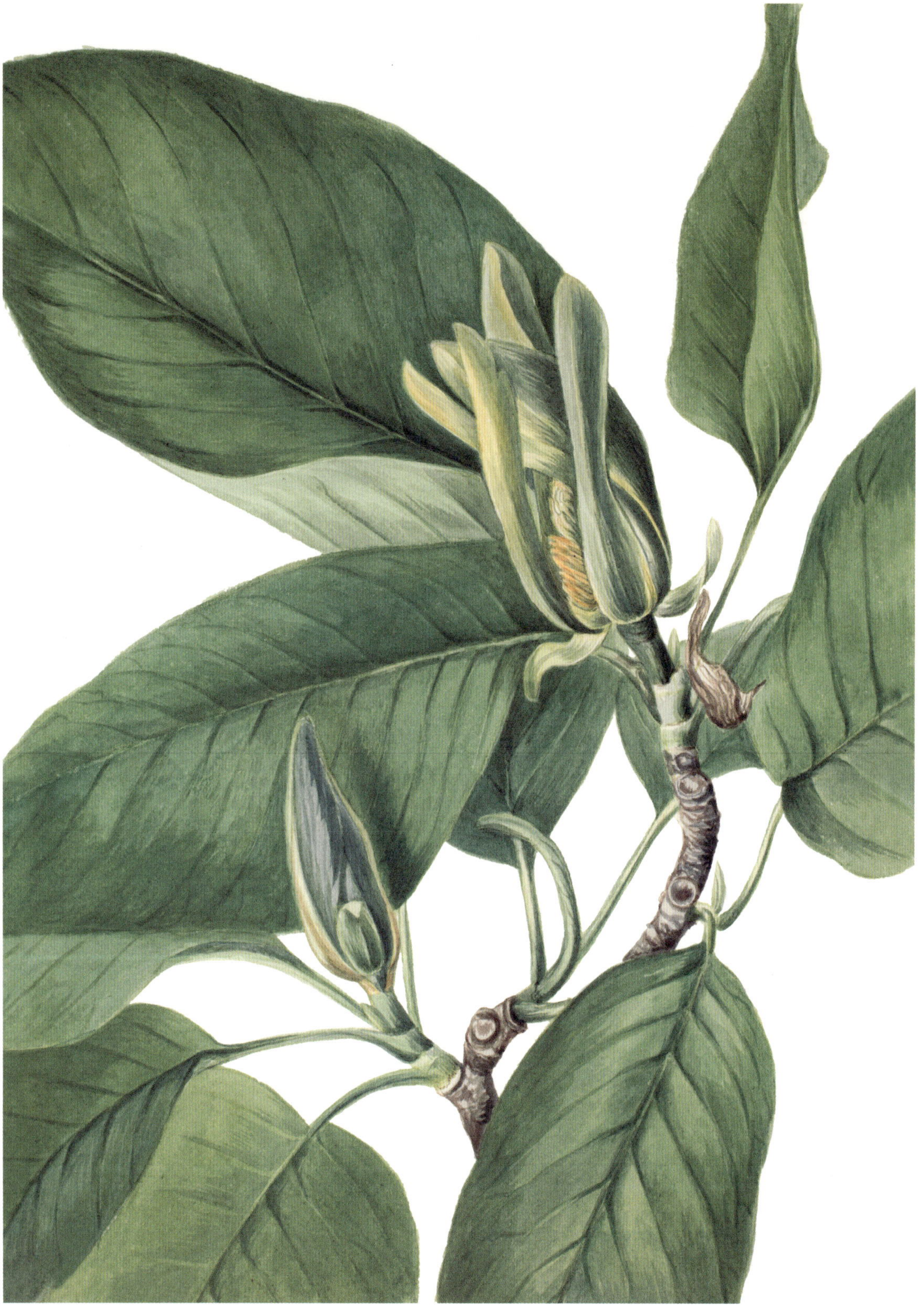

Magnolia acuminata
by Mary Vaux Walcott

cucumber tree | cucumber magnolia | blue magnolia

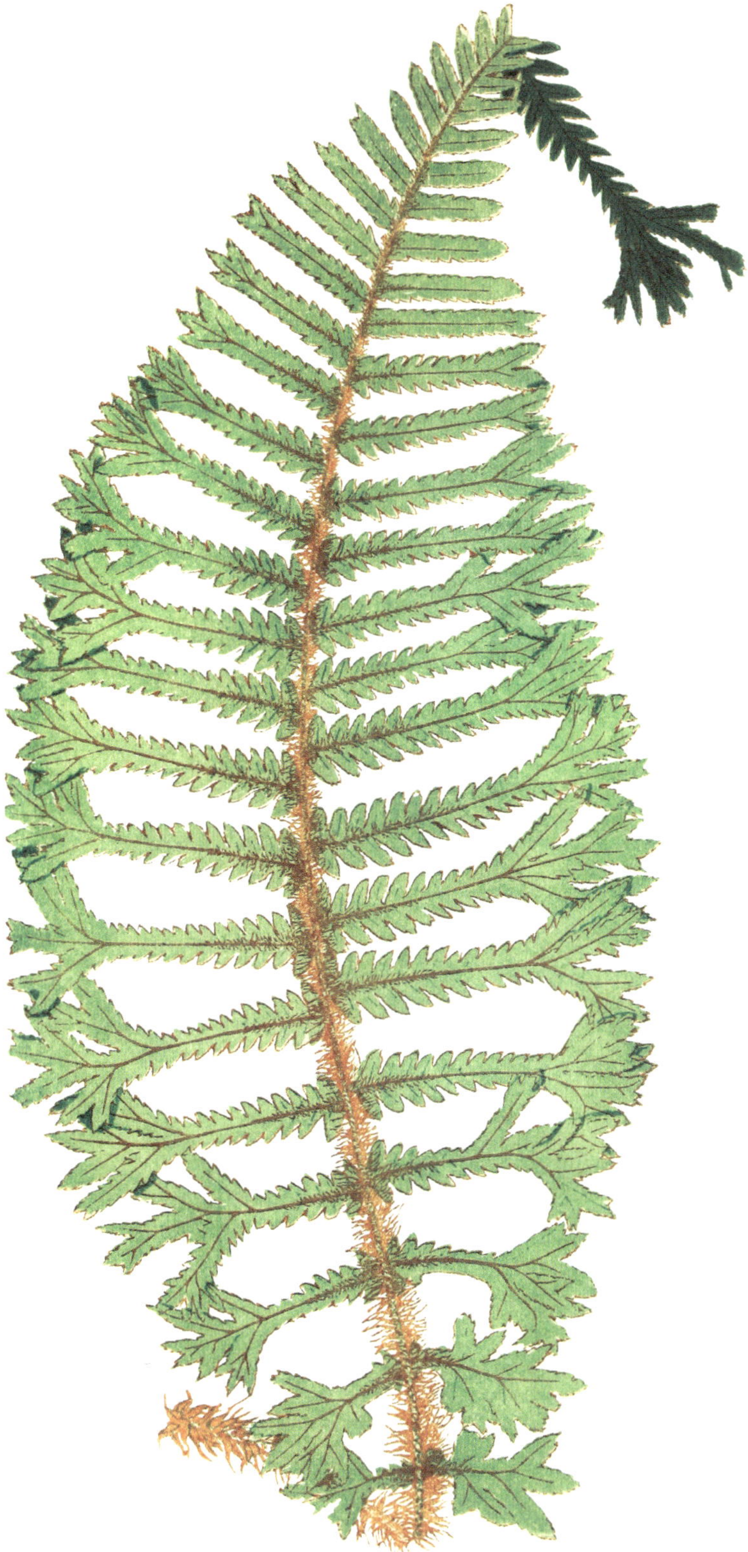

Dryopteris filix–mas
by Edward Joseph Lowe

male fern | worm fern

Salix
by William Morris

willow | sallow | osier

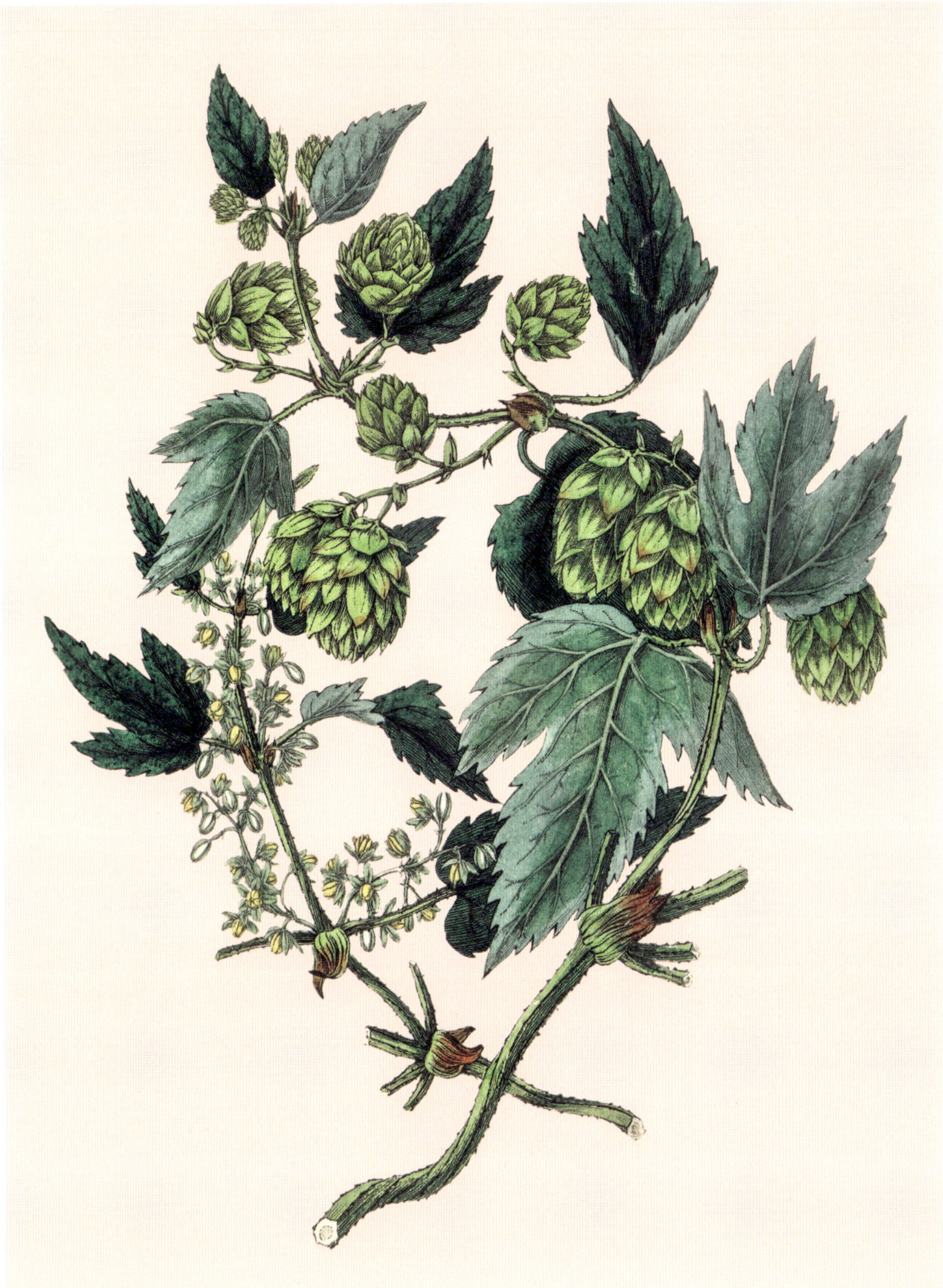

Humulus lupulus
by JOHN STEPHENSON & JAMES MORSS CHURCHILL

common hops

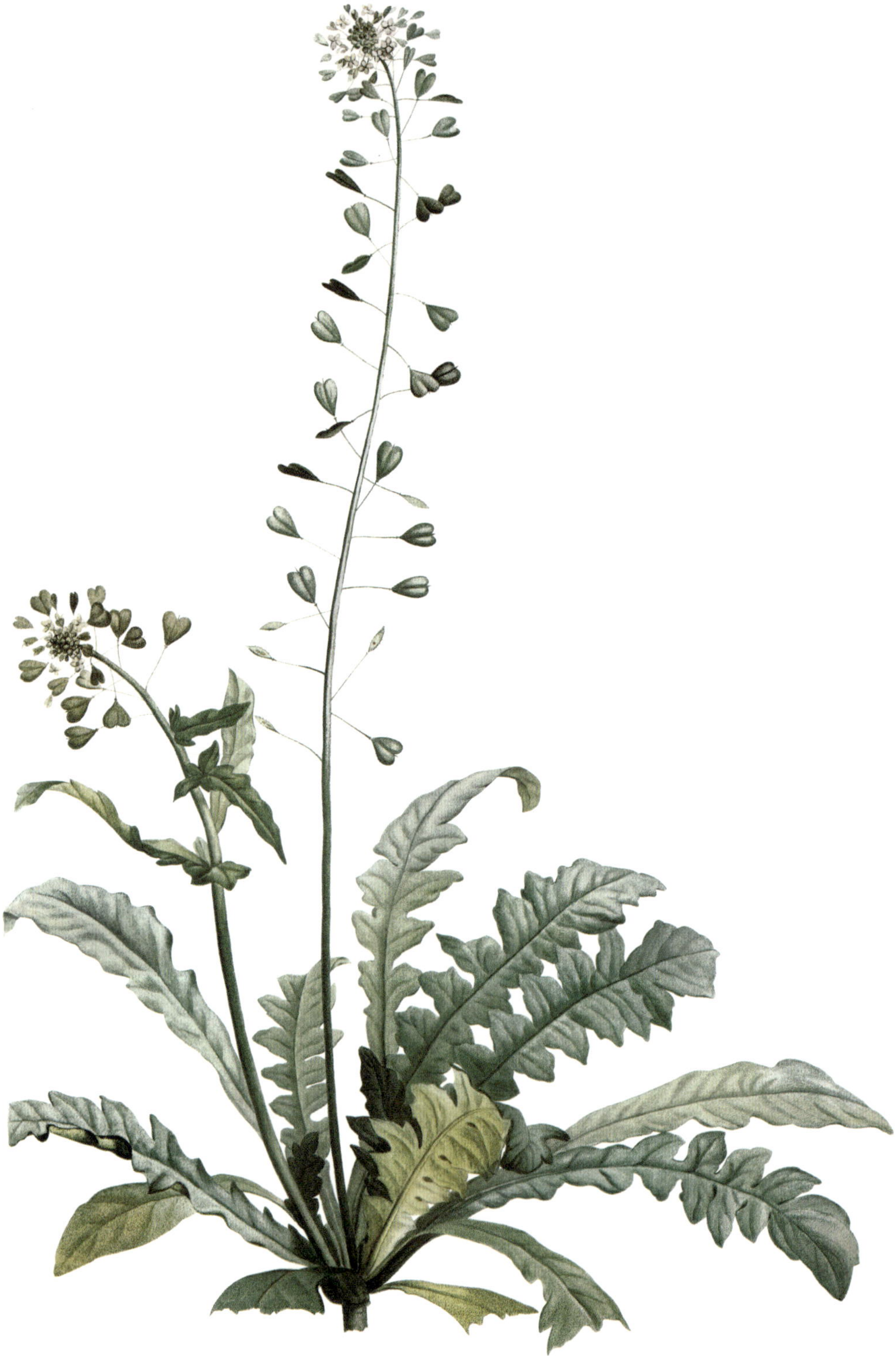

Capsella bursa-pastoris
by Pierre-Joseph Redouté

shepherd's purse | lady's purse

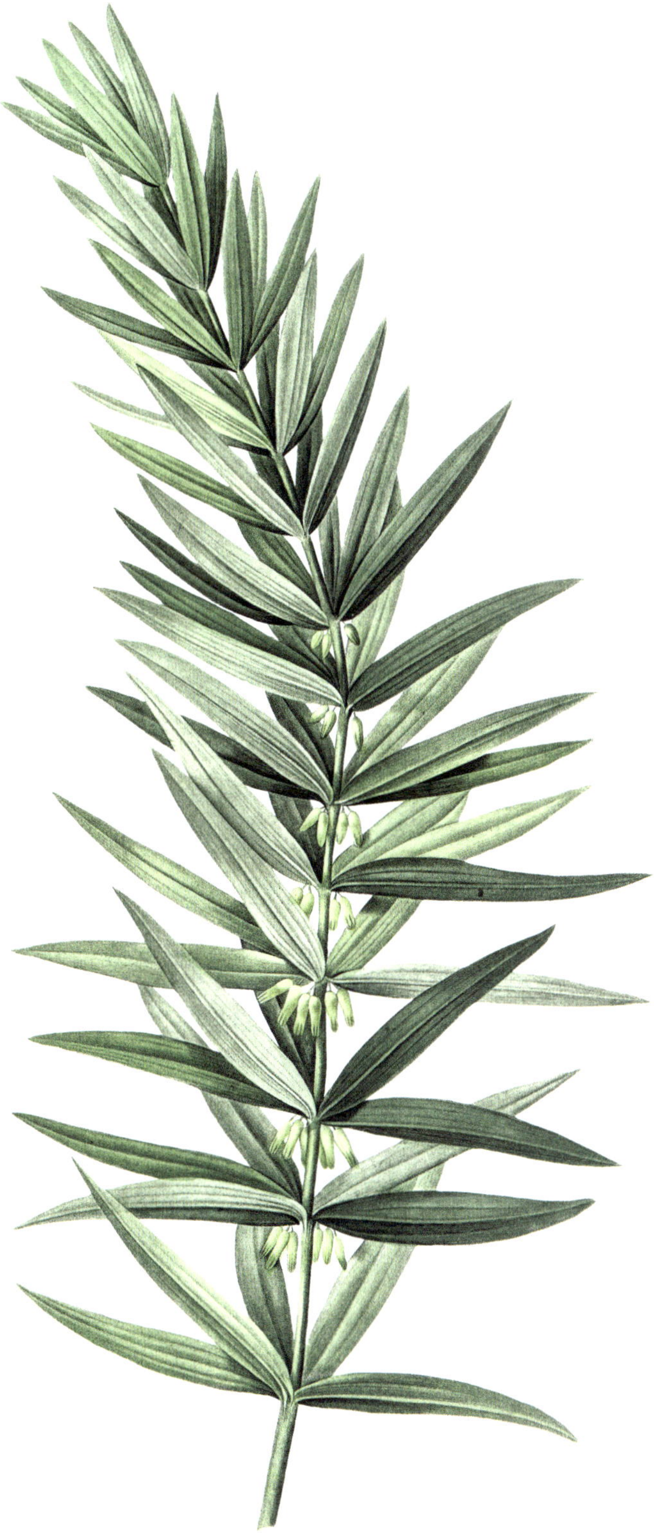

Polygonatum verticillatum
by Pierre-Joseph Redouté

whorled Solomon's seal

I believe a leaf
of grass is no less than
the journey-work
of the stars.

FROM 'Song of Myself' BY WALT WHITMAN

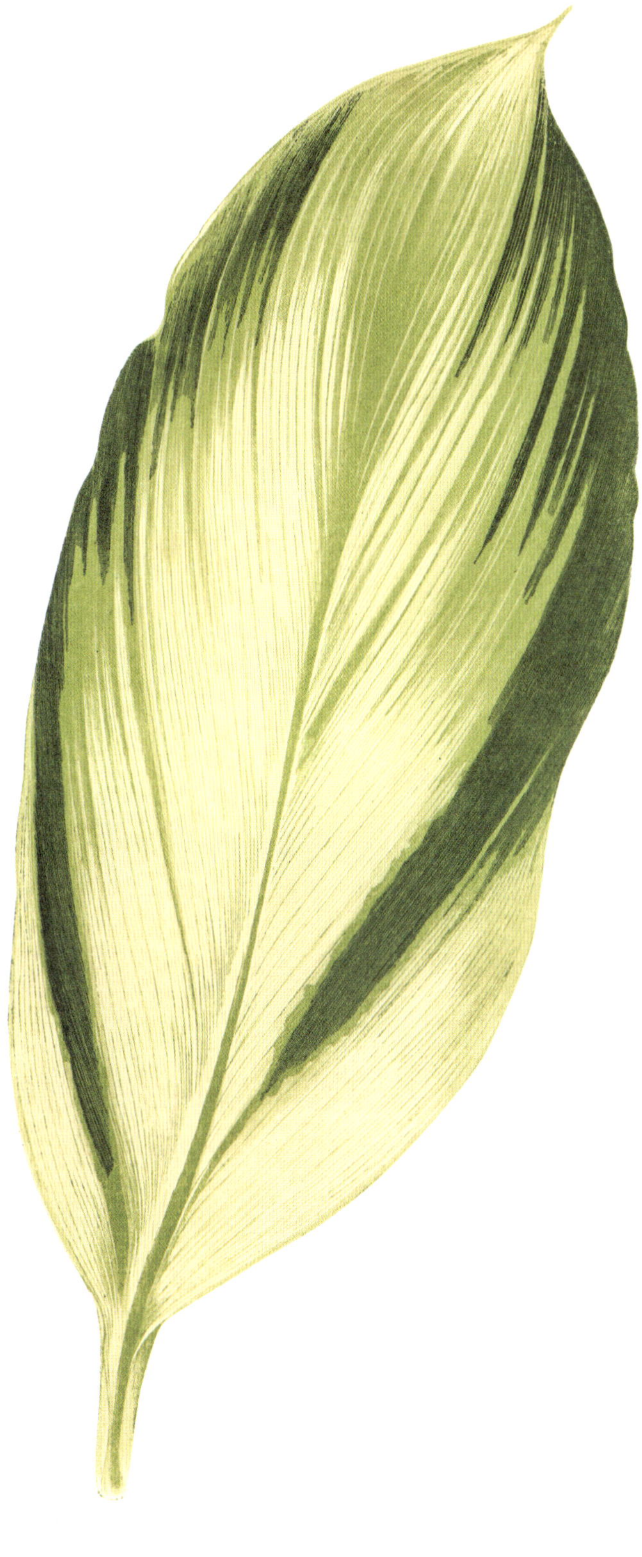

Dracaena
by BENJAMIN FAWCETT

dracaena (unknown variety)

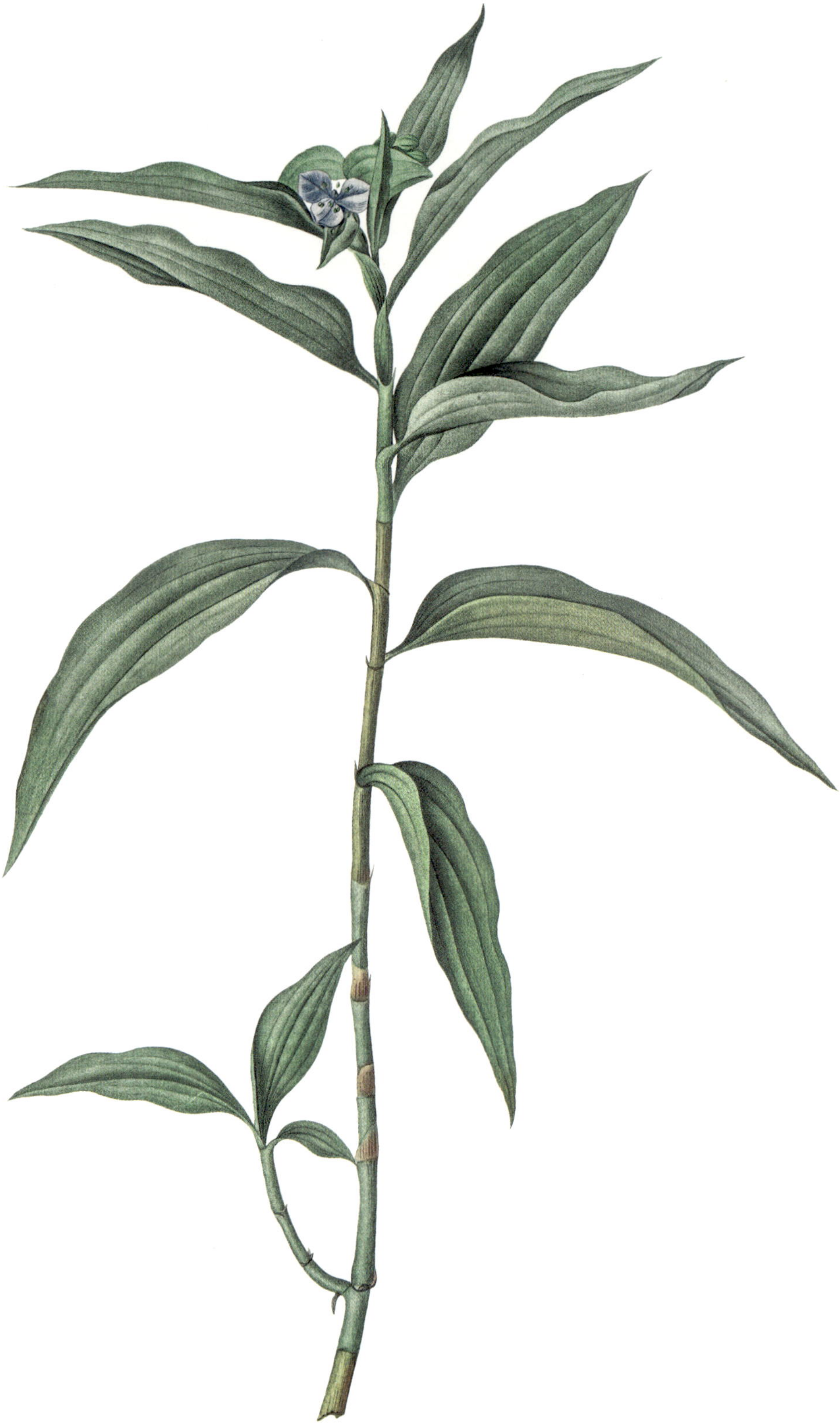

Commelina
by Pierre Joseph Redouté

dayflower (unknown variety)

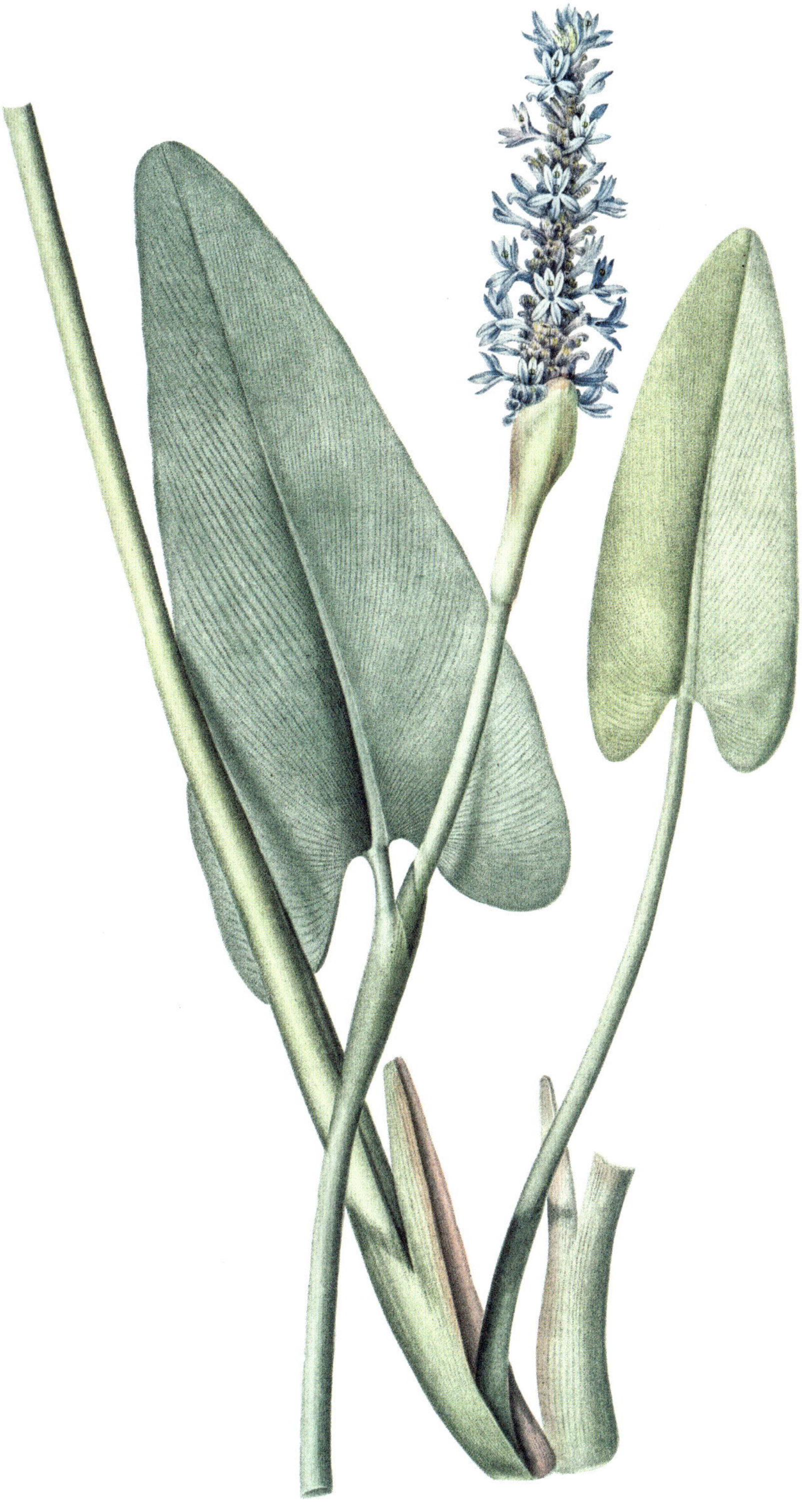

Pontederia cordata
by Pierre-Joseph Redouté

pickerelweed

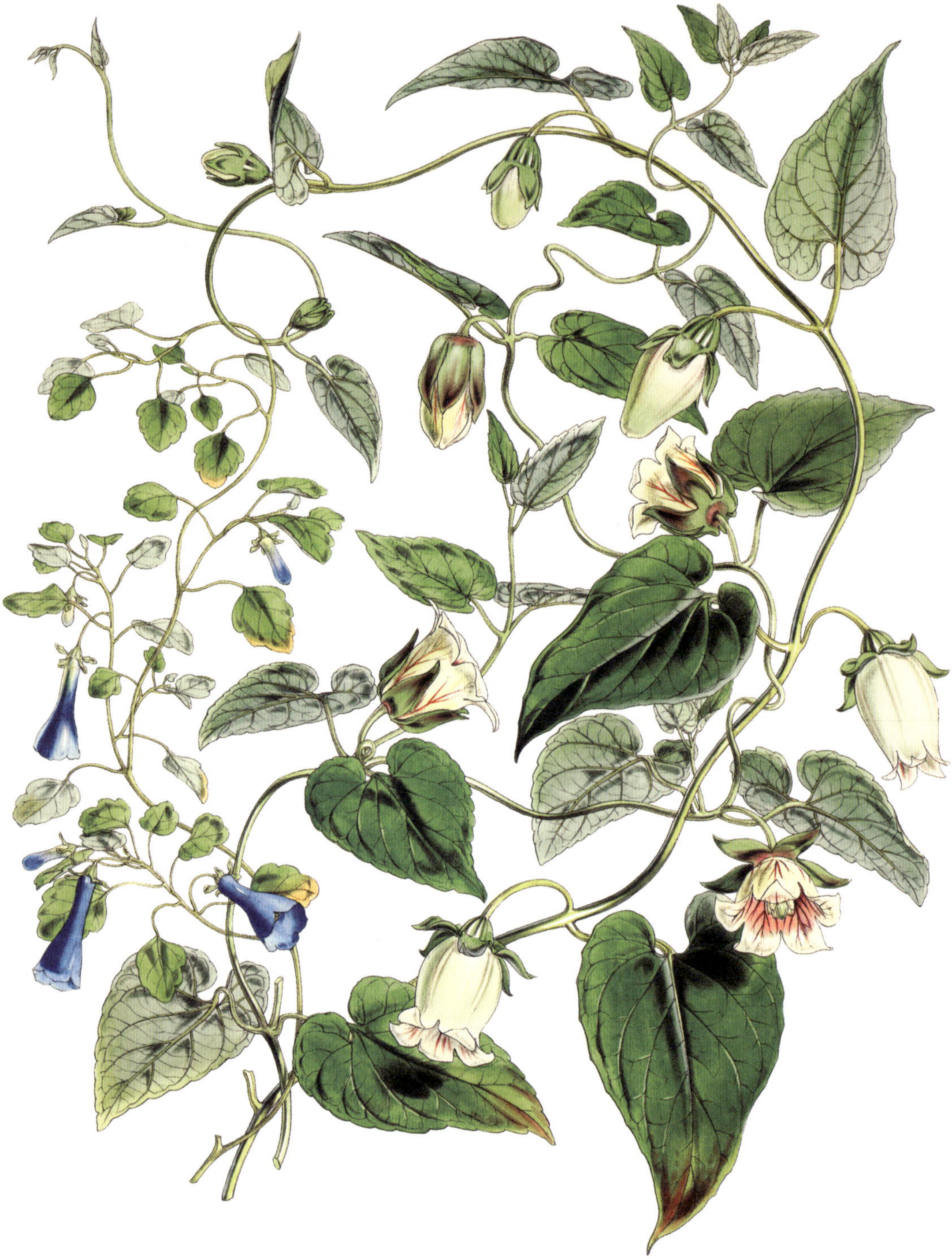

Lobelia inflata
BY WALTER HOOD FITCH

Indian tobacco | puke weed

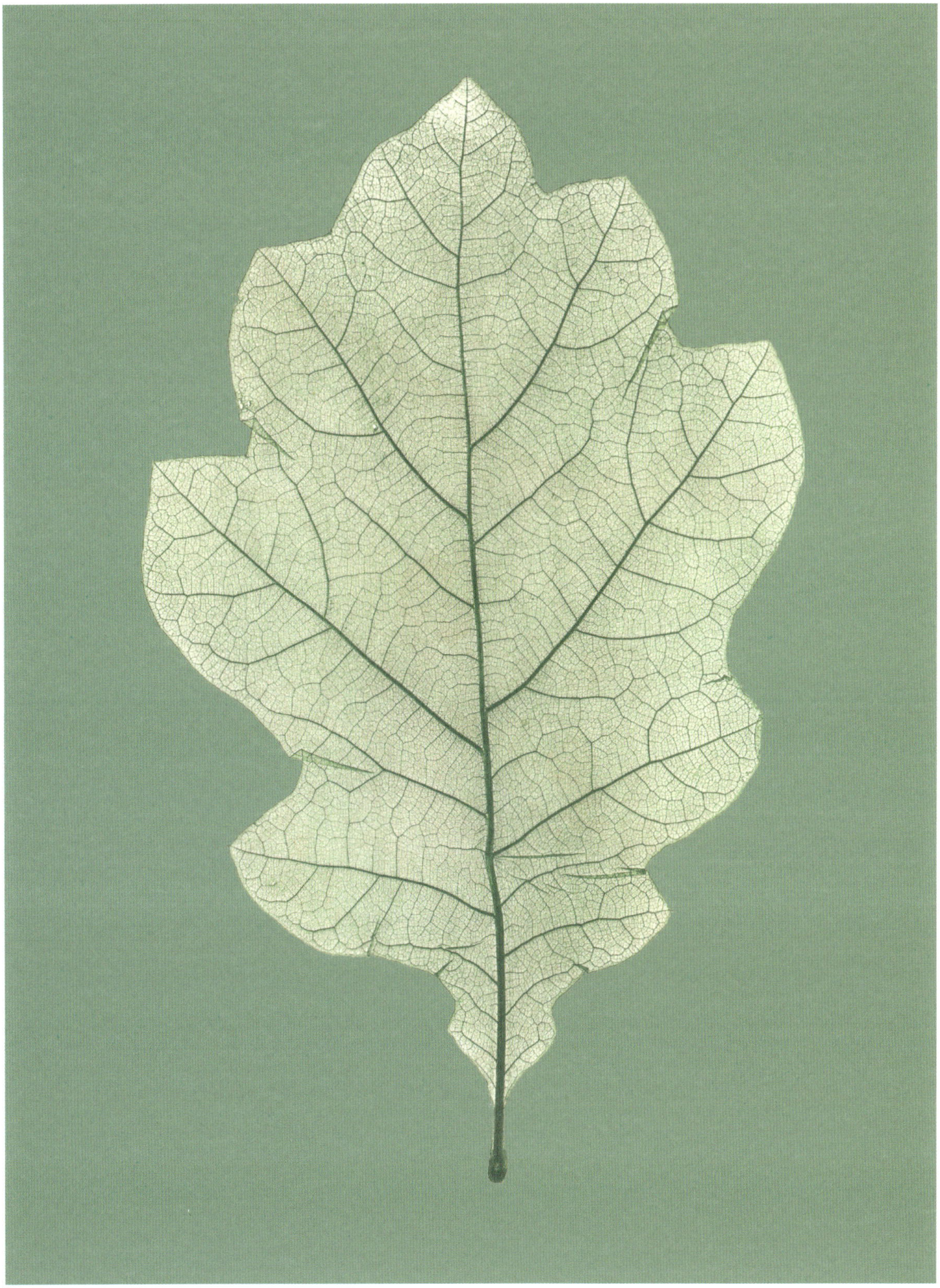

Quercus robur subsp. *robur*
by Alois Auer

common oak | English oak | pedunculate oak

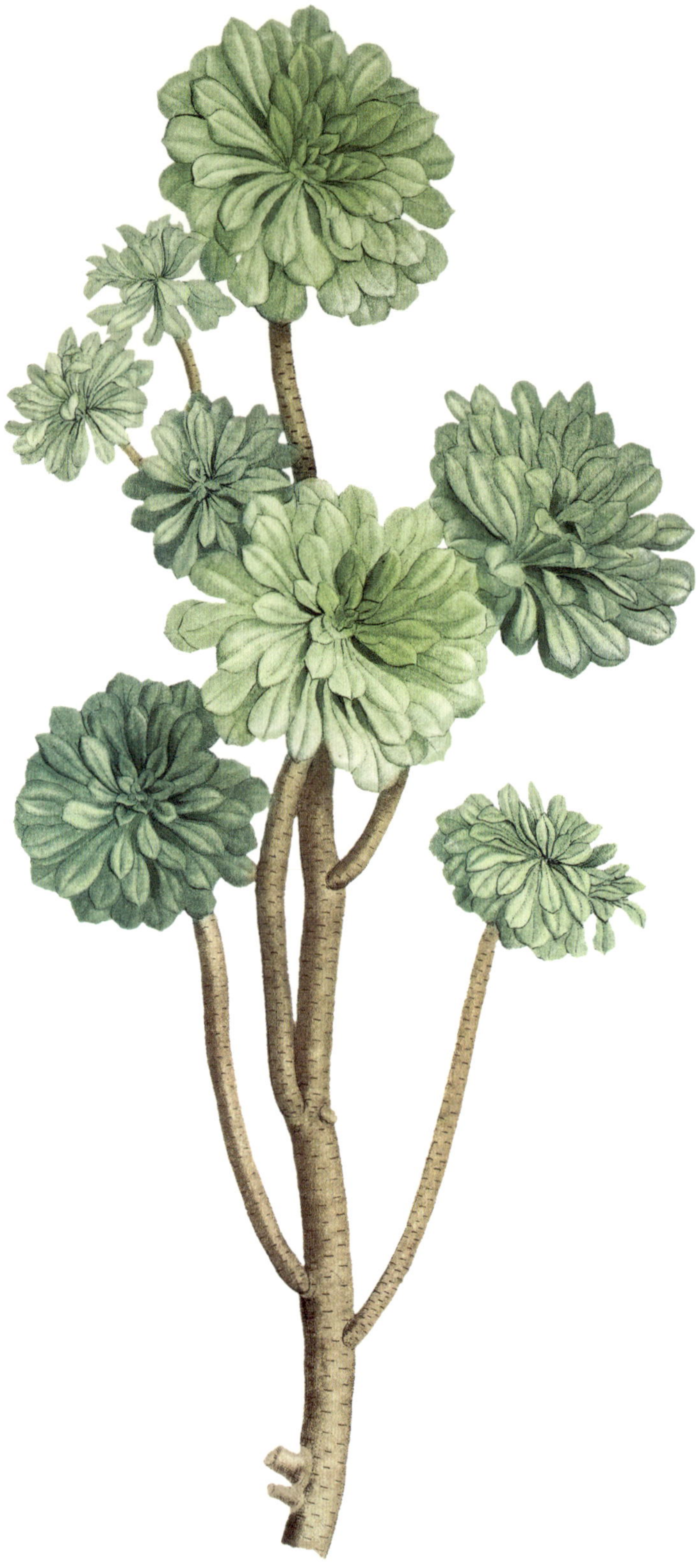

Aeonium arboreum
by Pierre-Joseph Redouté

tree aeonium | tree houseleek | Irish rose

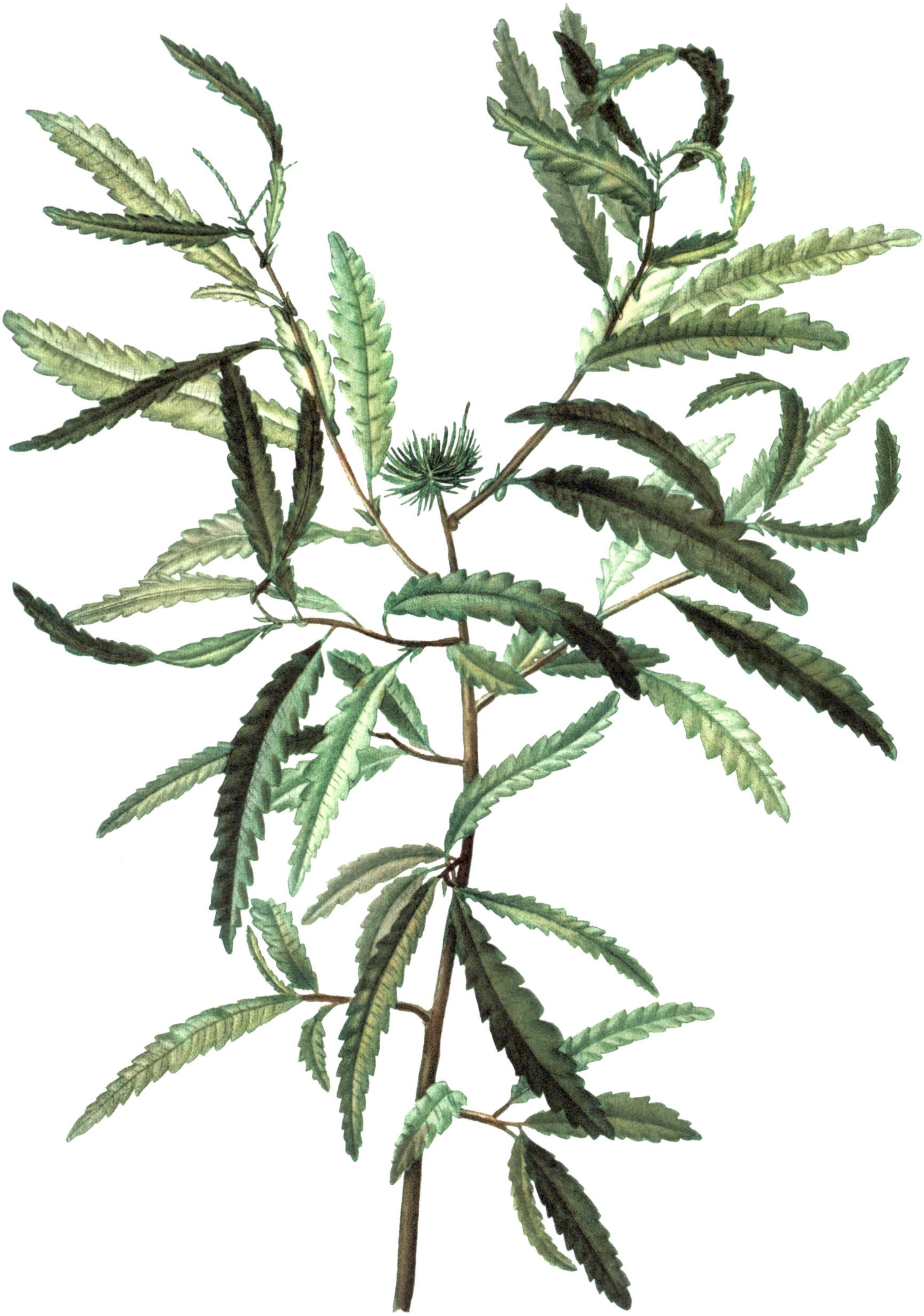

Comptonia peregrina
by Pierre-Joseph Redouté

sweetfern

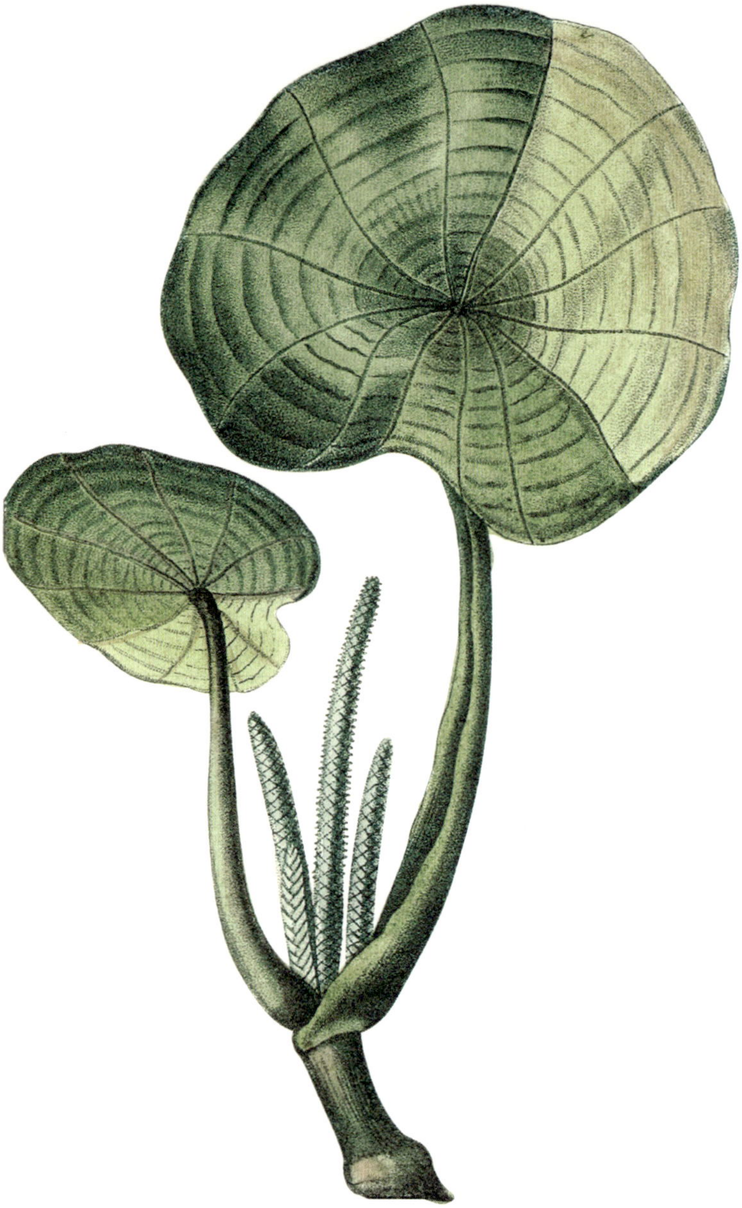

Piper peltatum
from BIODIVERSITY HERITAGE LIBRARY

monkey's hand | pakina | Santa Maria plant

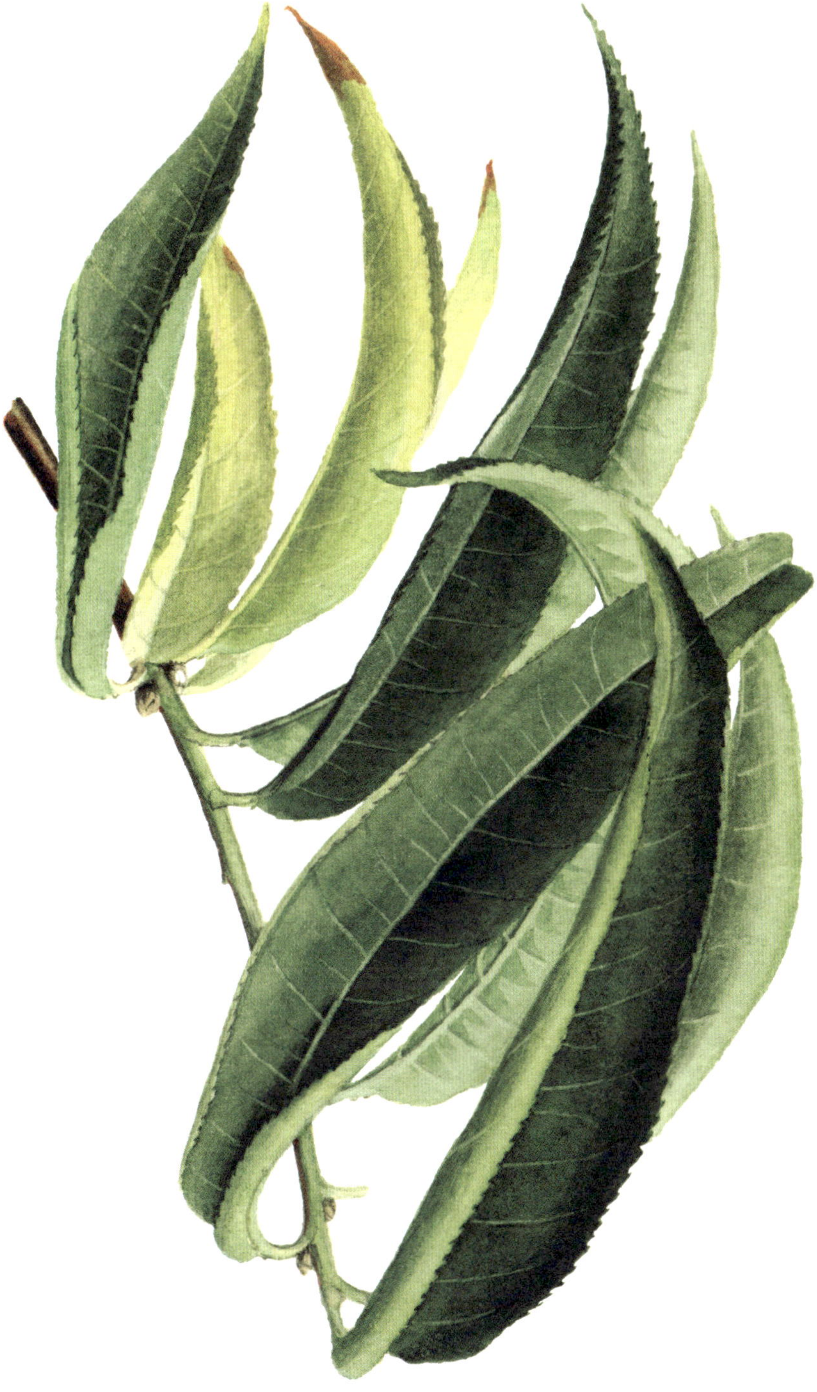

Prunus persica
by James Marion Shull

common peach

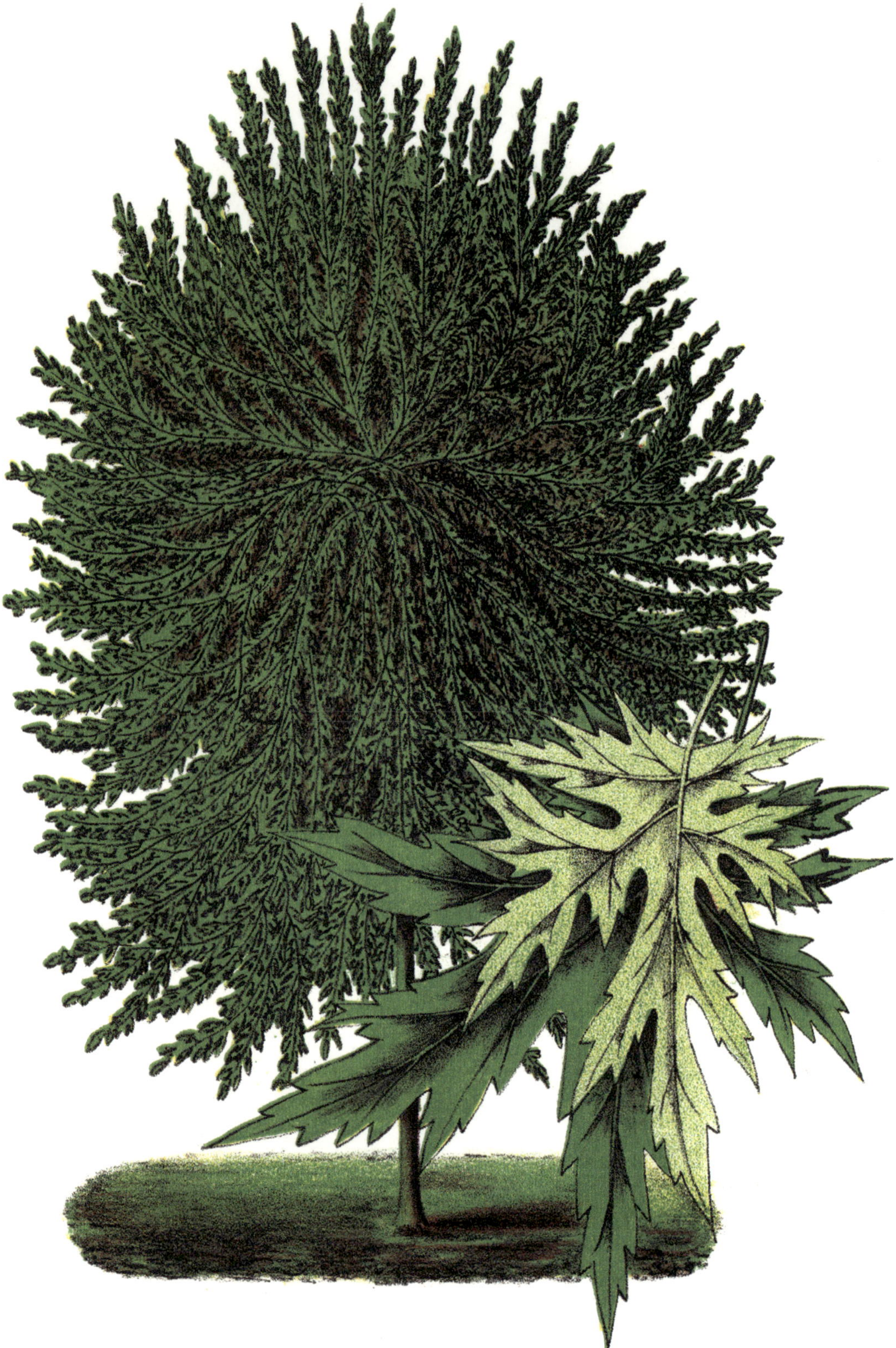

Acer saccharinum
from *Botanical Specimen*

silver maple | creek maple | silverleaf maple

The Maple with its tassell flowers of green
That turns to red, a stag horn shapèd seed
Just spreading out its scalloped leaves is seen,
Of yellowish hue yet beautifully green.

FROM 'The Maple Tree' BY JOHN CLARE

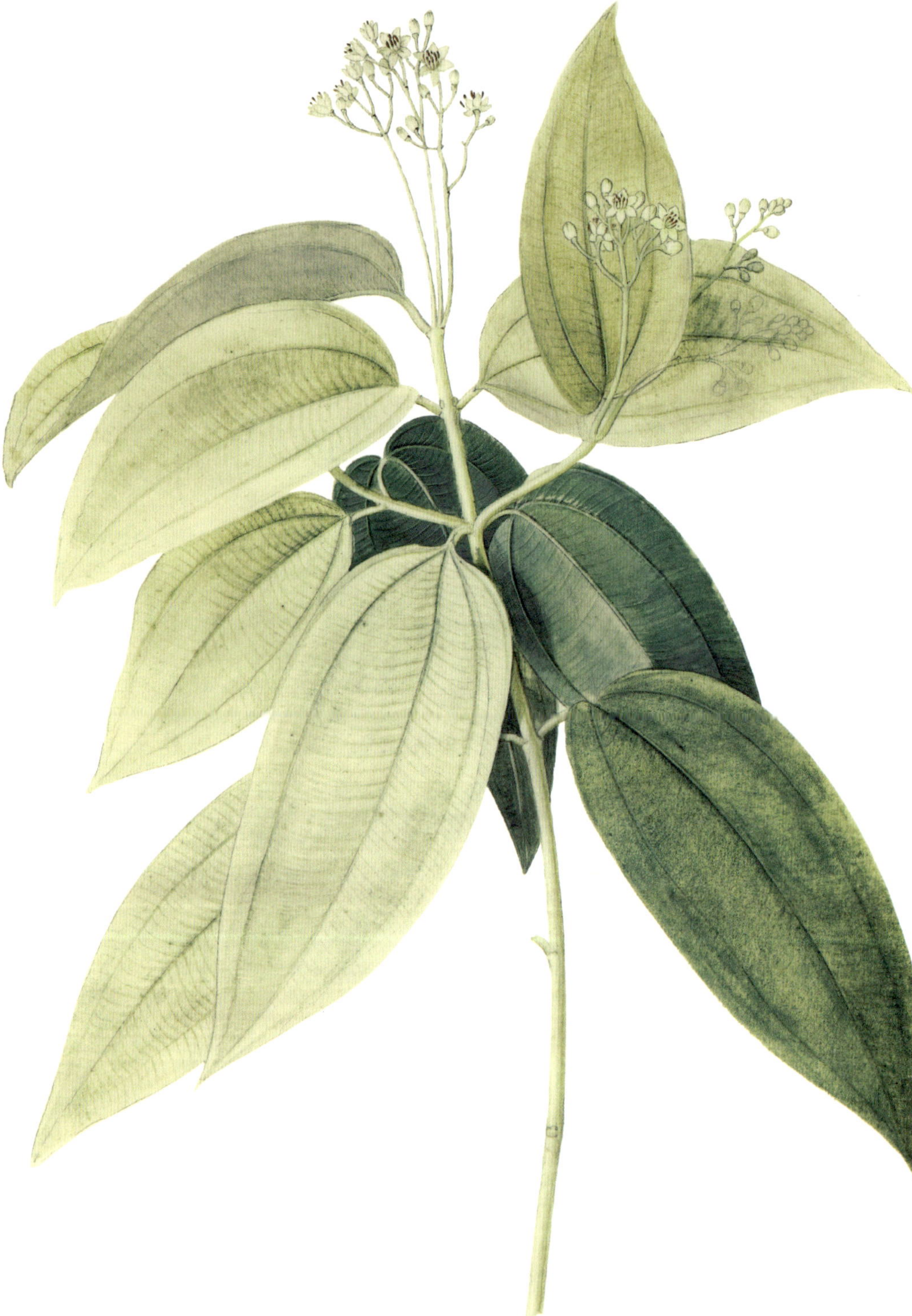

Cinnamomum verum
by Georg Dionysius Ehret

true cinnamon | Ceylon cinnamon

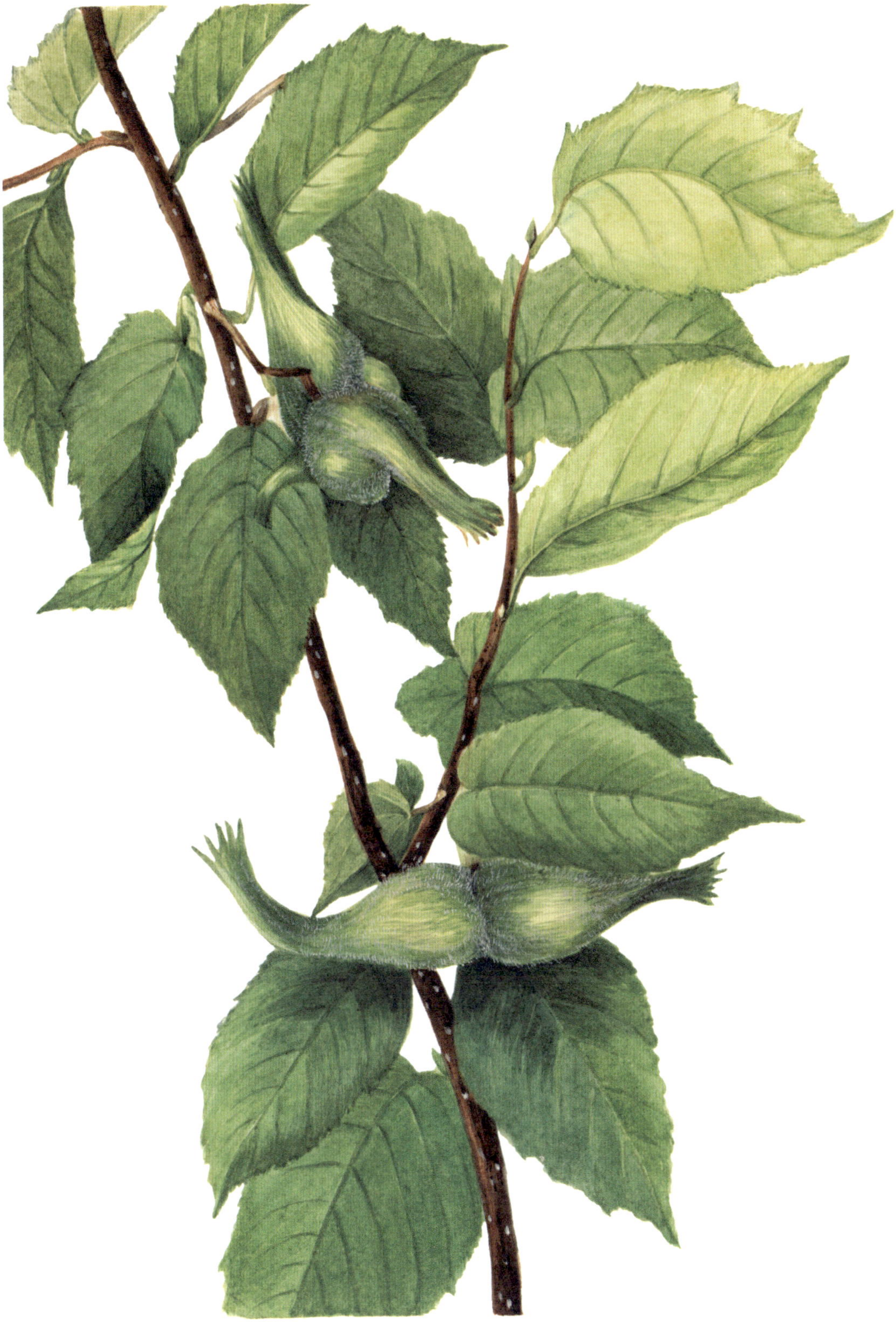

Corylus cornuta
by MARY VAUX WALCOTT

beaked hazelnut

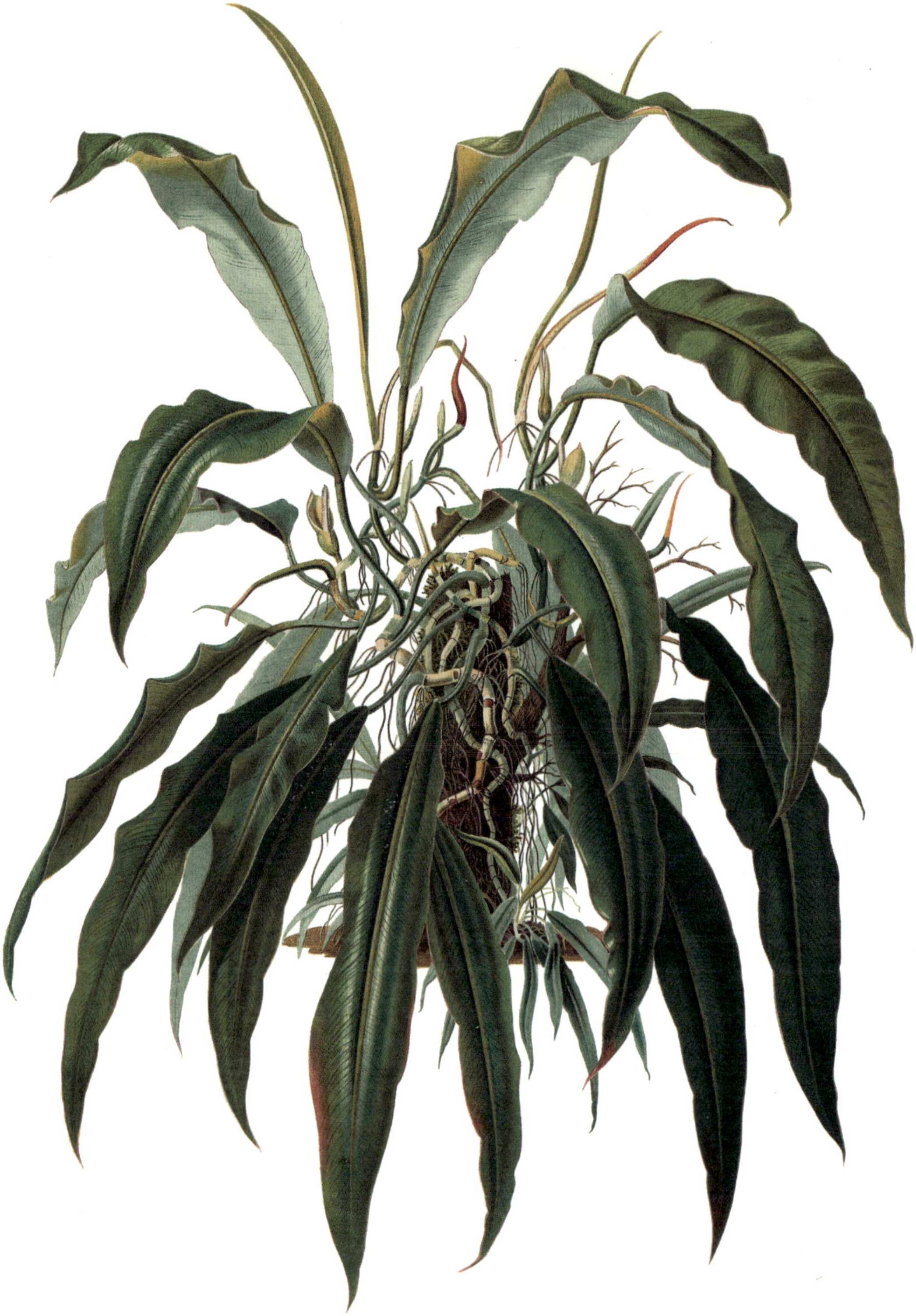

Philodendron longilaminatum
by HEINRICH WILHELM SCHOTT

philodendron longilaminatum

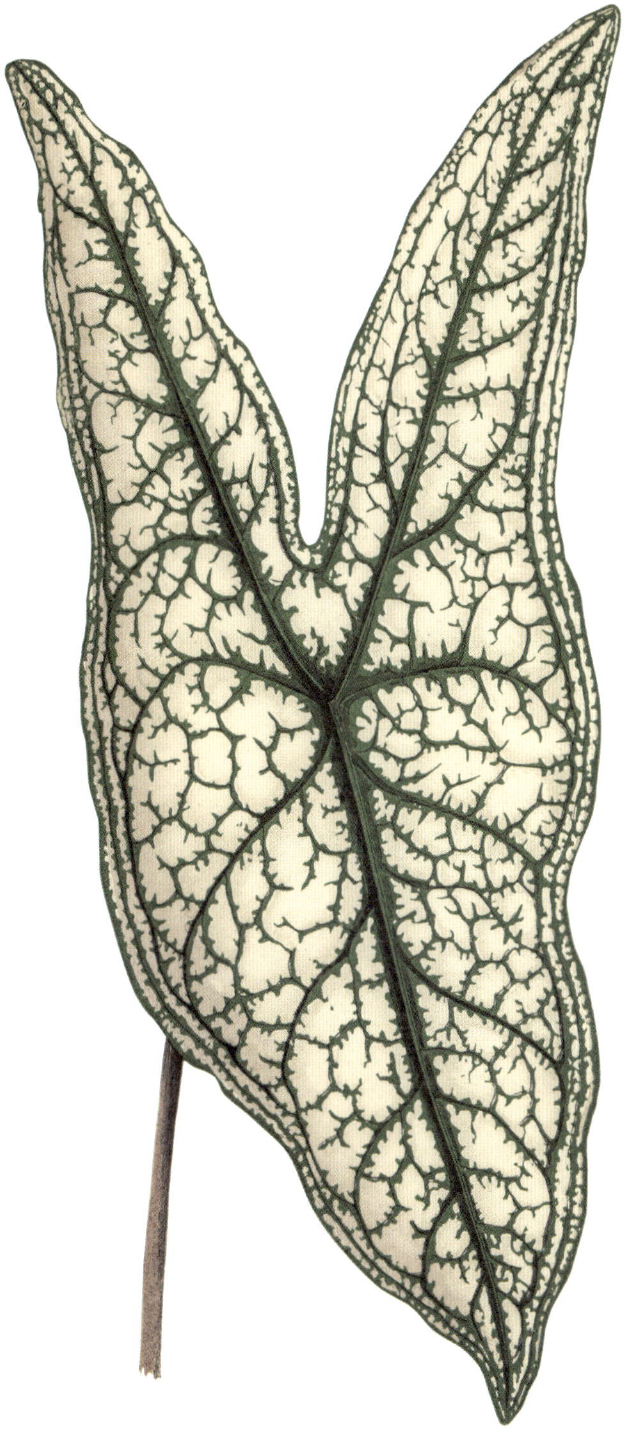

Caladium bicolor
by John Stephenson & James Morss Churchill

Heart of Jesus | elephant ear | angel wings

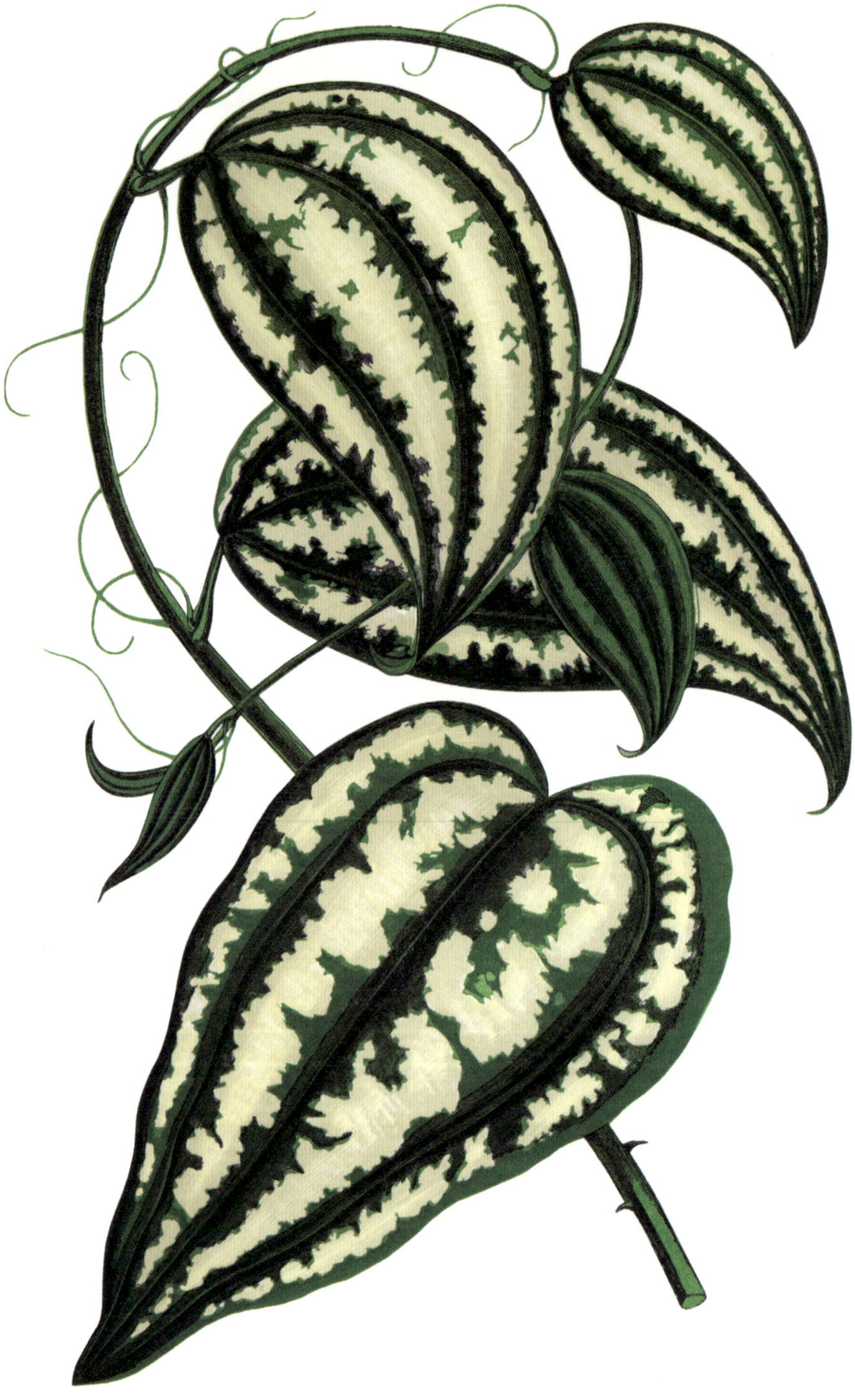

Smilax
by Alexander Francis Lydon & Benjamin Fawcett

greenbriers (unknown variety)

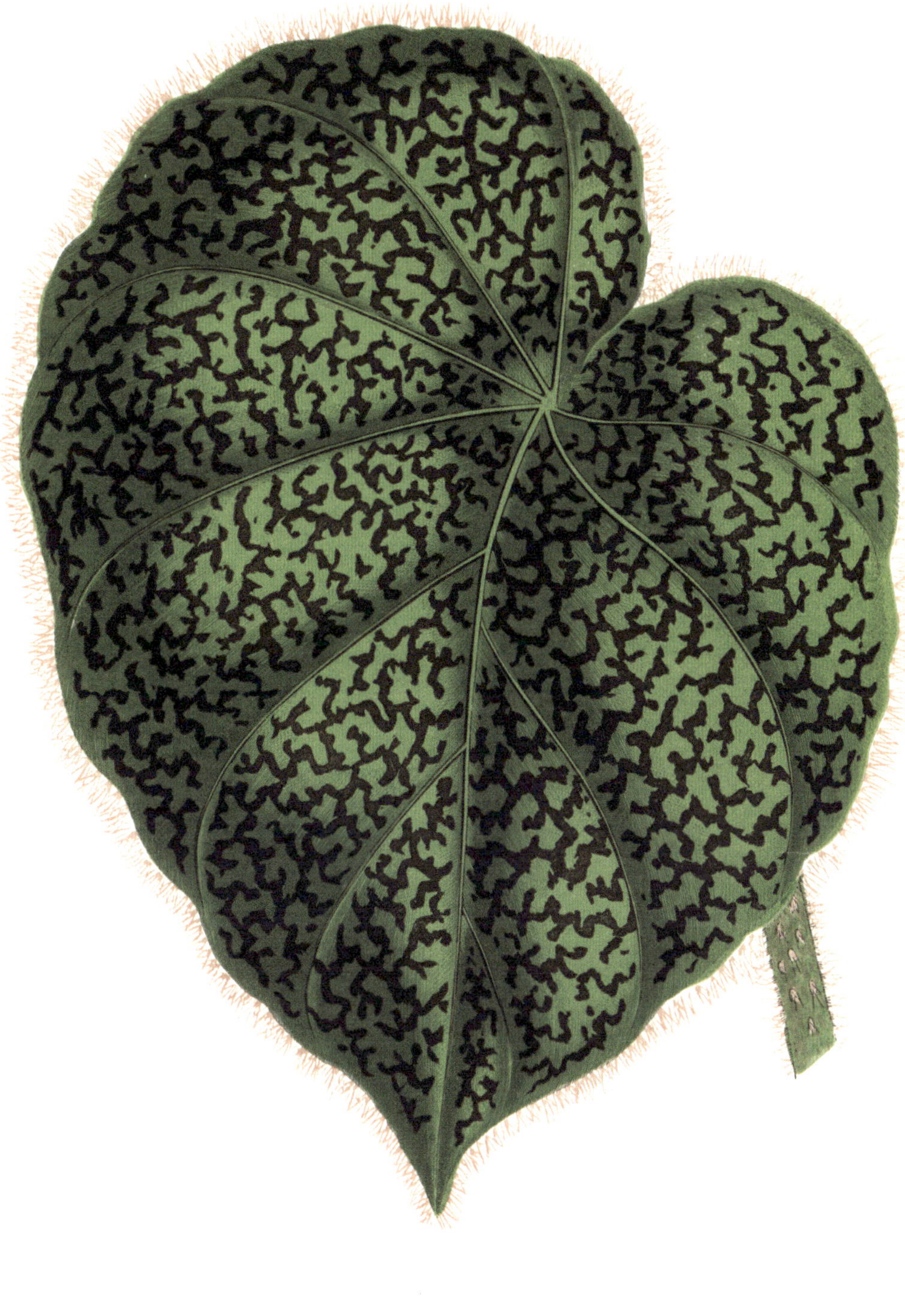

Begonia strigillosa
by Benjamin Fawcett & James Shirley Hibberd

begonia

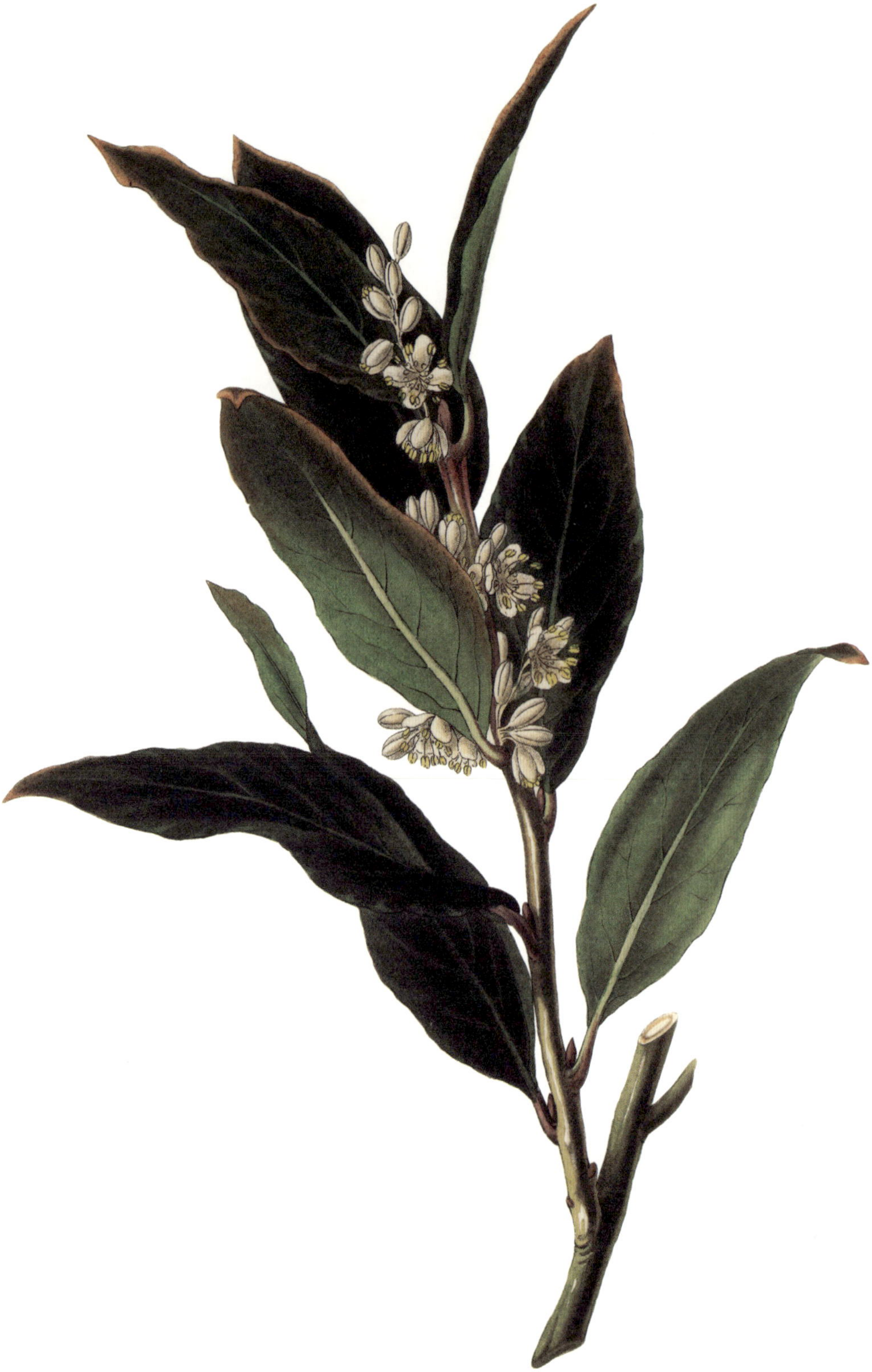

Laurus nobilis
by John Stephenson & James Morss Churchill

bay laurel | sweet bay tree

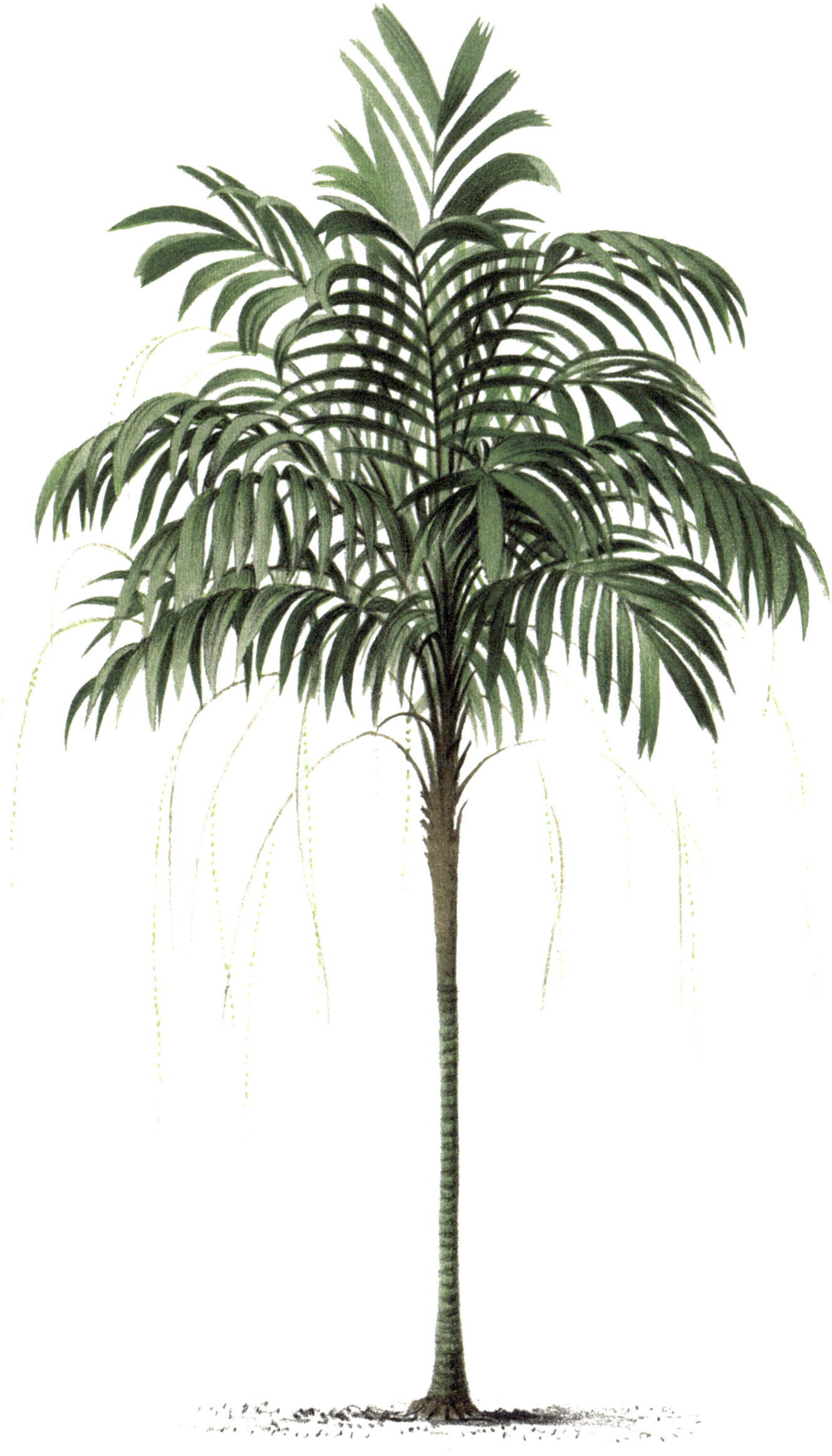

Linospadix monostachyos
by OSWALD DE KERCHOVE DE DENTERGHEM

walking stick palm

Whole ages have fled and their works decayed,
And nations have scattered been;
But the stout old Ivy shall never fade,
From its hale and hearty green.
The brave old plant, in its lonely days,
Shall fatten upon the past:
For the stateliest building man can raise,
Is the Ivy's food at last.
Creeping on, where time has been,
A rare old plant is the Ivy green.

FROM 'The Ivy Green' BY CHARLES DICKENS

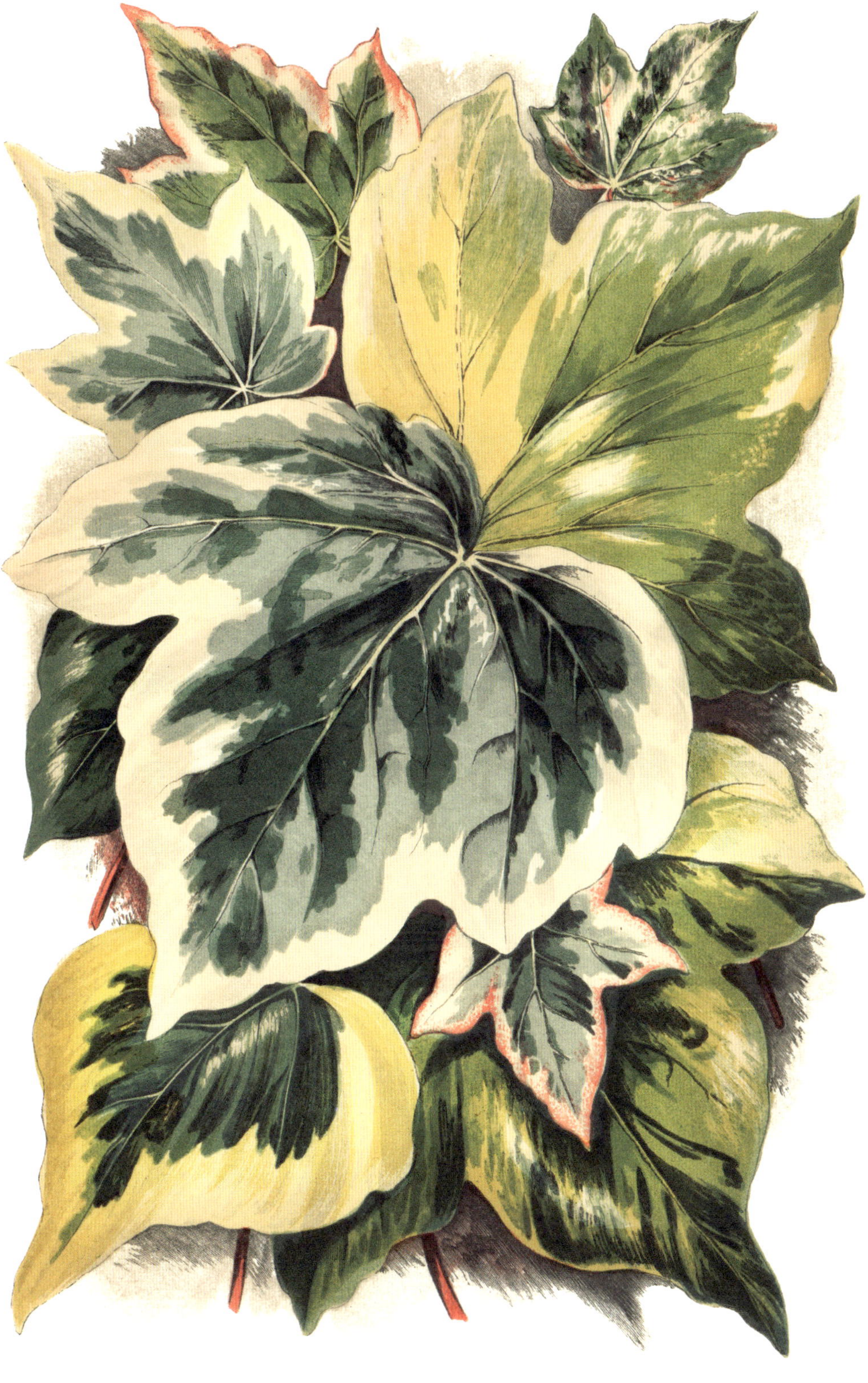

Hedera
by James Shirley Hibberd

ivy (various)

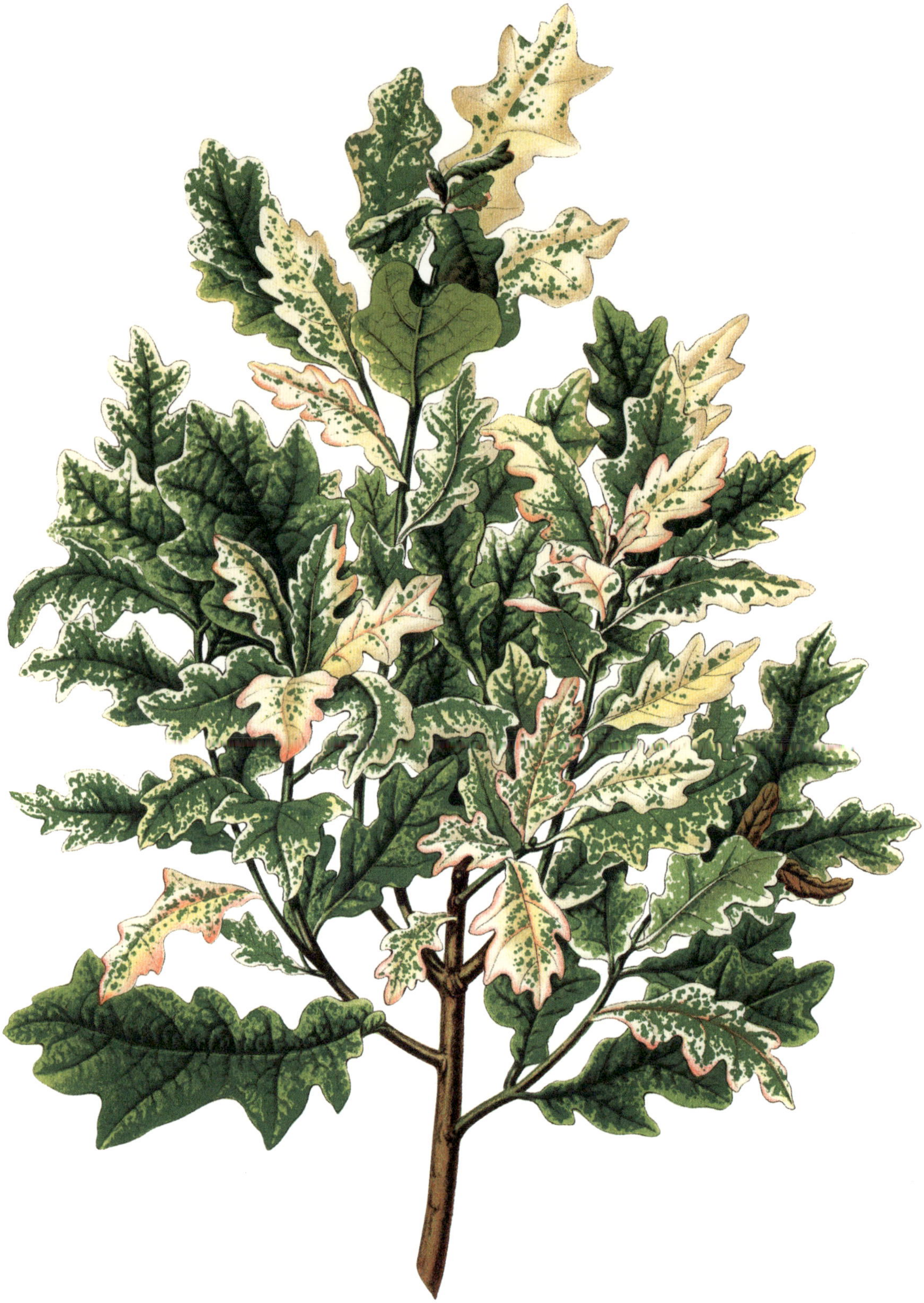

Quercus robur 'Fastigiata'
by Abraham Jacobus Wendel

upright English oak

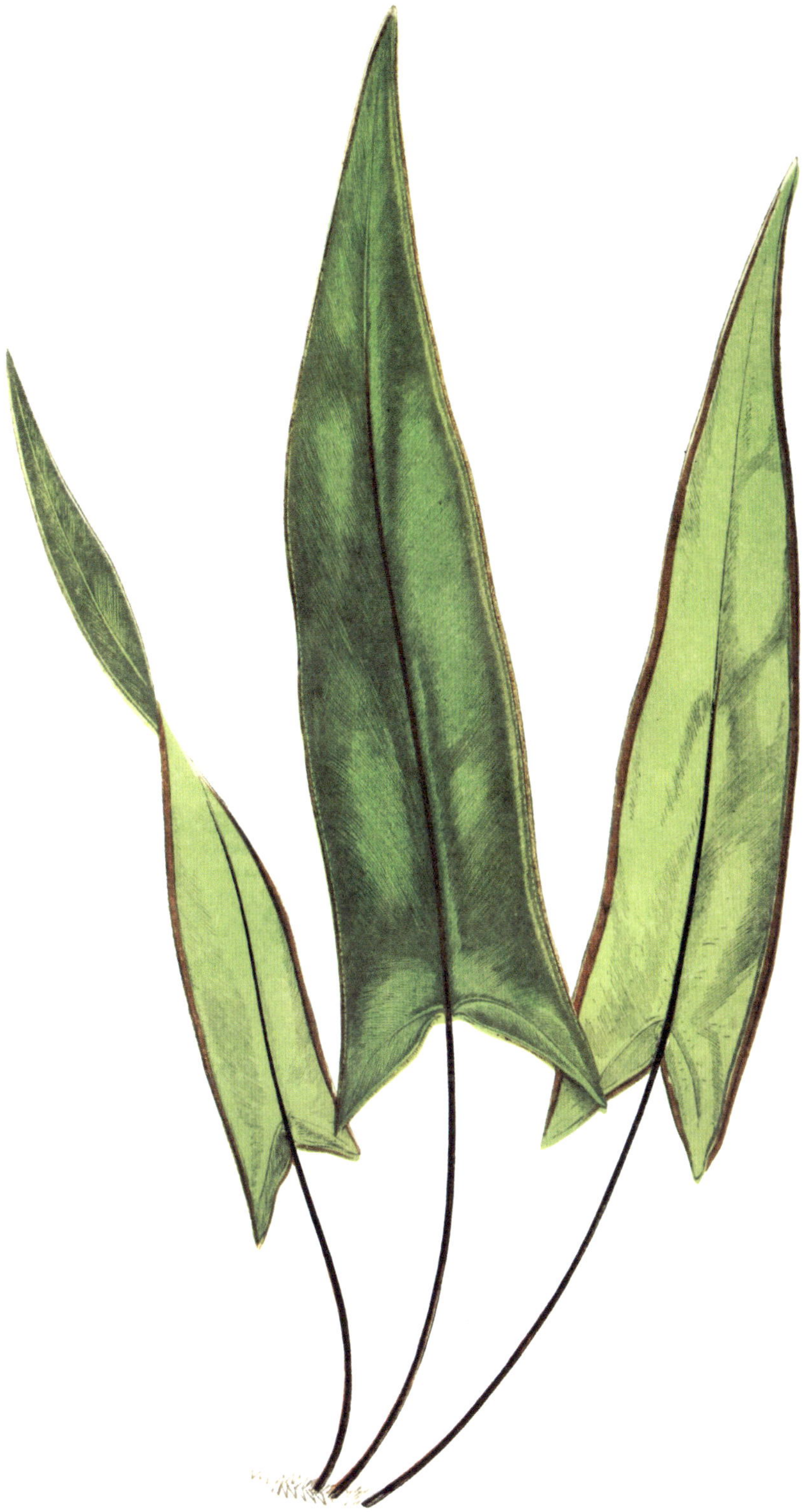

Hemionitis sagittifolia
by EDWARD JOSEPH LOWE

heart fern

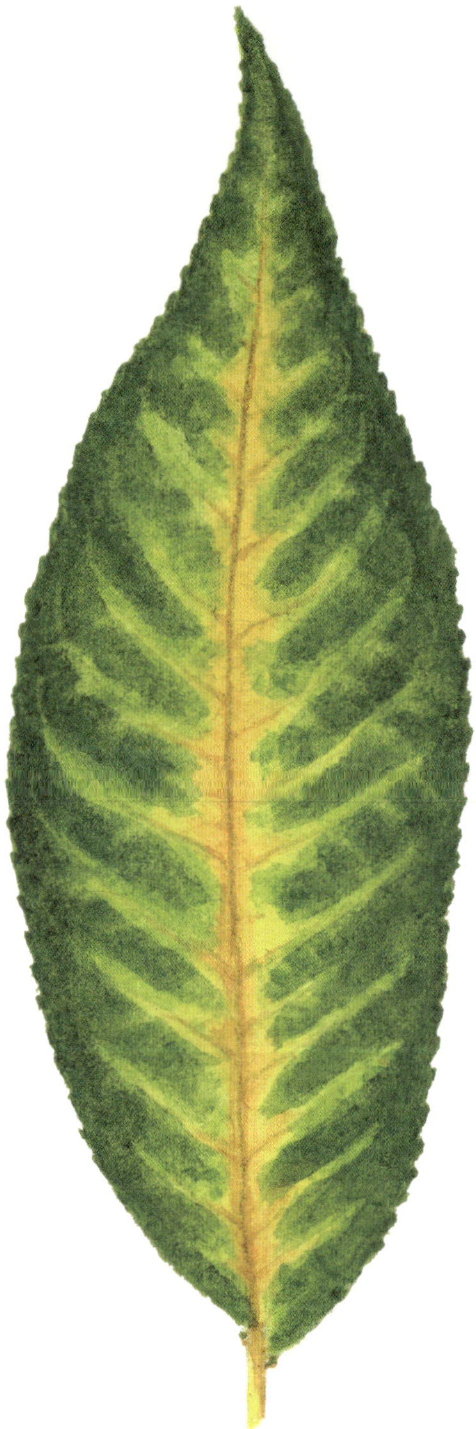

Prunus persica
by James Marion Shull

peach

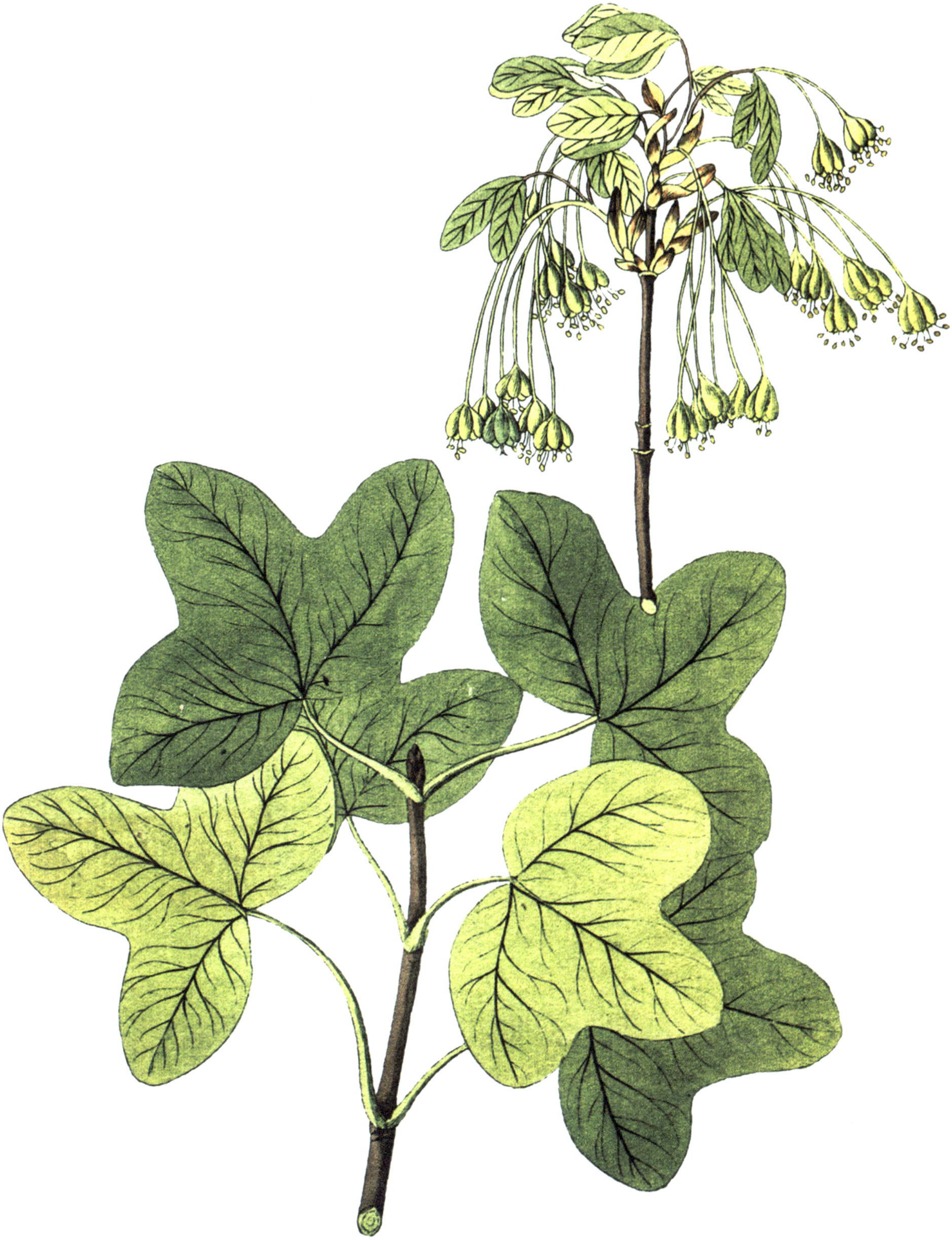

Acer monspessulanum
from BIODIVERSITY HERITAGE LIBRARY

Montpellier maple

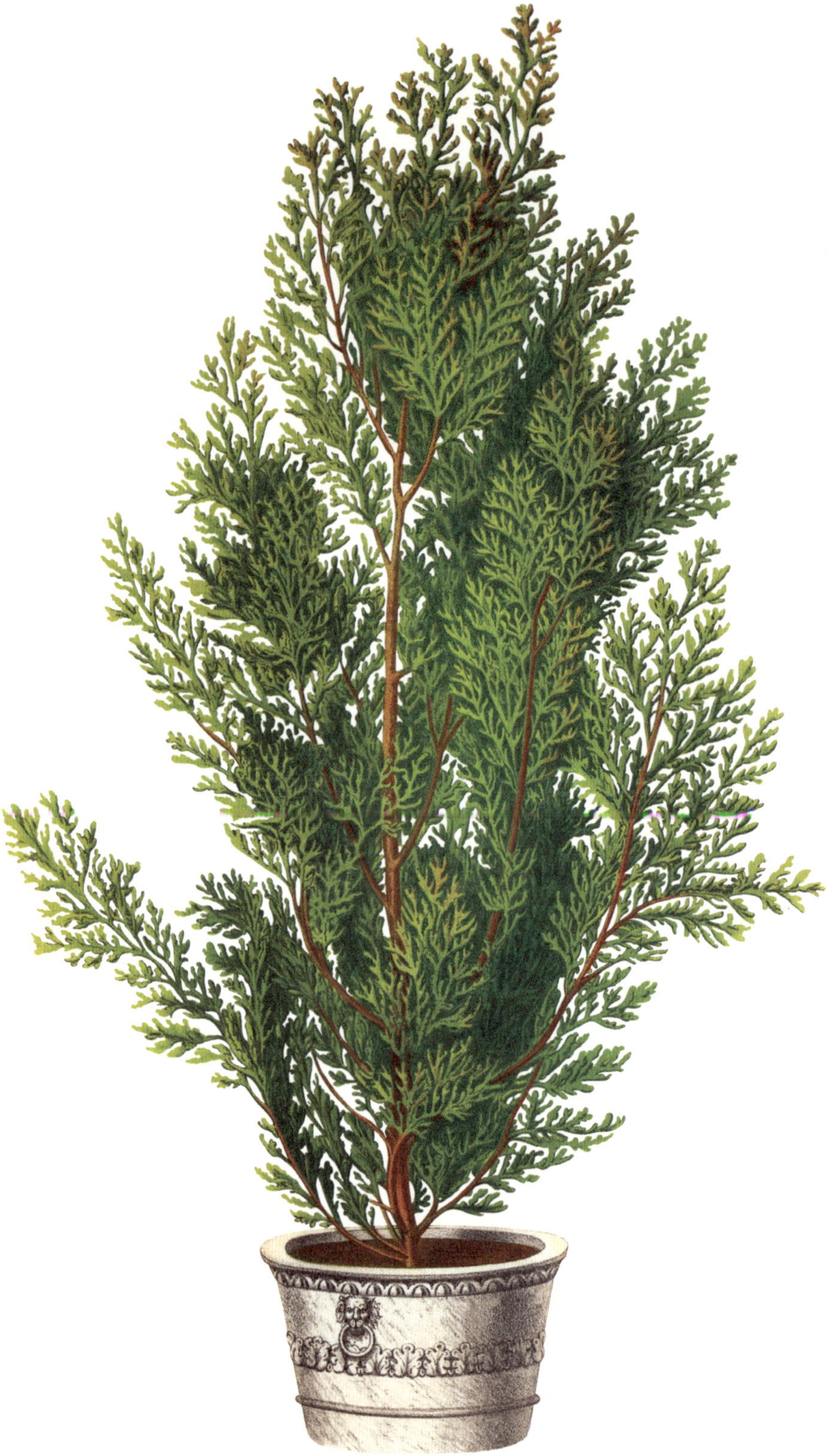

Chamaecyparis lawsoniana
by ABRAHAM JACOBUS WENDEL

Lawson's cypress | Port Orford cedar

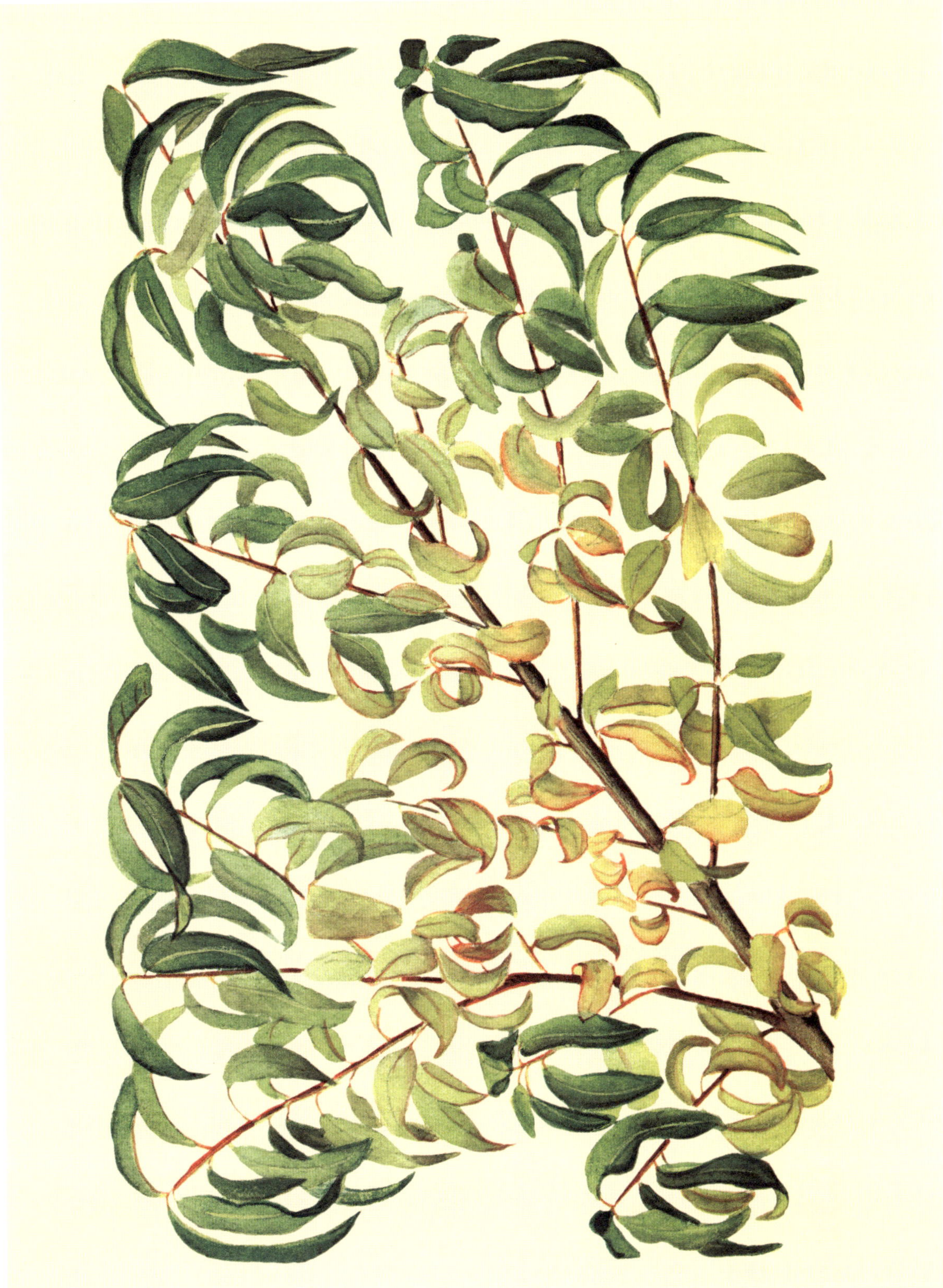

Prunus persica
from U.S. Department of Agriculture Pomological Watercolor Collection

peach

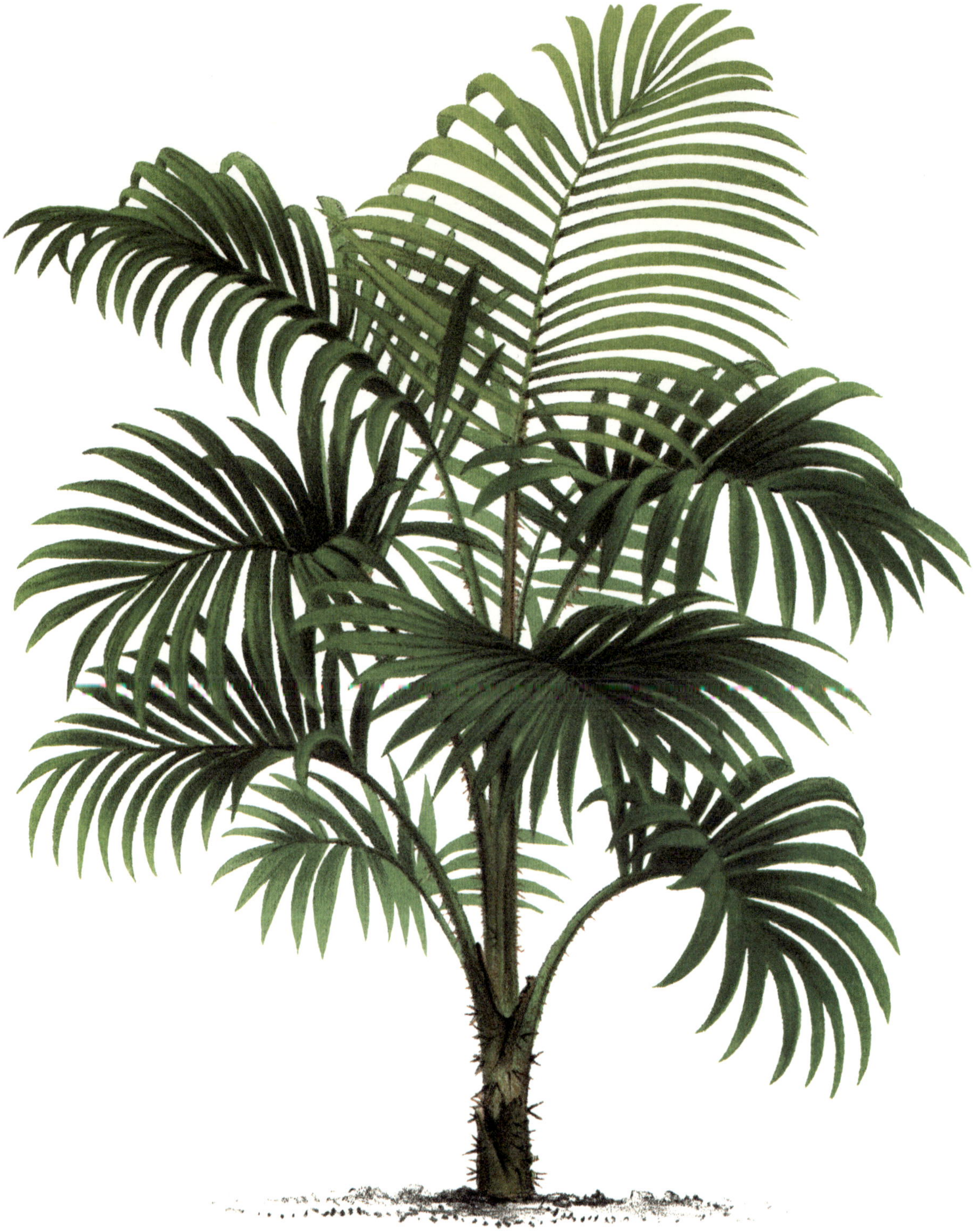

Calamus melanochaetes
by Oswald de Kerchove de Denterghem

yellow rattan palm | giant devil palm | chocolate rattan

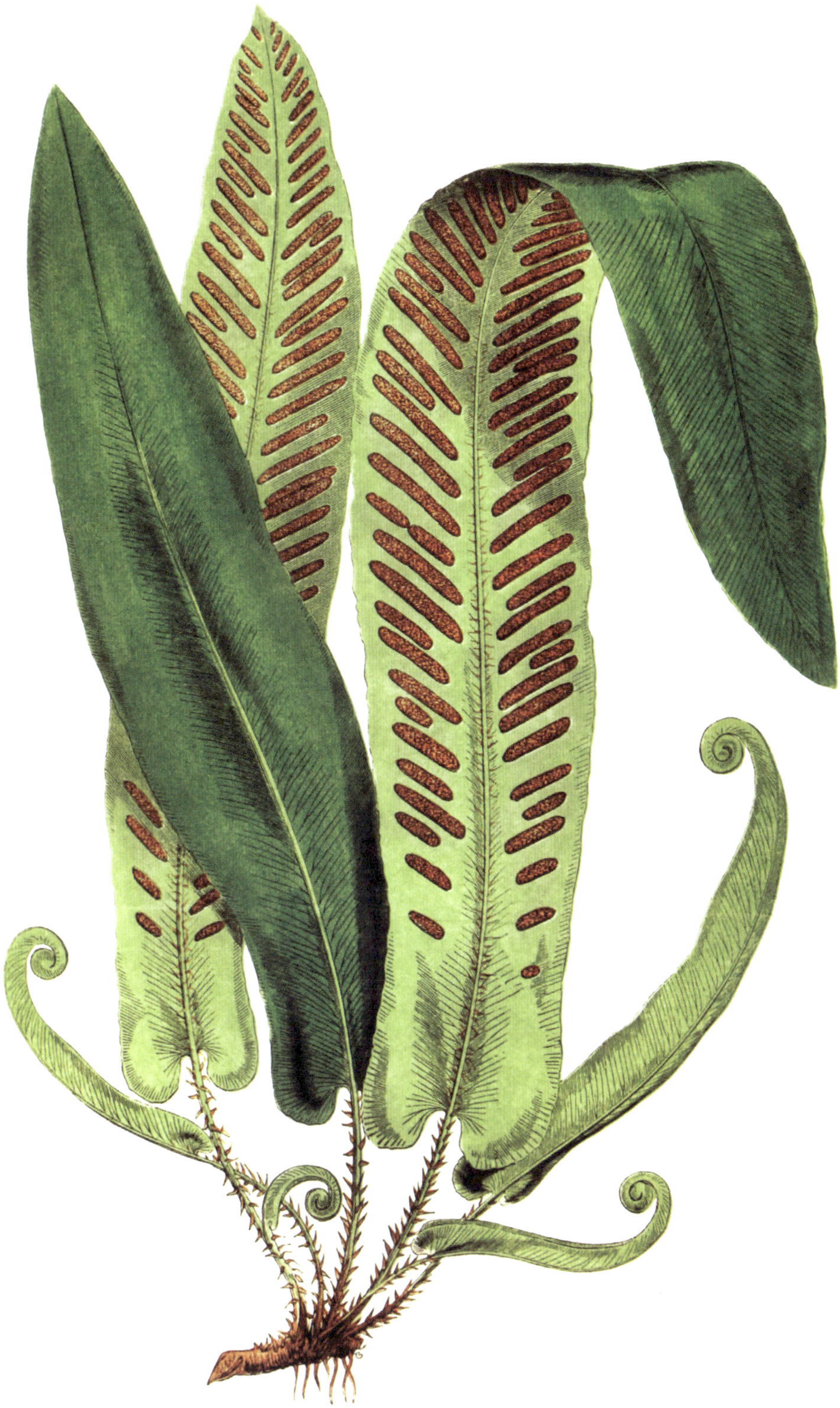

Asplenium scolopendrium
by Edward Joseph Lowe

Hart's tongue fern

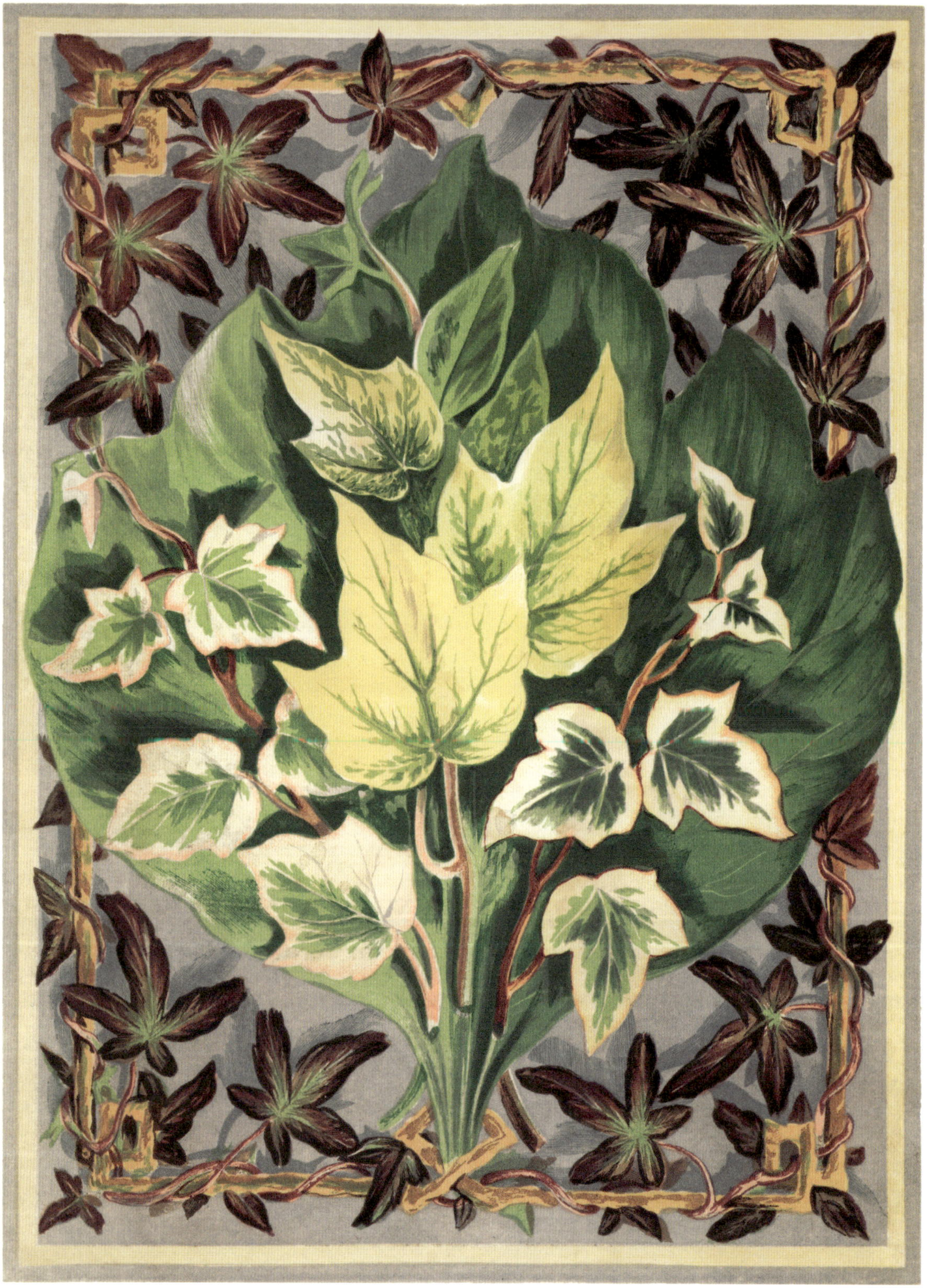

Hedera
by James Shirley Hibberd

ivy (various)

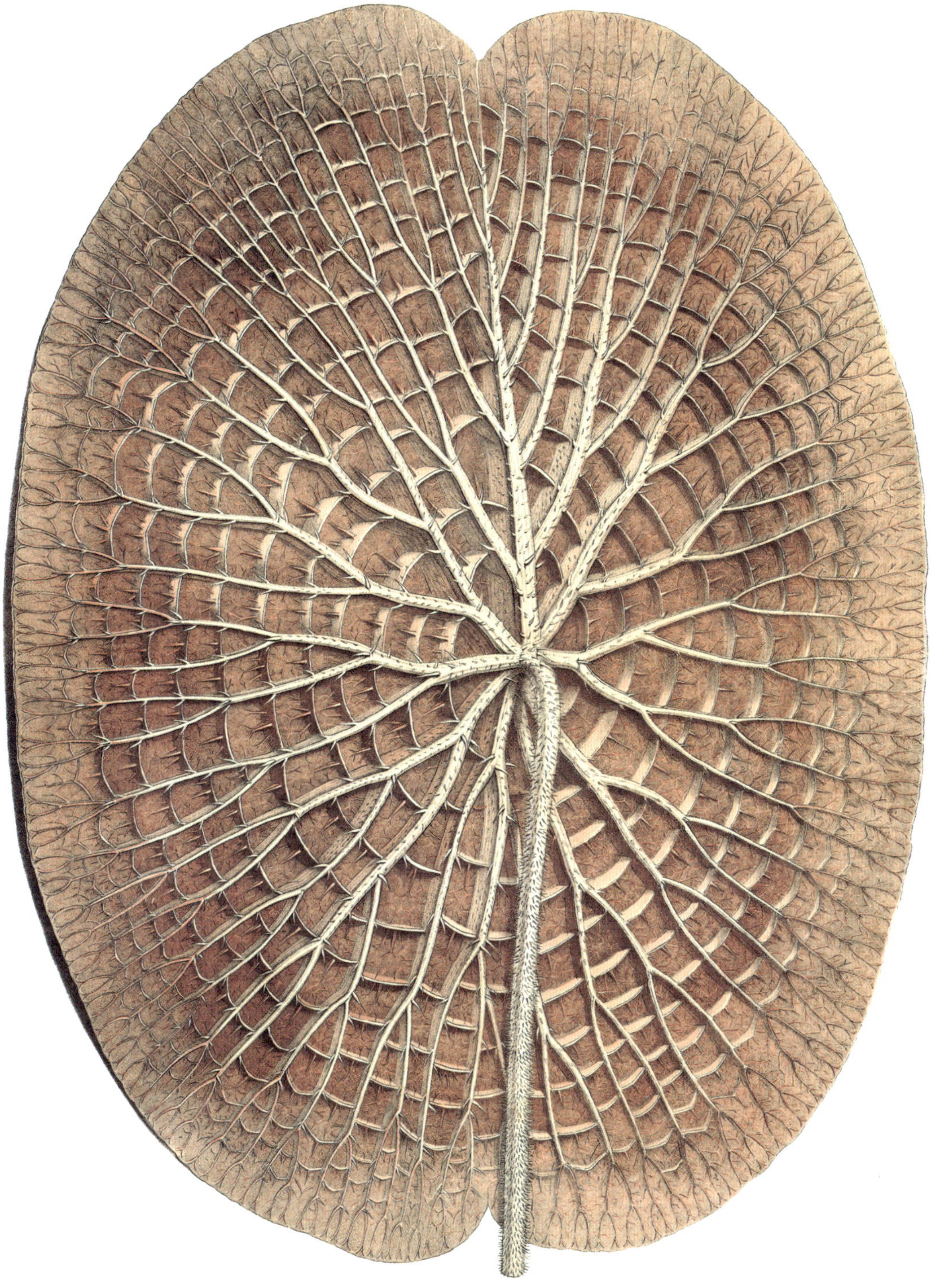

Victoria amazonica
by William Sharp

giant water lily | Amazon water lily | royal water lily

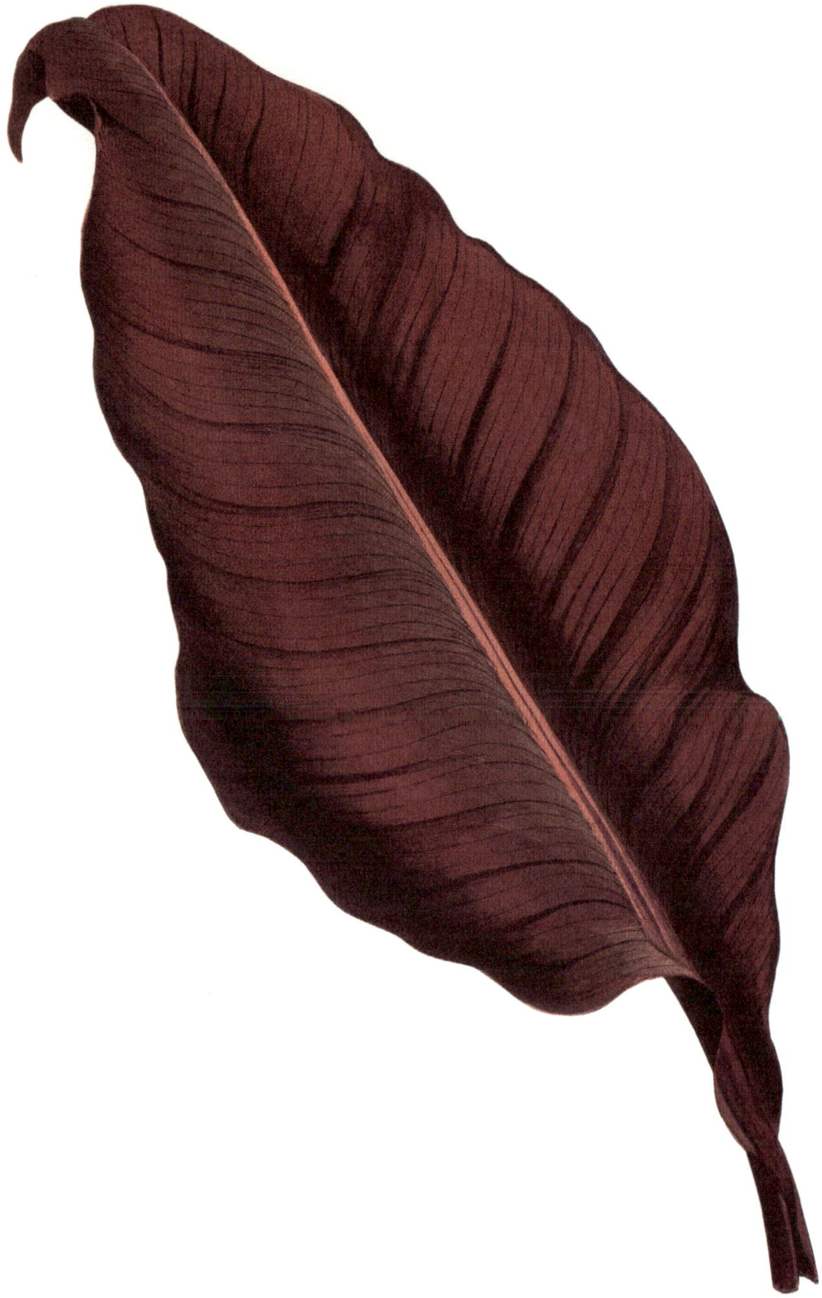

Canna indica
by Alexander Francis Lydon & Benjamin Fawcett

Indian shot | African arrowroot | edible canna | purple arrowroot

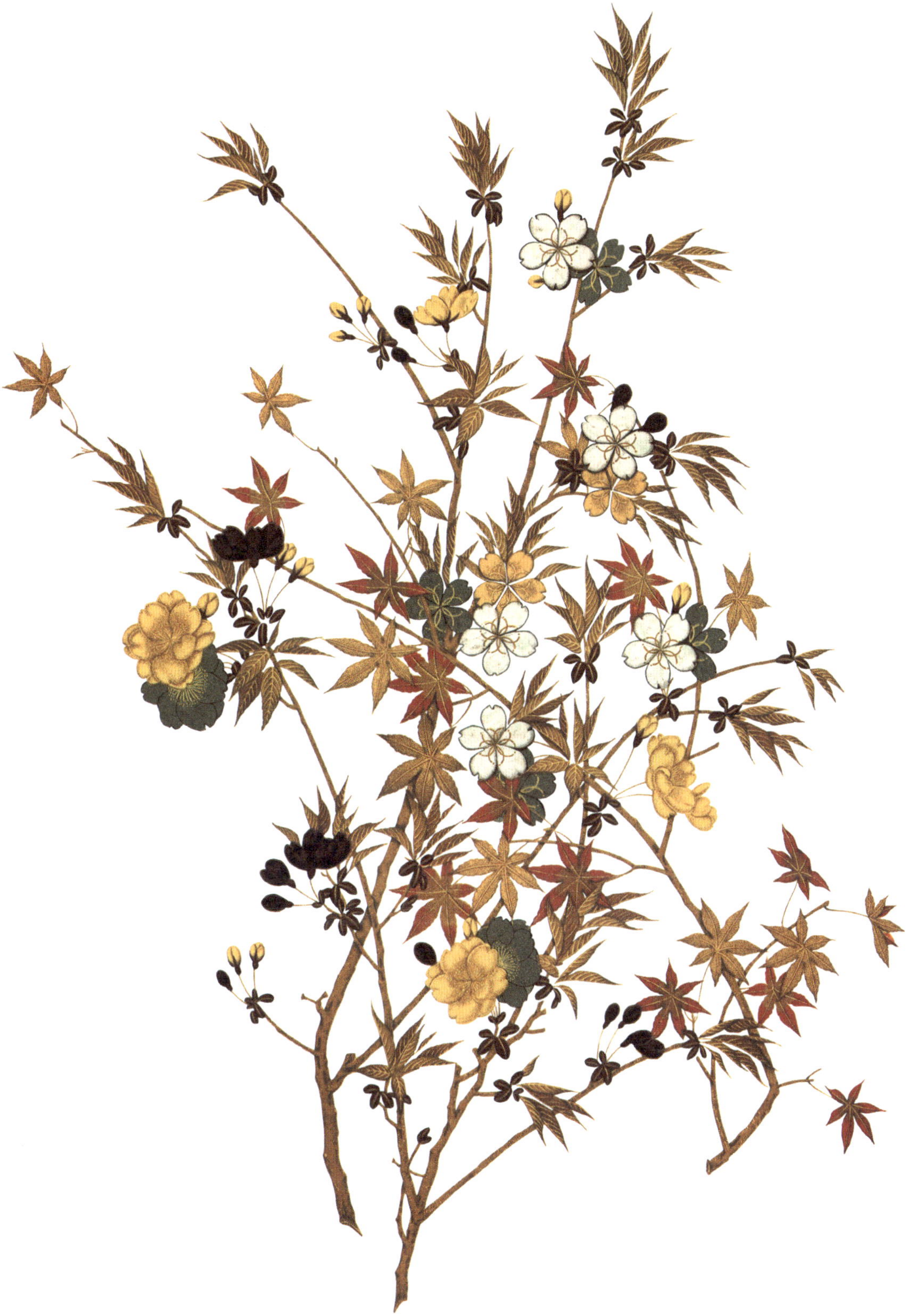

Acer
from *The Ornamental Arts of Japan*

maple (unknown variety)

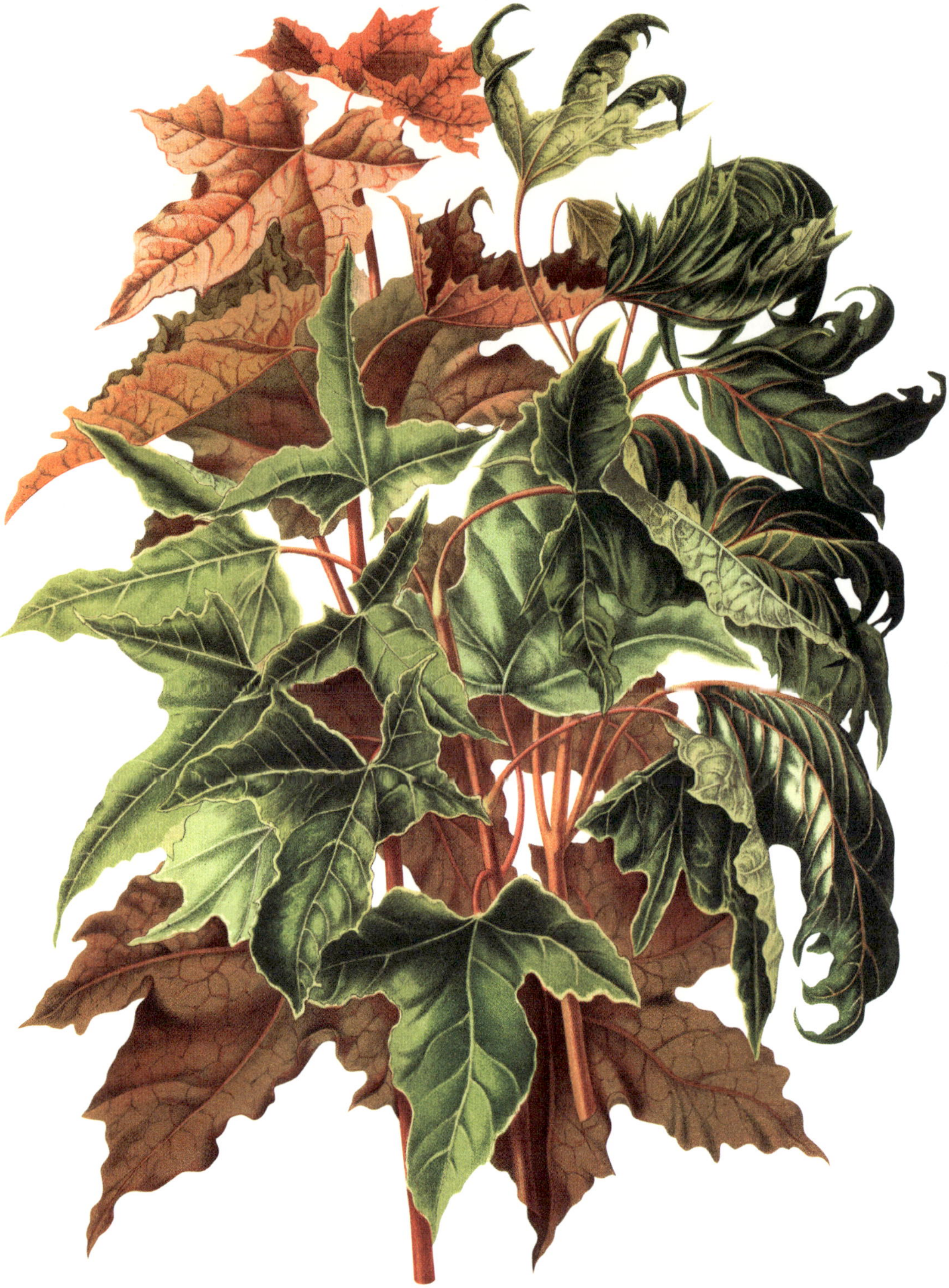

Acer platanoides
by Abraham Jacobus Wendel

Norway maple

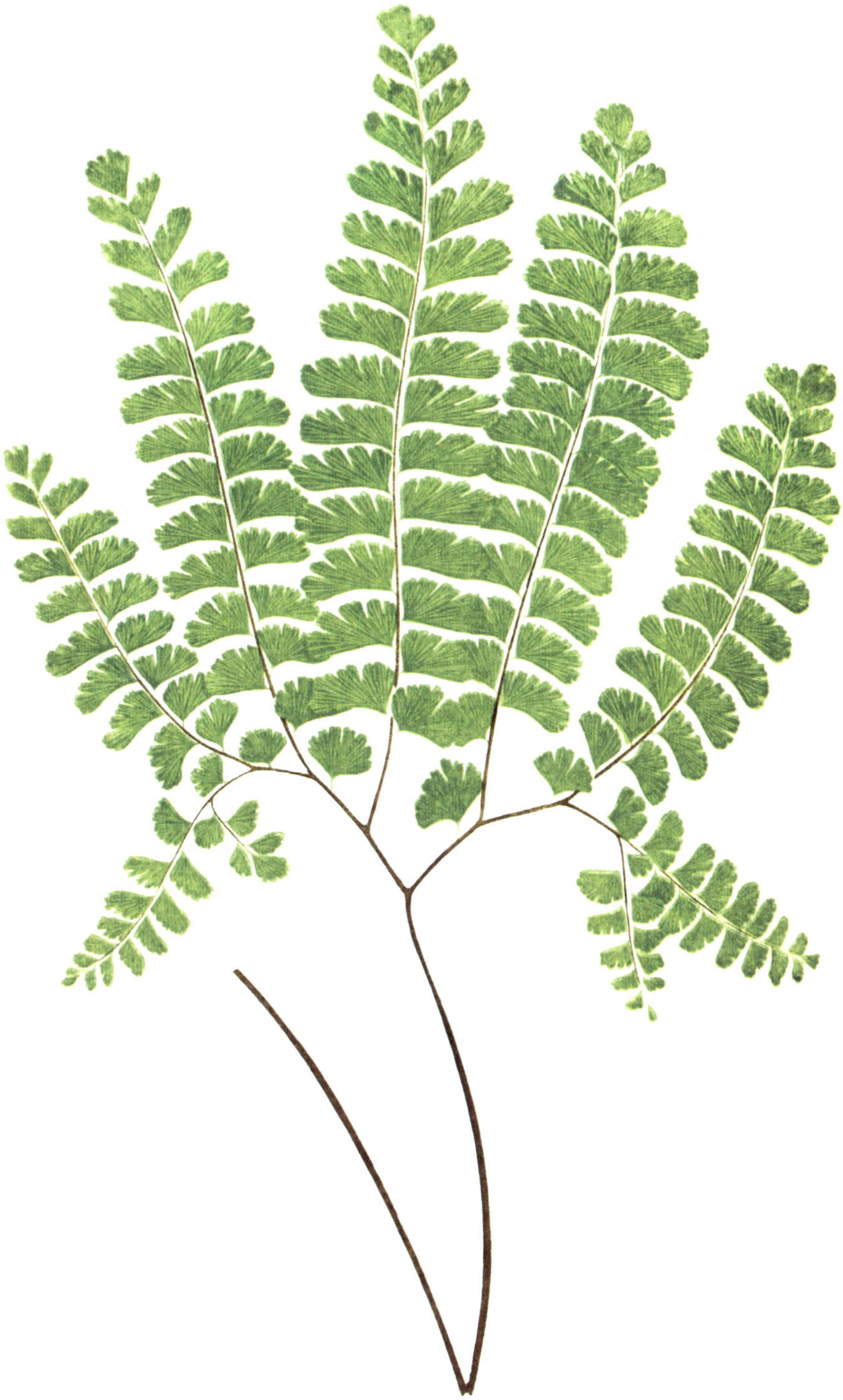

Adiantum pedatum
by Edward Joseph Lowe

northern maidenhair fern

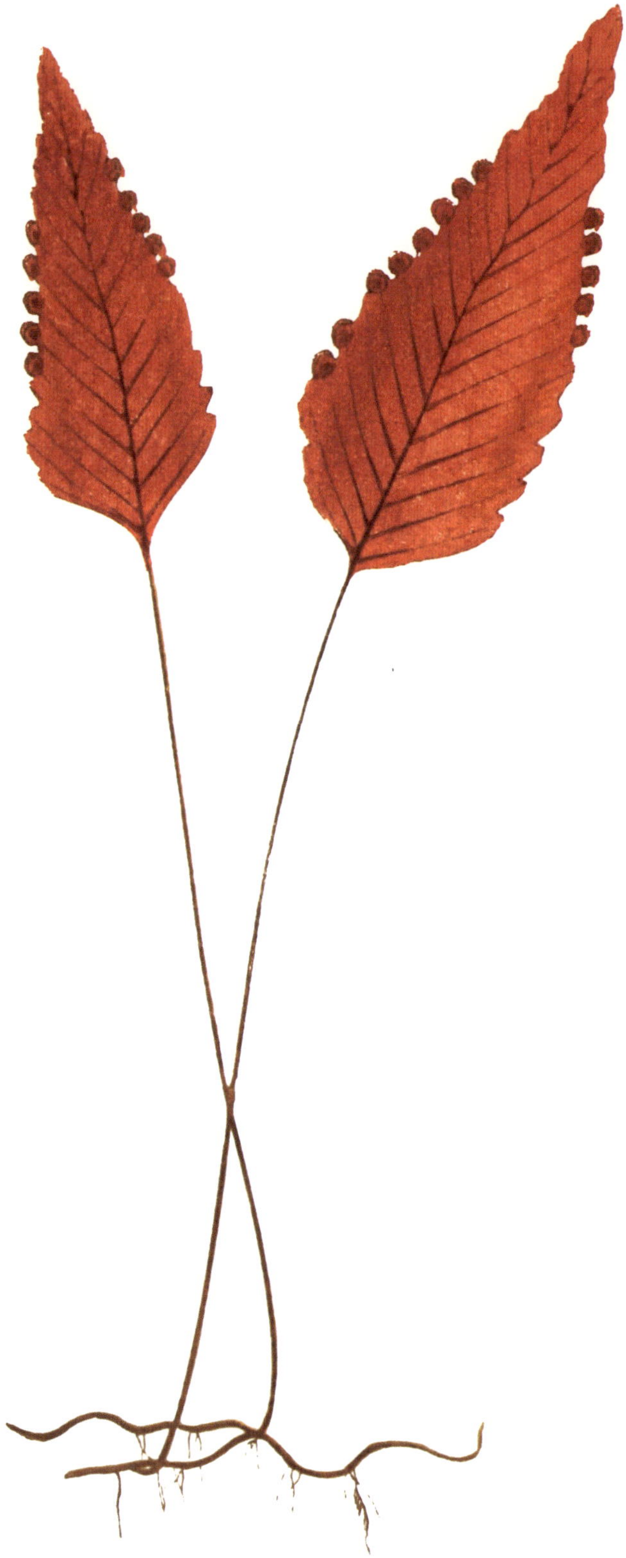

Hymenophyllum cruentum
by Edward Joseph Lowe

hymenophyllum cruentum

Quercus
by William Morris

oak (unknown variety)

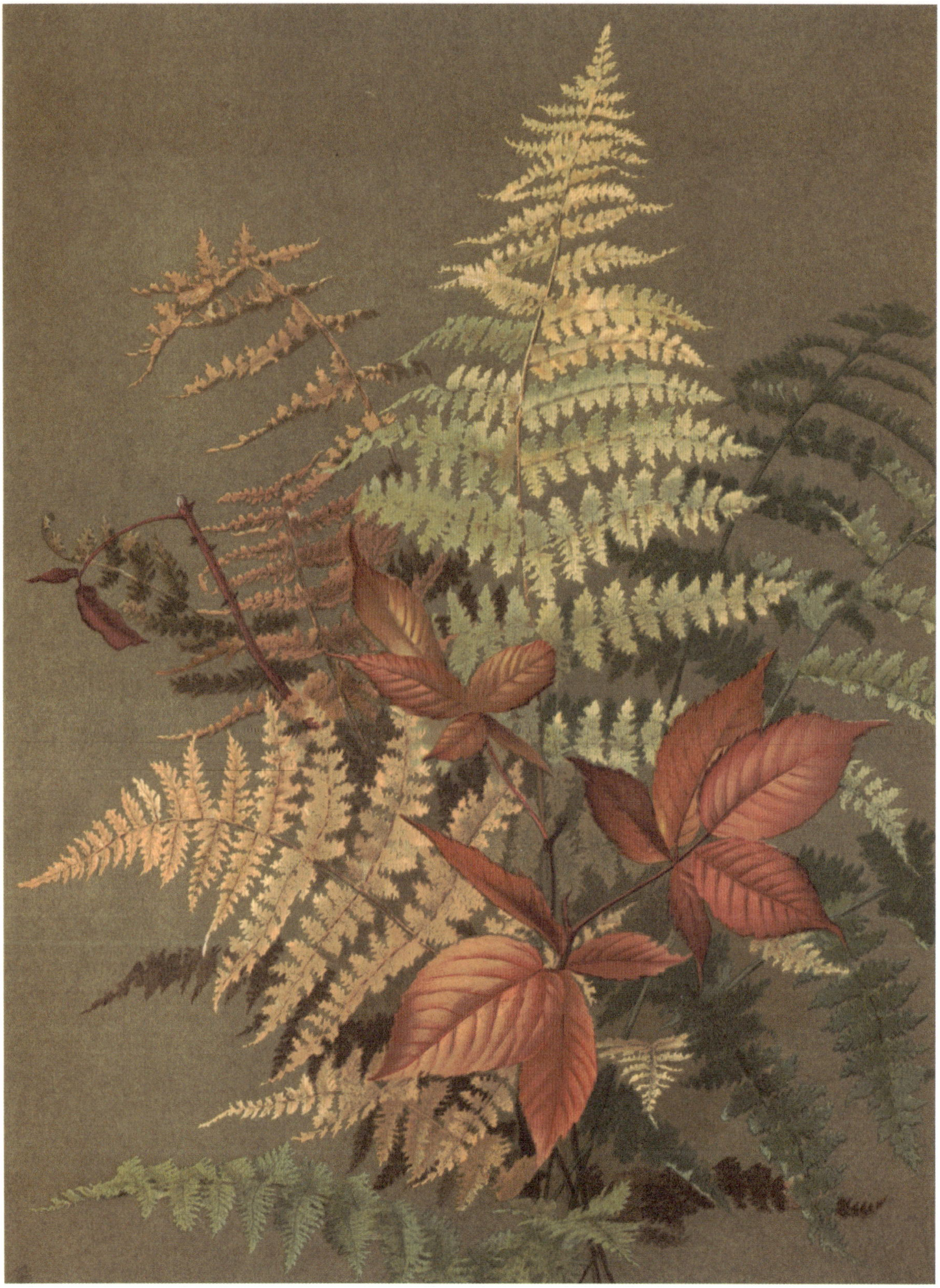

Polypodiopsida
by ELLEN T. FISHER

fern (various)

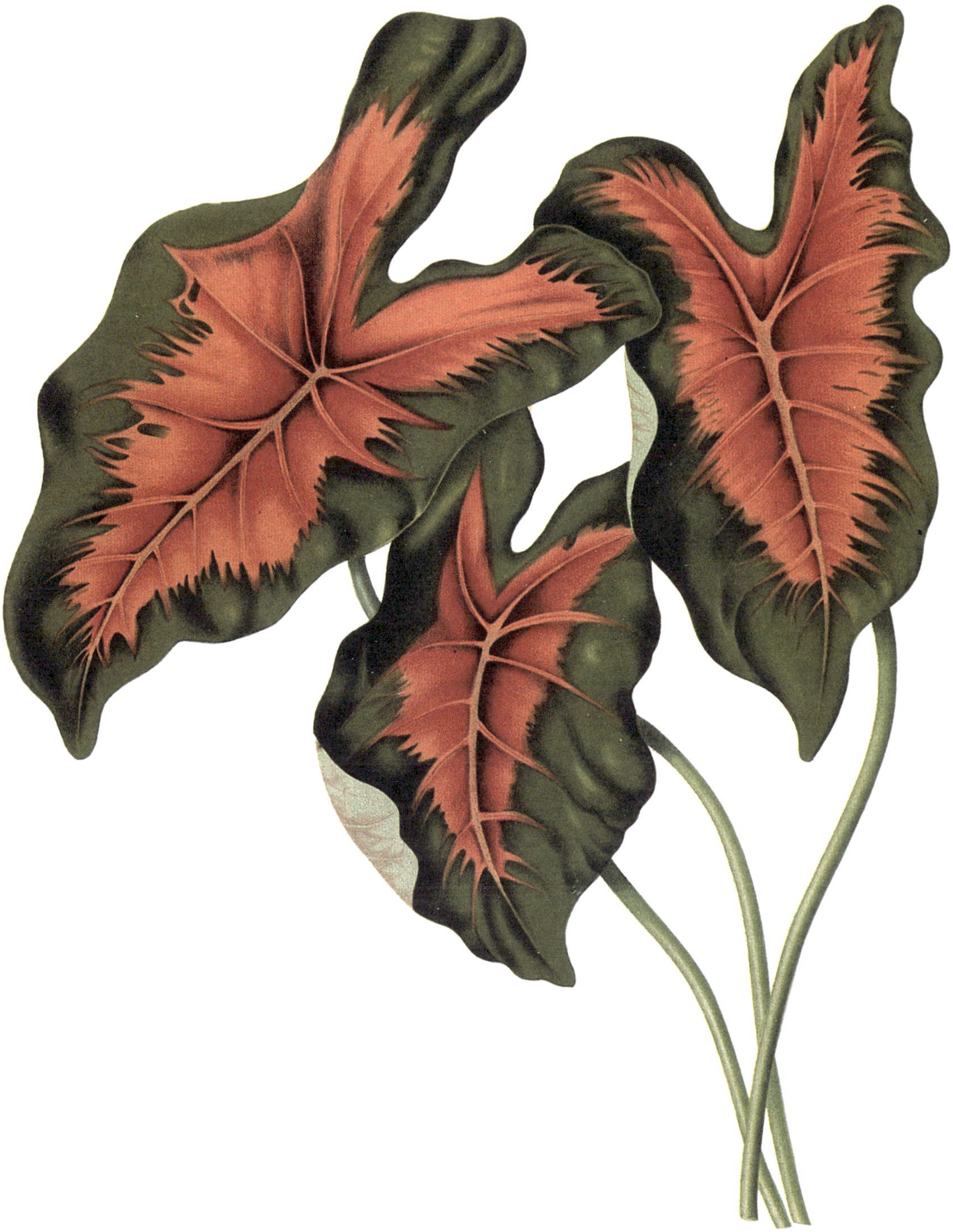

Caladium bicolor
by PIETER DE PANNEMAEKER

Heart of Jesus | elephant ear | angel wings

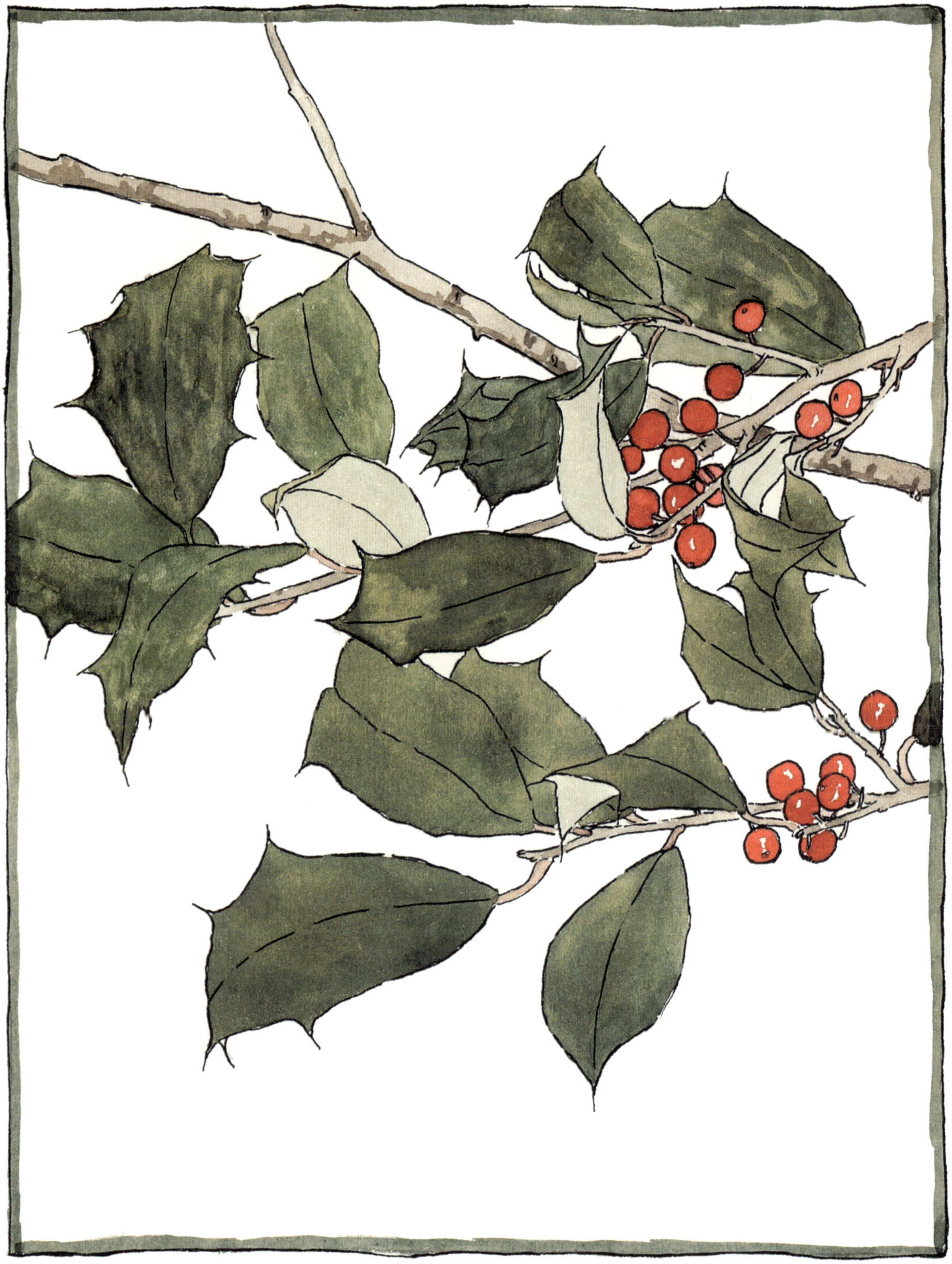

Ilex aquifolium
by HANNAH BORGER OVERBECK

common holly | English holly

While we laugh and carouse
'neath its glitt'ring boughs,
To the Christmas holly we'll sing.

FROM 'The Christmas Holly' BY ELIZA COOK

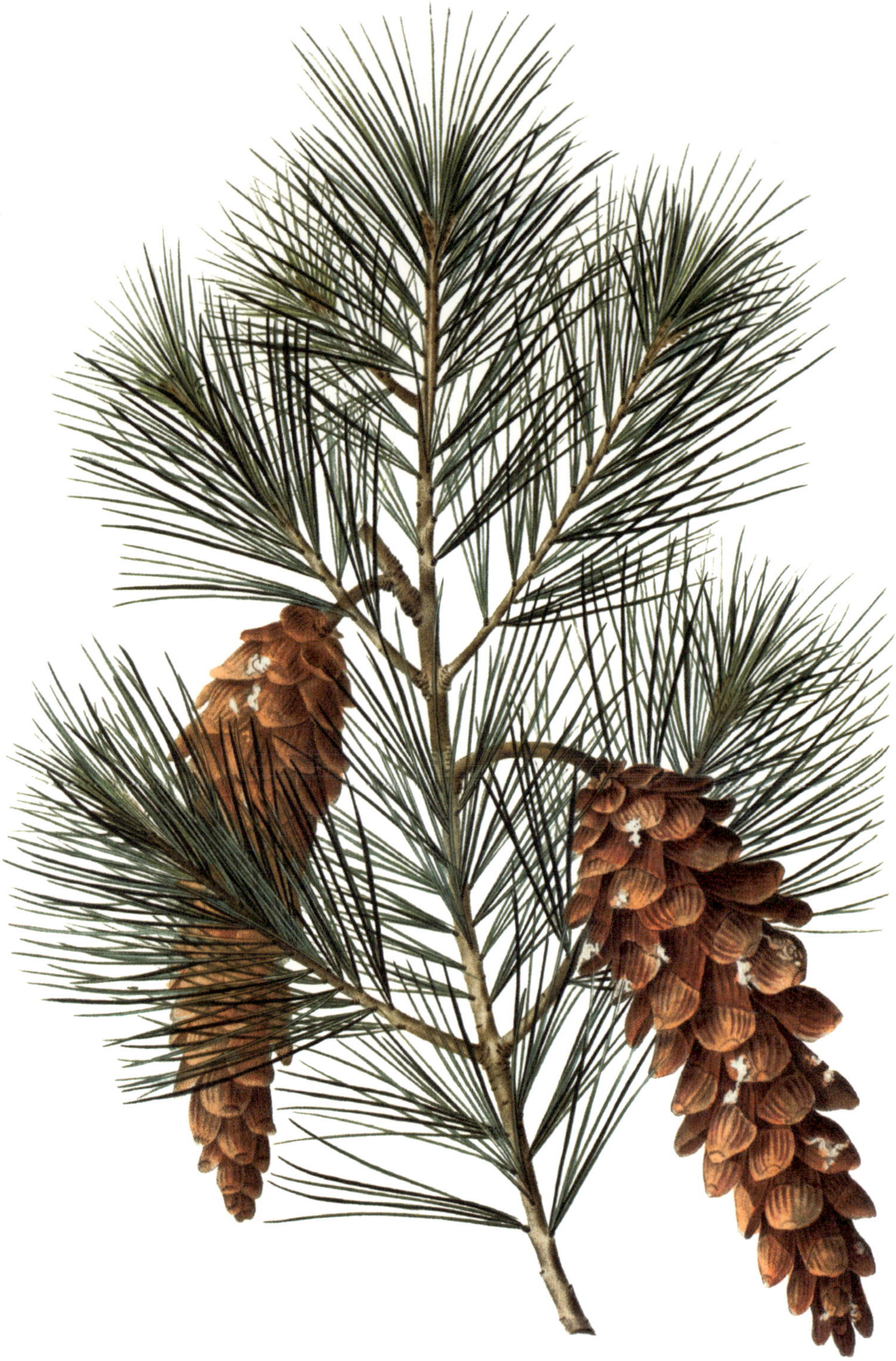

Pinus strobus
by Pierre-Joseph Redouté

white pine | Weymouth pine | soft pine | eastern white pine

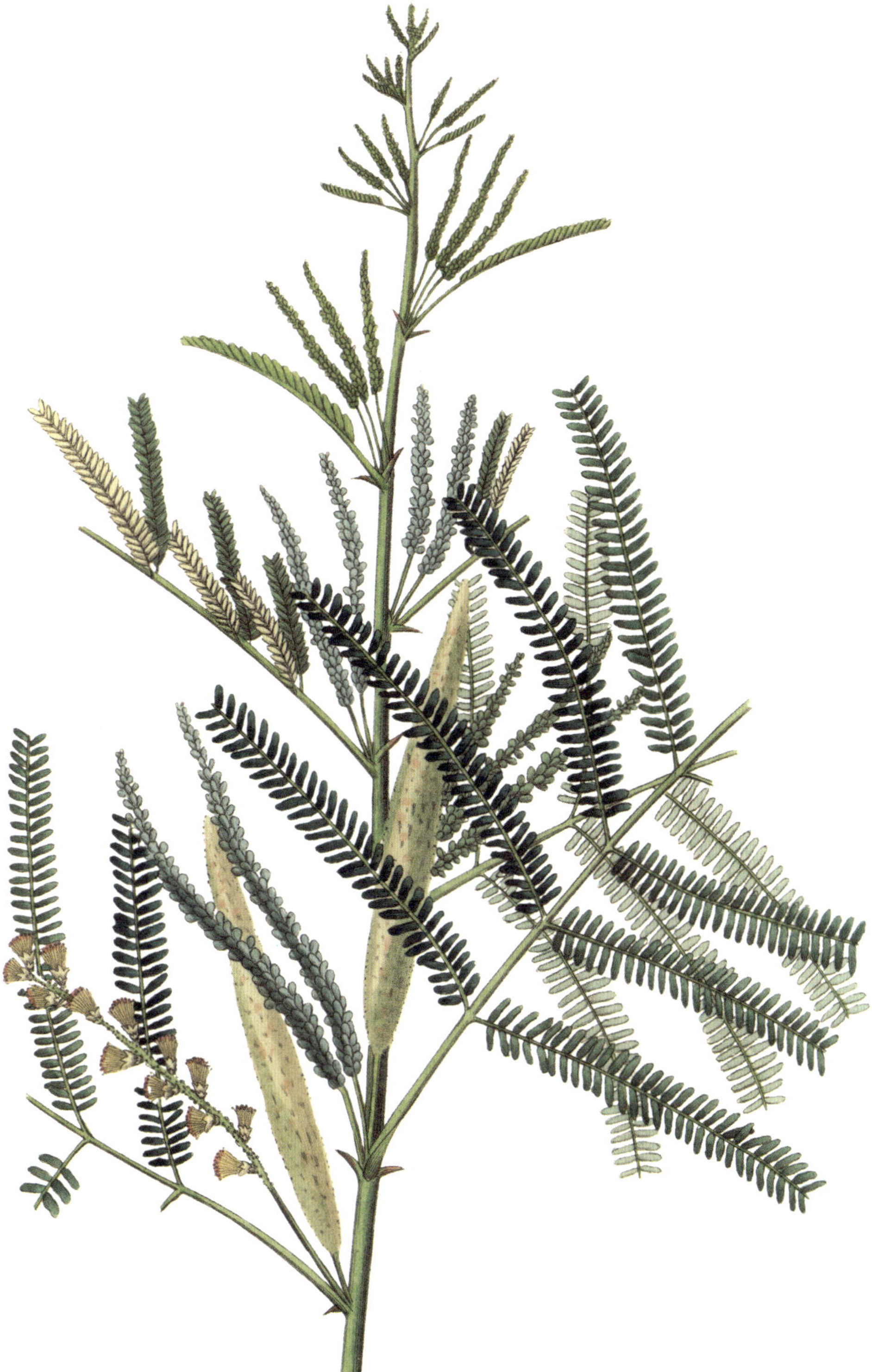

Senegalia catechu
by John Stephenson & James Morss Churchill

black cutch | black catechu | catechu | cutch tree

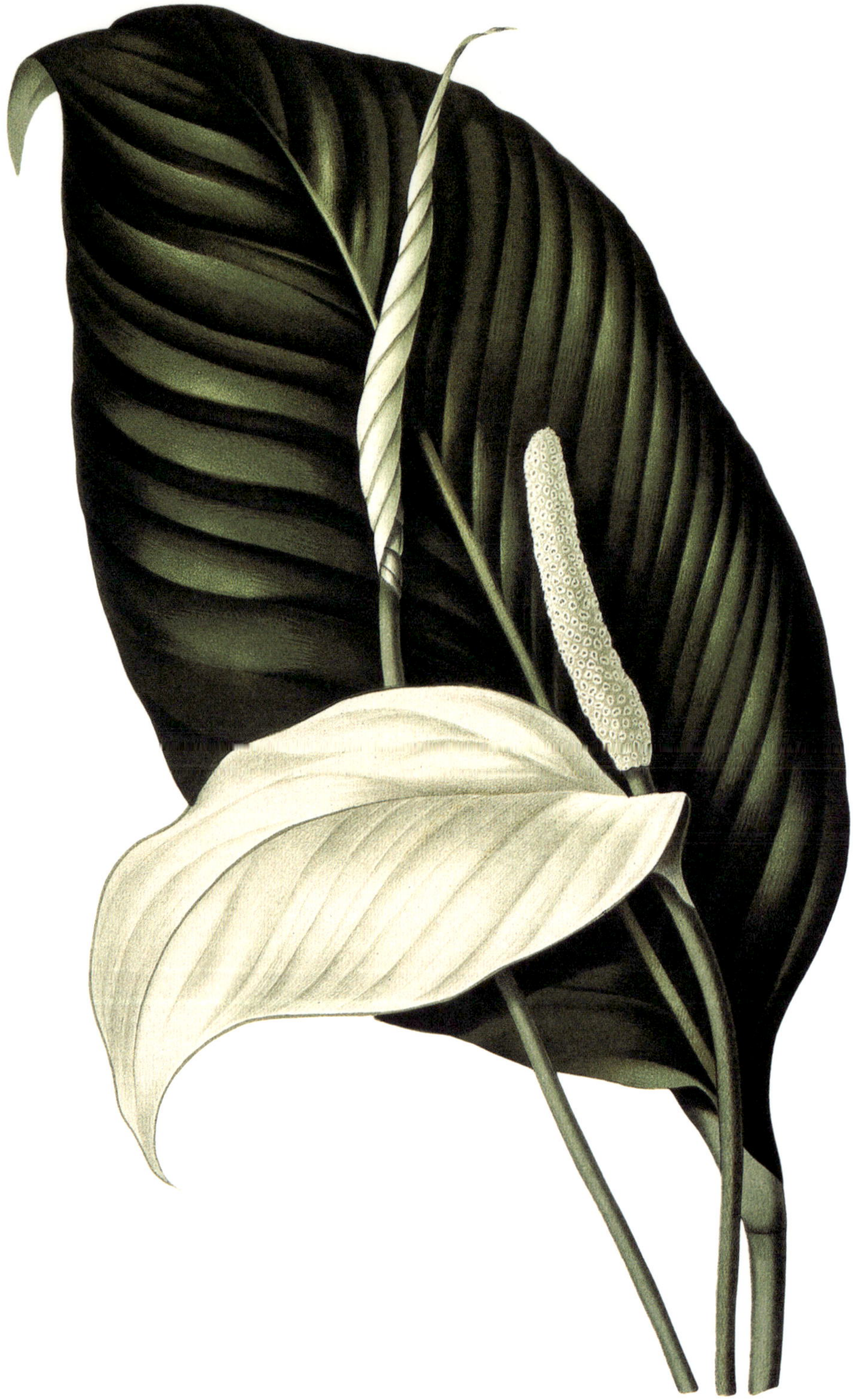

Spathiphyllum
by Berthe Hoola van Nooten

Peace lily

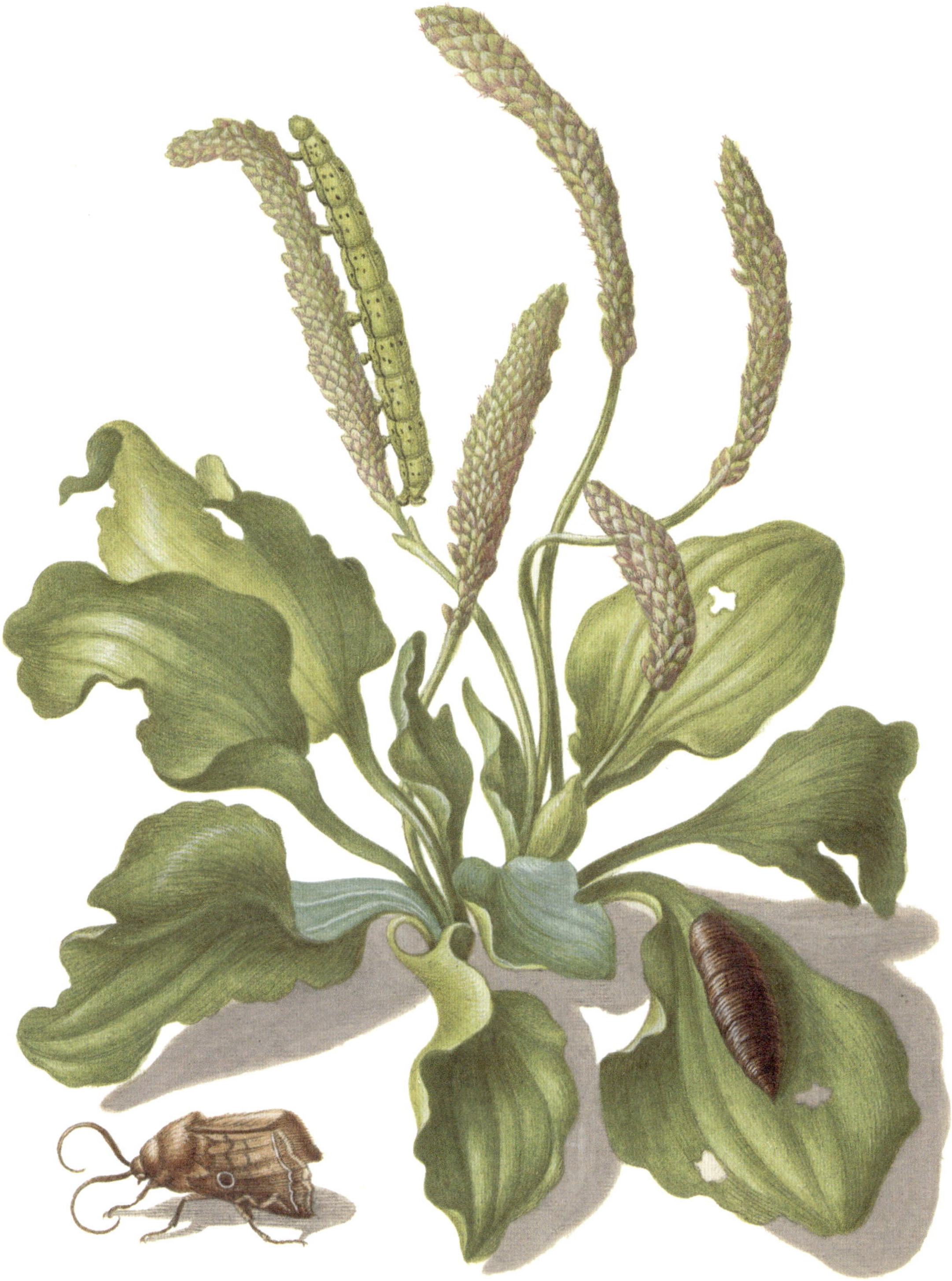

Plantago major
by Maria Sibylla Merian

broadleaf plantain | waybread | greater plantain

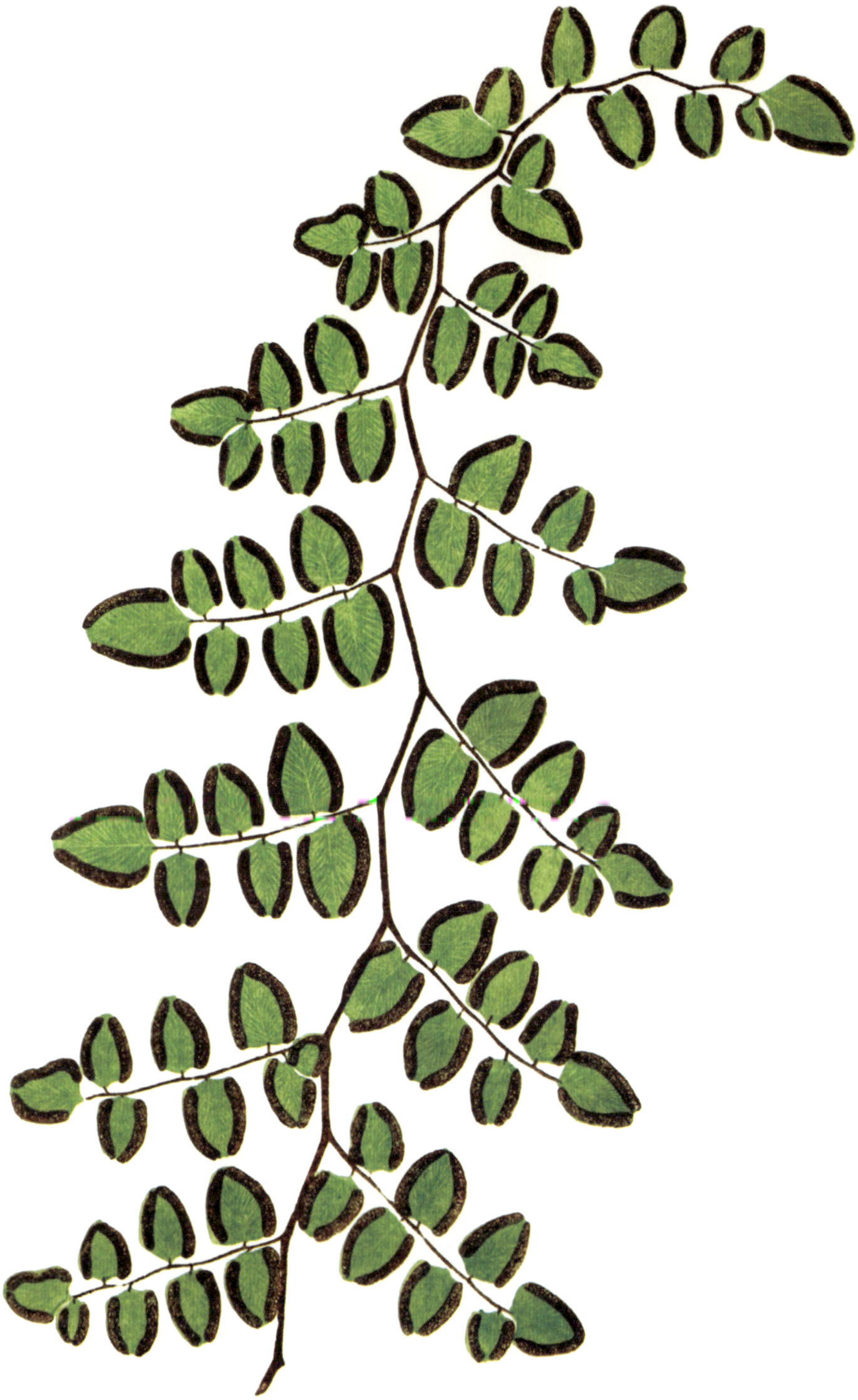

Pellaea ovata
by Edward Joseph Lowe

ovate-leaf cliff brake | flexuous cliff brake

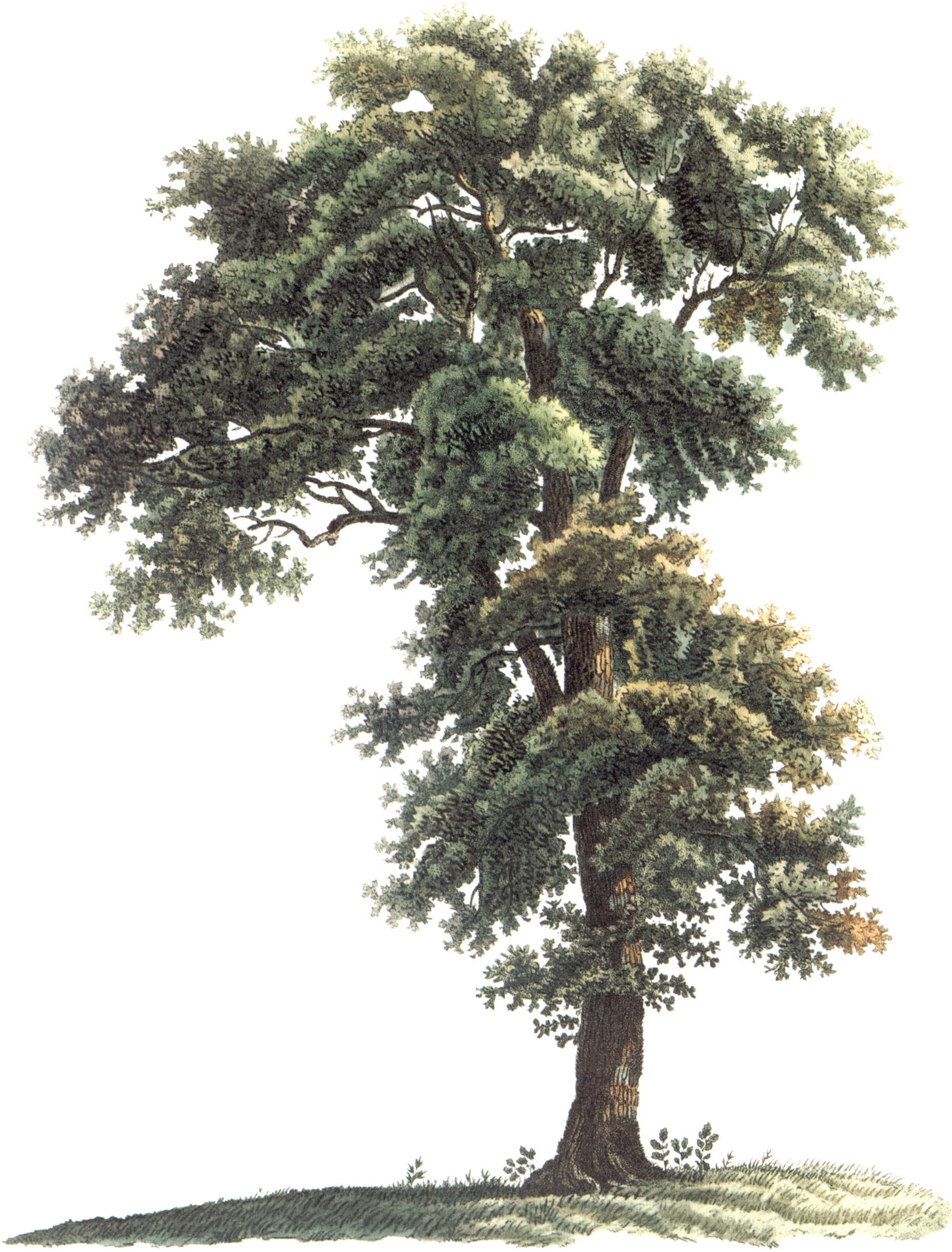

Quercus
by Pierre-Joseph Redouté

oak (unknown variety)

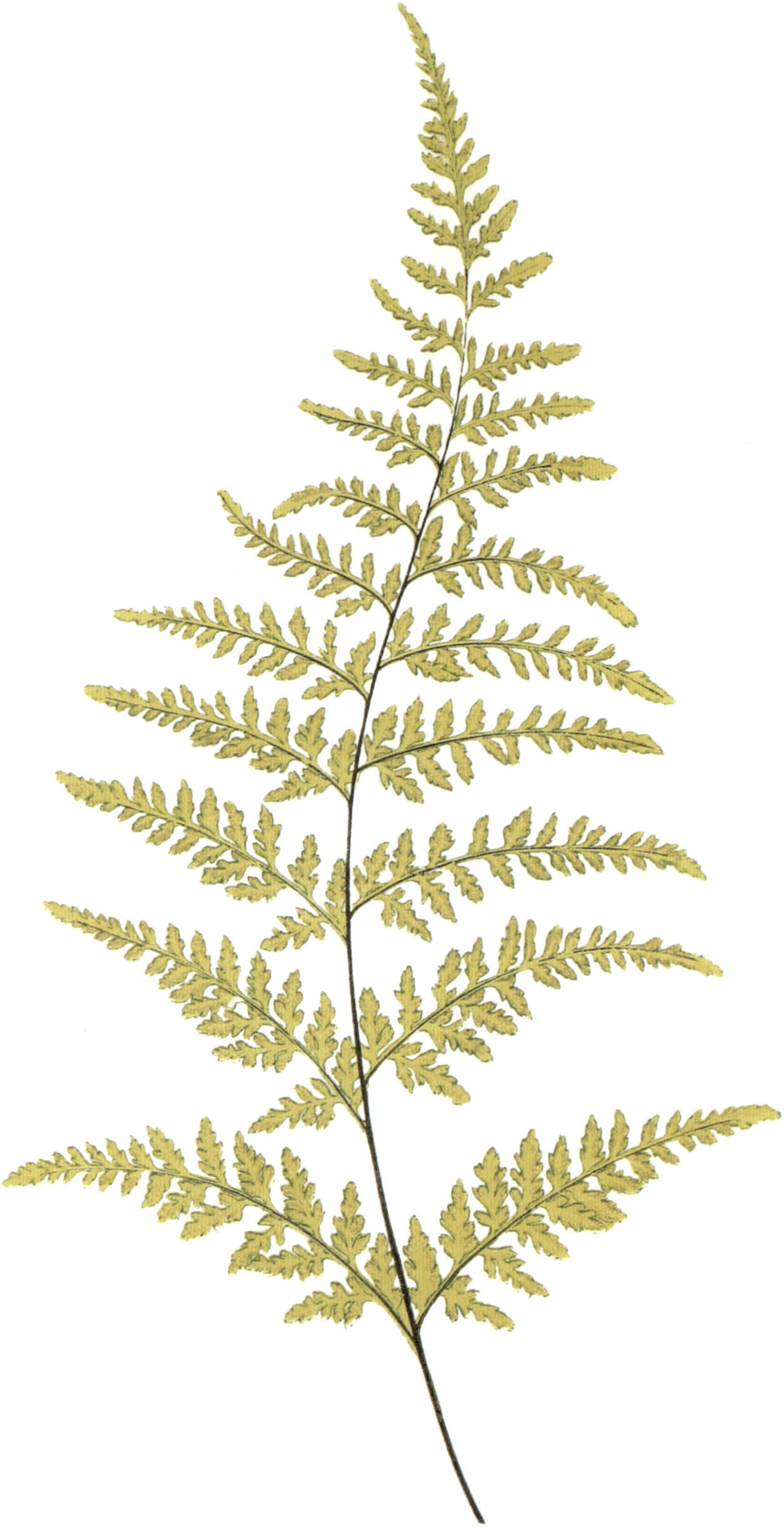

Pityrogramma chrysophylla
by Edward Joseph Lowe

goldback fern

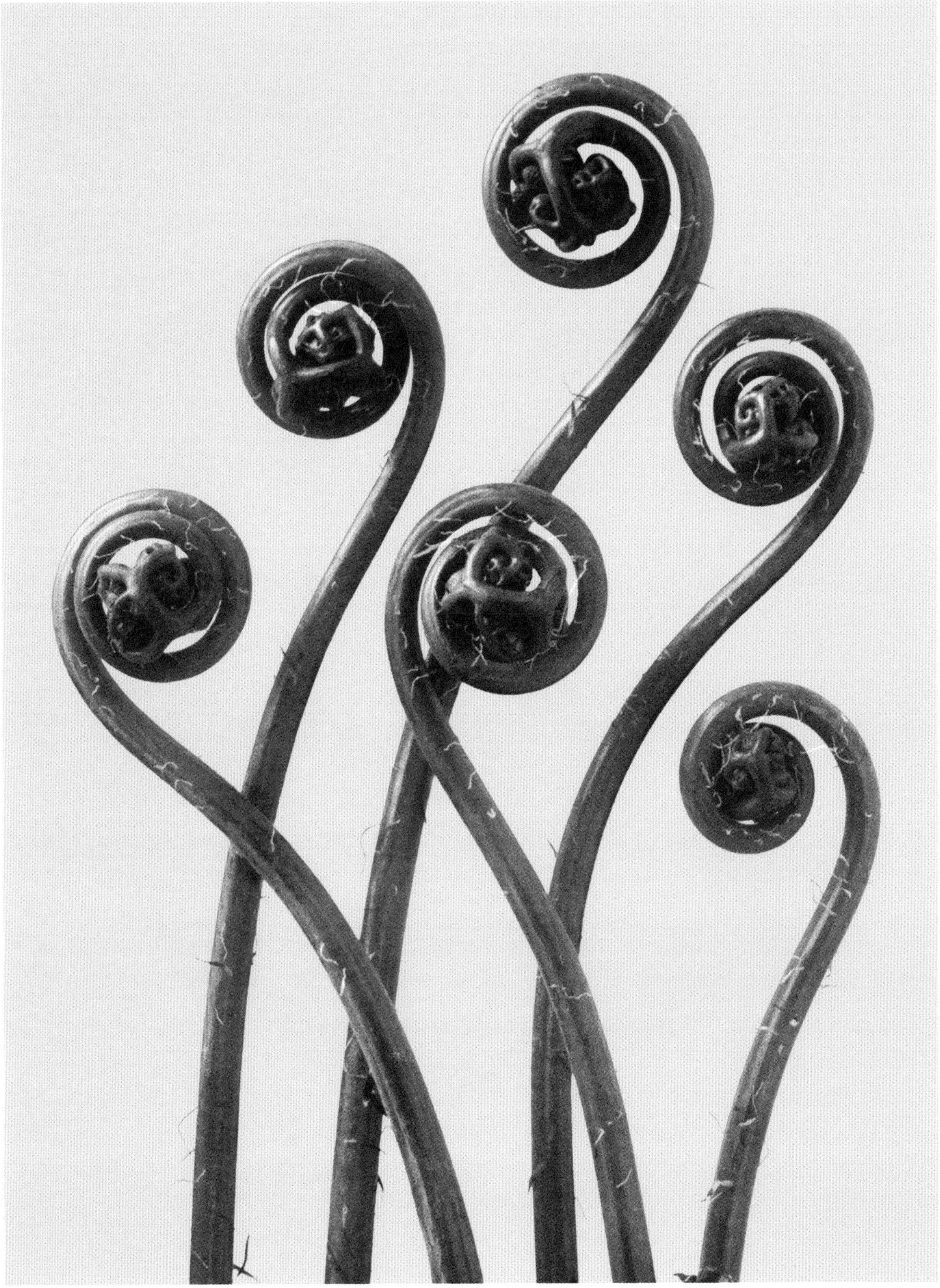

Adiantum pedatum
by Karl Blossfeldt

northern maidenhair fern

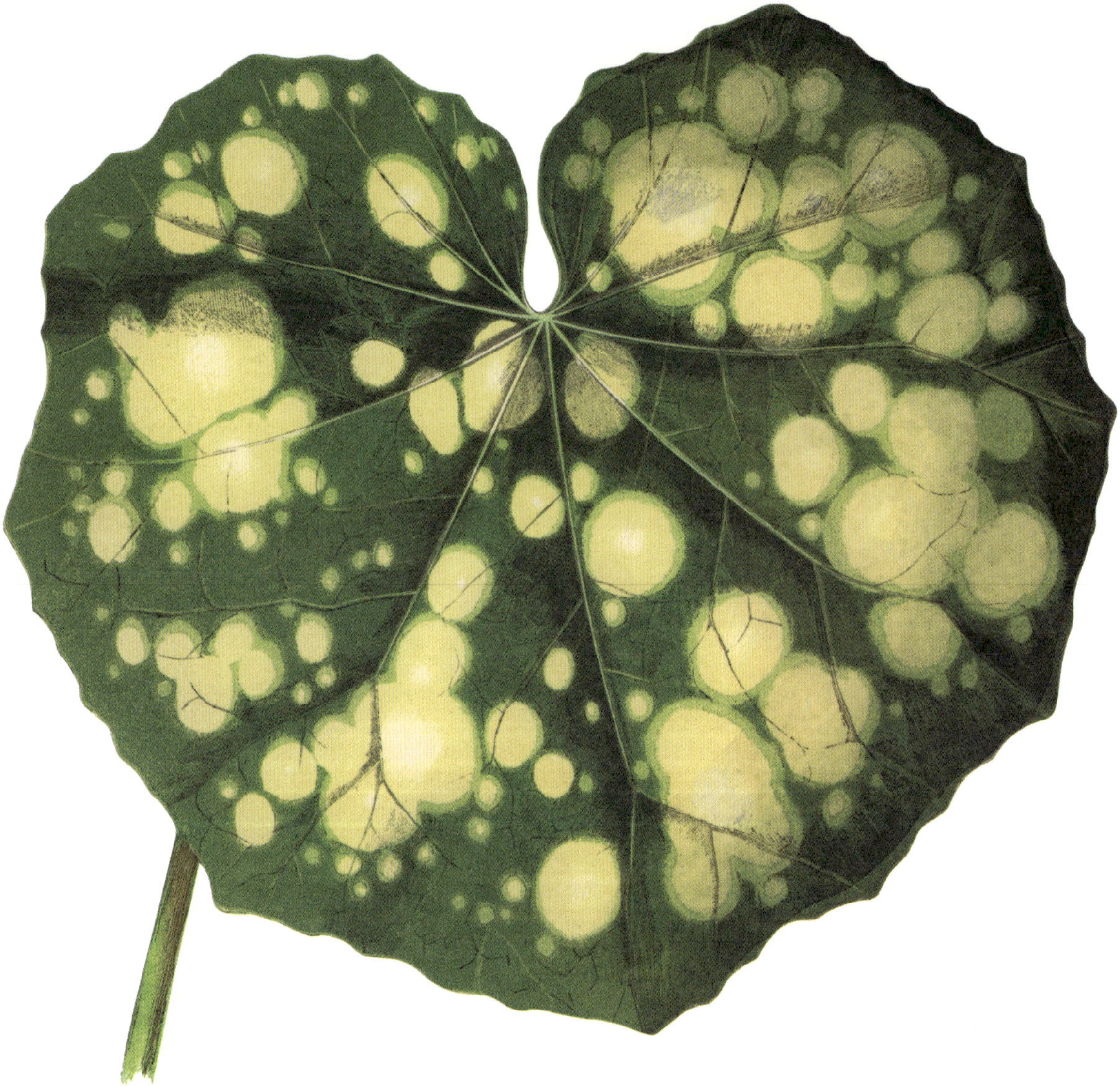

Farfugium japonicum
by Alexander Francis Lydon & Benjamin Fawcett

leopard plant | green leopard plant | tractor seat plant

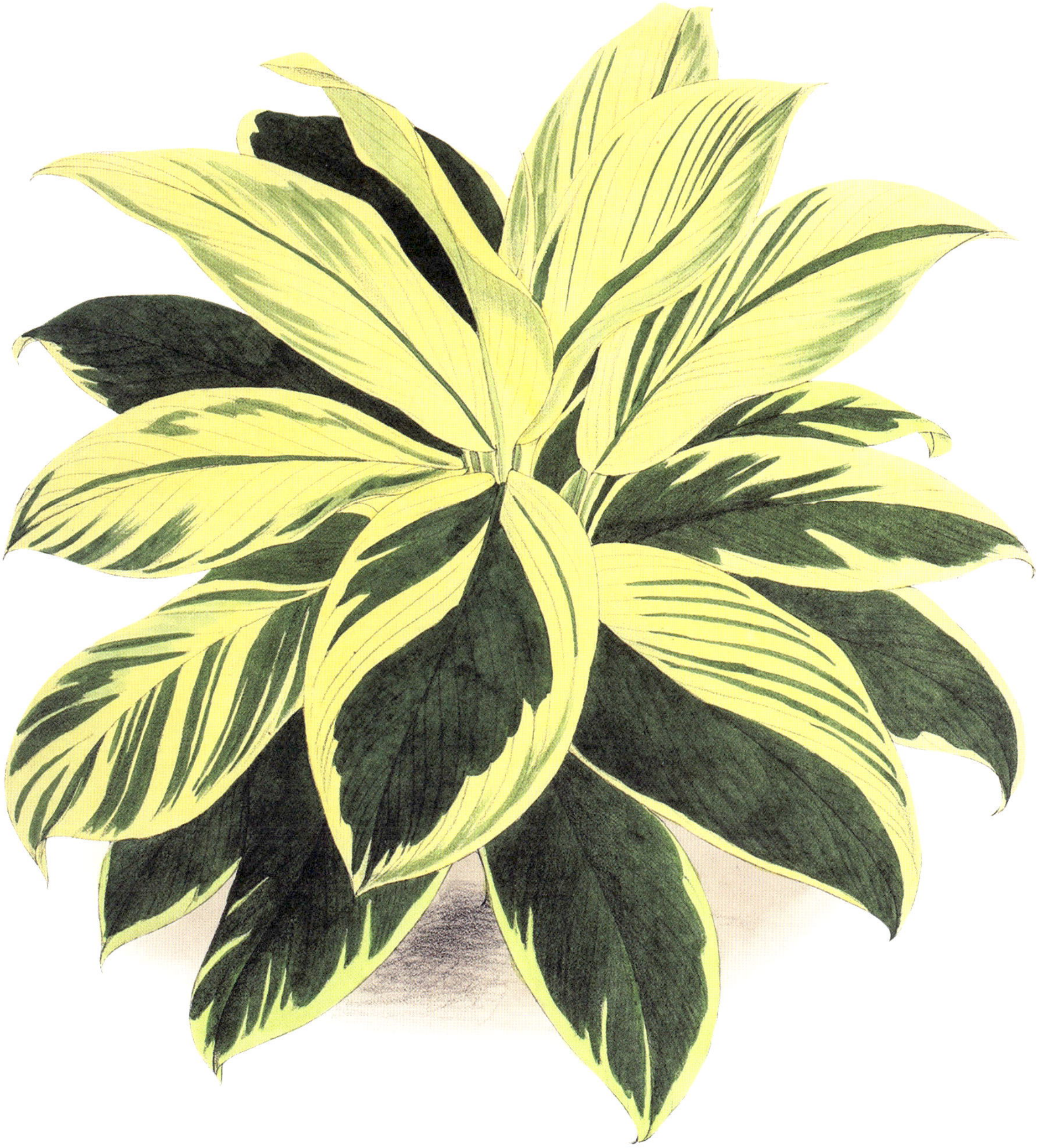

Dracaena
from BIODIVERSITY HERITAGE LIBRARY

dracaena (unknown variety)

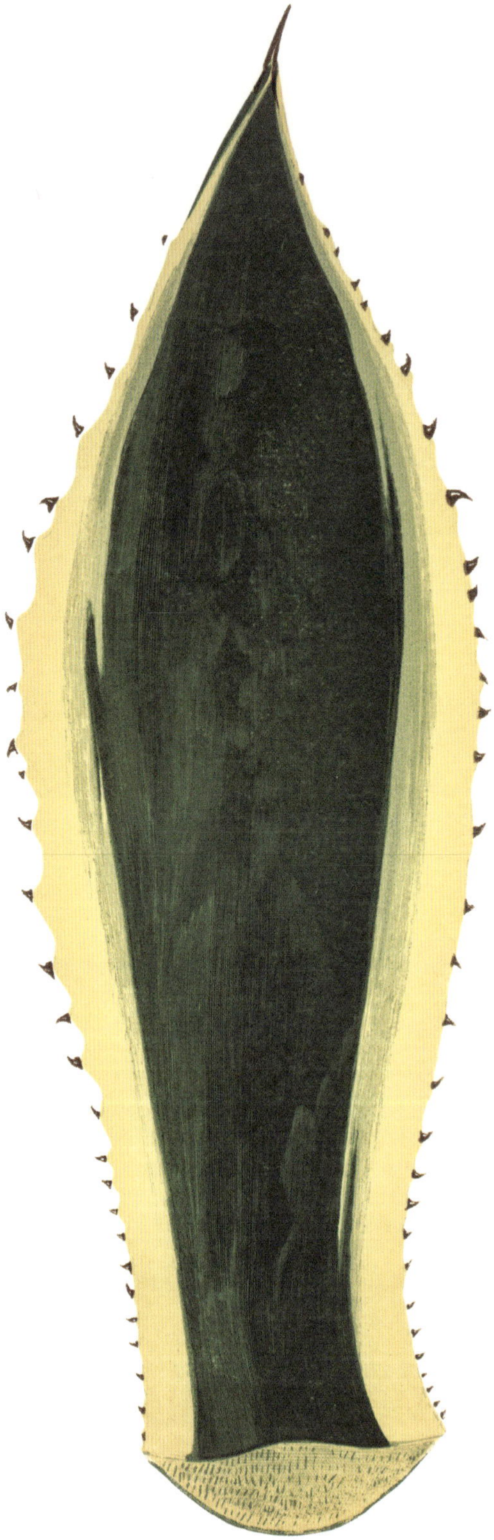

Agave americana
by Benjamin Fawcett & James Shirley Hibberd

century plant | maguey | American aloe

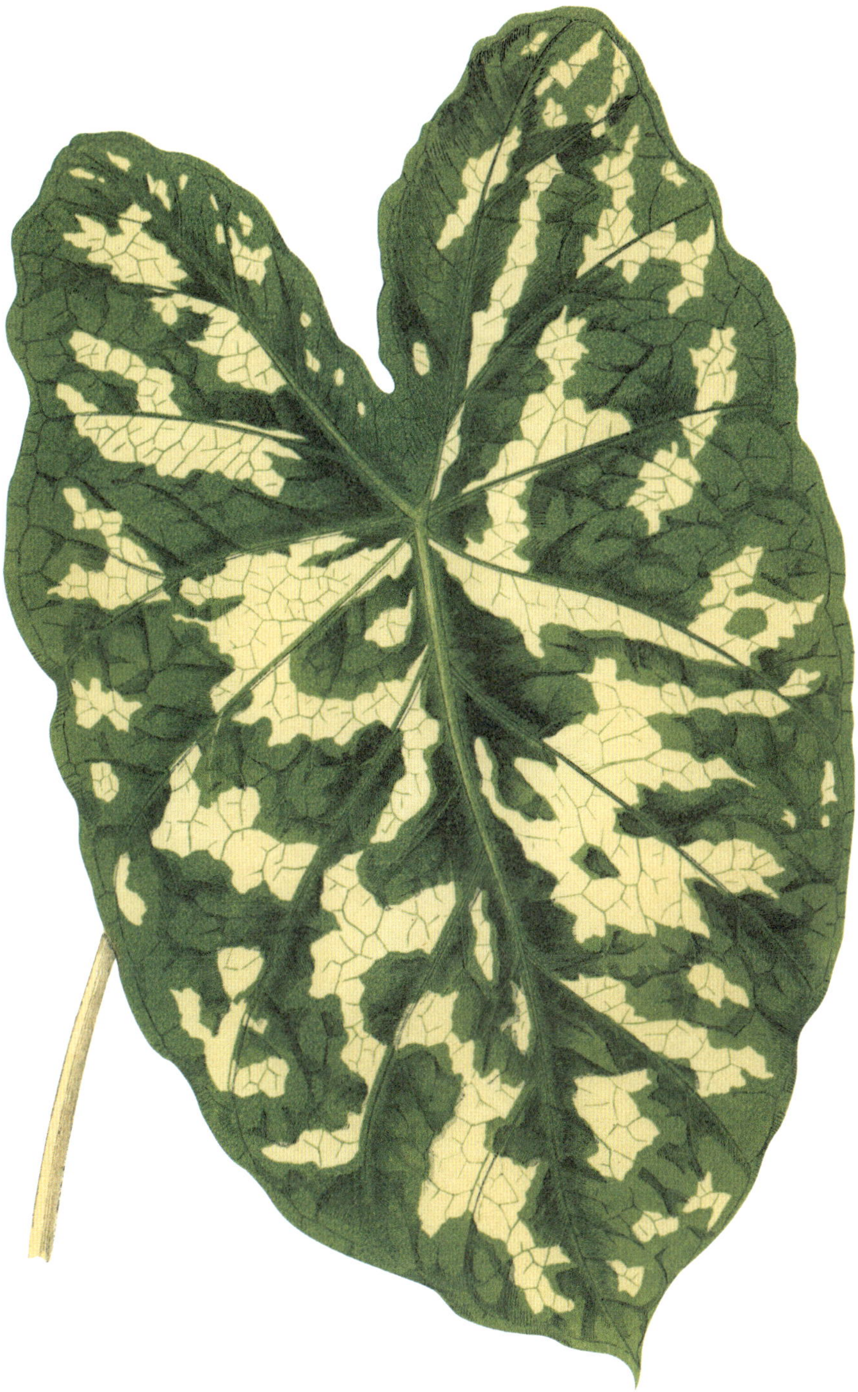

Caladium bicolor
by ALEXANDER FRANCIS LYDON & BENJAMIN FAWCETT

Heart of Jesus | elephant ear | angel wings

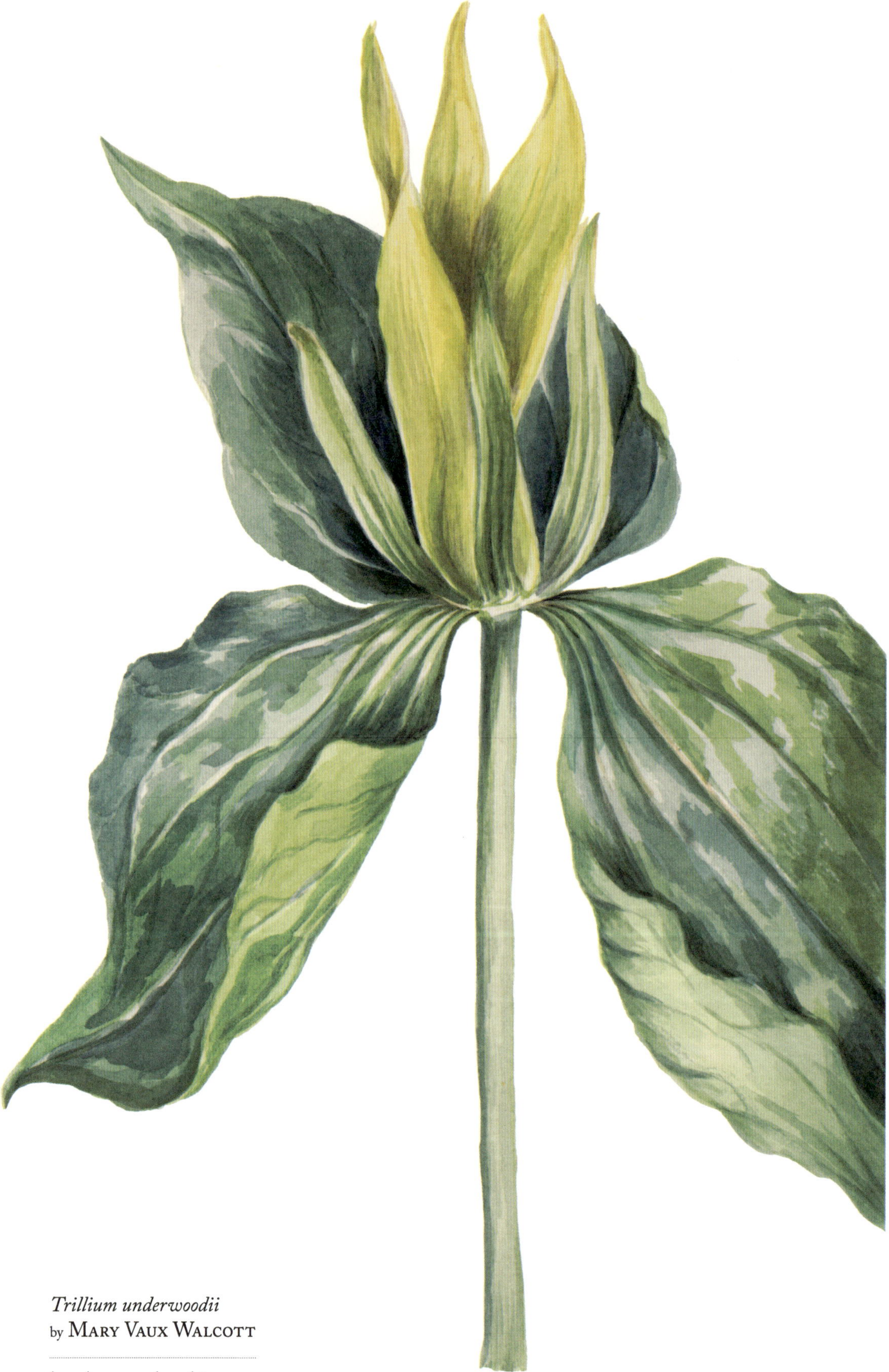

Trillium underwoodii
by MARY VAUX WALCOTT

longbract wakerobin

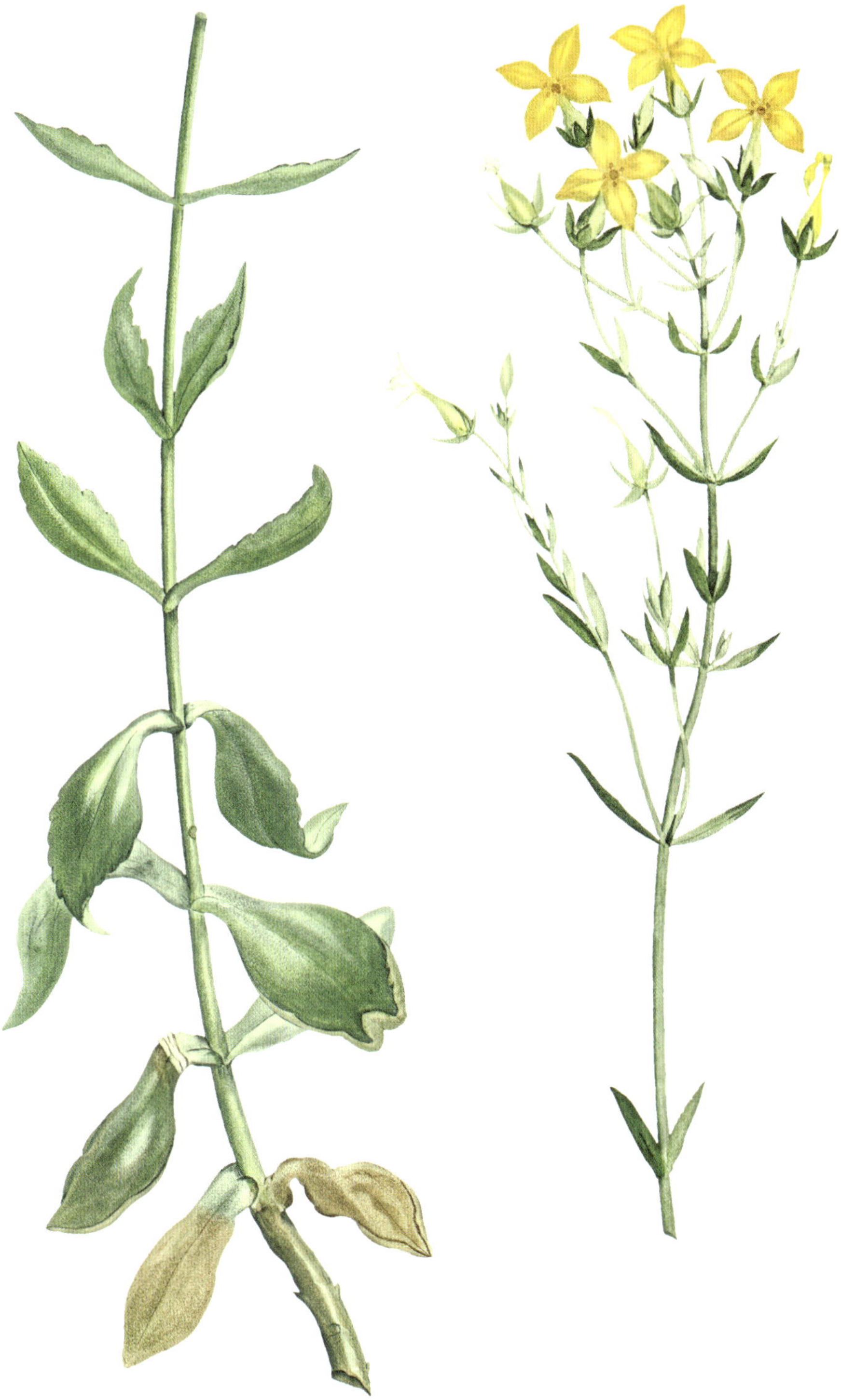

Kalanchoe integra
by Pierre-Joseph Redouté

never-die

The cactus in the desert stands
Like time's inviolate sentinel,
Watching the sun-washed waste of sands
Lest they their ancient secrets tell.
And the lost lore of mournful lands
It knows alone and guards too well.

Wiser than Sphynx or pyramid,
It points a stark hand at the sky,
And all the stars alight or hid
It counts as they go rolling by;
And mysteries the gods forbid
Darken its heavy memory.

FROM 'The Giant Cactus of Arizona' BY HARRIET MONROE

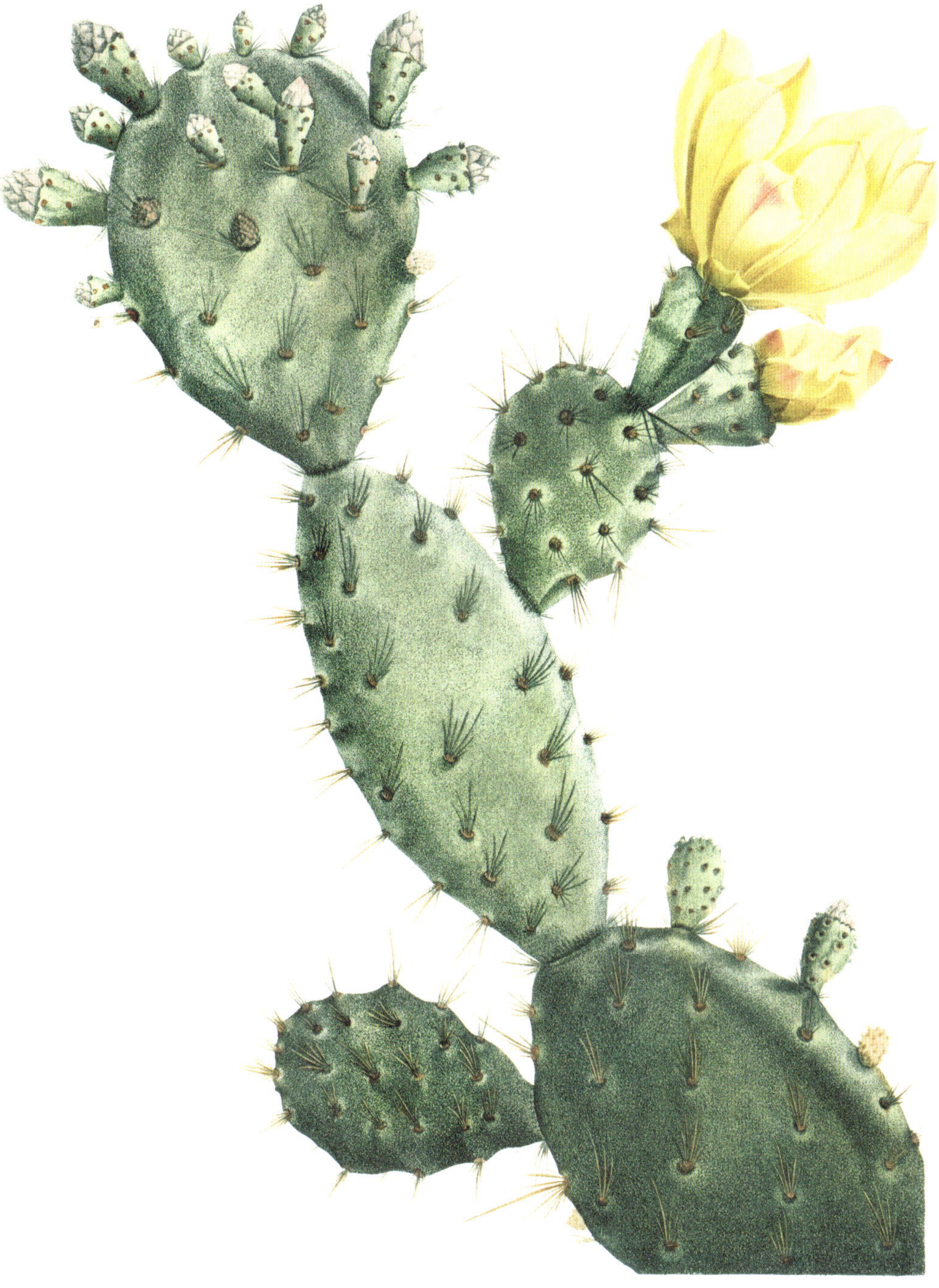

Opuntia polyacantha
by PIERRE-JOSEPH REDOUTÉ

plains pricklypear | starvation pricklypear | hairspine cactus

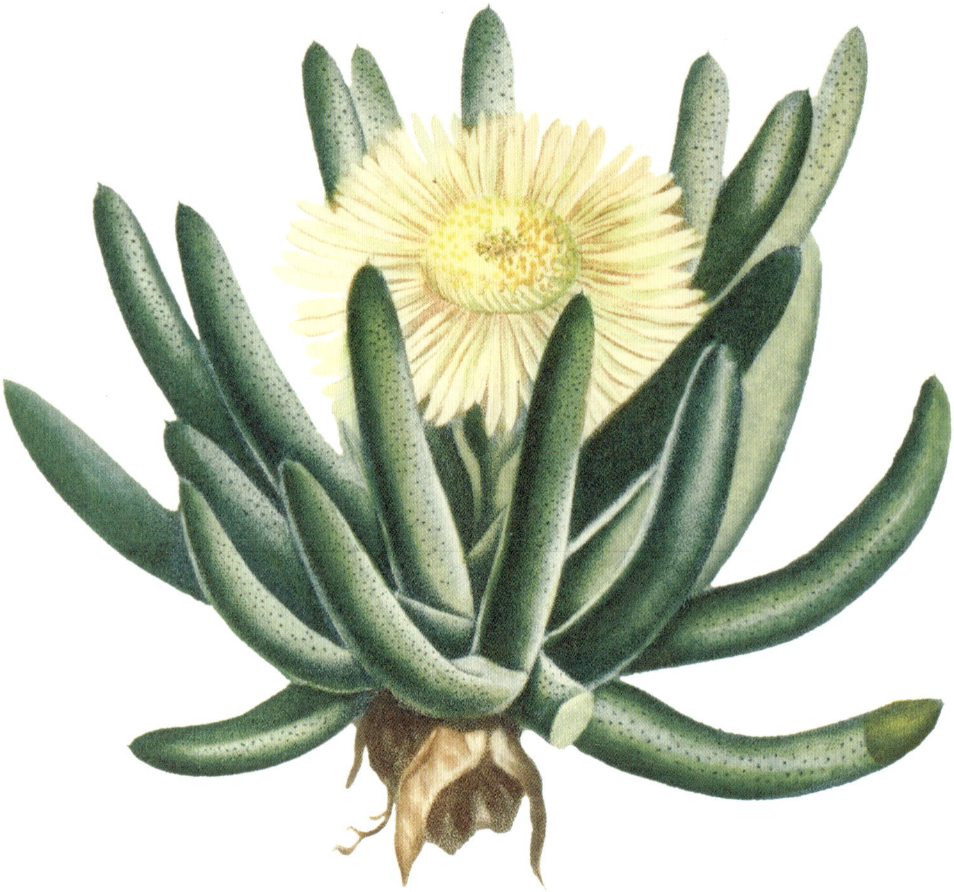

Glottiphyllum linguiforme
by Pierre-Joseph Redouté

tongue plant

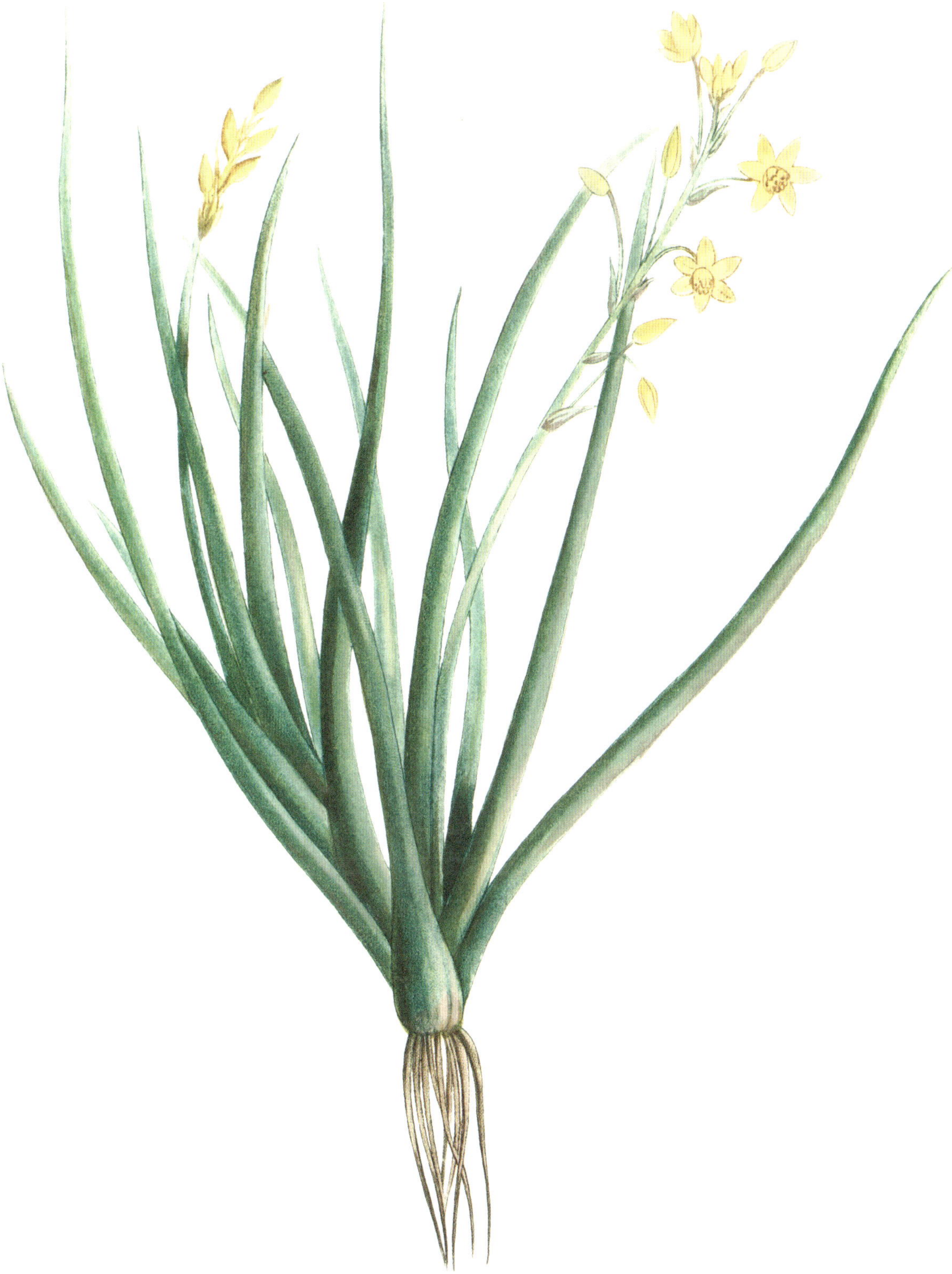

Bulbine annua
by Pierre-Joseph Redouté

bulbine annua

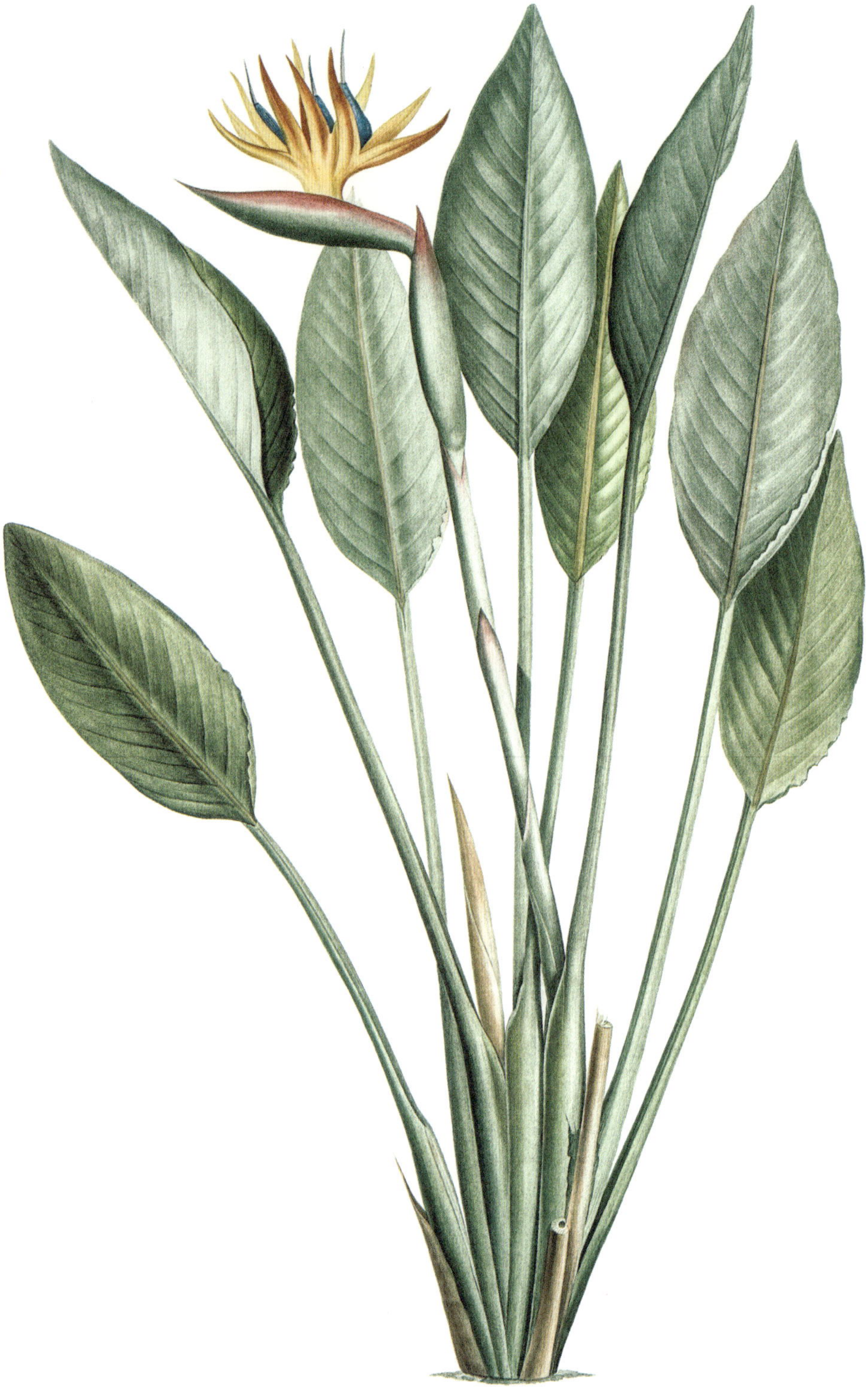

Strelitzia
by Pierre-Joseph Redouté

bird of paradise | crane flower

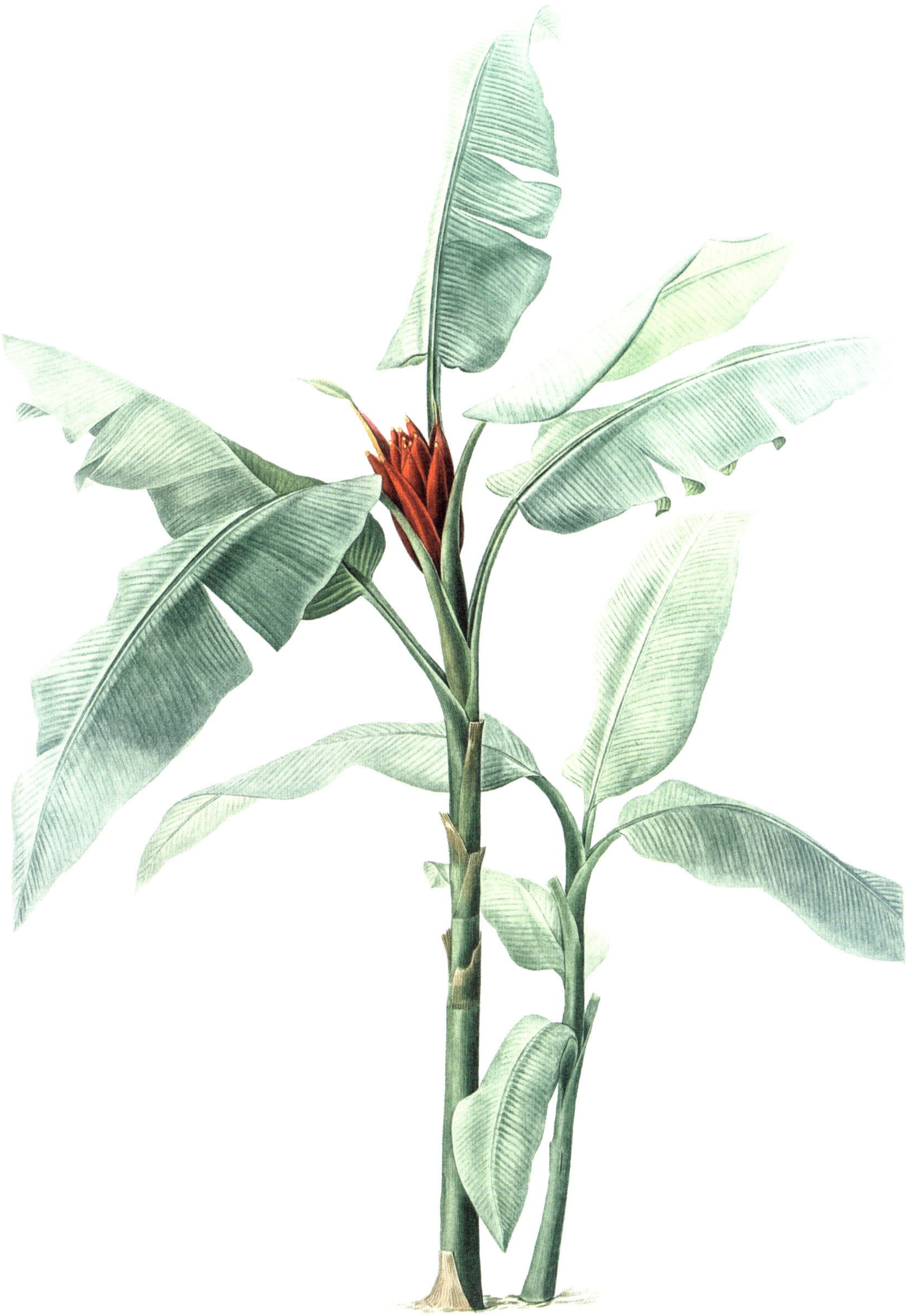

Musa coccinea
by Pierre-Joseph Redouté

scarlet banana | red-flowering banana

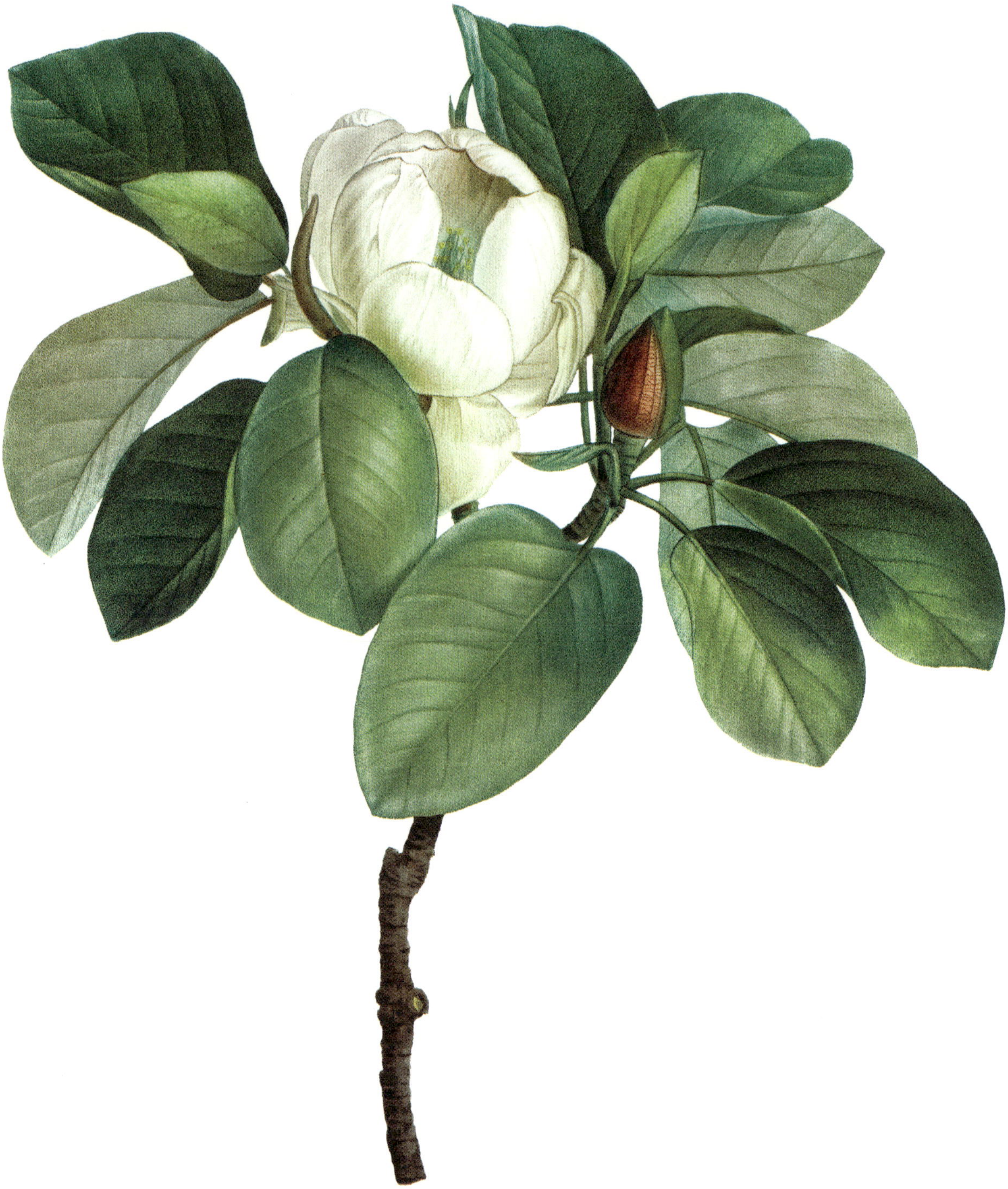

Magnolia Virginiana
by Pierre-Joseph Redouté

sweetbay magnolia

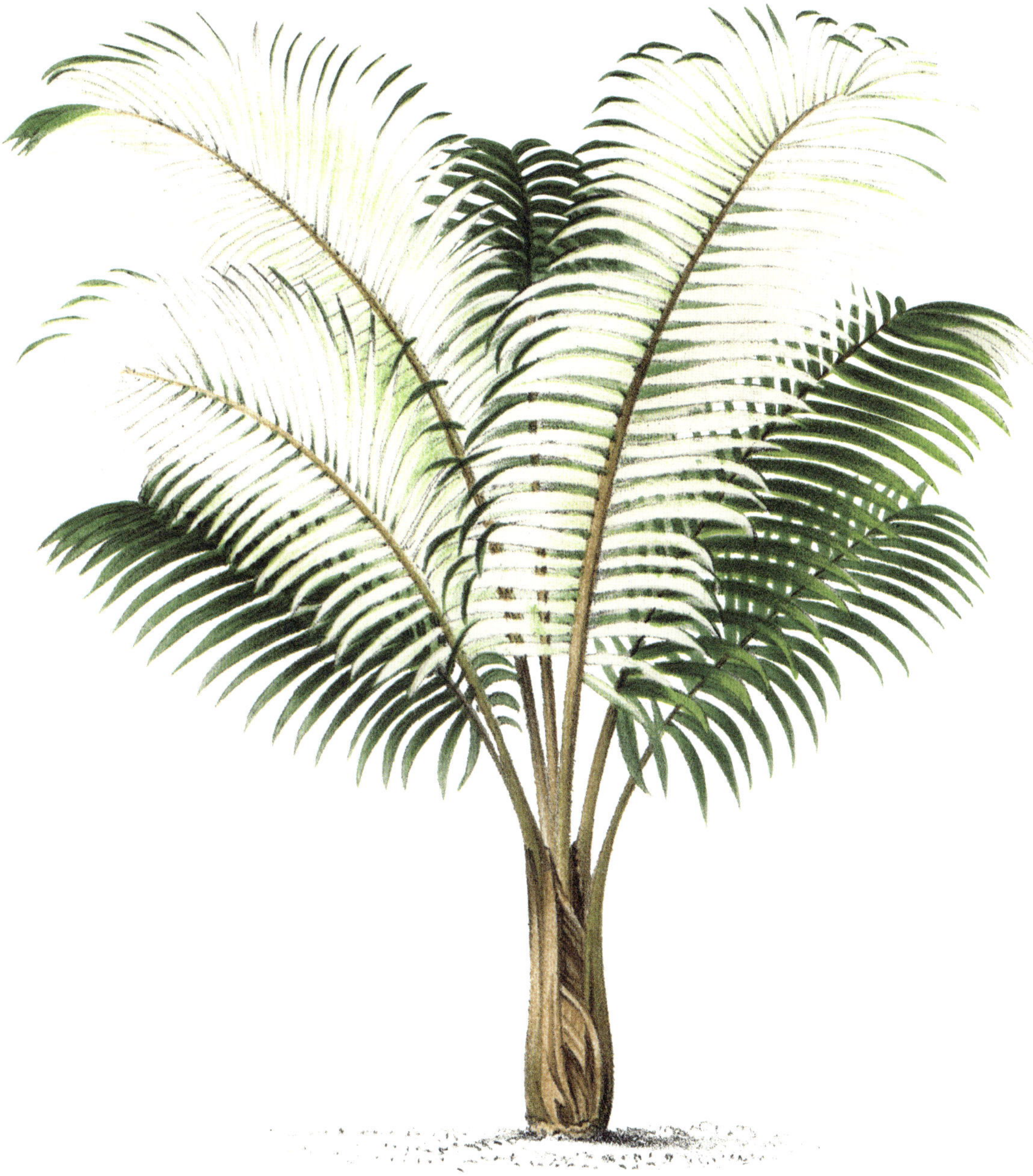

Ceroxylon
by Oswald de Kerchove de Denterghem

wax palm (unknown variety)

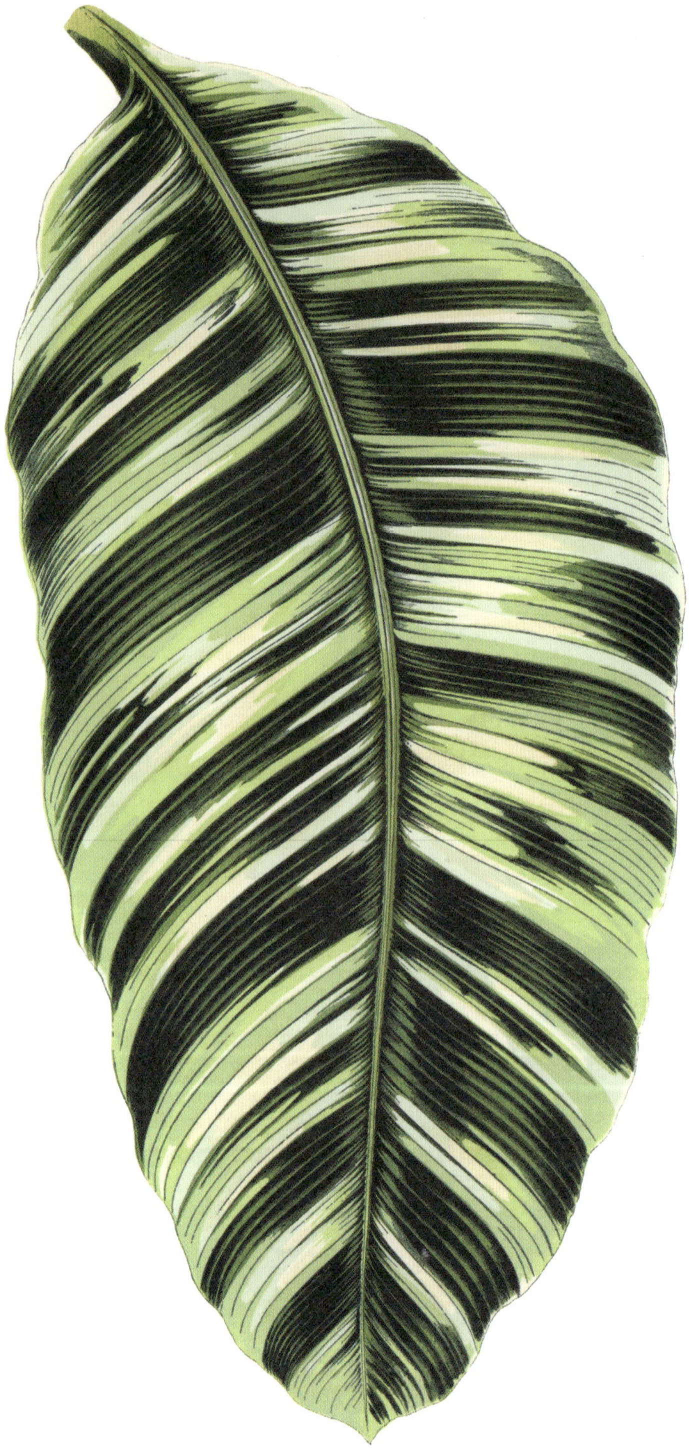

Musa × paradisiaca
by Alexander Francis Lydon & Benjamin Fawcett

plantain

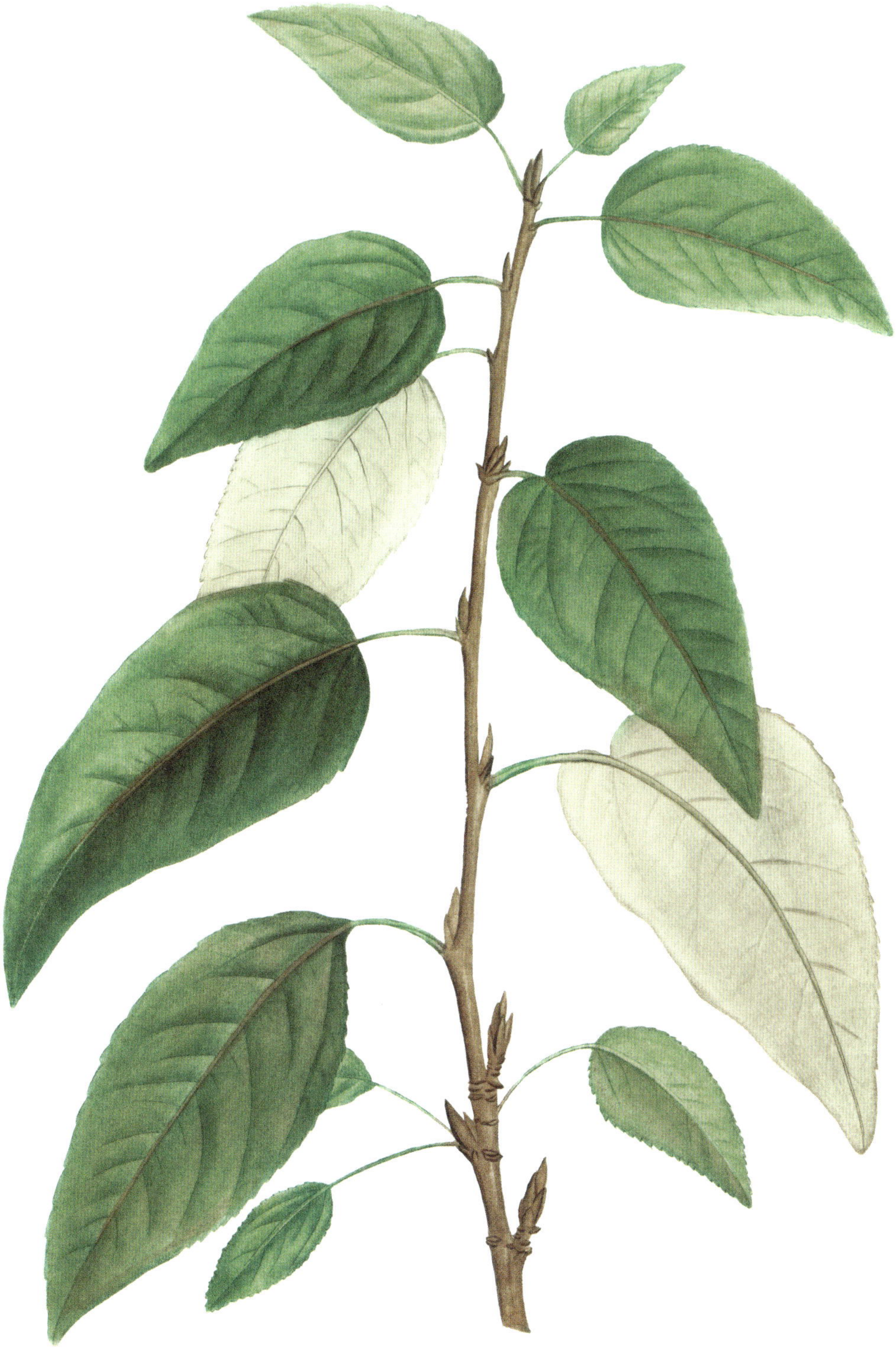

Populus balsamifera
by Pierre-Joseph Redouté

balsam poplar | bam | bamtree | eastern balsam-poplar

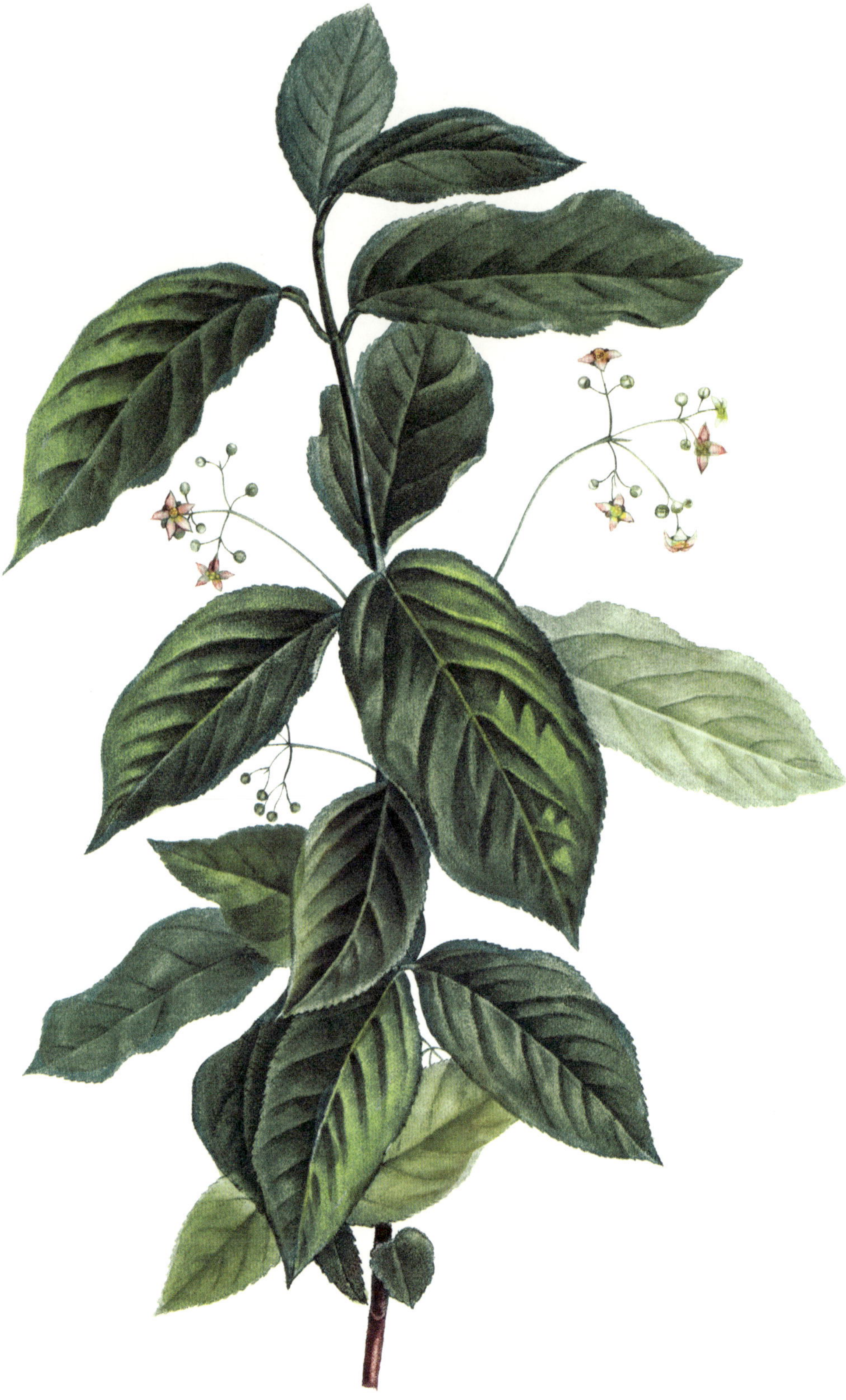

Euonymus latifolius
by Pierre-Joseph Redouté

broad-leaved spindle tree

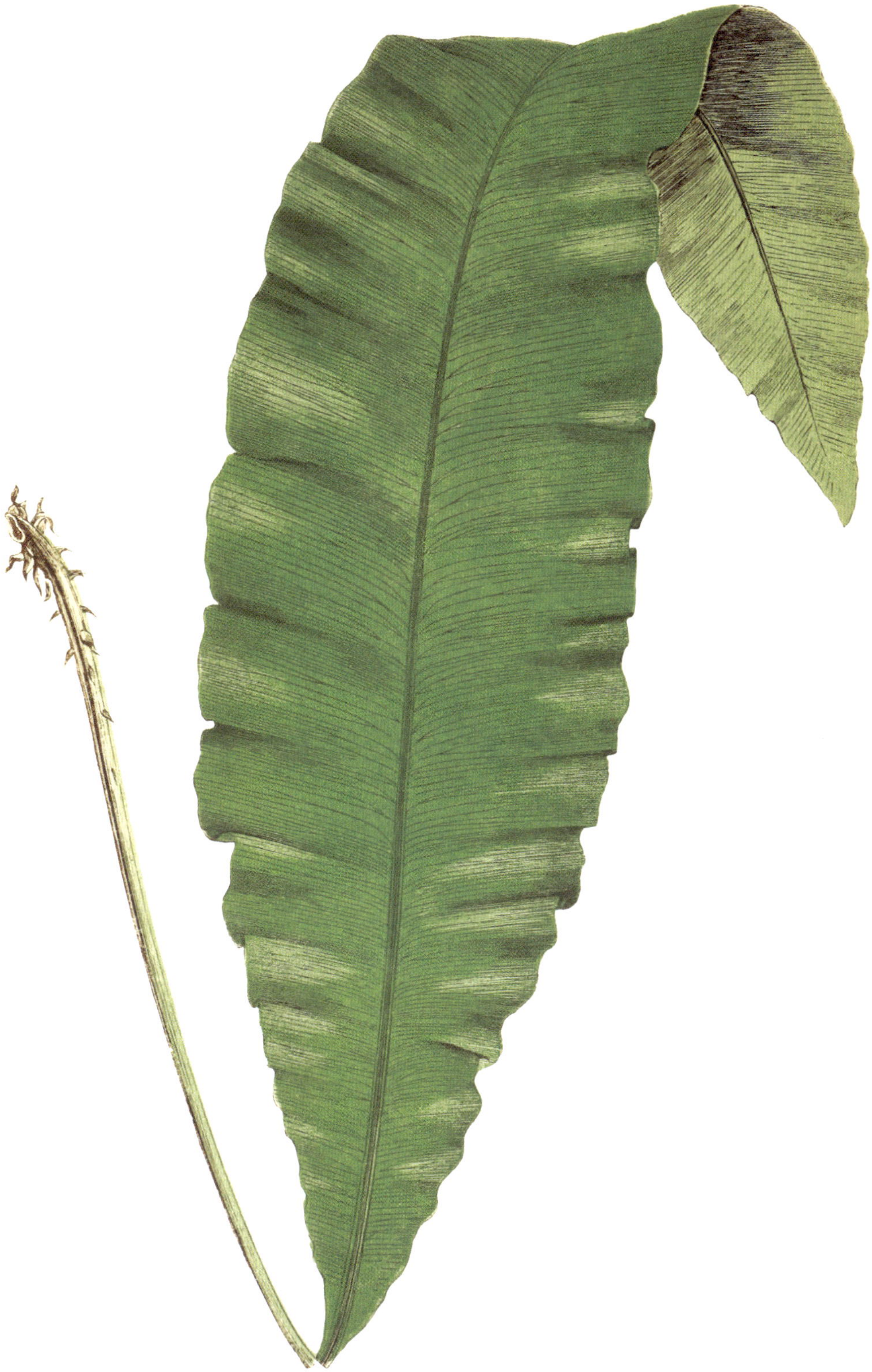

Elaphoglossum crassinerve
by EDWARD JOSEPH LOWE

tongue fern

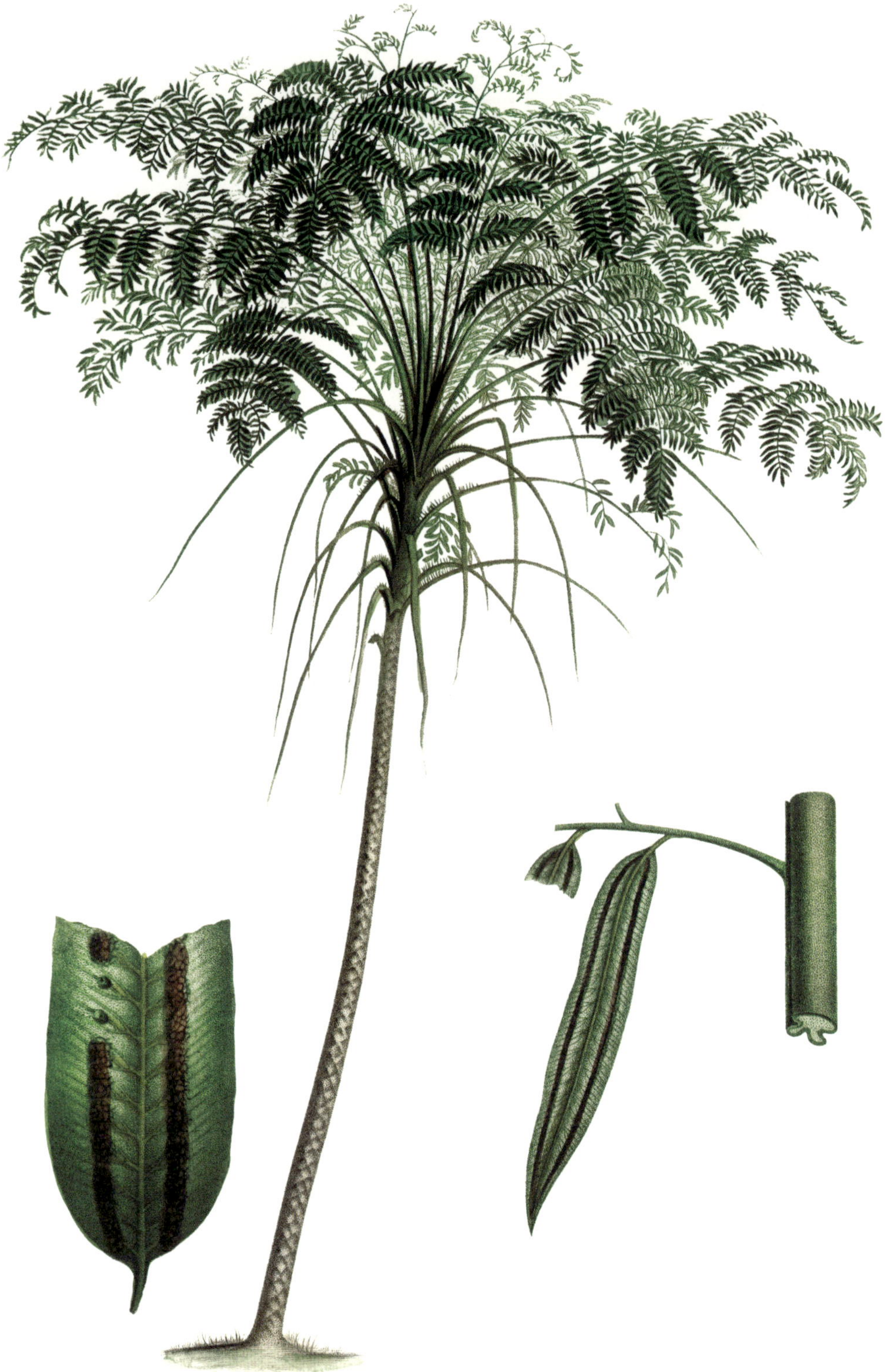

Sphaeropteris excelsa
by CHARLES DESSALINES D'ORBIGNY

Norfolk tree fern | smooth tree fern

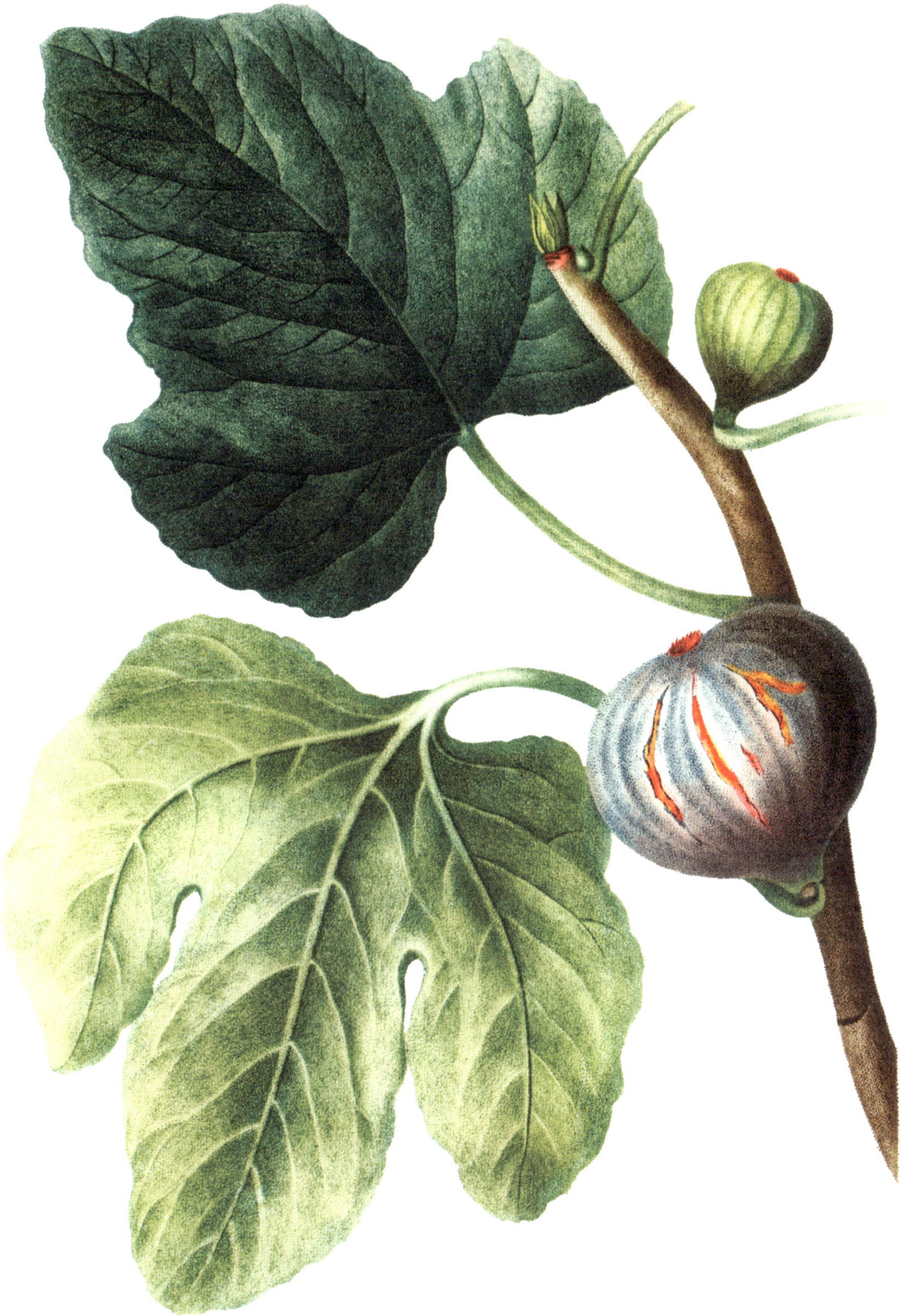

Ficus carica
by PIERRE-JOSEPH REDOUTÉ

common fig

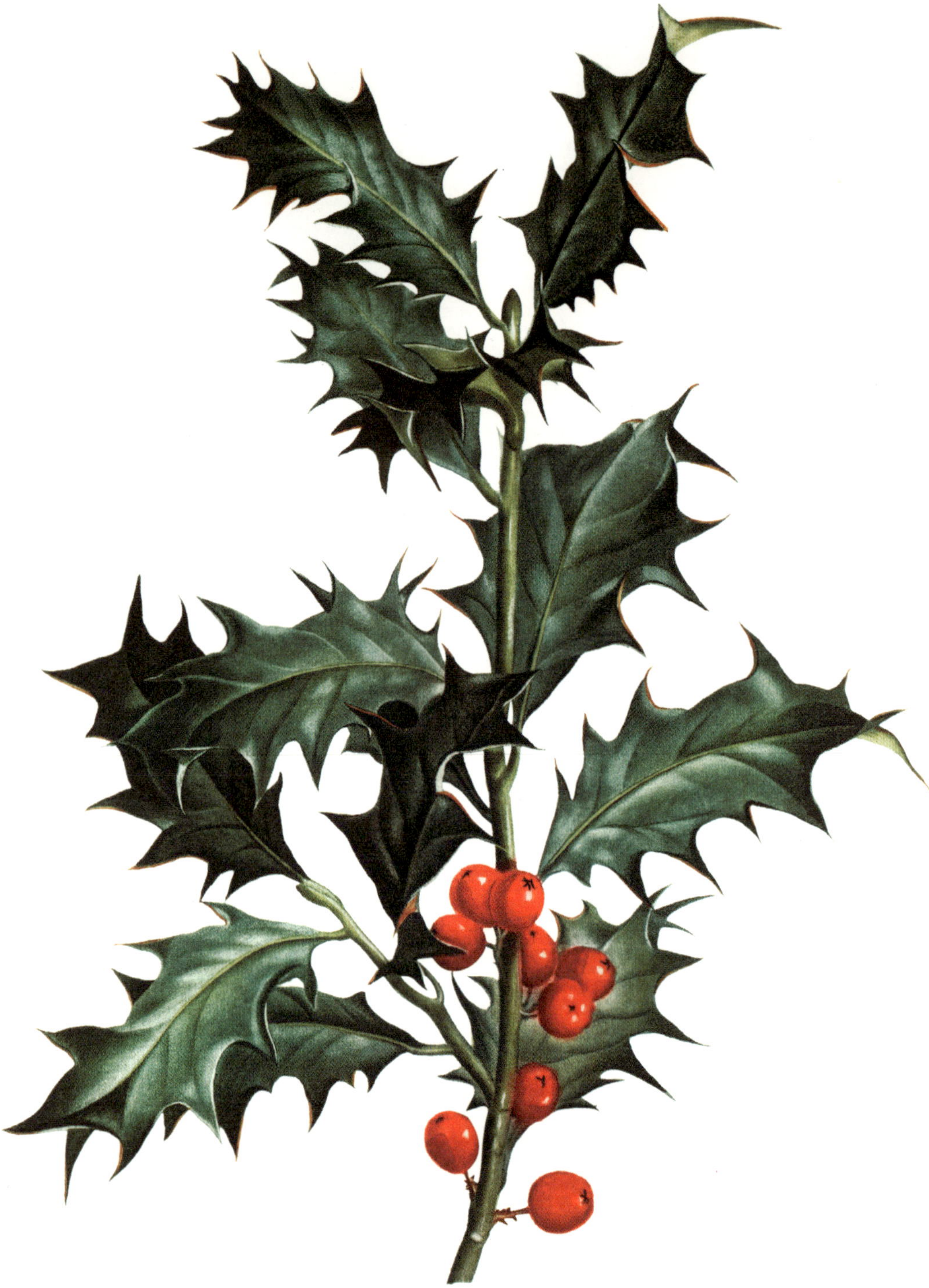

Ilex aquifolium
by Pierre-Joseph Redouté

common holly | English holly

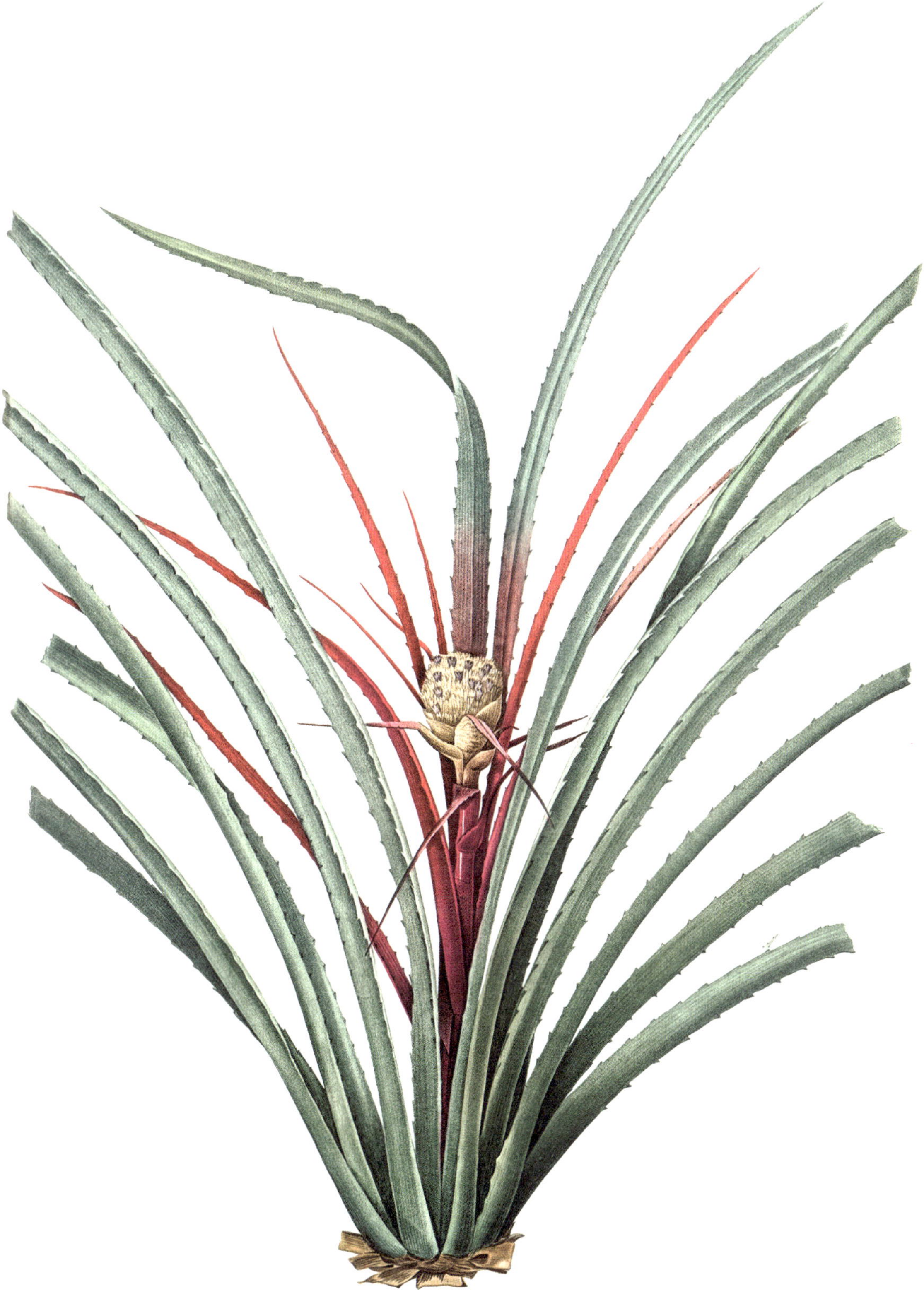

Bromelia karatas L.
by Pierre-Joseph Redouté

plumier's bromelia

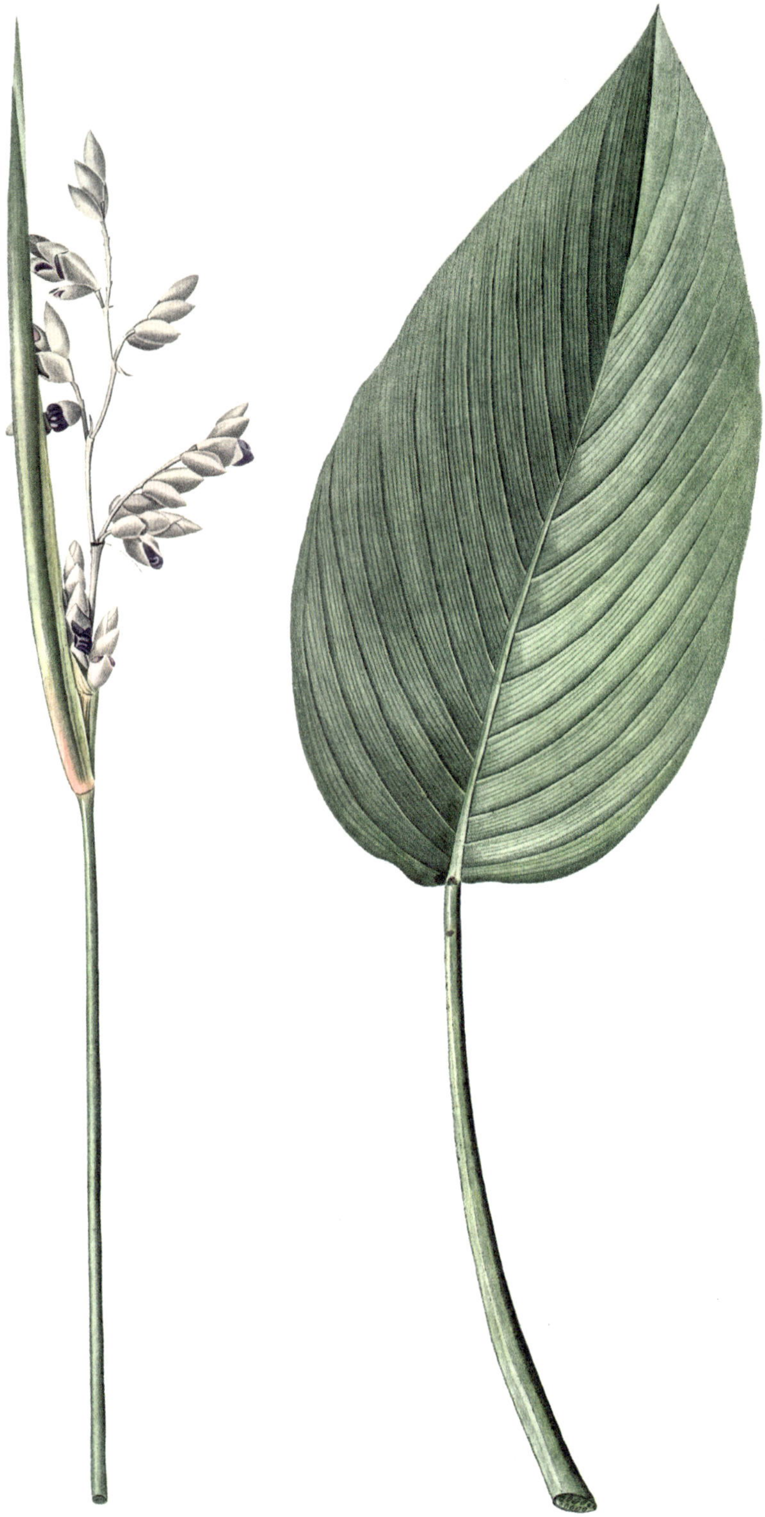

Thalia dealbata
by Pierre-Joseph Redouté

powdery alligator-flag | hardy canna | powdery thalia

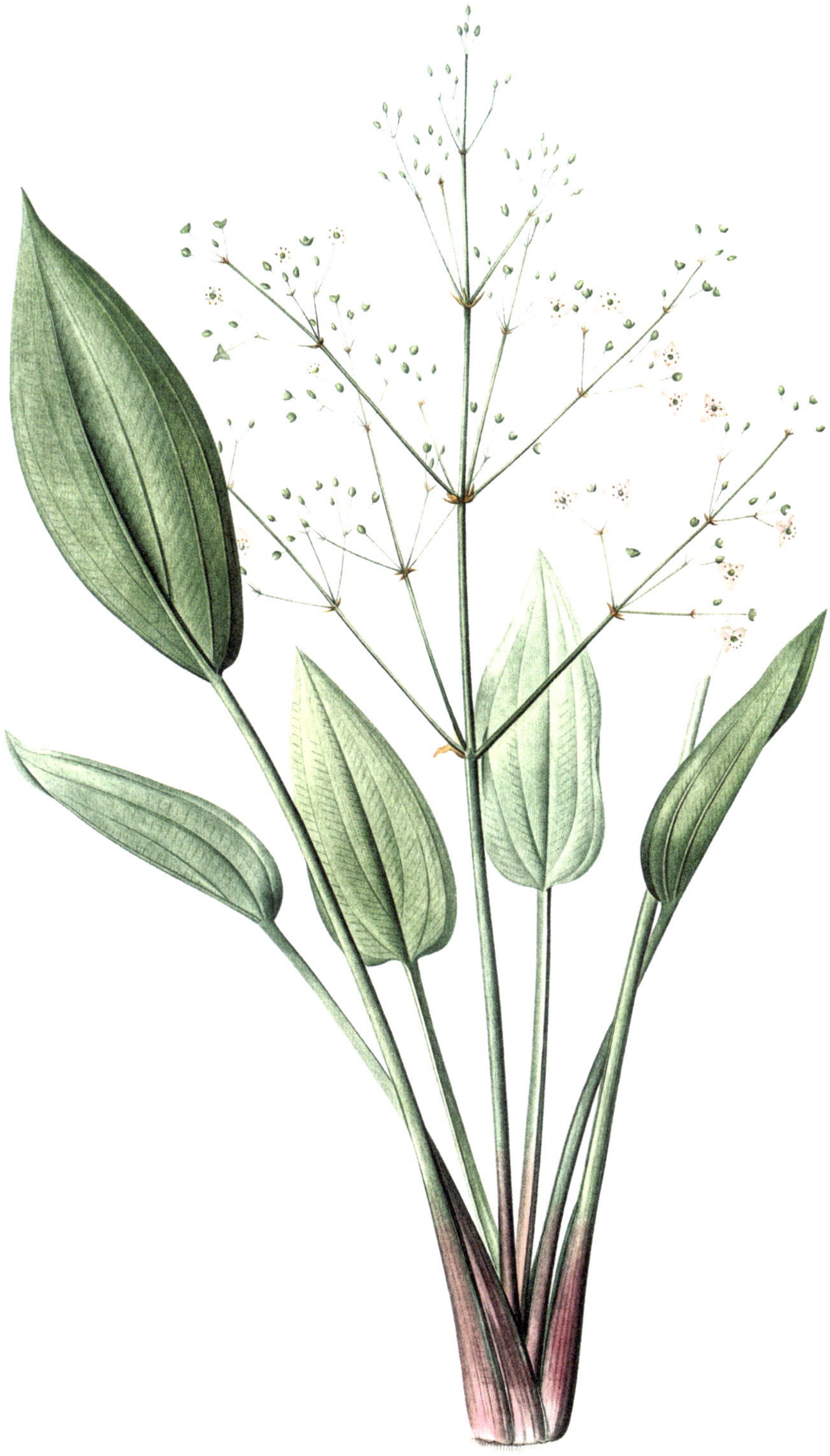

Alisma plantago-aquatica
by Pierre-Joseph Redouté

common water-plantain | European water-plantain | mad-dog weed

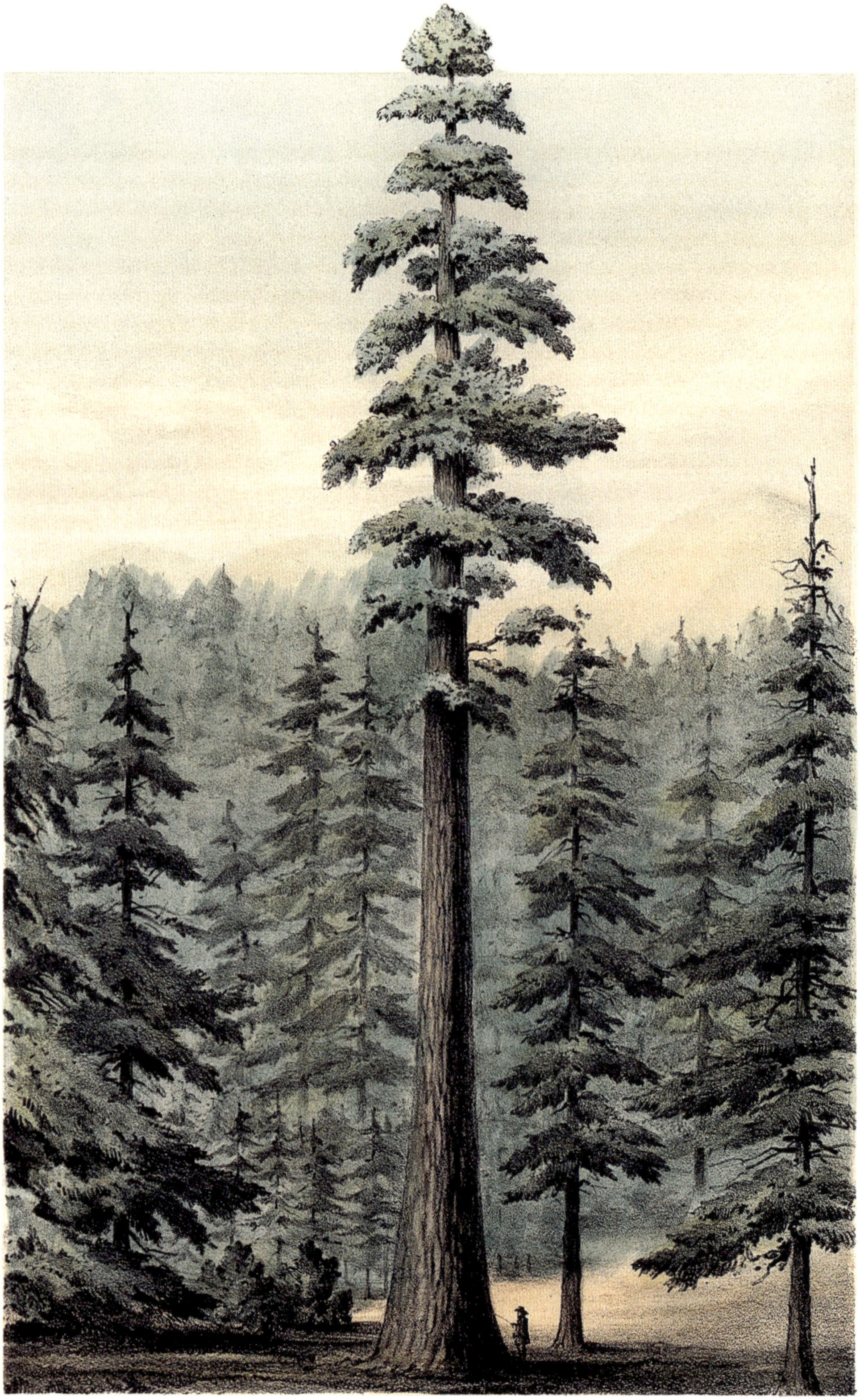

Sequoiadendron giganteum
BY W.P. BLAKE

giant sequoia

In a forest of a
hundred thousand trees,
no two leaves are alike.
And no two journeys along
the same path are alike.

Paulo Coelho

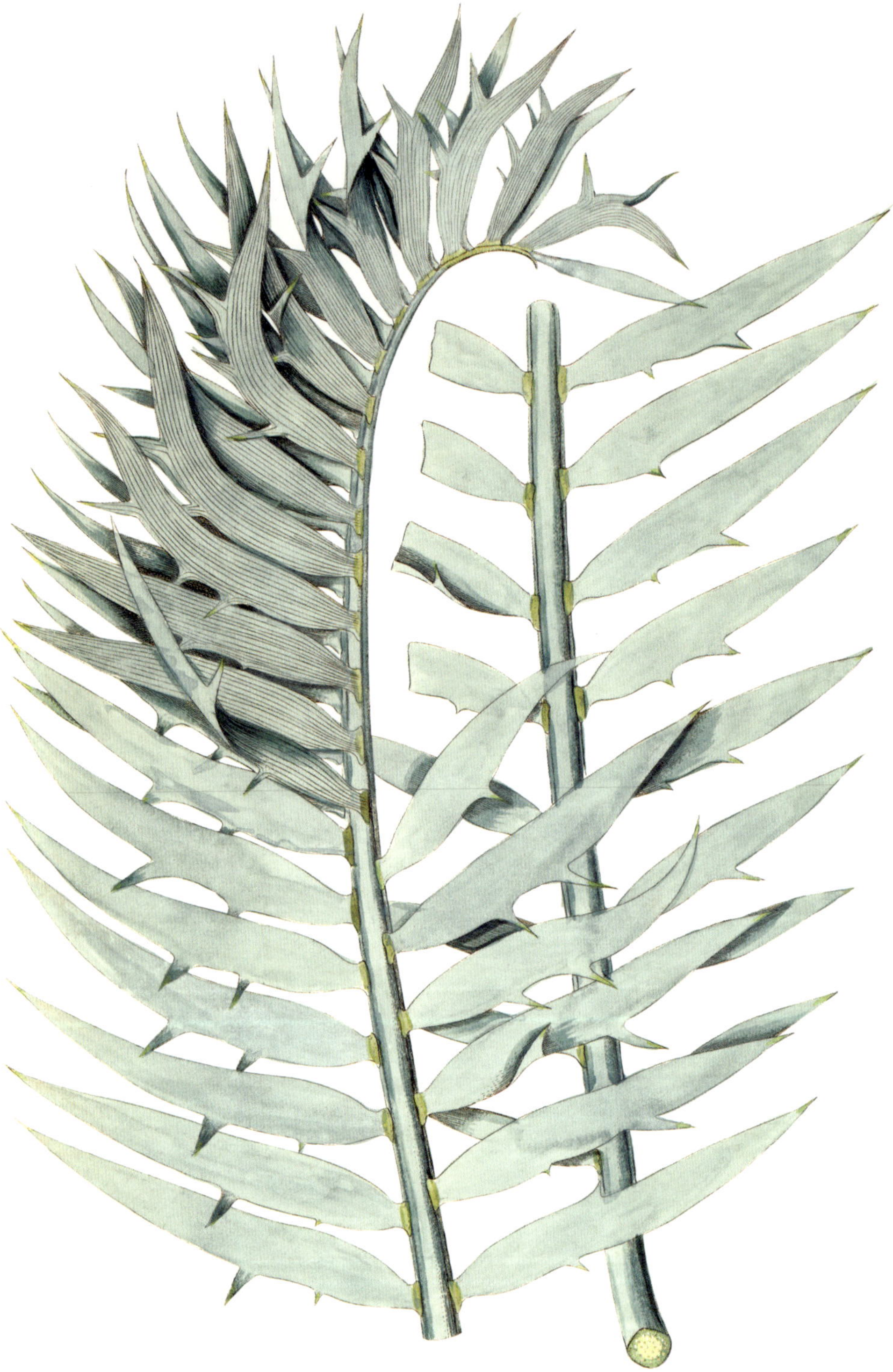

Encephalartos horridus
by Nikolaus Joseph von Jacquin

Eastern Cape blue cycad

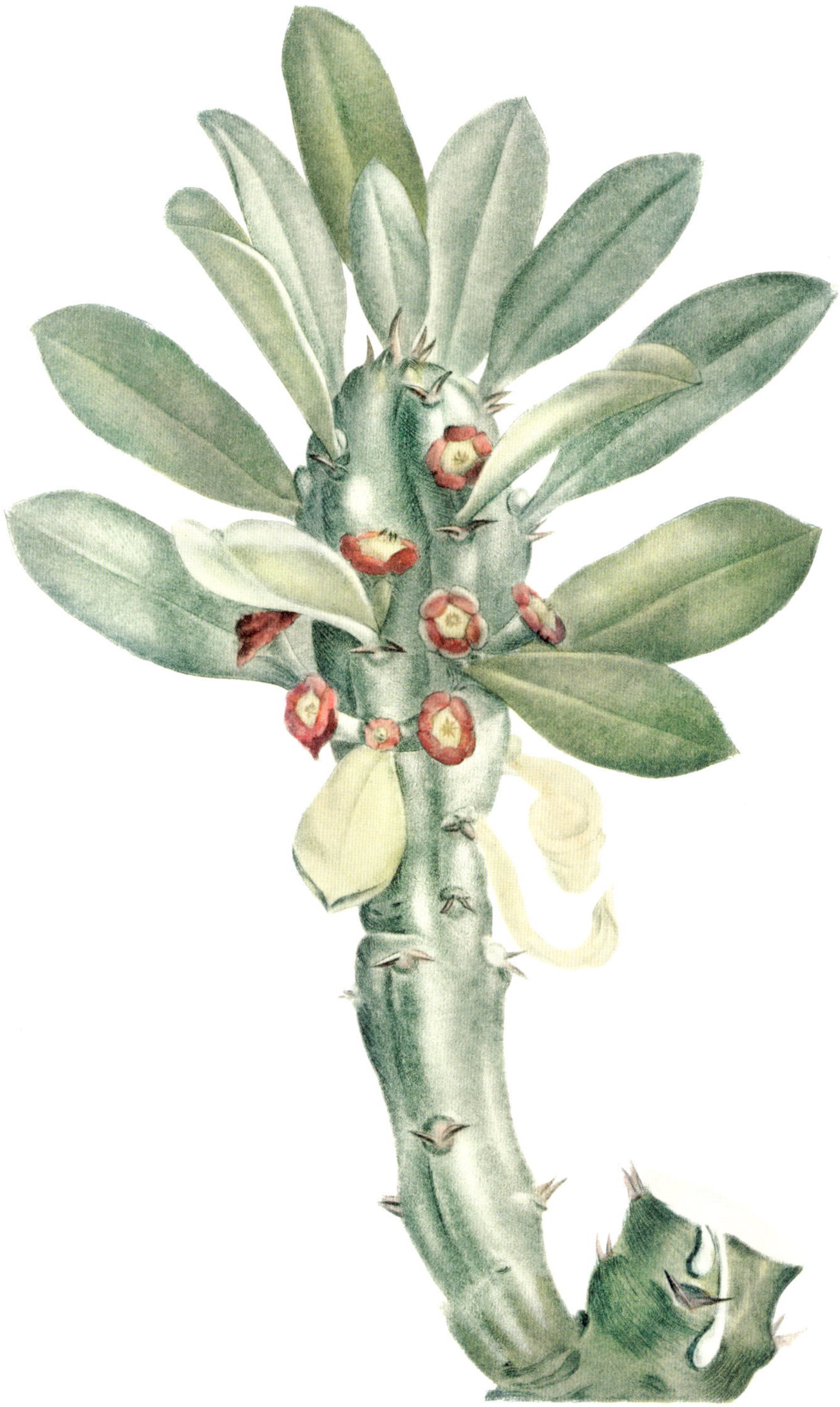

Euphorbia neriifolia
by Pierre-Joseph Redouté

Indian spurgetree

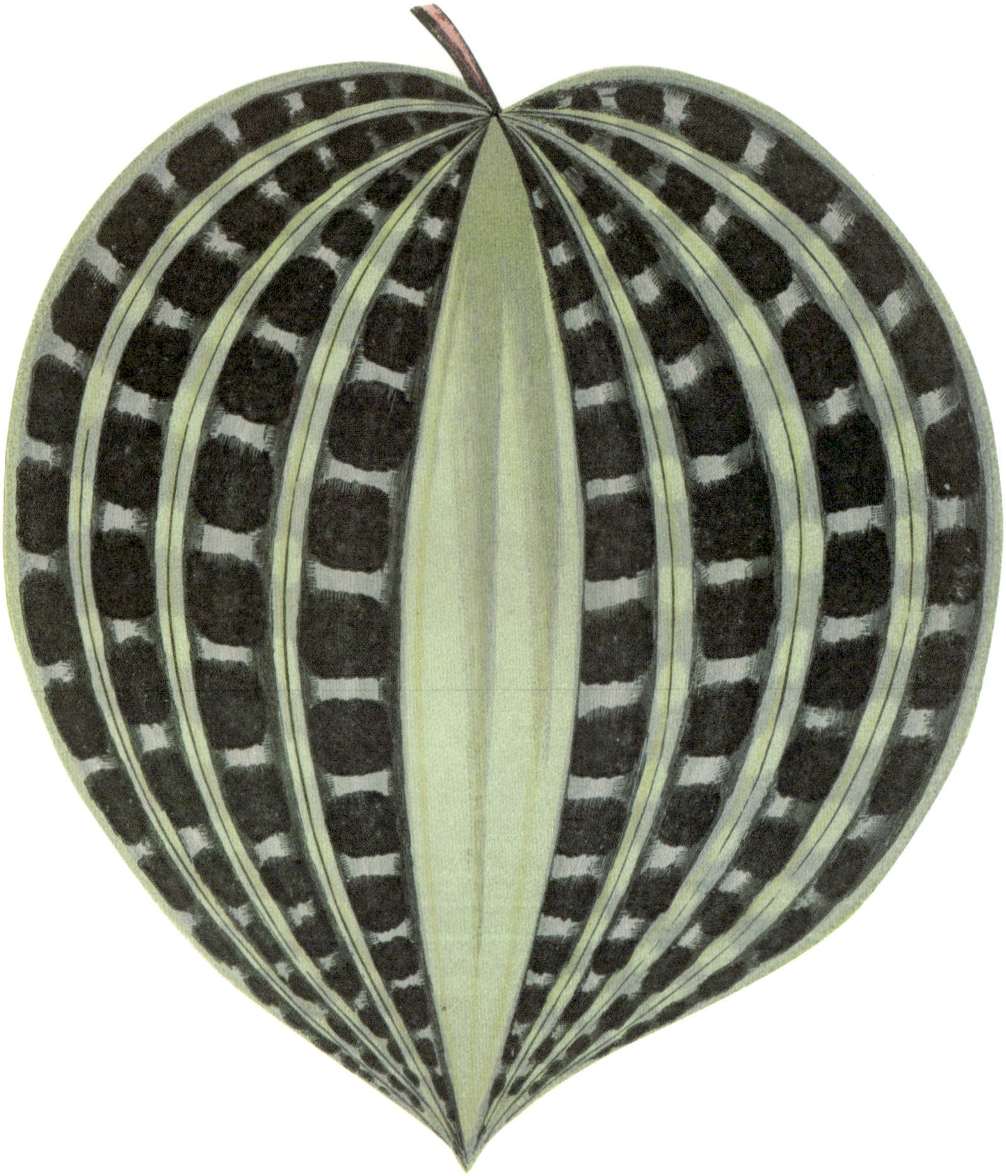

Geogenanthus poeppigii
by Benjamin Fawcett & James Shirley Hibberd

seersucker plant

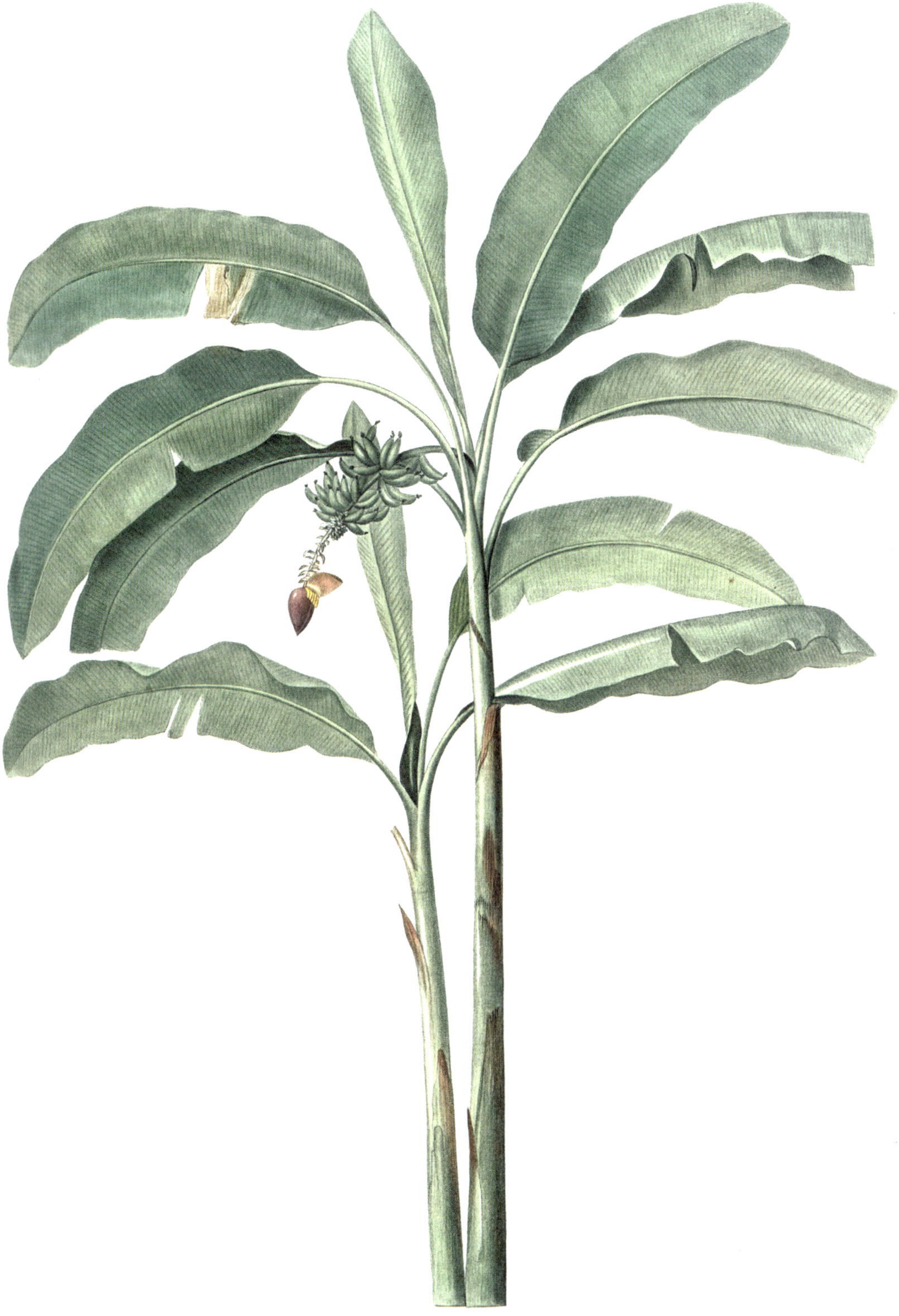

Musa acuminata
by PIERRE JOSEPH REDOUTÉ

banana

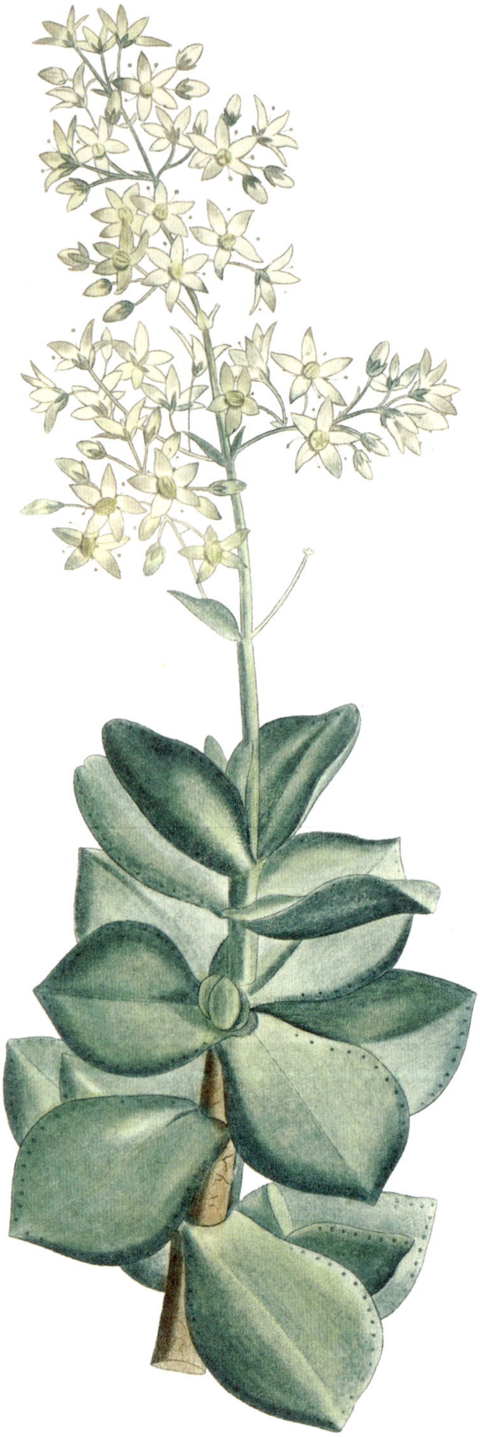

Crassula lactea
by Pierre-Joseph Redouté

Taylor's parches | tailor's patch | white many-flowering crassula | knysna crassula

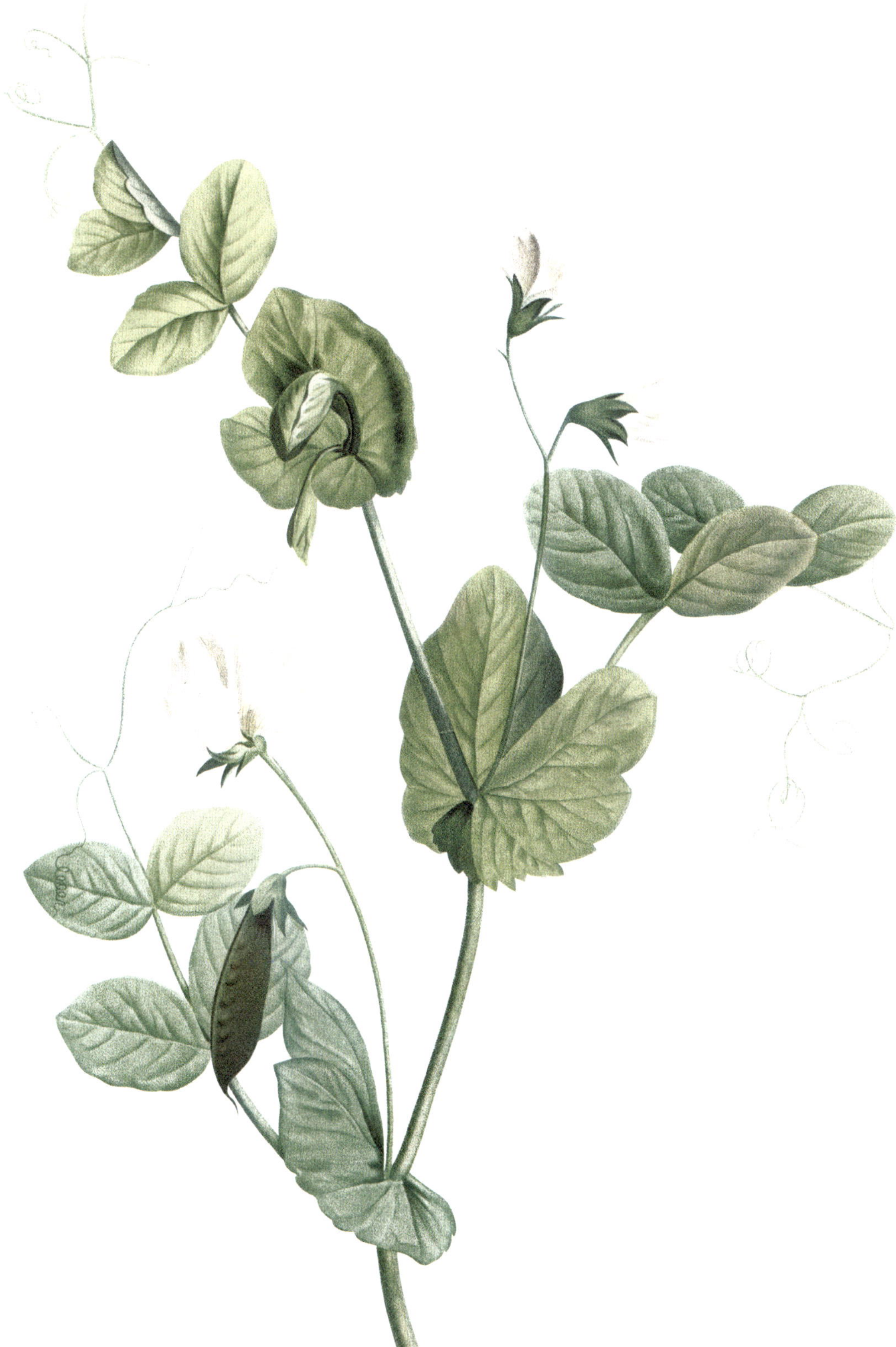

Clitoria ternatea
by Pierre-Joseph Redouté

butterfly pea | blue pea | Darwin pea | Asian pigeonwings

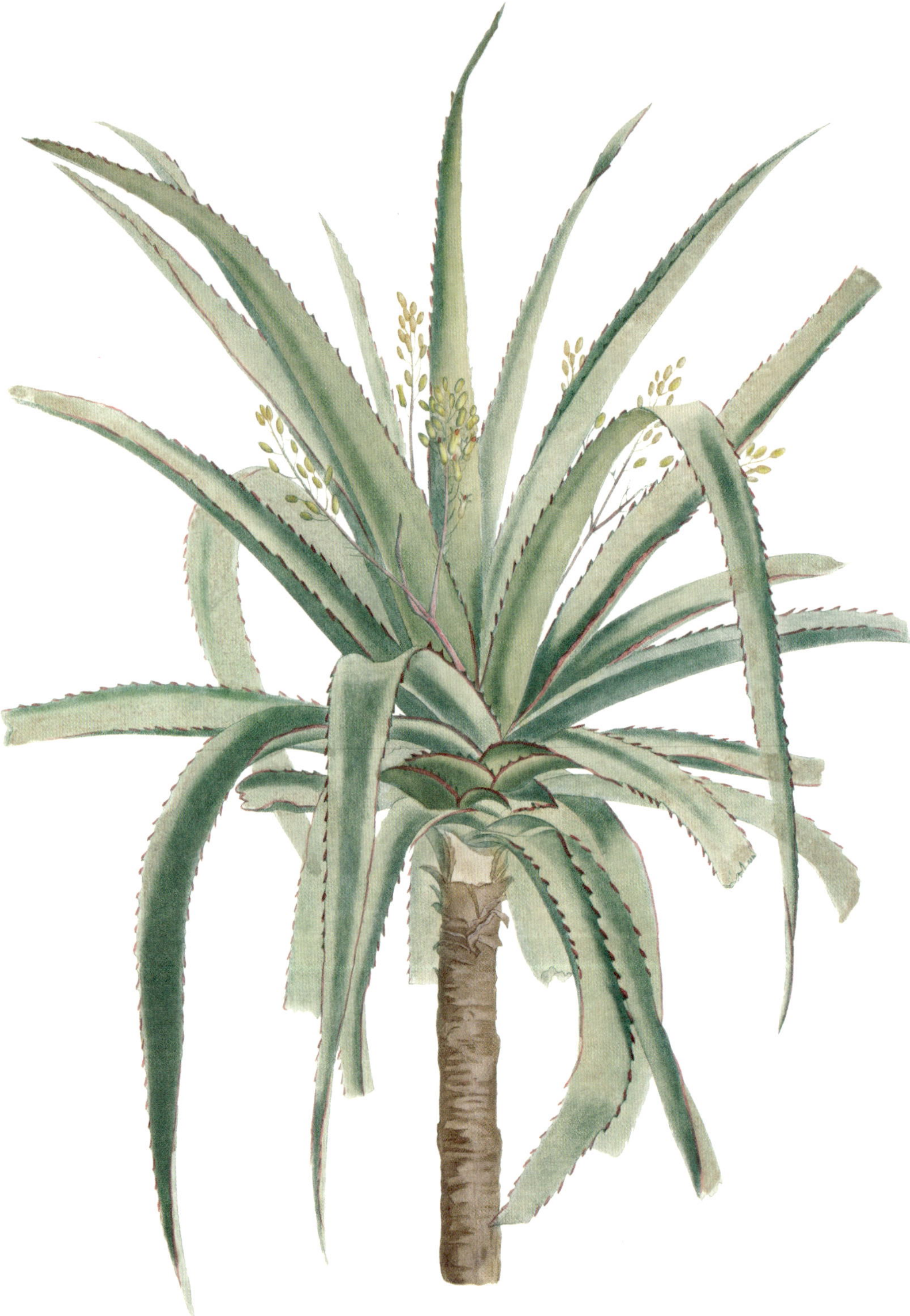

Aloe purpurea
by Pierre-Joseph Redouté

purple aloe | mazambron | socotrine du pays

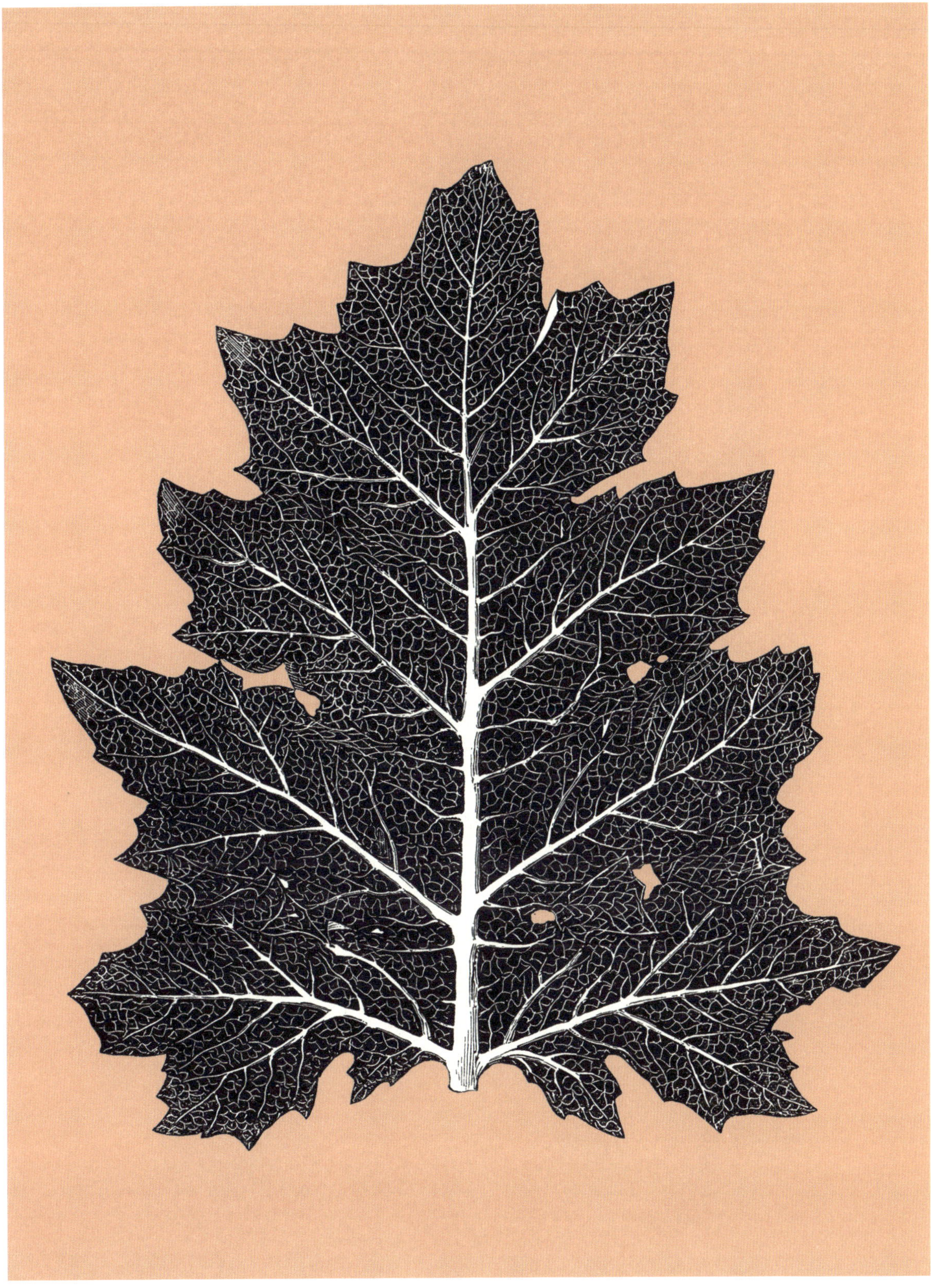

Acanthus mollis
by OWEN JONES

bear's breeches | oyster plant | sea dock

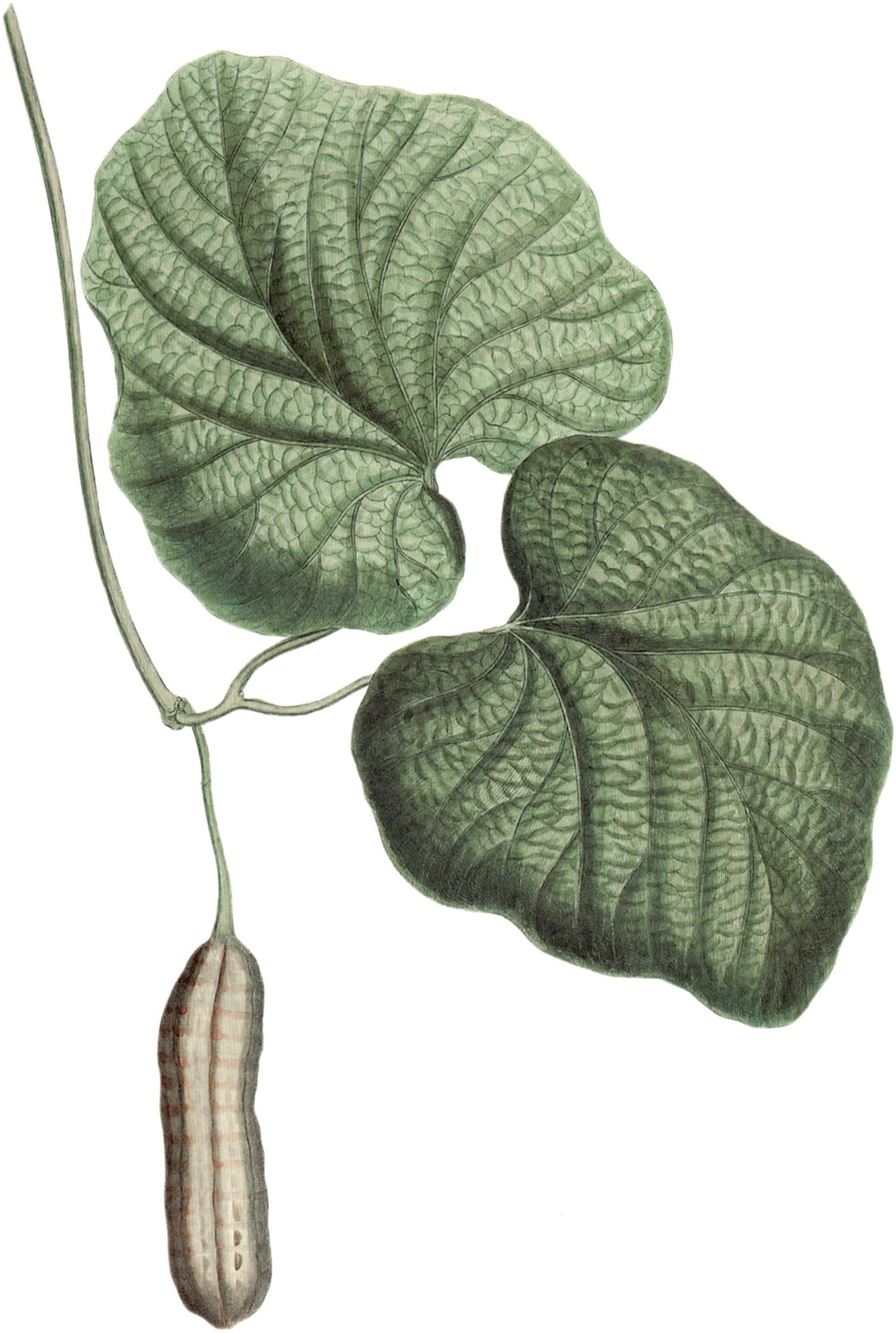

Aristolochia macrophylla
by Pierre-Joseph Redouté

Dutchman's pipe | pipevine

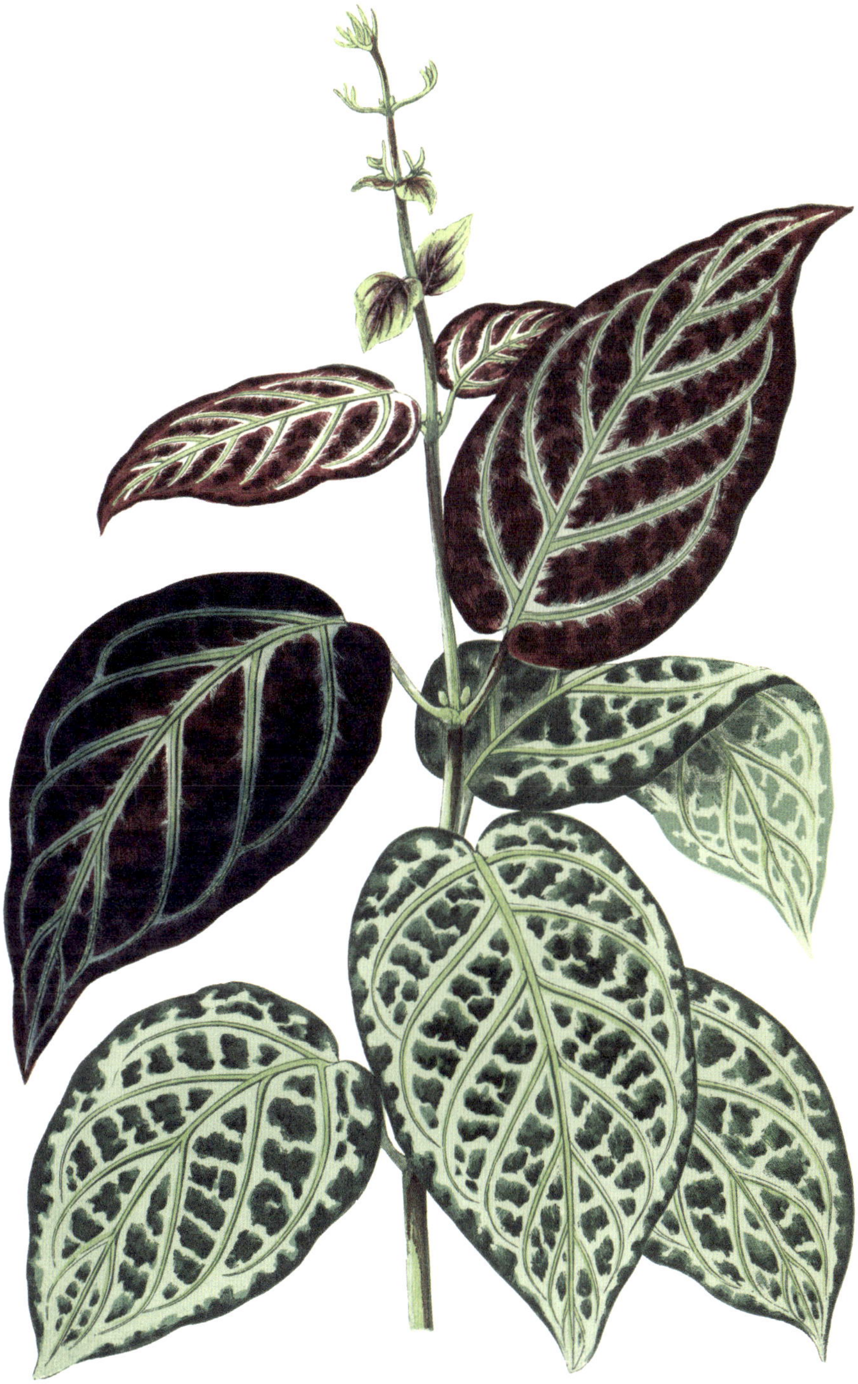

Bignonia argyro violacea
by Alexander Francis Lydon & Benjamin Fawcett

crossvine

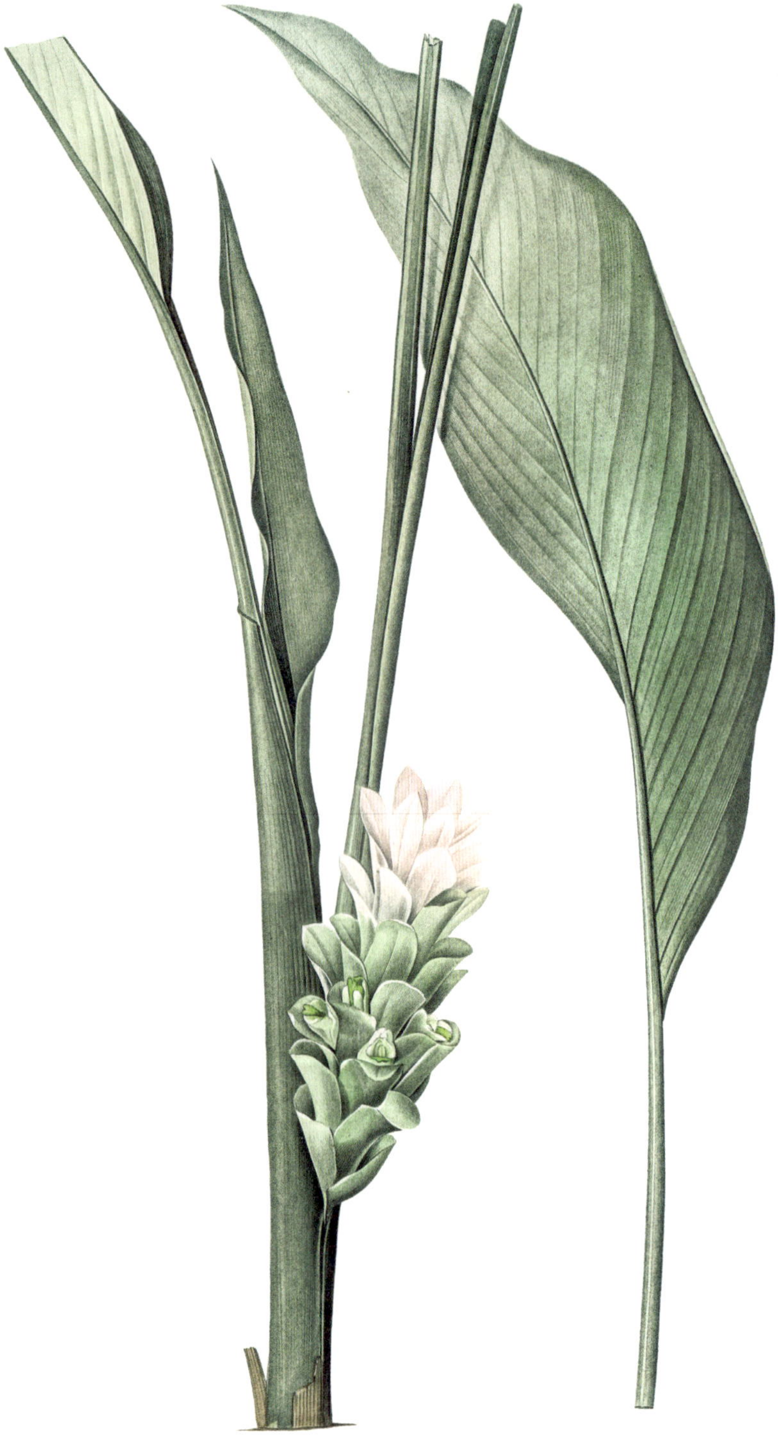

Curcuma longa
by Pierre-Joseph Redouté

turmeric

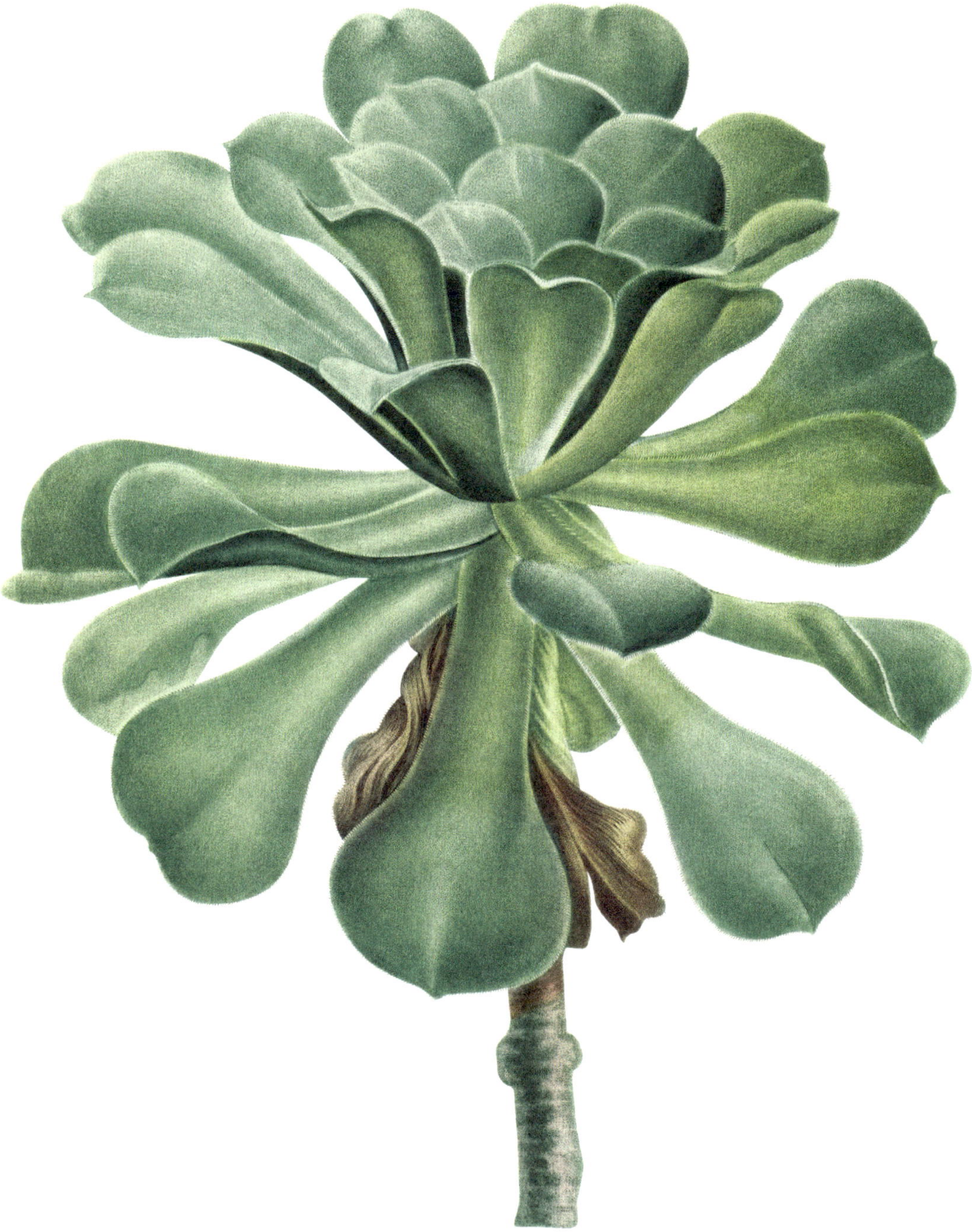

Aeonium canariense
by Pierre-Joseph Redouté

hen and chicks aeonium | giant velvet rose | canary aeonium

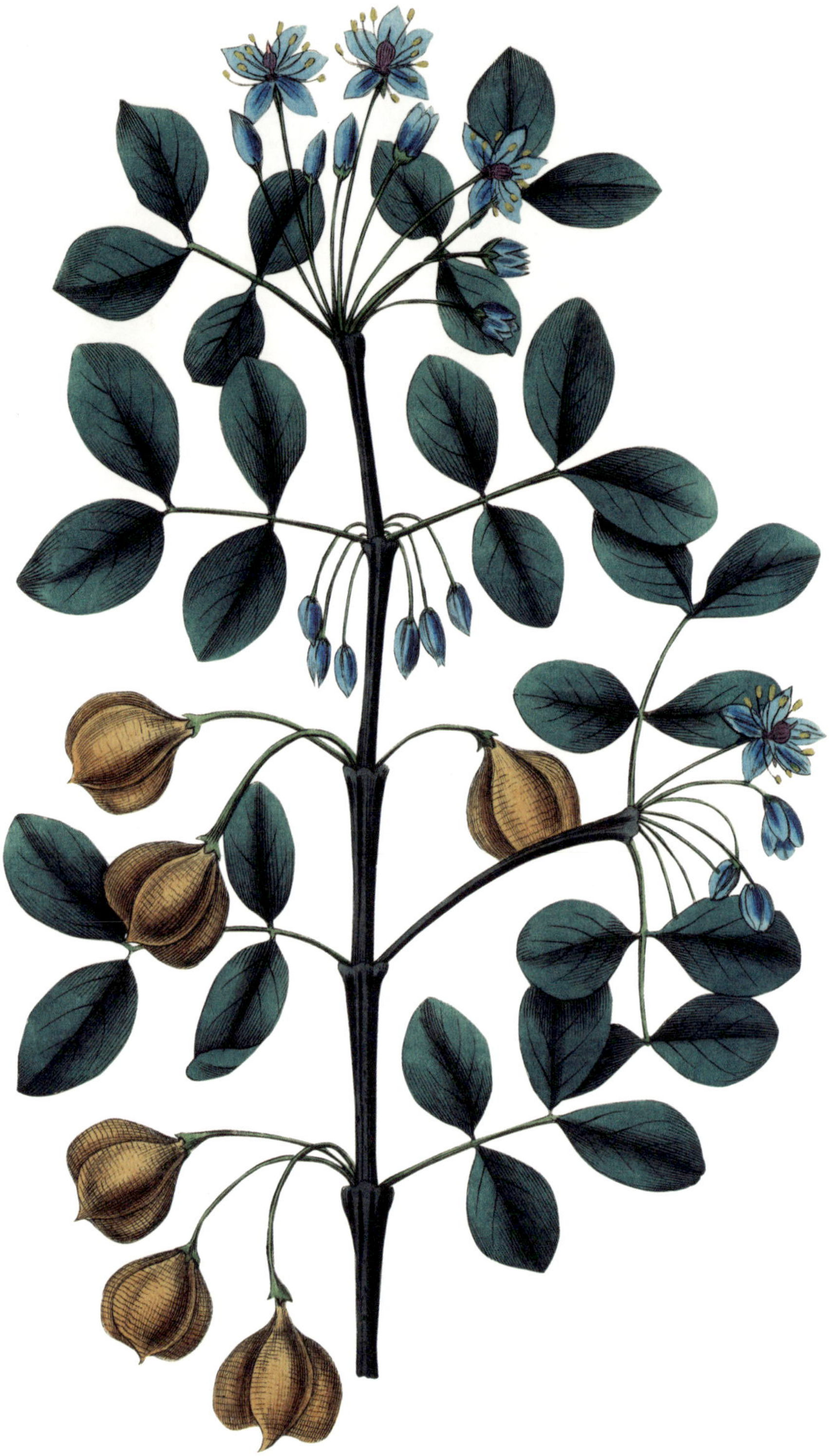

Guaiacum officinale
by John Stephenson & James Morss Churchill

roughbark lignum-vitae | guaiacwood | gaïacwood

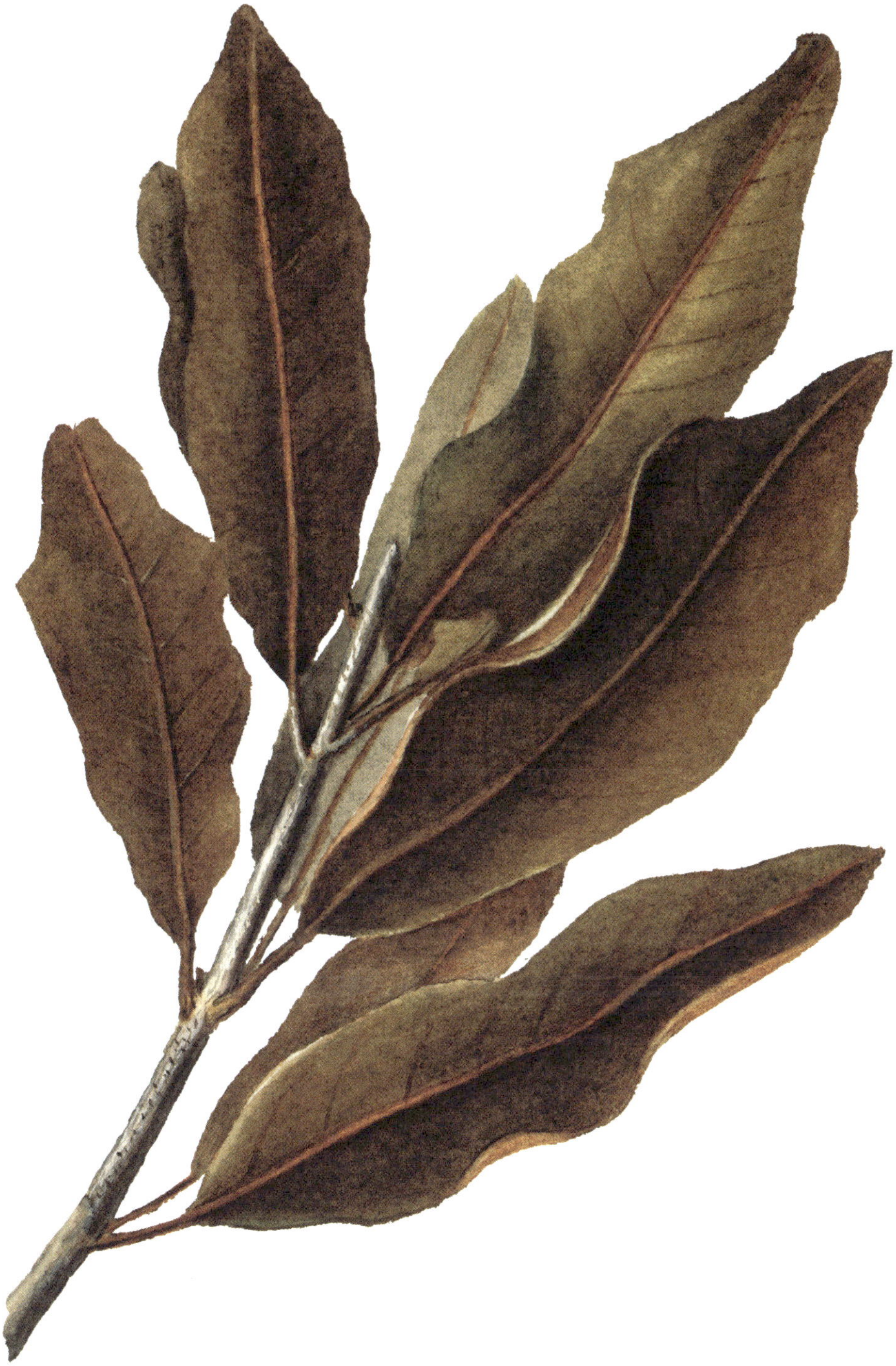

Macadamia ternifolia
by DEBORAH GRISCOM PASSMORE

small-fruited Queensland nut | Gympie nut

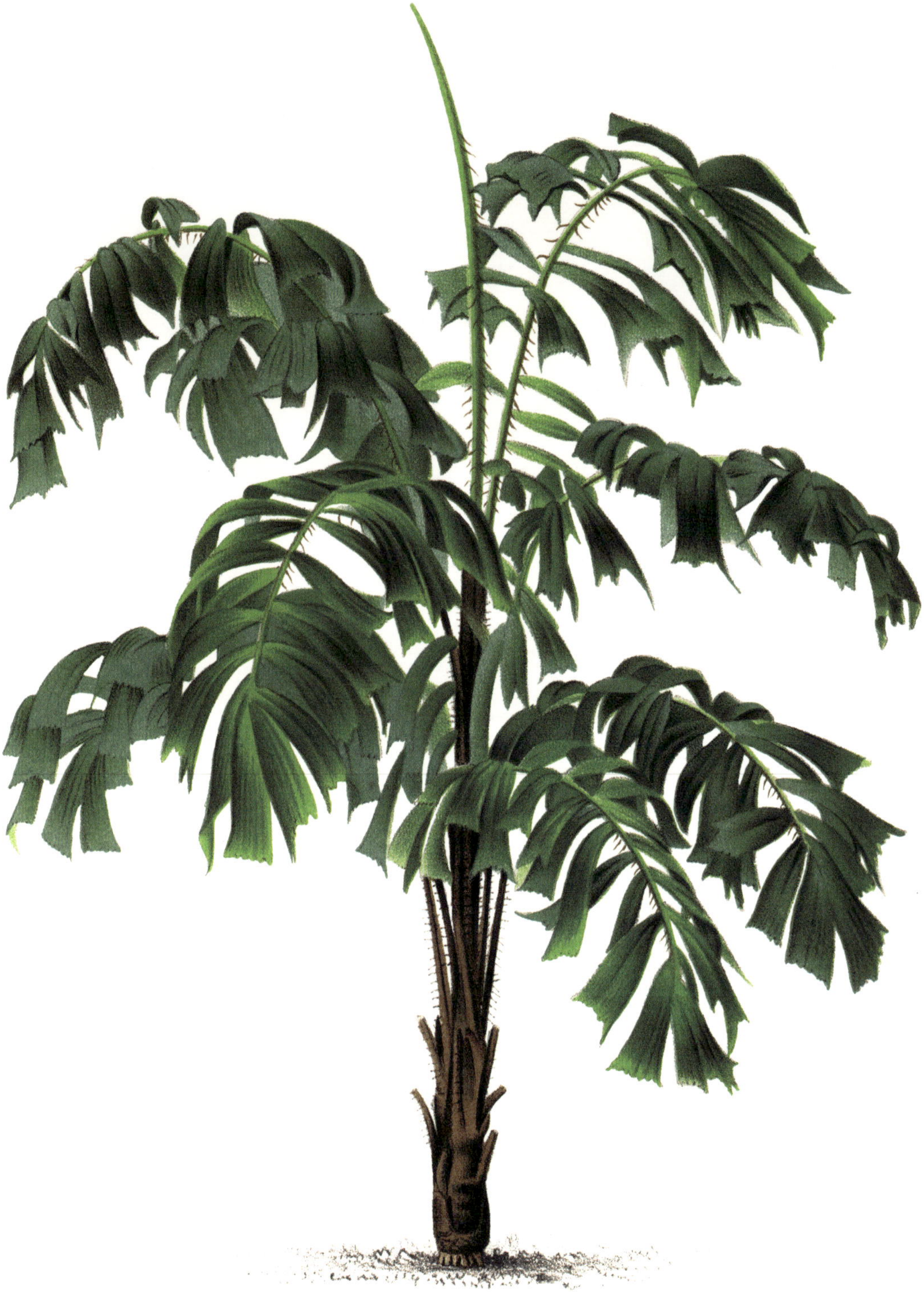

Aiphanes
by OSWALD DE KERCHOVE DE DENTERGHEM

spiny palm (unknown variety)

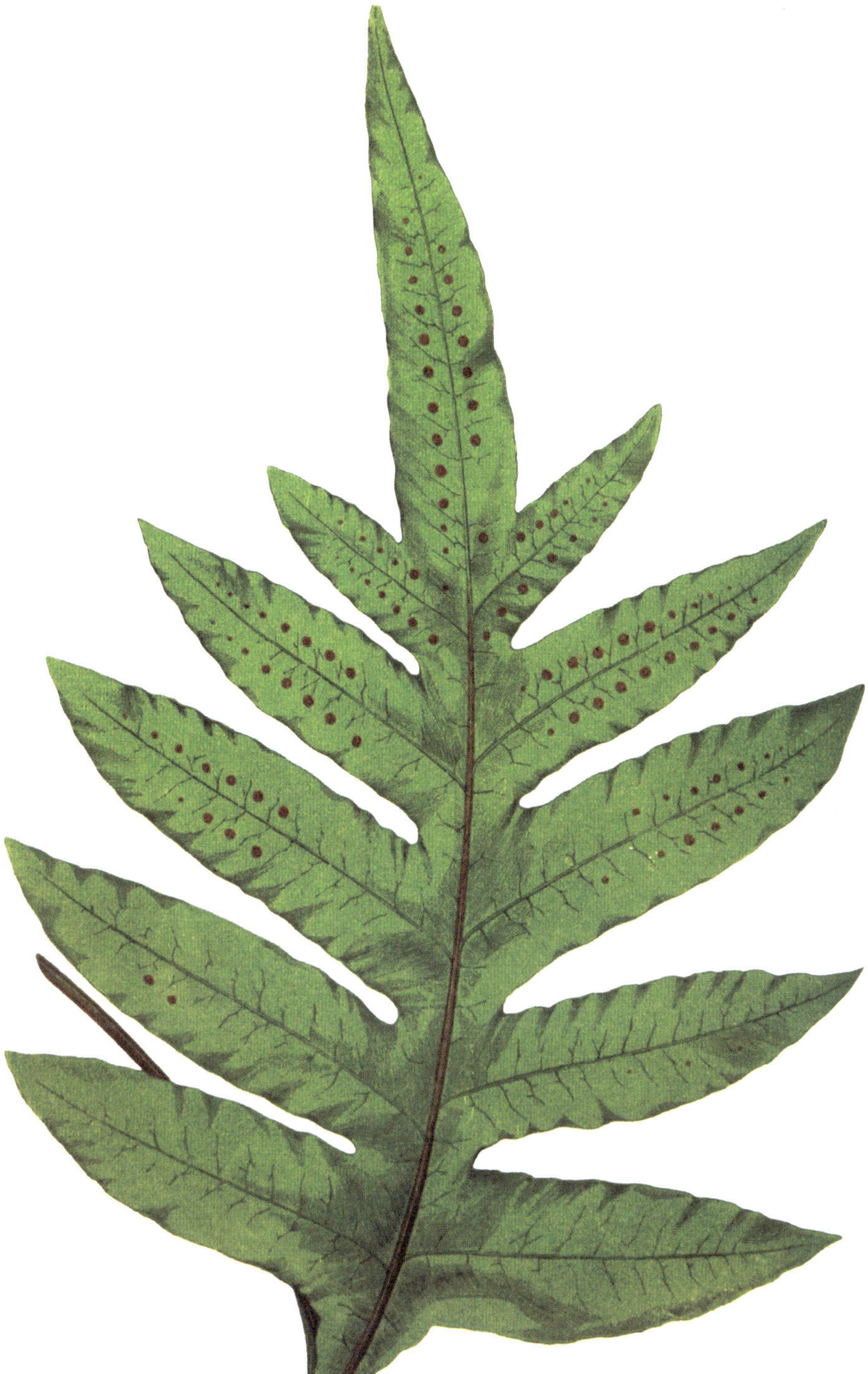

Lecanopteris pustulata subsp. *pustulata*
by Edward Joseph Lowe

kangaroo fern

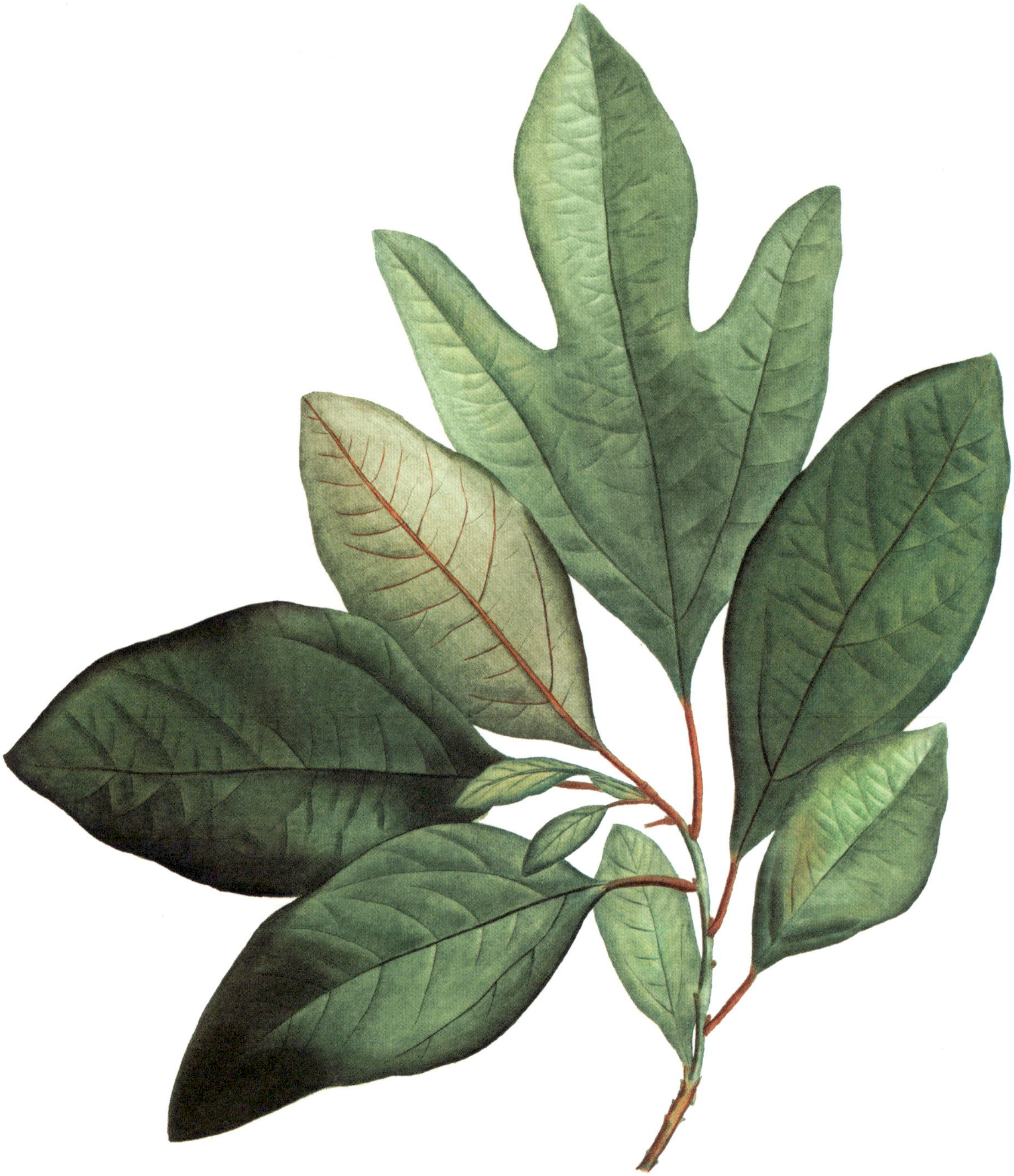

Sassafras albidum
by Pierre-Joseph Redouté

sassafras

Thus talking, hand in hand alone they passed
On to their blissful bower: it was a place
Chosen by the sovran Planter, when he framed
All things to Man's delightful use; the roof
Of thickest covert was inwoven shade
Laurel and myrtle, and what higher grew
Of firm and fragrant leaf; on either side
Acanthus, and each odorous bushy shrub,
Fenced up the verdant wall ...

FROM 'Paradise Lost' BY JOHN MILTON

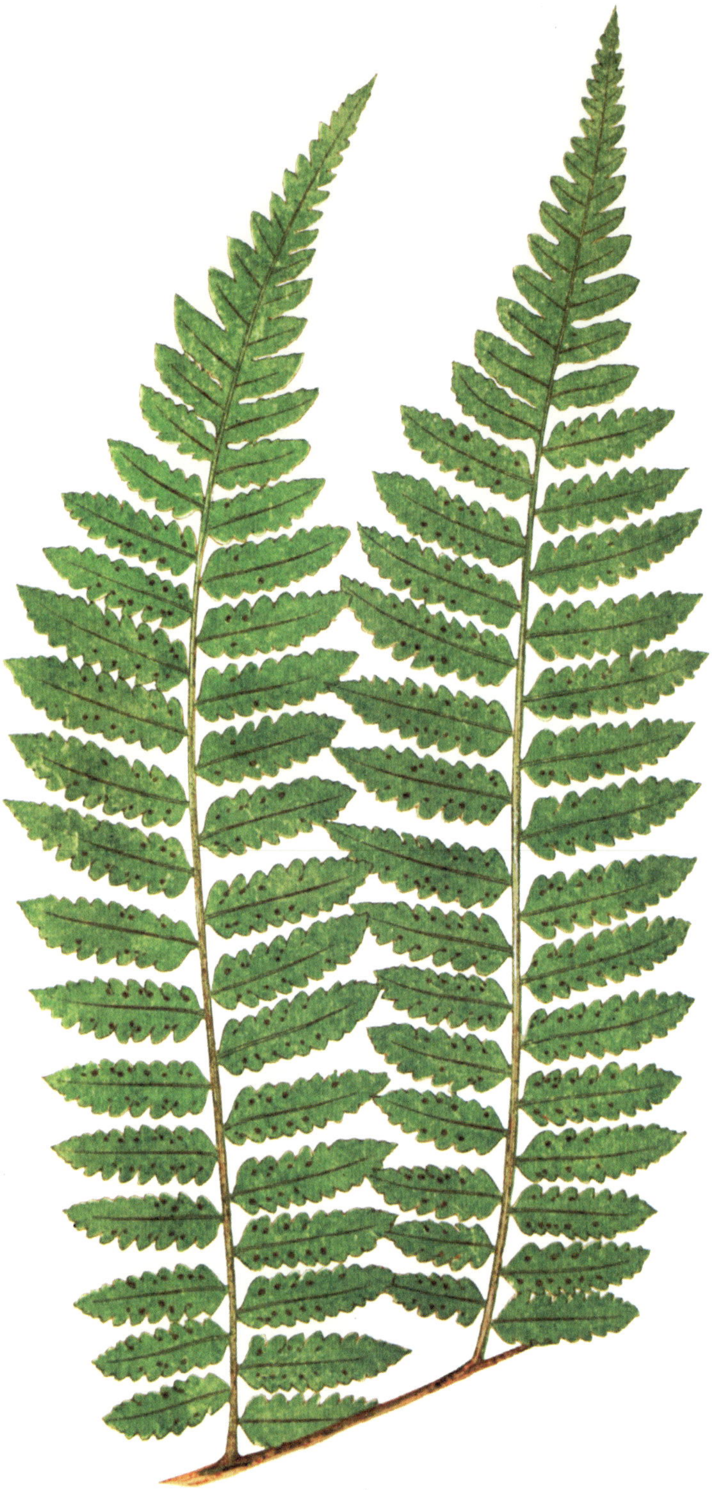

Cyathea atrovirens
by EDWARD JOSEPH LOWE

tree fern

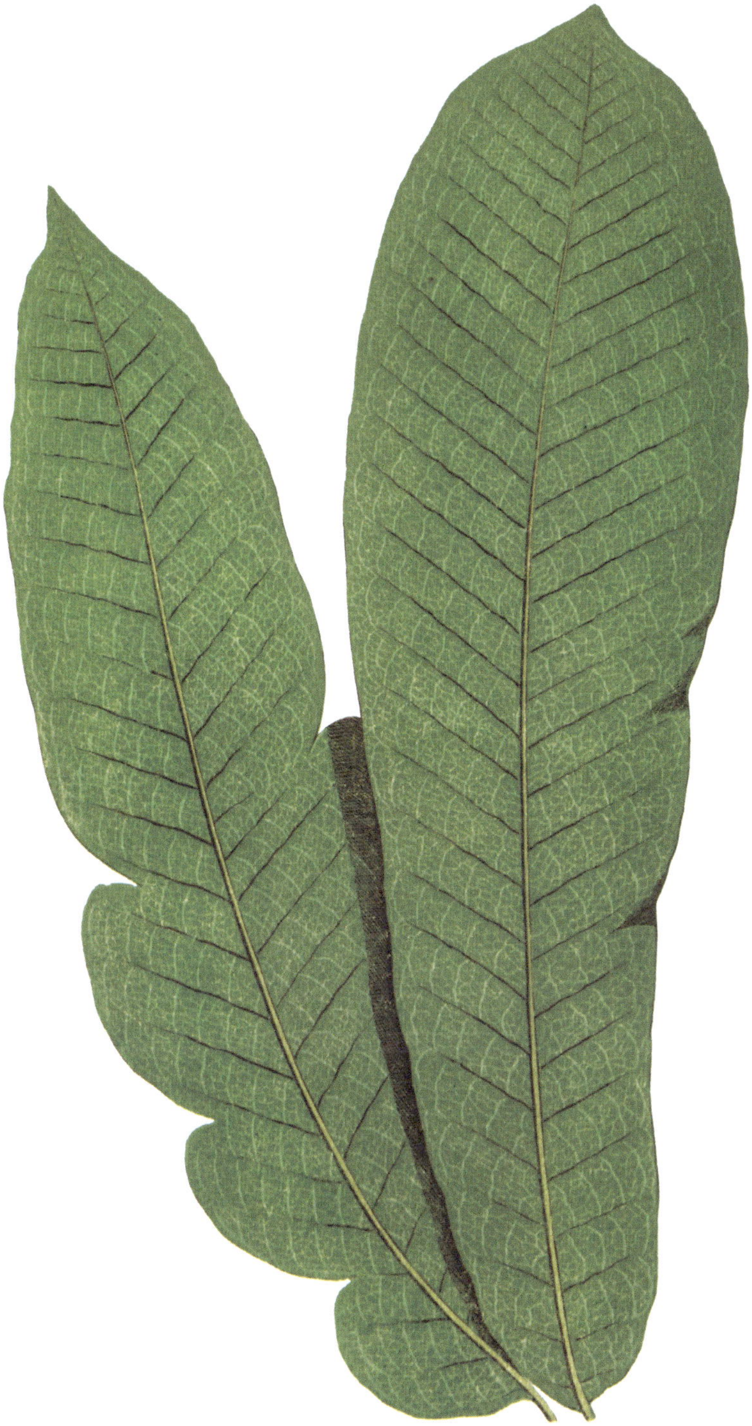

Microsorum musifolium
by Karl Blossfeldt

crocodile fern | alligator fern | crocodyllus fern

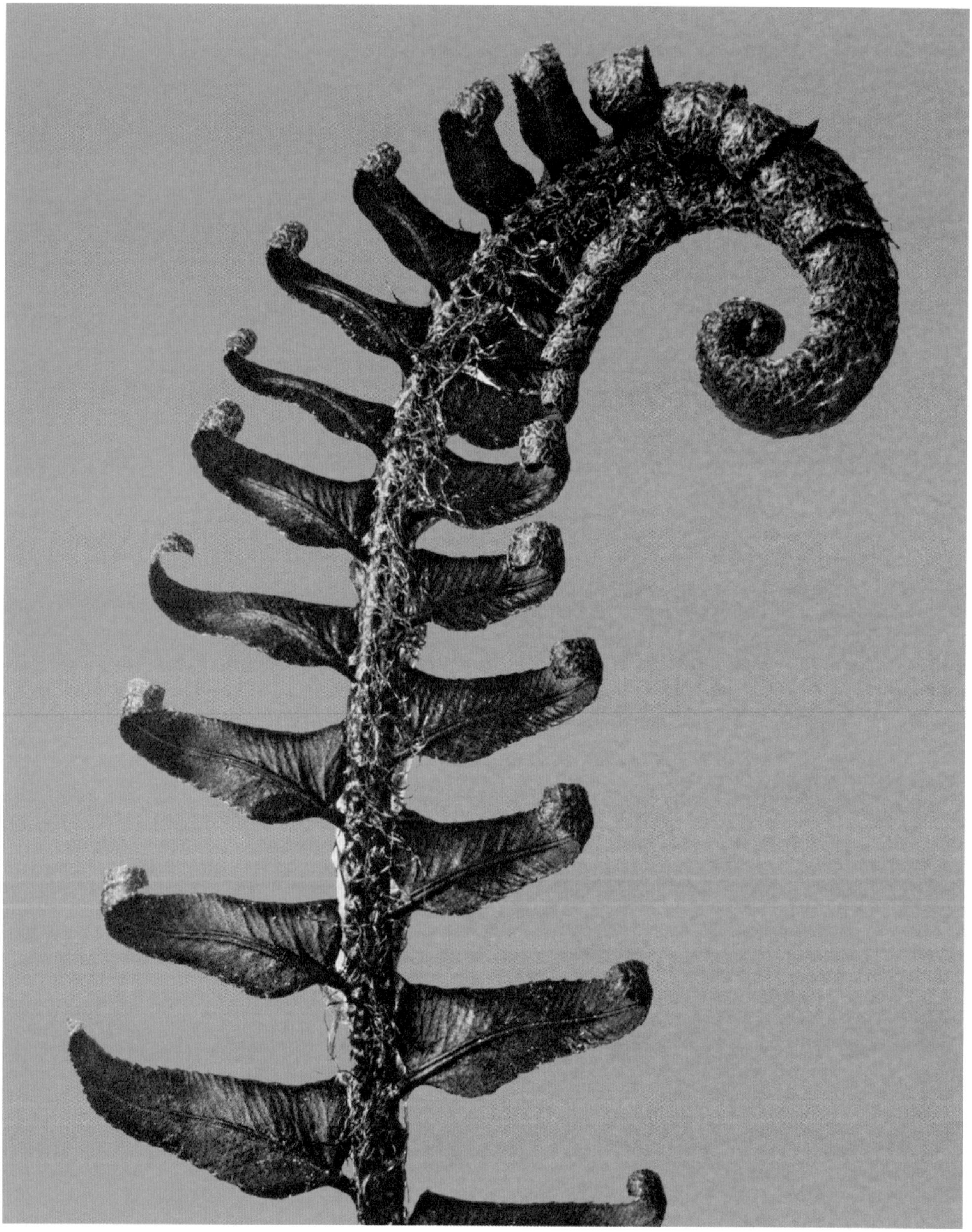

Polystichum vestitum
by KARL BLOSSFELDT

prickly shield fern

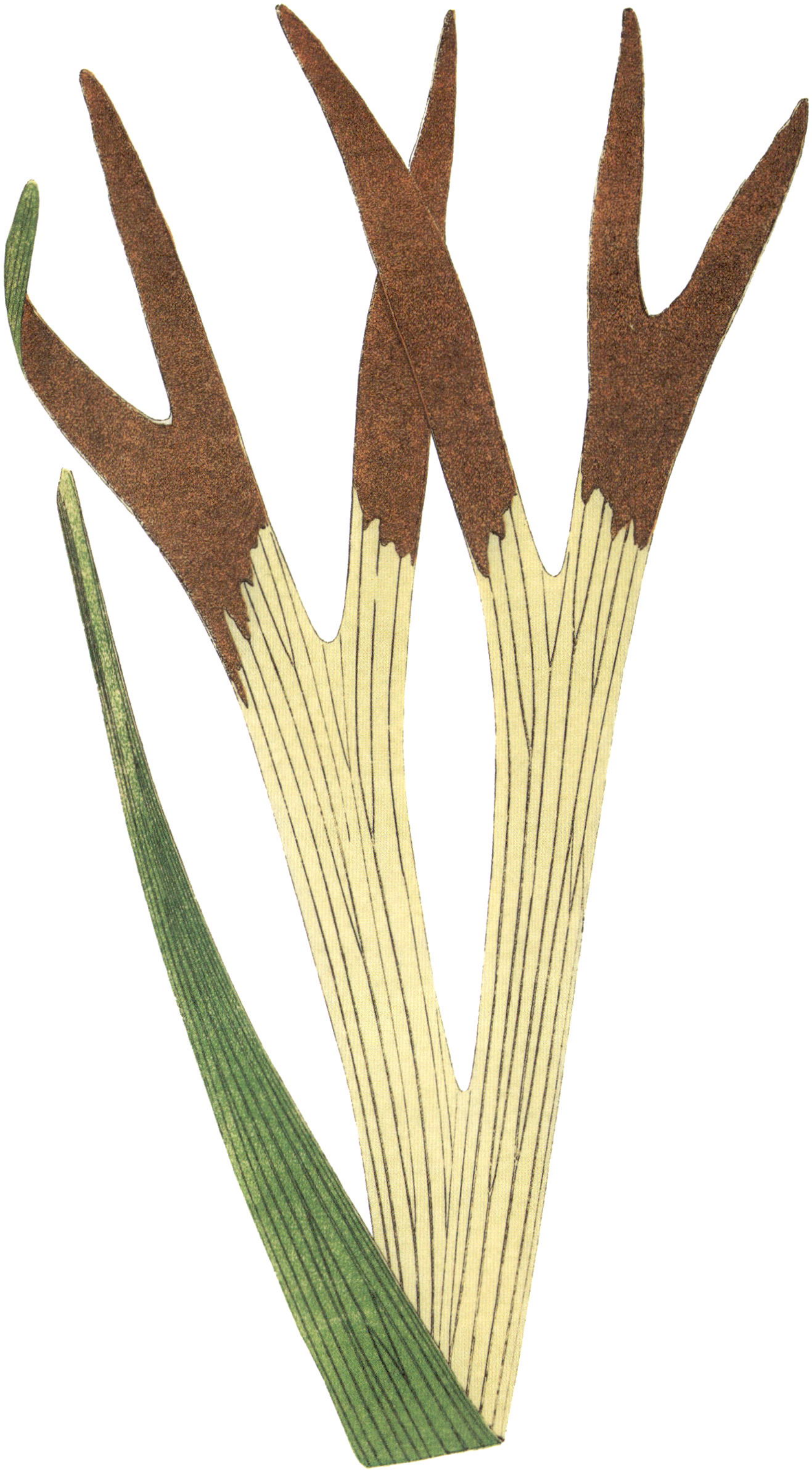

Platycerium alcicorne
by Edward Joseph Lowe

staghorn fern

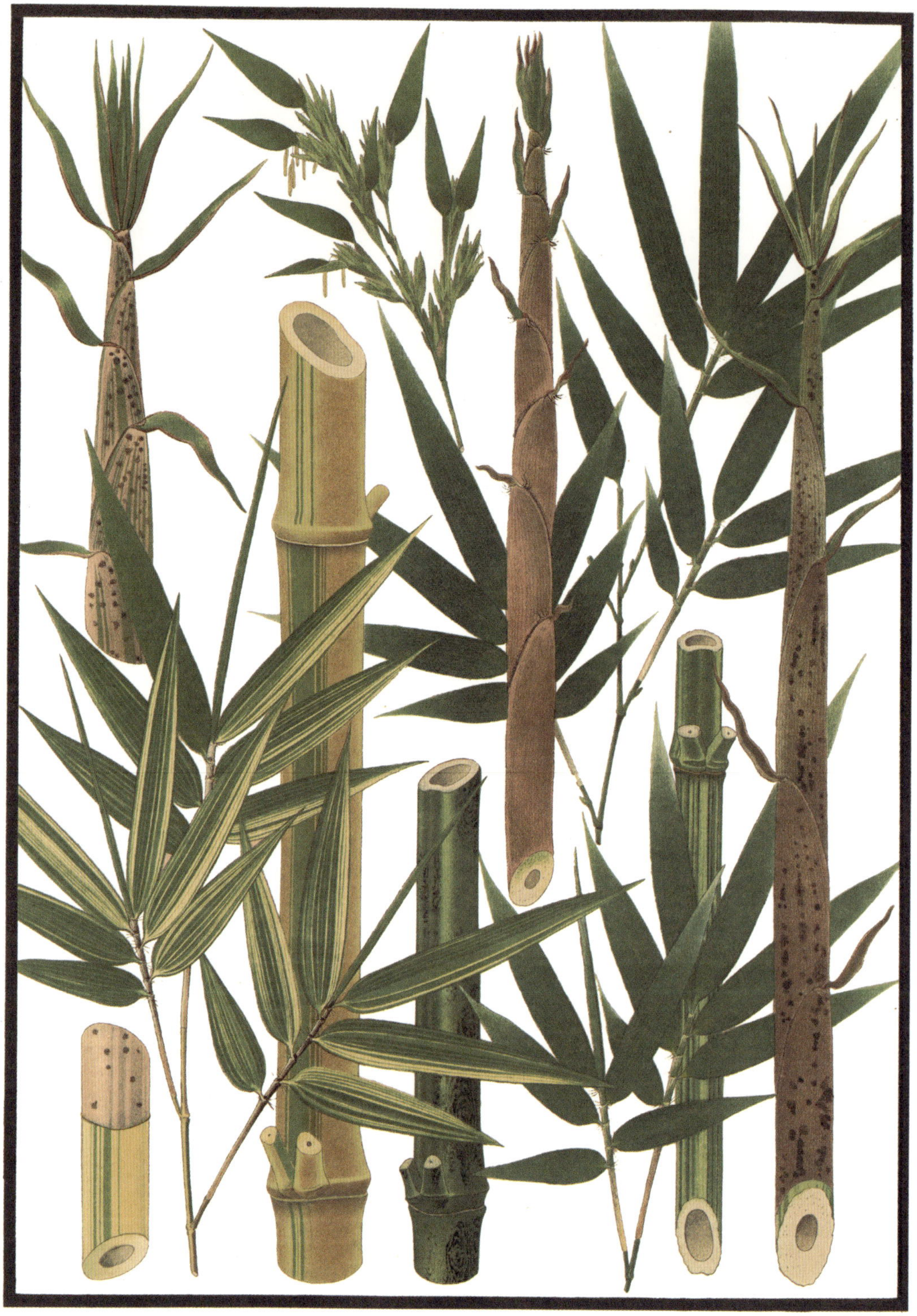

Phyllostachys
by Yasuyoshi Shirasawa

bamboo (various)

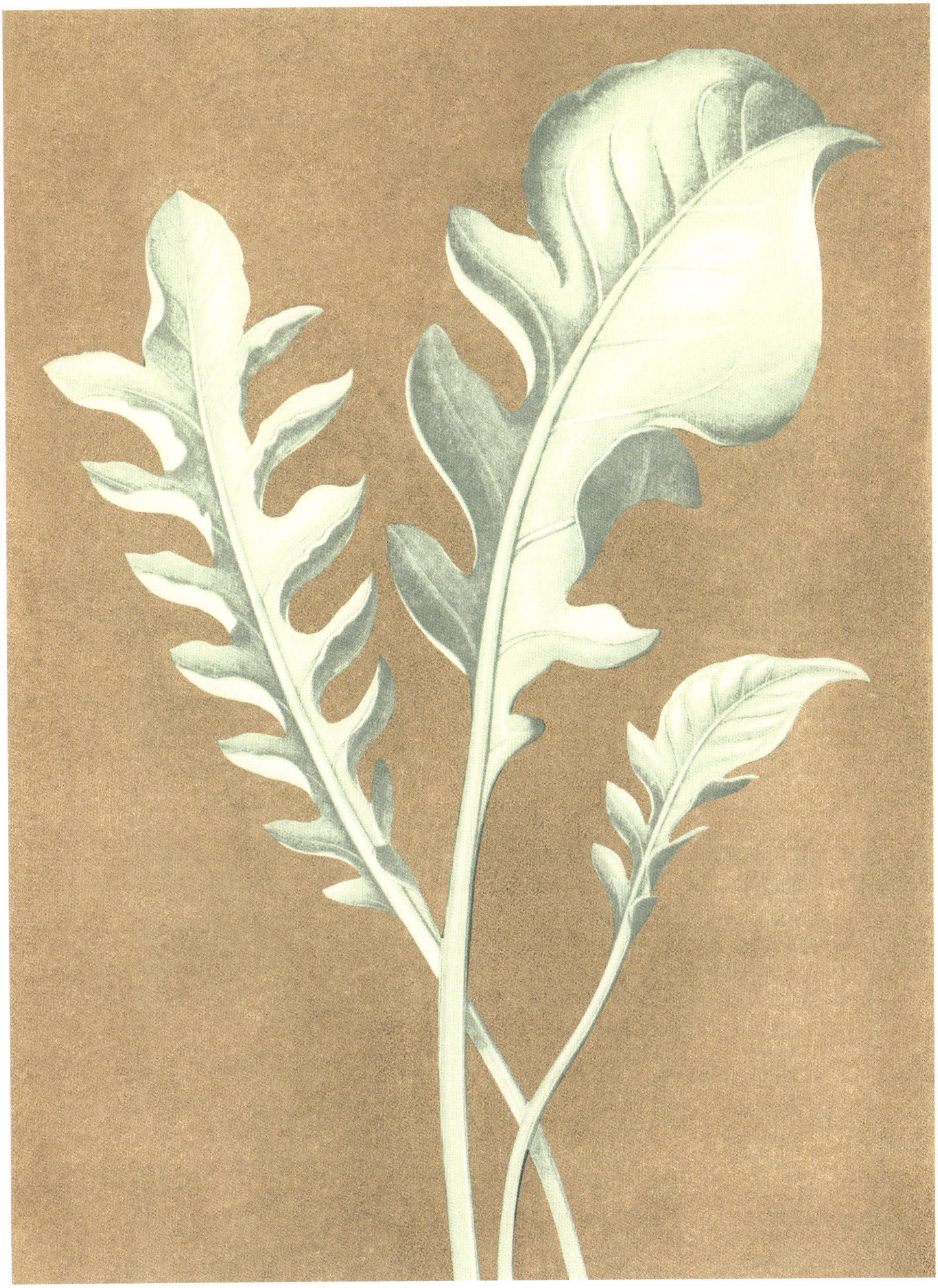

Centaurea cineraria
by Alexander Francis Lydon & Benjamin Fawcett

velvet centaurea | dusty miller | silver dust

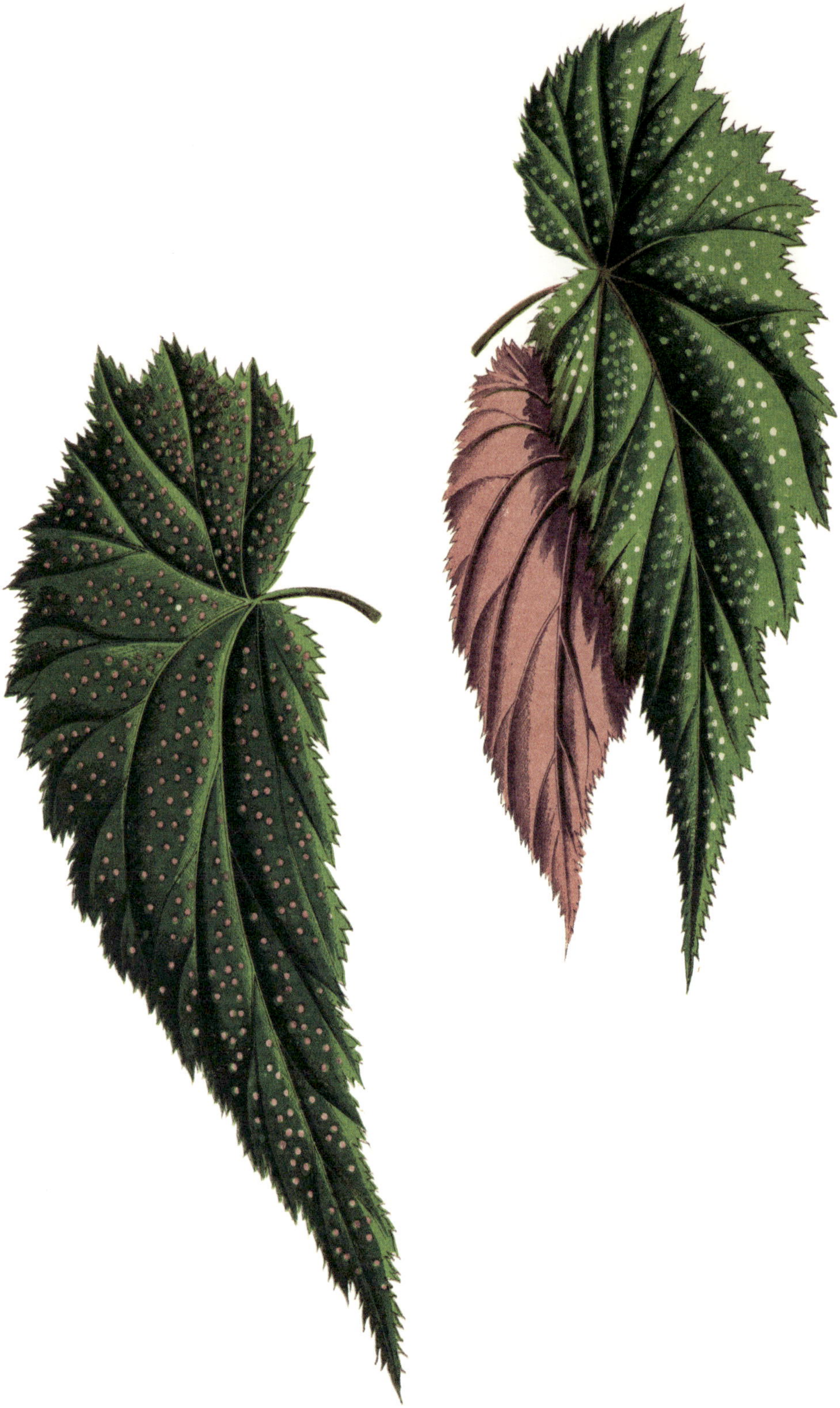

Begonia falcifolia
by Benjamin Fawcett & James Shirley Hibberd

begonia falcifolia

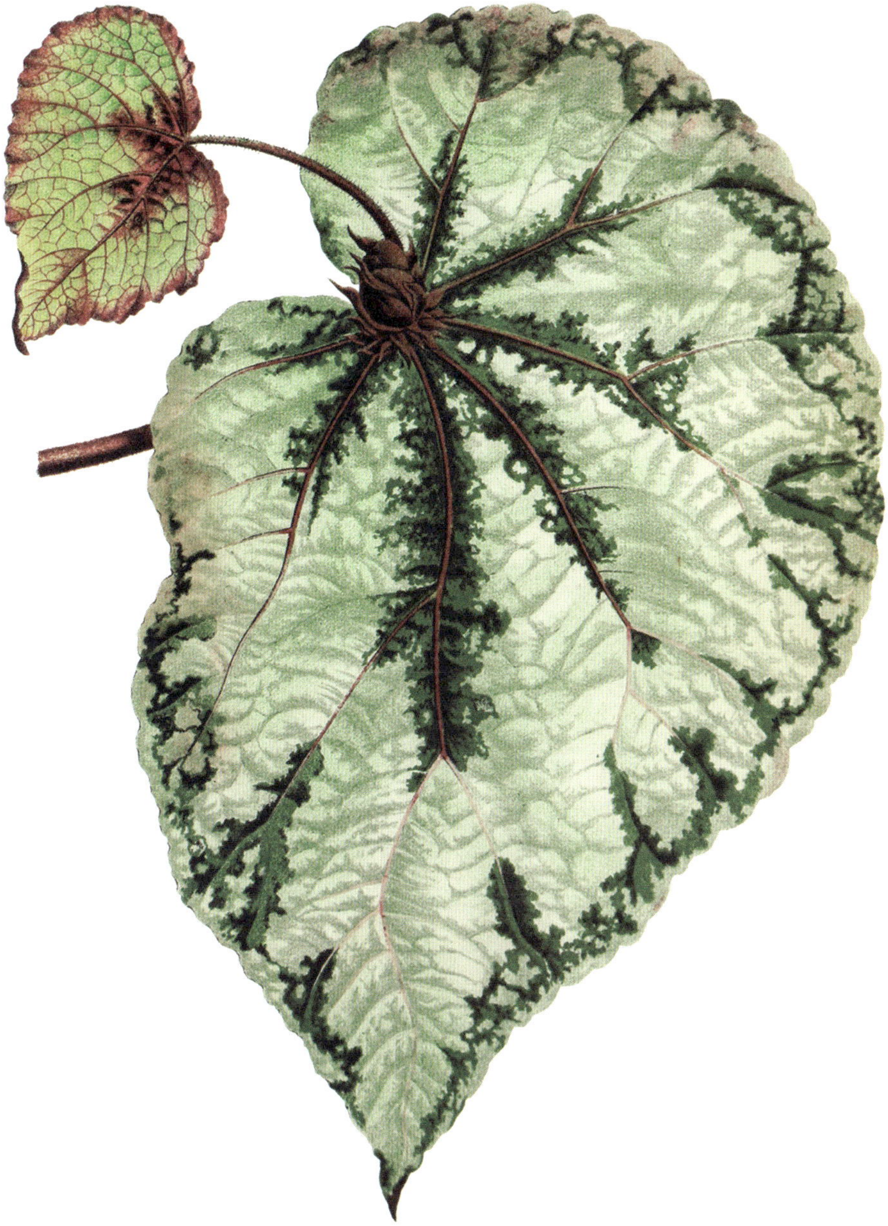

Begonia rex
by Alexander Francis Lydon

king begonia | fancy-leaf begonia | painted-leaf begonia

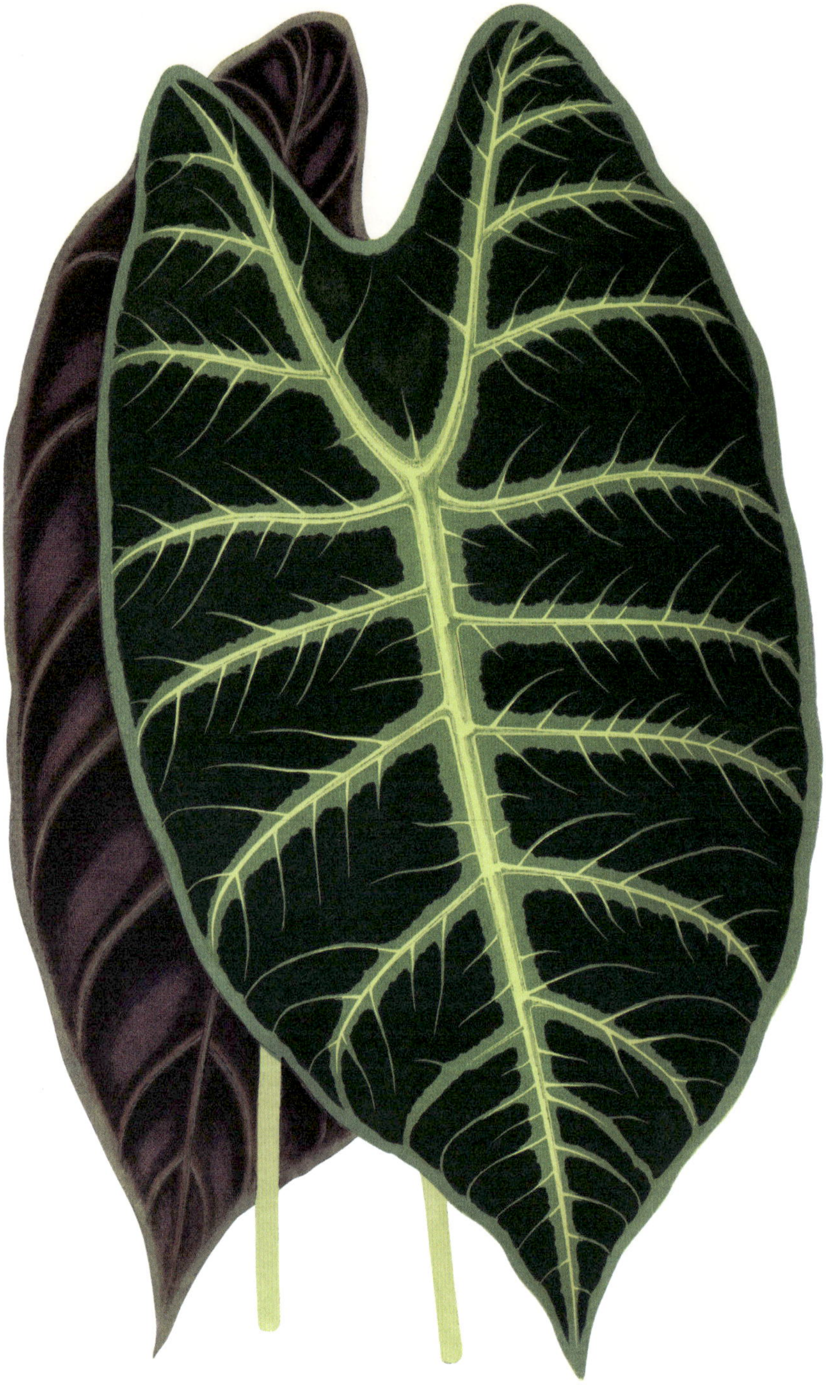

Alocasia longiloba
by ALEXANDER FRANCIS LYDON & BENJAMIN FAWCETT

elephant ear

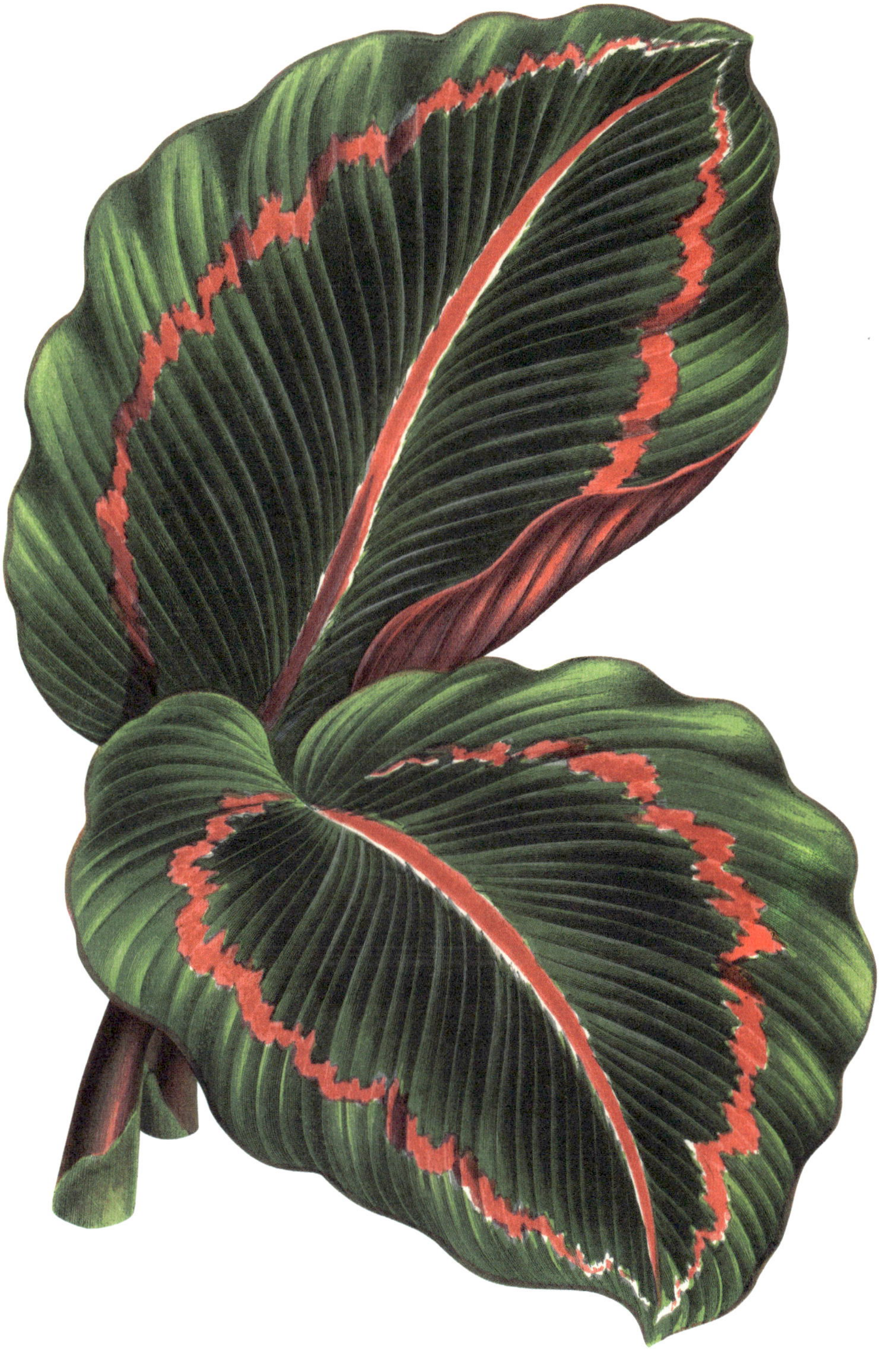

Goeppertia roseopicta
by ALEXANDER FRANCIS LYDON & BENJAMIN FAWCETT

rose-painted prayer plant | rose-painted calathea

The evergreen!
How beautiful,
how welcome,
how wonderful
the evergreen!

FROM *Mansfield Park* BY JANE AUSTEN

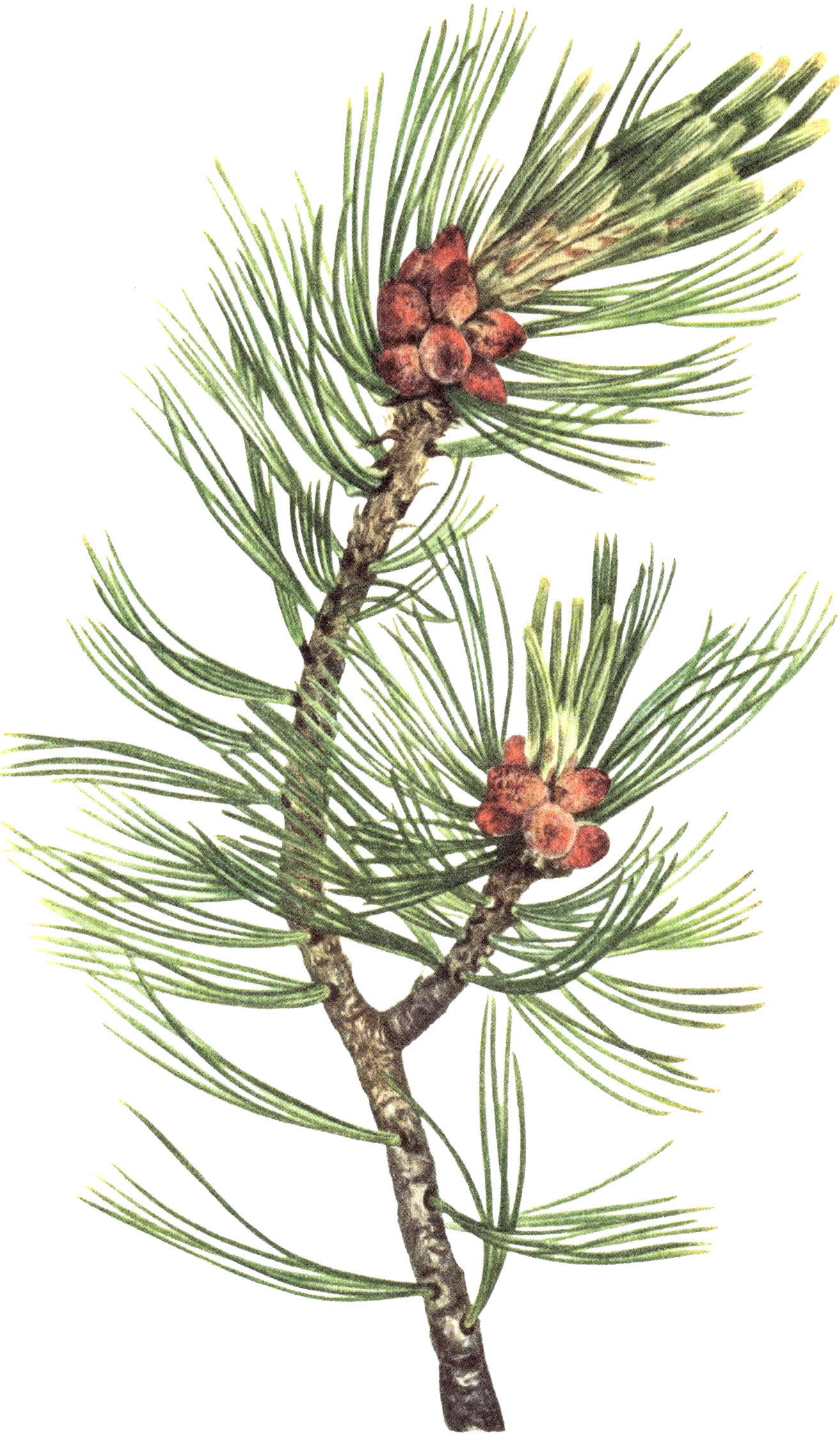

Pinus albicaulis
by MARY VAUX WALCOTT

whitebark pine | pitch pine | scrub pine | creeping pine

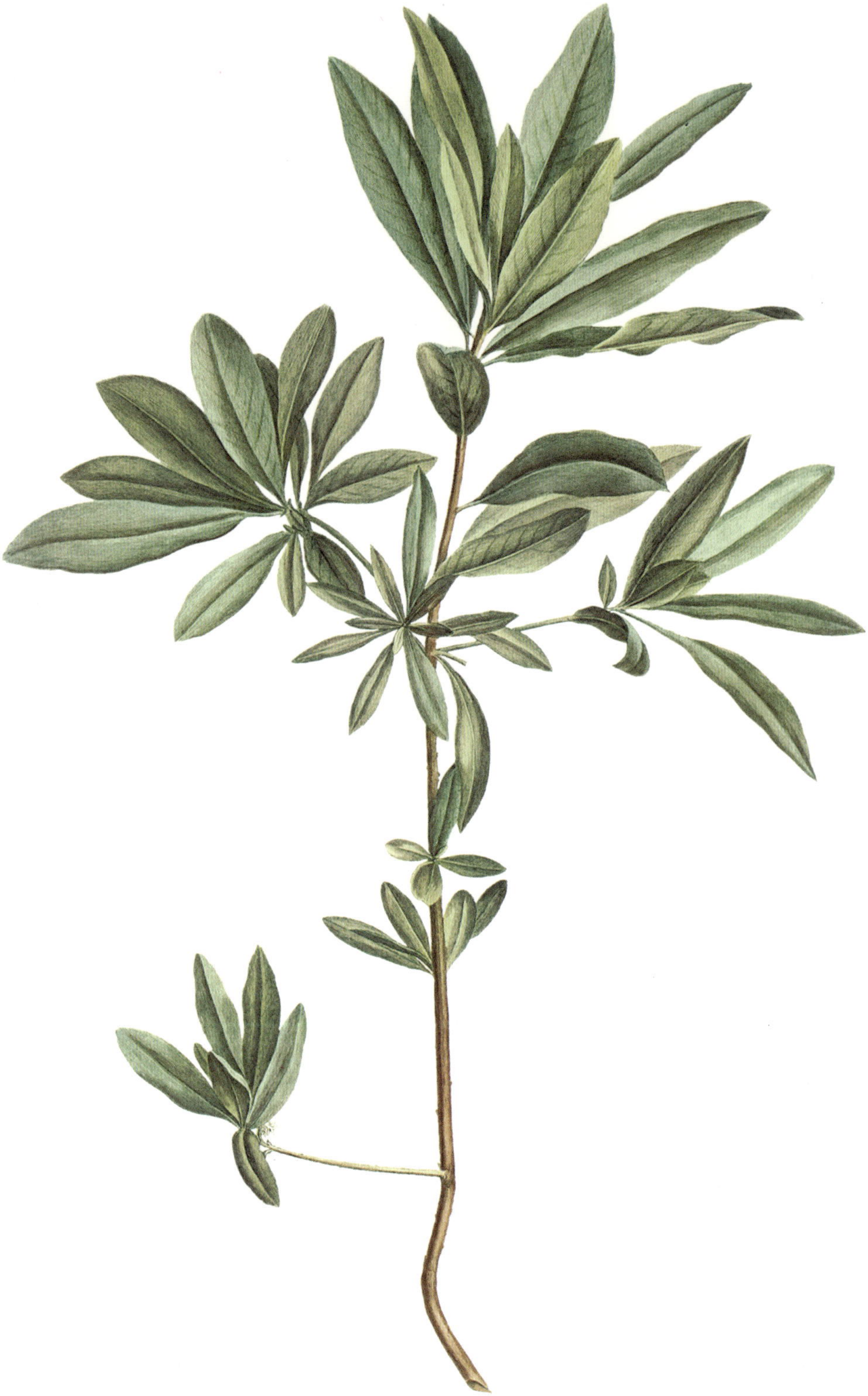

Cyrilla racemiflora
by Pierre-Joseph Redouté

swamp cyrilla | swamp titi | leatherwood

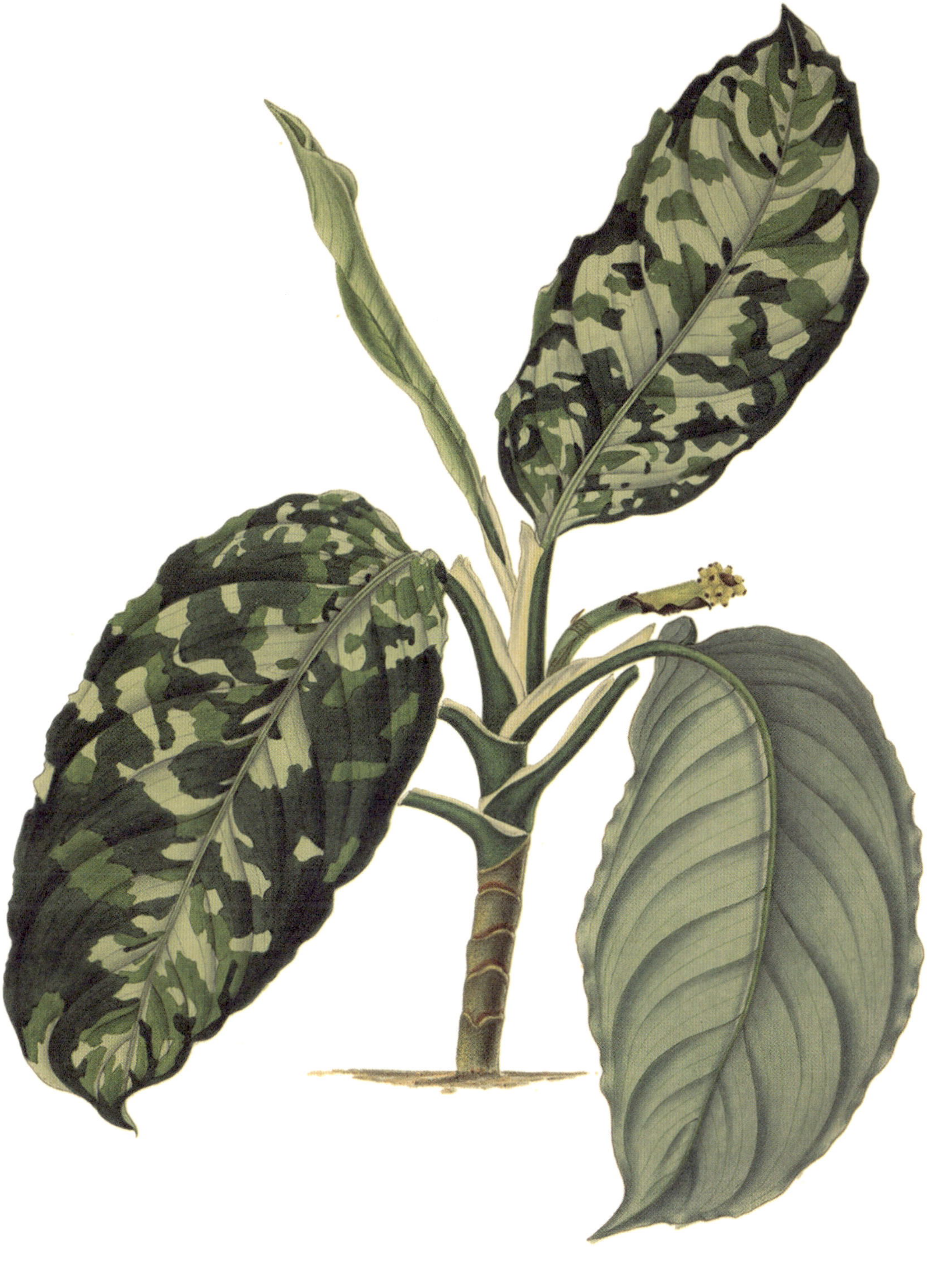

Aglaonema pictum
by George De Alwis

camouflage plant

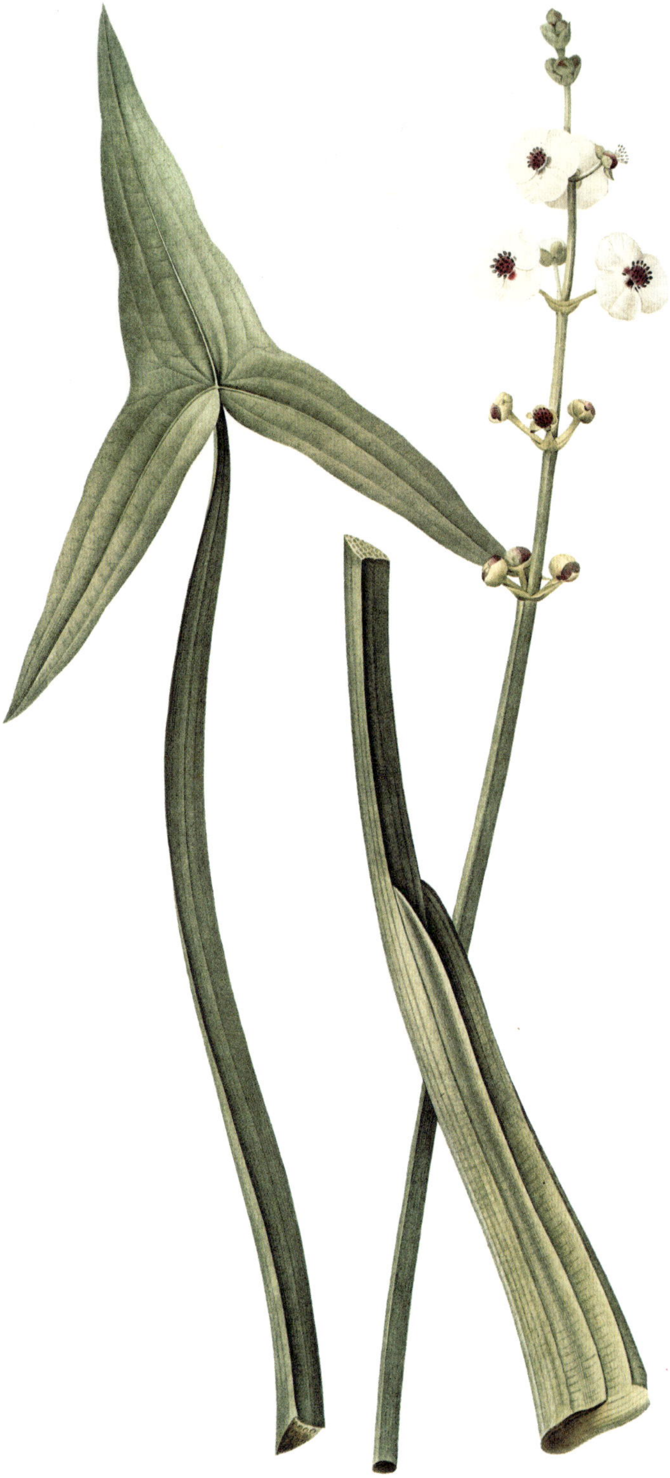

Sagittaria sagittifolia
by Pierre-Joseph Redouté

arrowhead

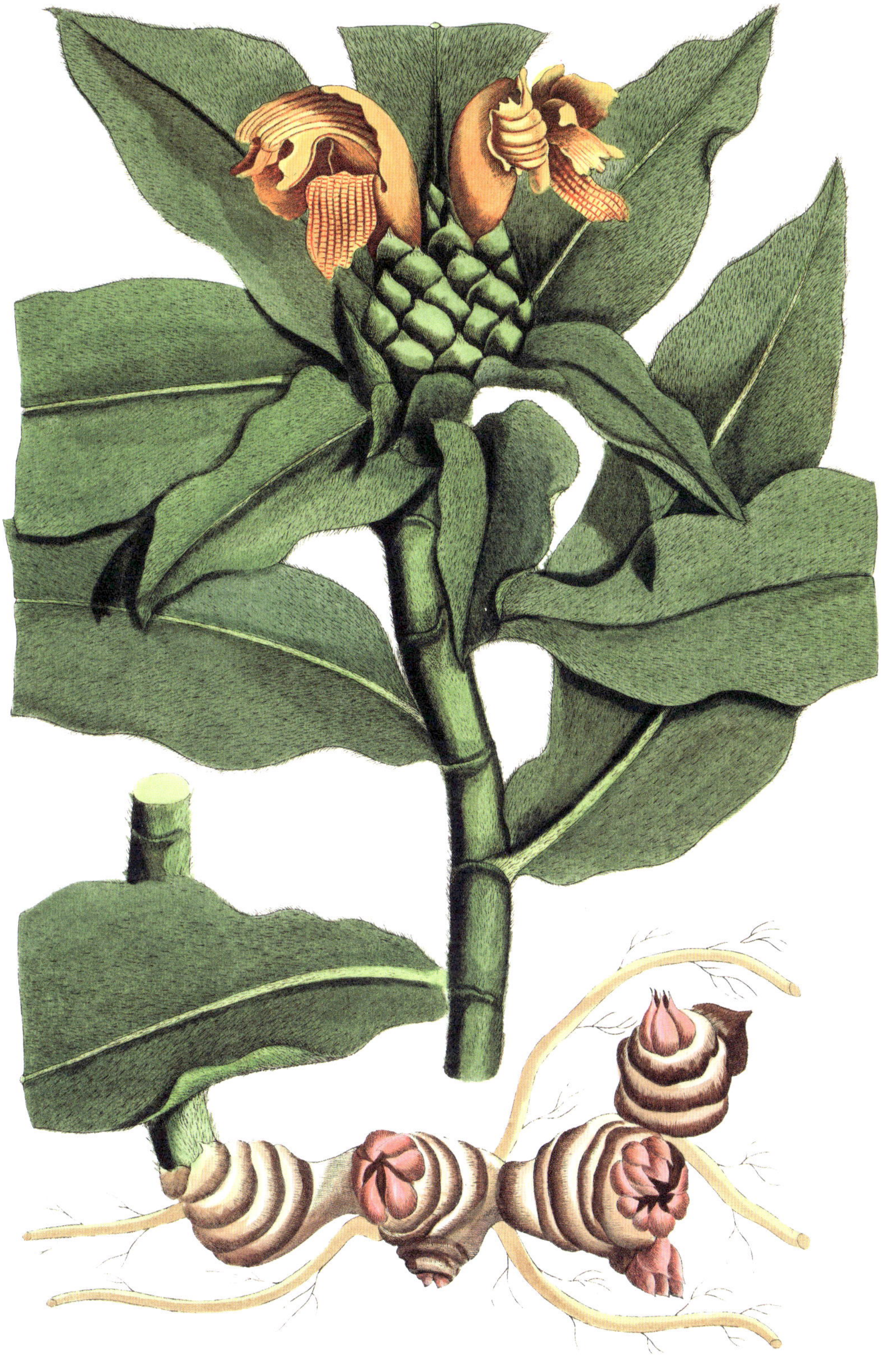

Costus villosissimus
by Nikolaus Joseph von Jacquin

porcupine spiral ginger | costus flower | spiral flag

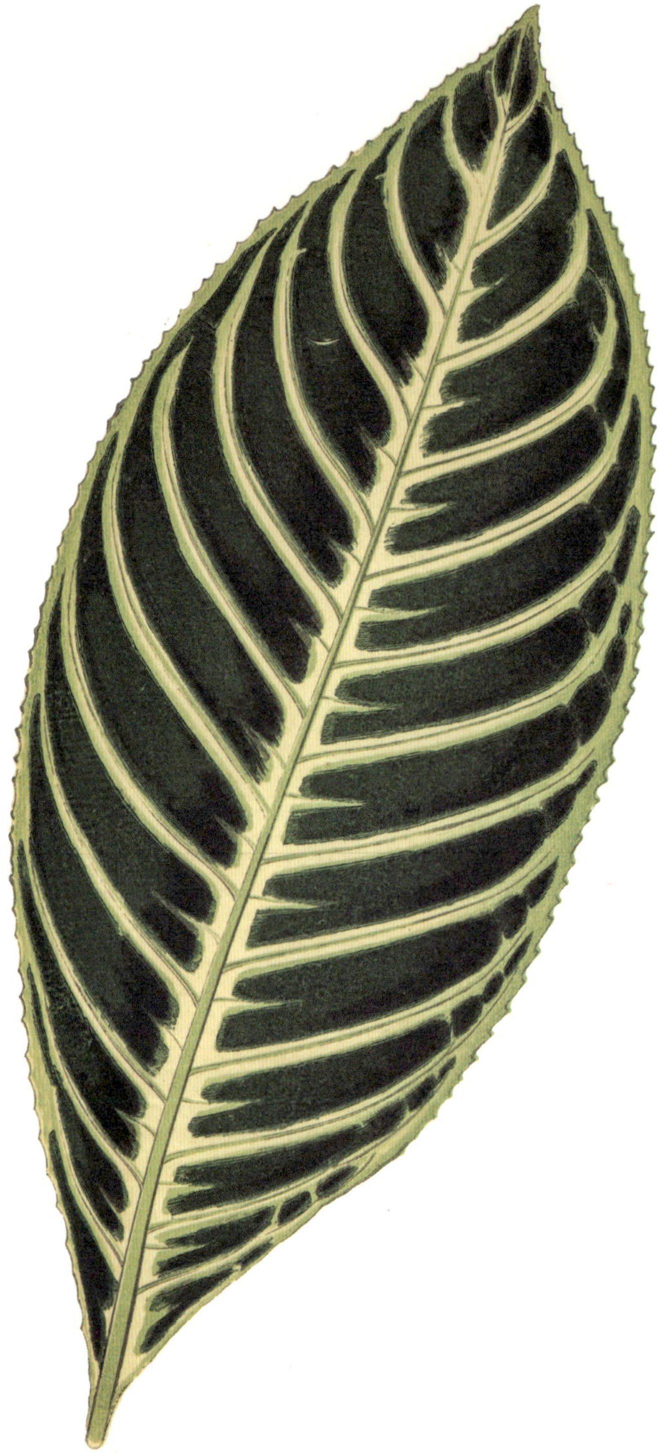

Sanchezia nobilis
by Benjamin Fawcett & James Shirley Hibberd

tiger plant | yellow Sanchezia

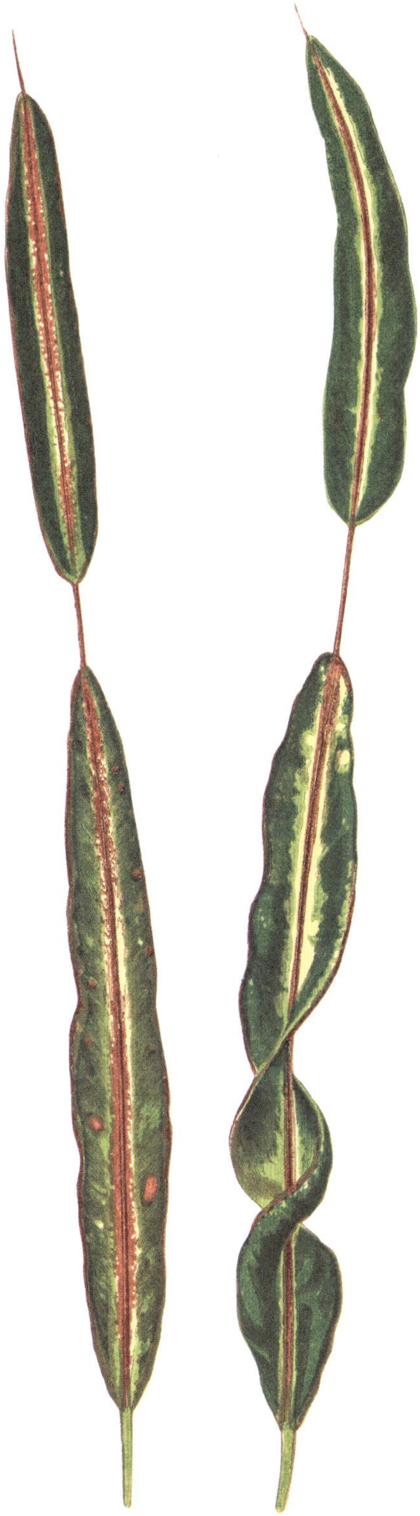

Codiaeum variegatum 'Interruptum'
by Benjamin Fawcett & James Shirley Hibberd

croton | garden croton

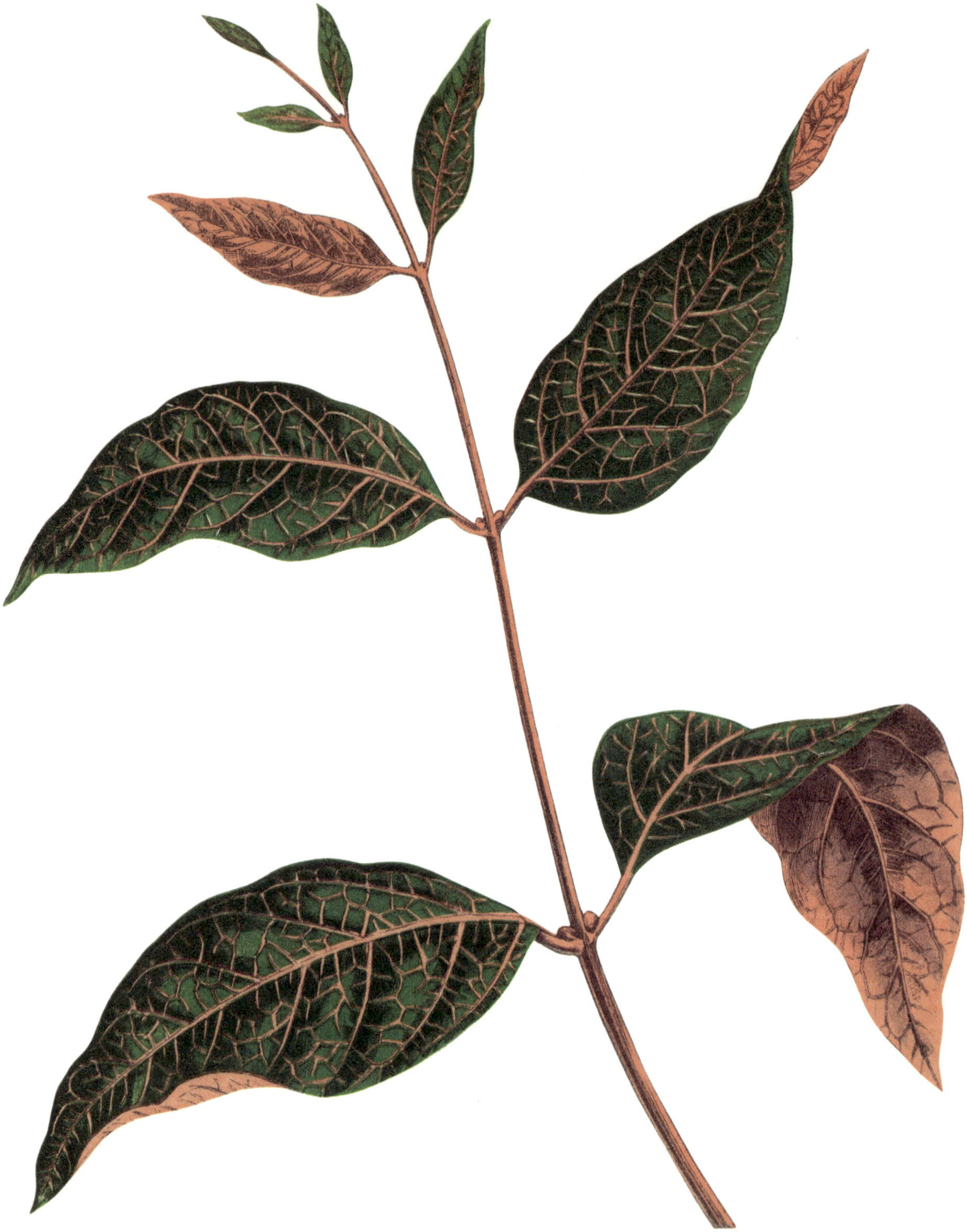

Prestonia quinquangularis
by ALEXANDER FRANCIS LYDON & BENJAMIN FAWCETT

echites nutans

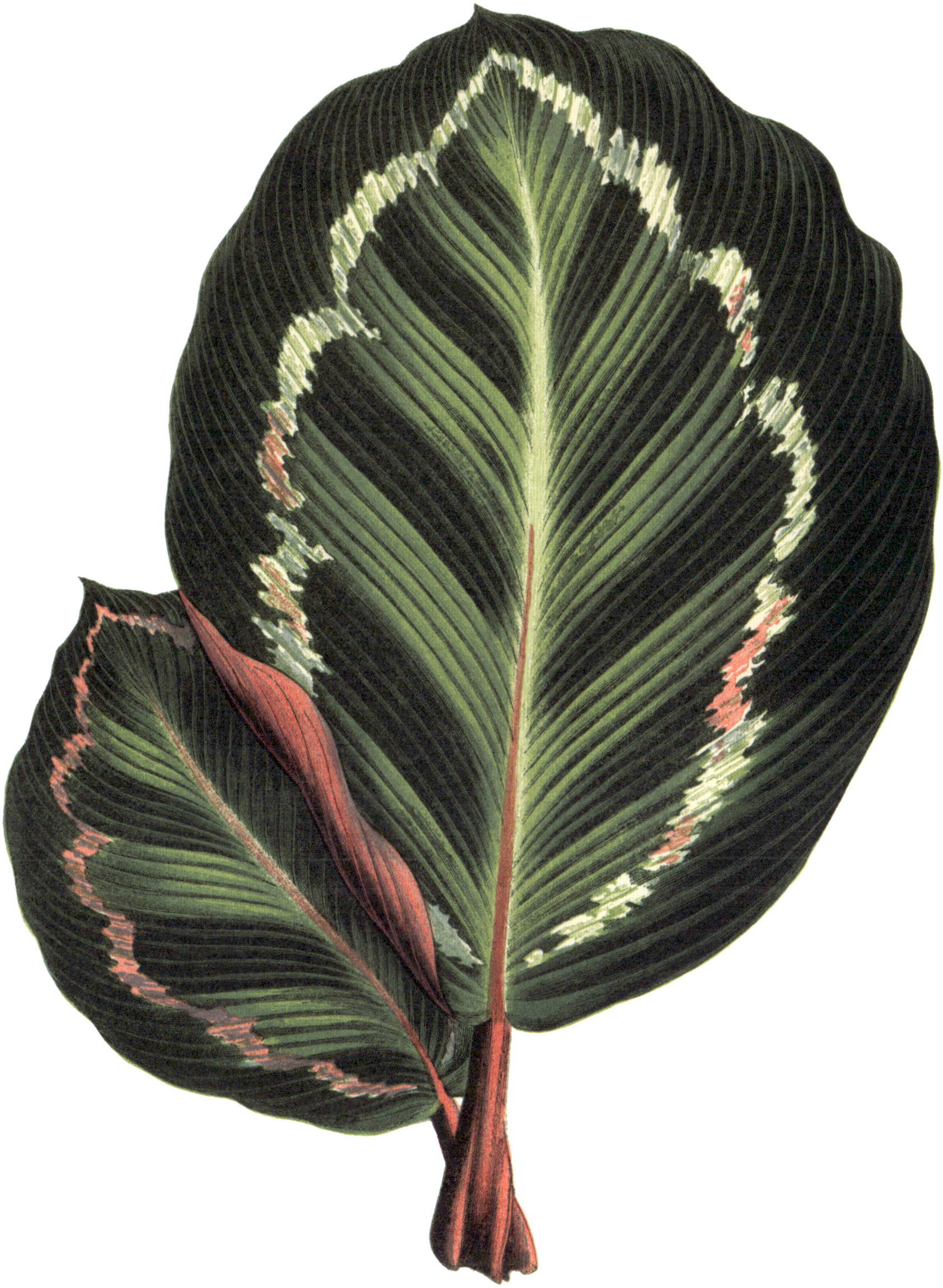

Maranta leuconeura
by Alexander Francis Lydon & Benjamin Fawcett

prayer plant

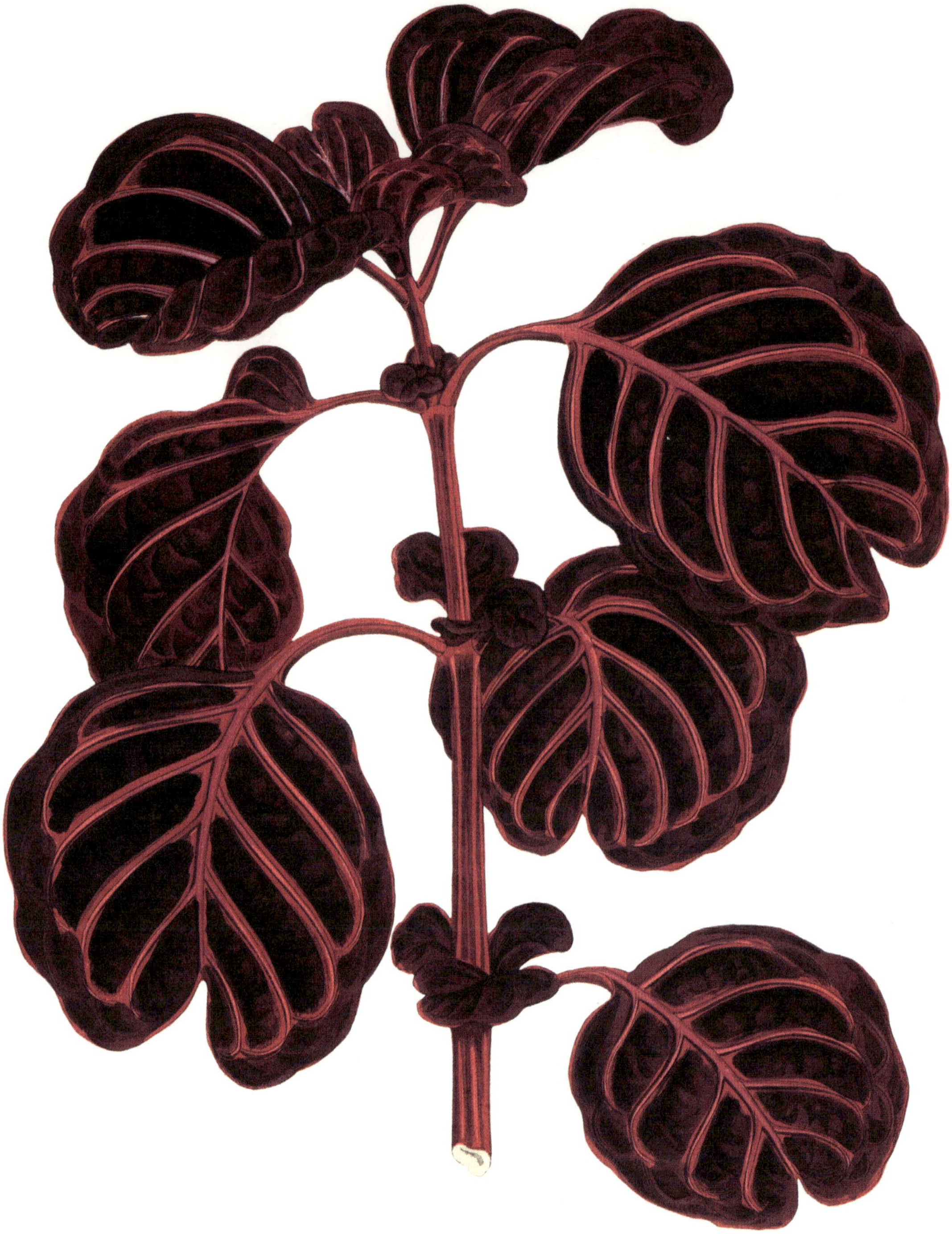

Iresine diffusa f. *herbstii*
by ALEXANDER FRANCIS LYDON & BENJAMIN FAWCETT

Herbst's bloodleaf | beefsteak plant | chicken gizzard plant

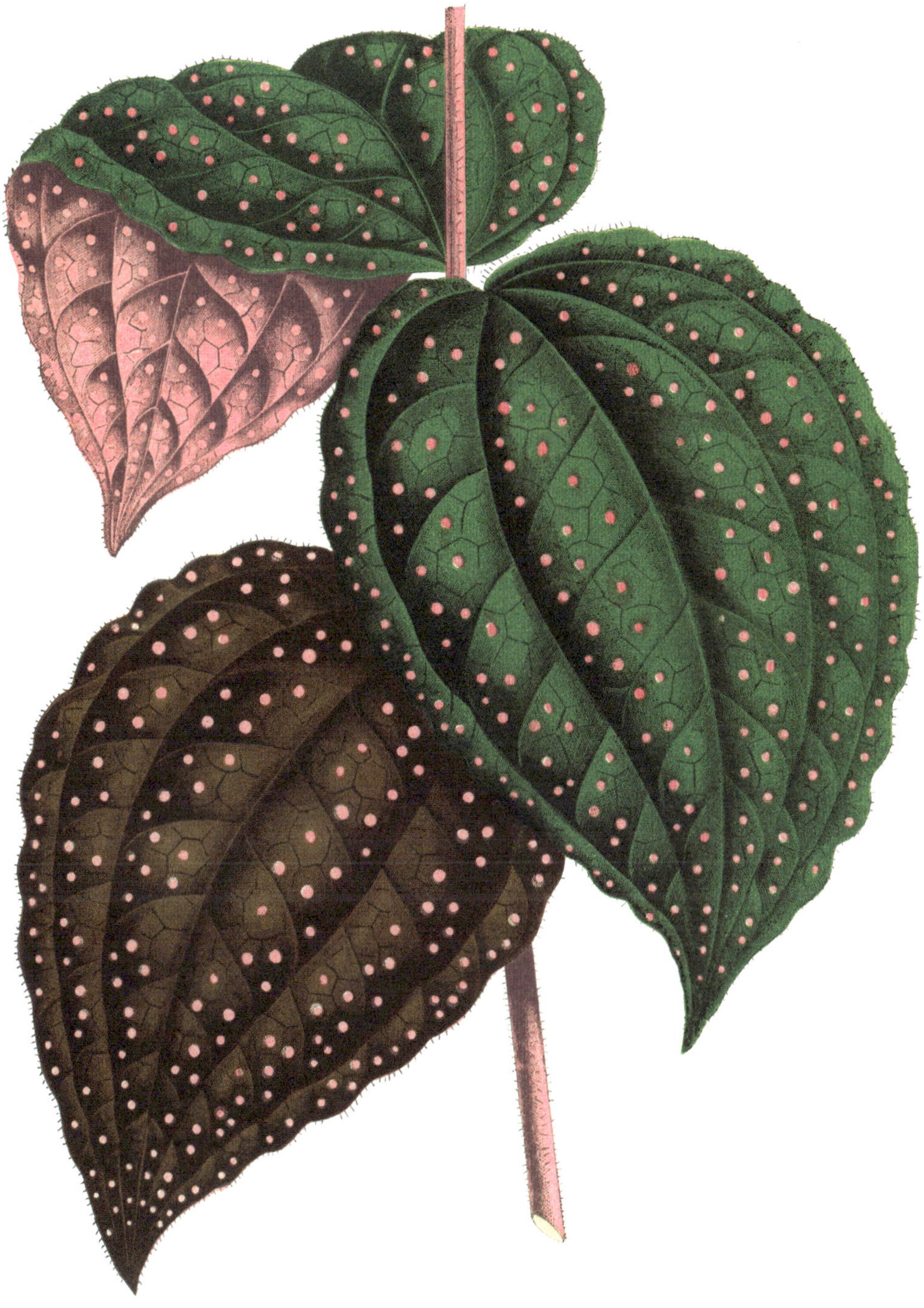

Gravesia guttata
by Alexander Francis Lydon & Benjamin Fawcett

gravesia guttata

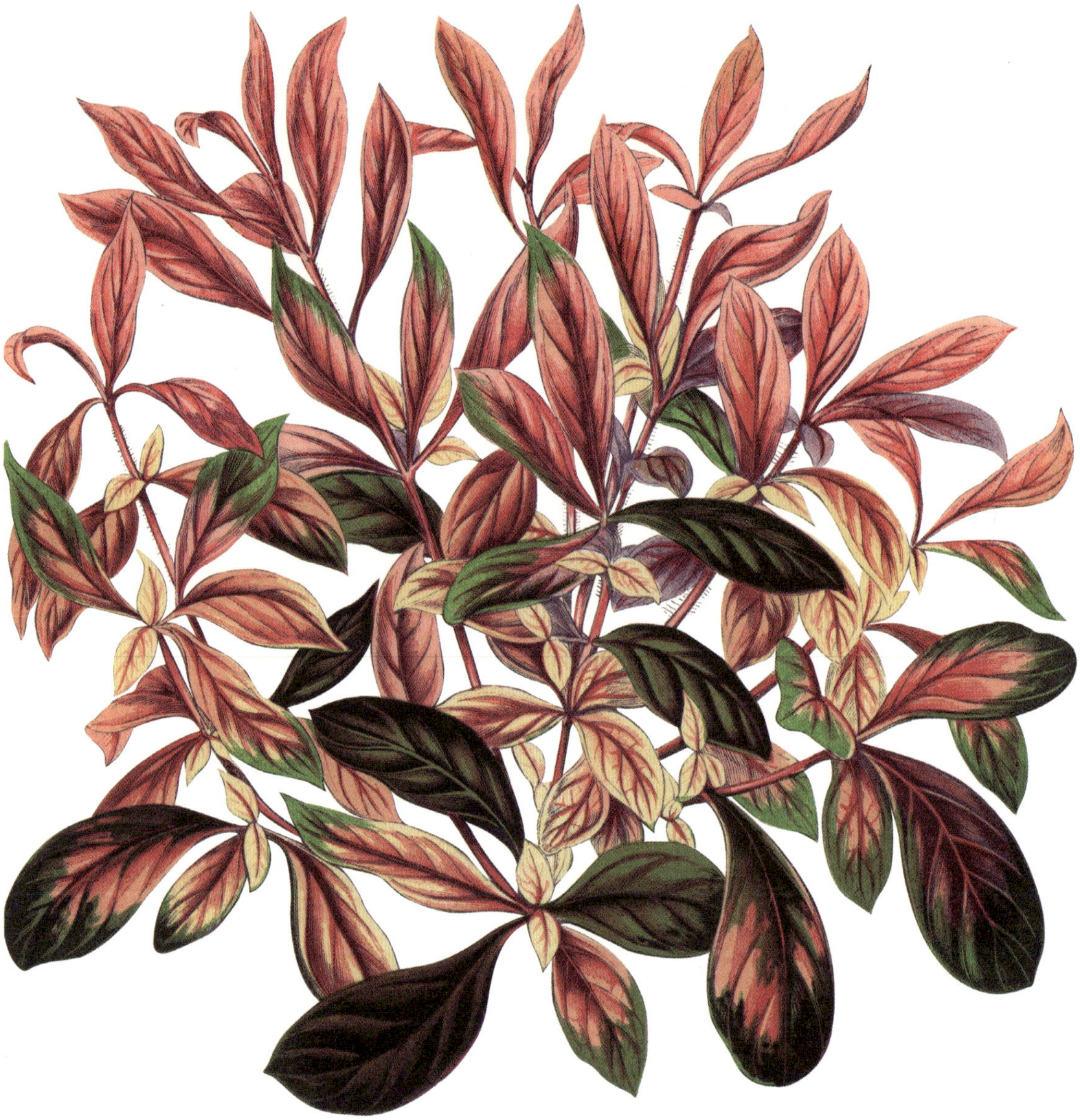

Alternanthera
by Alexander Francis Lydon & Benjamin Fawcett

joyweeds | Joseph's coat

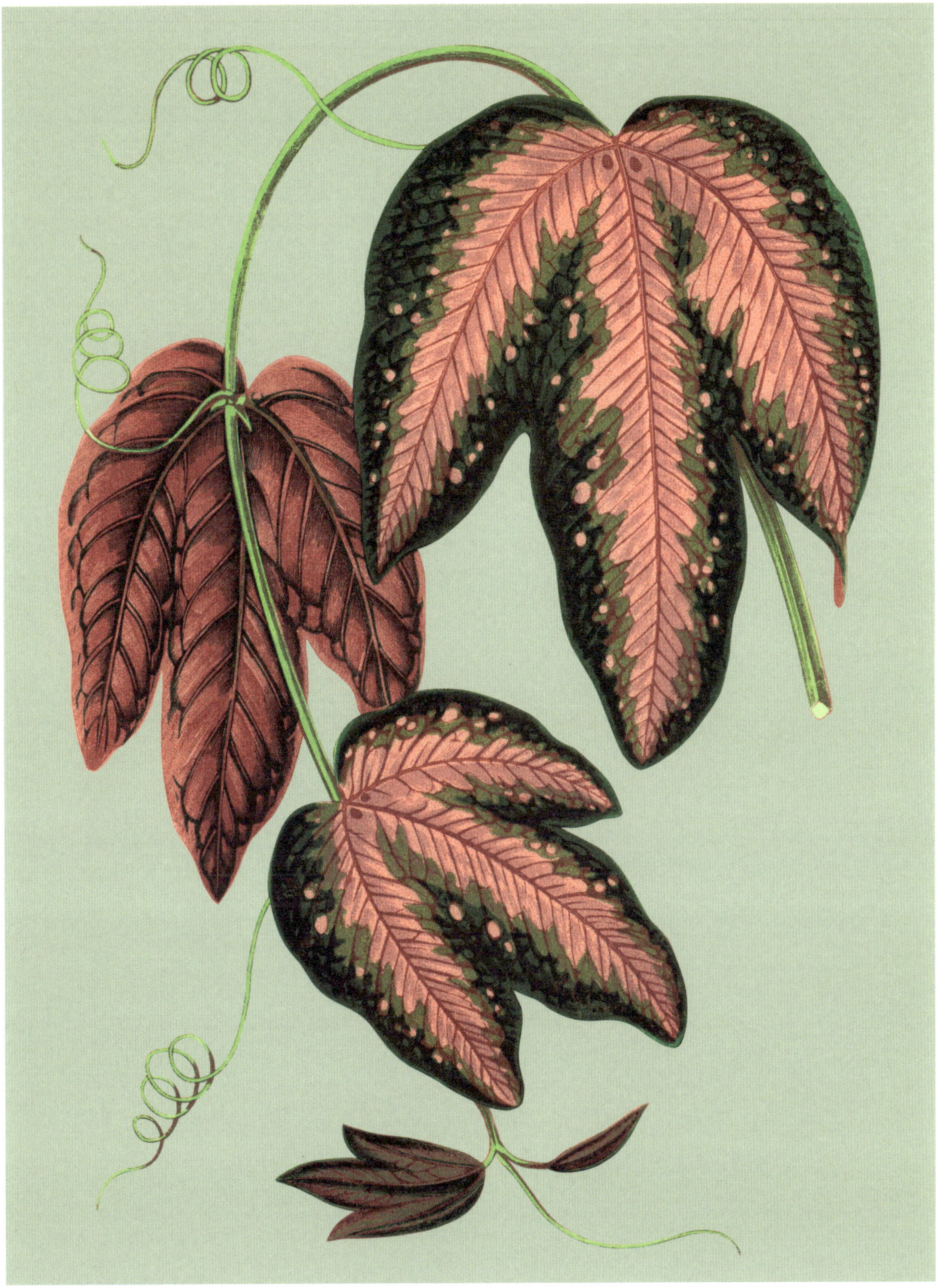

Passiflora trifasciata
by Alexander Francis Lydon & Benjamin Fawcett

passion flower | passion vine

The leaves, like women, interchange
Sagacious confidence;
Somewhat of nods, and somewhat of
Portentous inference,
The parties in both cases
Enjoining secrecy,—
Inviolable compact
To notoriety.

'Gossip' by Emily Dickinson

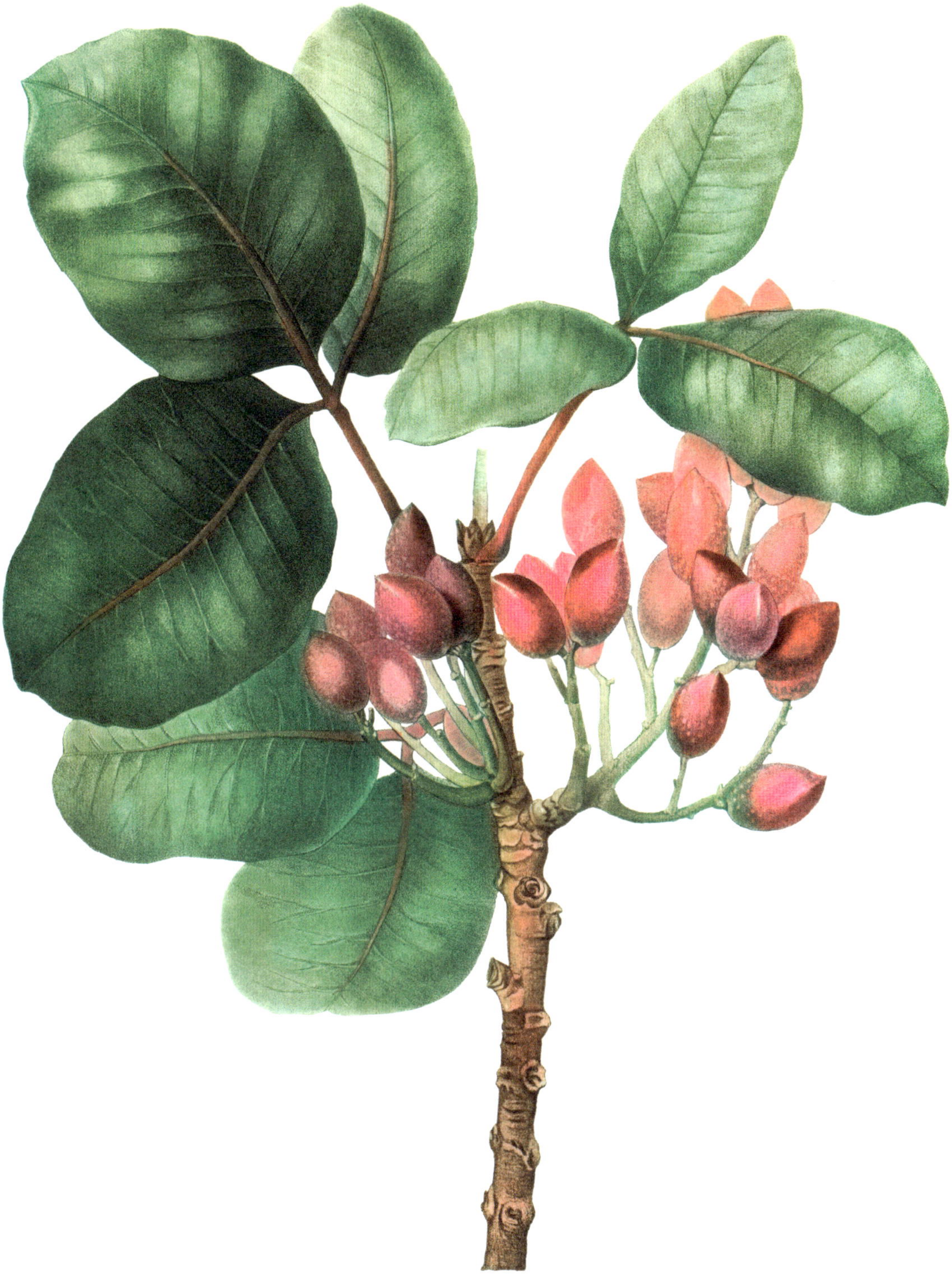

Pistacia vera
by PIERRE-JOSEPH REDOUTÉ

pistachio

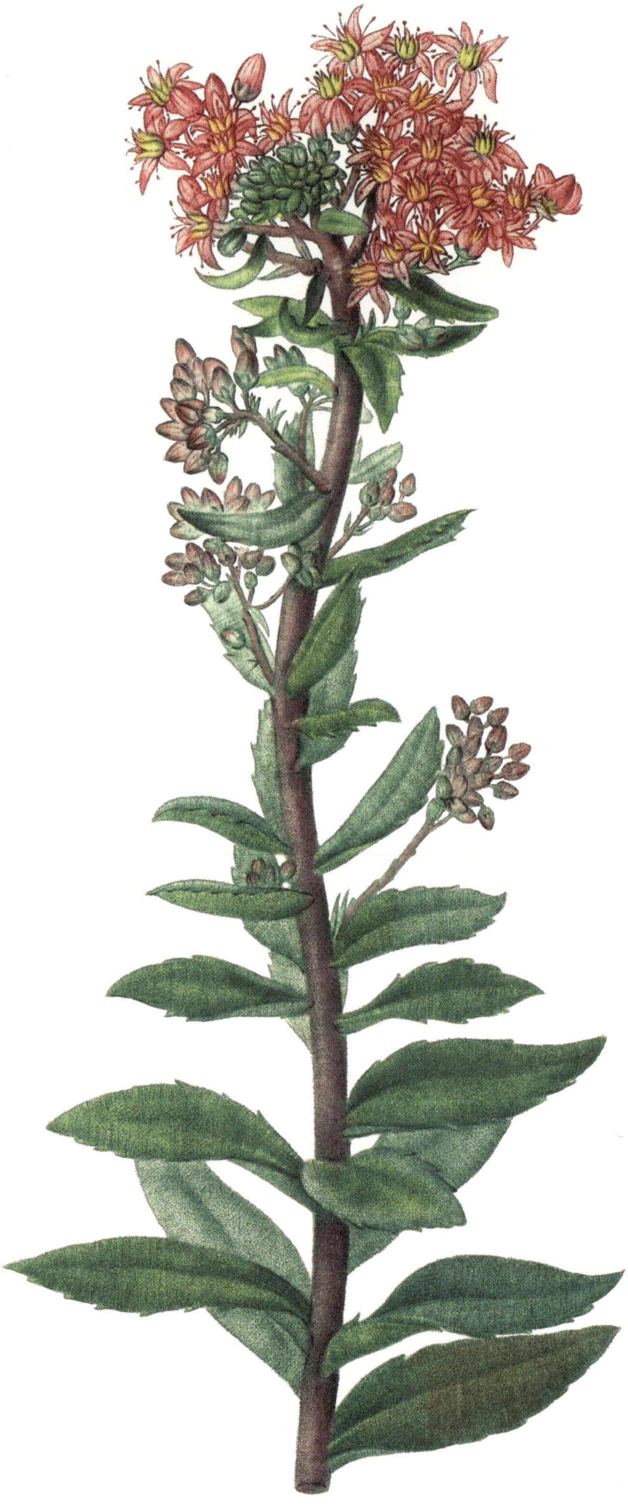

Hylotelephium telephium
by Pierre-Joseph Redouté

orpine | live-forever | stonecrop | livelong

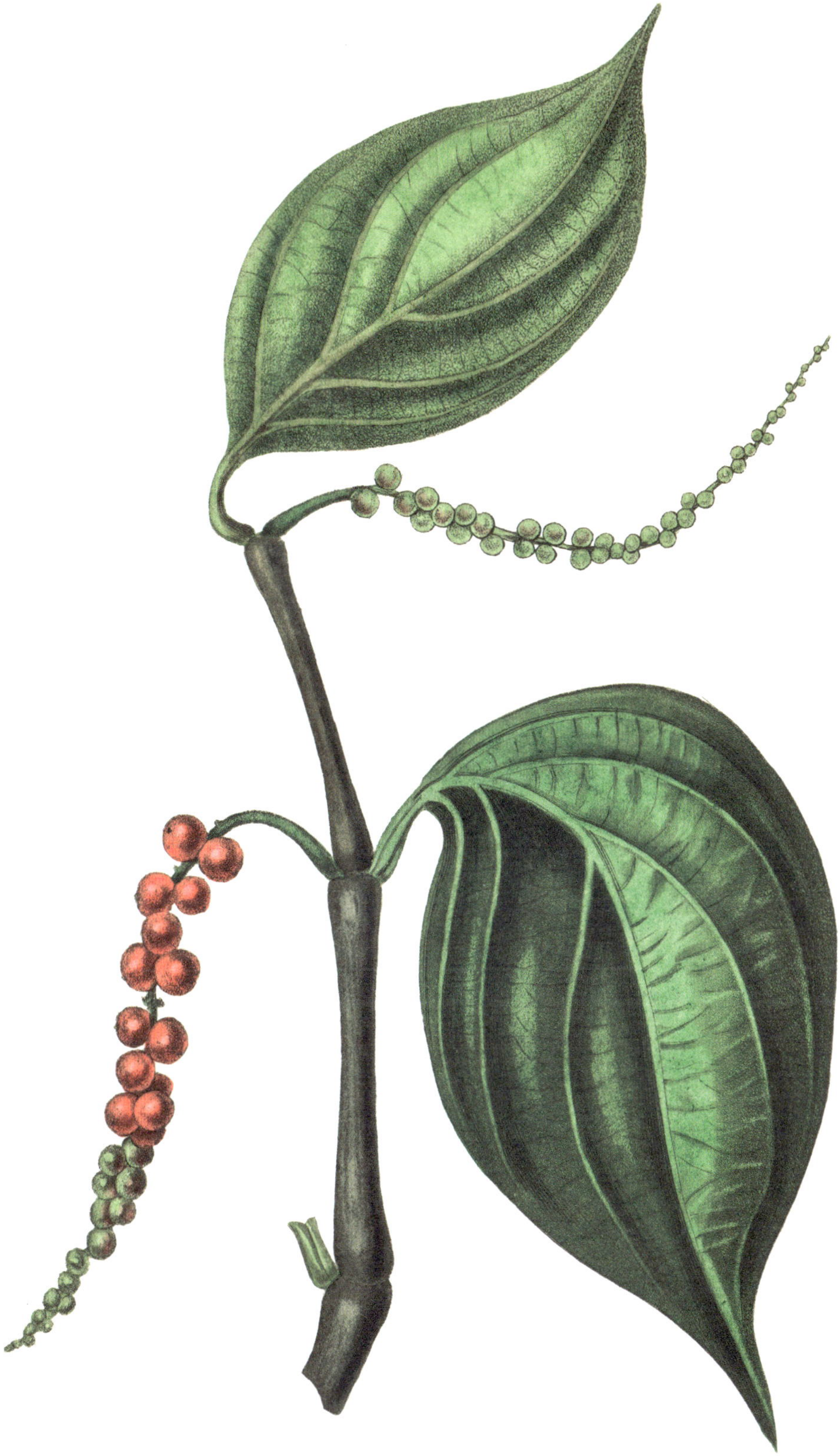

Piper nigrum
by John Stephenson & James Morss Churchill

black pepper

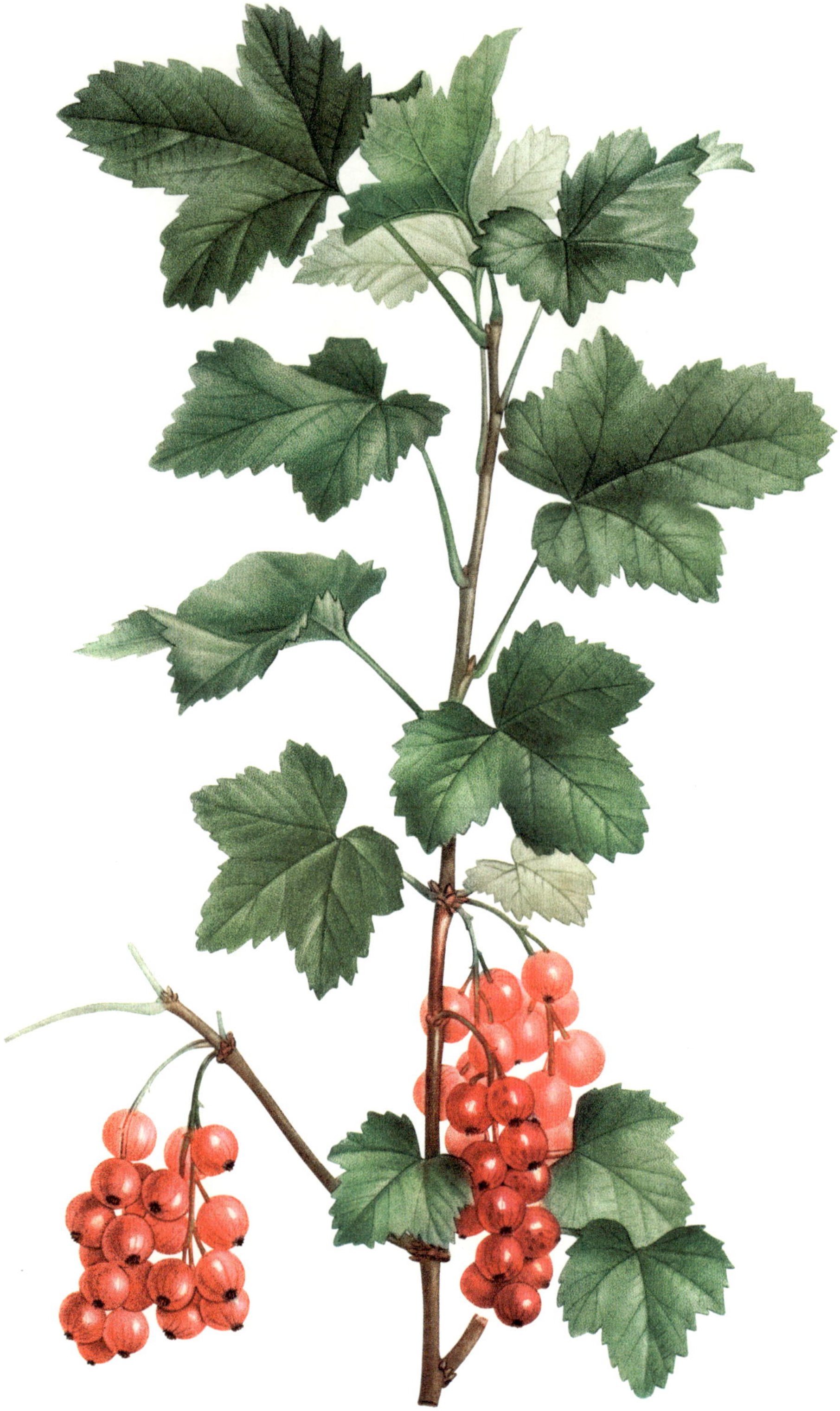

Ribes rubrum
by Pierre-Joseph Redouté

redcurrant

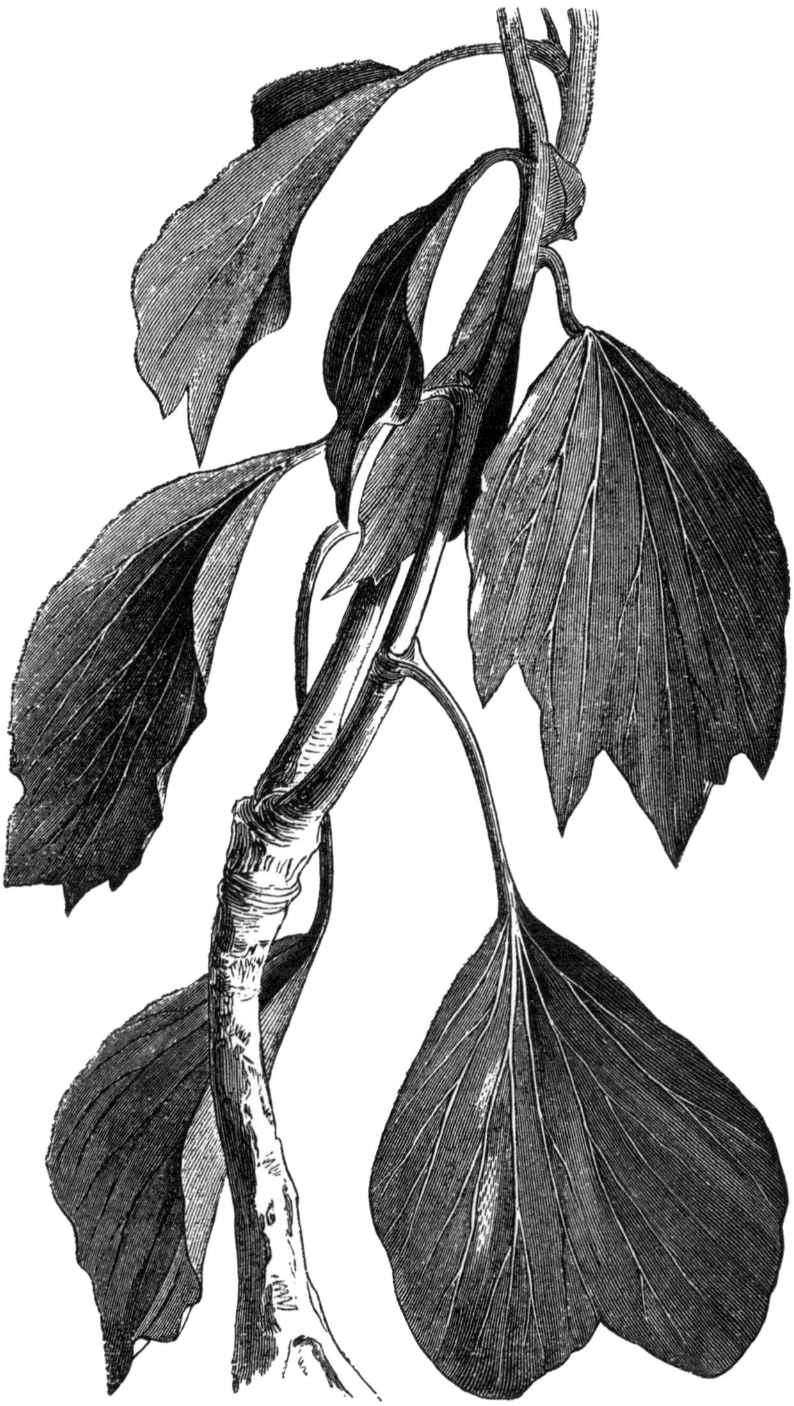

Hedera helix f. *helix*
by James Shirley Hibberd

common ivy | English ivy | European ivy

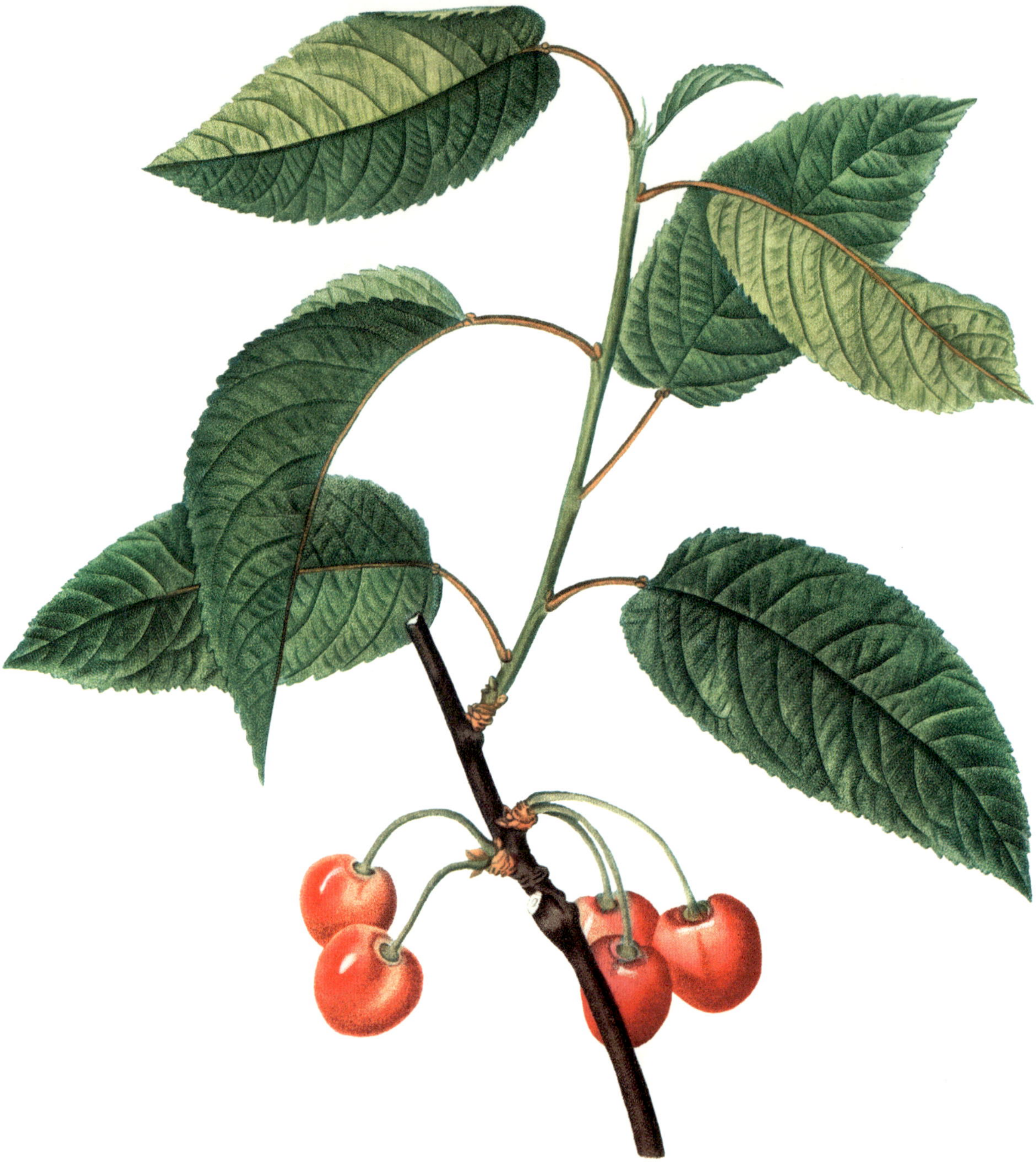

182

Prunus cerasus
by Pierre-Joseph Redouté

sour cherry

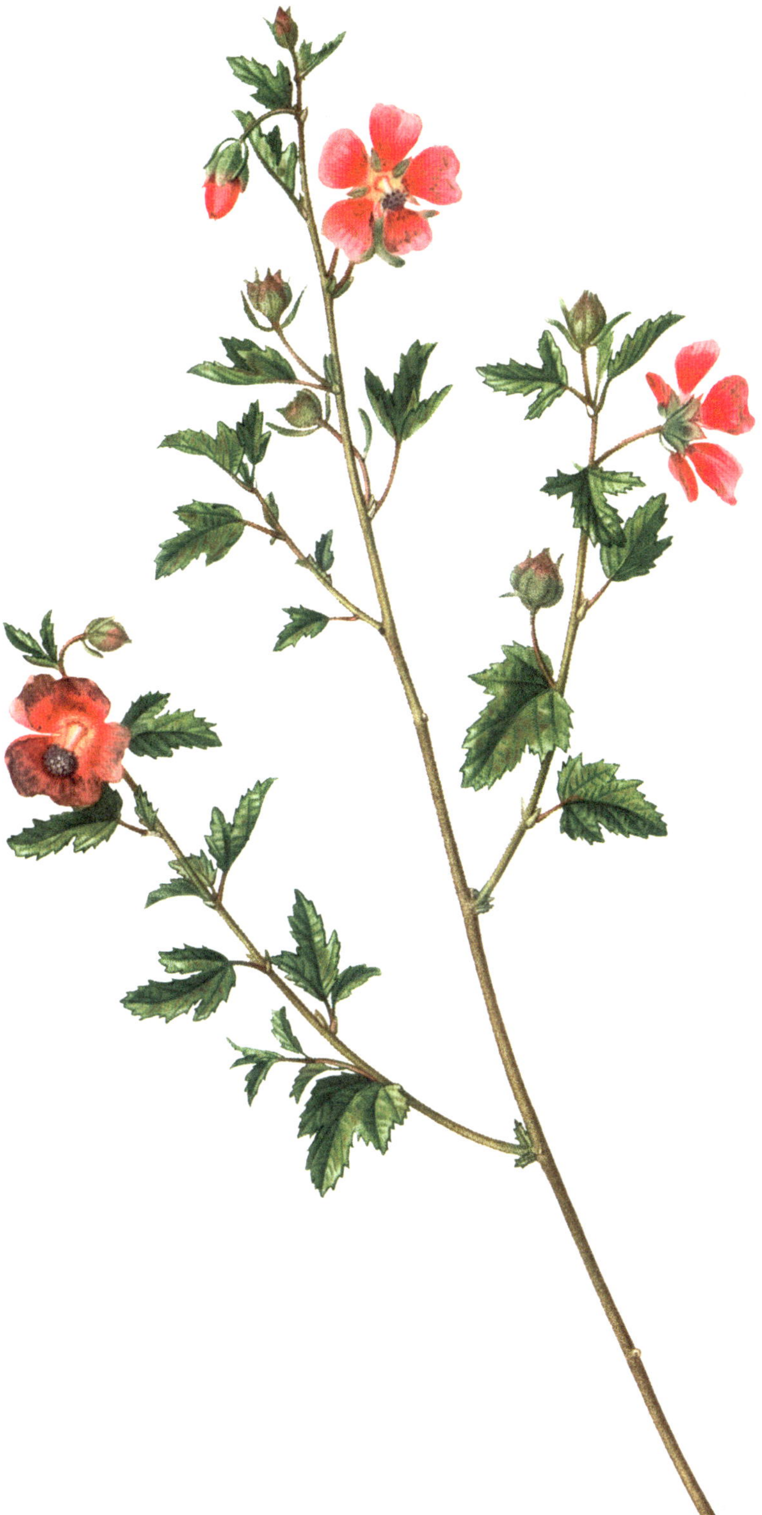

Anisodontea capensis
by Pierre-Joseph Redouté

African mallow | dwarf hibiscus | Cape mallow | Cape Africian queen

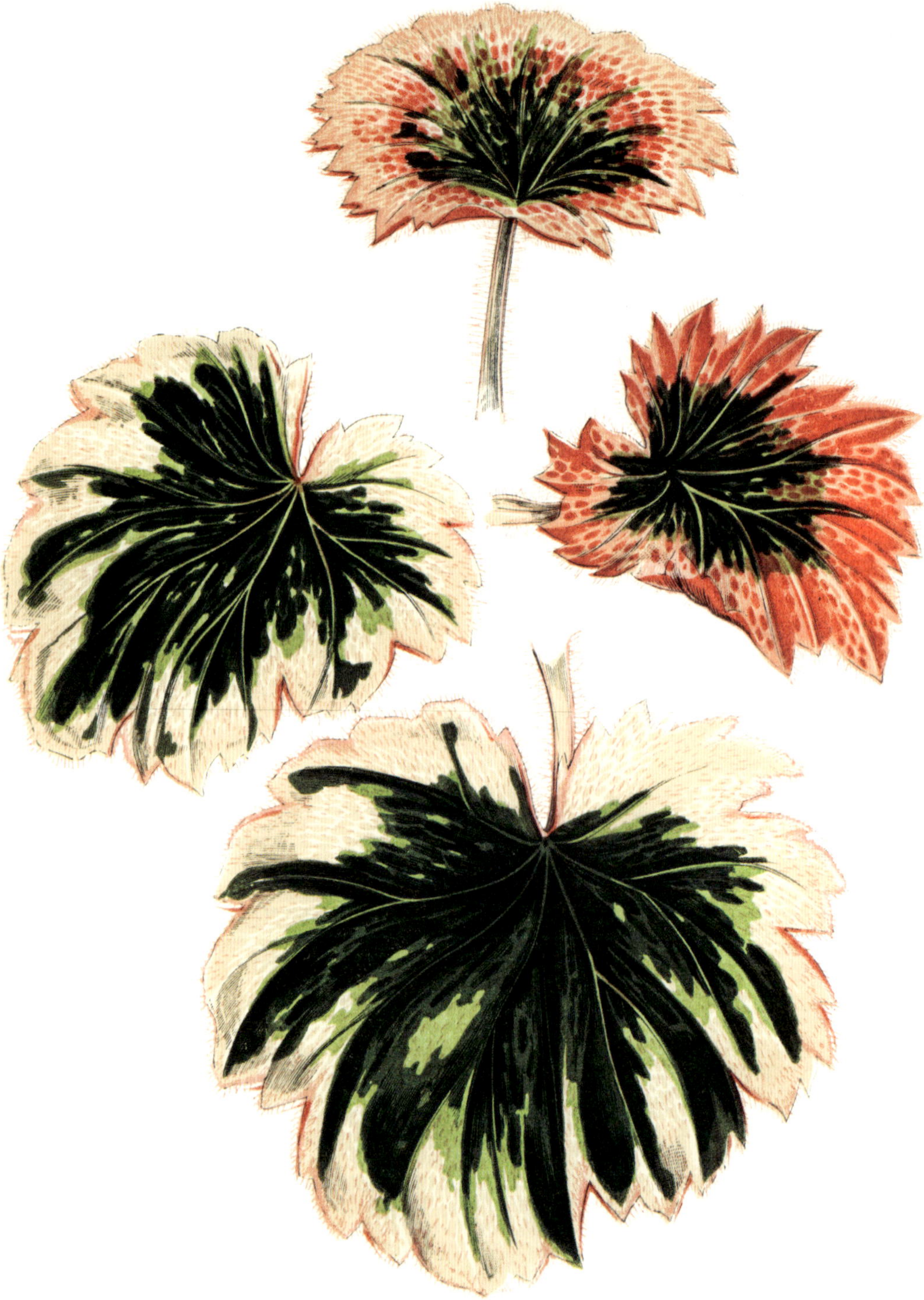

Saxifraga fortunei
by Benjamin Fawcett & James Shirley Hibberd

fortune saxifrage

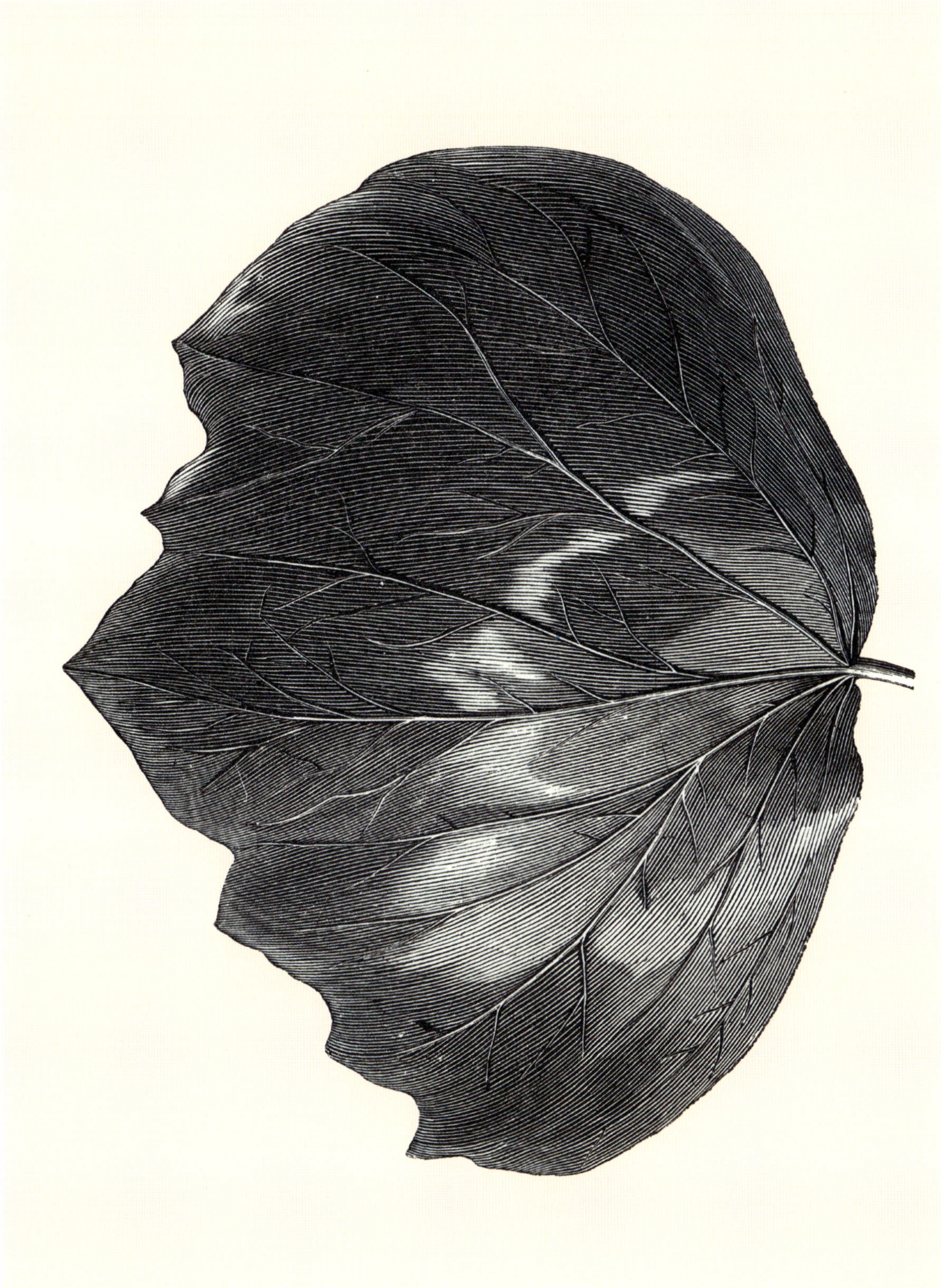

185

Hedera canariensis
by JAMES SHIRLEY HIBBERD

Canary Island ivy

No pen can describe the turning of the leaves—
the insurrection of the tree-people against the waning year.
A little maple began it, flaming blood-red of a sudden
where he stood against the dark green of a pine-belt.
Next morning there was an answering signal
from the swamp where the sumacs grow.
Three days later, the hill-sides as far as the eye could range
were afire, and the roads paved, with crimson and gold.

FROM *Letters of Travel (1982–1913)* BY RUDYARD KIPLING

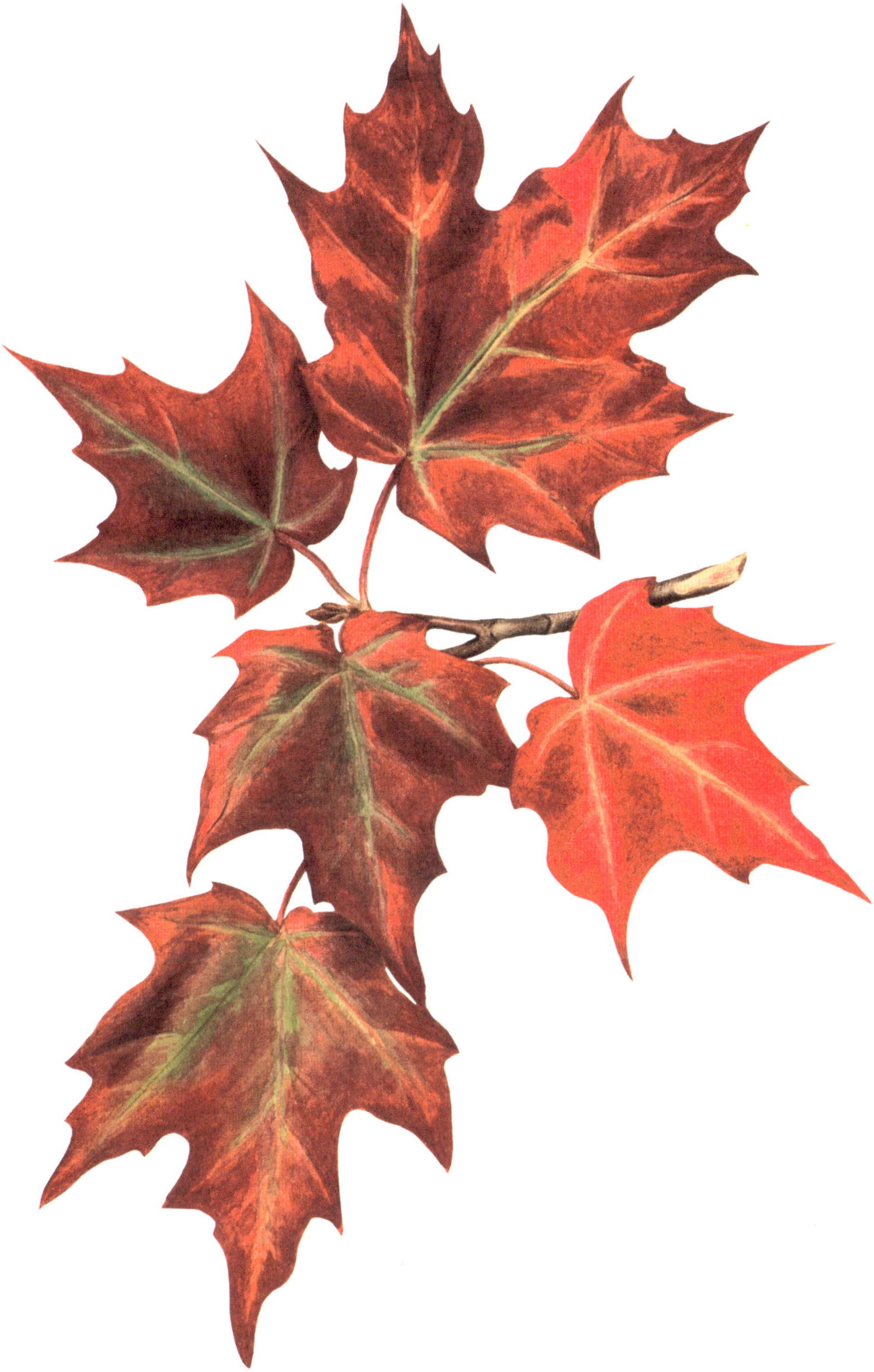

Acer
by Mary Vaux Walcott

maple (unknown variety)

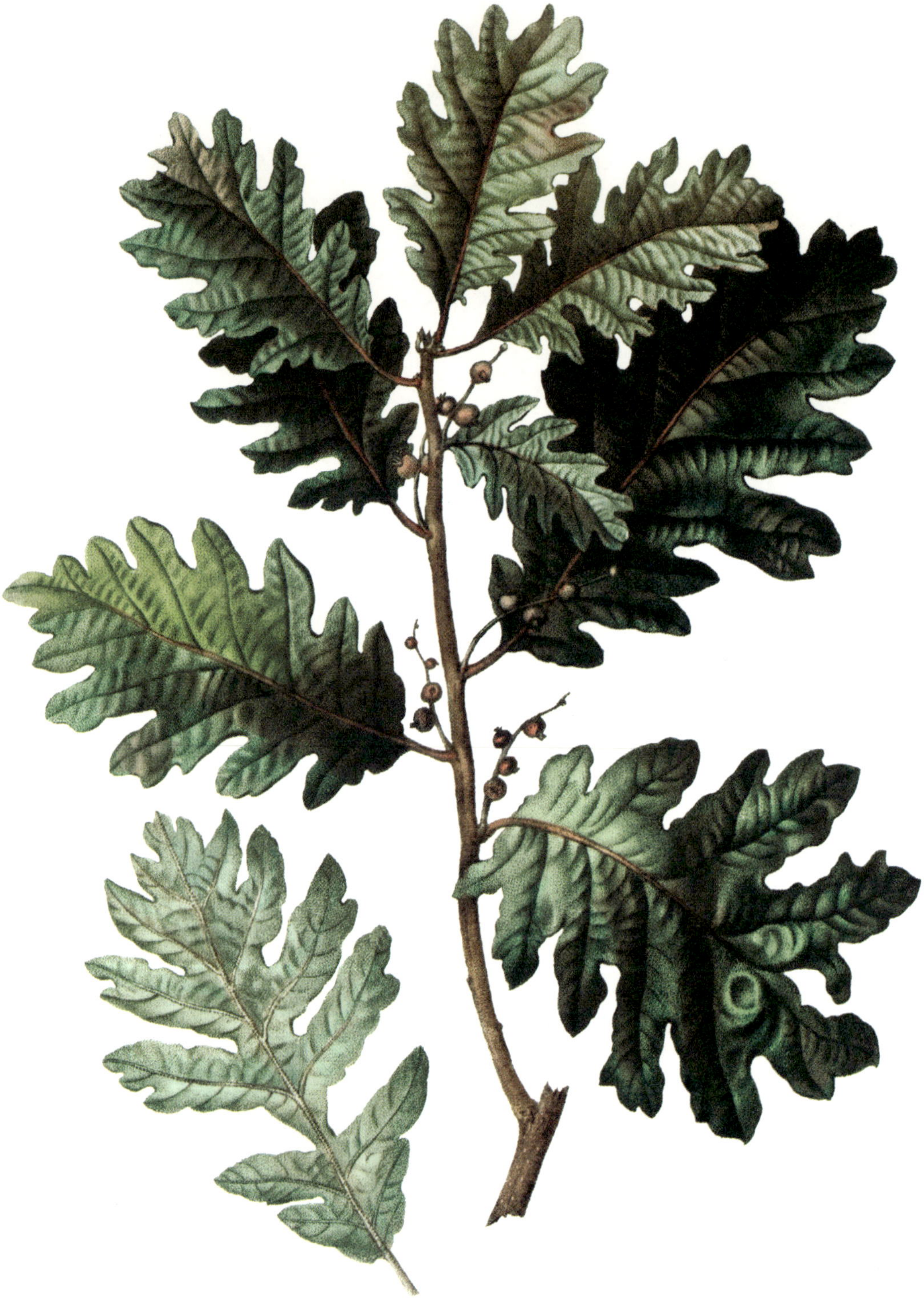

Quercus frainetto
by Pierre-Joseph Redouté

Hungarian oak

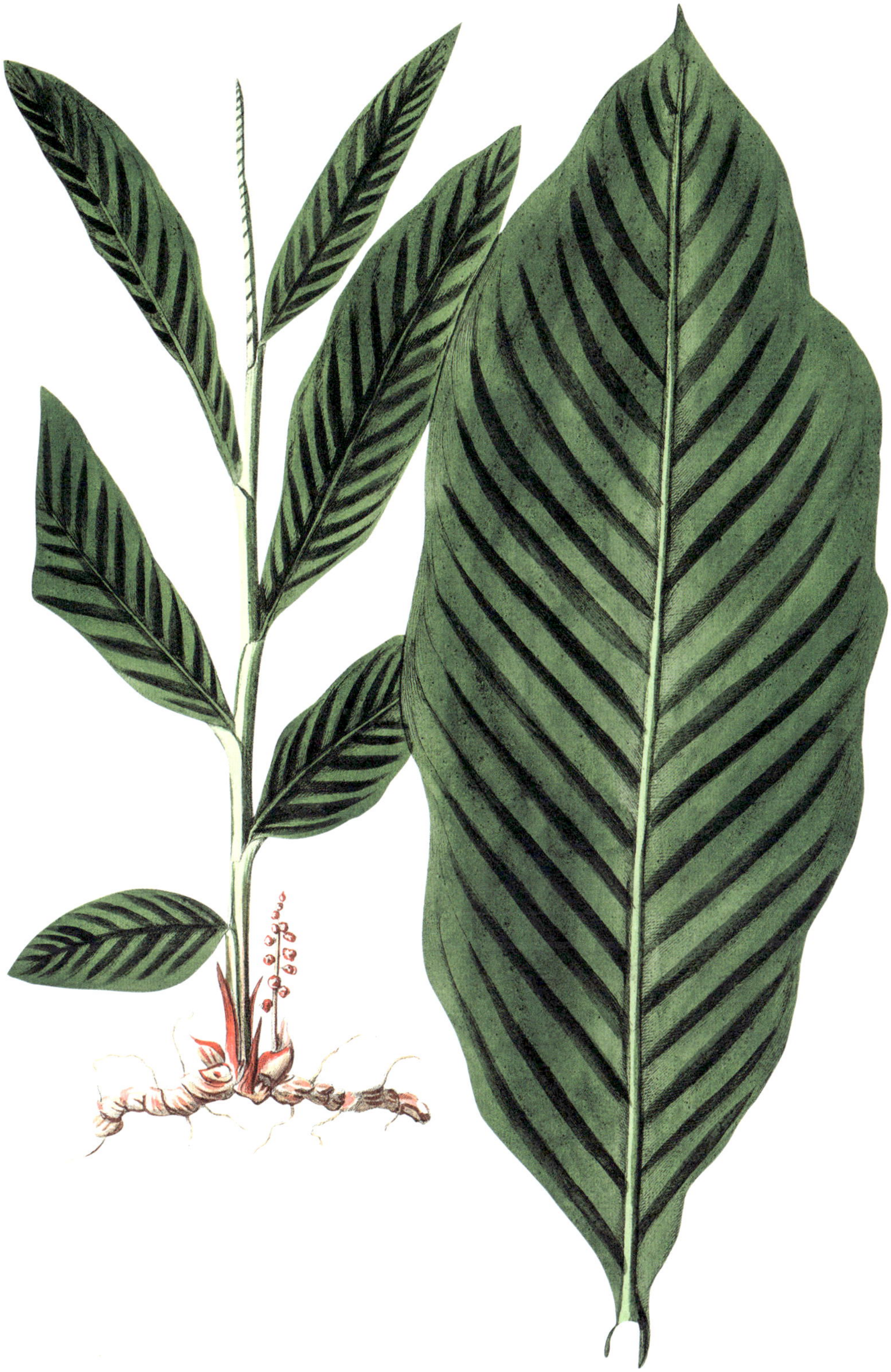

Alpinia zerumbet
from Biodiversity Heritage Library

shell ginger

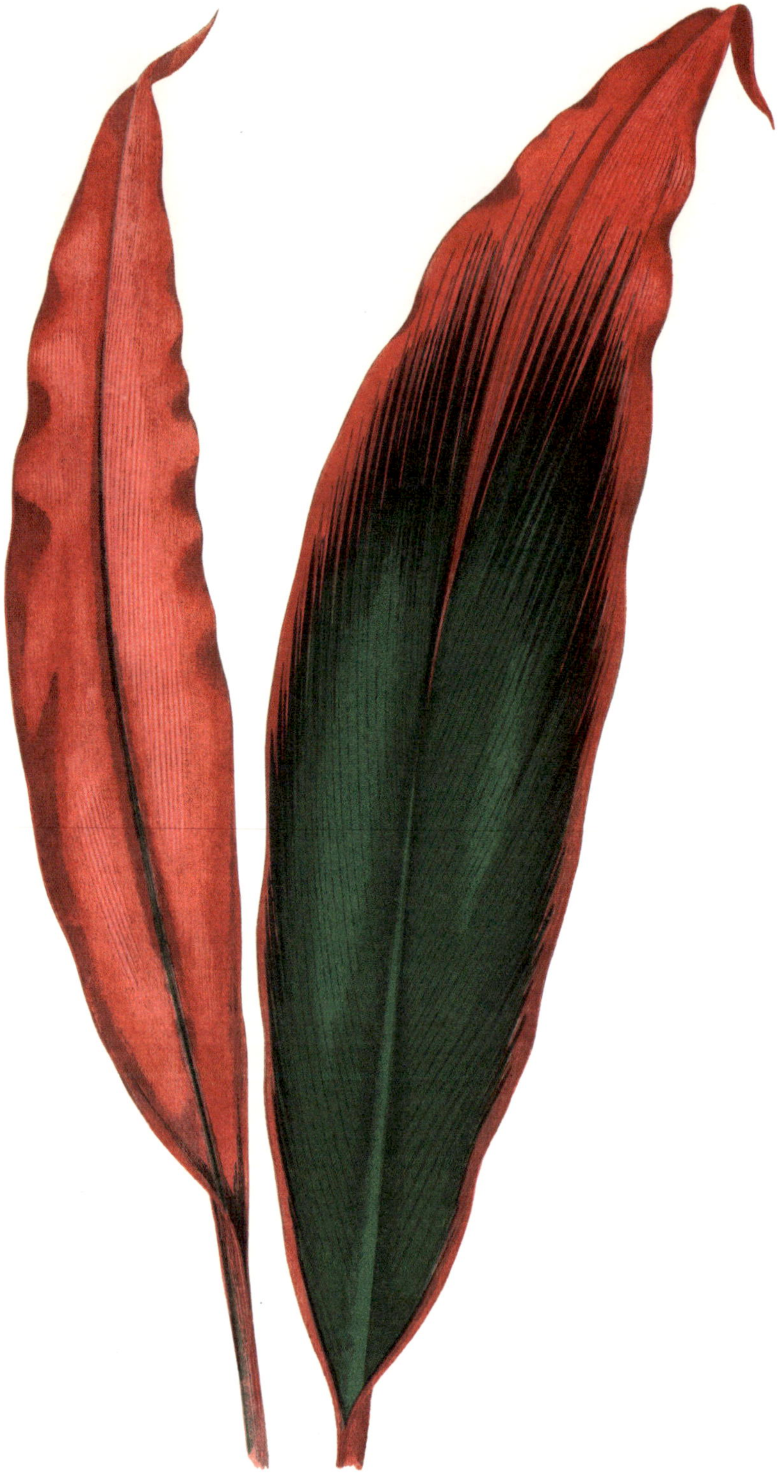

190

Dracaena marginata
by Alexander Francis Lydon & Benjamin Fawcett

Madagascar dragon tree | dragon tree | red-edge dracaena

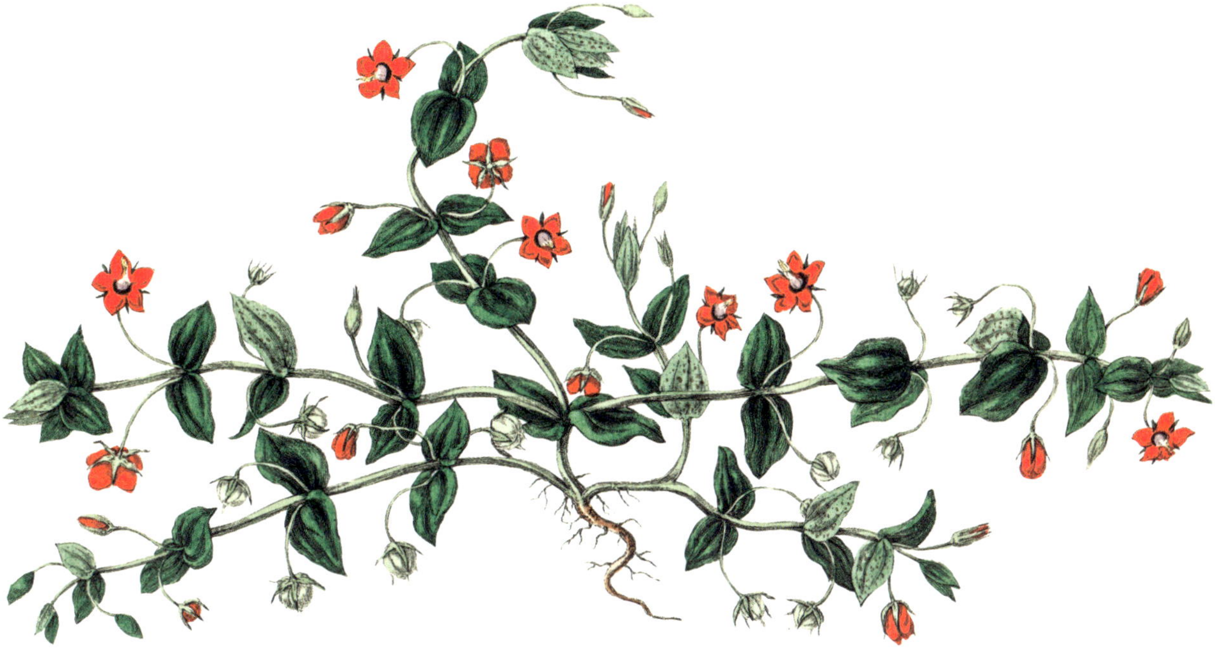

Lysimachia arvensis
by JOHN STEPHENSON & JAMES MORSS CHURCHILL

scarlet pimpernel | red chickweed | shepherd's weather glass

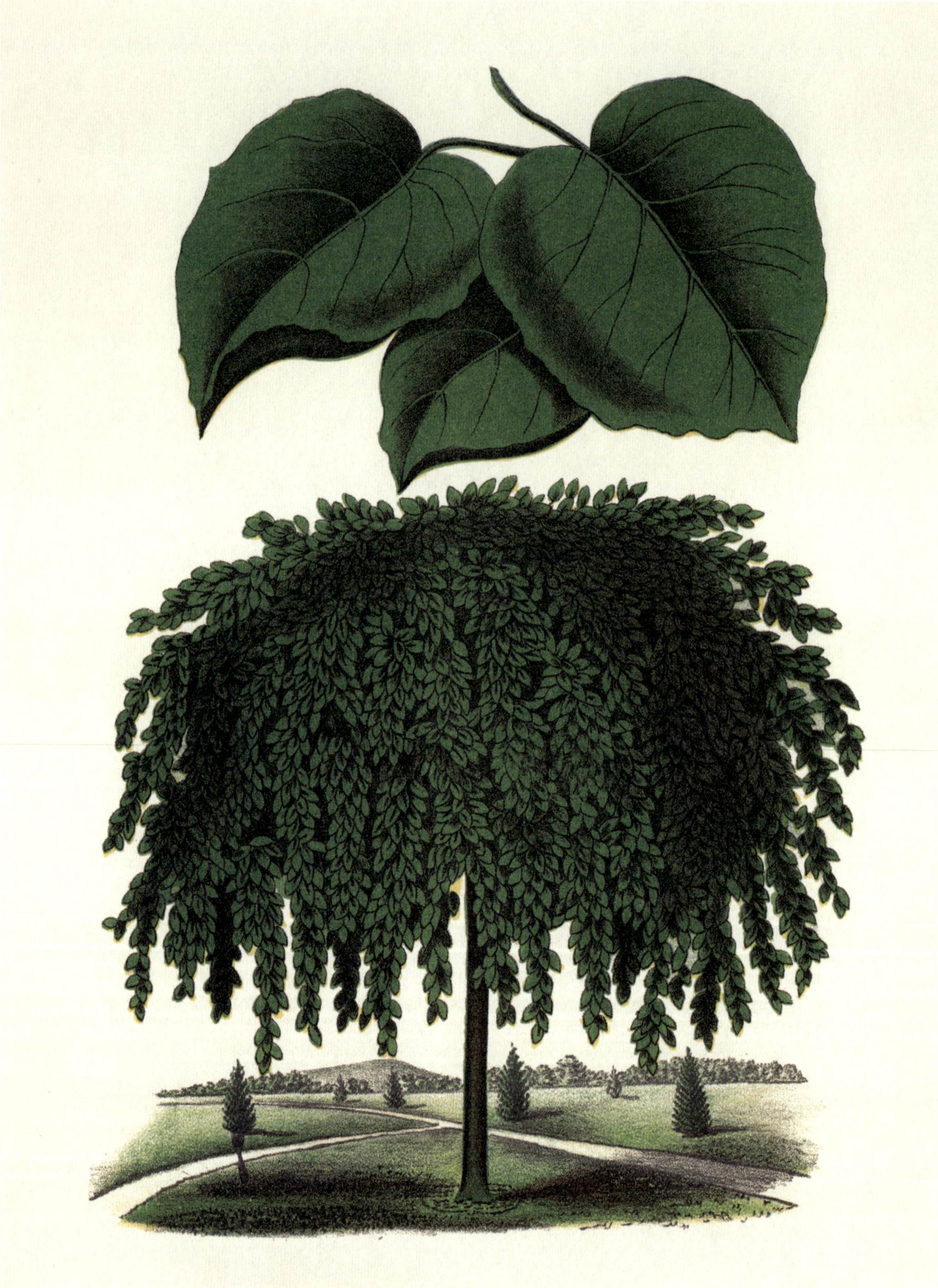

Ulmus glabra 'Camperdownii'
by Rochester Lithographing & Printing Company

Camperdown elm

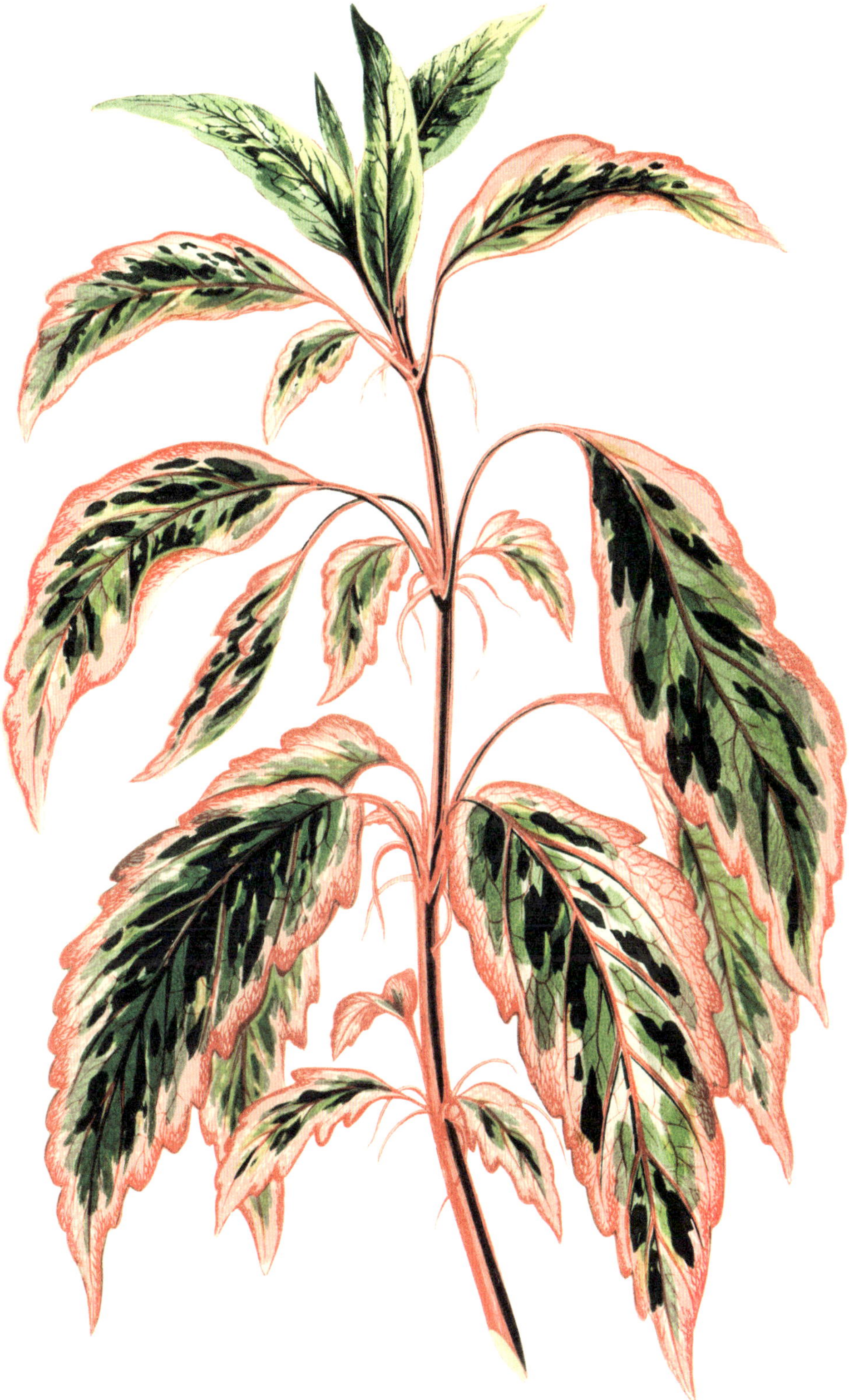

Hibiscus cooperi
by Benjamin Fawcett and James Shirley Hibberd

checkered hibiscus | Cooper's snowflake hibiscus

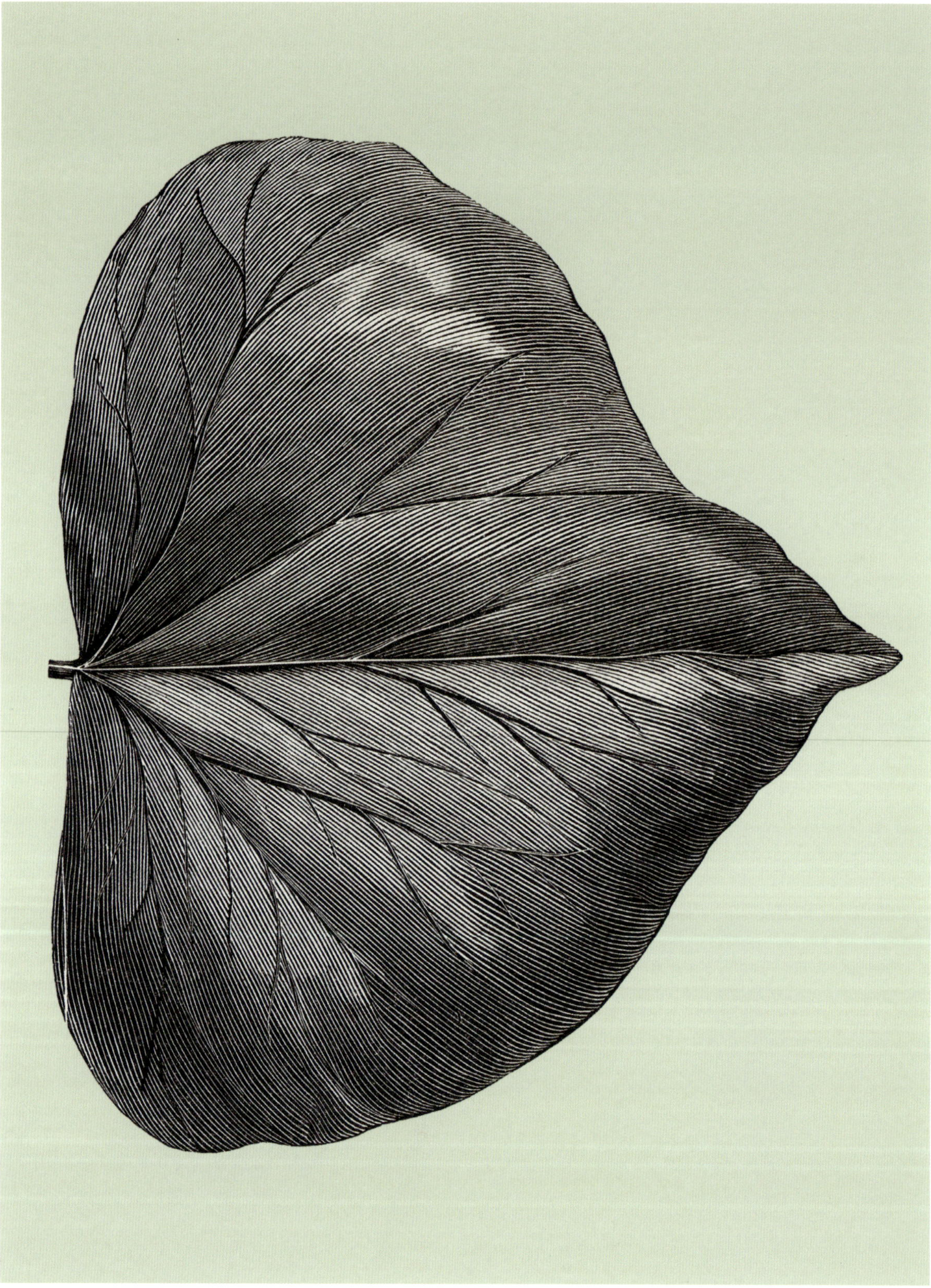

Hedera helix 'Arborescens'
by James Shirley Hibberd

tree ivy

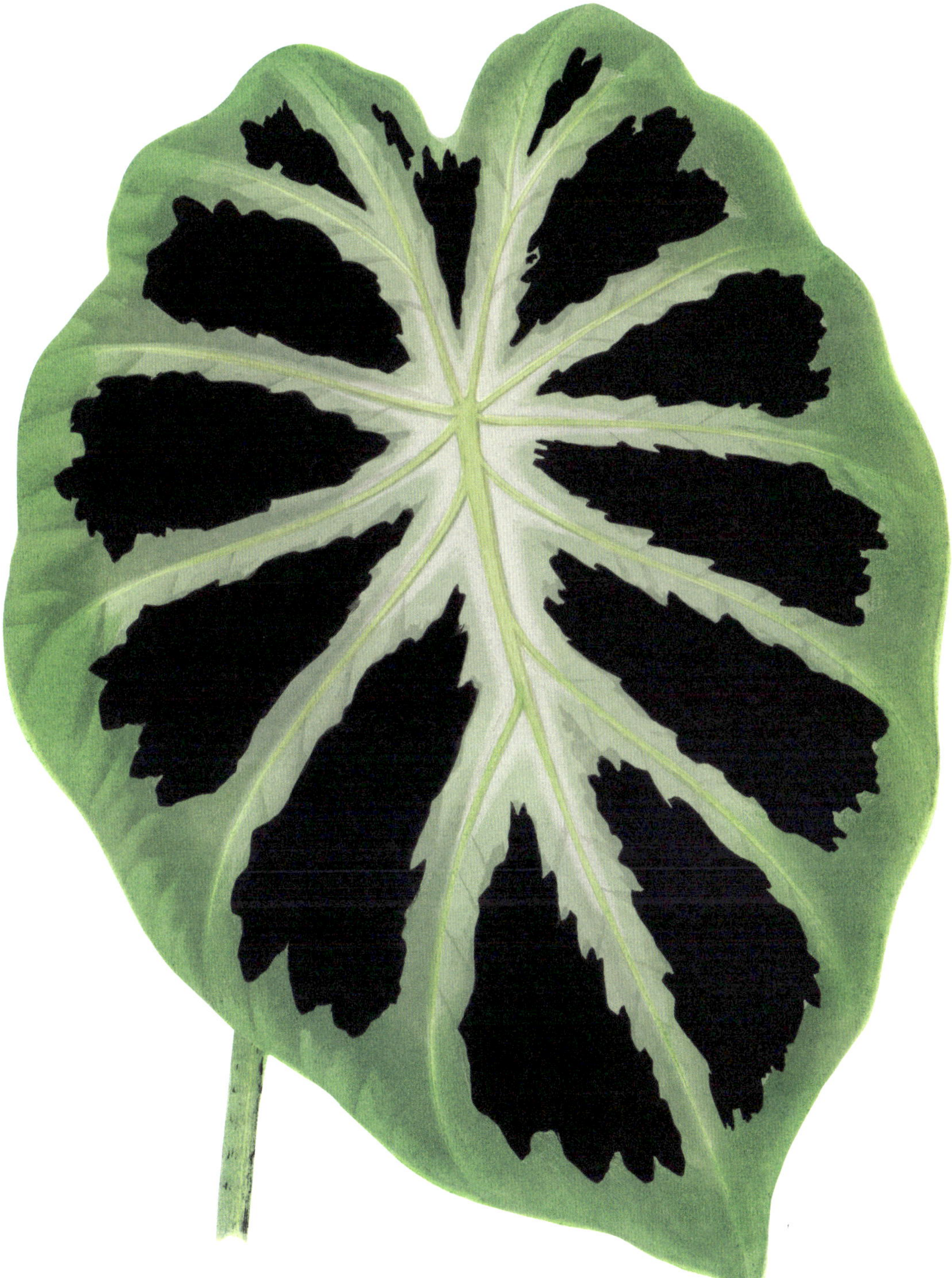

Alocasia longiloba
by Alexander Francis Lydon & Benjamin Fawcett

elephant ear

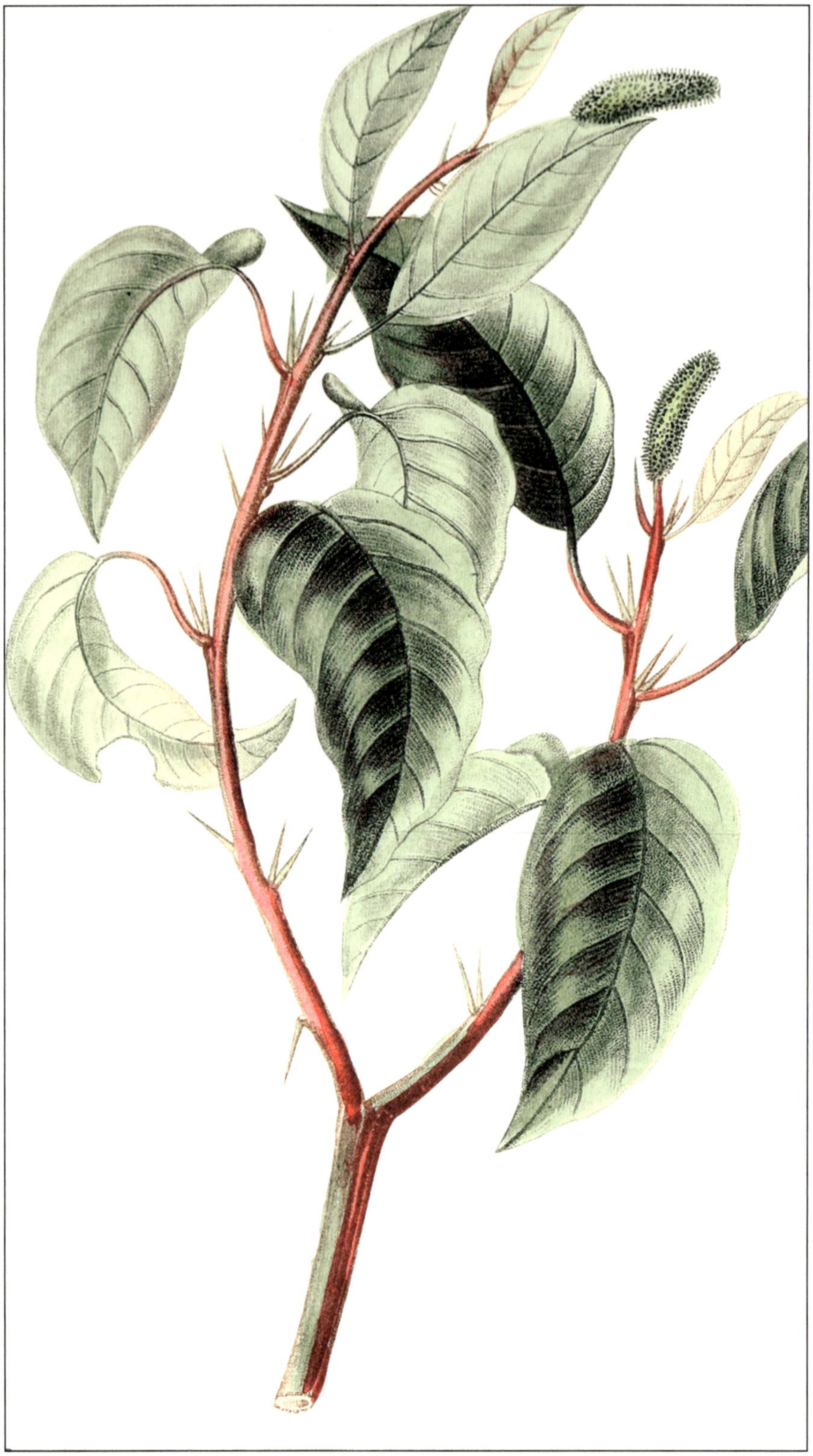

Amaranthus spinosus
by Georg Dionysius Ehret

spiny amaranth | spiny pigweed | prickly amaranth | thorny amaranth

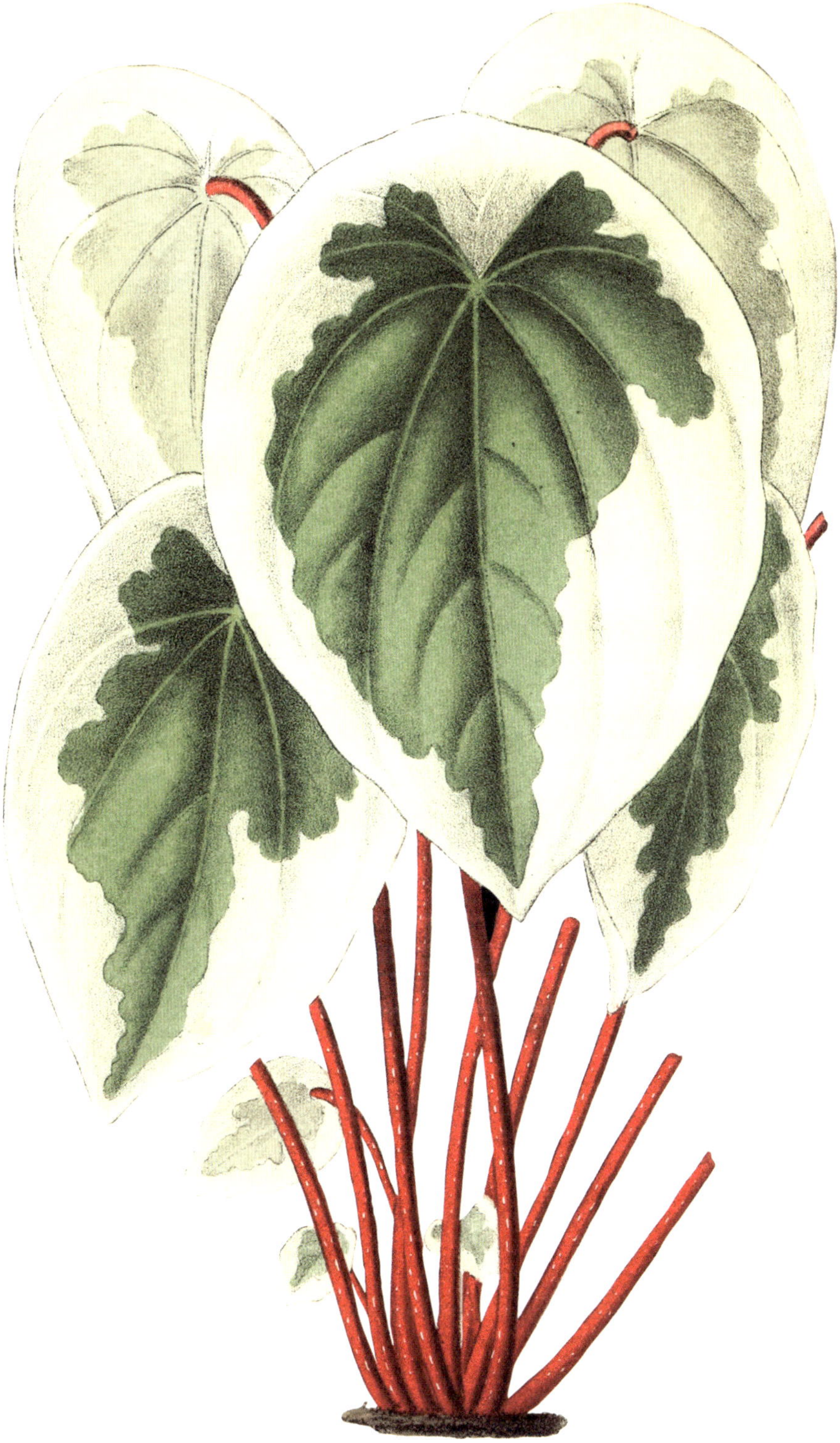

Peperomia argyreia
from BIODIVERSITY HERITAGE LIBRARY

watermelon peperomia

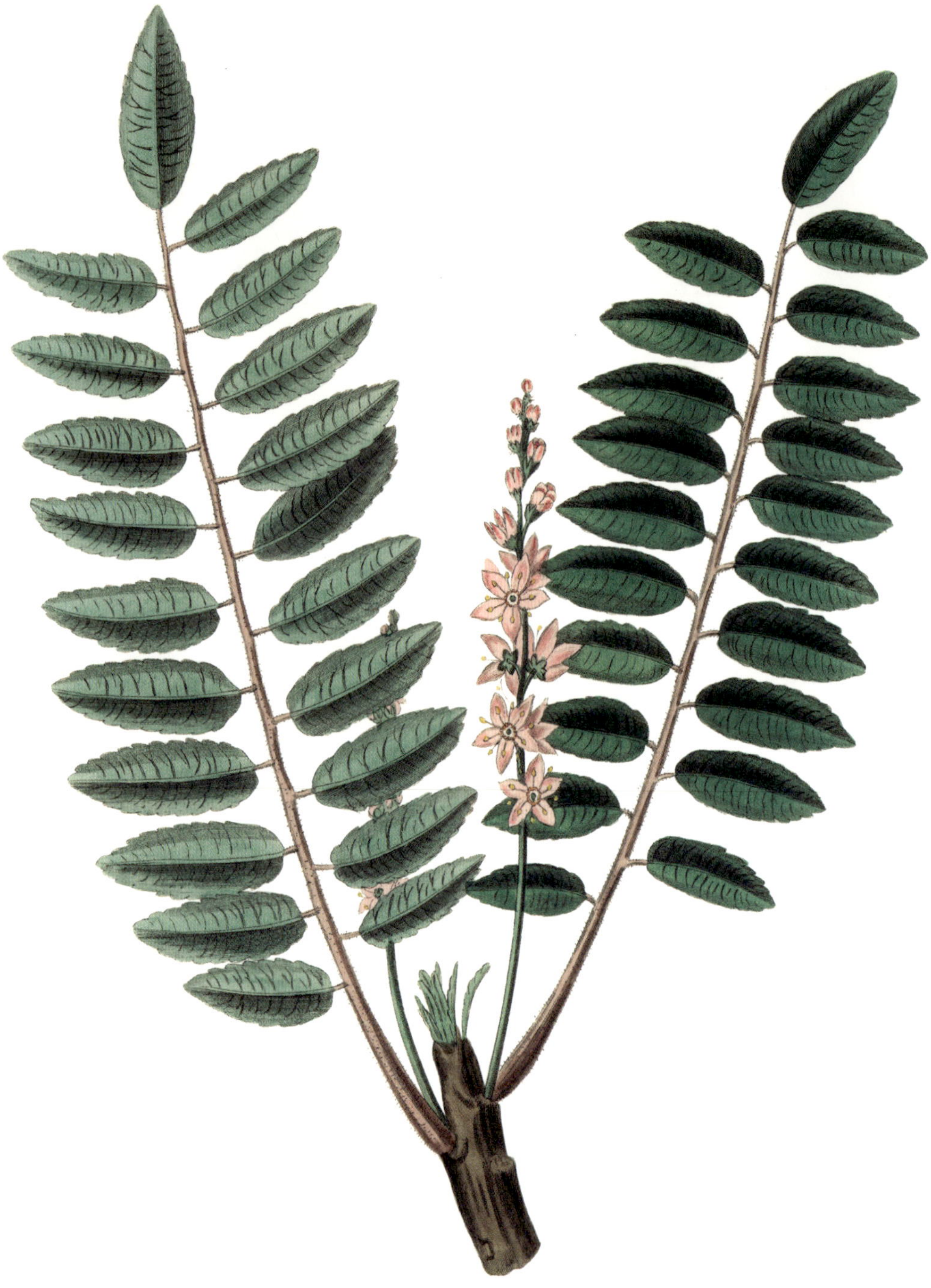

Boswellia serrata
by JOHN STEPHENSON & JAMES MORSS CHURCHILL

Indian frankincense

I pray with mosses, ferns and flowers shy
That hide like gentle nuns from human eye
To lift adoring perfumes to the sky.
I hear faint bridal-sighs of brown and green
Dying to silent hints of kisses keen
As far lights fringe into a pleasant sheen.
I start at fragmentary whispers, blown
From undertalks of leafy souls unknown,
Vague purports sweet, of inarticulate tone.
Dreaming of gods, men, nuns and brides, between
Old companies of oaks that inward lean
To join their radiant amplitudes of green
I slowly move, with ranging looks that pass
Up from the matted miracles of grass
Into yon veined complex of space
Where sky and leafage interlace
So close, the heaven of blue is seen
Inwoven with a heaven of green.

FROM 'Corn' BY SIDNEY LANIER

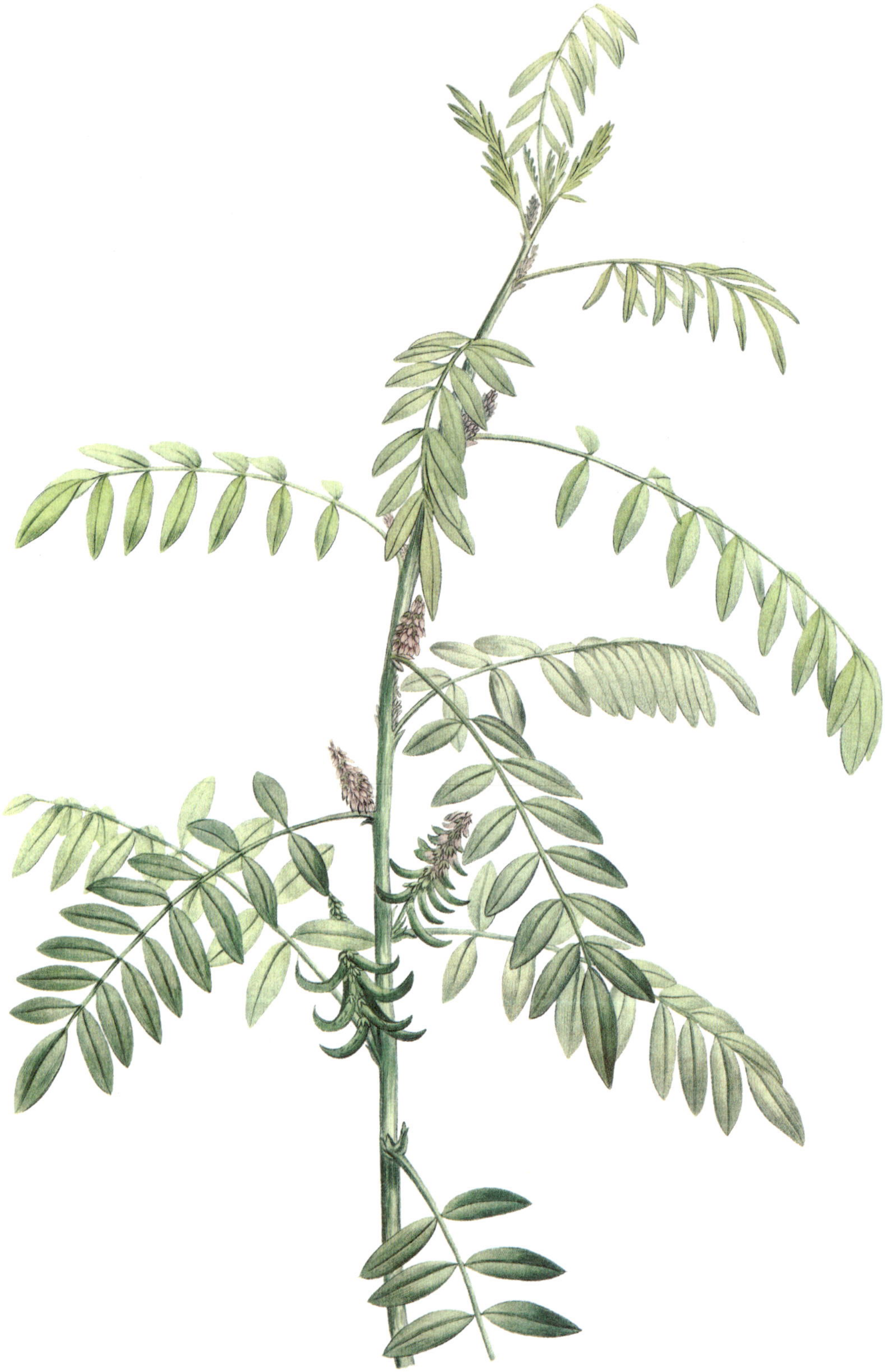

Indigofera tinctoria
by Pierre-Joseph Redouté

true indigo

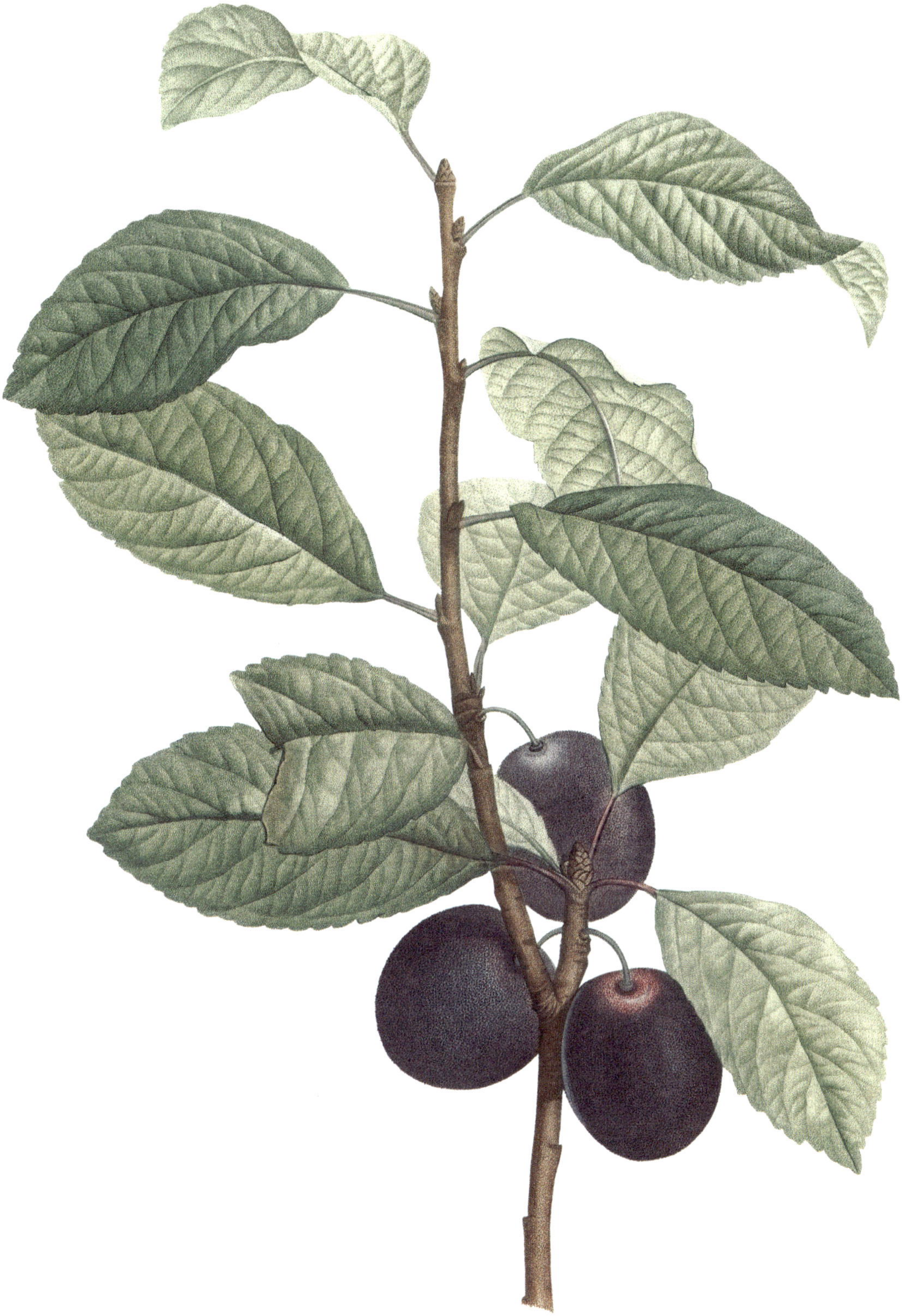

Prunus domestica
by Pierre-Joseph Redouté

garden plum

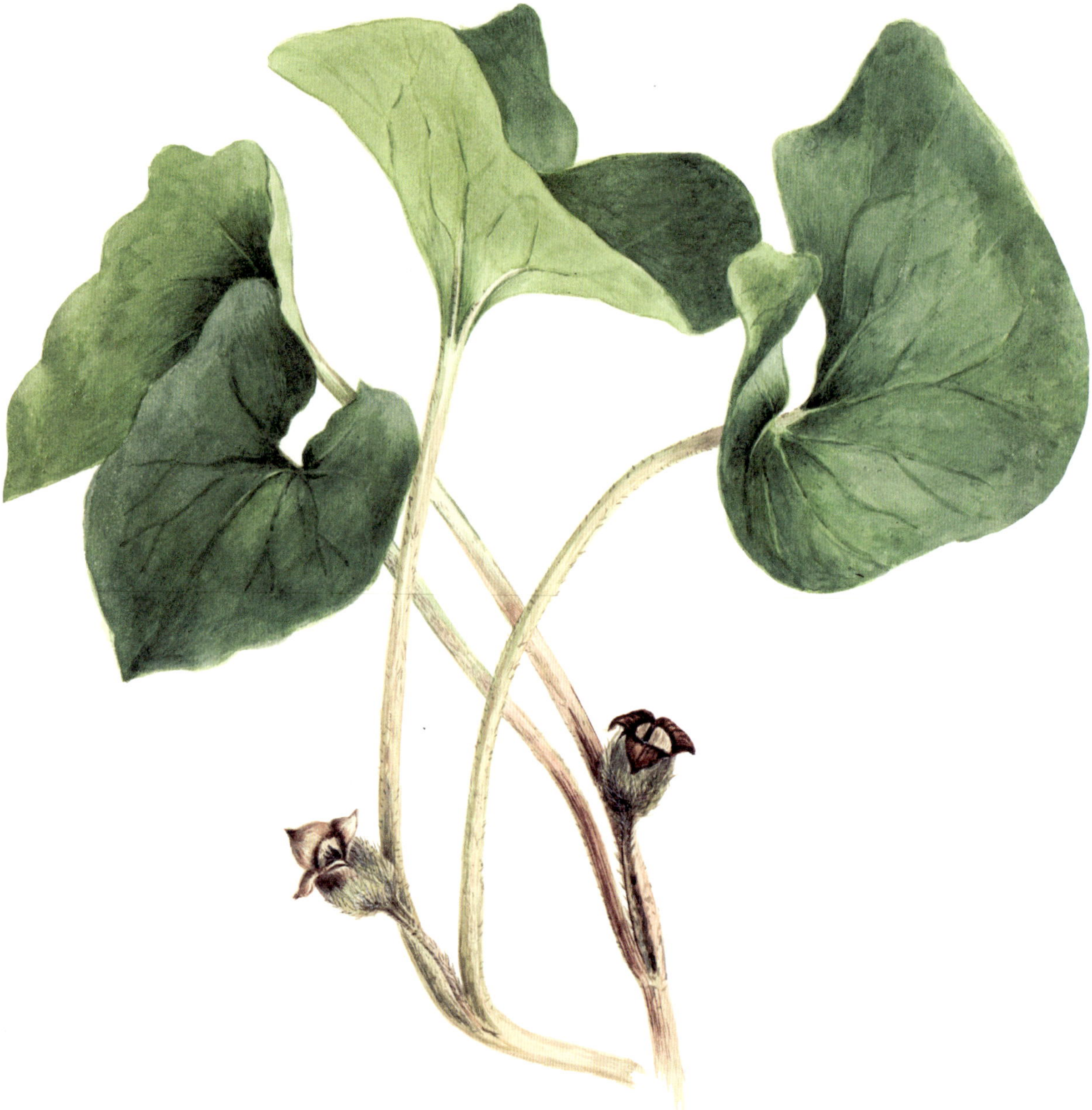

Asarum canadense
by Mary Vaux Walcott

Canadian wild ginger | Canadian snakeroot | broad-leaved asarabacca

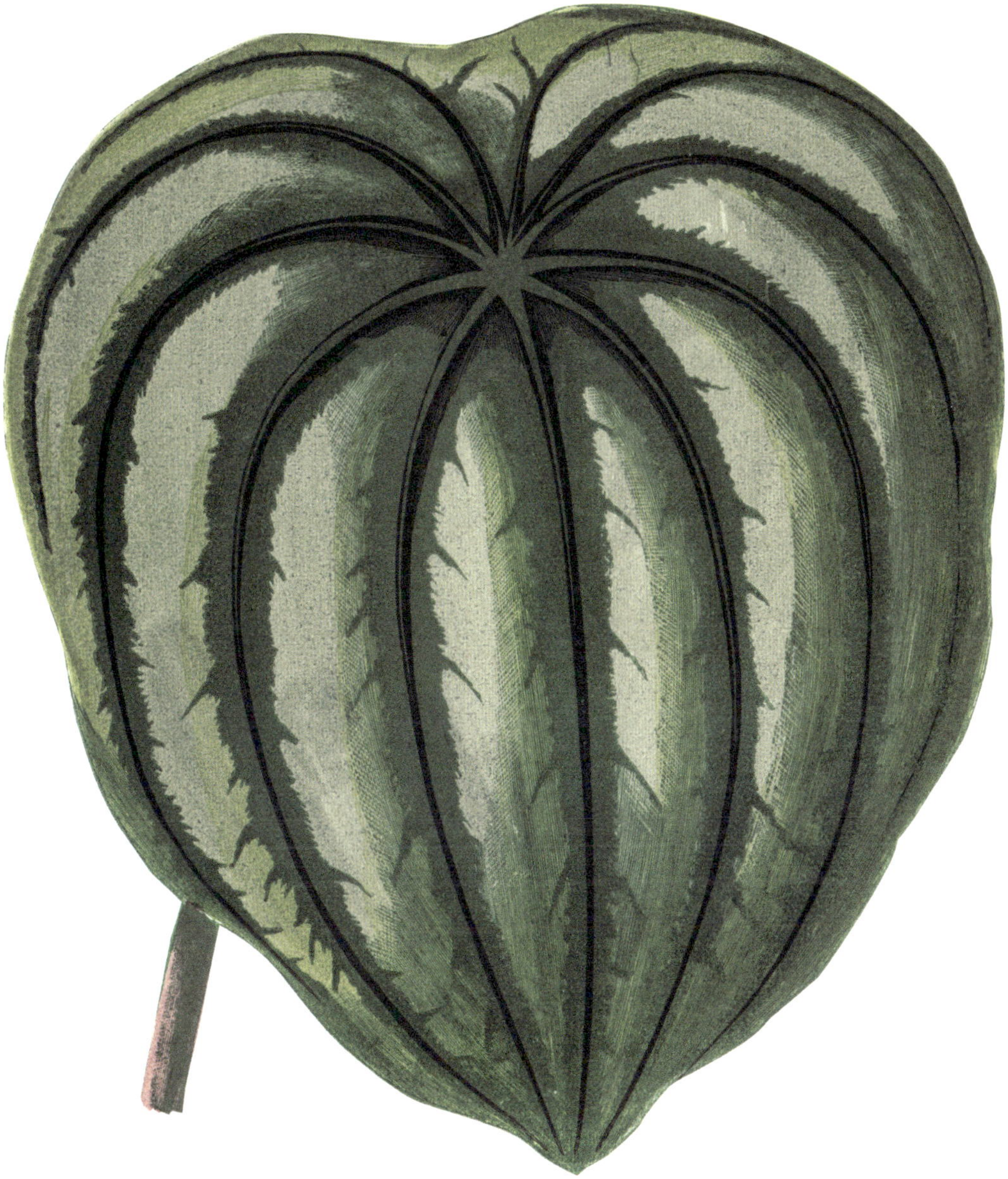

Peperomia argyreia
by BENJAMIN FAWCETT & JAMES SHIRLEY HIBBERD

watermelon peperomia

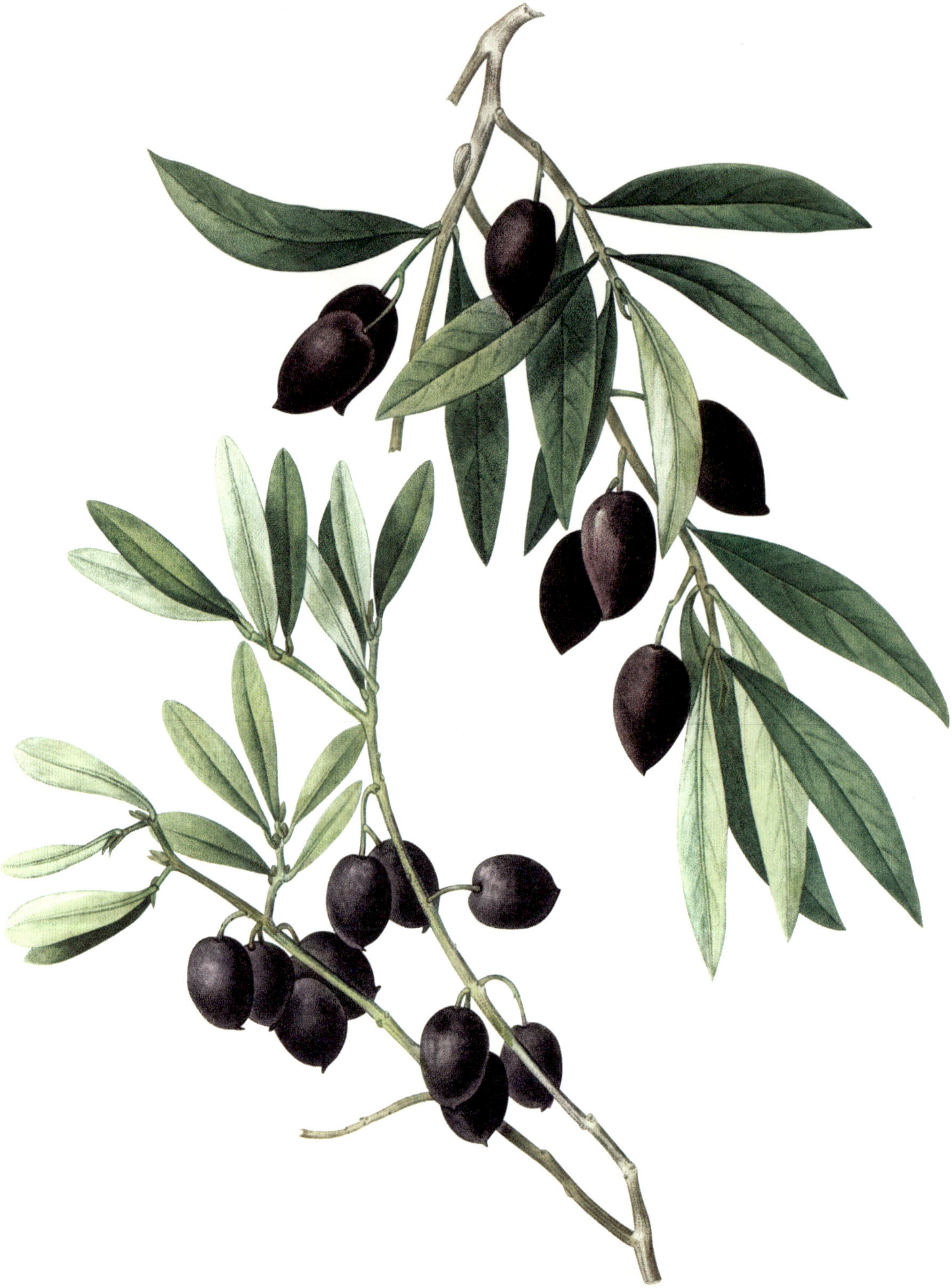

Olea europaea
by Pierre-Joseph Redouté

European olive

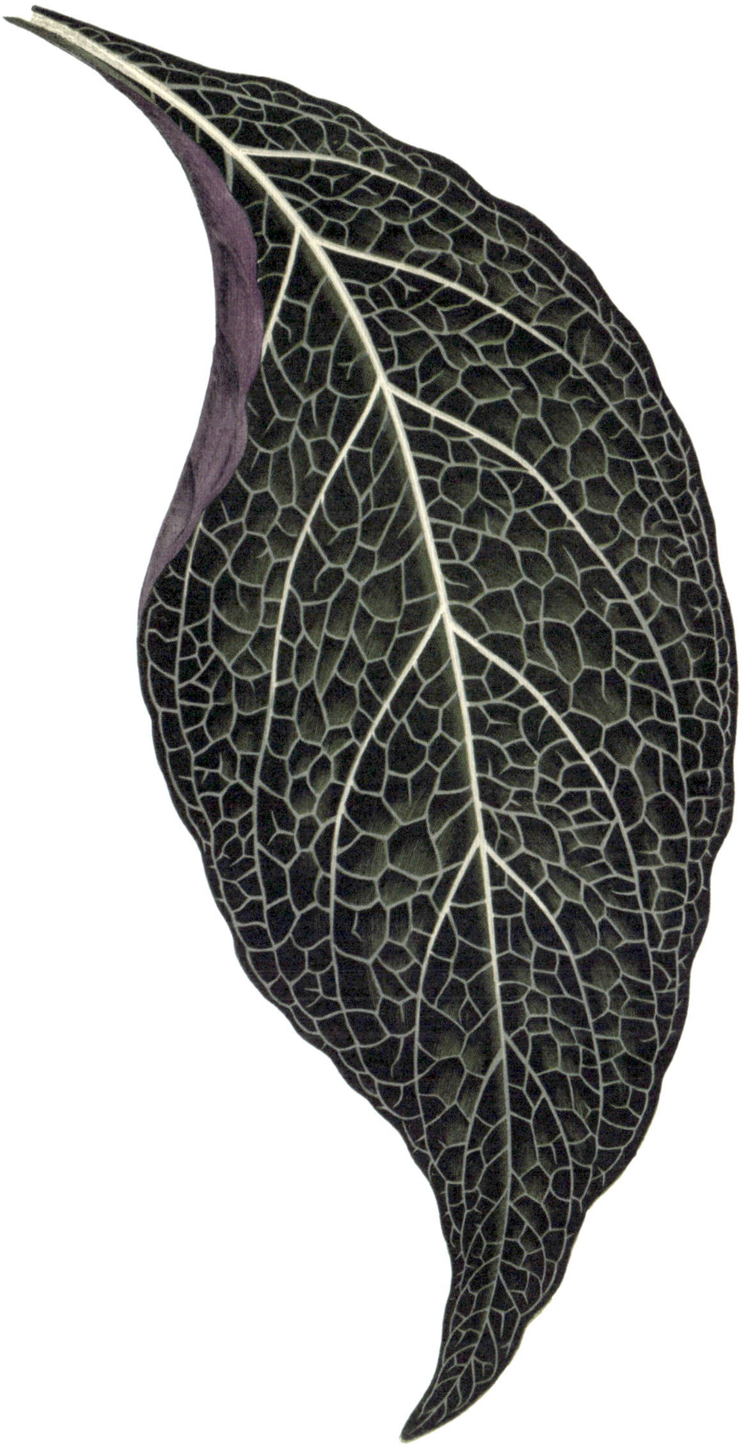

Fittonia albivenis
by Benjamin Fawcett & James Shirley Hibberd

nerve plant | mosaic plant

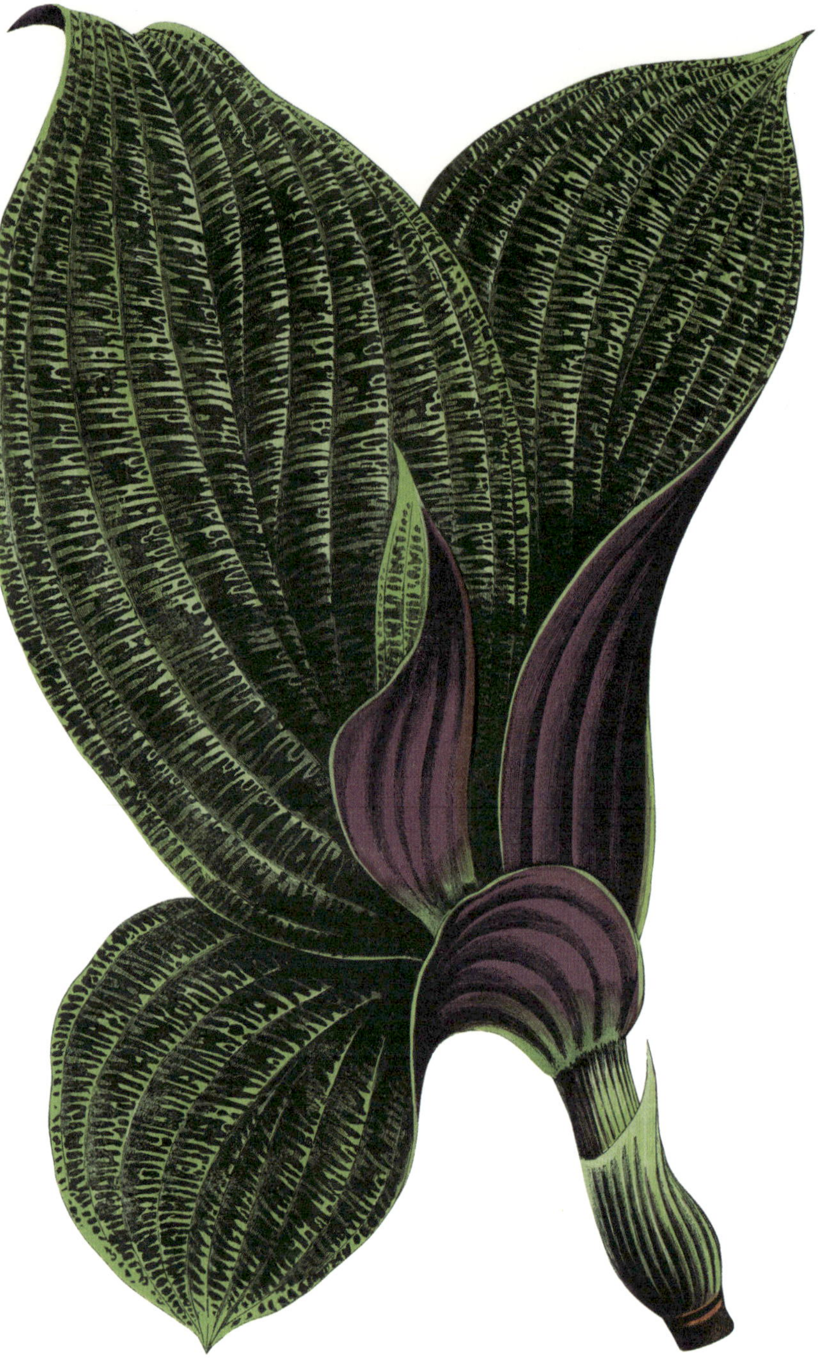

206

Dichorisandra musaica
by Alexander Francis Lydon & Benjamin Fawcett

queen's spiderwort

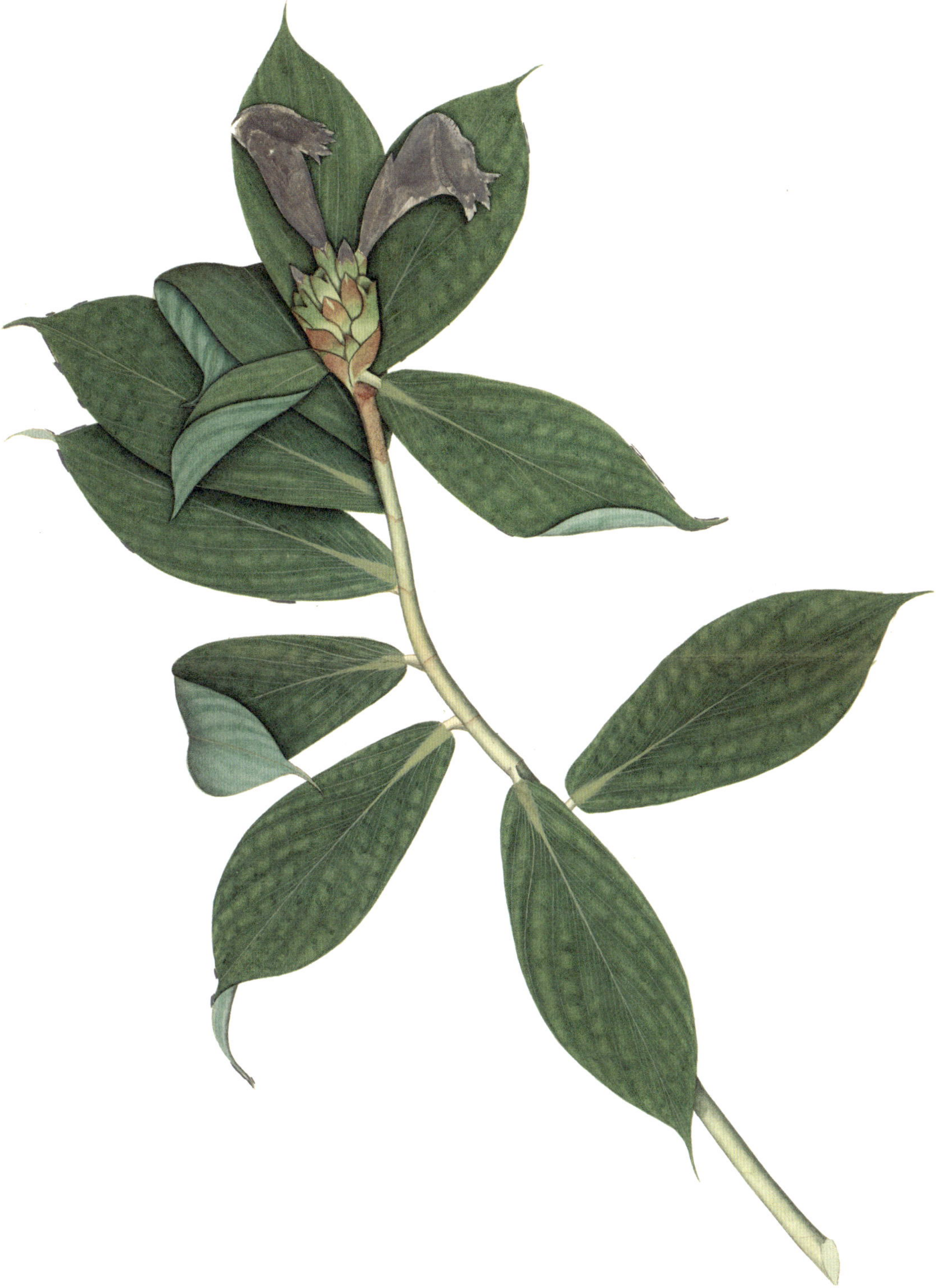

Hellenia speciosa
by SHEIKH ZAIN AL-DIN

crêpe ginger

For what has made the sage or poet write
But the fair paradise of Nature's light?
In the calm grandeur of a sober line,
We see the waving of the mountain pine;
And when a tale is beautifully staid,
We feel the safety of a hawthorn glade:
When it is moving on luxurious wings,
The soul is lost in pleasant smotherings:
Fair dewy roses brush against our faces,
And flowering laurels spring from diamond vases;
O'erhead we see the jasmine and sweet briar,
And bloomy grapes laughing from green attire;
While at our feet, the voice of crystal bubbles
Charms us at once away from all our troubles:
So that we feel uplifted from the world,
Walking upon the white clouds wreath'd and curl'd.

FROM 'I Stood Tip-toe Upon a Little Hill' BY JOHN KEATS

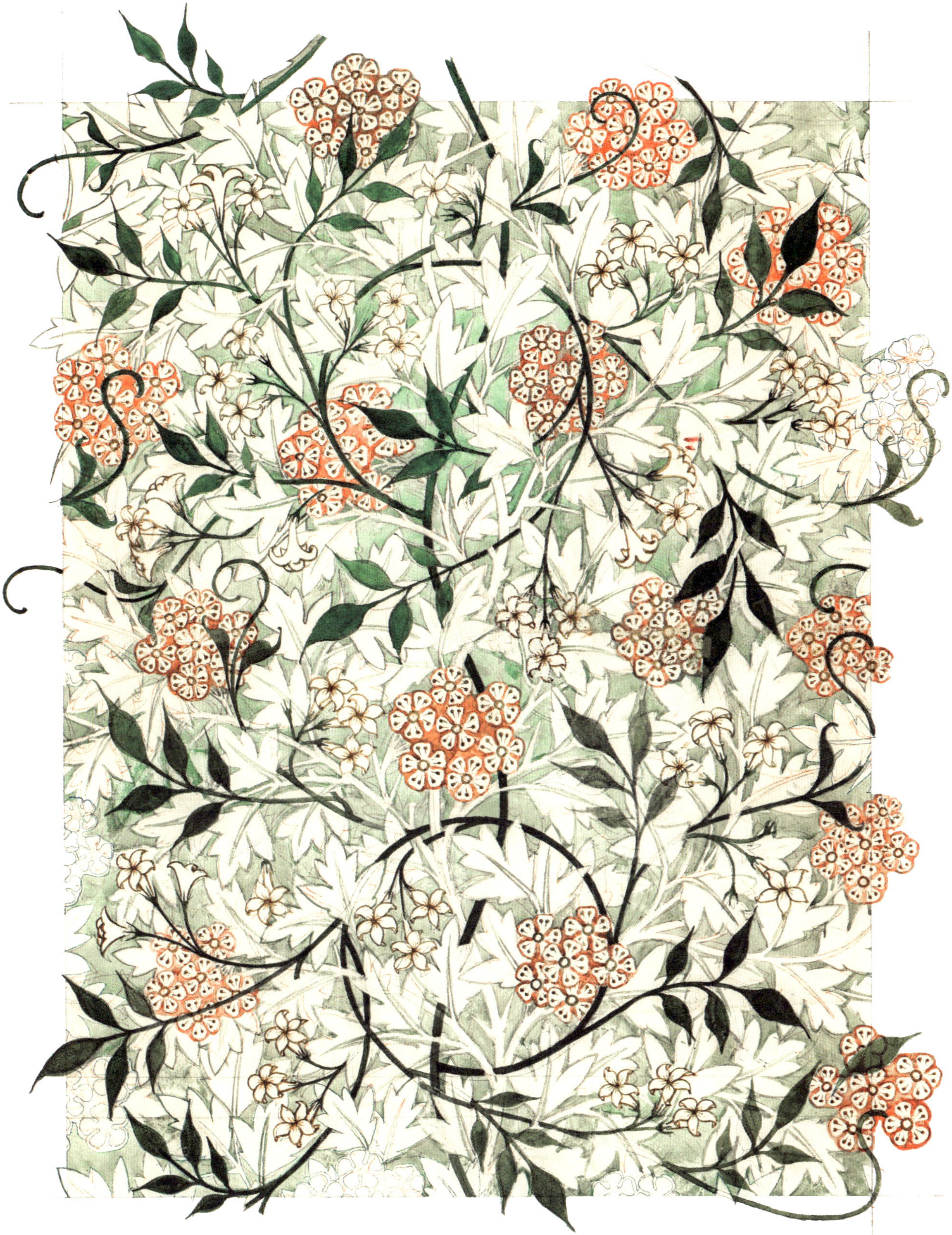

Crataegus monogyna
by WILLIAM MORRIS

common hawthorn

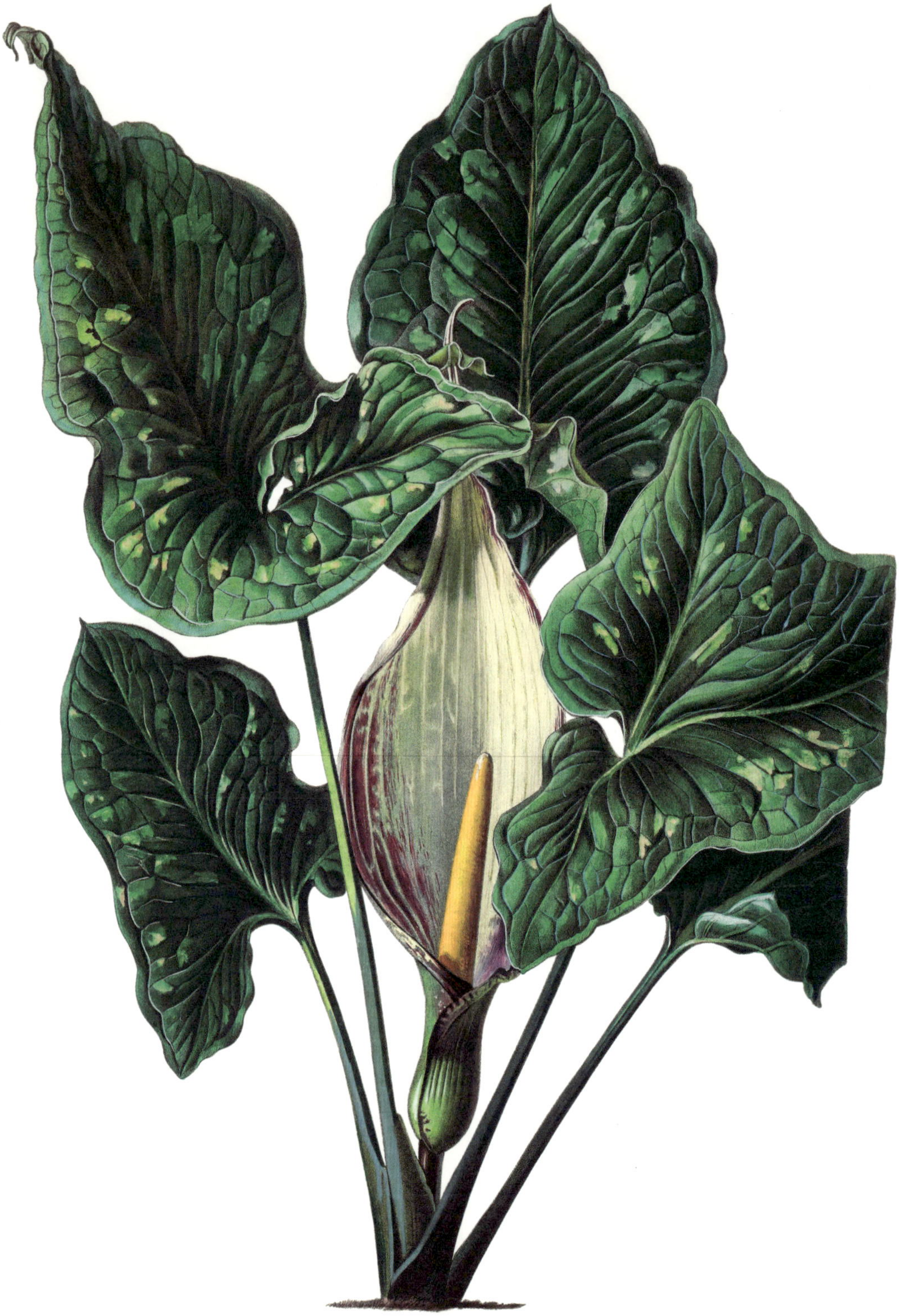

Arum concinnatum
by Heinrich Wilhelm Schott

Crete arum

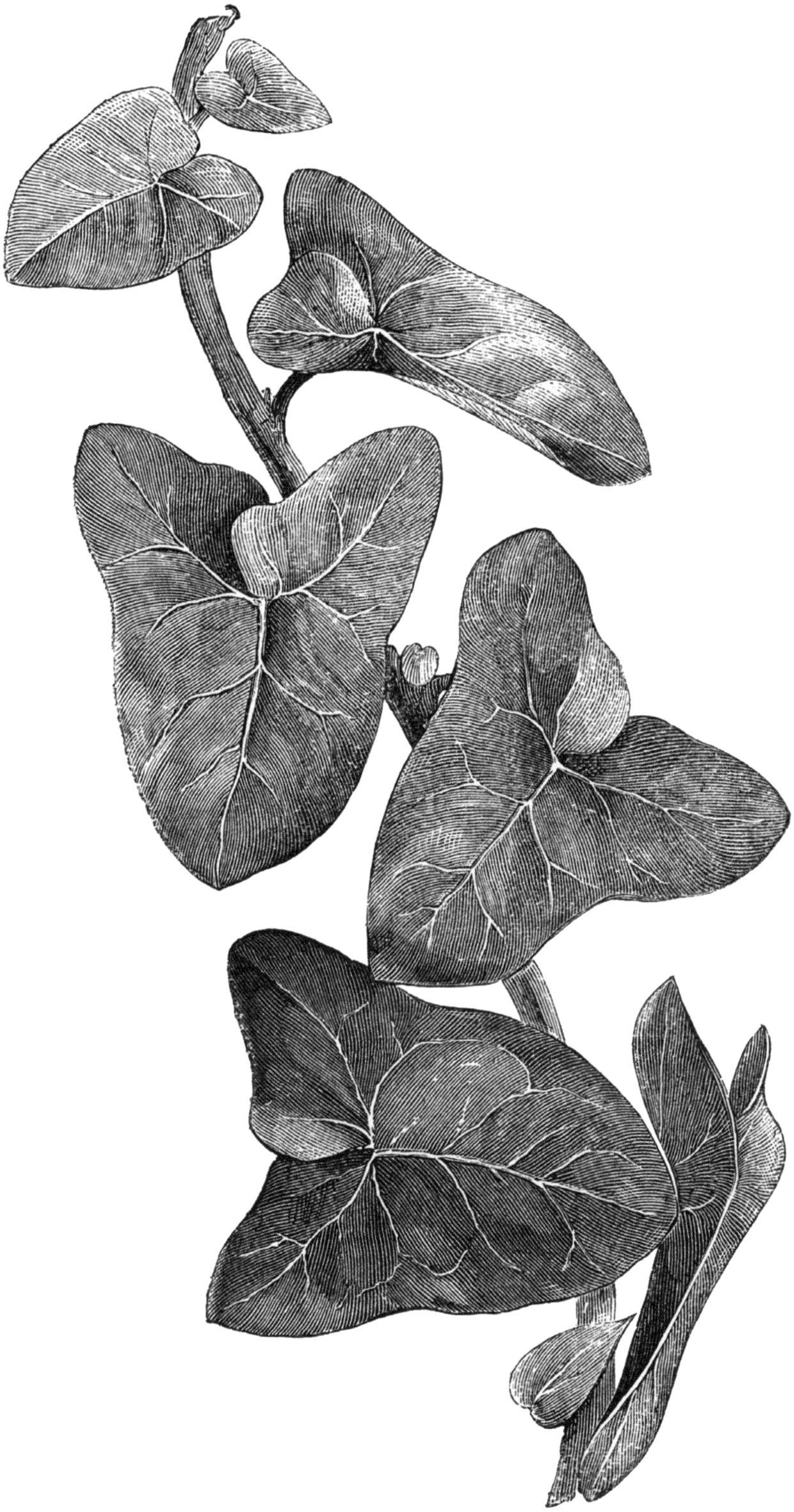

Hedera hibernica 'Deltoidea'
by James Shirley Hibberd

shield ivy | sweetheart ivy

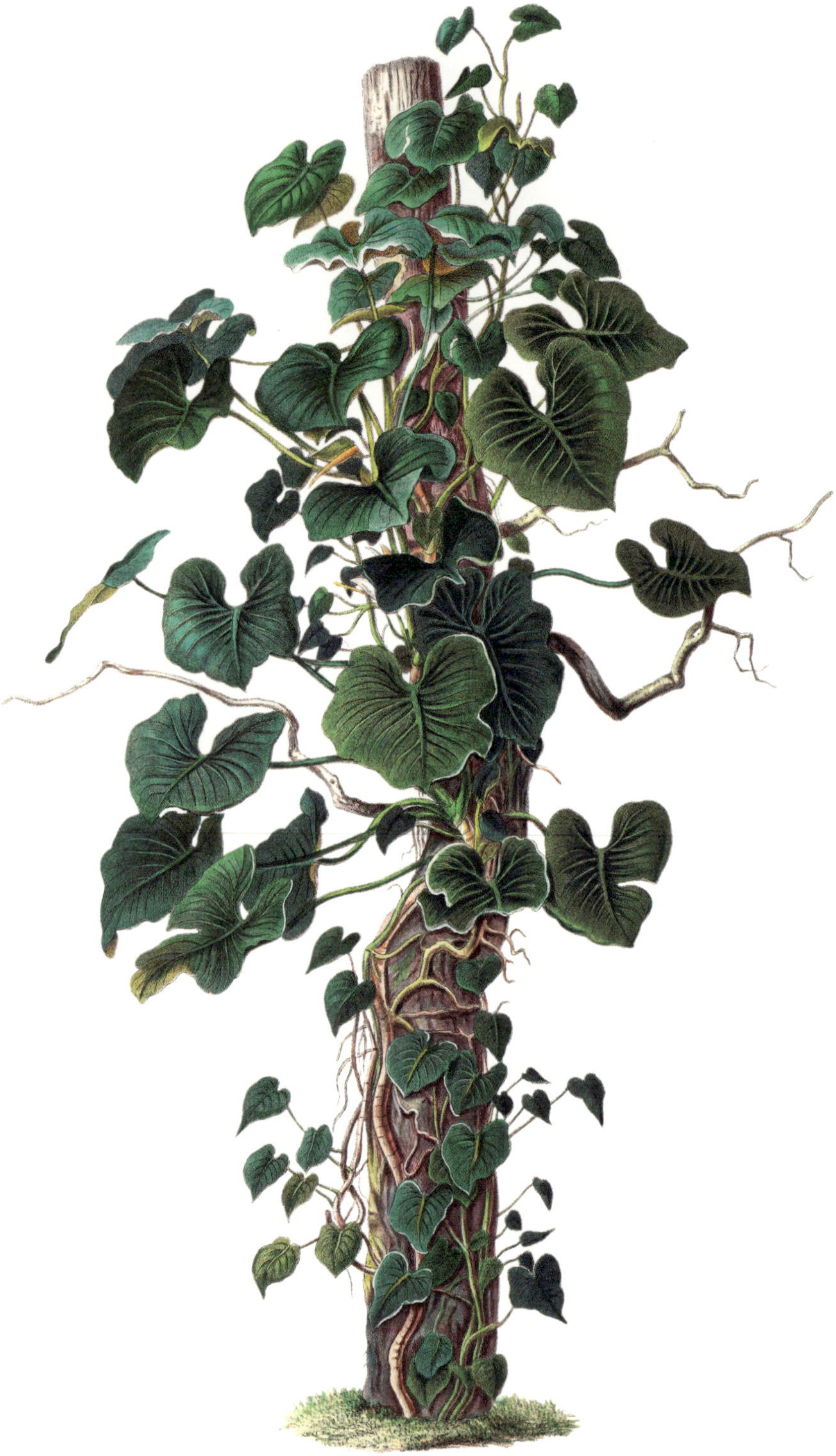

Philodendron eximium
by Heinrich Wilhelm Schott

philodendron

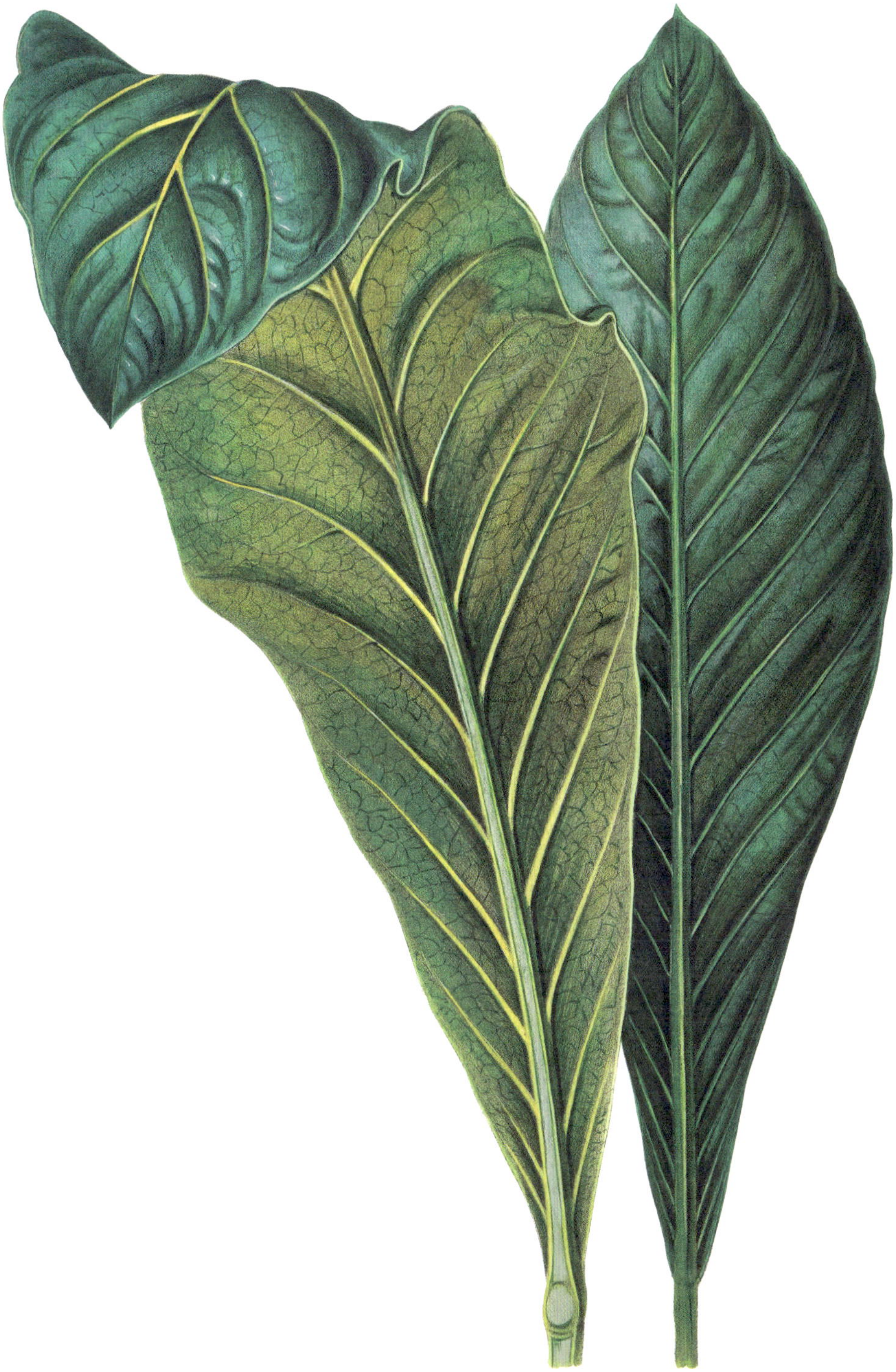

Anthurium hookeri
by Heinrich Wilhelm Schott

bird's nest anthurium

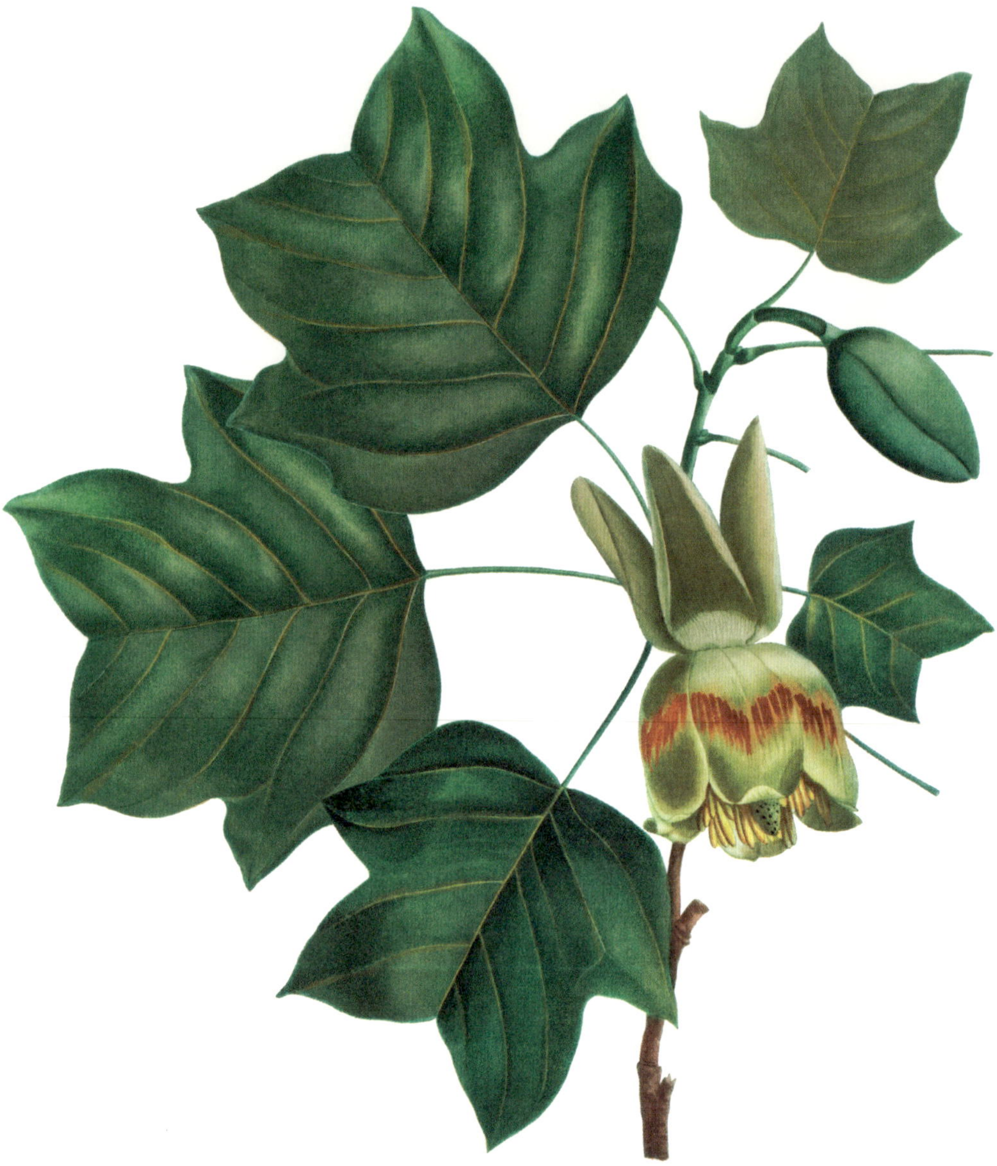

Liriodendron tulipifera
by Pierre-Joseph Redouté

tulip tree | tulip poplar | yellow poplar |whitewood

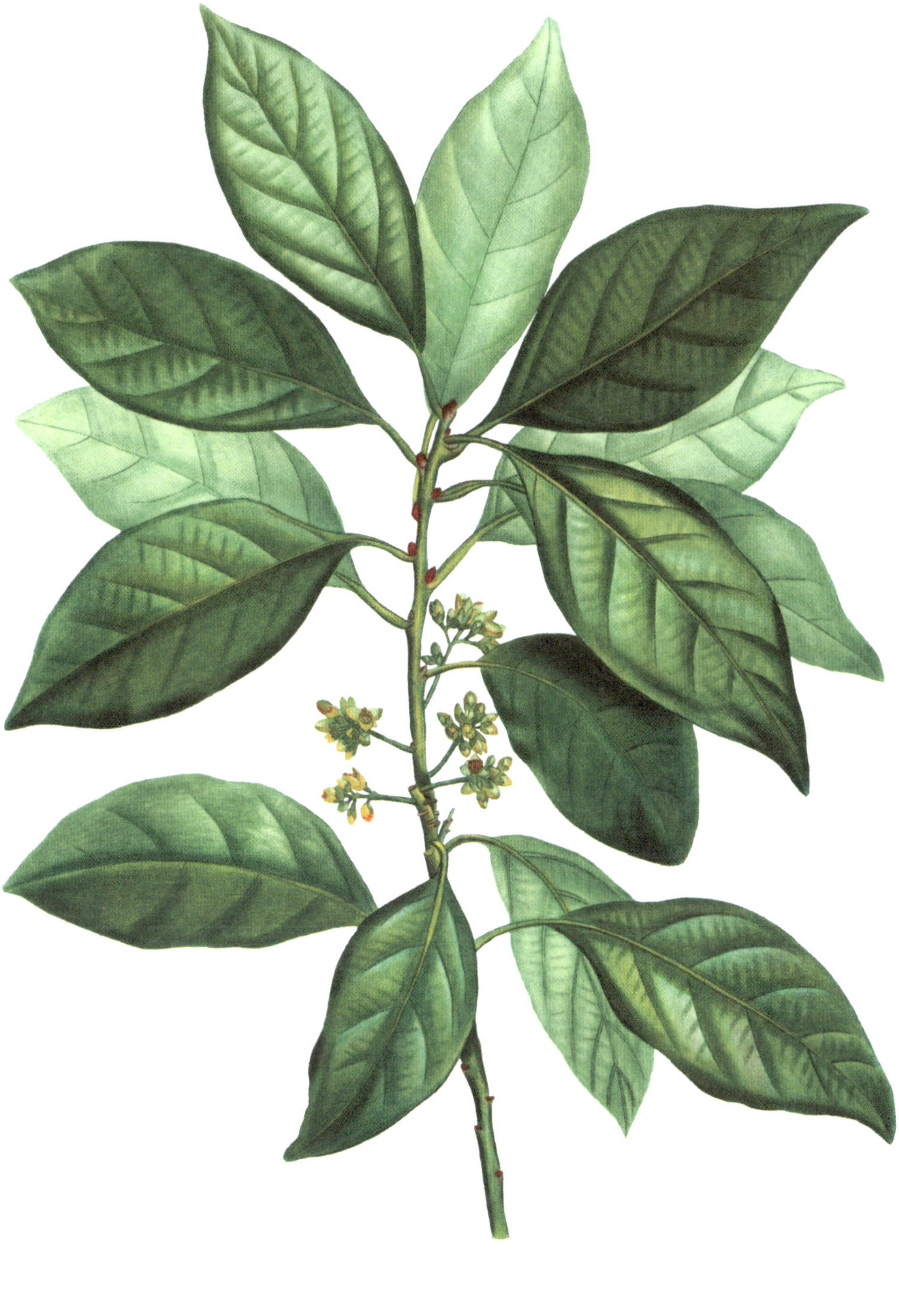

Tamala borbonia
by PIERRE-JOSEPH REDOUTÉ

redbay | tisswood | scrubbay | shorebay

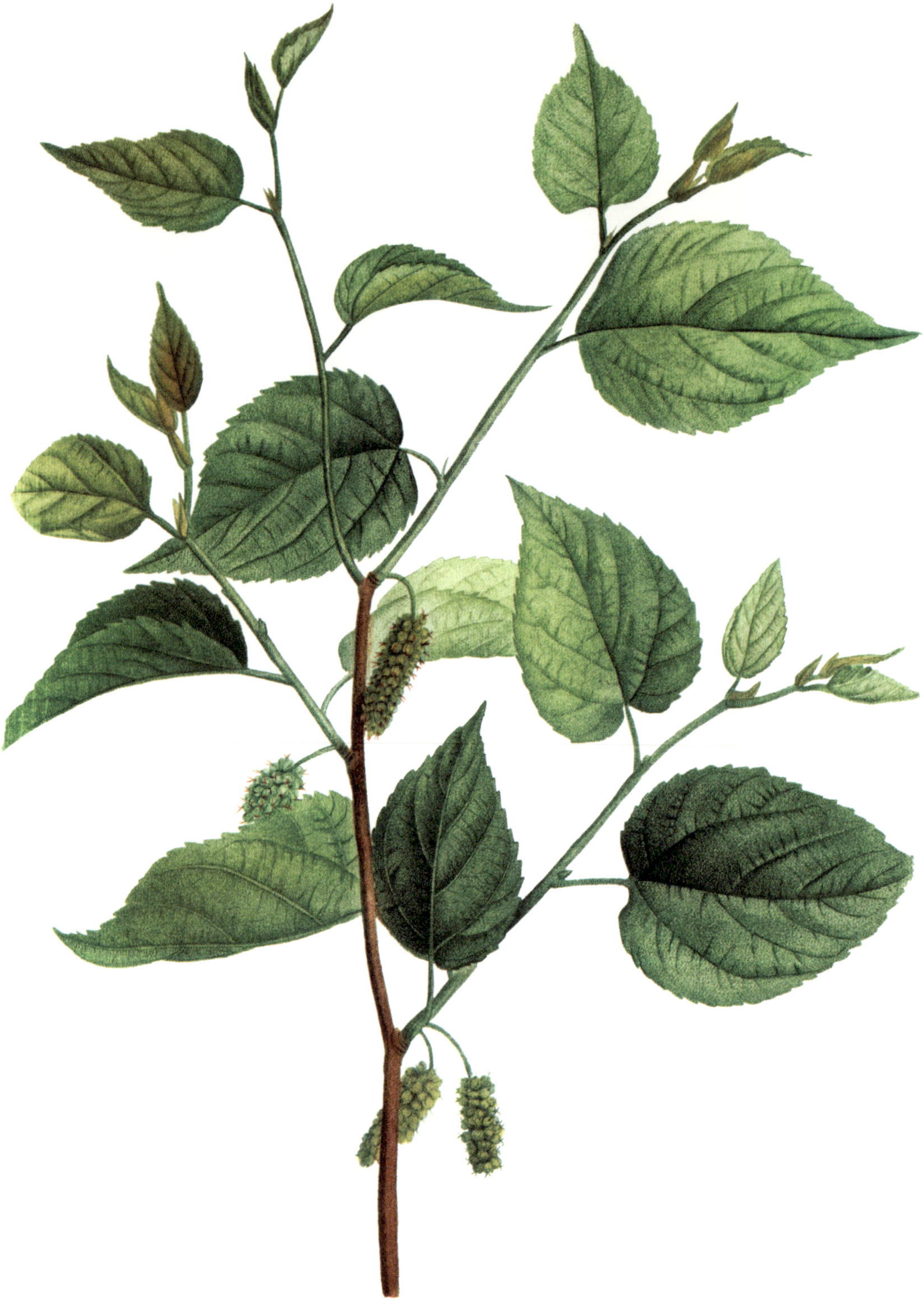

Morus rubra
by Pierre-Joseph Redouté

red mulberry

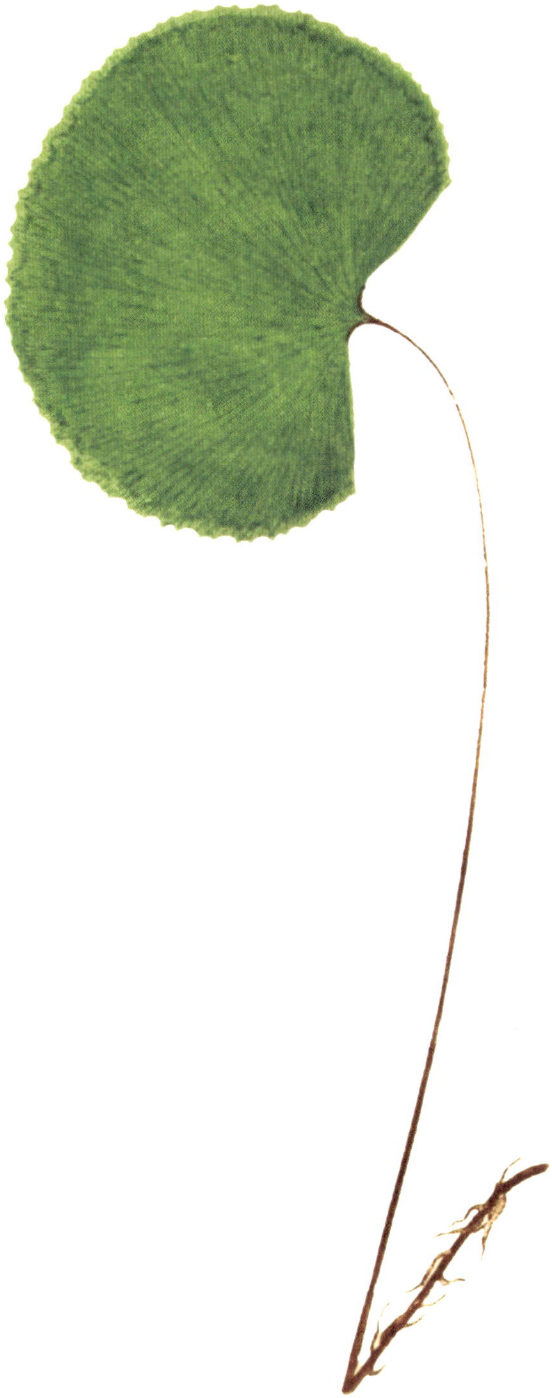

Adiantum reniforme
by EDWARD JOSEPH LOWE

kidney-leaved maidenhair fern

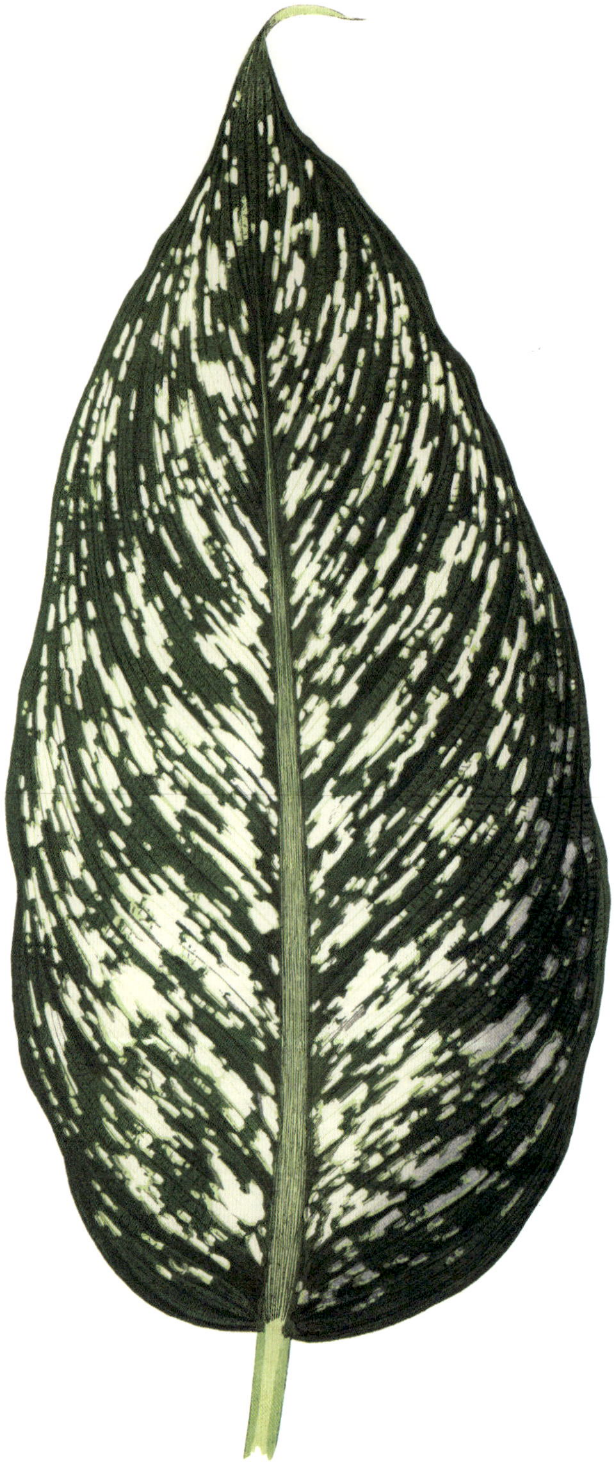

Dieffenbachia seguine
by Alexander Francis Lydon & Benjamin Fawcett

dumb cane | leopard lily | tuftroot

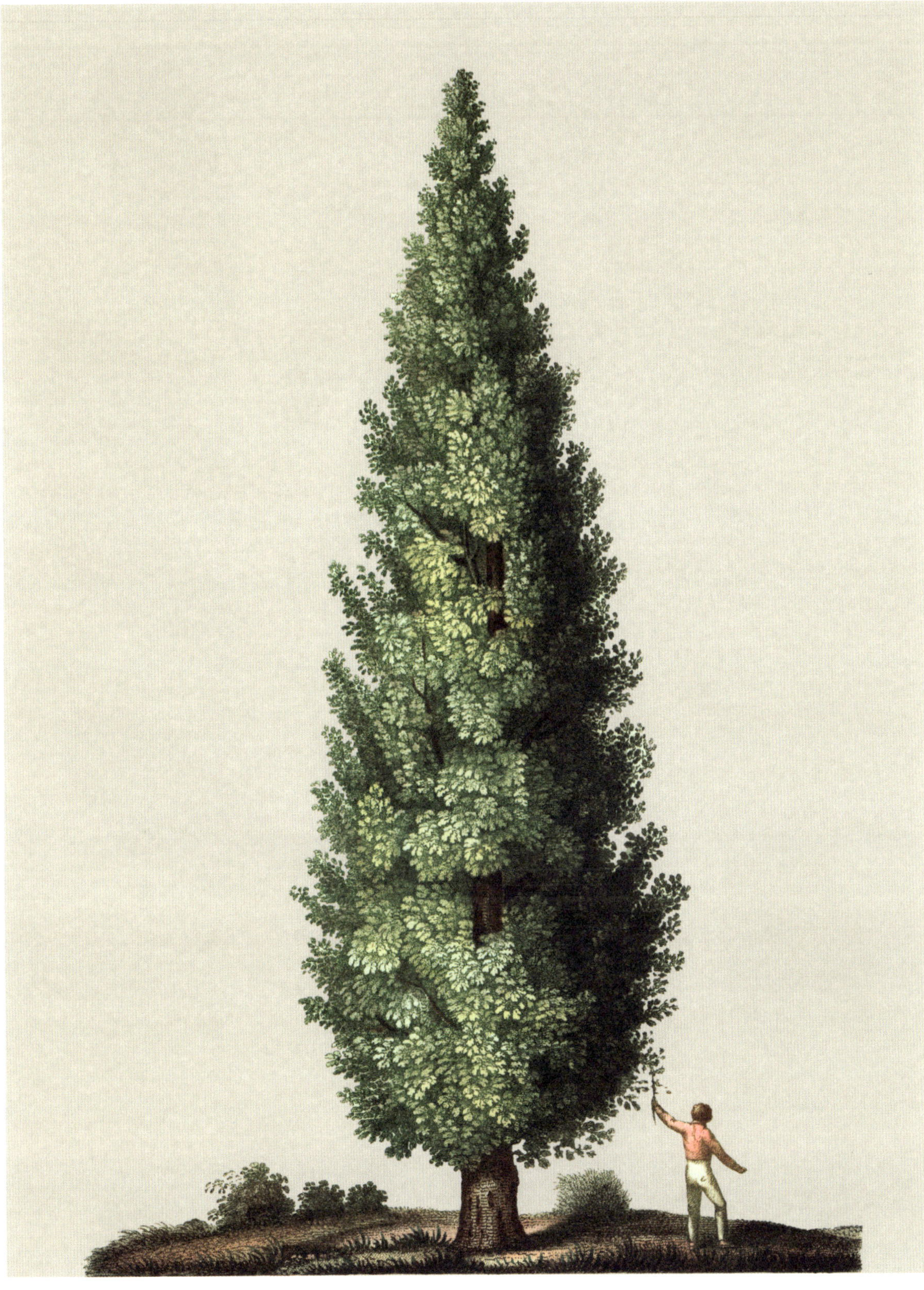

Quercus robur 'Fastigiata'
by Pierre-Joseph Redouté

upright English oak

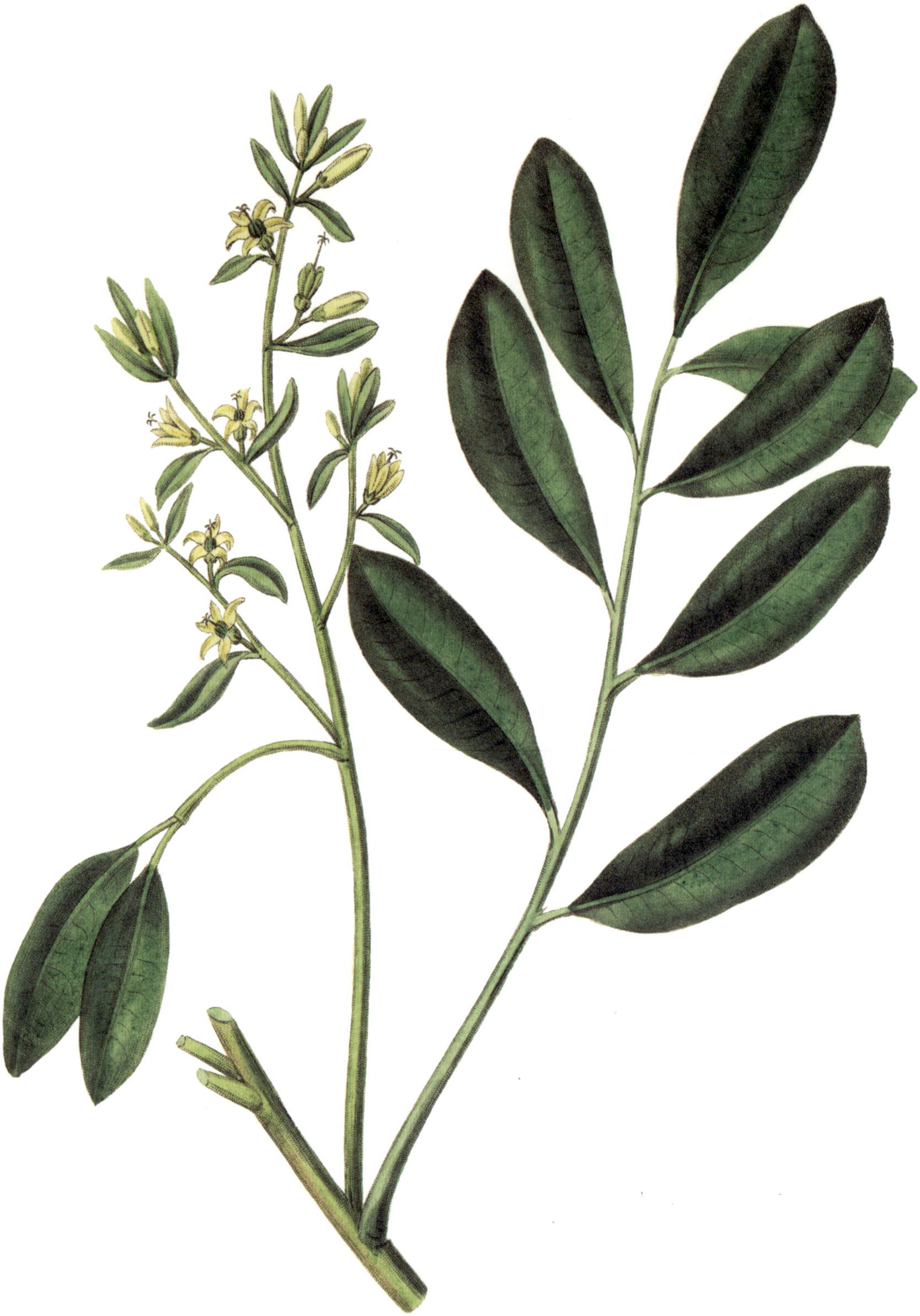

Simarouba amara
by JOHN STEPHENSON & JAMES MORSS CHURCHILL

simarupa | paradise tree

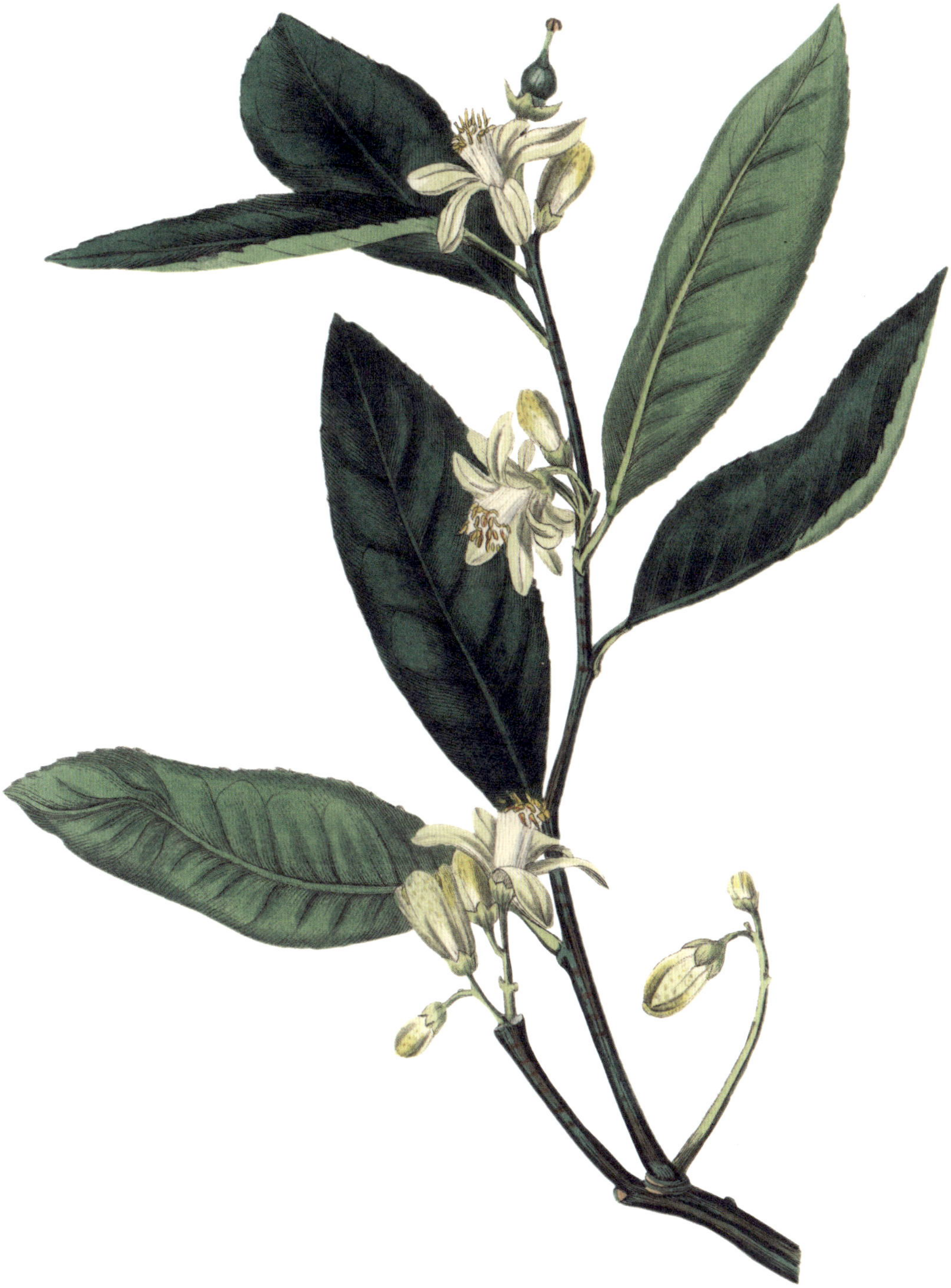

Citrus medica
by John Stephenson & James Morss Churchill

citron

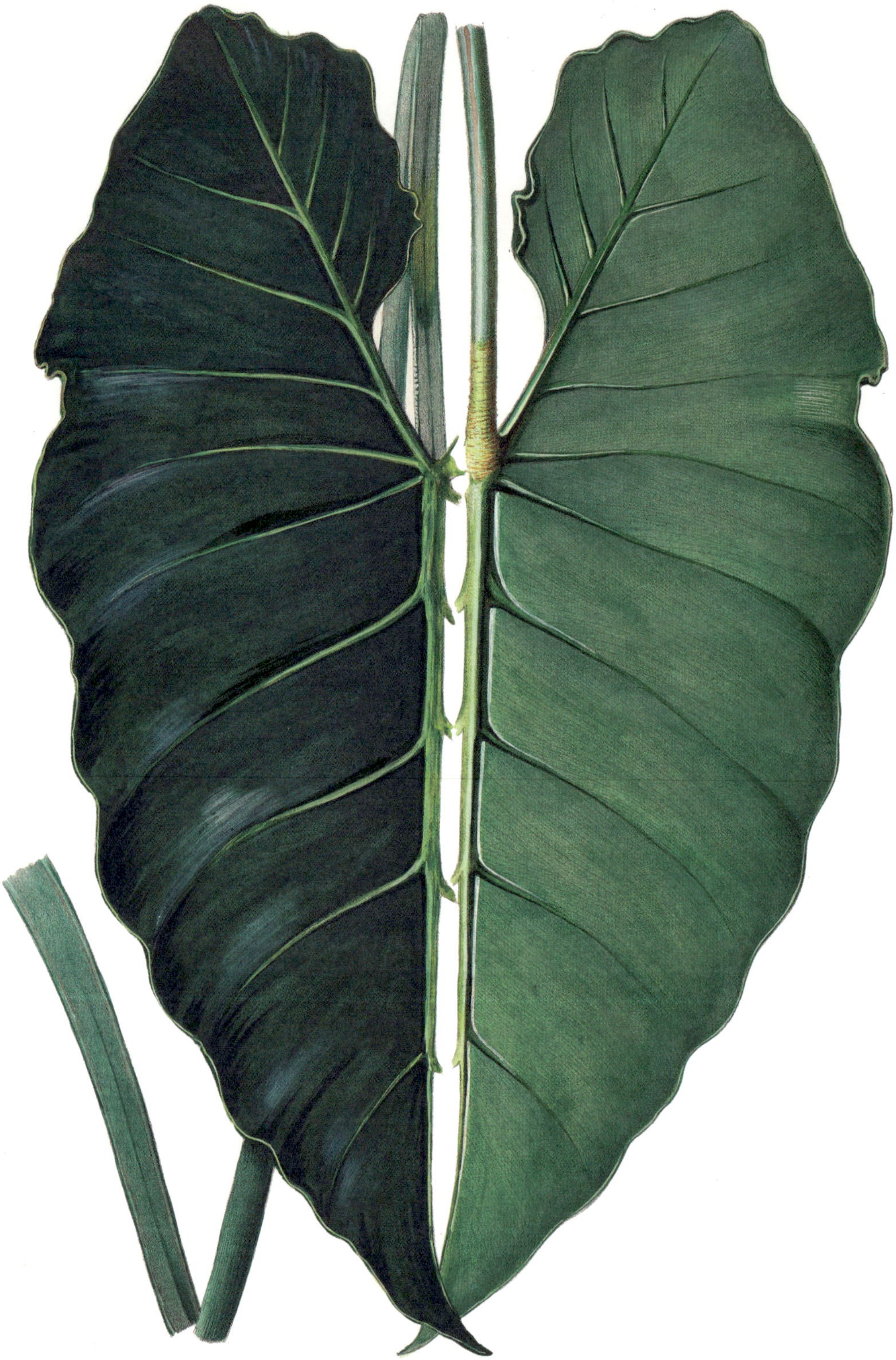

Philodendron speciosum
by HEINRICH WILHELM SCHOTT

king of philodendrons

By leaves we live.

Patrick Geddes

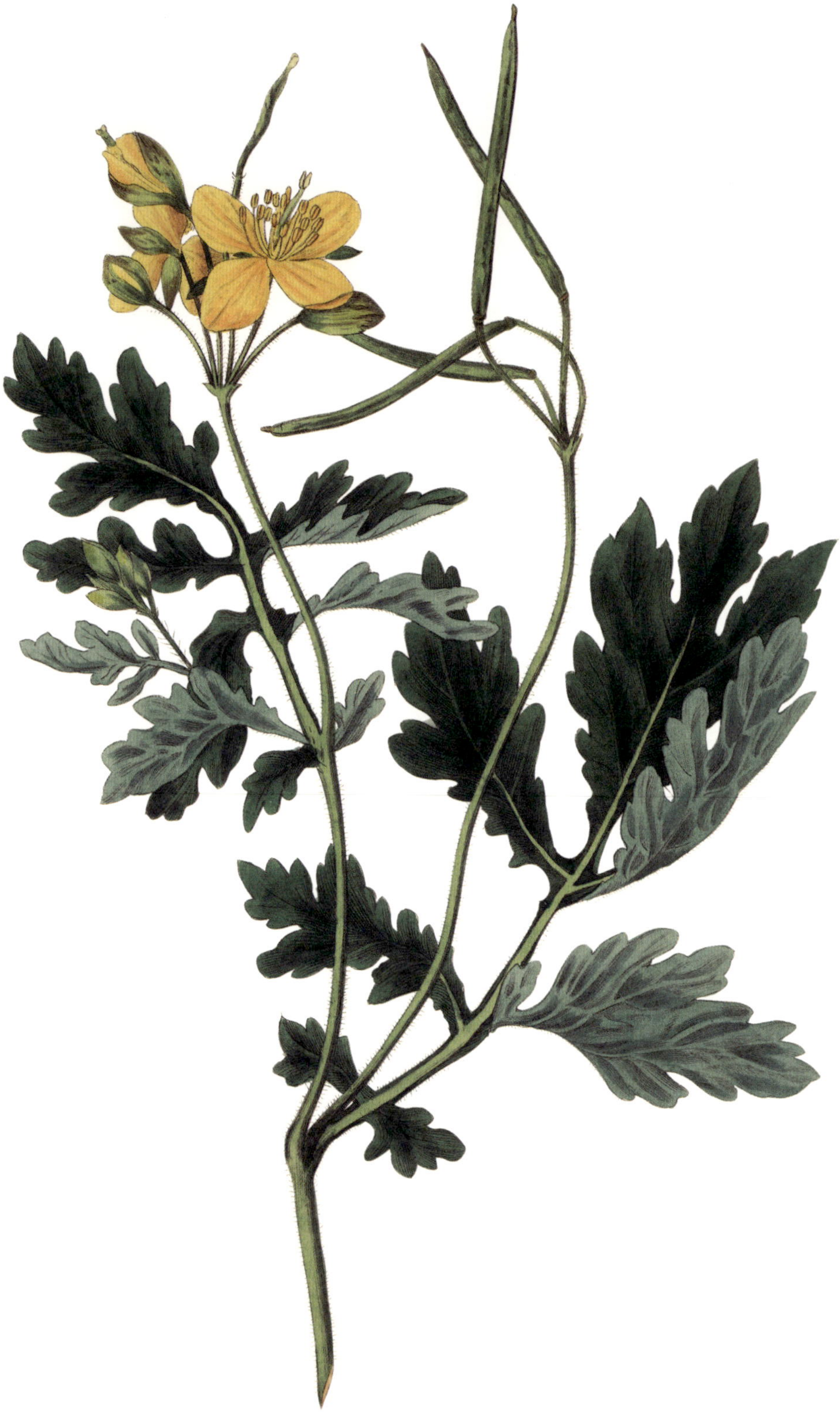

Chelidonium majus
by JOHN STEPHENSON & JAMES MORSS CHURCHILL

greater celandine

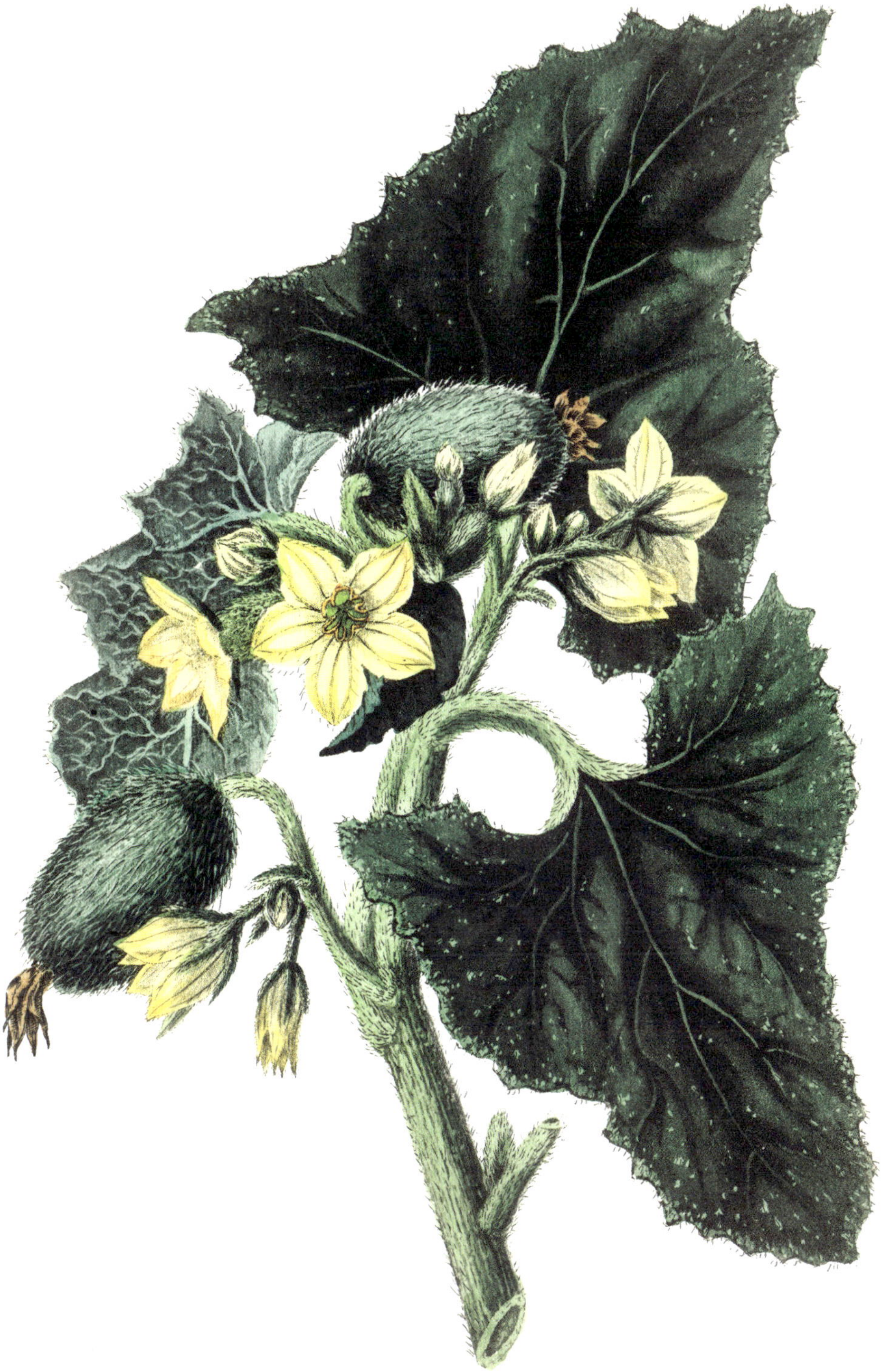

Ecballium elaterium
by JOHN STEPHENSON & JAMES MORSS CHURCHILL

squirting cucumber

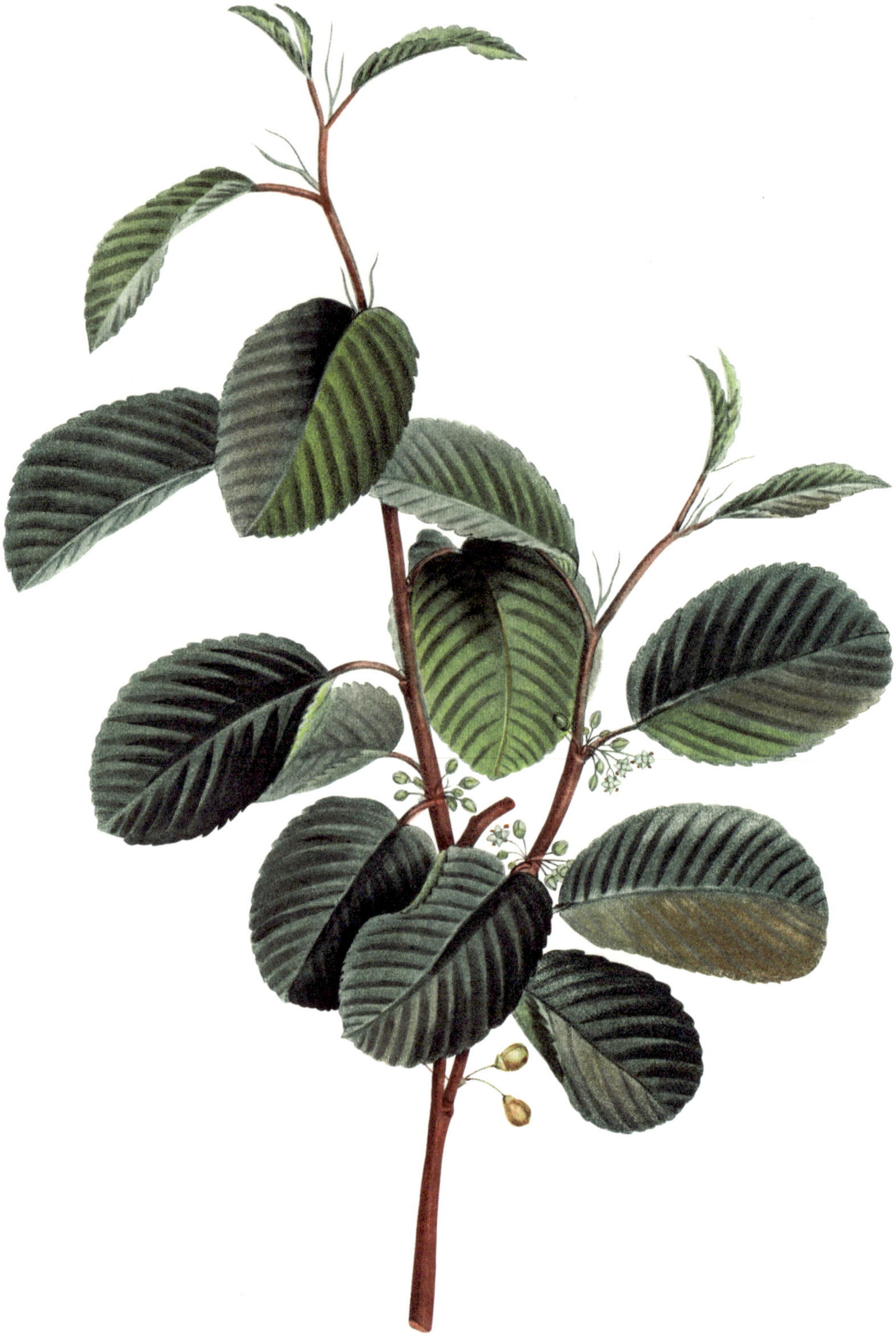

Rhamnus alpinus
by PIERRE-JOSEPH REDOUTÉ

alpine buckthorn

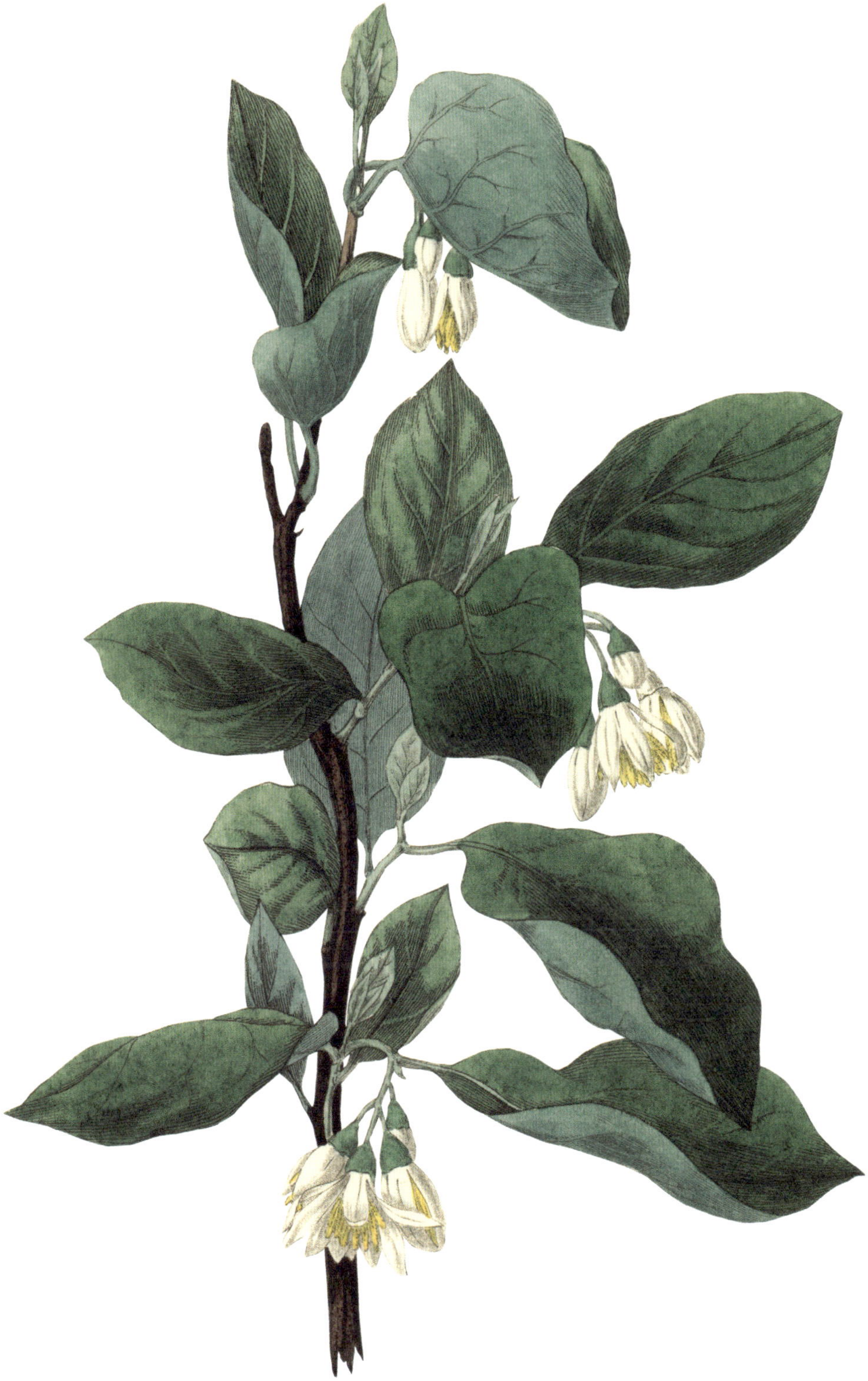

Styrax officinalis
by John Stephenson & James Morss Churchill

storax tree | snowdrop bush

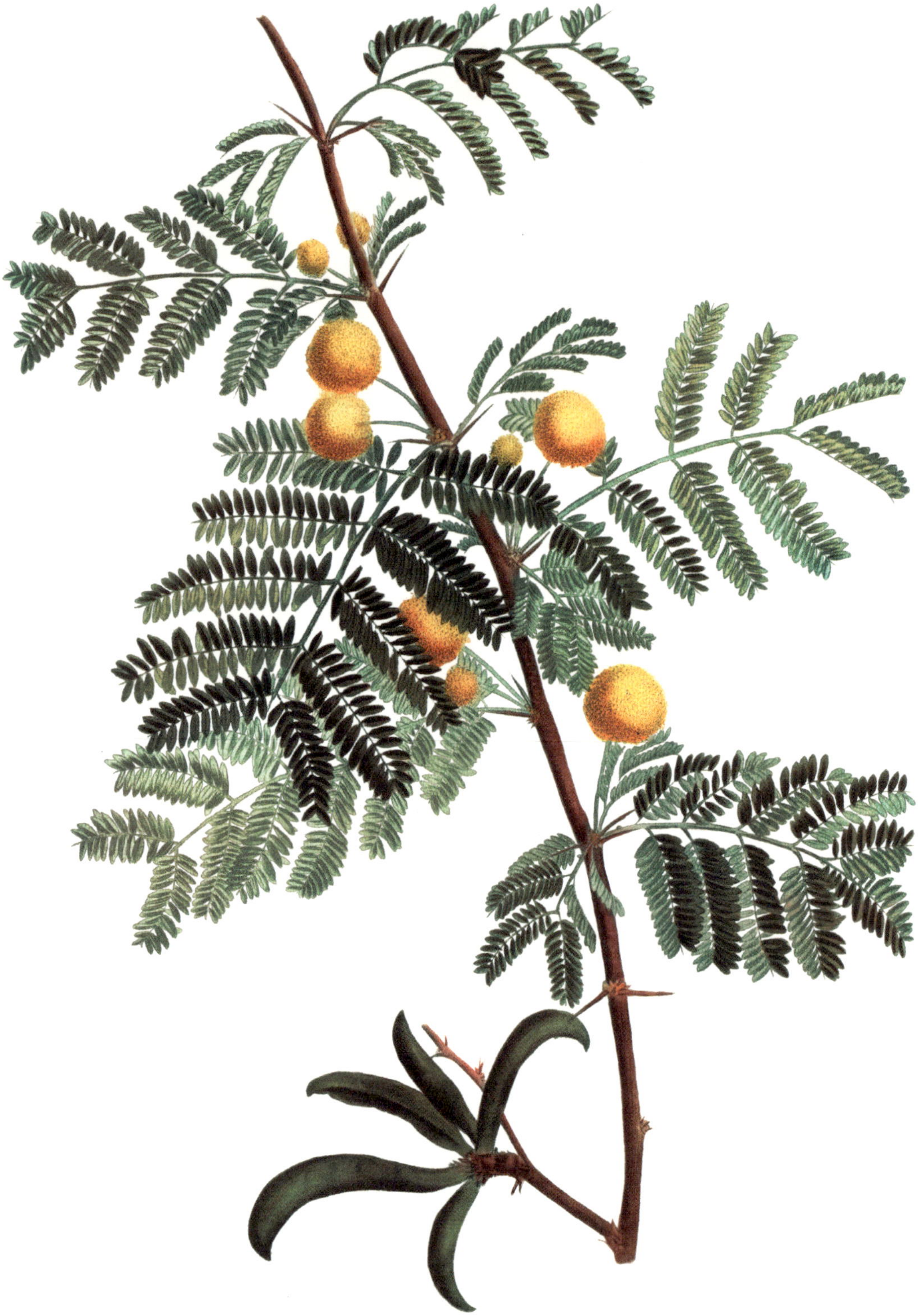

228

Vachellia farnesiana
by Karl Blossfeldt

sweet acacia | huisachel casha tree | needle bush

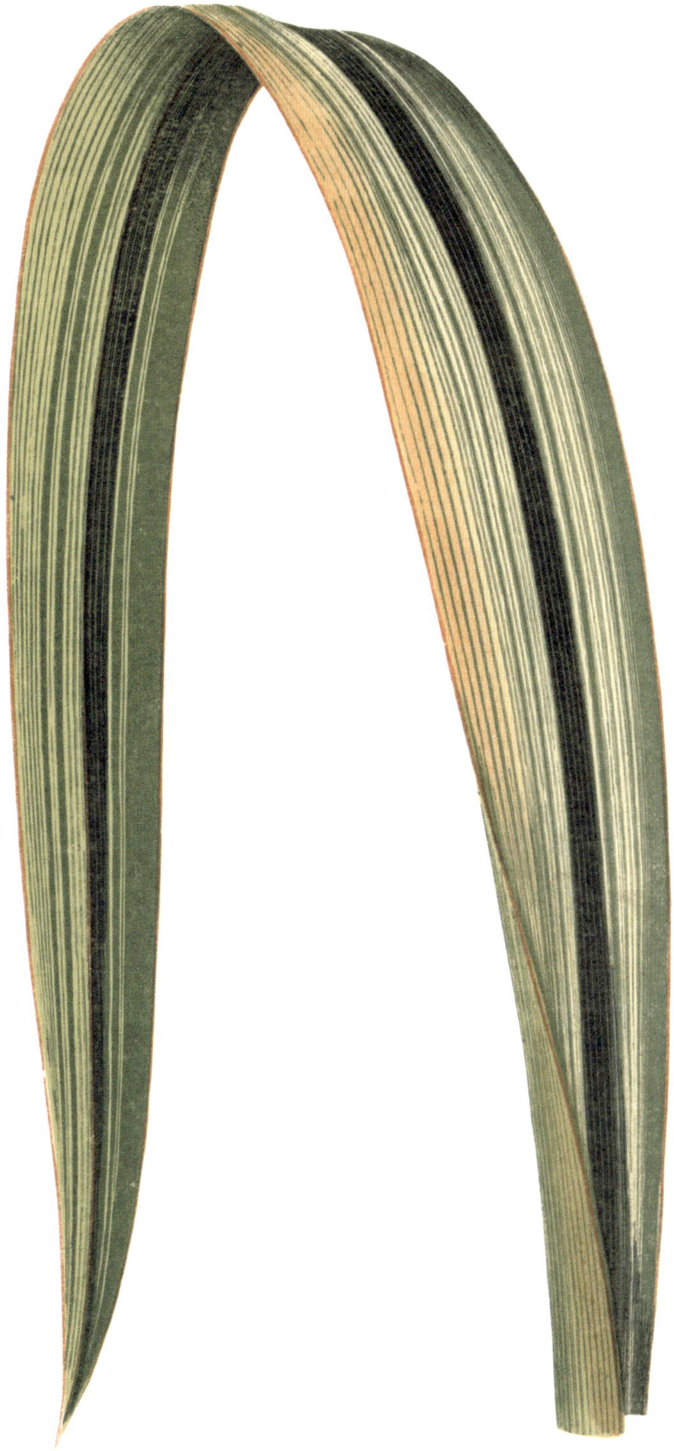

Phormium tenax
by BENJAMIN FAWCETT & JAMES SHIRLEY HIBBERD

New Zealand flax | New Zealand hemp

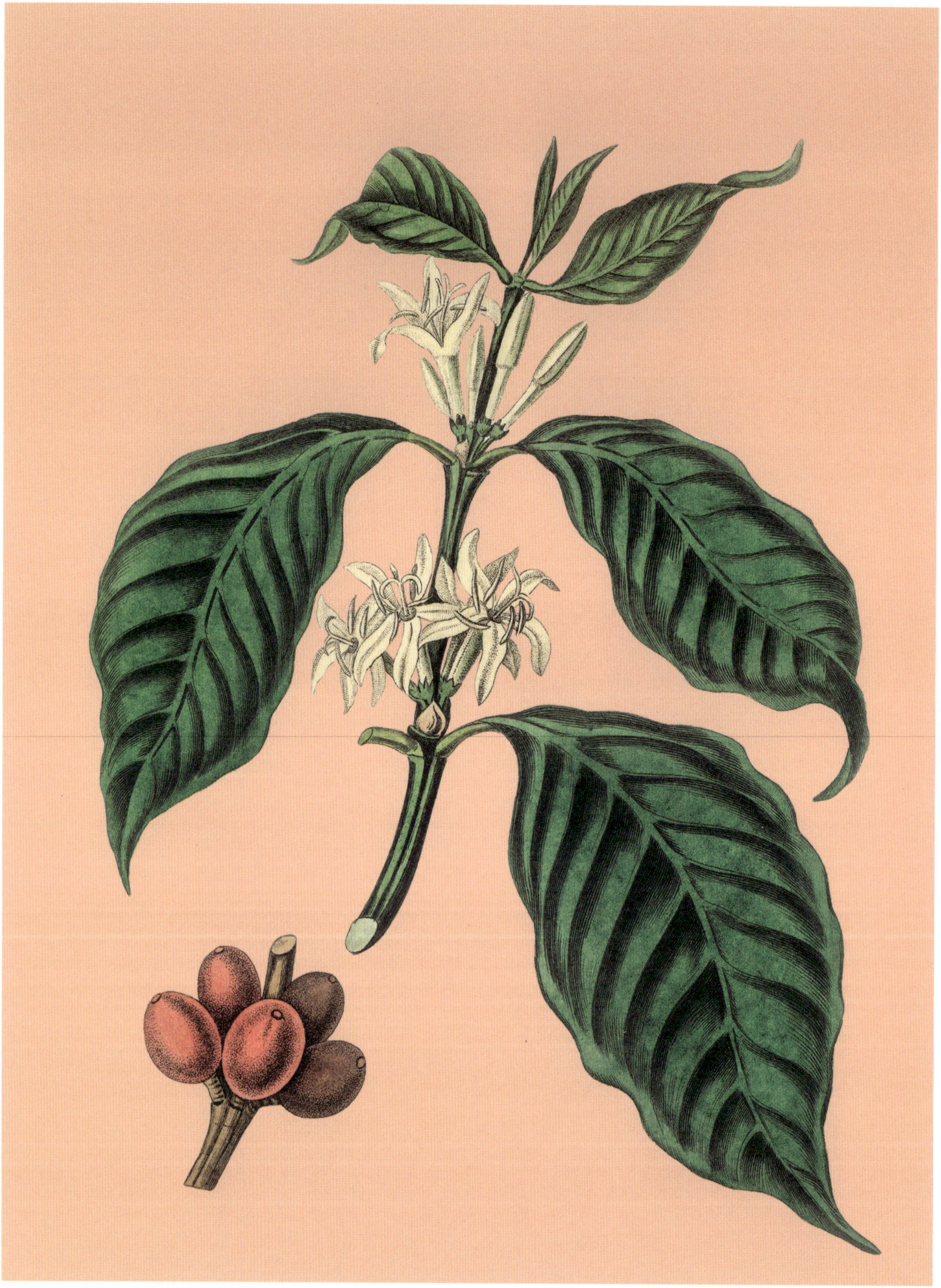

Coffea arabica
by JOHN STEPHENSON & JAMES MORSS CHURCHILL

Arabica coffee plant

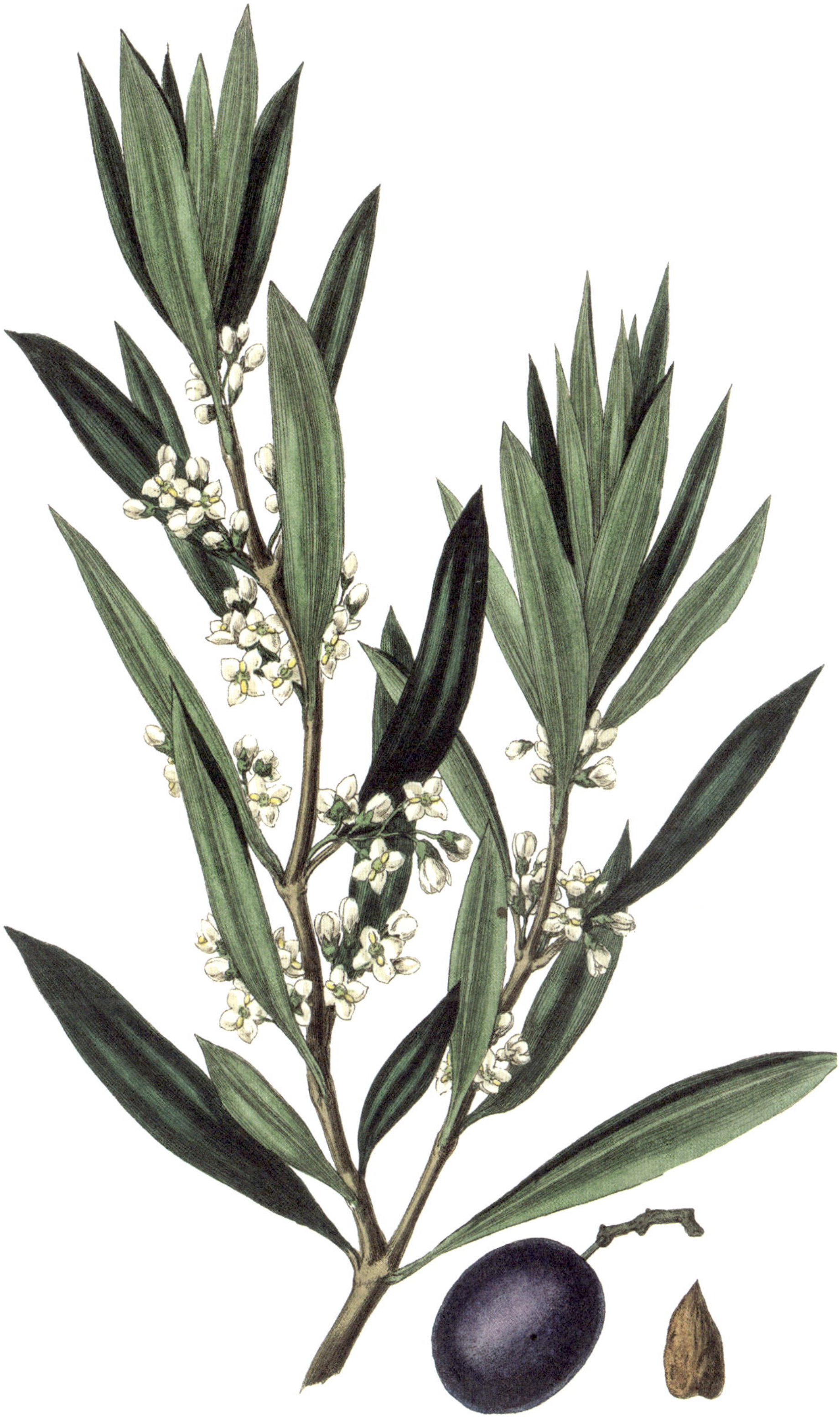

Olea europaea
by John Stephenson & James Morss Churchill

olive

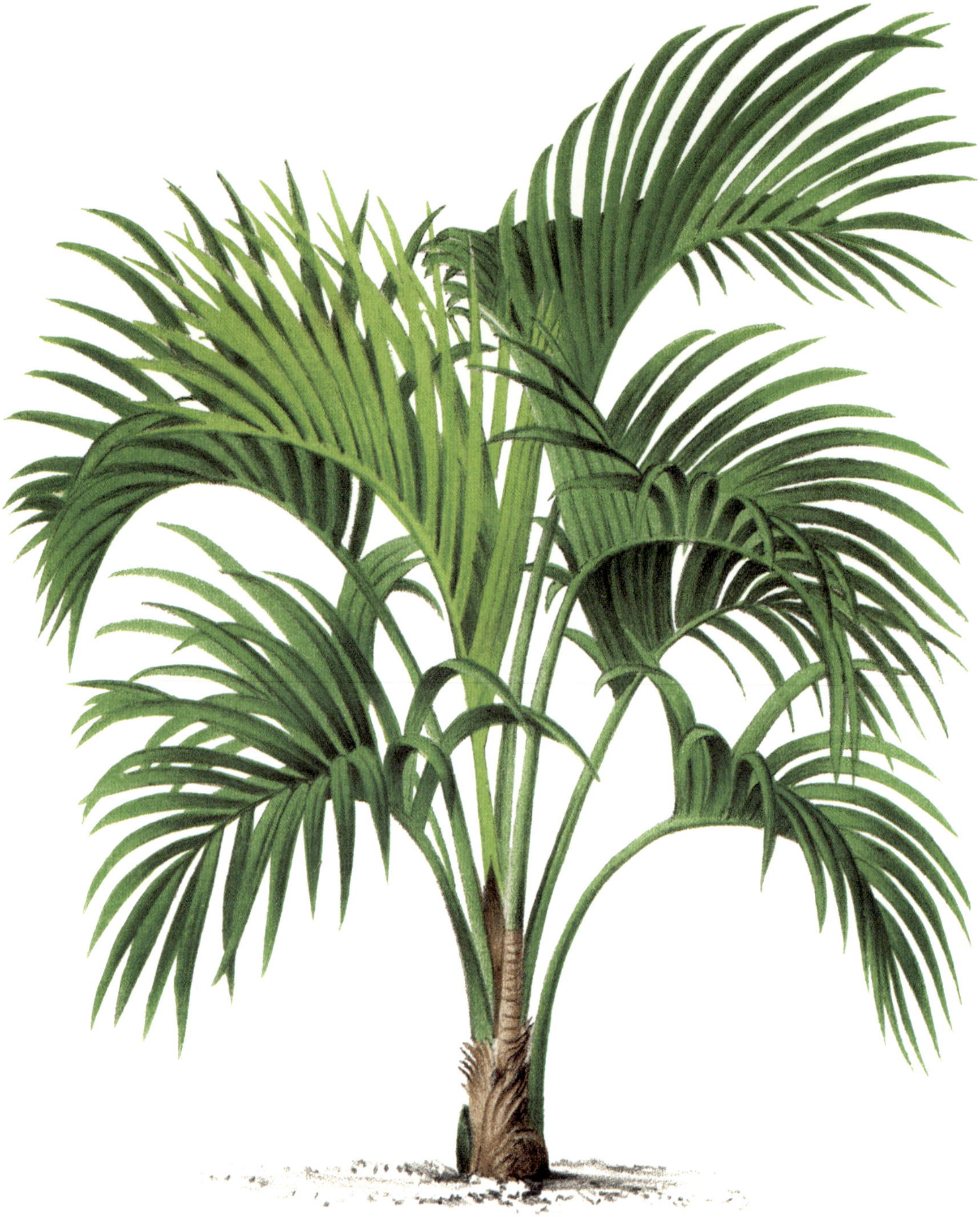

Howea belmoreana
by Oswald de Kerchove de Denterghem

curly palm | kentia palm | Belmore sentry palm

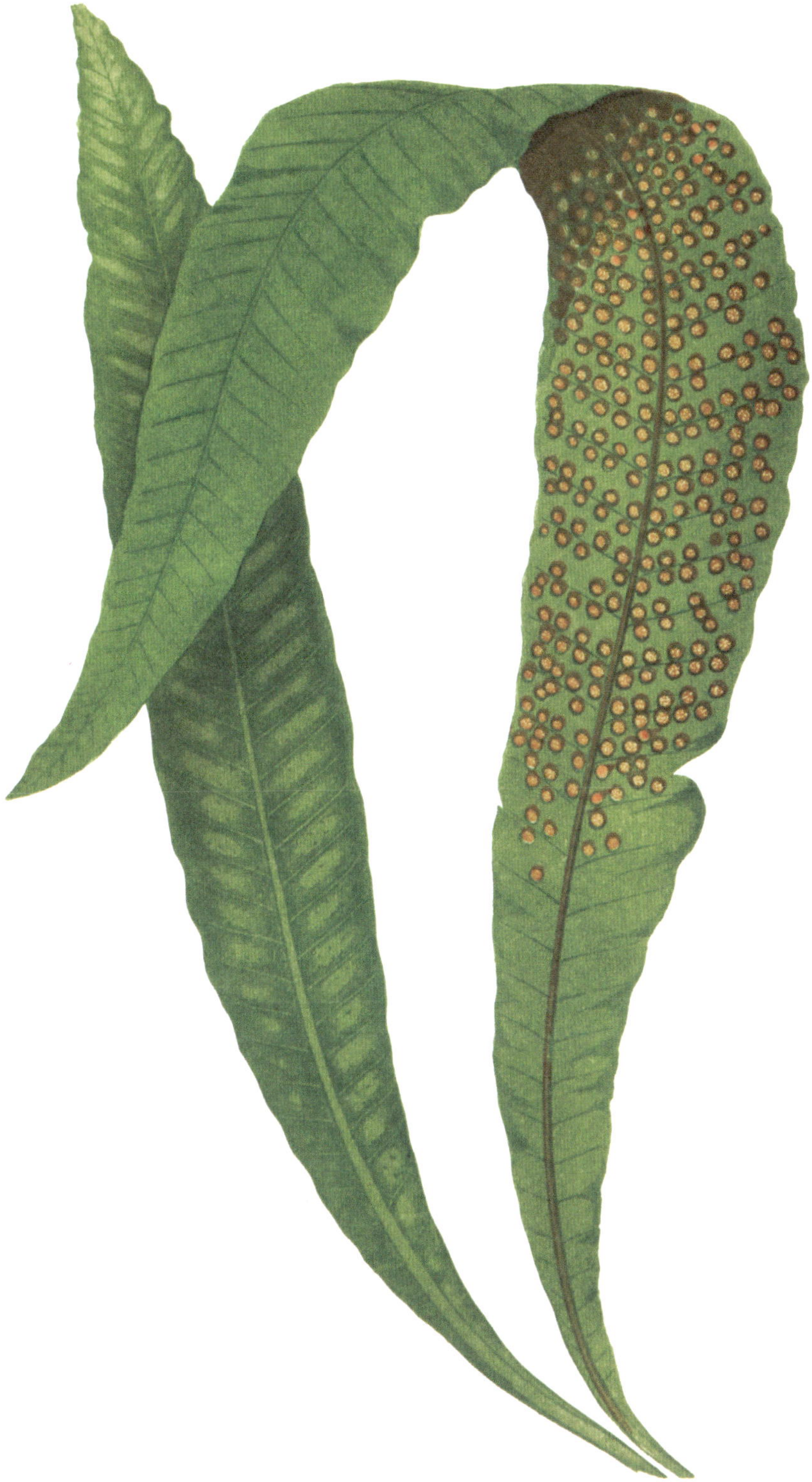

Campyloneurum nitidum
by Edward Joseph Lowe

strap fern

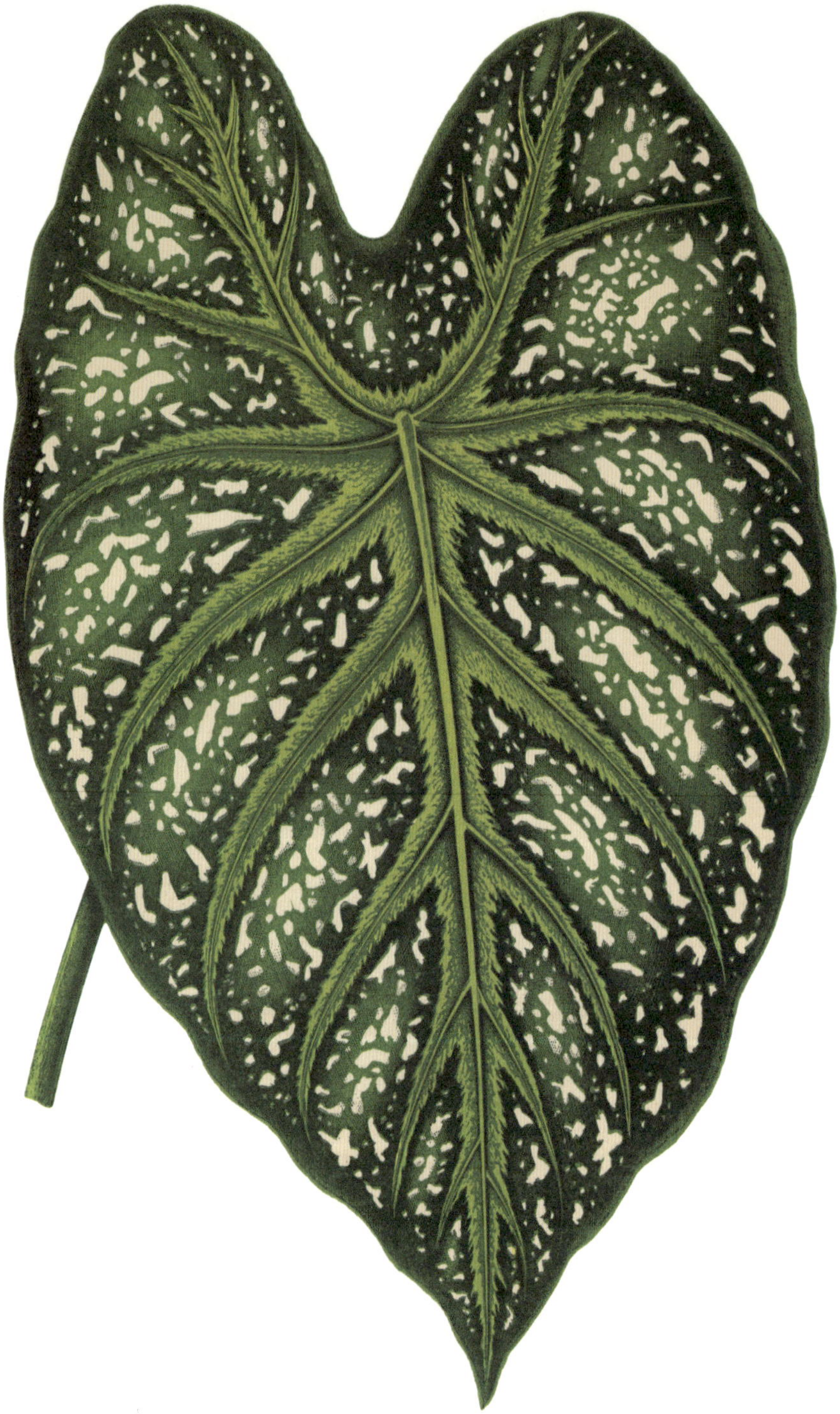

Caladium bicolor
by ALEXANDER FRANCIS LYDON & BENJAMIN FAWCETT

Heart of Jesus | elephant ear | angel wings

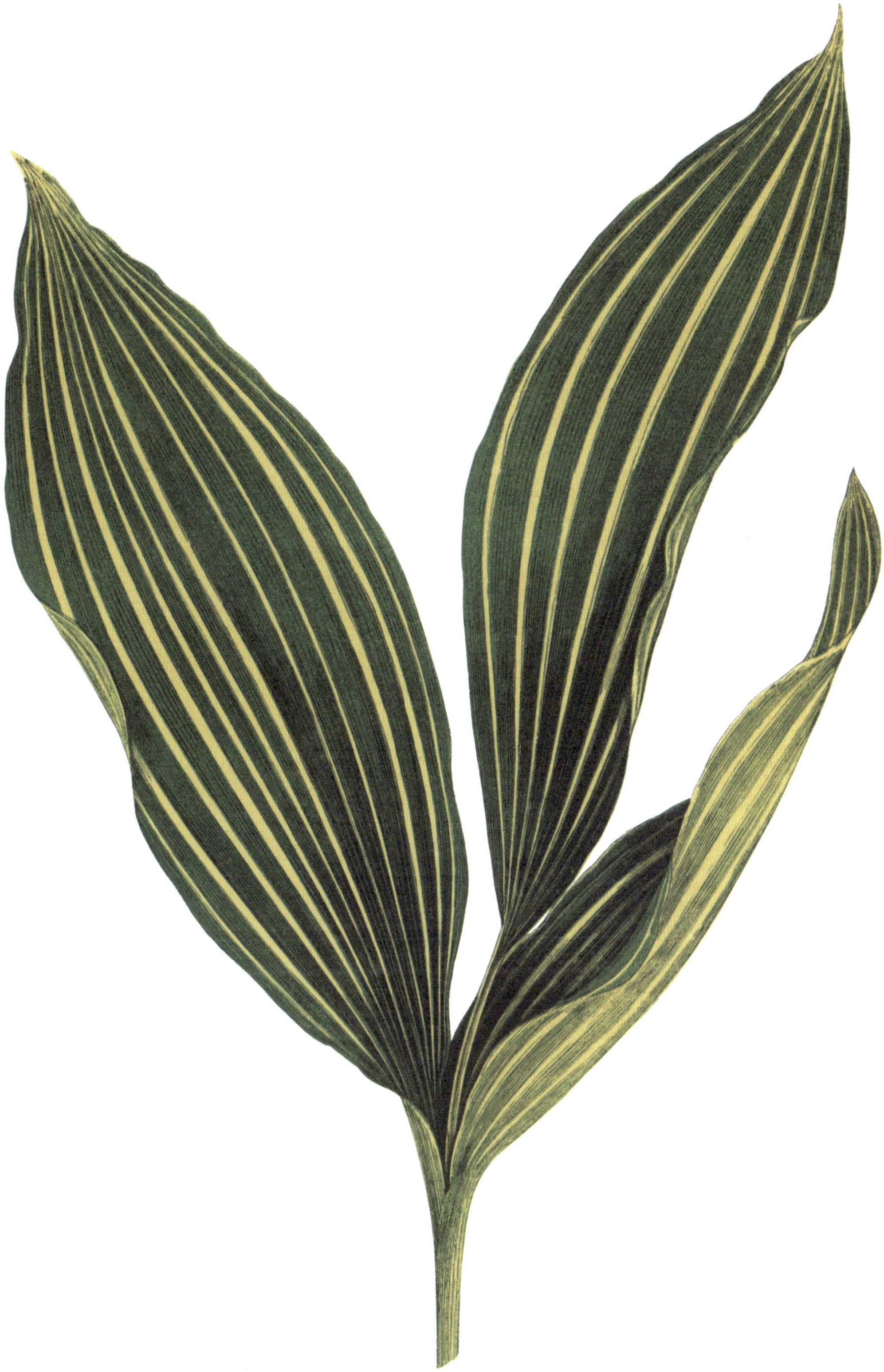

Convallaria majalis
by Alexander Francis Lydon & Benjamin Fawcett

lily of the valley

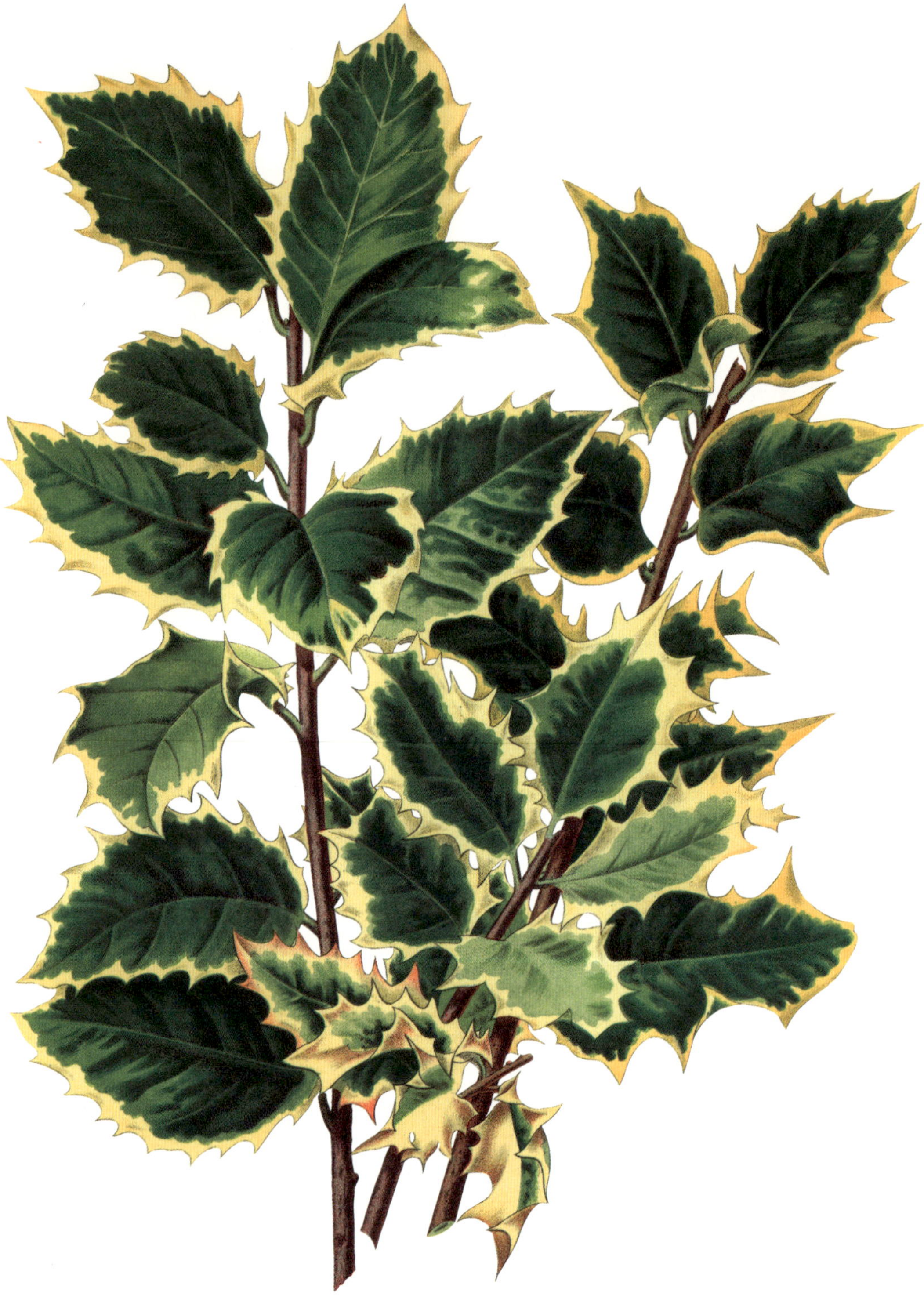

Ilex aquifolium
by Abraham Jacobus Wendel

common holly | English holly

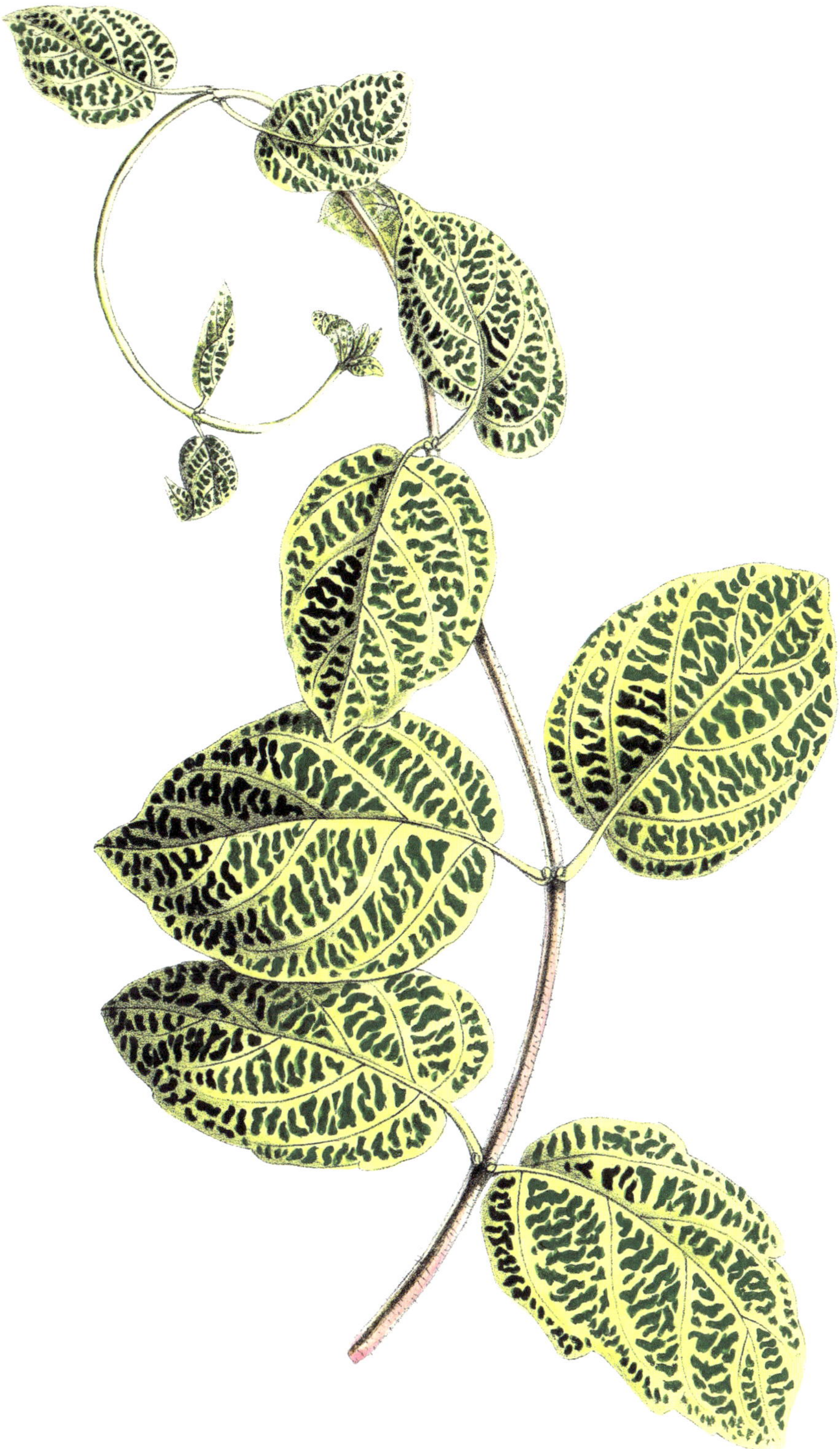

Lonicera japonica
by Worthington G. Smith, John N. Fitch & Walter H. Fitch

Japanese honeysuckle | golden-and-silver honeysuckle

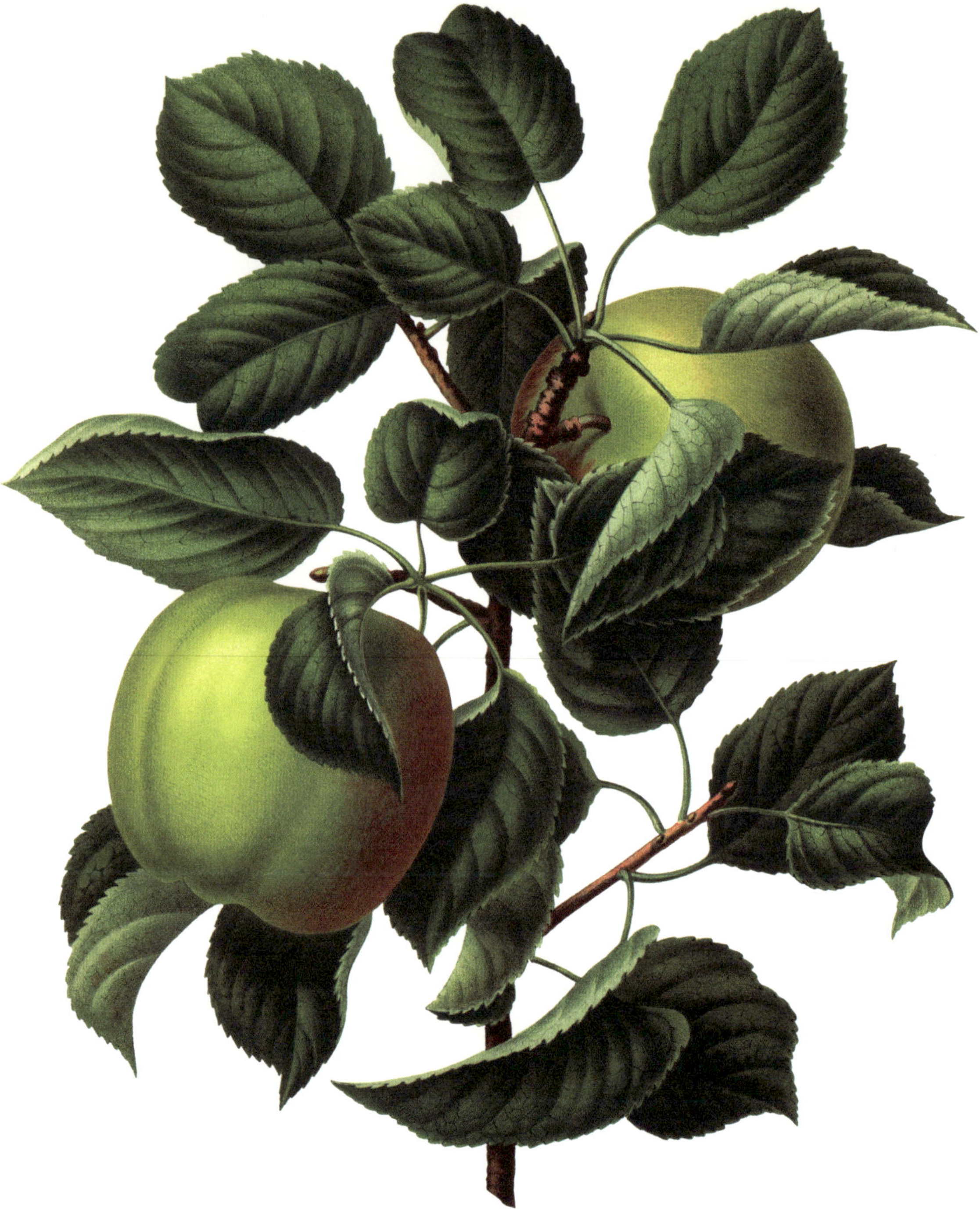

Malus domestica 'Ribston Pippin' × 'Nonpareil'
by Abraham Jacobus Wendel

Sturmer Pippin apple

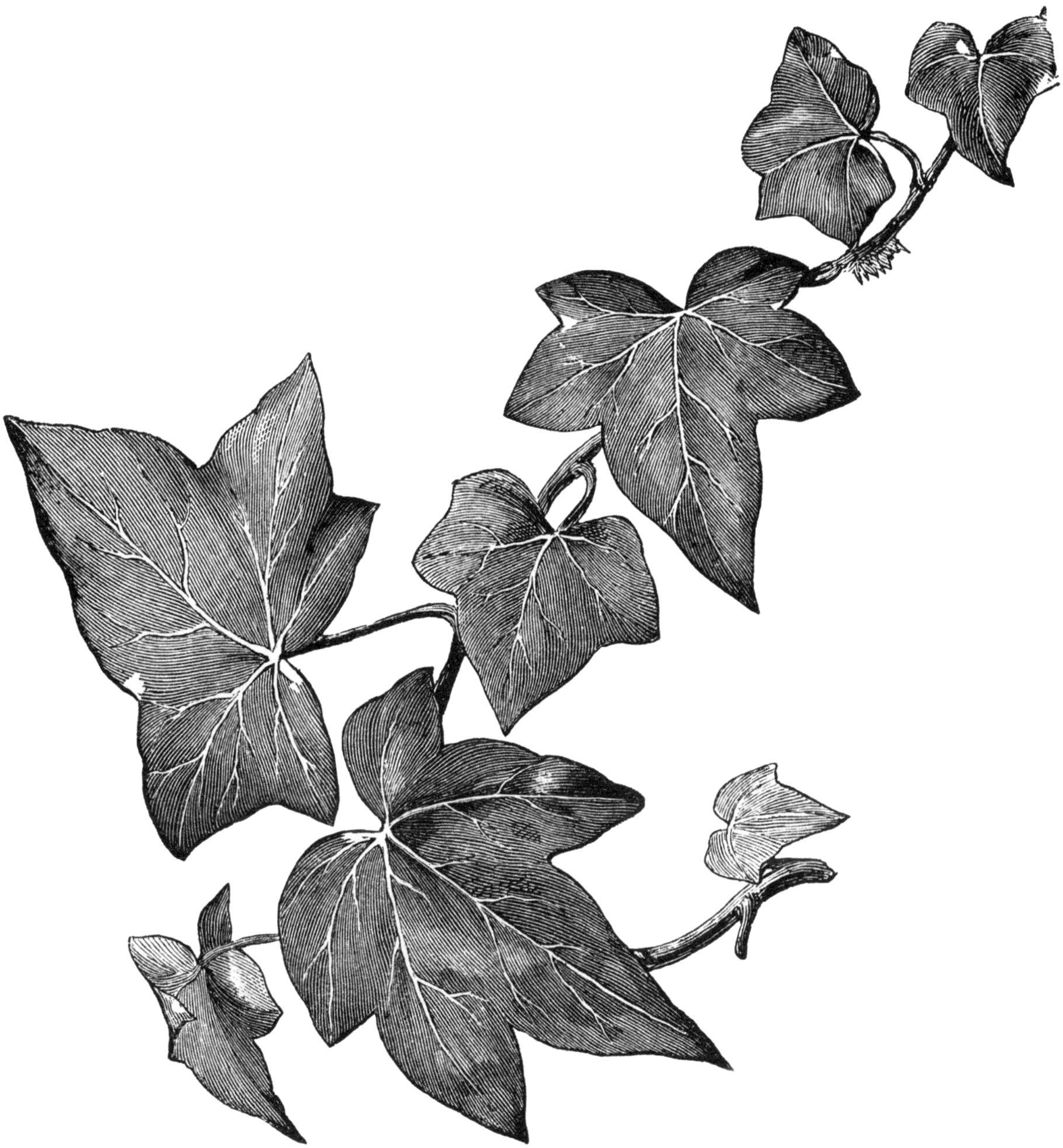

Hedera helix
by James Shirley Hibberd

common ivy | English ivy | European ivy

Chrysanthemum
by William Morris

chrysanthemum | mums

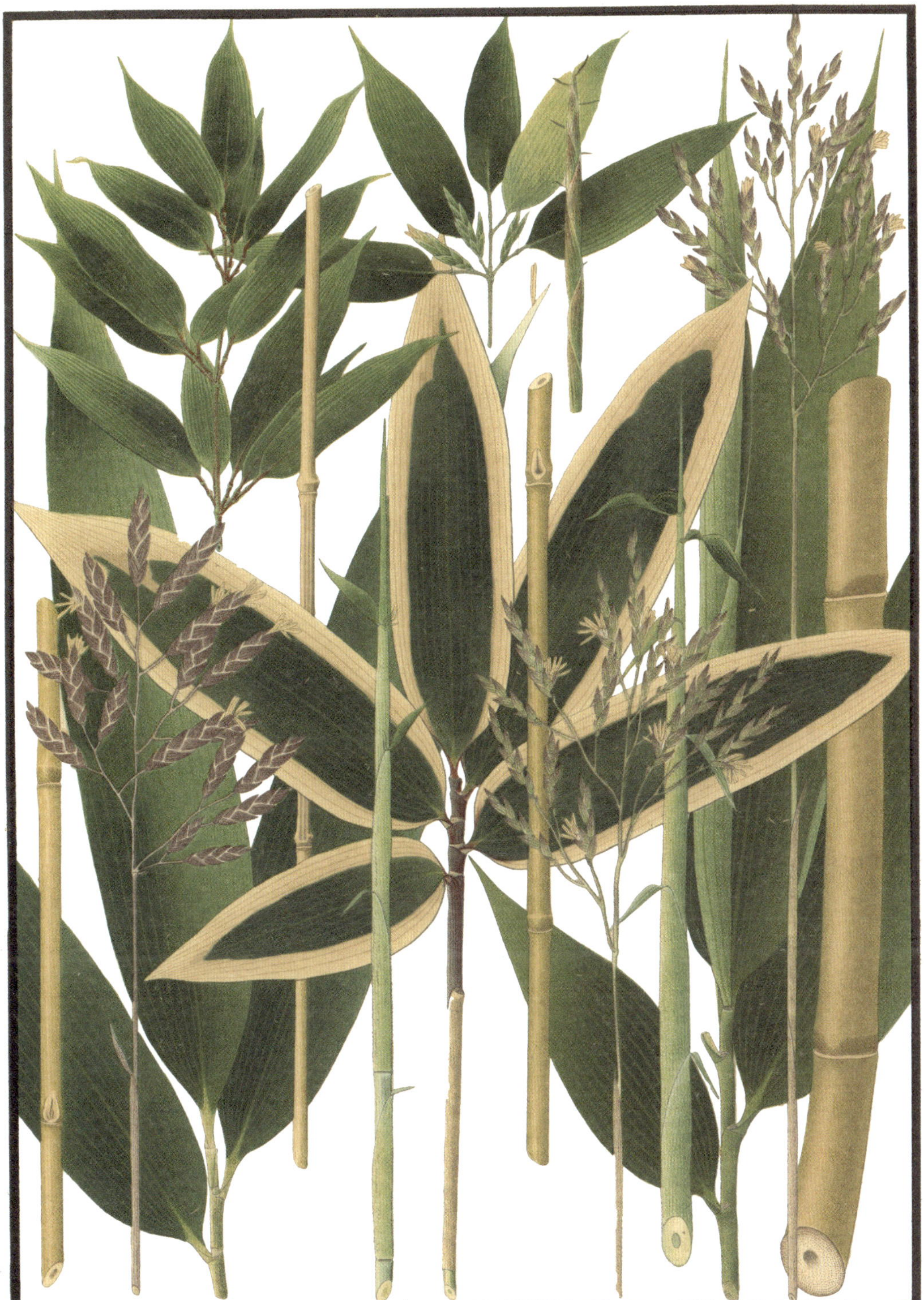

Phyllostachys and *Sasa*
by Yasuyoshi Shirasawa

bamboo (various)

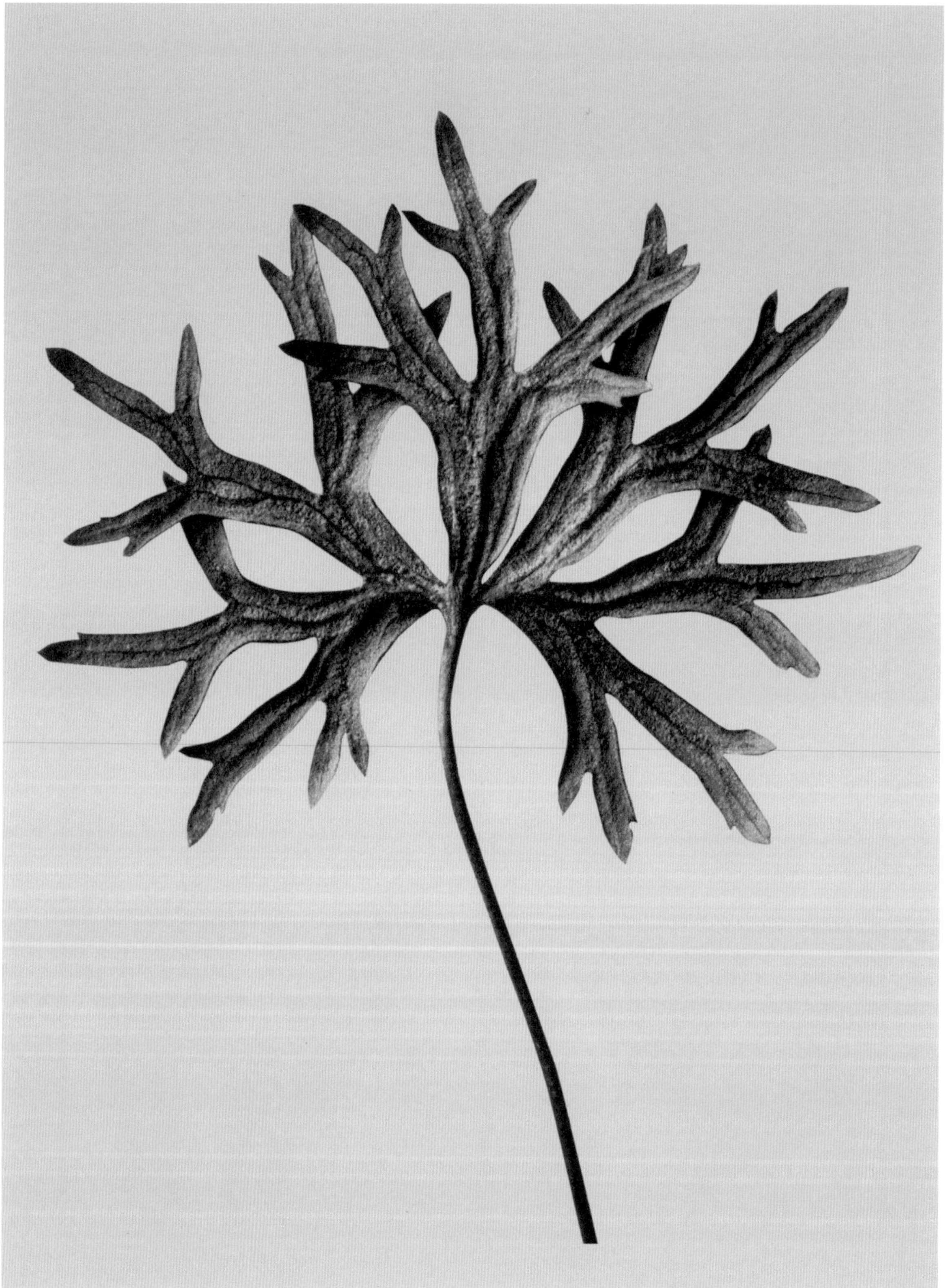

Aconitum anthora
by Karl Blossfeldt

yellow monkshood | yellow helmetflower | wholesome wolf's bane

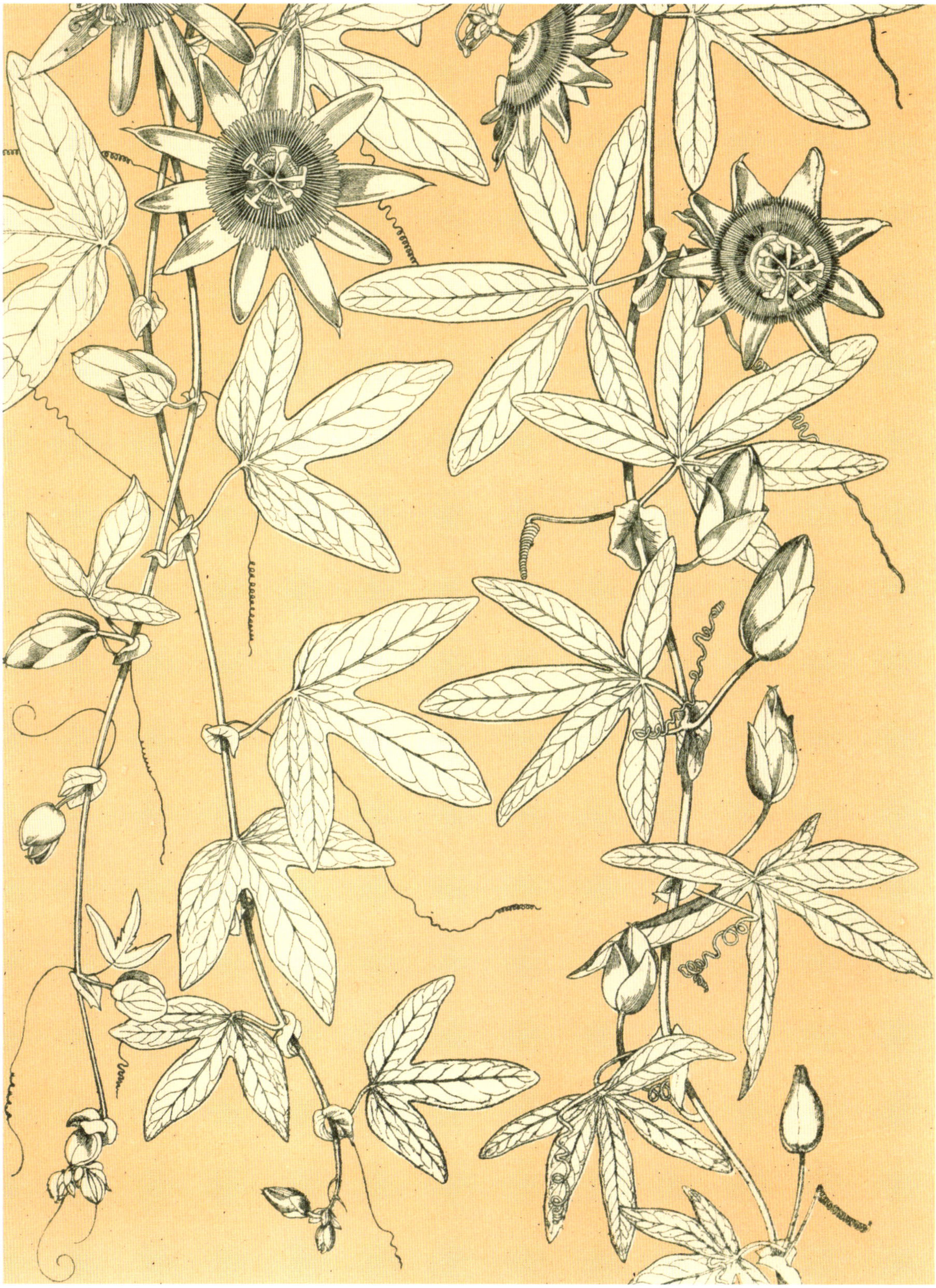

Passiflora
by Owen Jones

passion flower | passion vine

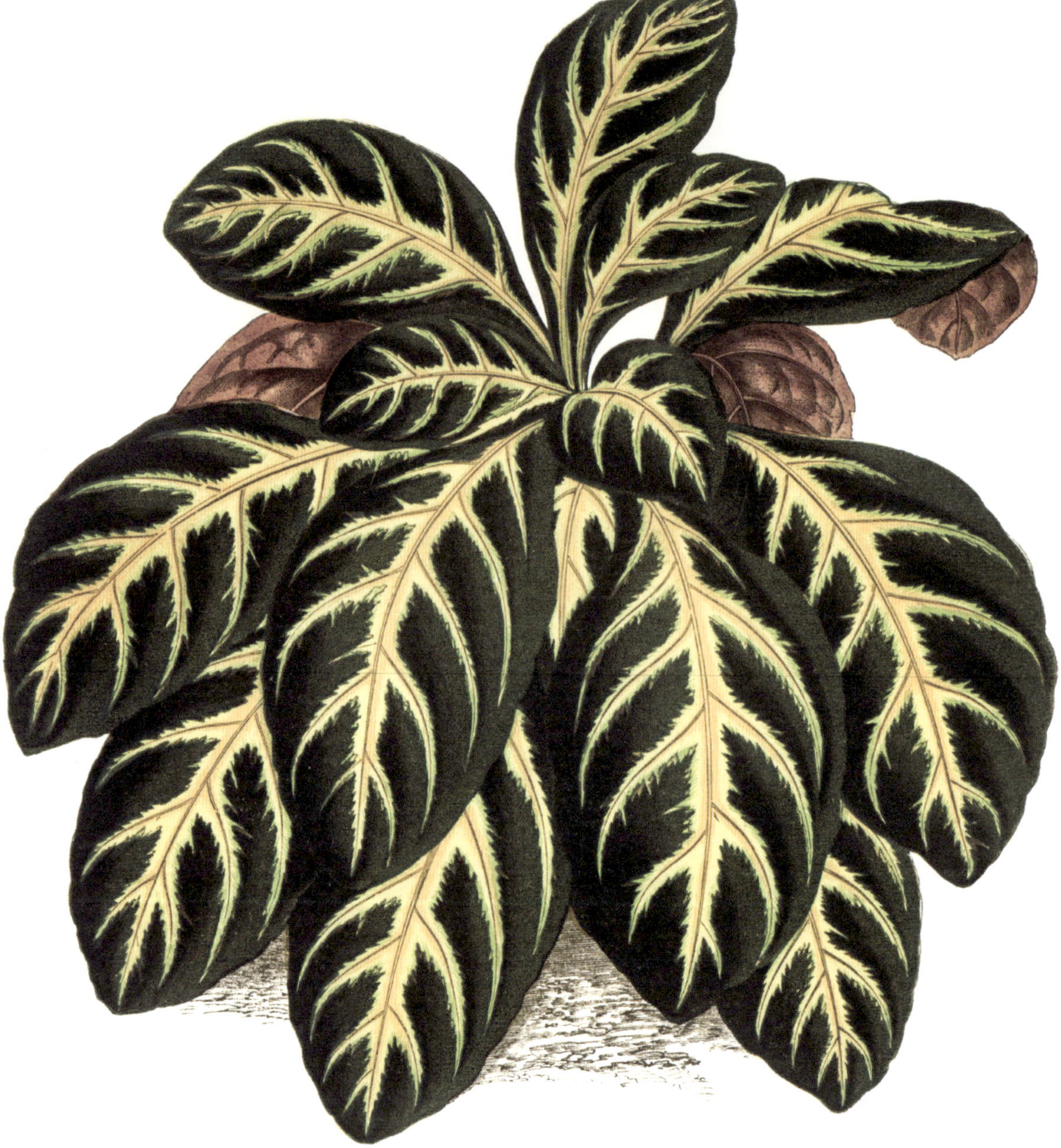

Xantheranthemum igneum
by Benjamin Fawcett & James Shirley Hibberd

golden vein plant | bronze vein plant

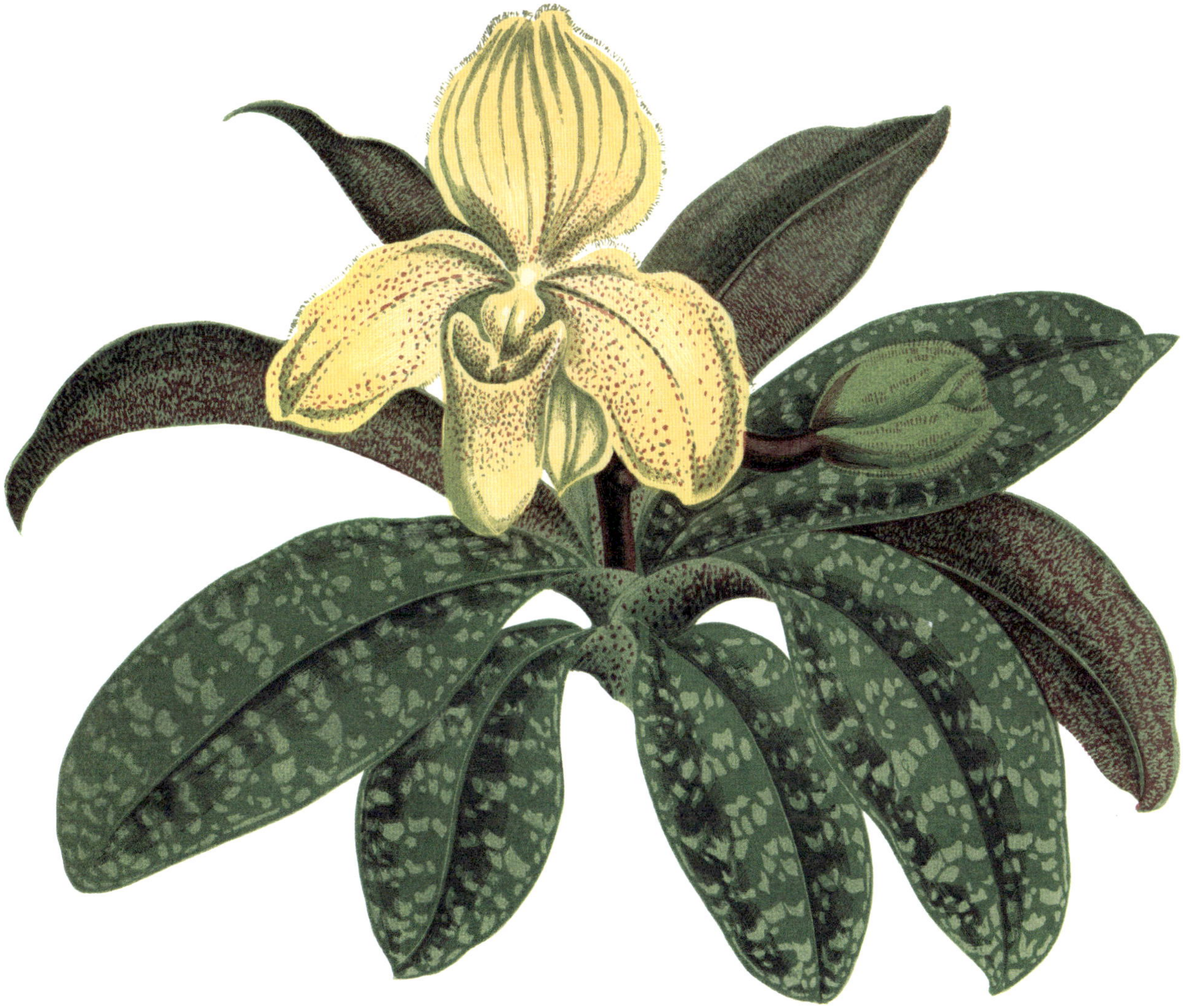

Paphiopedilum concolor
by Alexander Francis Lydon & Benjamin Fawcett

one-coloured paph | yellow slipper orchid | lady slipper orchid

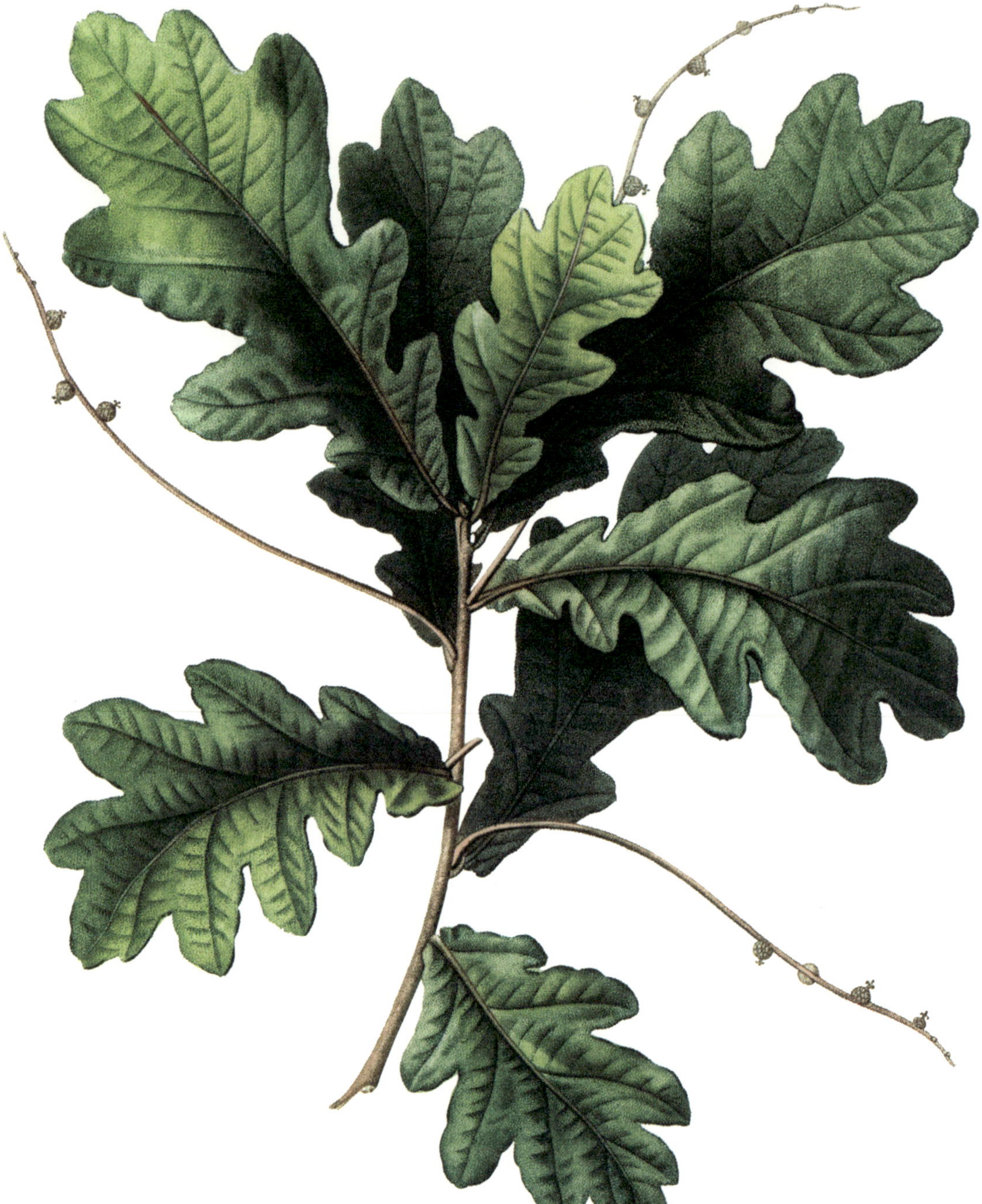

Quercus robur subsp. *robur*
by PIERRE-JOSEPH REDOUTÉ

common oak | English oak | pedunculate oak

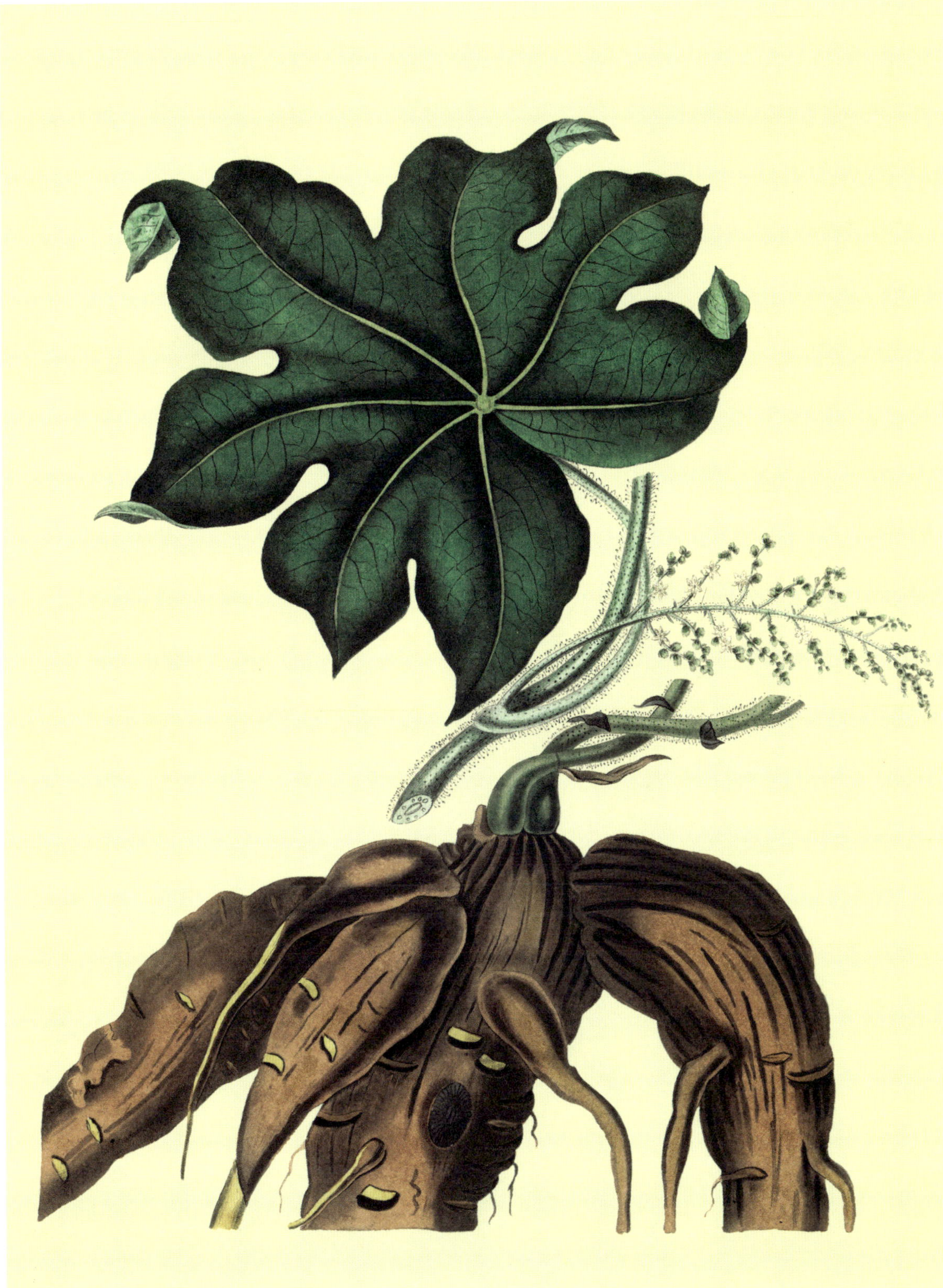

Jateorhiza palmata
by JOHN STEPHENSON & JAMES MORSS CHURCHILL

calumba | colombo

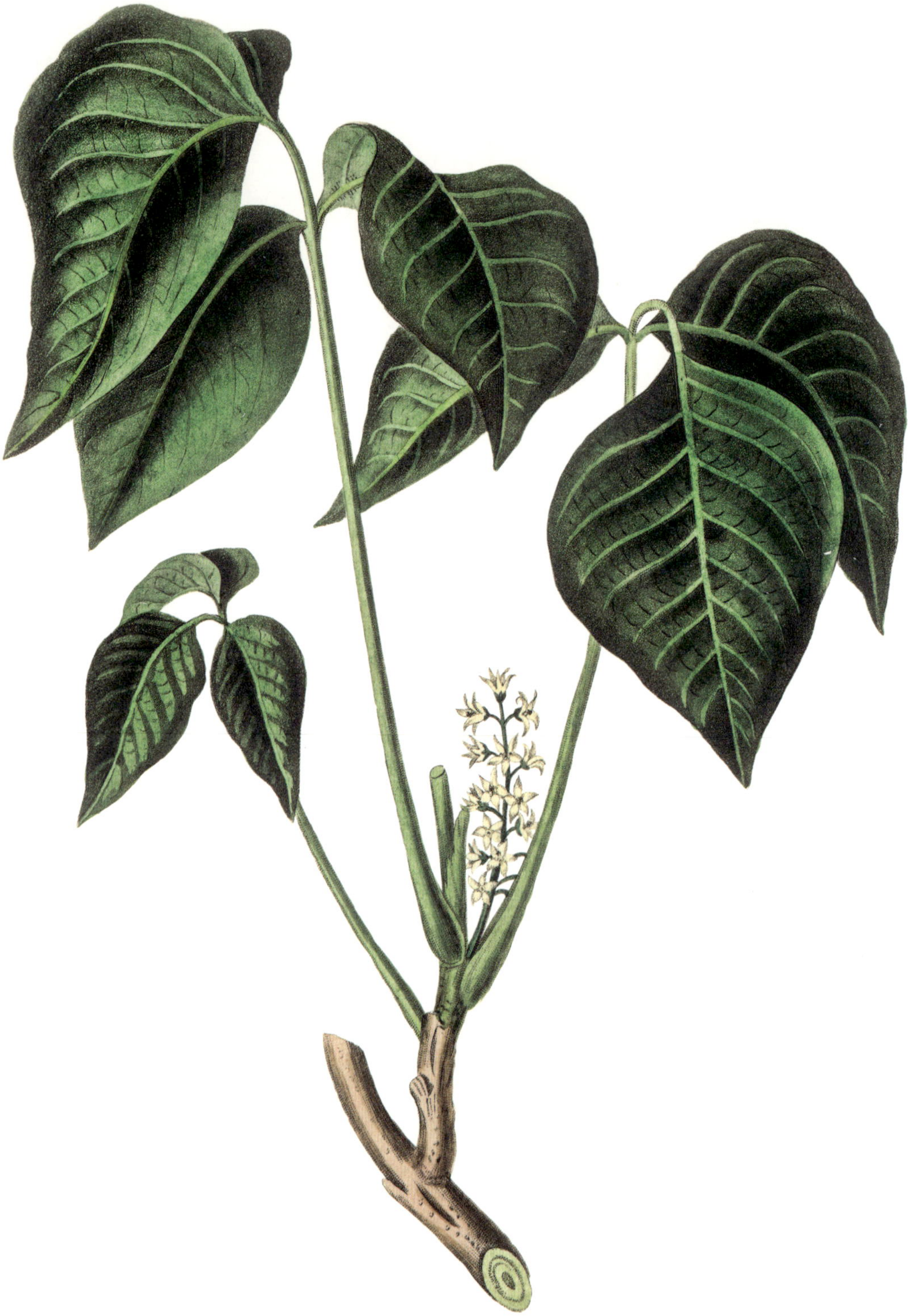

Toxicodendron radicans
by JOHN STEPHENSON & JAMES MORSS CHURCHILL

poison ivy

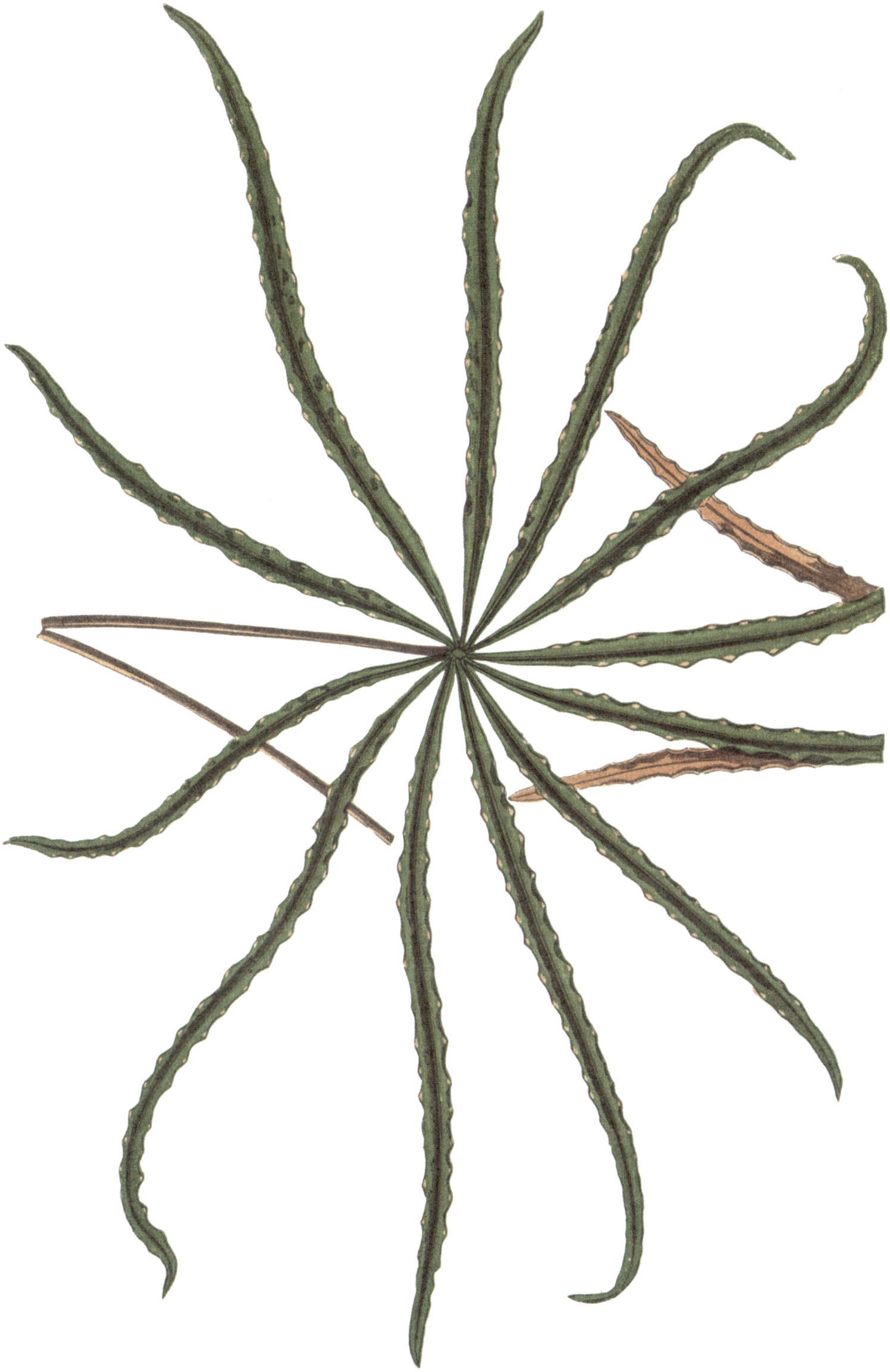

Plerandra veitchii
by BENJAMIN FAWCETT & JAMES SHIRLEY HIBBERD

plerandra veitchii

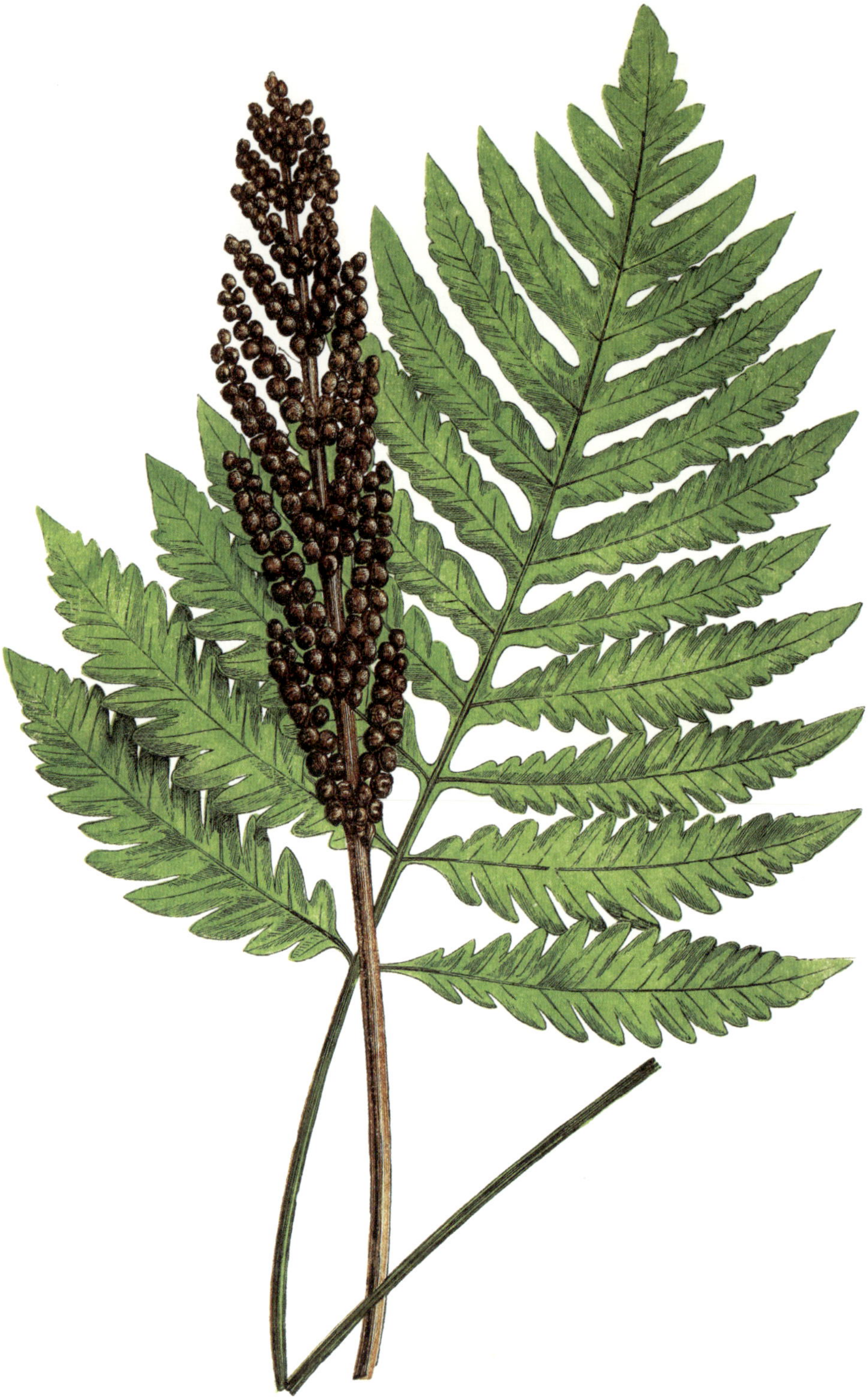

Onoclea sensibilis
by Edward Joseph Lowe

sensitive fern | bead fern

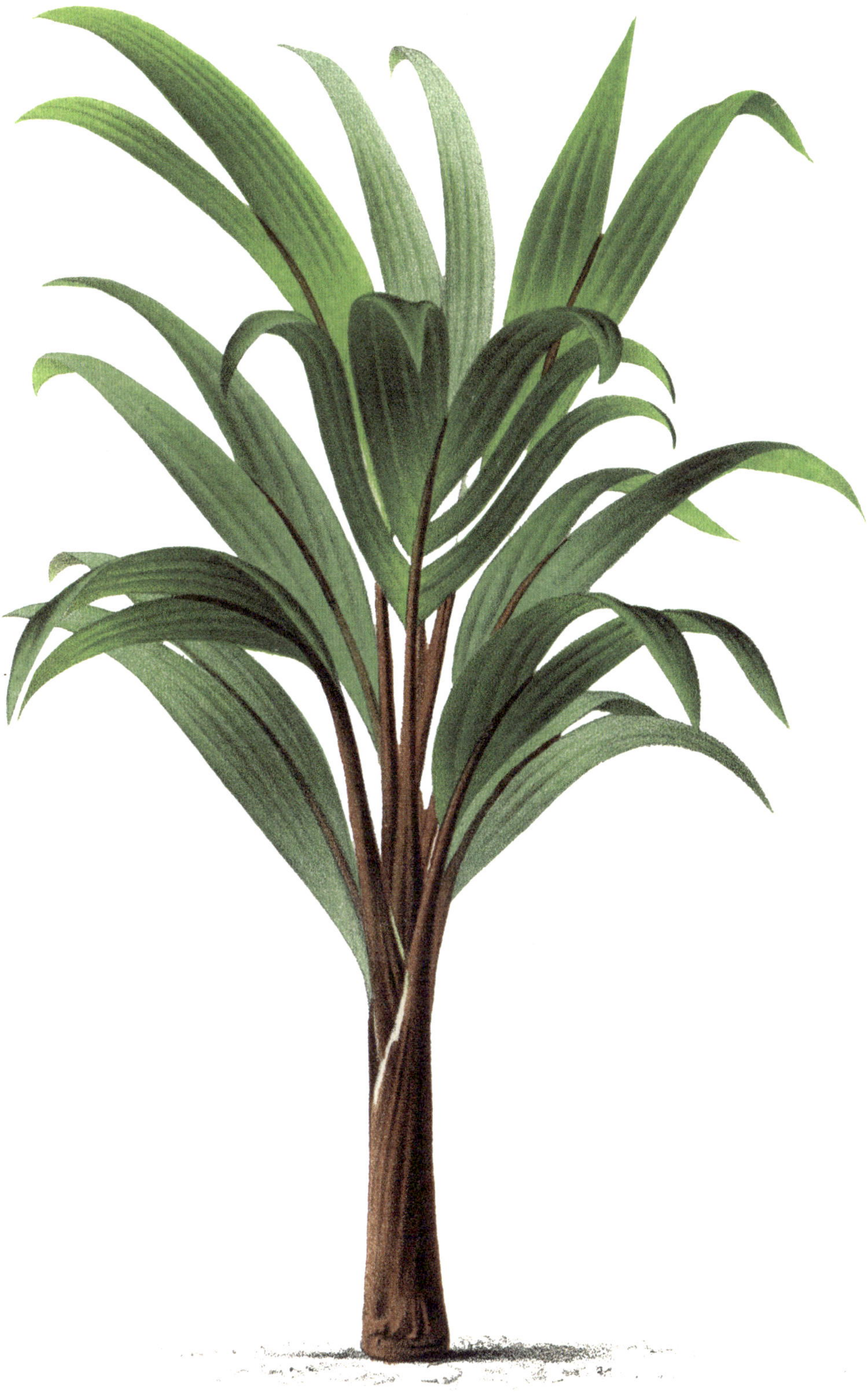

Hyophorbe amaricaulis
by Oswald de Kerchove de Denterghem

loneliest palm

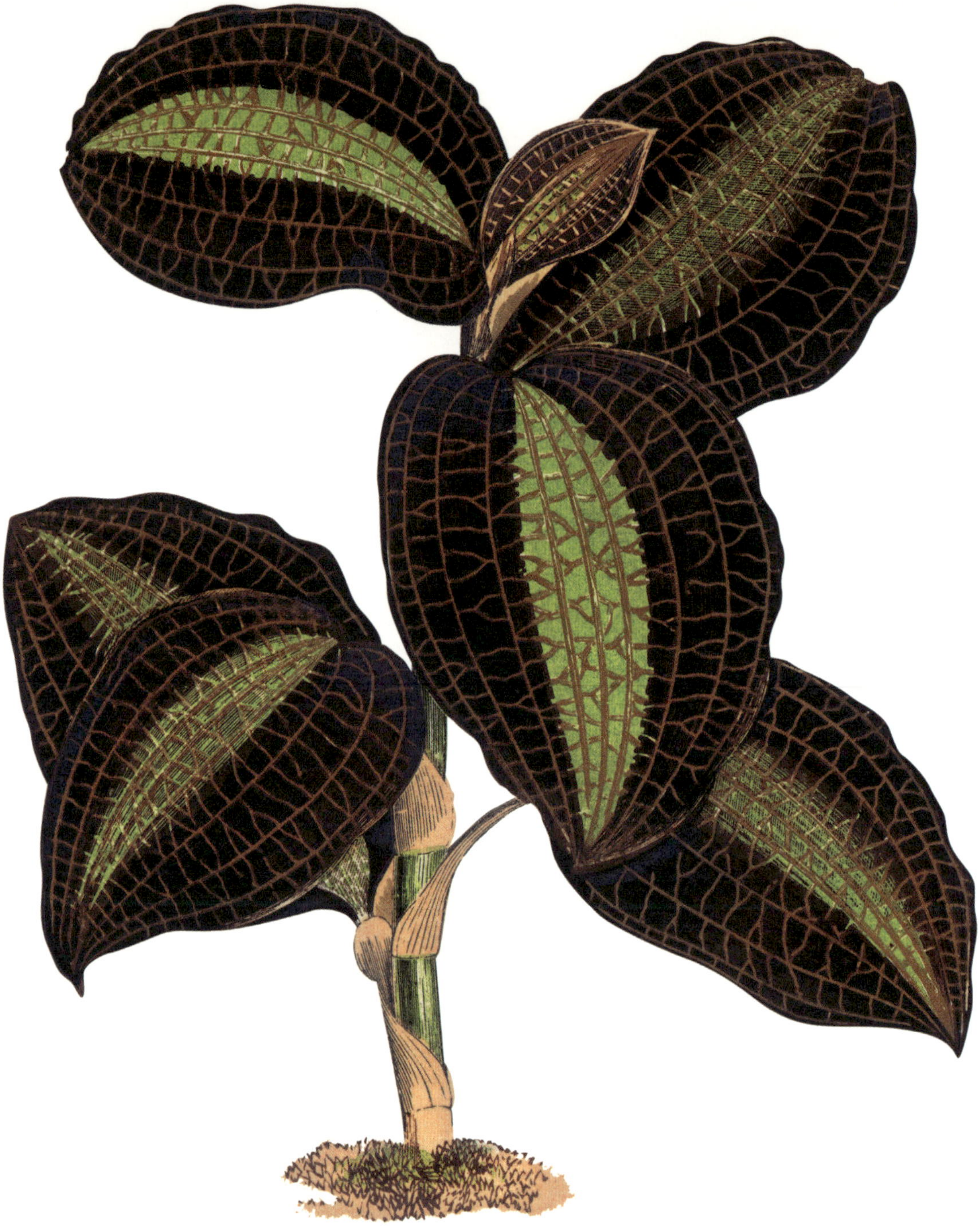

Anoectochilus roxburghii
by Alexander Francis Lydon & Benjamin Fawcett

golden vein jewel orchid

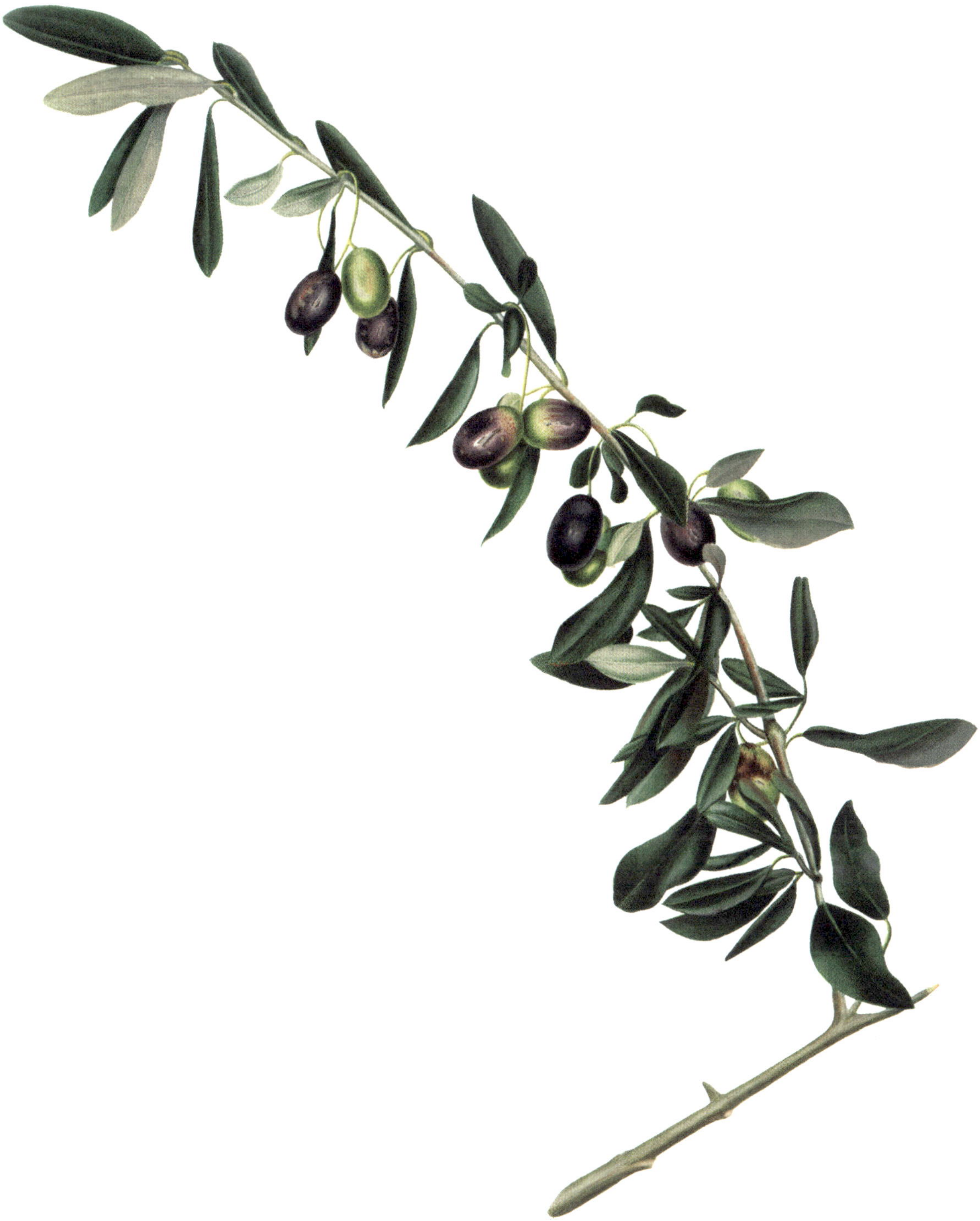

Olea europaea var. *sativa*
by Giorgio Gallesio

olive | garden olive

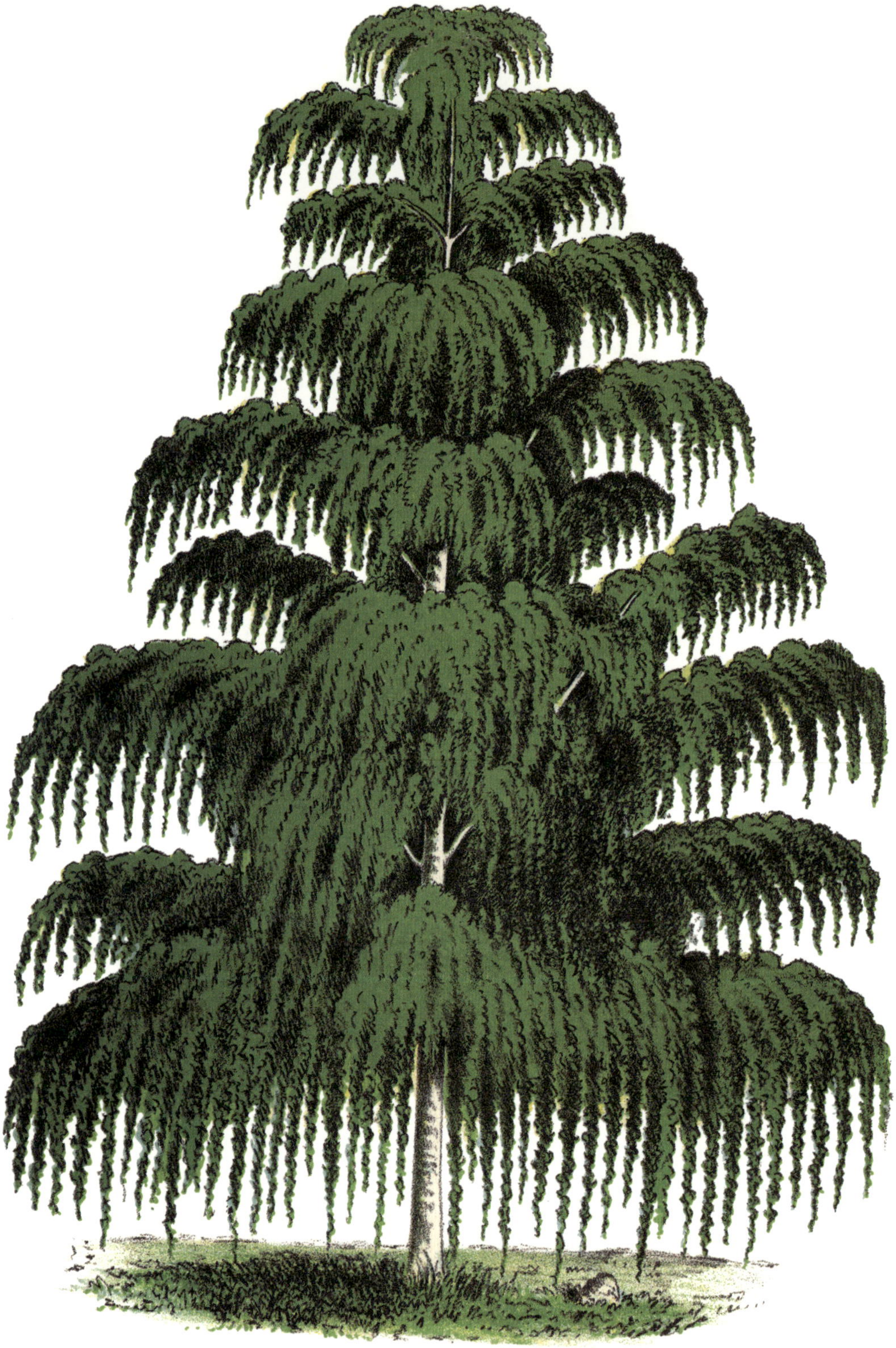

Betula pendula
by Rochester Lithographing & Printing Company

weeping birch | silver birch | European white birch | East Asian white birch

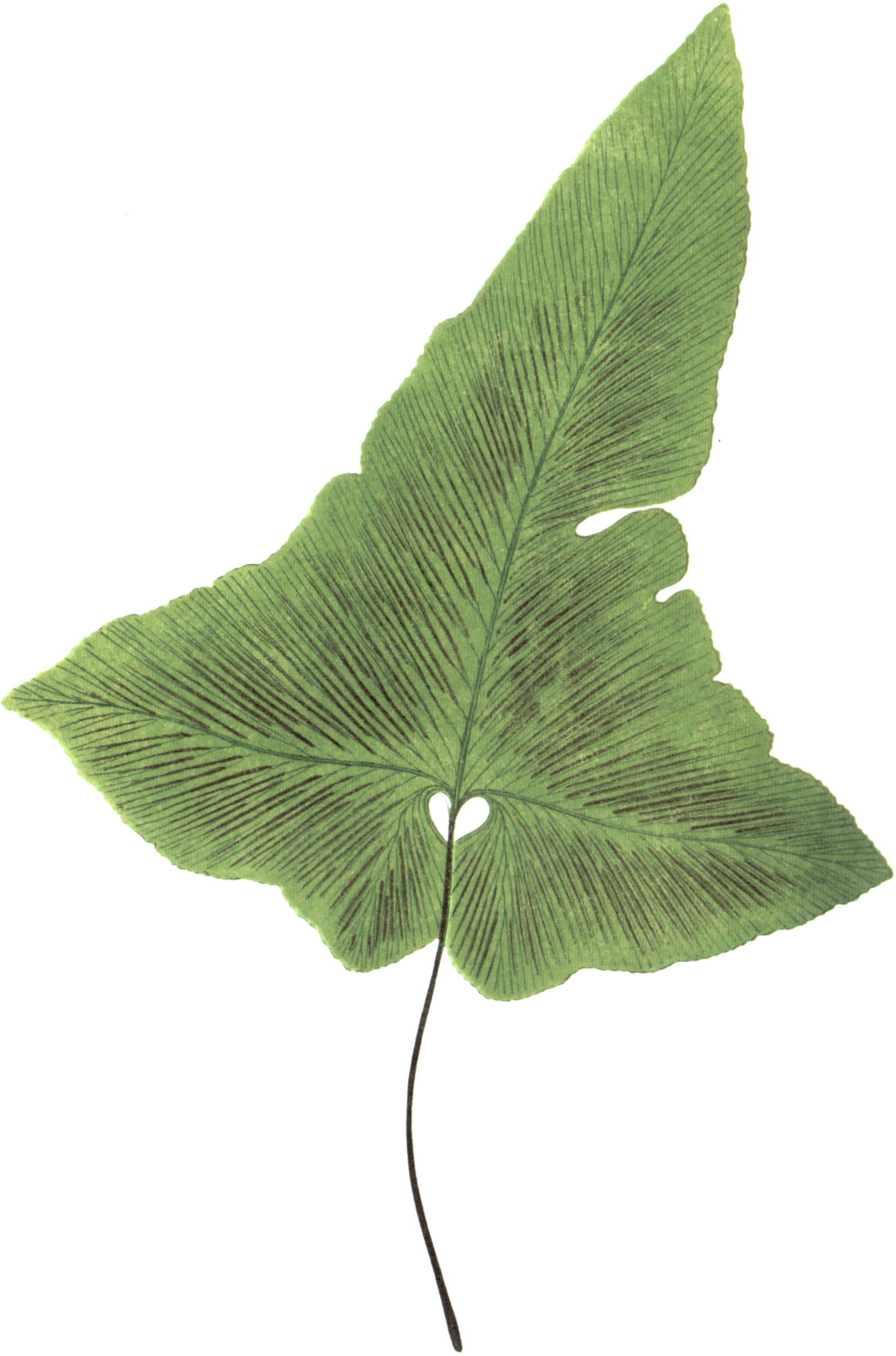

Asplenium hemionitis
by Edward Joseph Lowe

heart fern | heart-leaf fern

The clearest way into
the Universe is through
a forest wilderness.

JOHN MUIR

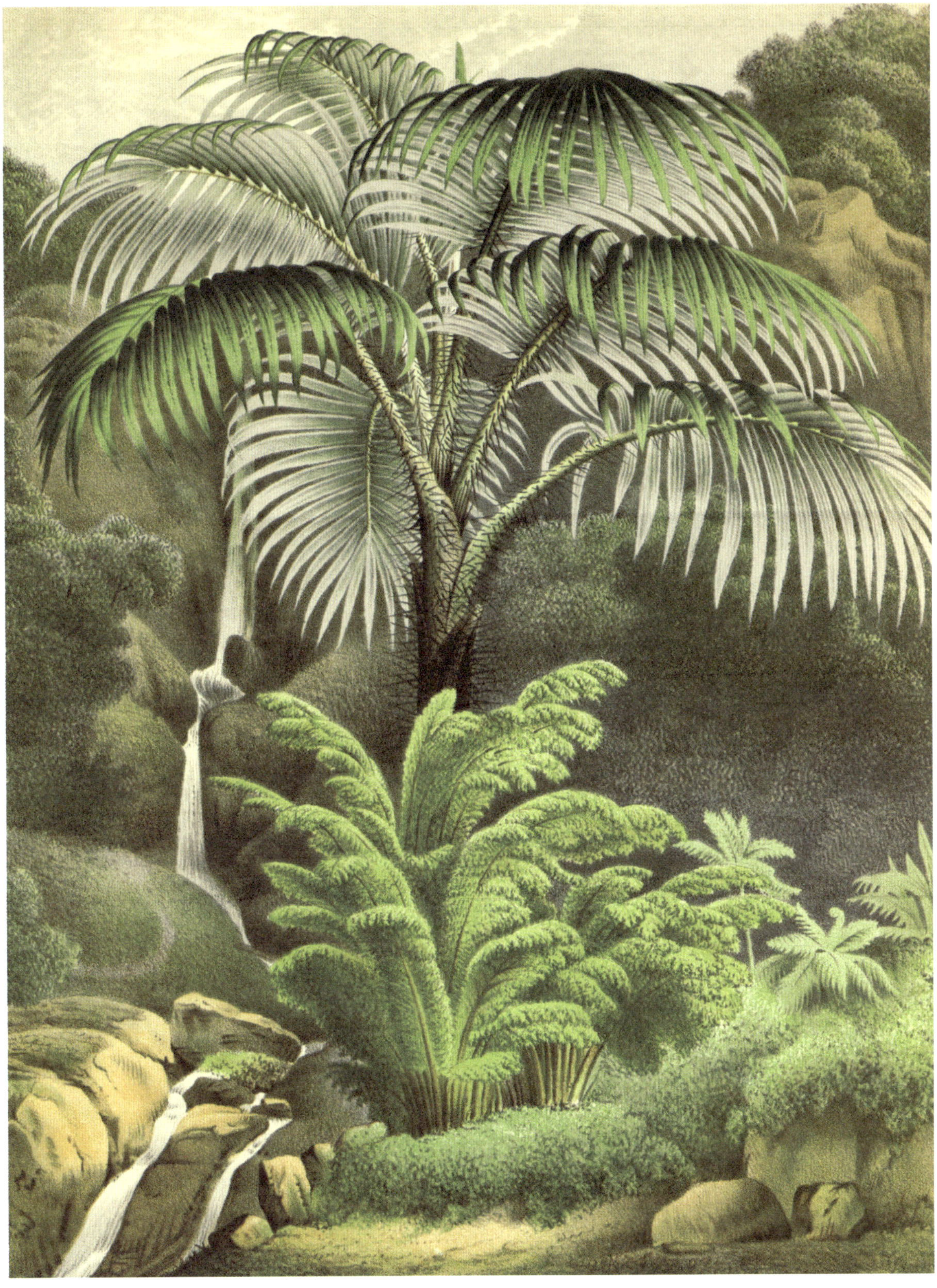

Acanthophoenix crinita
by Louis van Houtte

white barbel palm

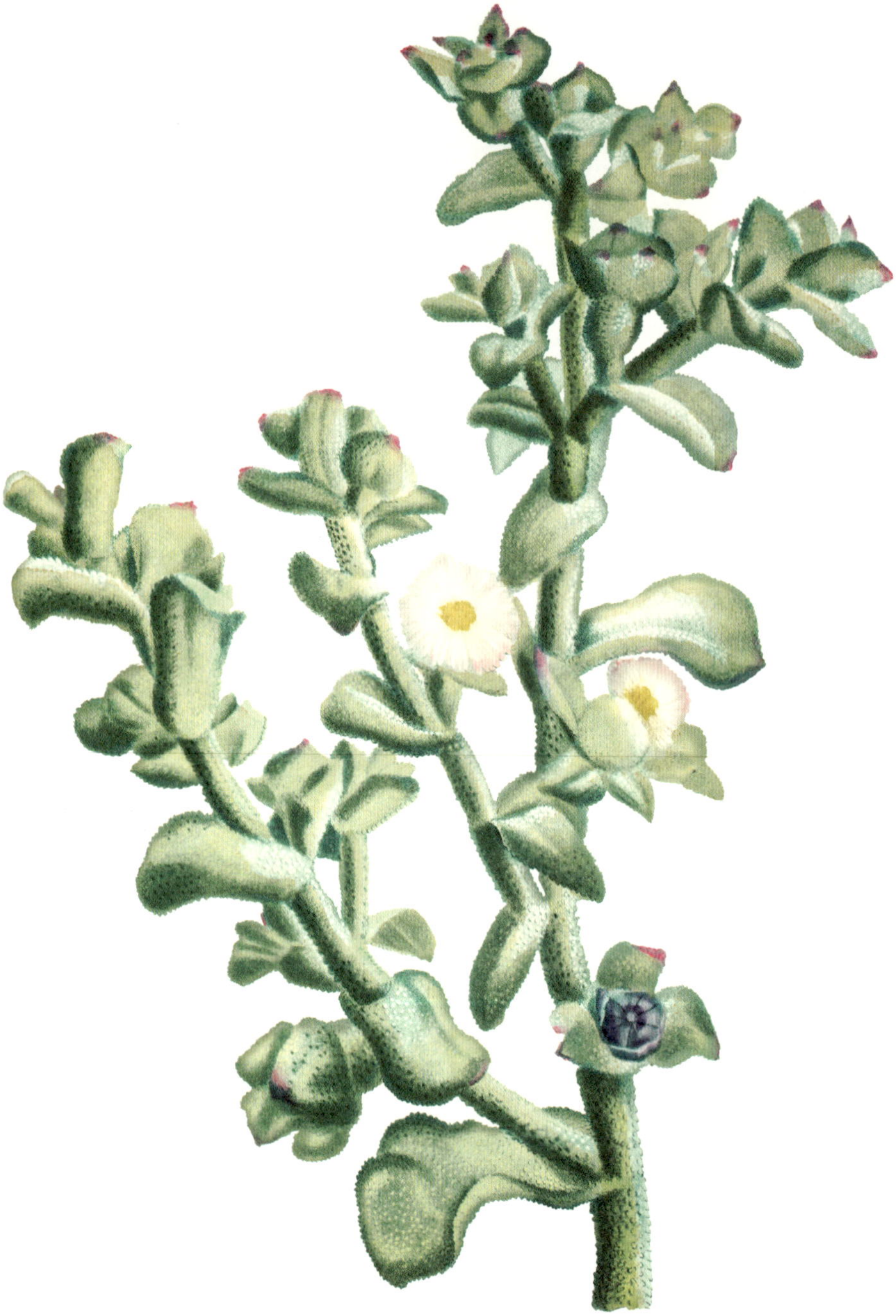

Mesembryanthemum crystallinum
by Pierre-Joseph Redouté

common iceplant

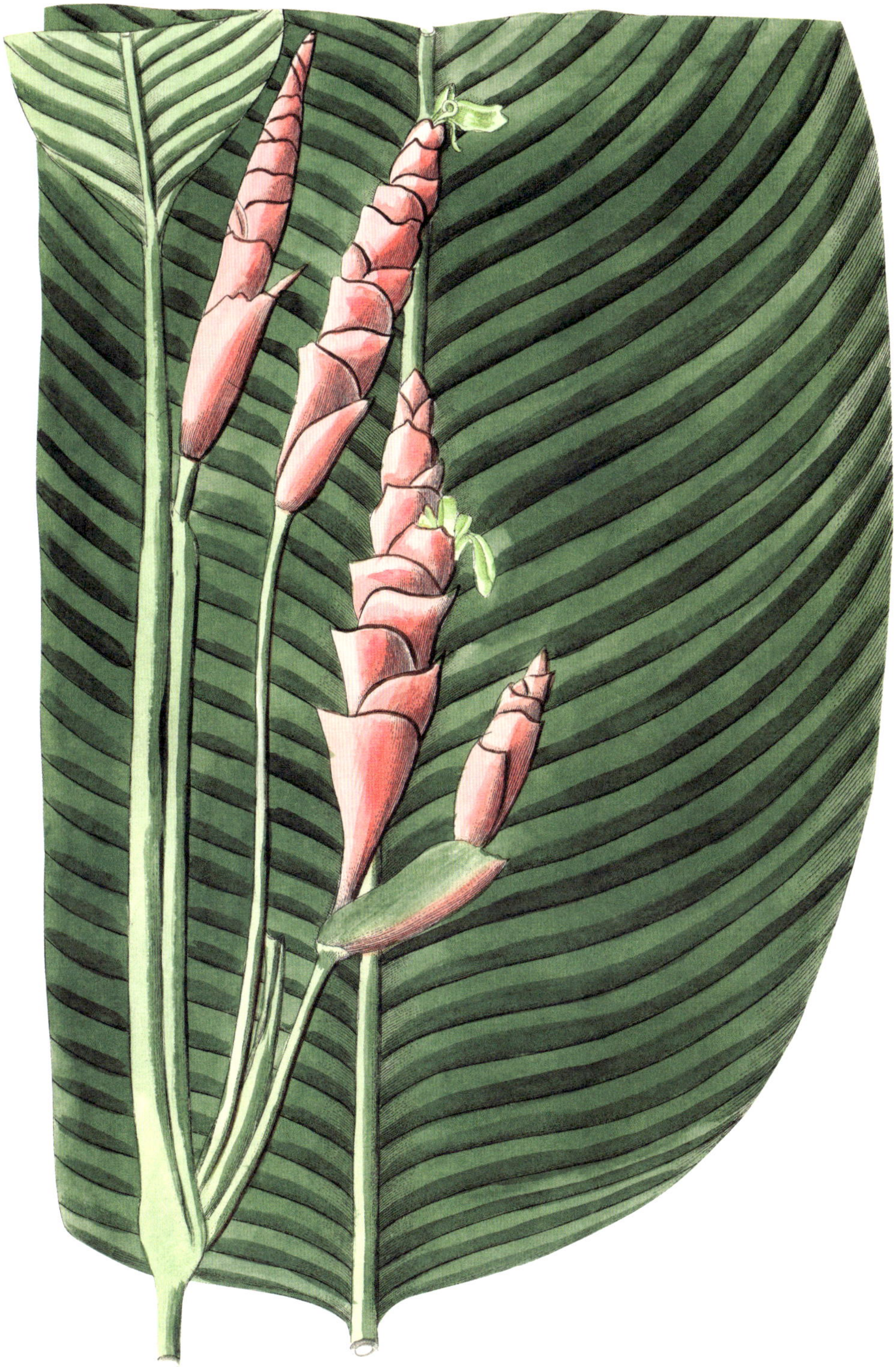

Calathea lutea
by Karl Blossfeldt

bijao | cigar calathea | Cuban cigar | Mexican cigar plant

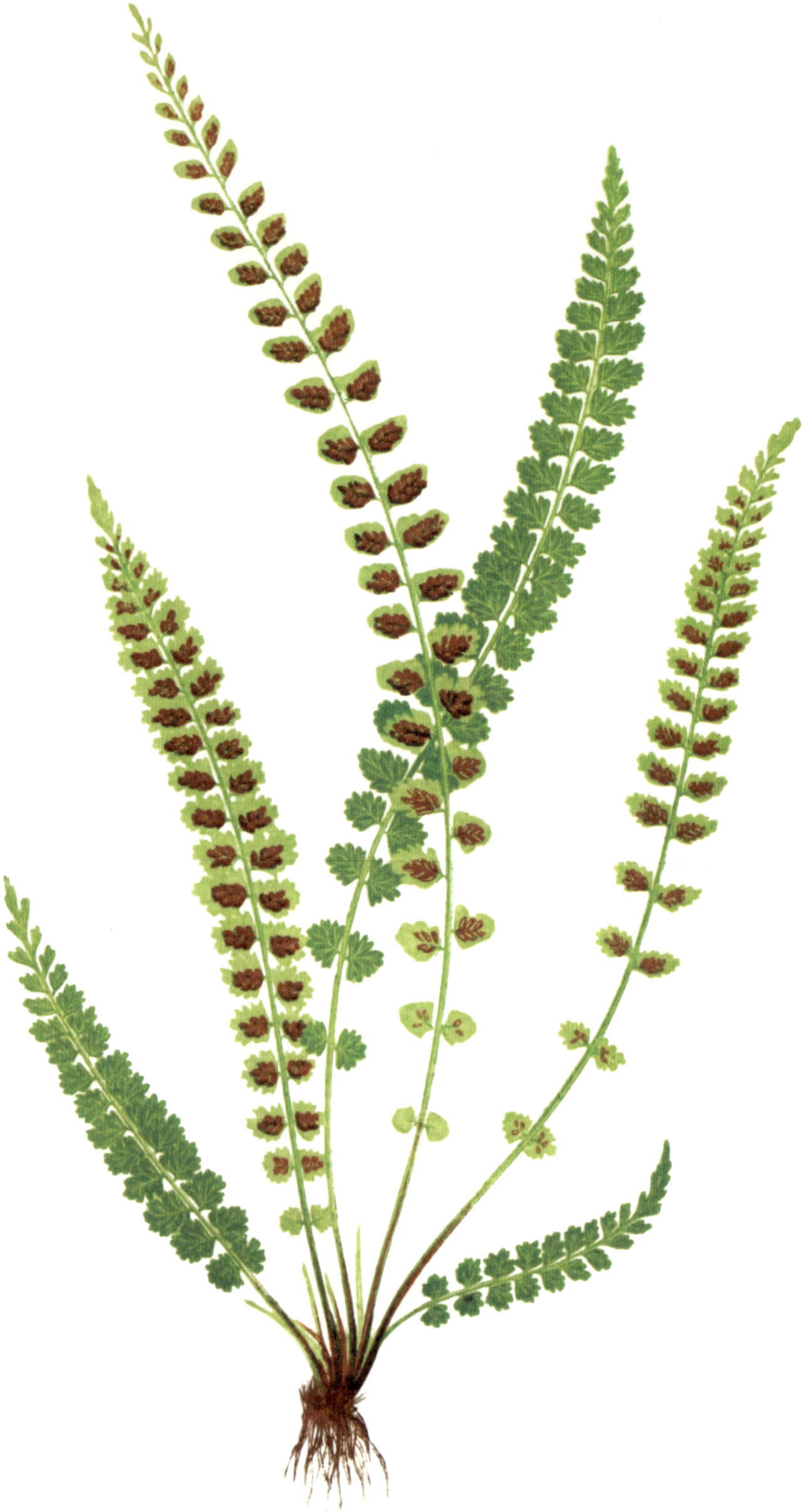

Asplenium viride
by Edward Joseph Lowe

green spleenwort

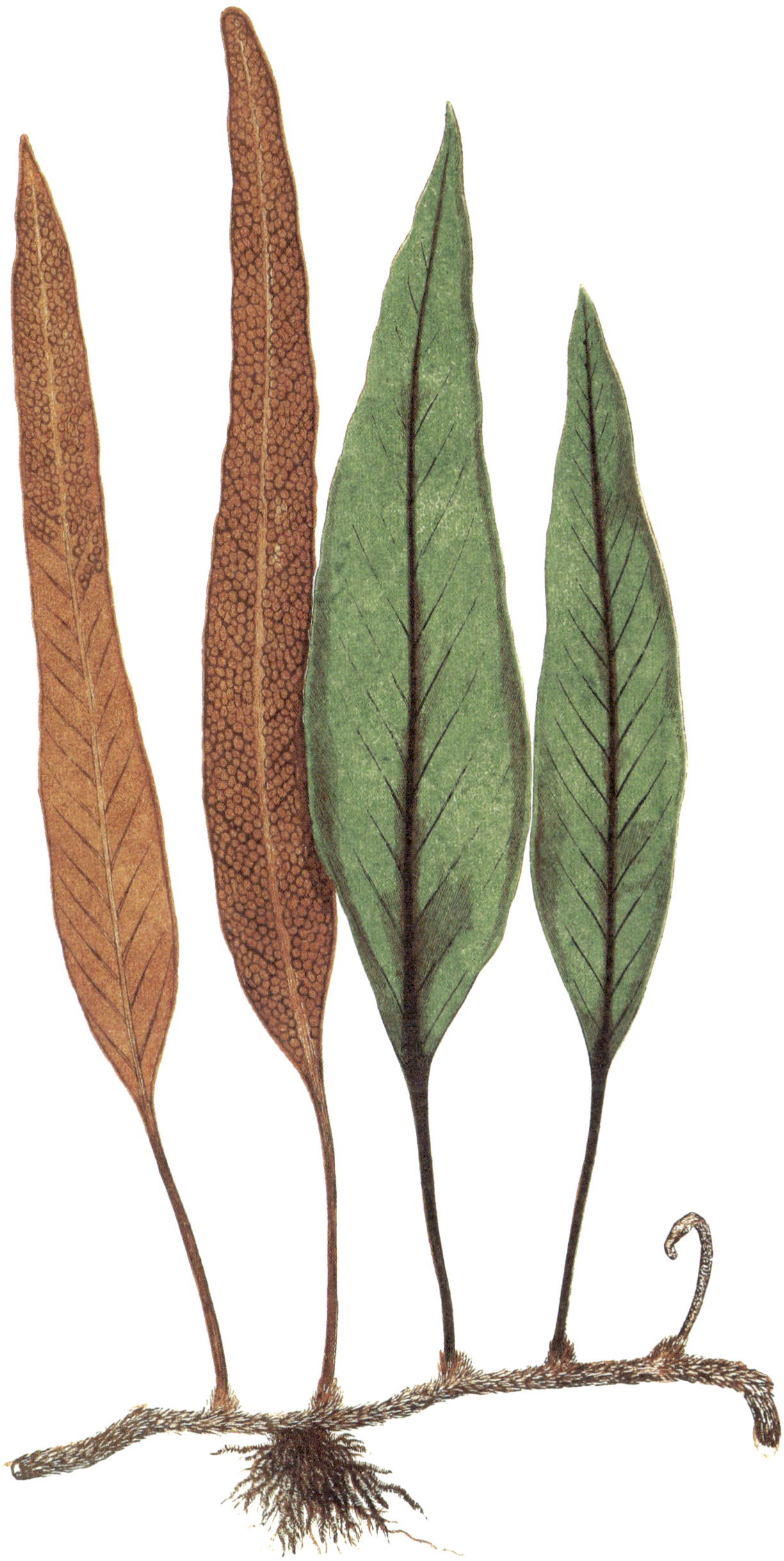

Pyrrosia lingua
by Edward Joseph Lowe

tongue fern | Japanese felt fern

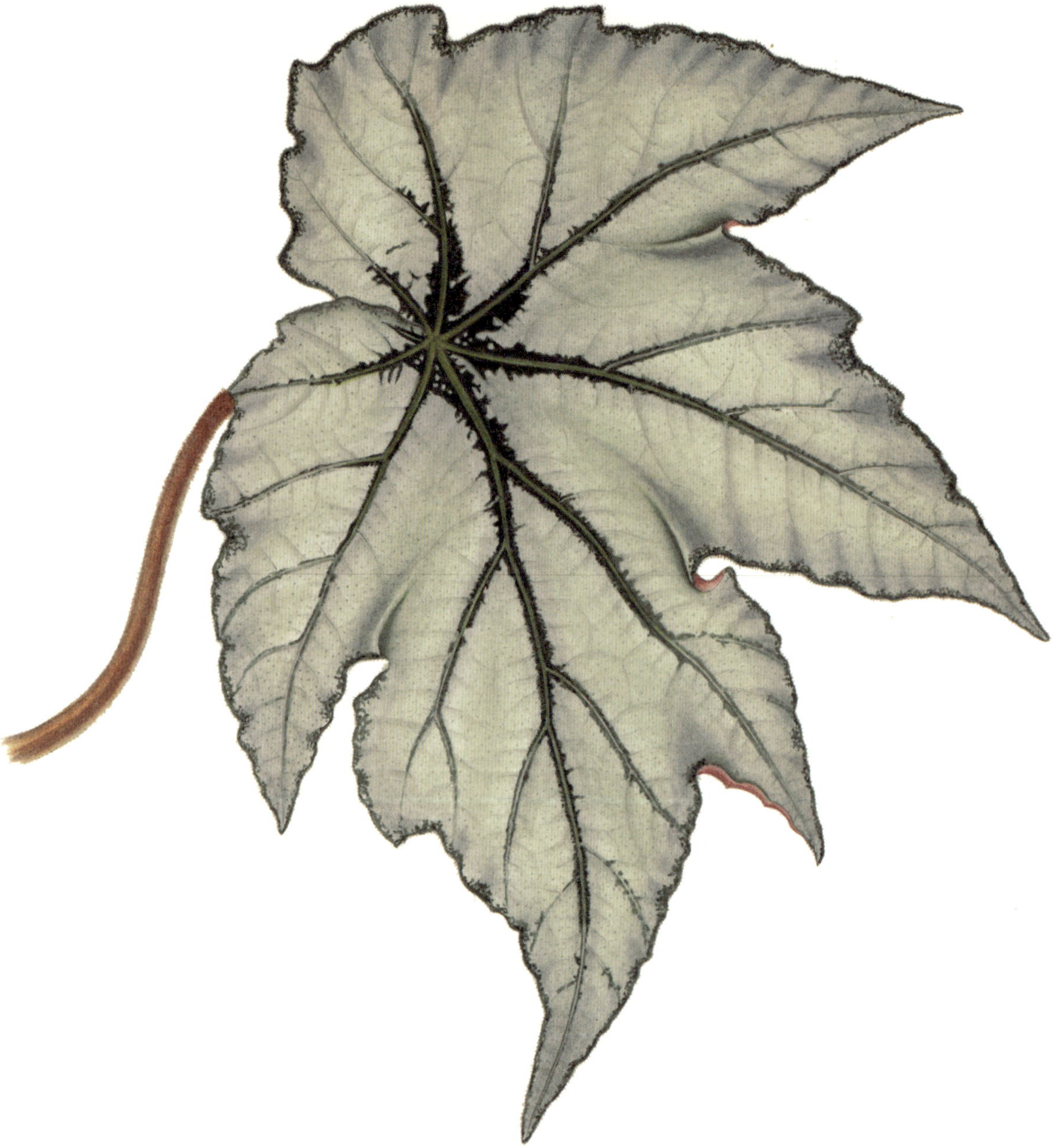

262

Begonia 'ricinifolia'
by George De Alwis

castor bean begonia | bronze-leaf begonia

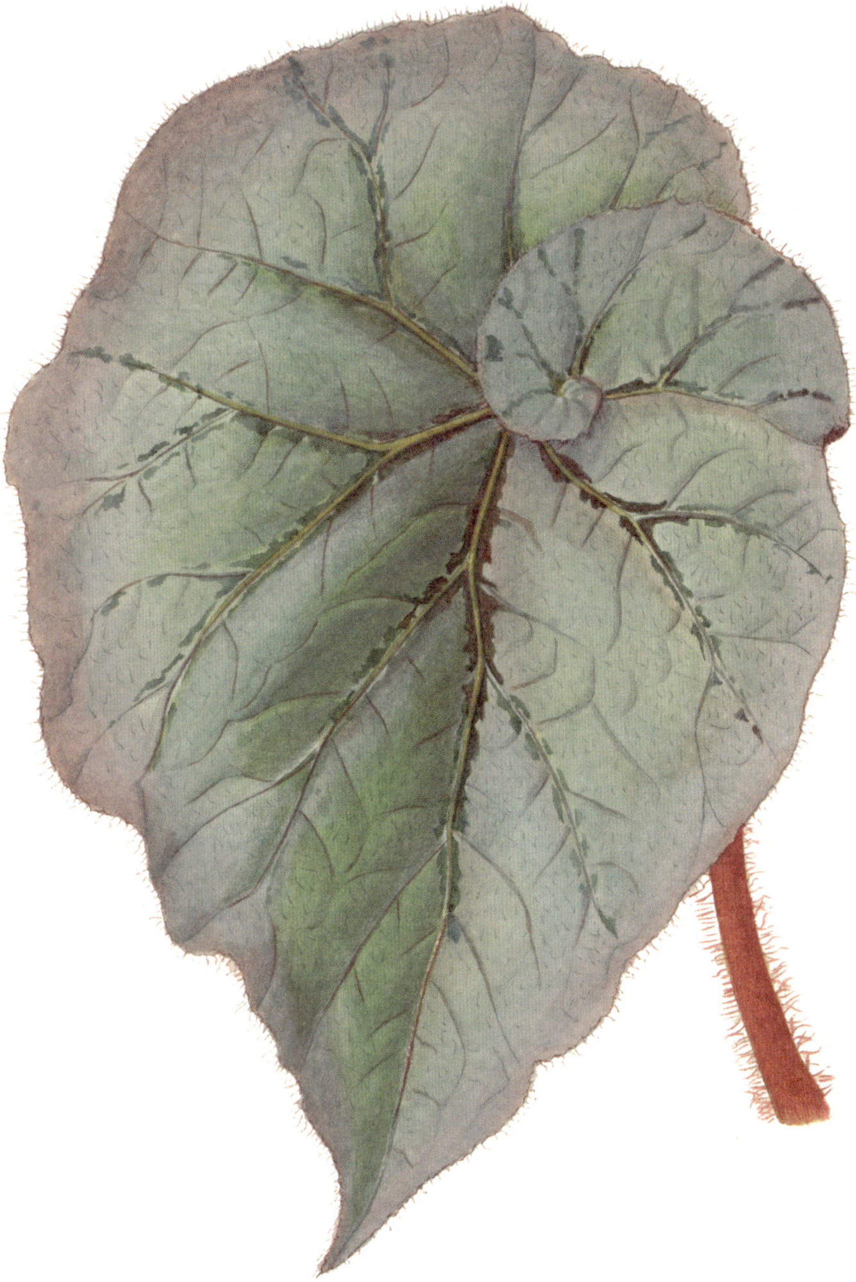

Begonia rex
by GEORGE DE ALWIS

king begonia | fancy-leaf begonia | painted-leaf begonia

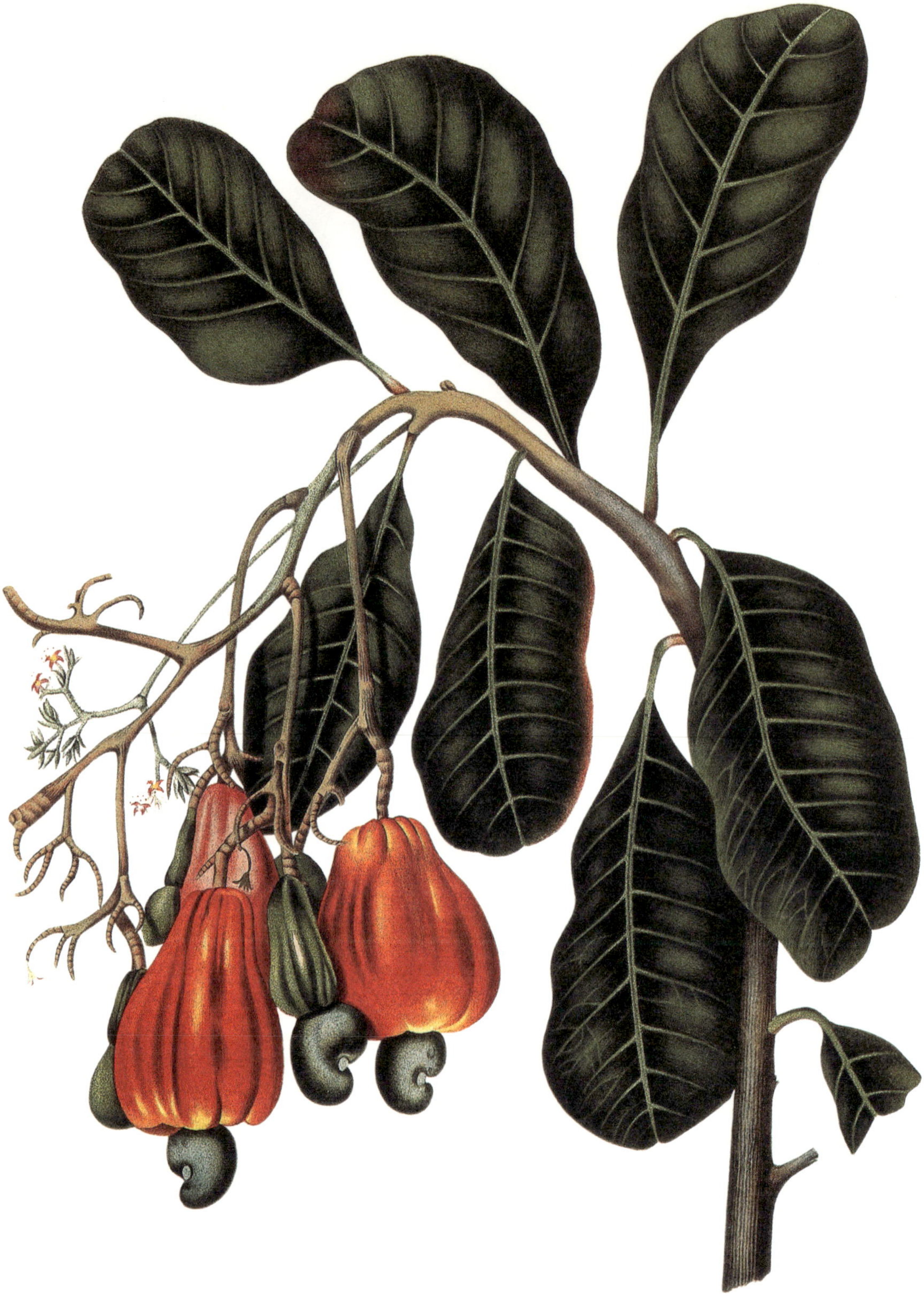

Anacardium occidentale L.
by Pieter de Pannemaeker

cashew nut tree

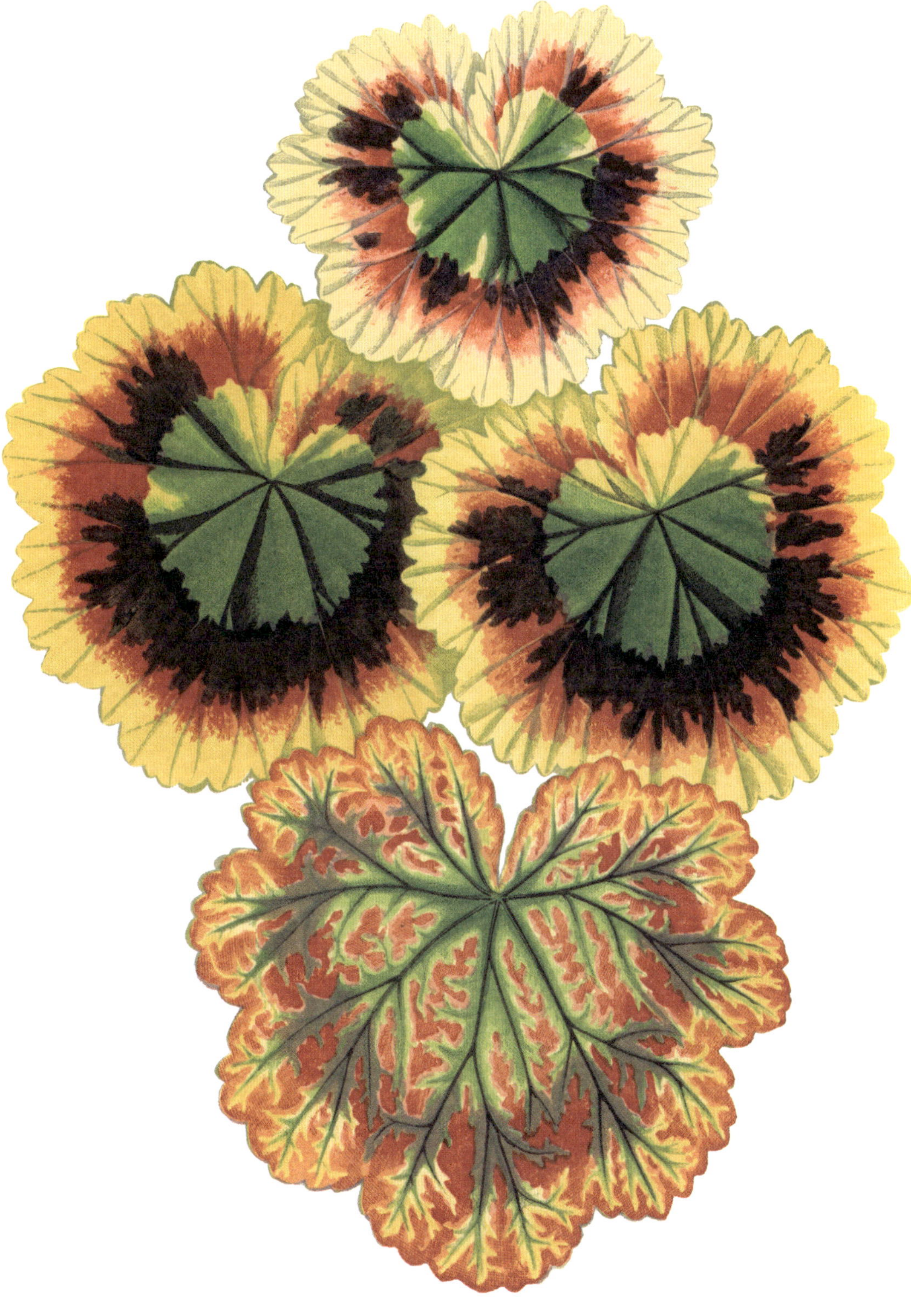

Geranium
by Benjamin Fawcett & James Shirley Hibberd

geranium (various)

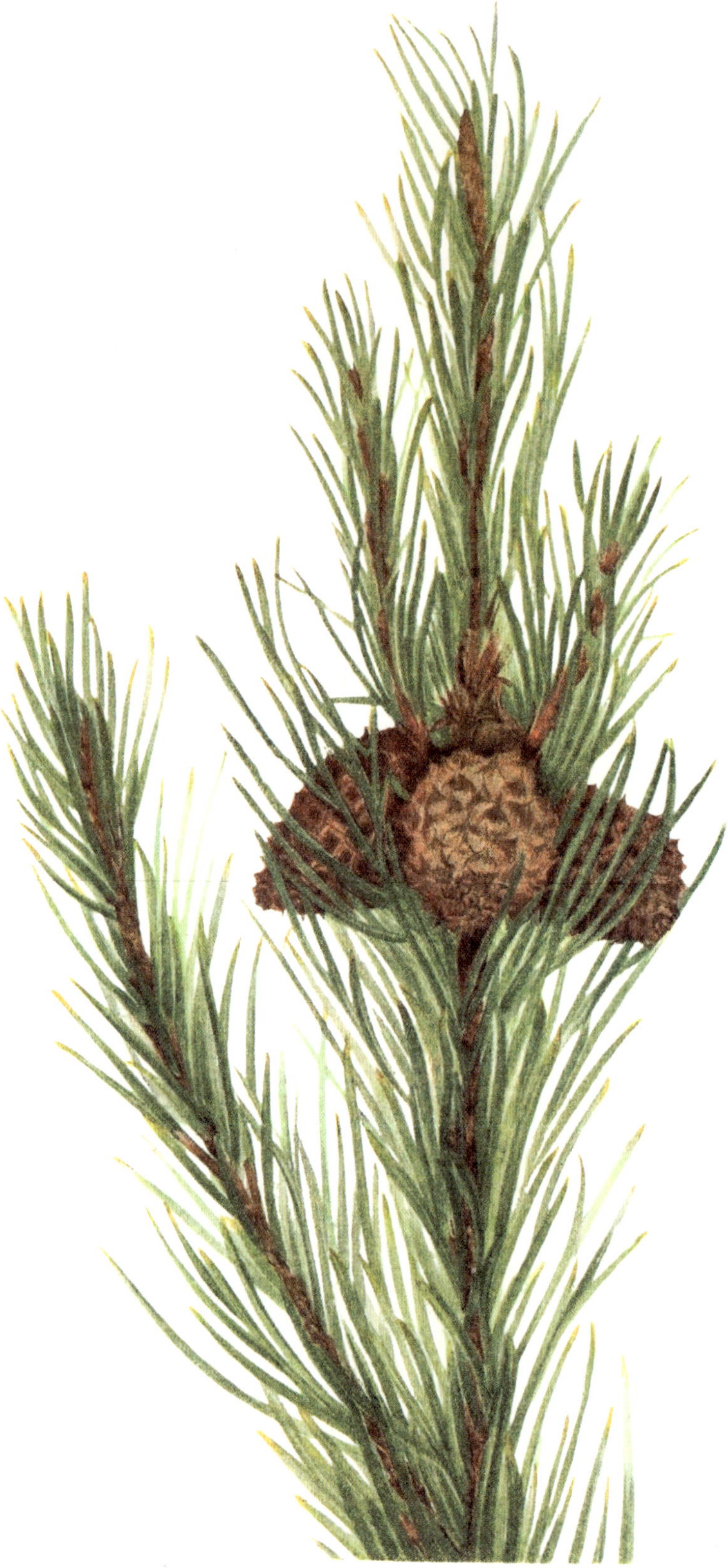

Pinus contorta
by Mary Vaux Walcott

lodgepole pine | shore pine | twisted pine | contorta pine

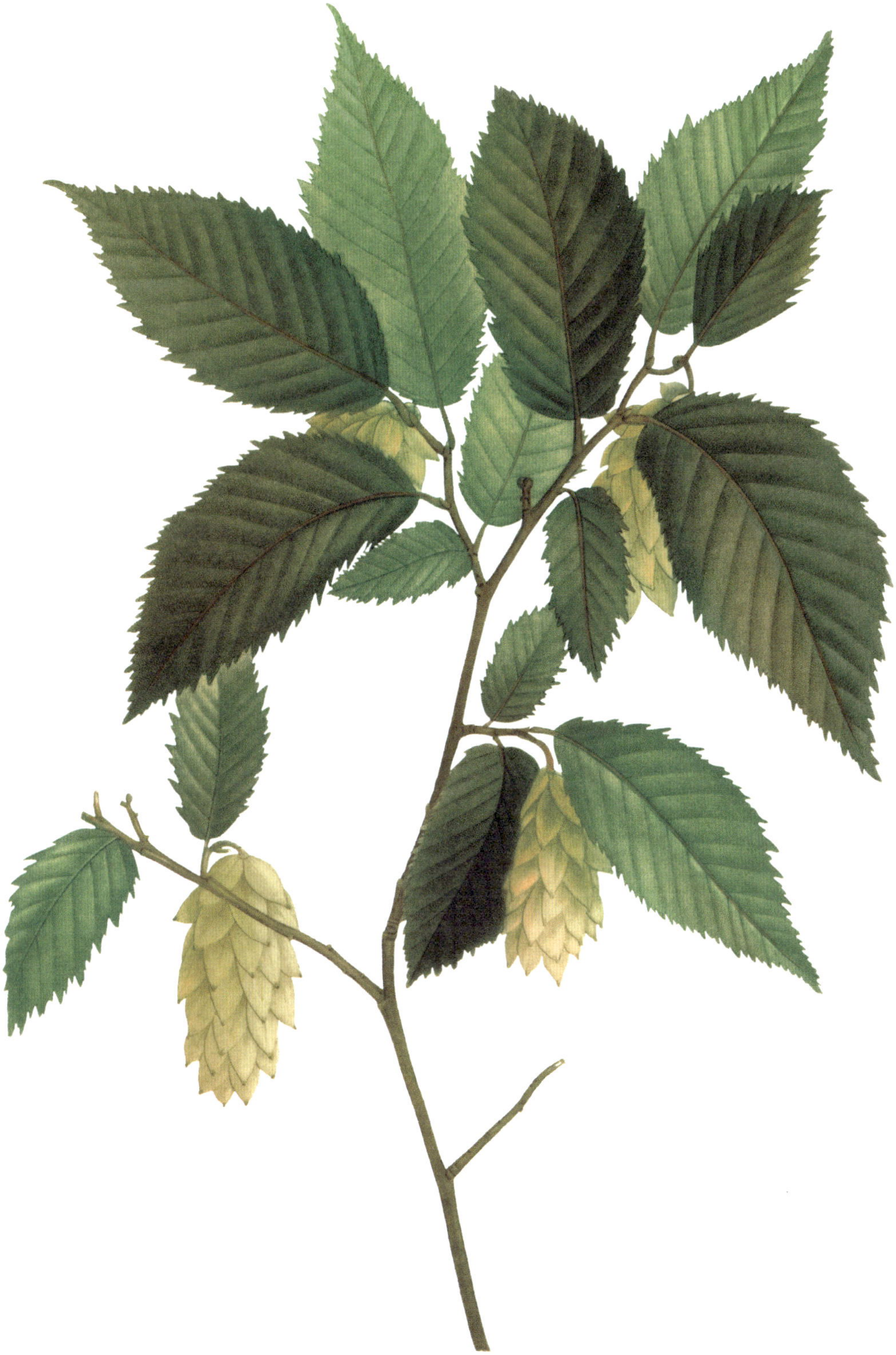

Ostrya virginiana
by Pierre-Joseph Redouté

American hophornbeam | eastern hophornbeam | leverwood

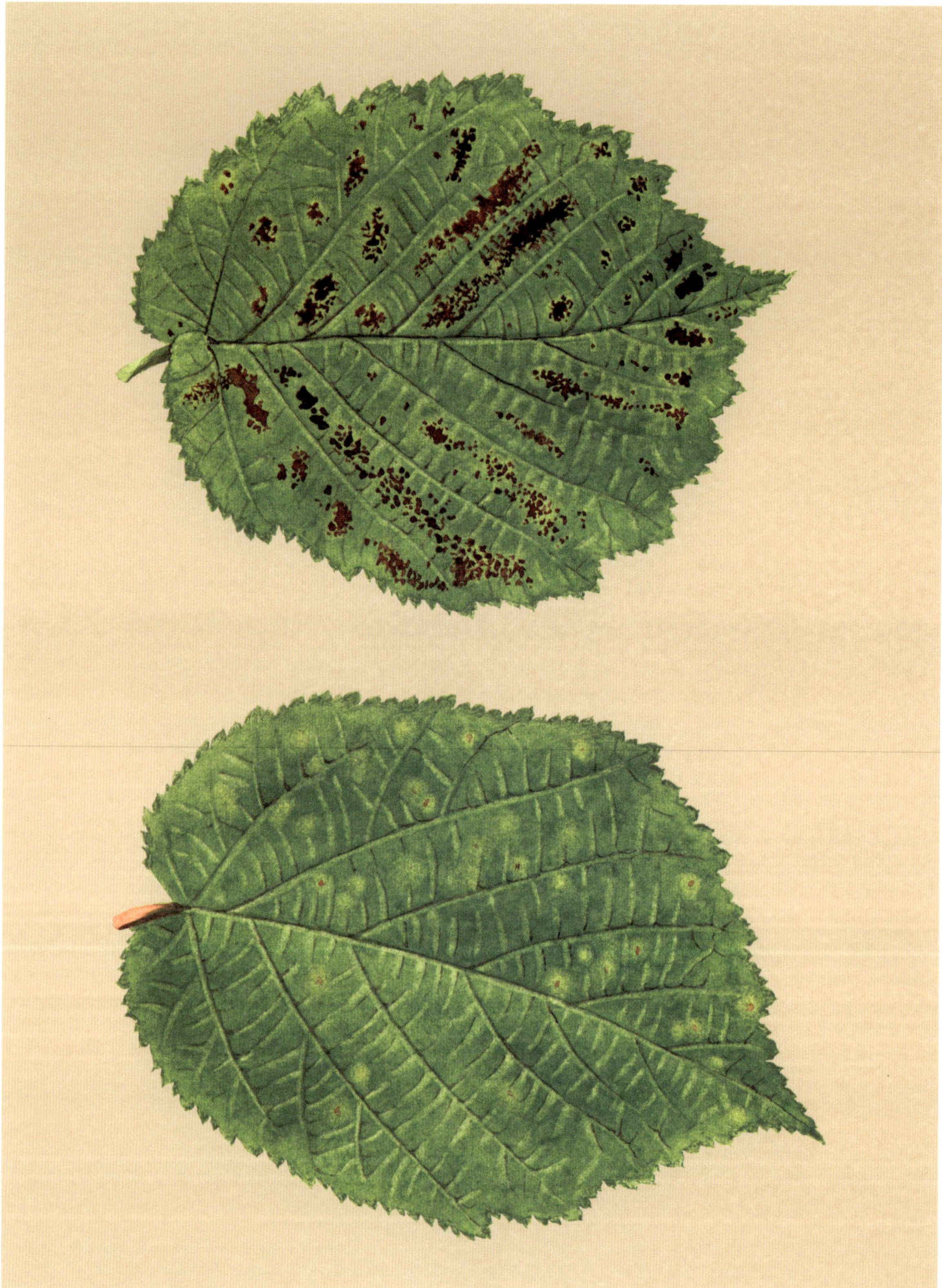

Corylus avellana
by James Marion Shull

common hazel

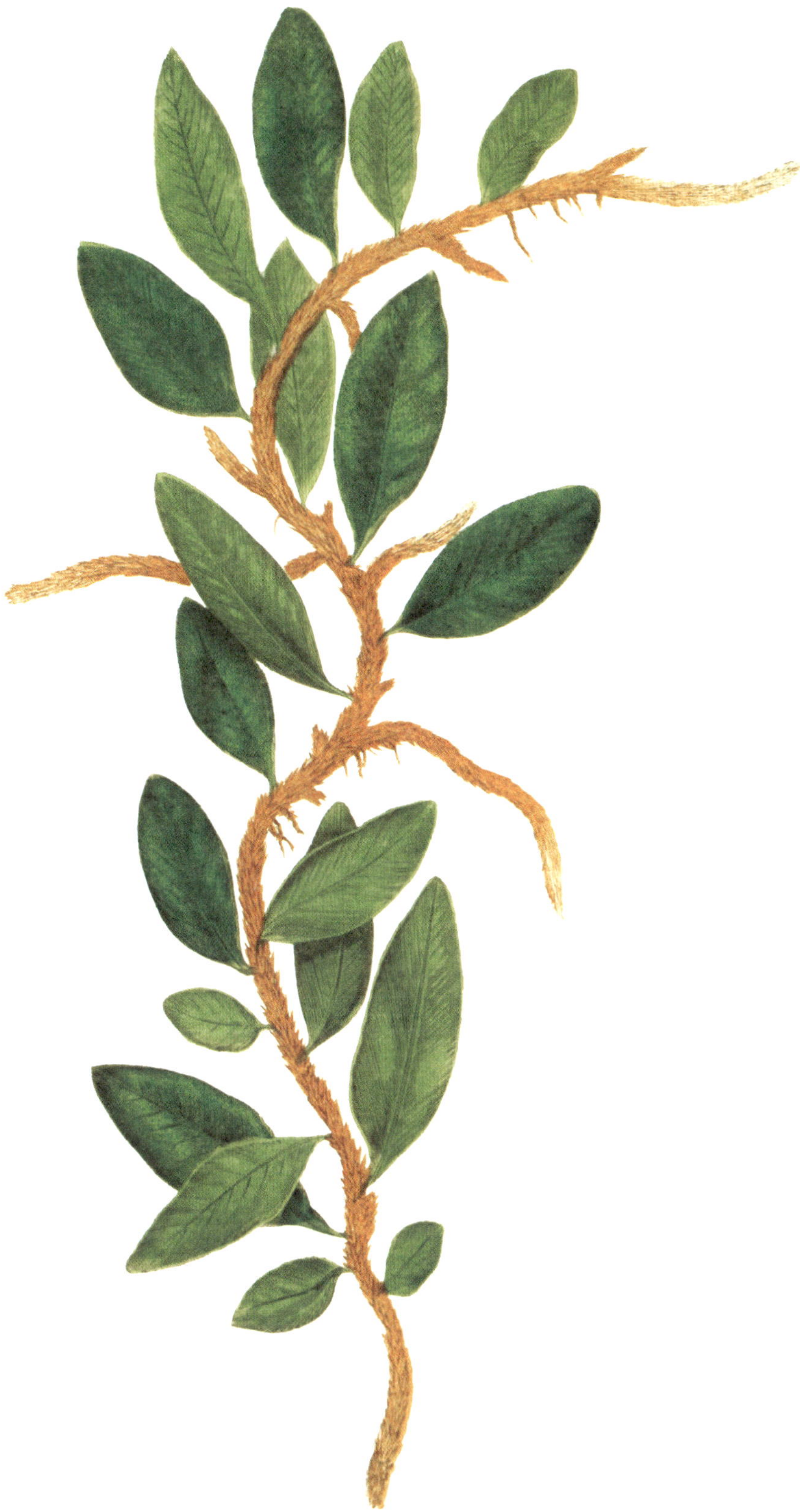

Microgramma mauritiana
by Edward Joseph Lowe

vine fern | snakefern | rockrunner

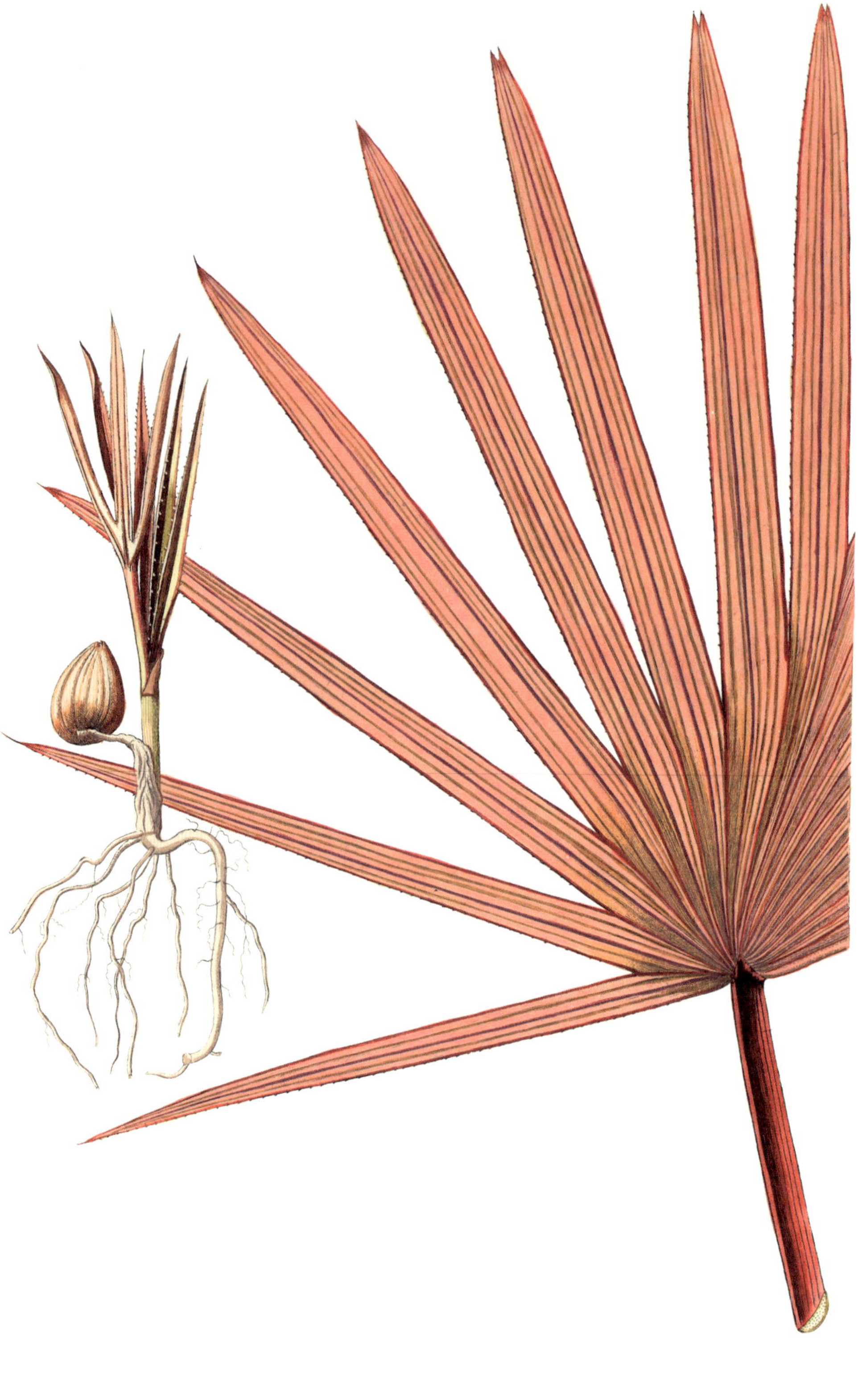

Latania lontaroides
by Carl Friedrich Philipp von Martius

red latan | latanier de la Réunion | latanier rouge

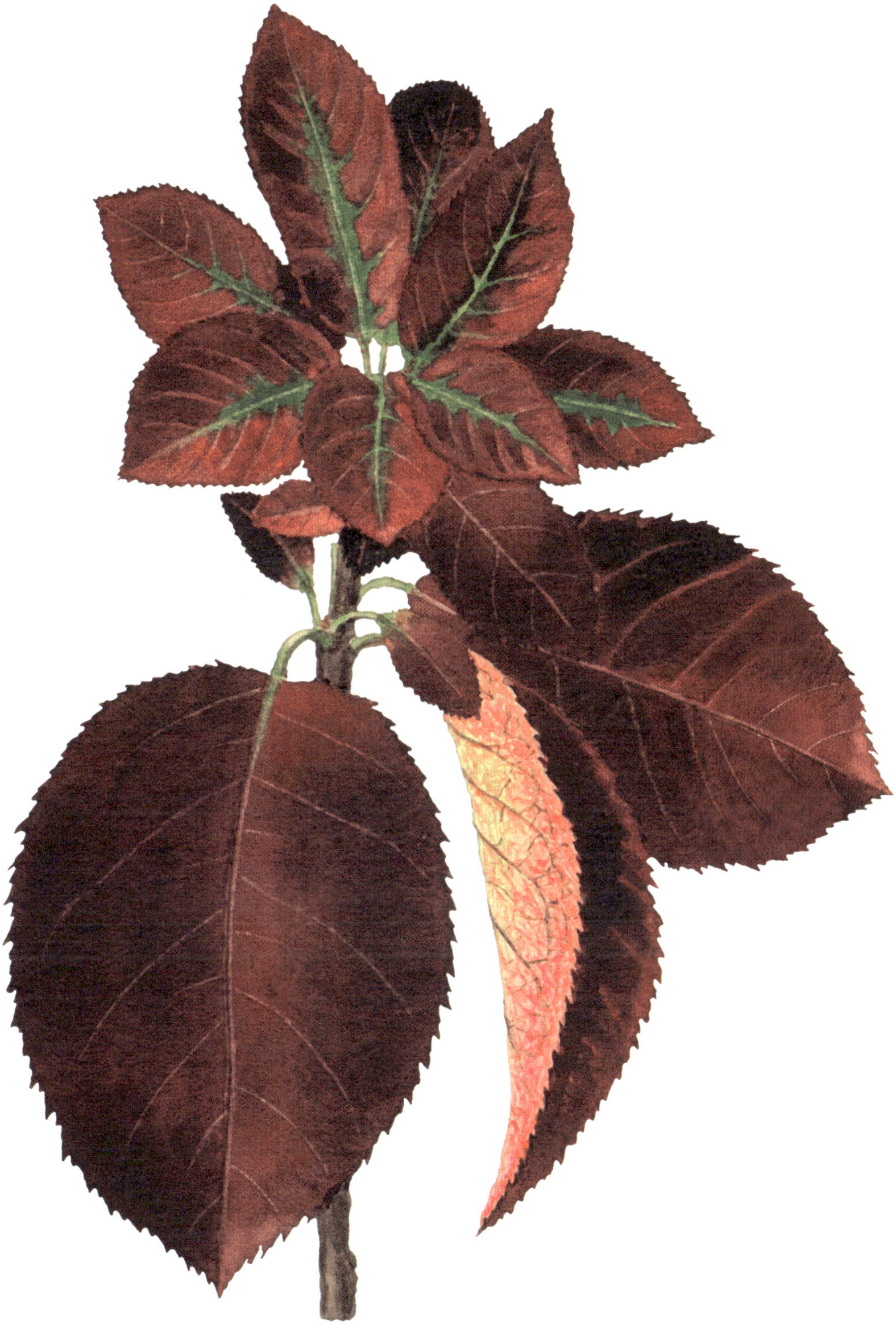

Prunus virginiana
by JAMES MARION SHULL

bitter-berry | chokecherry | Virginia bird cherry | western chokecherry

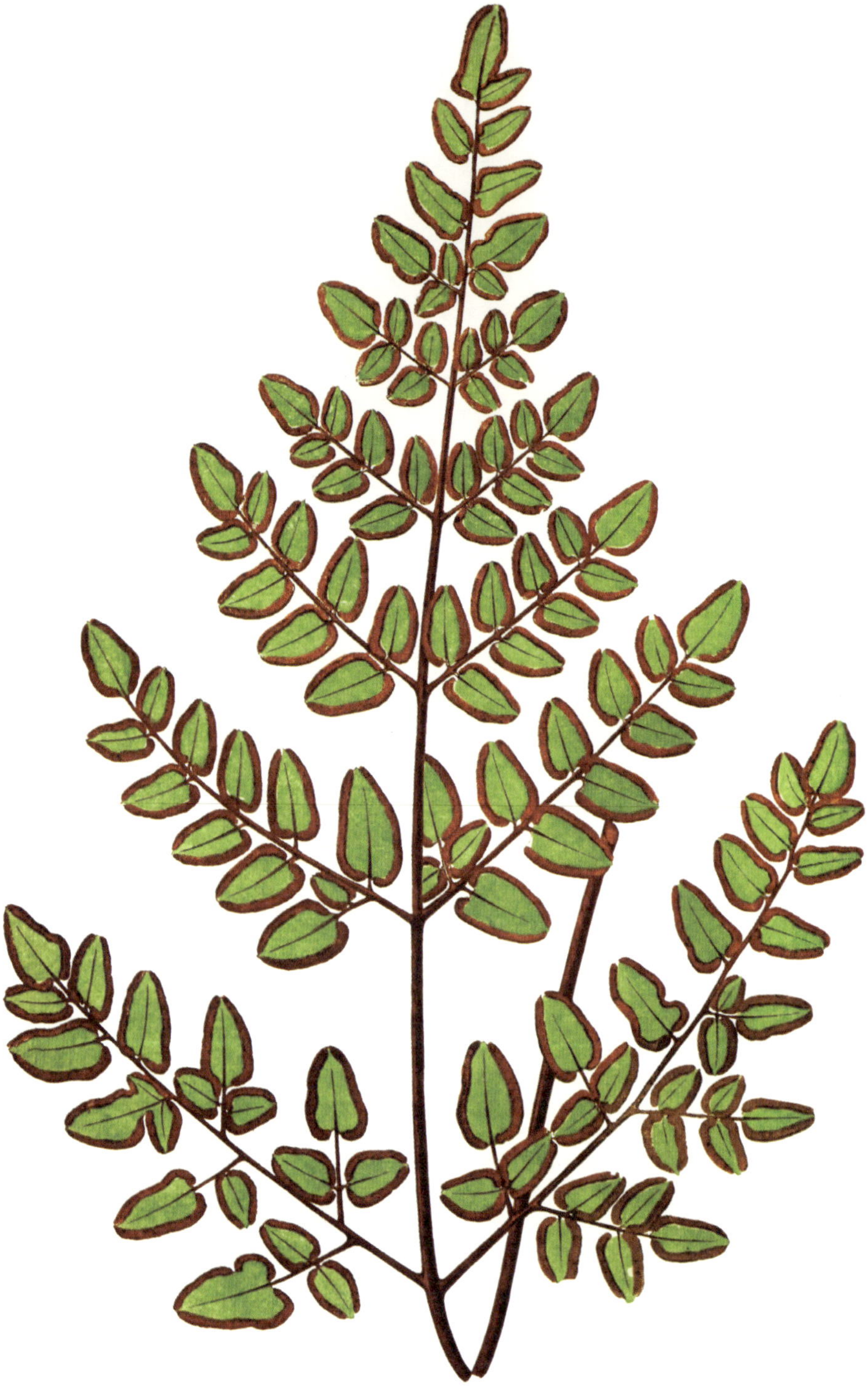

Cheilanthes pteroides
by Edward Joseph Lowe

lip fern

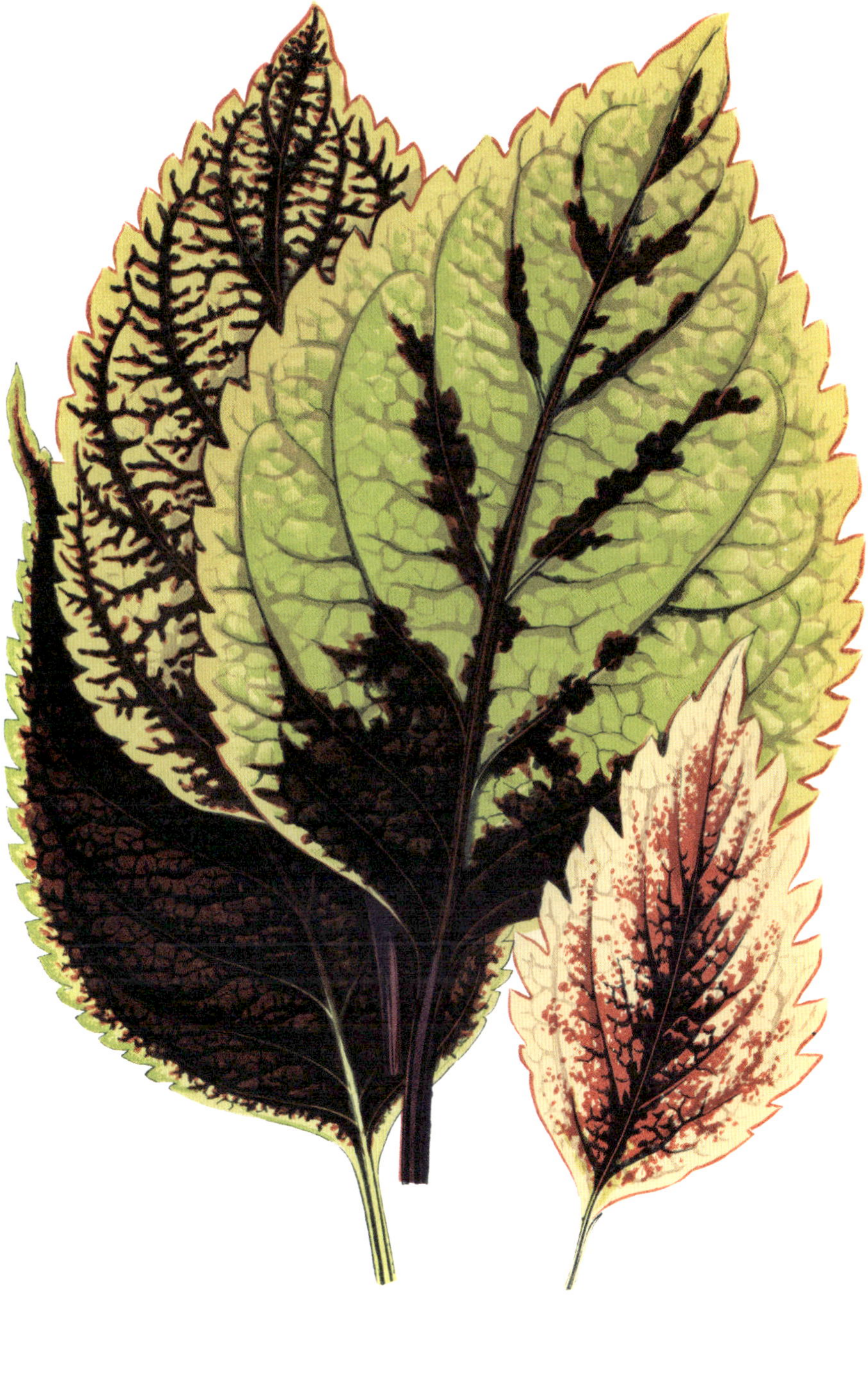

Coleus scutellarioides 'Murrayi'
by BENJAMIN FAWCETT & JAMES SHIRLEY HIBBERD

coleus | painted nettle

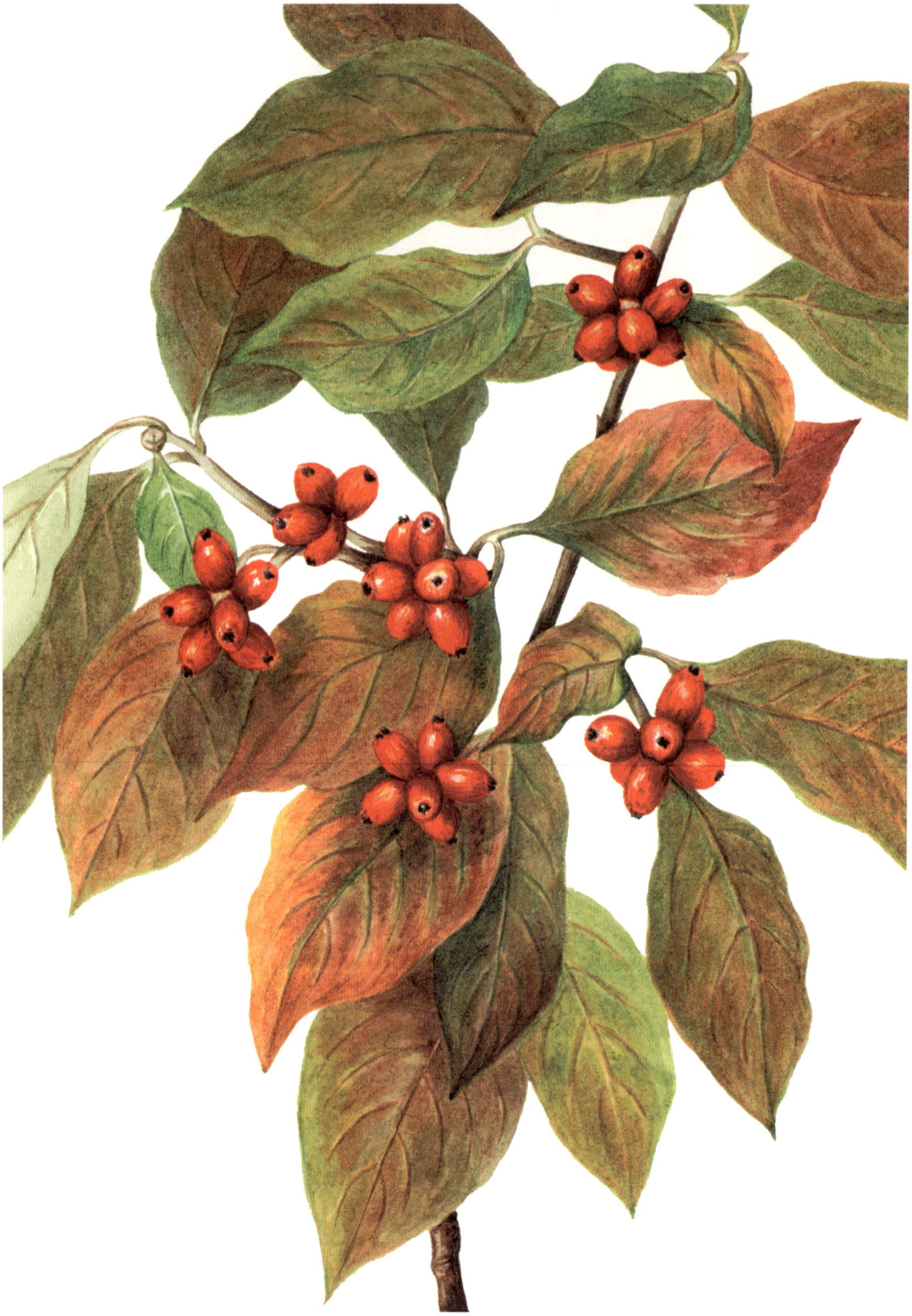

Cornus florida
by Mary Vaux Walcott

flowering dogwood | American dogwood

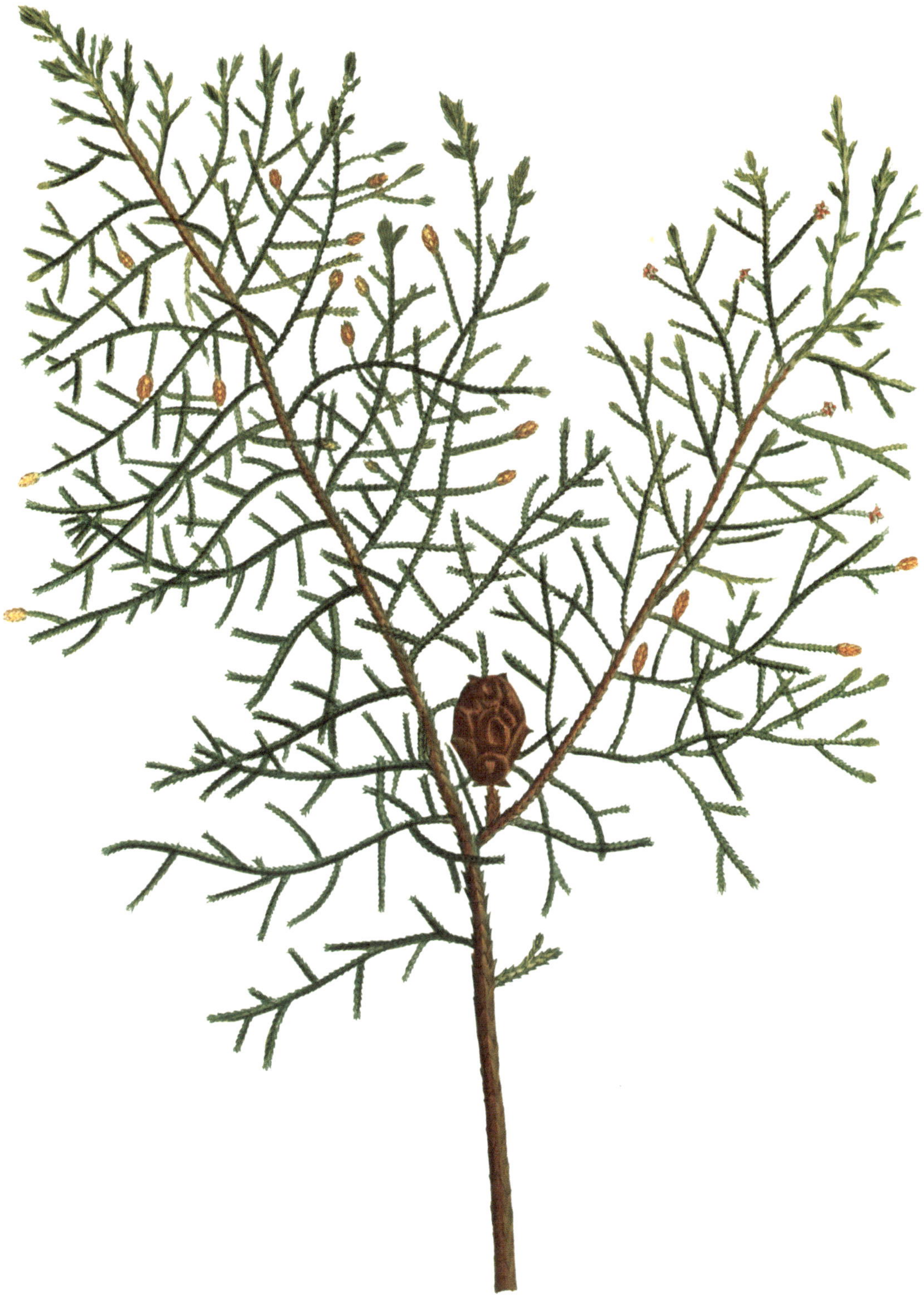

Cupressus funebris
by Pierre-Joseph Redouté

Chinese weeping cypress

Nature's first green is gold,
Her hardest hue to hold.
Her early leaf's a flower;
But only so an hour.
Then leaf subsides to leaf.
So Eden sank to grief,
So dawn goes down to day.
Nothing gold can stay.

FROM 'Nothing Gold Can Stay' BY ROBERT FROST

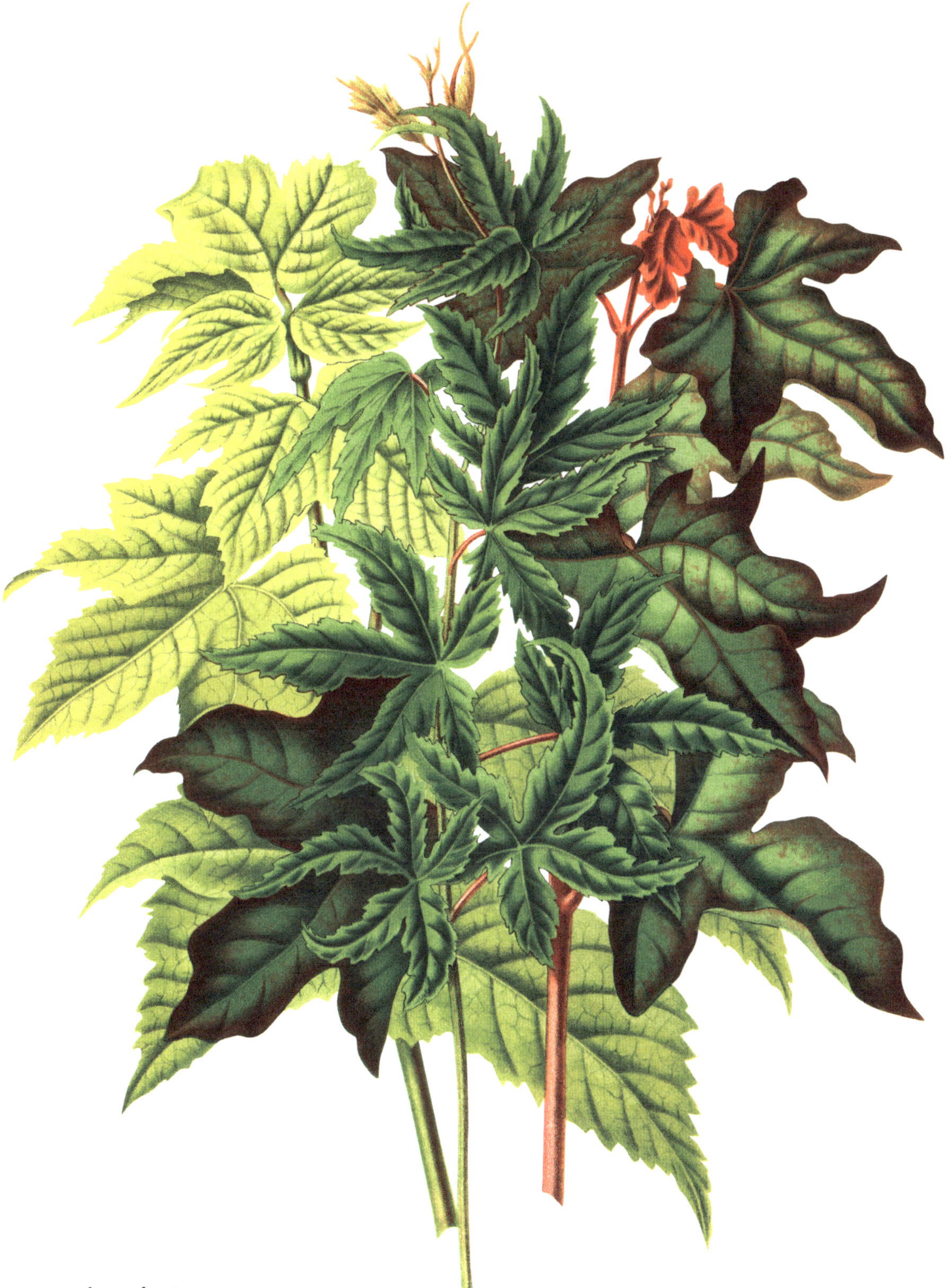

Acer palmatum
by Abraham Jacobus Wendel

Japanese maple | palmate maple | smooth Japanese maple

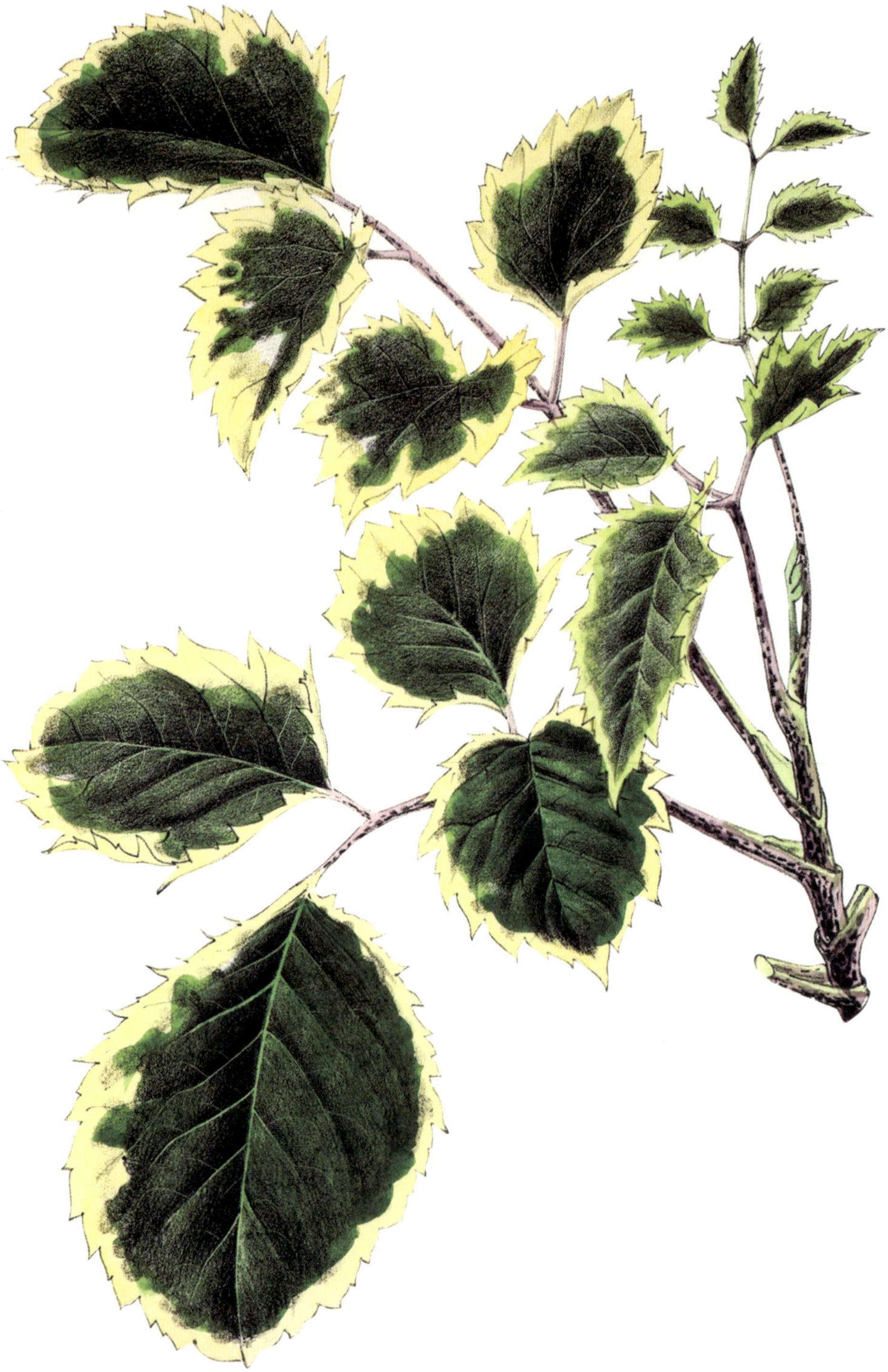

Polyscias guilfoylei
by Worthington G. Smith

geranium aralia | wild coffee

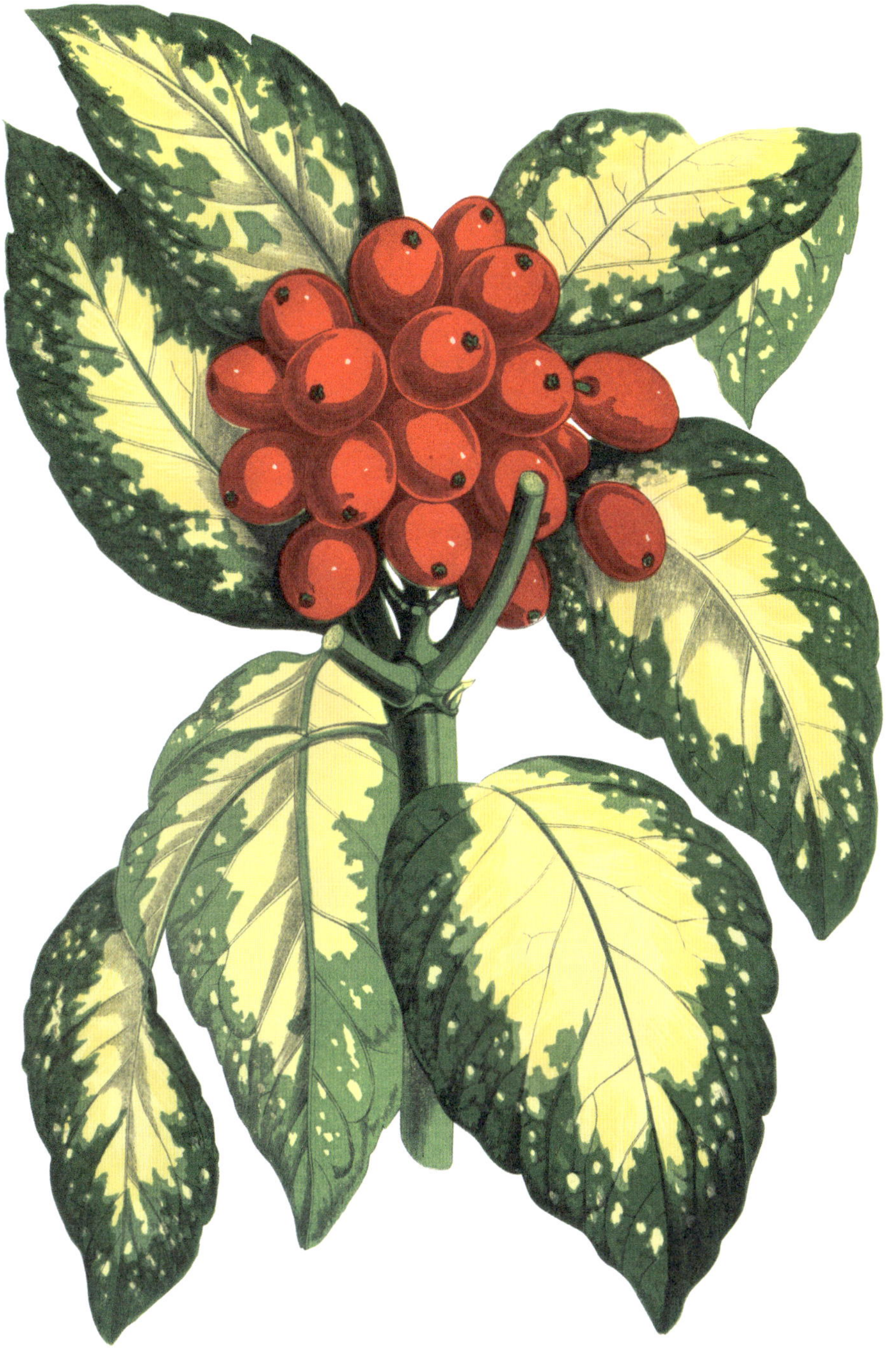

Aucuba japonica
by Alexander Francis Lydon & Benjamin Fawcett

spotted laurel | Japanese laurel | Japanese aucuba | gold dust plant

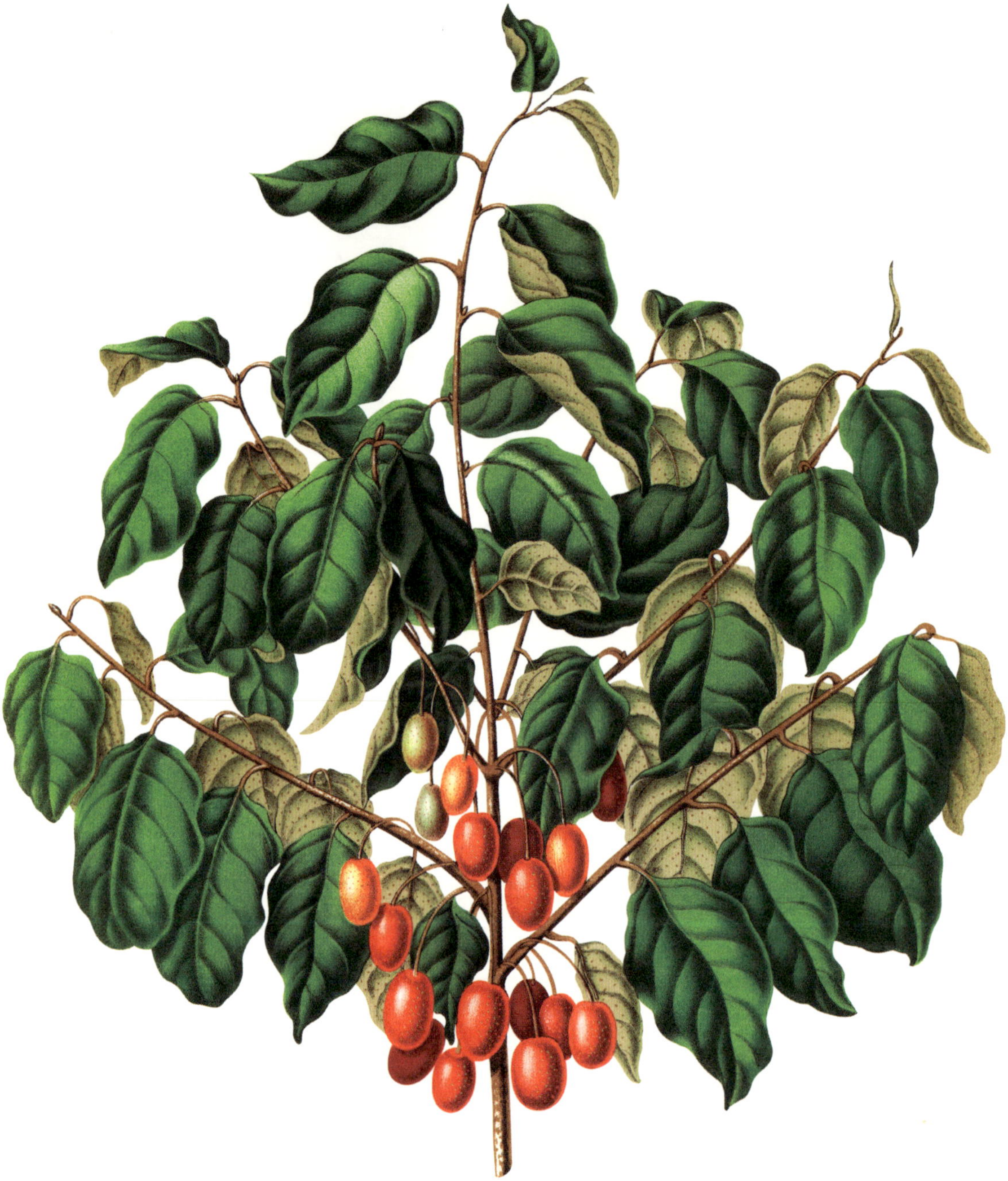

Elaeagnus × submacrophylla
by Abraham Jacobus Wendel

Ebbinge's silverberry

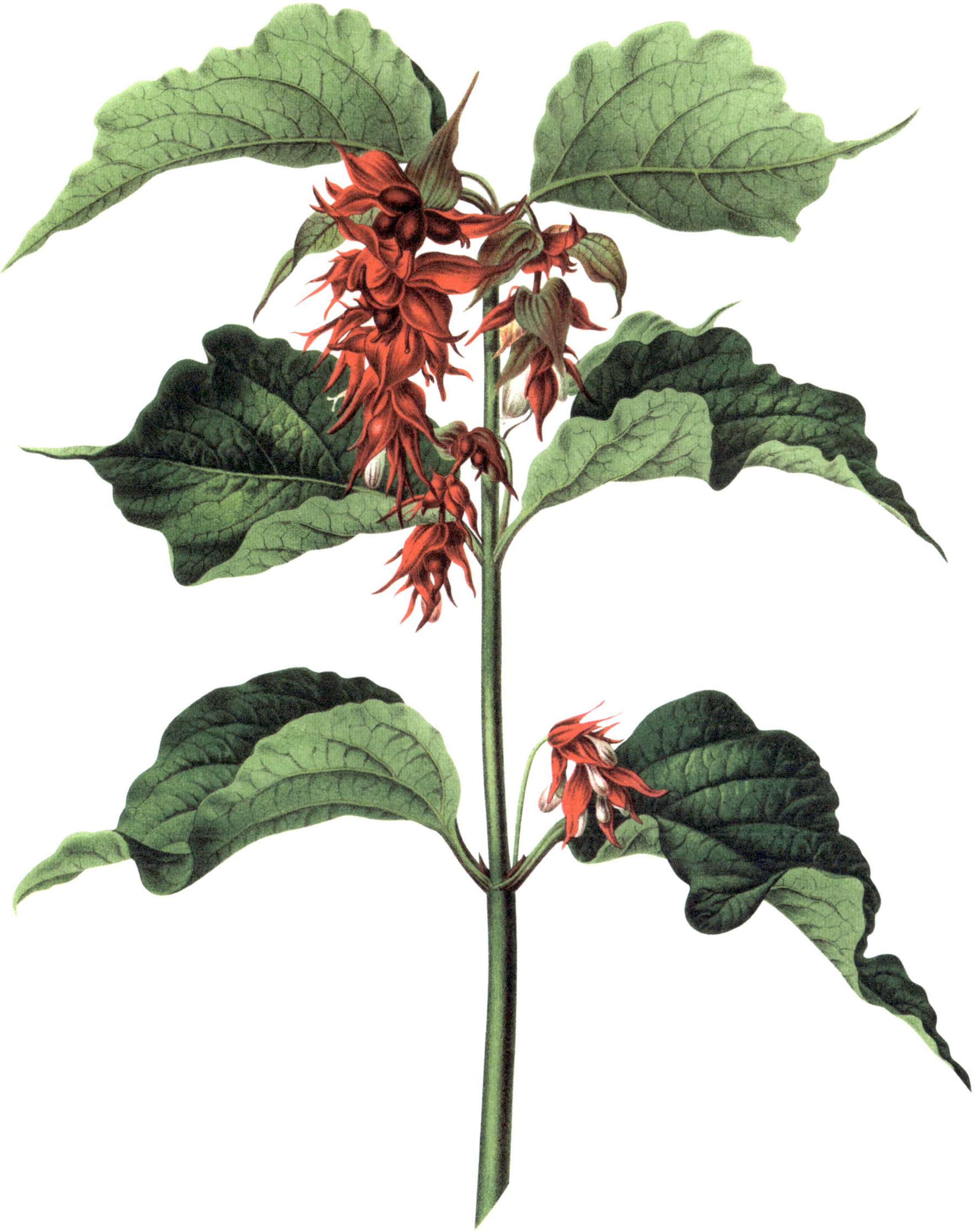

Leycesteria formosa
by ABRAHAM JACOBUS WENDEL

pheasant berry | Himalayan honeysuckle

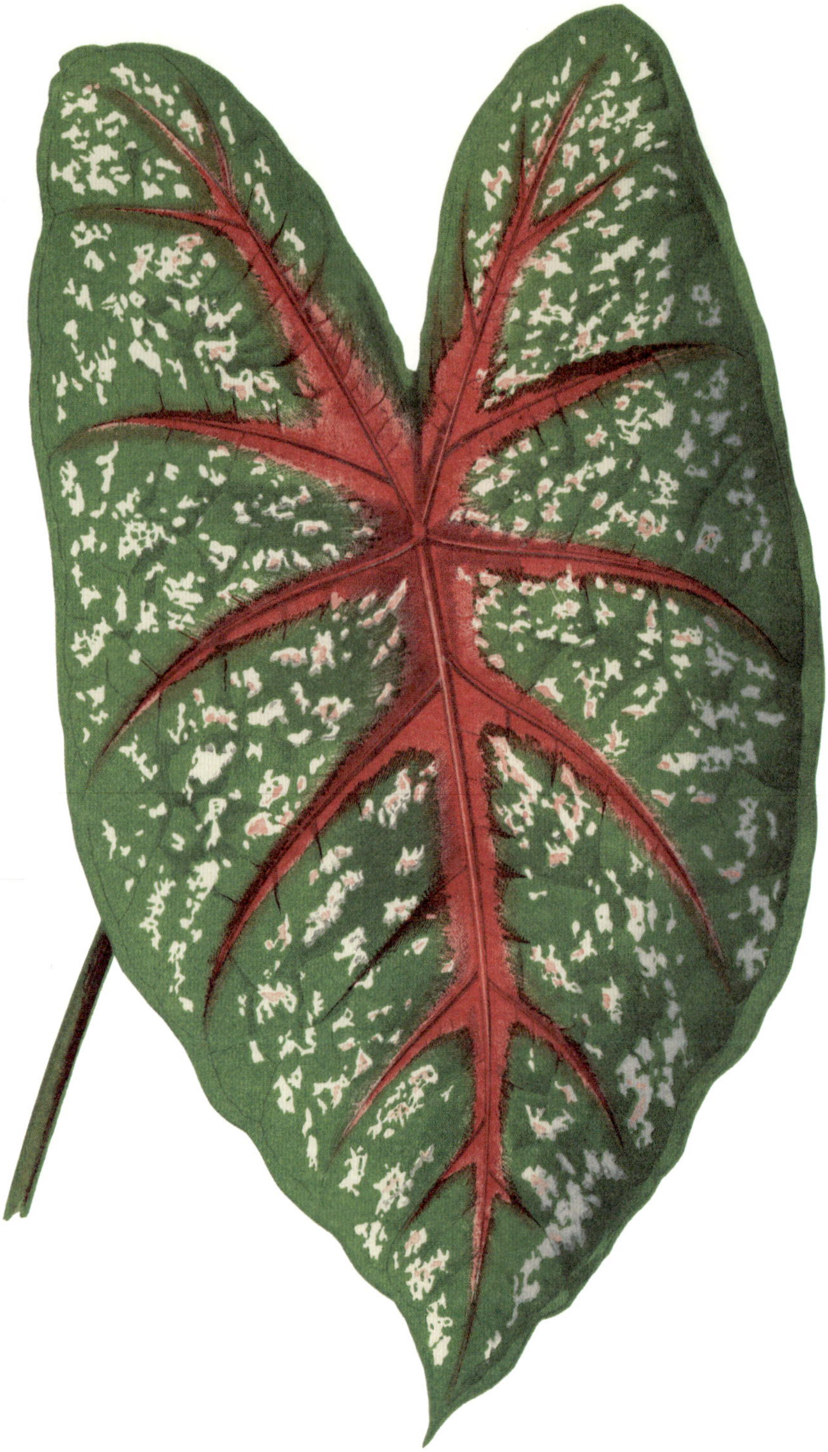

Caladium bicolor
by ALEXANDER FRANCIS LYDON & BENJAMIN FAWCETT

Heart of Jesus | elephant ear | angel wings

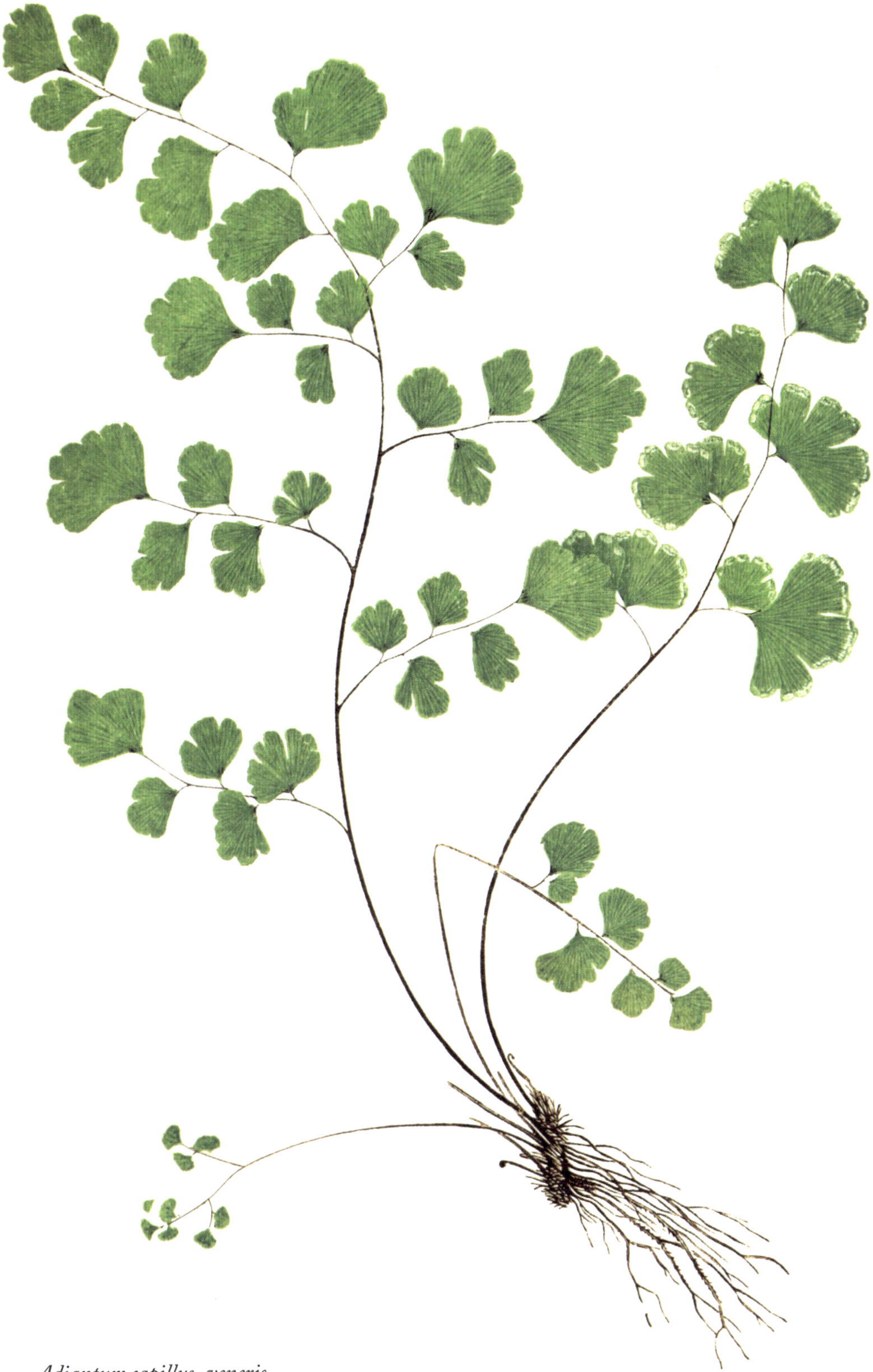

Adiantum capillus–veneris
by Edward Joseph Lowe

maidenhair fern | southern maidenhair fern | black maidenhair fern | Venus hair fern

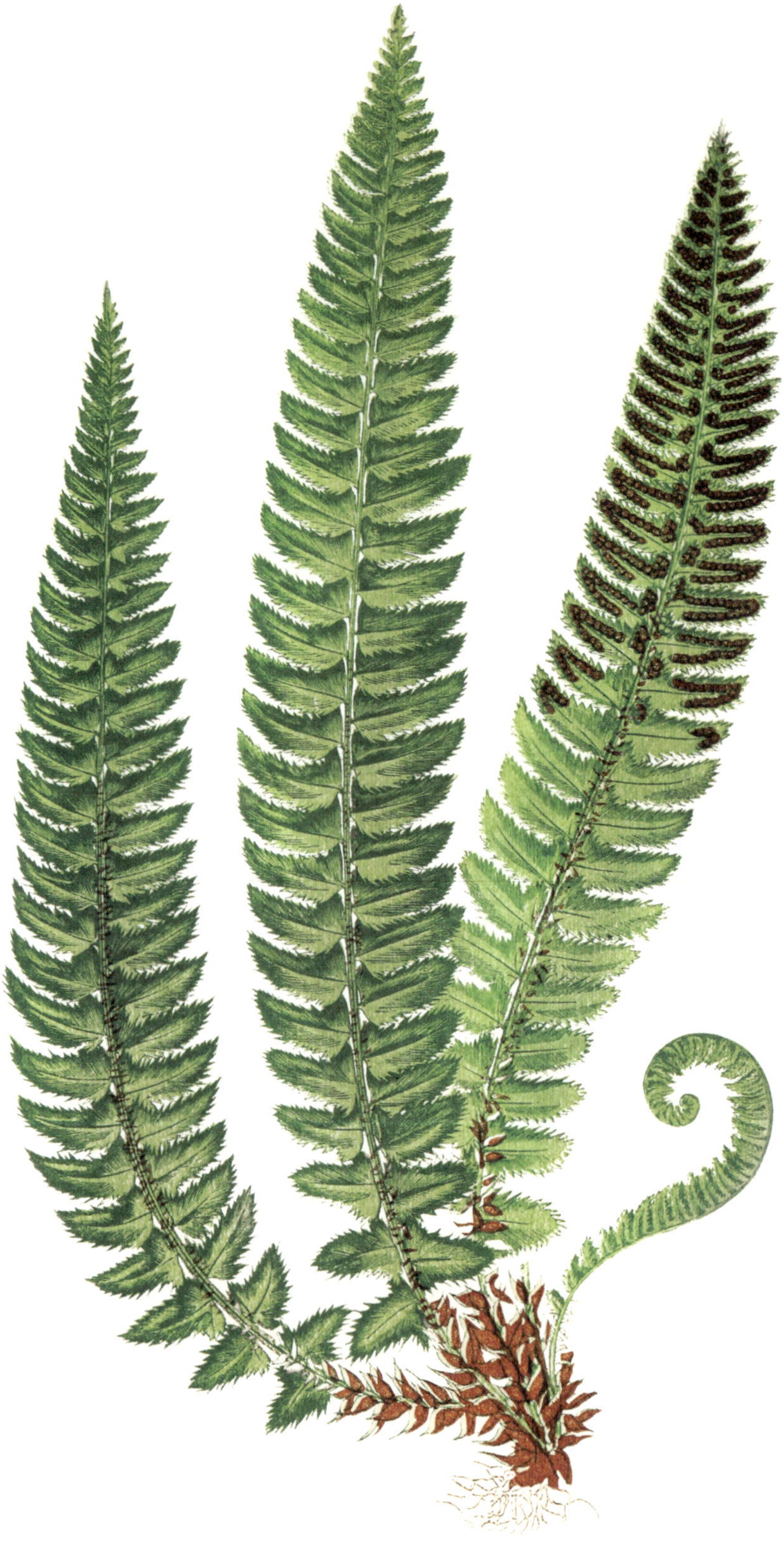

Polystichum lonchitis
by Edward Joseph Lowe

northern holly fern | holly fern

Only spread a fern-frond over a man's head and worldly cares are cast out, and freedom and beauty and peace come in.

John Muir

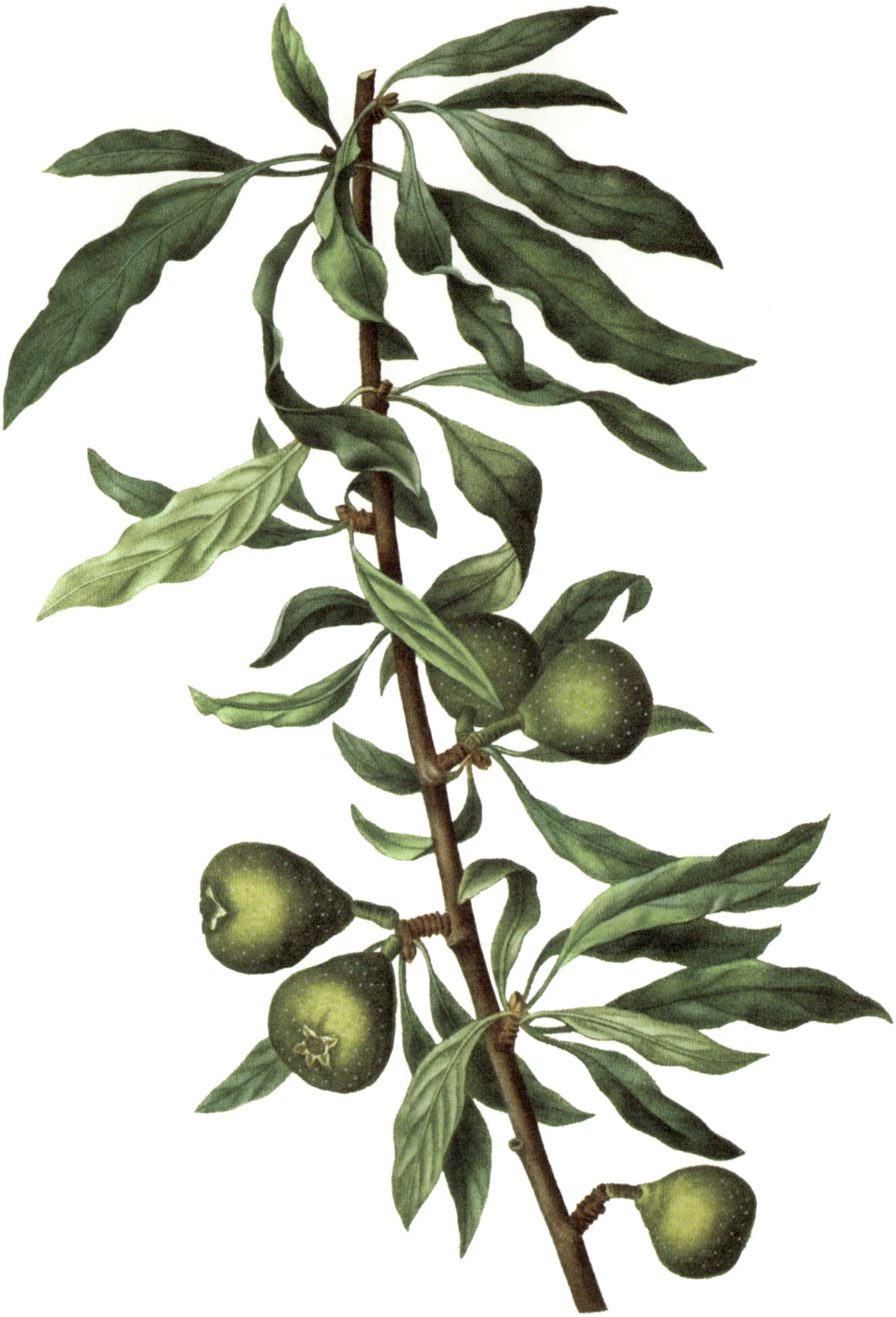

Pyrus salicifolia
by Pierre-Joseph Redouté

willow-leaved pear | weeping pear | weeping silver pear

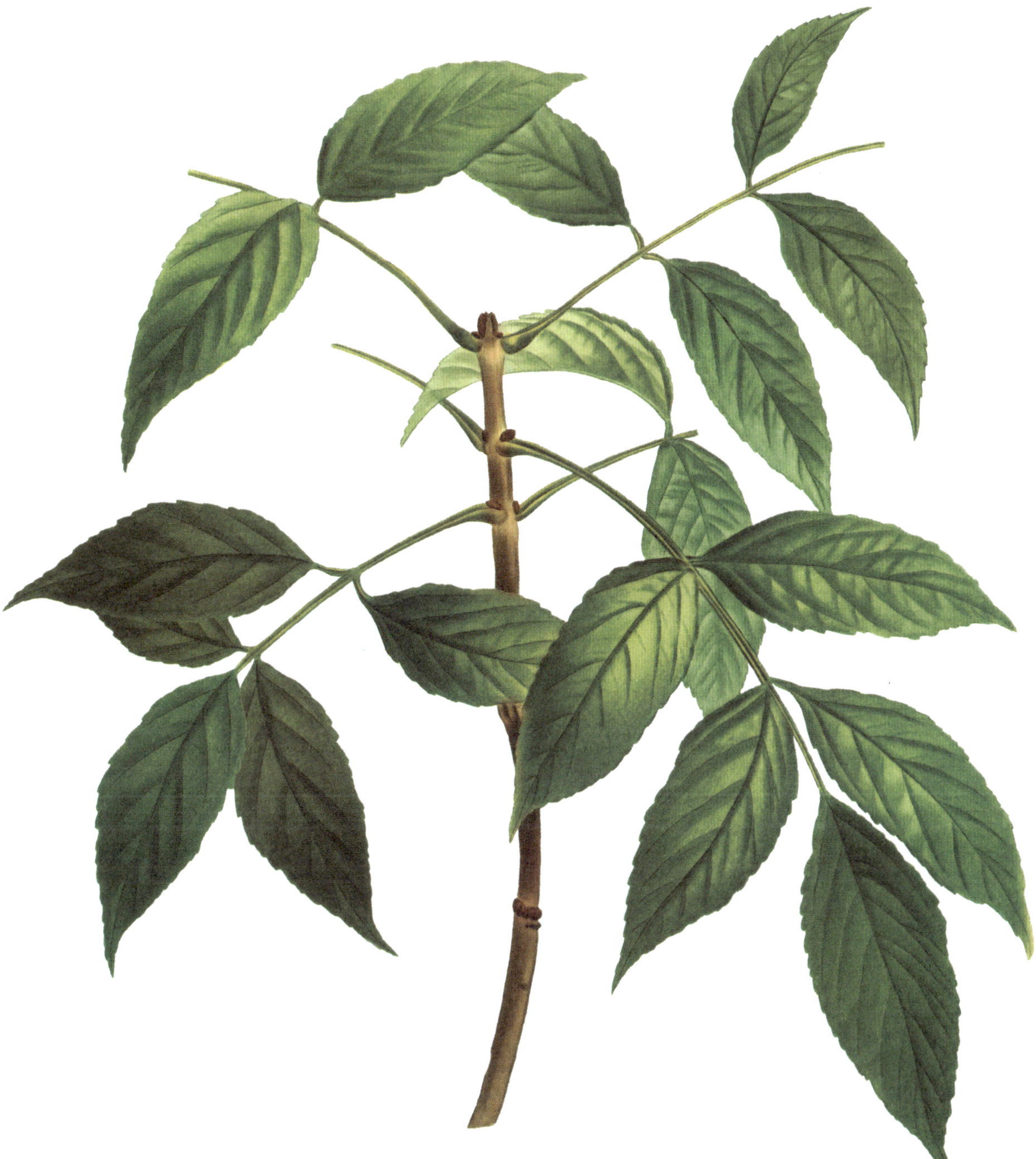

Fraxinus americana
by PIERRE-JOSEPH REDOUTÉ

American ash | white ash

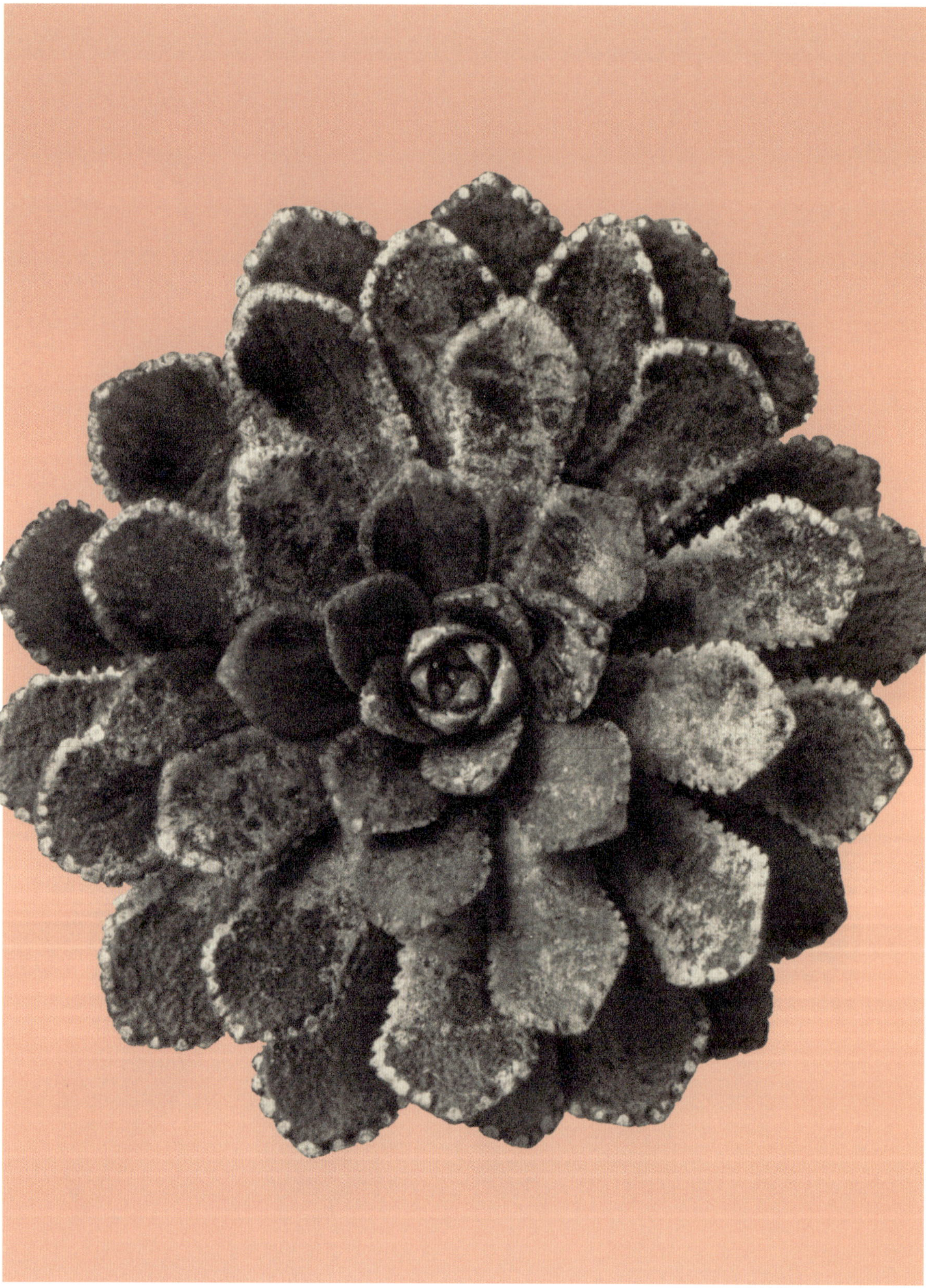

Saxifraga paniculata
by KARL BLOSSFELDT

alpine saxifrage | encrusted saxifrage | lifelong saxifrage

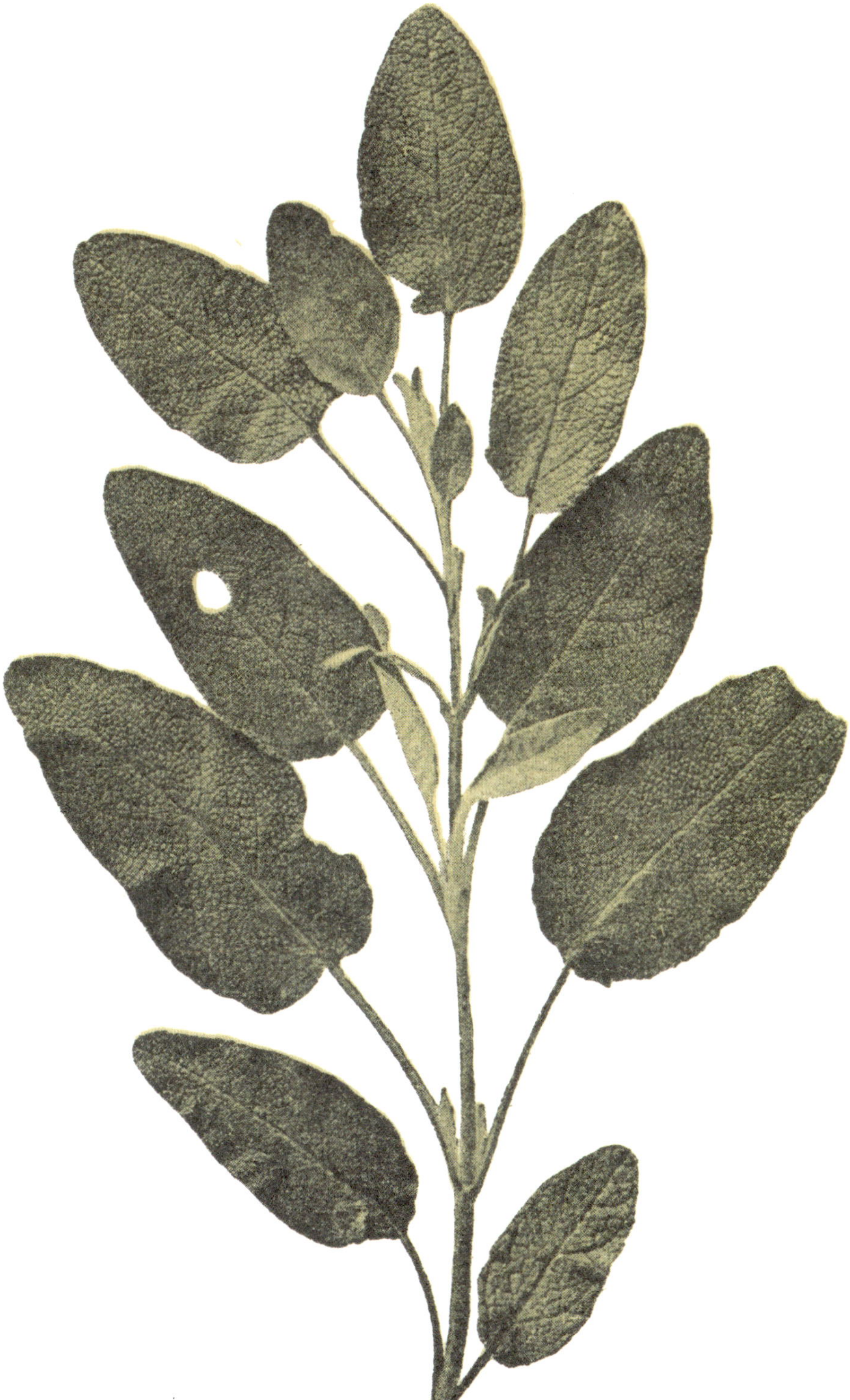

Salvia officinalis
by Sebastian Kneipp

sage

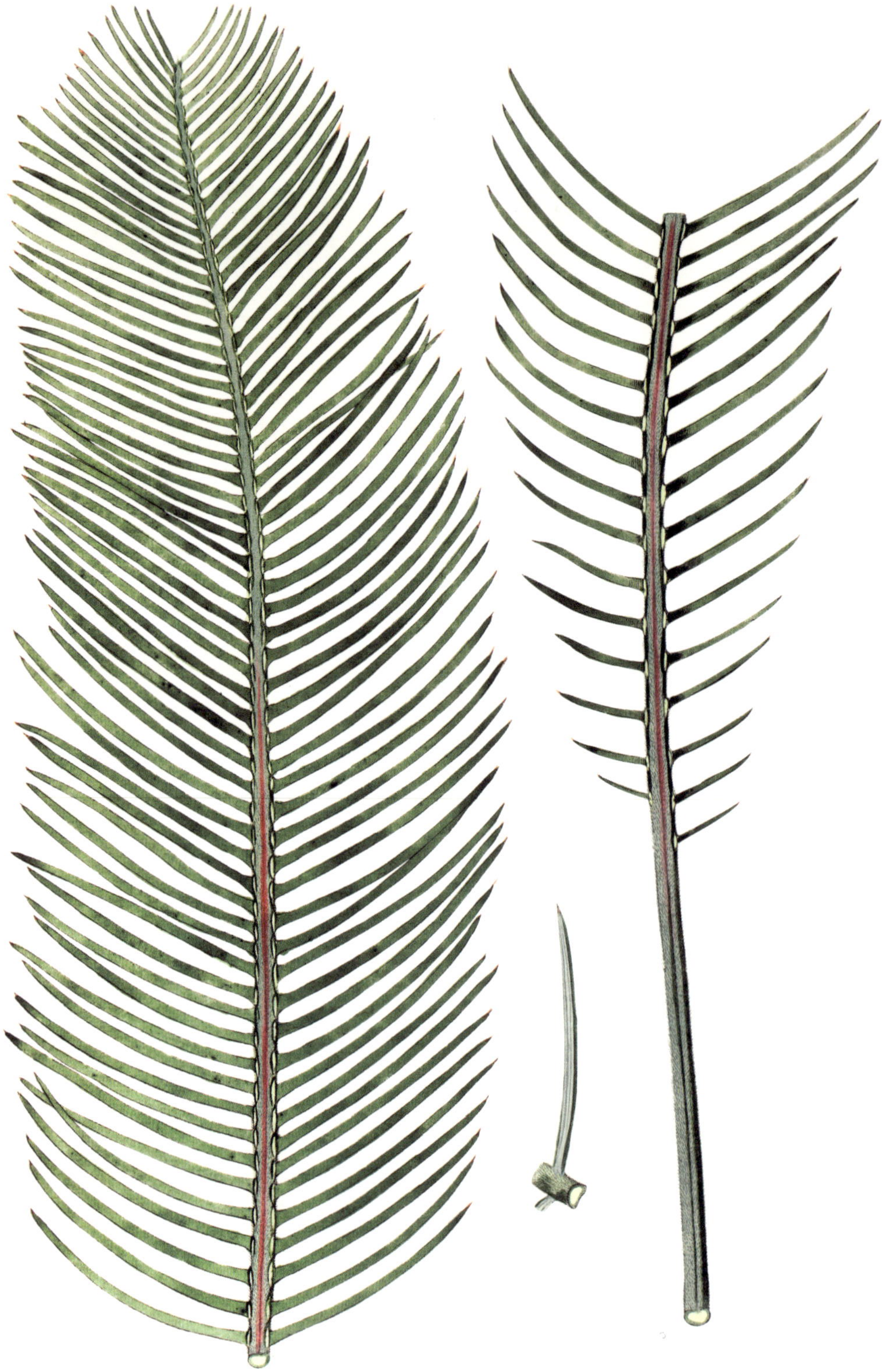

Encephalartos cycadifolius
by Edward Joseph Lowe

Winterberg cycad | Bedford cycad | bread palm

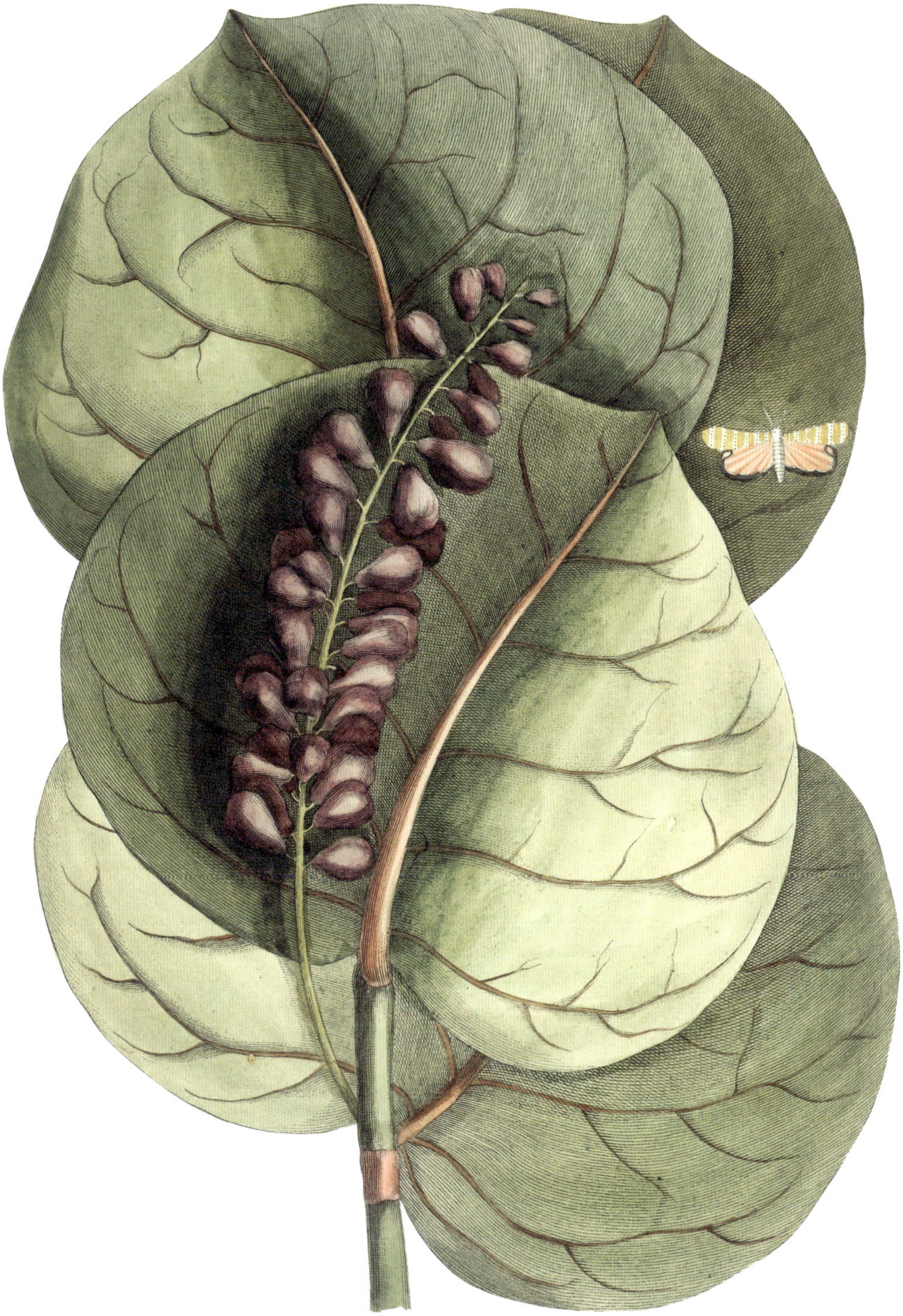

Coccoloba uvifera
by Mark Catesby

seaside grape | sea grape | bay grape

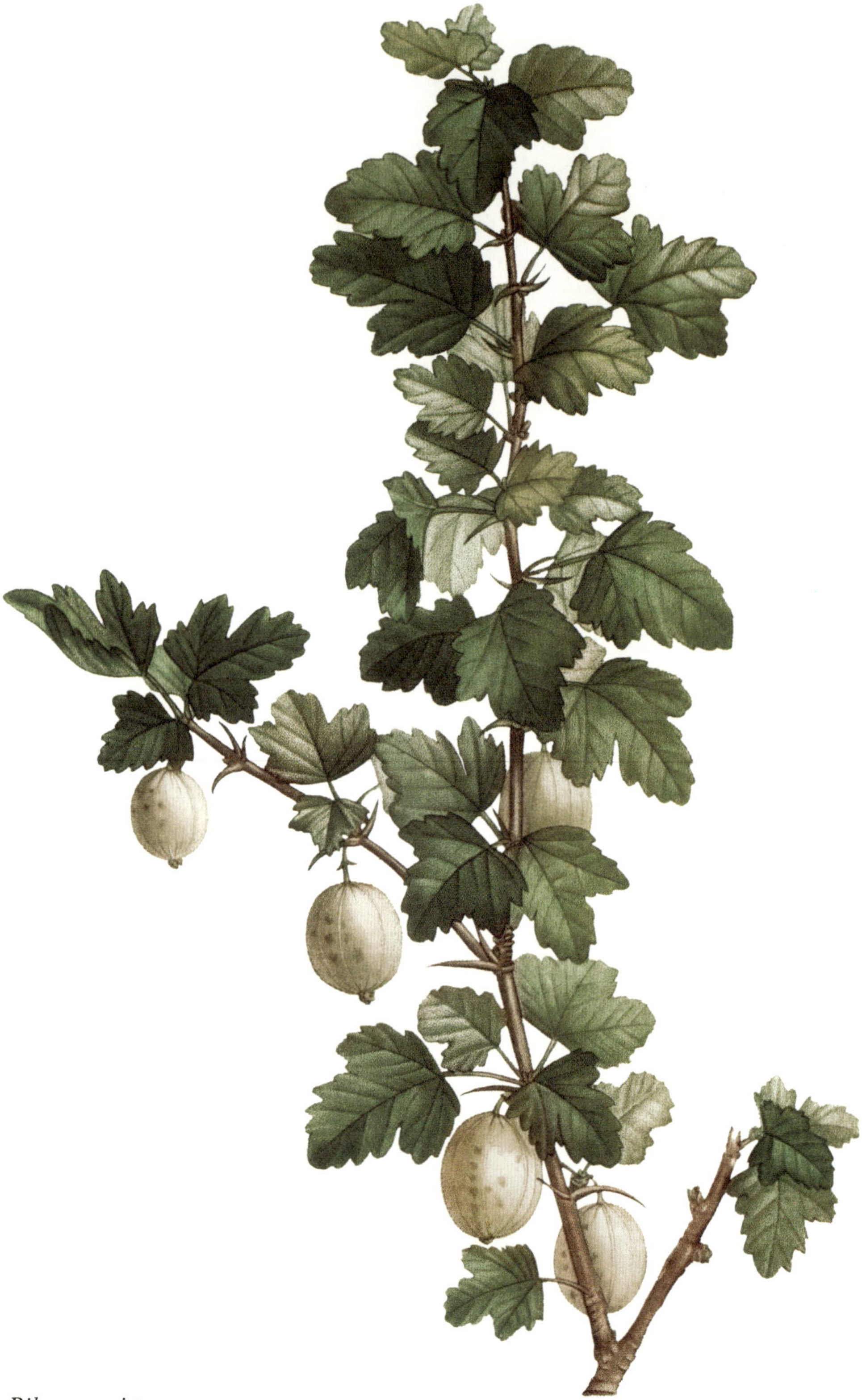

Ribes uva-crispa
by Pierre-Joseph Redouté

gooseberry | European gooseberry

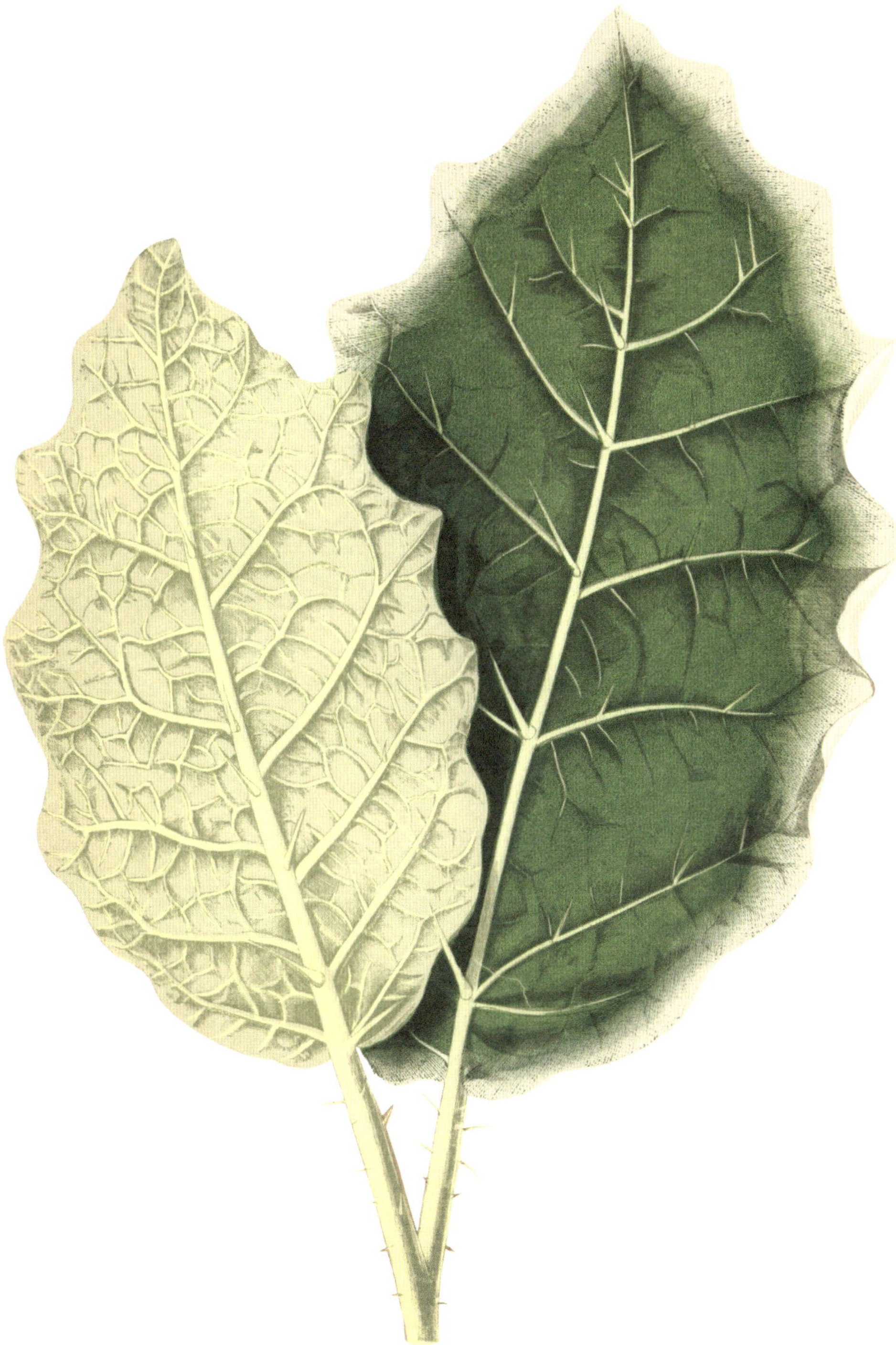

Solanum marginatum
by Alexander Francis Lydon & Benjamin Fawcett

purple African nightshade | white-margined nightshade

'Come, little leaves,' said the wind one day,
'Come o'er the meadows with me and play;
Put on your dresses of red and gold,
For summer is gone and the days grow cold.'

FROM 'Come, Little Leaves' BY GEORGE COOPER

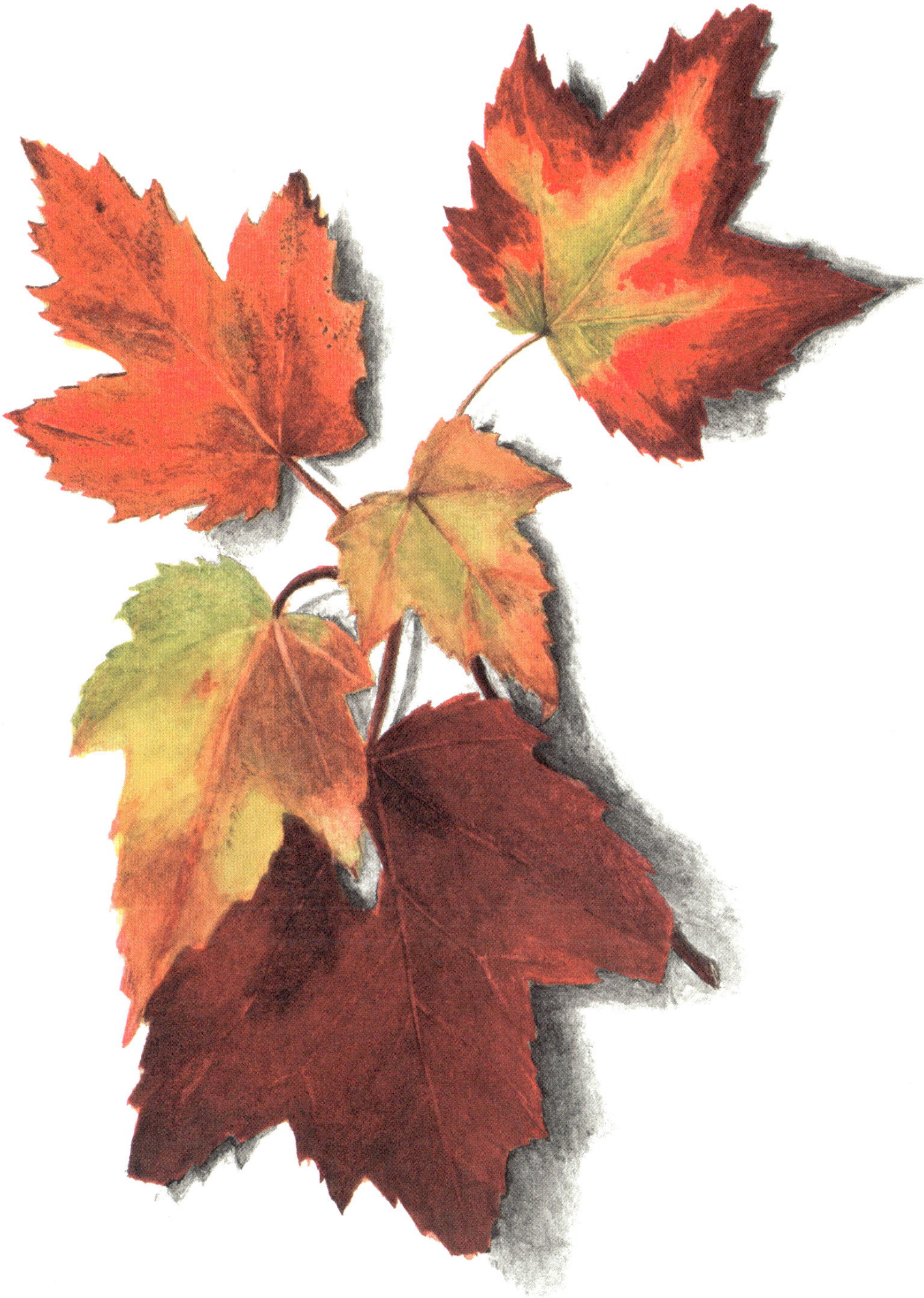

Acer
by Mary Vaux Walcott

maple (unknown variety)

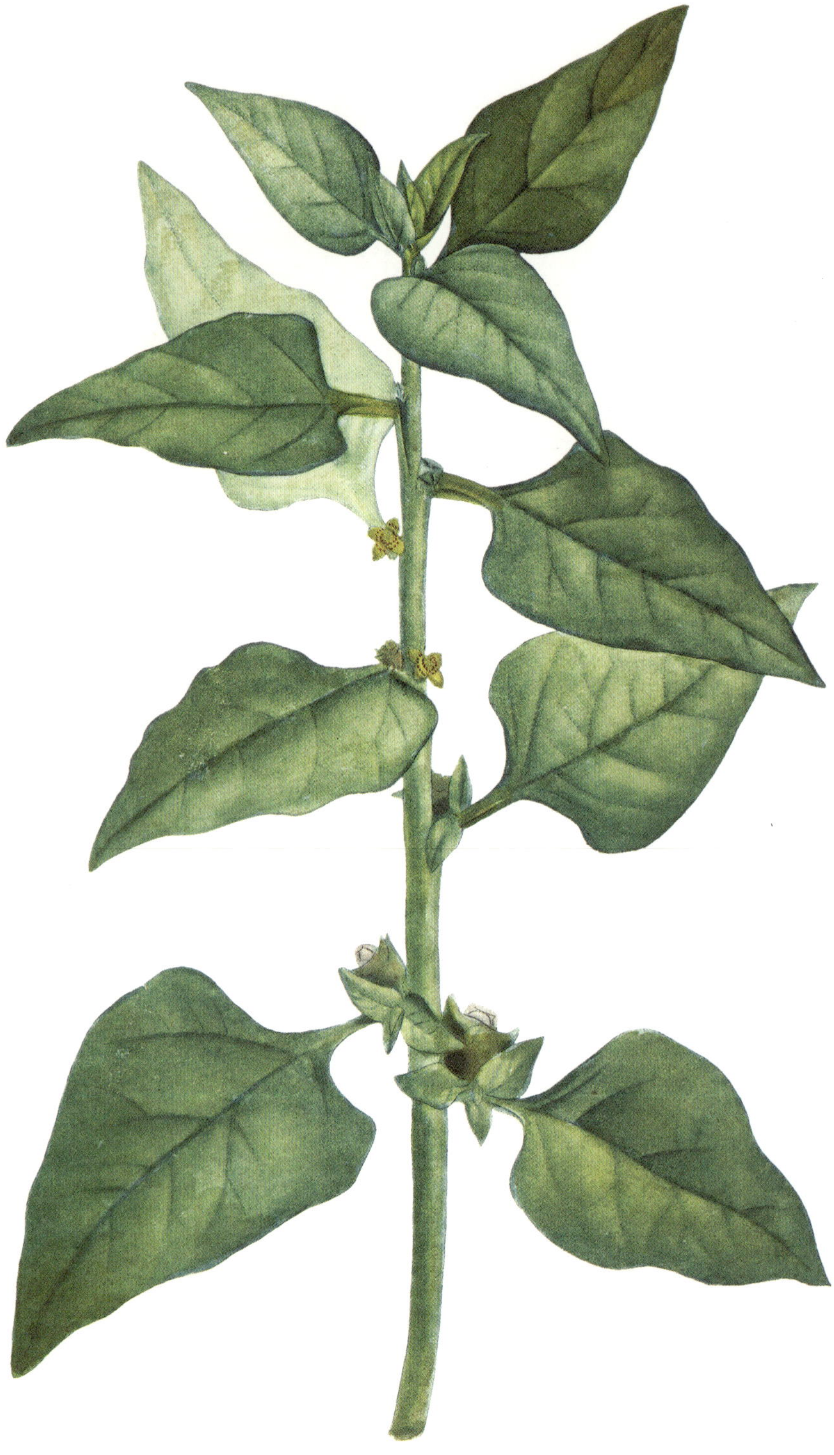

Tetragonia tetragonioides
by Pierre-Joseph Redouté

New Zealand spinach | warrigal greens

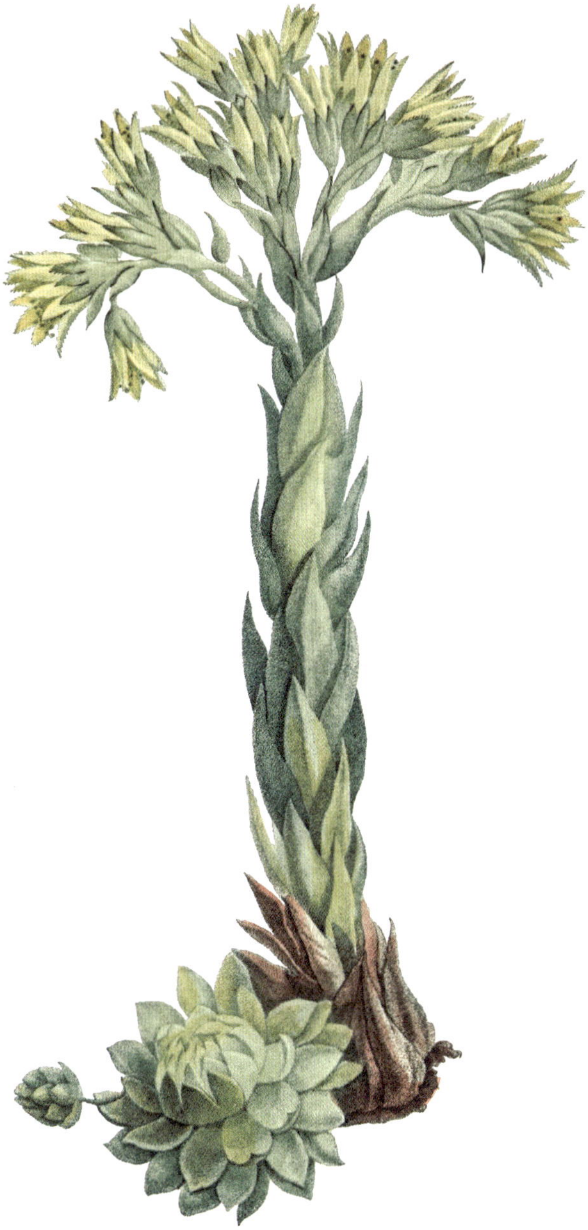

Sempervivum globiferum subsp. *hirtum*
by Pierre-Joseph Redouté

rolling hen and chicks

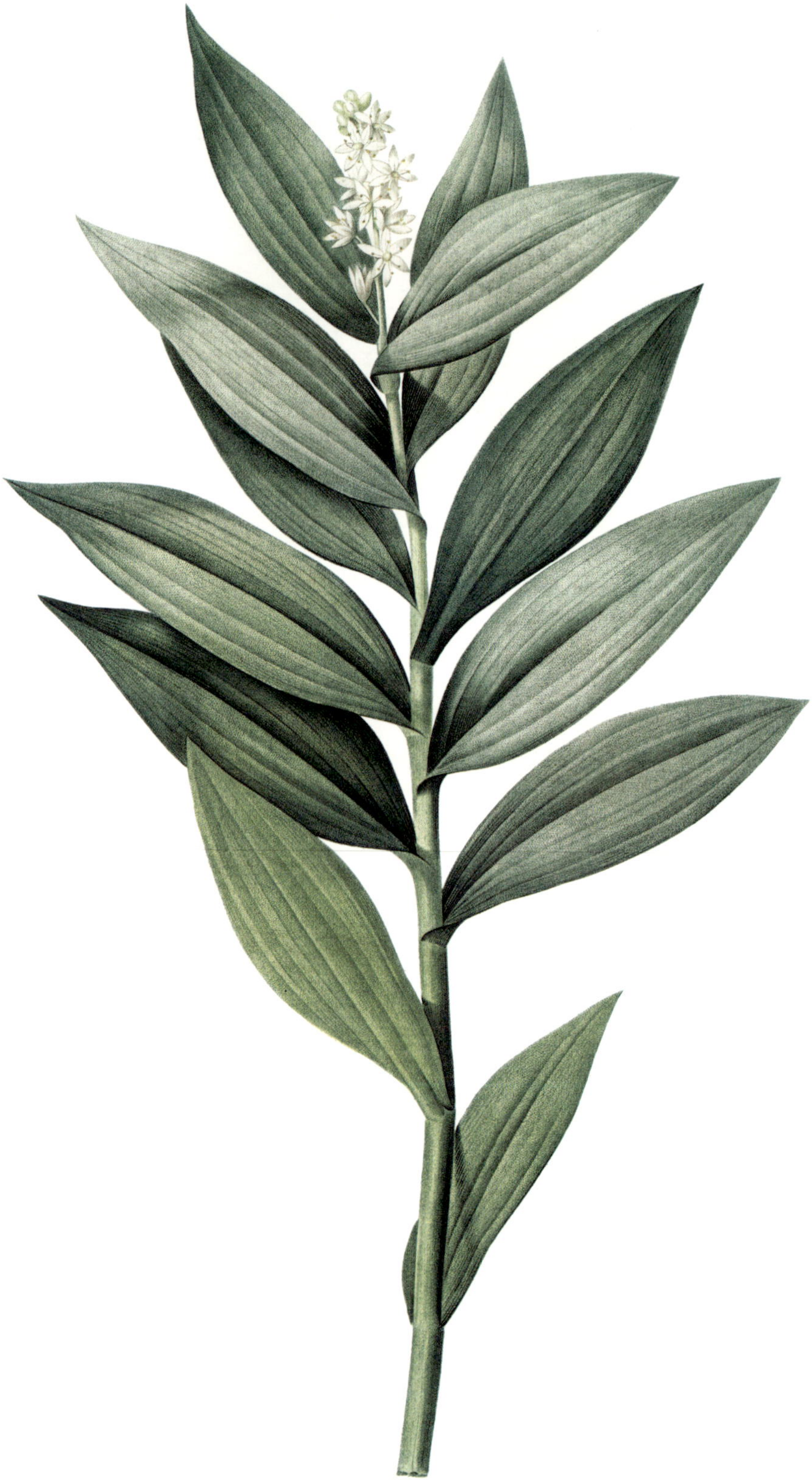

Maianthemum stellatum
by PIERRE-JOSEPH REDOUTÉ

star-flowered lily of the valley | star-like false Solomon's seal

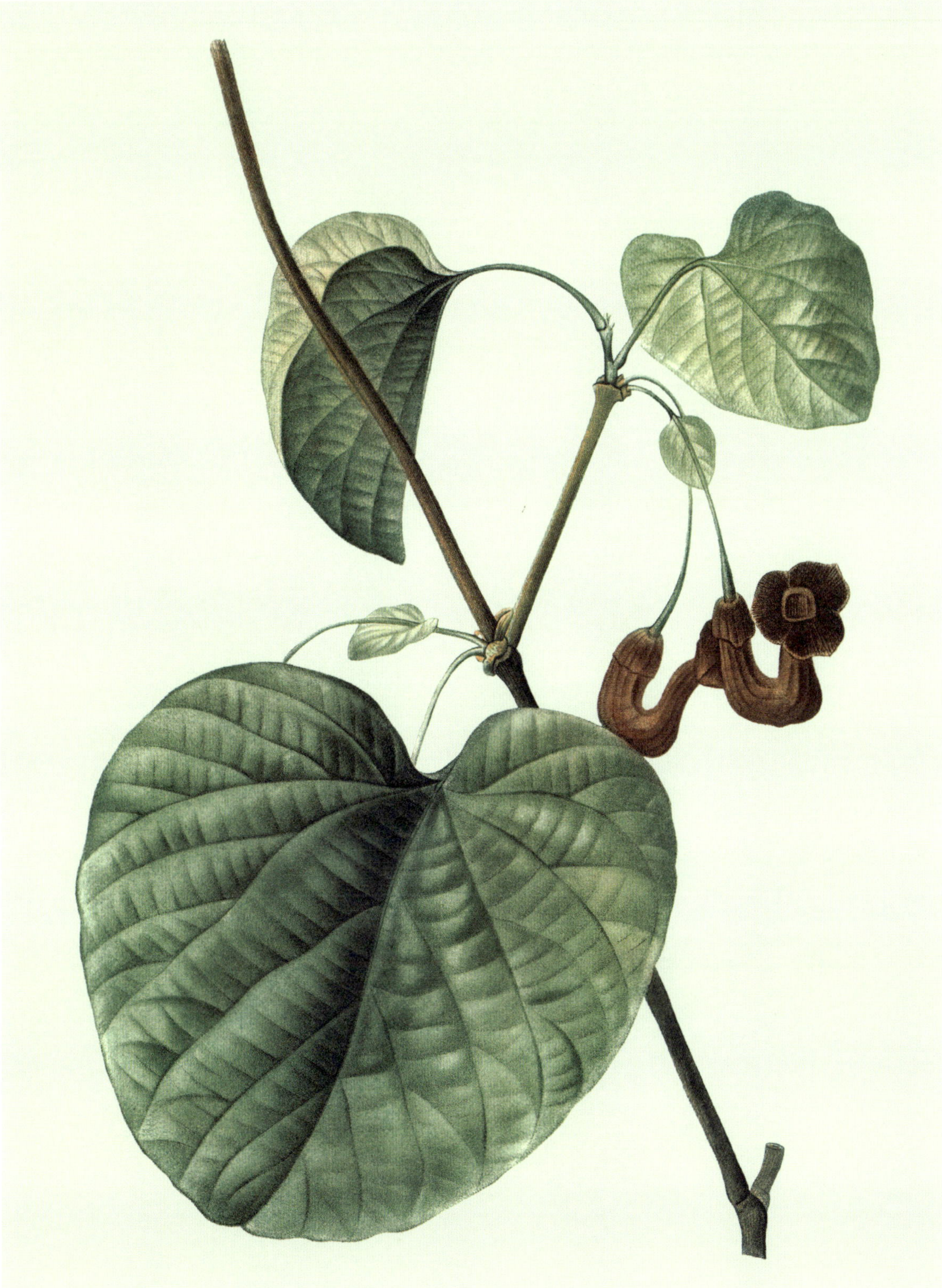

Aristolochia macrophylla
by Pierre-Joseph Redouté

Dutchman's pipe | pipevine

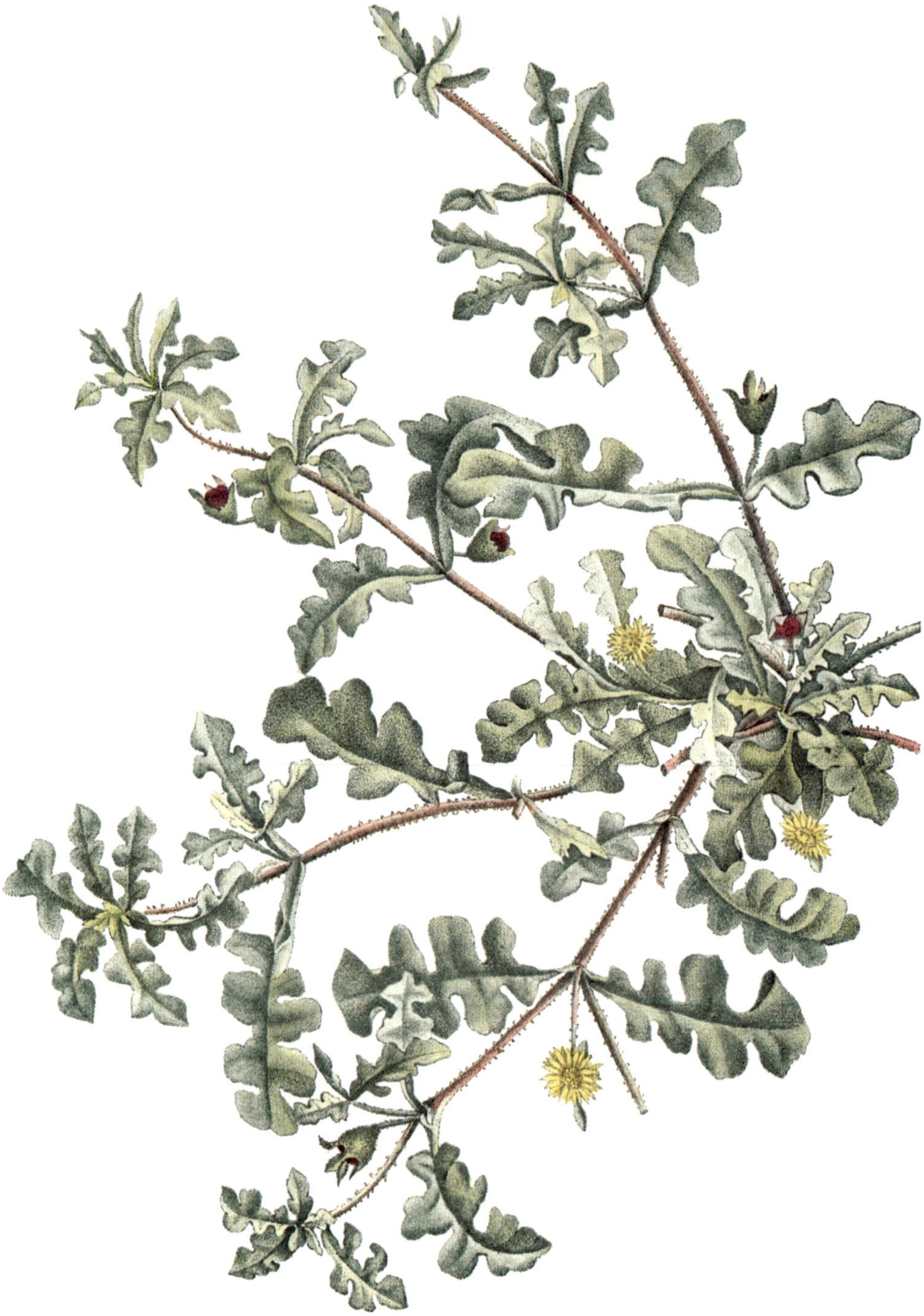

Cleretum pinnatifidum
by Pierre-Joseph Redouté

strangeleaf sandfig

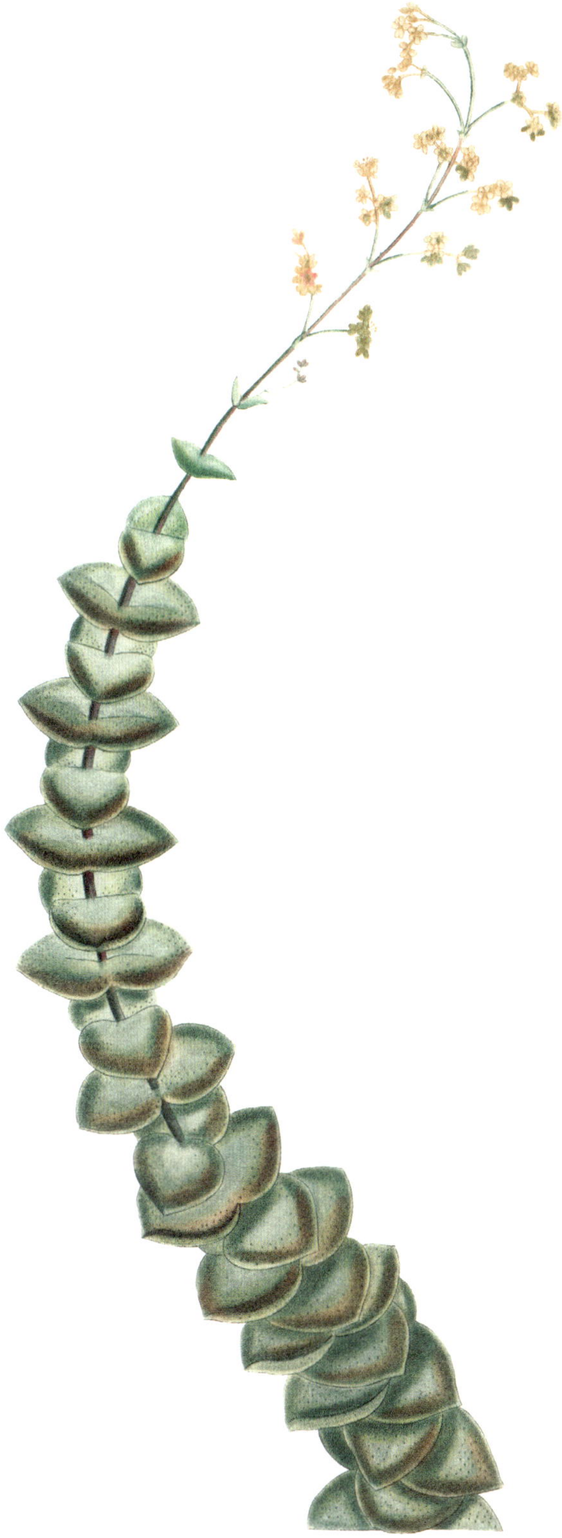

Crassula perforata
by Pierre-Joseph Redouté

string of buttons

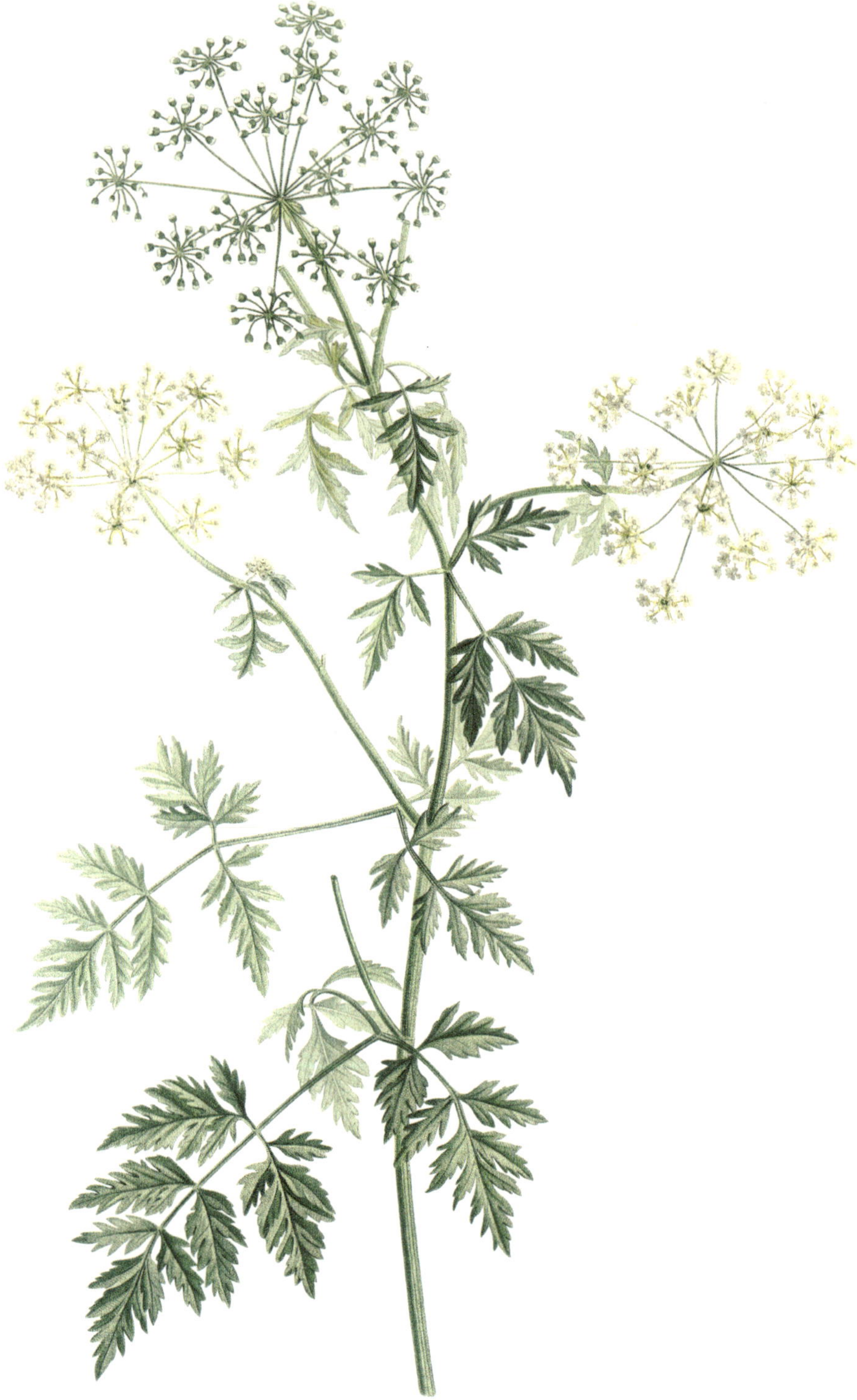

Conium maculatum
by Pierre-Joseph Redouté

hemlock

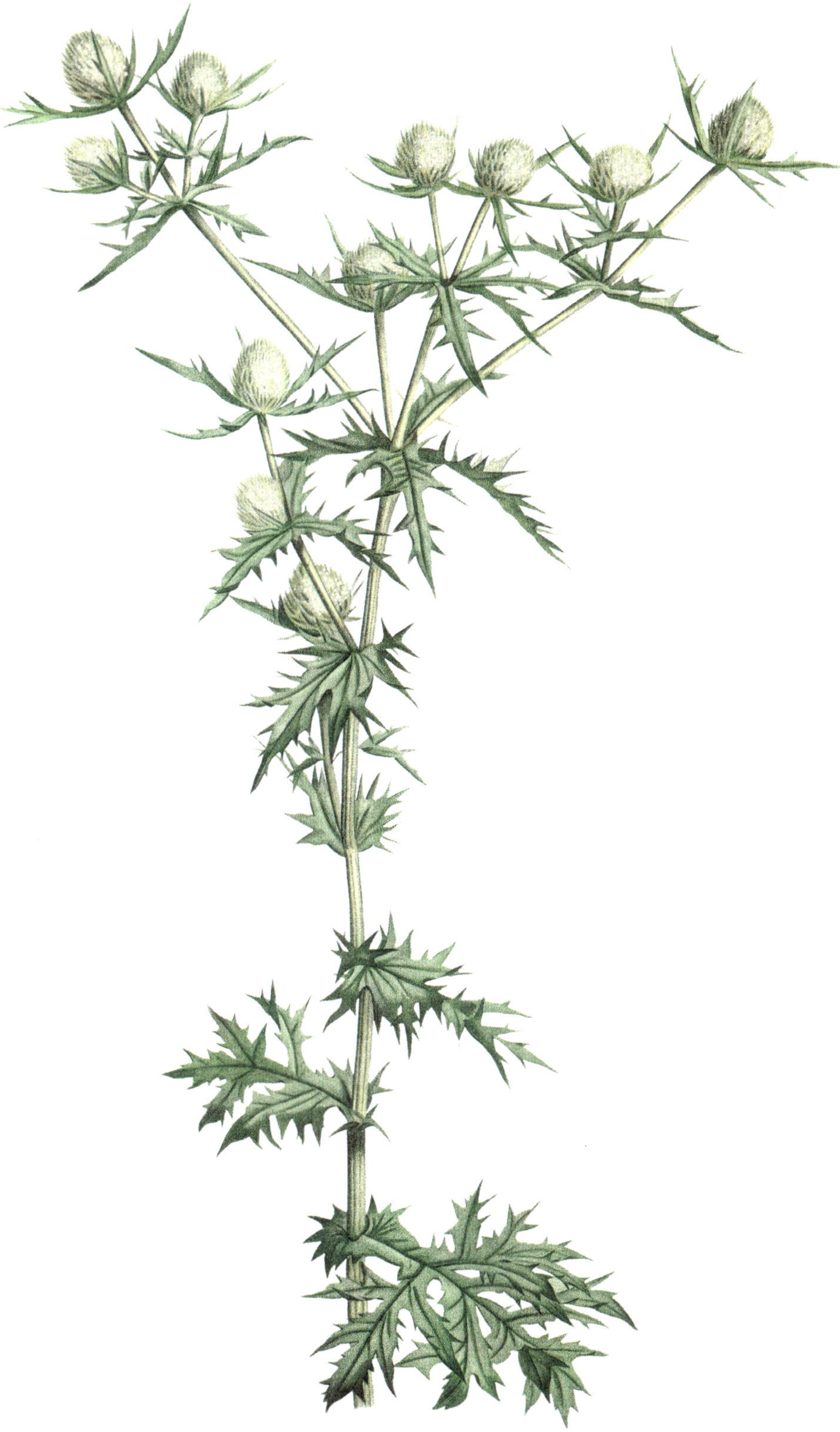

Eryngium amethystinum
by Pierre-Joseph Redouté

amethyst eryngo | amethyst sea holly | Italian eryngo

Smith Street Books

Published in 2026 by Smith Street Books
Naarm (Melbourne) | Australia
smithstreetbooks.com

Distributed outside of ANZ, North & Latin America by
Thames & Hudson Ltd., 6–24 Britannia Street, London, WC1X 9JD
thamesandhudson.com

EU Authorised Representative: Interart S.A.R.L.
19 rue Charles Auray, 93500 Pantin, Paris, France
productsafety@thameshudson.co.uk; www.interart.fr

ISBN: 978-1-9235-0316-8

Smith Street Books respectfully acknowledges the Wurundjeri People of the Kulin Nation, who are the Traditional Owners of the land on which we work, and we pay our respects to their Elders past and present.

Publisher: Hannah Koelmeyer
Design: Aaron Beehre
Design layout: Heather Menzies, Studio31 Graphics
Proofreader: Pamela Dunne
Prepress: Megan Ellis
Production manager: Aisling Coughlan

Printed & bound in China by C&C Offset Printing Co., Ltd.

Book 468

10 9 8 7 6 5 4 3 2 1

FSC www.fsc.org
MIX
Paper | Supporting responsible forestry
FSC® C008047

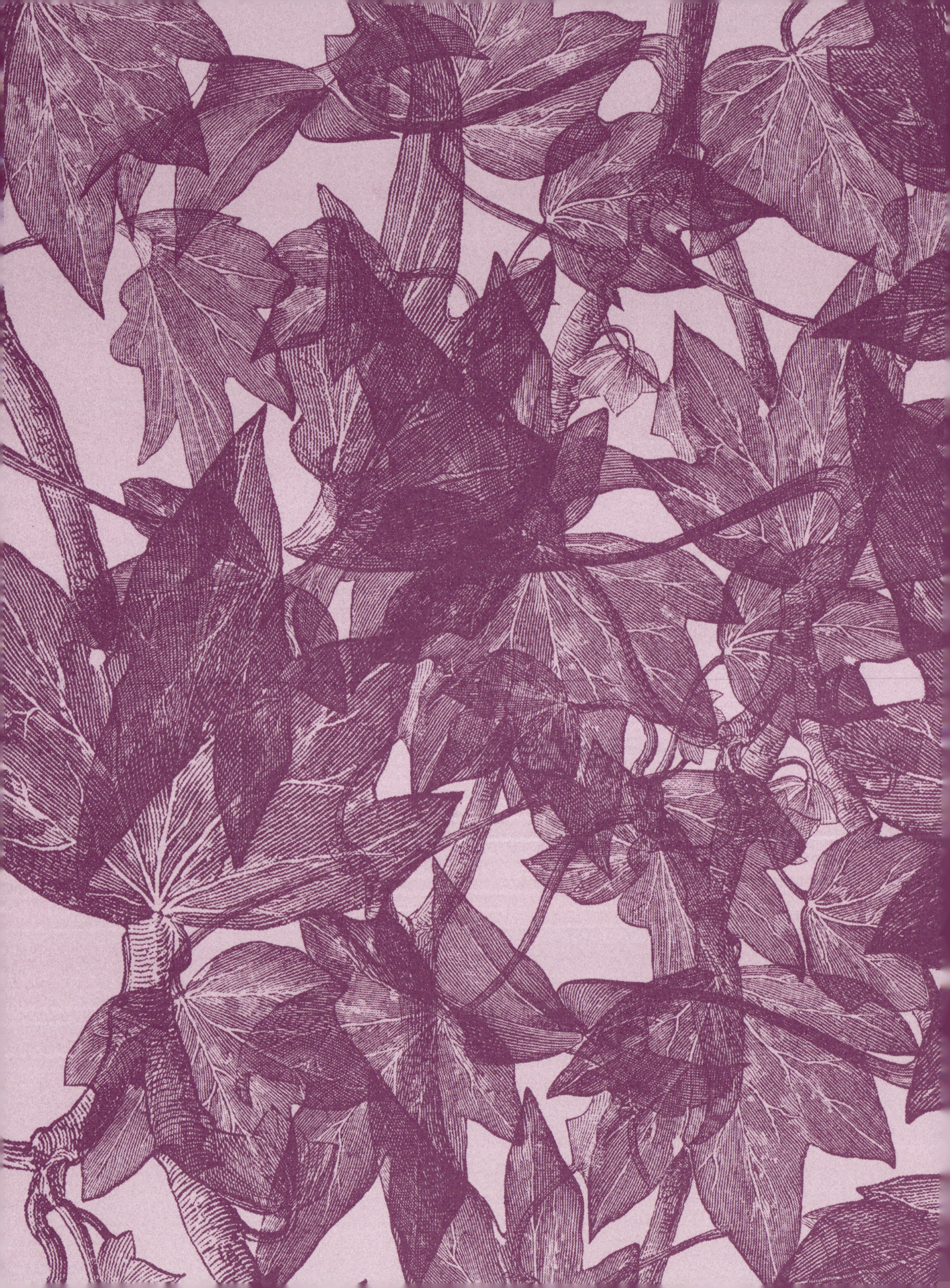